ENCYCLOPEDIA OF

Folklore

AND

Literature

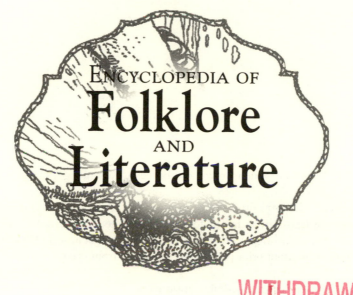

ENCYCLOPEDIA OF
Folklore
AND
Literature

EDITORS
MARY ELLEN BROWN
INDIANA UNIVERSITY

BRUCE A. ROSENBERG
BROWN UNIVERSITY

EDITORIAL ASSISTANTS
PETER HARLE
KATHY SITARSKI

ABC-CLIO

Santa Barbara, California
Denver, Colorado
Oxford, England

Library of Congress Cataloging-in-Publication Data
Encyclopedia of folklore and literature / Mary Ellen Brown and
    Bruce A. Rosenberg, editors ; Peter Harle, Kathy Sitarski,
    editorial assistants.
        p.   cm.
    Includes bibliographical references and index.
    Summary: Contains entries for authors, titles, national
literatures, themes, and motifs in literature and folklore.
    ISBN 1-57607-003-4 (hc)—1-57607-124-3 (pbk) (alk. paper)
    1. Literature—Encyclopedias.   2. Folklore—Encyclopedias.
[1. Literature—Encyclopedias.   2. Folklore—Encyclopedias.]
I. Brown, Mary Ellen, 1939– . II. Rosenberg, Bruce A.
PN41.E48   1998
803—dc21   98-19904
                                                                CIP
                                                                AC

04 03 02 01 00 99   10 9 8 7 6 5 4 3 2

ABC-CLIO, Inc.
130 Cremona Drive, P.O. Box 1911
Santa Barbara, California 93116–1911

To all who have helped make this encyclopedia possible

Contents

Encyclopedia of
Folklore
and
Literature, 1

CONTRIBUTORS

Cynthea L. Ainsworth
University of Alaska
Anchorage, AK

Richard W. Anderson
Independent Scholar
Hillsboro, OR

Mohammed S. Ansari
Indiana University
Bloomington, IN

Christopher Antonsen
The Ohio State University
Columbus, OH

Jennifer Eastman Attebery
Idaho State University
Pocatello, ID

Cristina Bacchilega
University of Hawaii
Honolulu, HI

Ronald L. Baker
Indiana State University
Terre Haute, IN

Amanda Carson Banks
Vanderbilt University
Nashville, TN

Linda Barwick
University of Sydney
Sydney, Australia

Richard Bauman
Indiana University
Bloomington, IN

Karen E. Beardslee
Independent Scholar
Cinnaminson, NJ

Margaret Hiebert Beissinger
University of Wisconsin
Madison, WI

Robert D. Bethke
University of Delaware
Newark, DE

Gene Bluestein
California State University
Fresno, CA

Valentina Bold
University of Aberdeen, King's College
Aberdeen, Scotland

Betsy Bowden
Rutgers, The State University of New
*   Jersey*
New Brunswick, NJ

Donald Braid
Butler University
Indianapolis, IN

Mary Ellen Brown
Indiana University
Bloomington, IN

Jan Harold Brunvand
University of Utah
Salt Lake City, UT

Contributors

Michael Buonanno
Manatee Community College
Bradenton, FL

Richard Allen Burns
Arkansas State University
State University, AR

Josie Campbell
University of Rhode Island
Kingston, RI

John Cash
Indiana University
Bloomington, IN

John Cawelti
University of Kentucky
Lexington, KY

William M. Clements
Arkansas State University
State University, AR

Krista Comer
Rice University
Houston, TX

Jesus Contreras
San Francisco State University
San Francisco, CA

†Daniel J. Crowley
University of California, Davis
Davis, CA

Anne J. Cruz
University of Illinois, Chicago
Chicago, IL

Anastasios Daskalopoulos
University of Missouri
Columbia, MO

Jody Davie
Brandeis University
Waltham, MA

Frank de Caro
Louisiana State University
Baton Rouge, LA

Luisa Del Giudice
University of California, Los Angeles
Los Angeles, CA

Sandra K. Dolby
Indiana University
Bloomington, IN

James R. Dow
Iowa State University
Ames, IA

Sam Driver
Brown University
Providence, RI

Dianne Dugaw
University of Oregon
Eugene, OR

Elizabeth C. Fine
Virginia Polytechnic Institute
Blacksburg, VA

Gary Alan Fine
University of Georgia
Athens, GA

Mary Catherine Flannery
University of Louisville
Louisville, KY

John Miles Foley
University of Missouri
Columbia, MO

Douglas Freake
York University
North York, Ontario, Canada

Lawrence S. Friedman
Indiana University, Fort Wayne
Fort Wayne, IN

Marcia Gaudet
University of Southwestern Louisiana
Lafayette, LA

David E. Gay
Indiana University
Bloomington, IN

Robert A. Georges
University of California, Los Angeles
Los Angeles, CA

Rachel Gholson
Memorial University of Newfoundland
St. John's, Newfoundland, Canada

Peter Gilet
Universitas Kristen Satya Wacana
Salatiga, Indonesia

Janet N. Gold
University of New Hampshire
Durham, NH

Christine Goldberg
Independent Scholar
Los Angeles, CA

Marjetka Golež
Slovene Academy of Sciences and Arts
Ljubljana, Slovenia

James Gollnick
St. Paul's United College
Waterloo, Ontario, Canada

Donald Haase
Wayne State University
Detroit, MI

William Hansen
Indiana University
Bloomington, IN

Debbie A. Hanson
Augustana College
Sioux Falls, SD

Lee Haring
Brooklyn College
Brooklyn, NY

Peter G. Harle
Indiana University
Bloomington, IN

Ilana Harlow
Queens Council on the Arts
Queens, NY

Joseph Harris
Harvard University
Cambridge, MA

Patricia Haseltine
Providence University
Taichung Hsien, Taiwan

Maria Herrera-Sobek
University of California, Santa Barbara
Santa Barbara, CA

Martha Hixon
University of Southwestern Louisiana
Lafayette, LA

Andrew J. Hoffman
Brown University
Providence, RI

Melanie K. Hutsell
Indiana University
Bloomington, IN

Bonnie D. Irwin
Eastern Illinois University
Charleston, IL

Carol Jamison
Armstrong Atlantic State University
Savannah, GA

John William Johnson
Indiana University
Bloomington, IN

Contributors

Charles Greg Kelley
East Georgia College
Swainsboro, GA

Sonia I. Ketchian
Harvard University
Cambridge, MA

James W. Kirkland
East Carolina University
Greenville, NC

John Kolsti
University of Texas
Austin, TX

Natalie Kononenko
University of Virginia
Charlottesville, VA

Reimund Kvideland
University of Bergen
Bergen, Norway

Robert Lee
Brown University
Providence, RI

Valerie Lee
The Ohio State University
Columbus, OH

George Leonard
San Francisco State University
San Francisco, CA

A. Levitski
Brown University
Providence, RI

Anatoly Liberman
University of Minnesota
Minneapolis, MN

Carl Lindahl
University of Houston
Houston, TX

Liz Locke
Indiana University
Bloomington, IN

Martin Lovelace
Memorial University of Newfoundland
St. John's, Newfoundland, Canada

Mary Magoulick
Indiana University
Bloomington, IN

Jerome Mandel
Tel Aviv University
Tel Aviv, Israel

Kathleen E. B. Manley
University of Northern Colorado
Greeley, CO

John H. McDowell
Indiana University
Bloomington, IN

Sylvia McLaurin
University of Georgia
Athens, GA

W. K. McNeil
The Ozark Folk Center
Mountain View, AR

Joanne Pope Melish
Brown University
Providence, RI

Dan Merkur
University of Toronto
Toronto, Ontario, Canada

Wolfgang Mieder
University of Vermont
Burlington, VT

John Minton
Indiana University–Purdue University
Fort Wayne, IN

Robert Mondi
Weber State University
Ogden, Utah

Eric Montenyohl
Independent Scholar
Cary, NC

Pamela S. Morgan
University of California, Berkeley
Berkeley, CA

Patrick B. Mullen
The Ohio State University
Columbus, OH

Maureen Murphy
Hofstra University
Hempstead, NY

W. F. H. Nicolaisen
University of Aberdeen, King's College
Aberdeen, Scotland

John Niles
University of California, Berkeley
Berkeley, CA

Dorothy Noyes
The Ohio State University
Columbus, OH

Rafael Ocasio
Agnes Scott College
Decatur, GA

Joseph F. Patrouch
Florida International University
Miami, FL

Elaine Petrie
Falkirk College of Technology
Falkirk, Scotland

Kenneth D. Pimple
Indiana University
Bloomington, IN

Catherine Quick
University of Texas–Pan American
Edinburg, TX

Pirkko-Liisa Rausmaa
University of Helsinki
Helsinki, Finland

Sigrid Rieuwerts
Johannes Gutenburg Universität
Mainz, Germany

Donald A. Ringe
University of Kentucky
Lexington, KY

Susan Roach
Louisiana Tech University
Ruston, LA

Warren Roberts
Indiana University
Bloomington, IN

Danielle M. Roemer
Northern Kentucky University
Highland Heights, KY

Bruce A. Rosenberg
Brown University
Providence, RI

Anya Peterson Royce
Indiana University
Bloomington, IN

Patricia E. Sawin
University of Southwestern Louisiana
Lafayette, LA

Jennifer Schacker-Mill
Indiana University
Bloomington, IN

Alex Scobie
Victoria University
Wellington, New Zealand

Contributors

Carole Silver
Yeshiva University
New York, NY

Guntis Smidchens
University of Washington
Seattle, WA

Silvia Spitta
Dartmouth College
Hanover, NH

David Sprunger
Concordia College
Moorhead, MN

Sue Standing
Wheaton College
Norton, MA

Mary Beth Stein
The George Washington University
Washington, DC

Beverly J. Stoeltje
Indiana University
Bloomington, IN

Kay Stone
University of Winnipeg
Winnipeg, Manitoba, Canada

Michael Taft
University of North Carolina
Chapel Hill, NC

Victor Terras
Brown University
Providence, RI

Kenneth A. Thigpen
Pennsylvania State University
University Park, PA

Jeanne B. Thomas
Indiana State University
Terre Haute, IN

Ewa M. Thompson
Rice University
Houston, TX

Mary Beth Tierney-Tello
Wheaton College
Norton, MA

Elizabeth Tucker
State University of New York
Binghamton, NY

Robert E. Walls
Lafayette College
Easton, PA

Lorraine Walsh
Indiana University
Bloomington, IN

Donald Ward
University of California, Los Angeles
Los Angeles, CA

R. Kelly Washbourne
University of Massachusetts
Amherst, MA

Elizabeth E. Wein
Independent Scholar
Marlow, Bucks, United Kingdom

Clover Williams
Indiana University
Bloomington, IN

William A. Wilson
Brigham Young University
Provo, UT

Stephen Winick
University of Pennsylvania
Philadelphia, PA

Mark E. Workman
University of North Florida
Jacksonville, FL

LIST OF ENTRIES

Aarne, Antti
Achebe, Chinua
Aesop's Fables
Akhmatova, Anna
Anaya, Rudolfo Alfonso
Andersen, Hans Christian
Anderson, Walter
Angelou, Maya
Anzaldúa, Gloria
Apuleius
Archetype
Arenas, Reinaldo
Arguedas, José María
Arnim, Achim von
Arthur, King
Arthurian Tradition
Asturias, Miguel Angel
Atwood, Margaret
Aucassin and Nicolette
Azadovskii, Mark Konstantinovich
Baba Iaga (also Baba Yaga)
Bakhtin, Mikhail Mikhailovitch
Balkan Folklore and Literature
Ballad
Basile, Giambattista
Bédier, Joseph
Belief
Beowulf
Bible
Bierce, Ambrose Gwinnett
Bildungsroman
Blues
Boccaccio, Giovanni
Botkin, Benjamin A.

Brentano, Clemens
Briggs, Katharine
Bulosan, Carlos
Bunraku
Bunyan, Paul
Burns, Robert
Bylinas
Caedmon
Calvino, Italo
Camelot
Campbell, Joseph
Cante Fable
Canterbury Tales
Cardenal, Ernesto
Caribbean Folklore and Literature
Carter, Angela
Carvajal, Maria Isabel
Cather, Willa
Celtic Literature
Cervantes, Lorna Dee
Cervantes (Saavedra), Miguel de
Chapbook
Charlemagne
Chaucer, Geoffrey
Chesnutt, Charles Waddell
Chicago Folklore Society
Child, Francis James
Children's Literature
Chin, Frank
Chinese Opera
Ch'uan-ch'i
Cinderella
Cisneros, Sandra
Cofer, Judith Ortiz

ENTRIES BY CATEGORY

Munro, Alice
Narayan, Rasipuram Krish-
naswami
Nekrasov, Nikolay Alekseyevich
Oates, Joyce Carol
Peri Rossi, Cristina
Perrault, Charles
Piñon, Nélida
Poe, Edgar Allan
Poniatowska, Elena
P'u Sung-ling
Rabelais, François
Rossetti, Christina Georgina
Sandburg, Carl
Schiller, Johann Christoph
Friedrich
Scorza, Manuel
Scott, Sir Walter
Shakespeare, William
Silko, Leslie Marmon
Singer, Isaac Bashevis
Soto, Pedro Juan
Soyinka, Wole
Steinbeck, John
Stephens, James
Stoker, Bram
Straparola, Gian Francesco
Sturt, George
Synge, John Millington
Thompson, Flora
Tolkien, J. R. R. (John Ronald
Reuel)
Tutuola, Amos
Twain, Mark
Valdez, Luis Miguel
Valenzuela, Luisa
Walker, Alice
Welty, Eudora
Whittier, John Greenleaf
Wilder, Laura Ingalls
Yeats, William Butler

WORKS

Aesop's Fables
Aucassin and Nicolette
Balkan Folklore and Literature
Beowulf
Bible
Bunraku
Canterbury Tales
Caribbean Folklore and Literature
Celtic Literature
Children's Literature
Chinese Opera
Commedia dell'arte
Decameron
The Dragon Slayer
Edda, Poetic
Edda, Prose
Feng-shen yen-i
Gawain and the Green Knight, Sir
Genji, Tale of
Gesta Romanorum
Golden Ass
The Golden Bough
Greece, Ancient
Hamlet
Heike, Tale of the
Hindu Epics
Iliad
Jātaka
Kabuki
Kalevala
King Lear
Konjaku
Labor Folklore and Literature
Latino and Chicano Folklore and
Literature
Native American Writing
Nibelungenlied
Nō (Noh)
Nursery Rhymes

PREFACE

The *Encyclopedia of Folklore and Literature* offers an introduction to a subject that could potentially encompass all the world's literature and folklore. Here we have had to be selective, providing entries in four categories, each of which offers a way to begin understanding the fascinating complexity of the interrelationships between folklore and literature. There are entries that (1) discuss some of the world's writers and works of literature that have been identified as significant users of folklore as a resource or source; (2) describe a number of concepts that facilitate looking at folklore and literature together; (3) offer a selection of themes and characters that—while originating in oral literature—are also found in written literature; and (4) provide information on some of the scholars (for the most part excluding those whose life work is not yet complete) who have studied folklore and literature. You will find a list of entries by categories beginning on page xxi.

Each entry is followed by a brief list of references for further exploration; the works listed provide far more detailed studies of the subject in question than could be included as individual entries in this encyclopedia. Each entry is also followed by a *See also* section that cross-references the entry with others found in this work, pointing the reader to related entries: under Shakespeare, for example, readers are referred primarily to entries for individual plays as well as to those that describe particular genres of folklore found in his dramas. The individual entries and their relationships to one another are the very heart of this work.

The general introduction gives a short history of the scholarly interest in the connections between folklore and literature and ends with a bibliography that includes a sampling of specific and general studies relevant to the study of the world's literature and folklore, the vast and virtually inexhaustible study to which this encyclopedia is an invitation.

STANDARD FOLKLORE CITATIONS

Folklorists are particularly interested in recurring cultural phenomena; and folklorists who work with oral and written literatures identify familiar, repeated materials by referring to two concepts—the tale-type and the motif, both of which are defined in this encyclopedia. Two works in particular are frequently cited within the entries in the short forms shown in brackets.

Aarne, Antti, and Stith Thompson. *The Types of the Folktale*. Folklore Fellows Communication no. 184. Helsinki: Academia Scientiarum Fennica, 1964. [Cited as AT, type, tale-type, followed by the appropriate number.]

Thompson, Stith. *The Motif-Index of Folk-Literature*. 6 vols. Bloomington: Indiana University Press, 1955–1958. [Cited as Motif or motif and followed by the appropriate letter and numbers.]

INTRODUCTION

This encyclopedia offers an entrée into a vast subject that might include all the world's literature and folklore. Interestingly, the sustained study of the relationship between these two enormous areas—folklore and literature—has been predominantly the activity of folklorists, individuals trained in examining the array of traditional cultural and artistic processes that have come to be called folklore. They focus particularly on processes that are learned orally and/or by observation and imitation, perceived to be authorless and thus anonymous, usually inherited from earlier generations or transmitted horizontally in time, and showing signs of both continuity and change—stability and variation.

The approaches taken often reveal the concerns of the scholars and implicitly suggest the questions they ask, the areas that interest them. Behind many of the studies lie old concerns about origins: Where do ideas come from? Some scholars have interested themselves in questions about the artistic process; others have been concerned with adding to the stores of folklore by extrapolating materials from works of written literature. The approaches taken reflect various definitional assumptions as well, particularly around the meaning of the word *folklore* and the relation of that conception of folklore to literature. We "know" what literature is; ideas about *folklore* range from the "scientifically" exact to the more amorphous—assuming that folklore encompasses all themes and symbols (Hoffman 1961). Many of these characterizations have added something of value to the debate, yet approaches that see folklore as an all-purpose "other," against which literature defines itself, have largely failed the interdisciplinary challenge.

Scholars who have approached the study of folklore and literature, however those terms are perceived, have had their own particular foci and concerns, which, of course, have not remained the same over time. If literary scholars have been particularly interested in author and text, this focus has assumed the artistic quality of the materials under study and has been preoccupied with interpretation, meaning, and hermeneutics. Folklorists, on the other hand, who may have stressed performance and context, have been particularly interested in artistry—perhaps an already accepted base assumption of the more literarily trained. Thus, folklorists have looked at the building blocks of literary works, the base materials, sometimes folkloric (again, begging the definition and delimitation of that term), that a writer (or other artist) may transmute. Identifying folklore may help reveal the artistic process and can certainly point to the culturally available resources that have been employed in a literary work.

Writers' and speakers' communicative capabilities may be increased when they marshal familiar forms and contents. On the other hand, they may be constrained by the necessity to communicate using familiar materials. Some collectors of folklore have also been creative writers and, like Sir Walter Scott and Zora Neale Hurston, have consciously collected and/or remembered materials from their own cultural milieu, which in turn have become central elements in subsequent written endeavors.

Three major approaches have been taken, each with its own set of essential assumptions: folklore as ur, or original, literature; folklore in literature; and folklore and literature as parallel forms of art.

1. FOLKLORE AS UR LITERATURE

Some scholars have been particularly interested in folklore as the original literature, though oral, that existed prior to written literature and provided the basis for written works. In fact, written versions of originally oral material have sometimes been seen as canonical works of literature—the *Odyssey* and *Beowulf*, both epics, and ballads such as "Sir Patrick Spens" being cases in point. These examples implicitly interrogate the distinction between oral and written literature, for these works were based on oral stories, shaped to the contours of predominantly oral genres, and transmitted orally. Thus, they belong to the category of folklore rather than to literature if the distinction between the two is based on mode of transmission and, no doubt, the concept of authorship.

Sometimes the relationship between oral and written material is seen in an evolutionary or a developmental framework. The nineteenth-century Scottish antiquary, ballad collector/editor, and poet William Motherwell expressed the ideas of many eighteenth- and nineteenth-century commentators when he suggested that "poetry was the first vehicle of human thought." He went on to imply its prior status and the value of studying such early literatures:

> Few studies are more fascinating after a short time's application and none perchance accompanied with more solid advantages and edifying results than that of the ancient poetry of a country.

The philologist is thereby made acquainted with the gradations and changes the language of that country has undergone from its first formation until its latest improvements. The philosopher is thereby enabled to trace the progress of human intellect from its first rude efforts to its more exalted and perfect performances— the moralist is thereby furnished with means to ascertain what effects different circumstances have wrought in the opinions and judgments of men—the historian is supplied with hints and sketches of the prevalent fashions[,] vices[,] follies[,] manners[,] literature and domestic relations of Society in these distant periods of which no other record remains[;] and the man of taste and the Critic are put in possession of materials by which they can speculate & generalise with more certainty on the greater part of the subjects most intimately connected with their respective pursuits. (Motherwell)

For Motherwell and others then, ancient poetry is anterior; that is, came before; may well be that out of which subsequent literature has developed; and thus offers a means of historical reconstruction.

Johann Wolfgang von Goethe more specifically suggested that one particular kind of ancient poetry, the ballad, contained within itself the *Ur ei*, or "primal germ," of all poetry: he considered the ballad to be ur poetry, bearing within itself the seeds of the major genres—lyric, epic, and drama. Thus, the ballad is definitely prior (before), that from which the other forms of poetry are derived. The general assumption of many early commentators on the origins of literature was that poetry was prior to prose, that rhyme and rhythm were elementary, primary qualities. There was also the assumption that this early, ancient, and presumably oral material was natural, providing the model for later artificial literatures, the distinction then between *Naturpoesie* (natural poetry) and *Kunstpoesie* (literary poetry). The American poet Robert Frost suggested his own evolutionary view, that literary form came from folk speech, that written literature builds on proverbs and proverbial sayings. The oral precedes the written.

The massive sweep of H. Munro Chadwick and N. Kershaw Chadwick's *The Growth of Literature* (1968) affirms the prior existence of oral forms to canonical written literature. Genres may develop from other genres, and may reflect particular cultural stages, which are themselves not static but evolving. Heroic literature comes out of the heroic age, which the Chadwicks designated as barbaric. They suggested it was characterized by small communities that had a prince/leader, a member of the dominant warrior class, who became the central focus of the literature.

More recently, some of the work in oral formulaic composition—the idea that certain oral forms of art are formulated and reformulated in performance using learned patterns (particularly oral formulas: verbal clusters whose syntactic and semantic forms are repeated, sometimes only approximately, to express an idea or part of a narrative)—has tended to see such literature as existing prior to written forms where formulaic qualities and certainly themes may persist (Foley, Lord, Ong).

Naturally, some analysts have compared and contrasted oral and written literatures in an attempt to identify inherent qualities of style, content, and form—recognizing that the exigencies of oral and written performance enable certain styles. Oral style, for example, is often characterized as repetitive, redundant, even paratactic—reflecting an oral aesthetic and no doubt arising from the necessity of holding materials in memory. On the other hand, print culture, with its mechanical reproduction, is probably far more repetitive.

These disparate approaches share a common assumption about what folklore is—oral literature: ballads, prose narratives (folktales, *märchen*, legends), epics. This assumption in turn predetermines how folklore is seen in relation to literature—as evolutionarily prior, not the same as written literature but indeed similar. Folklore and literature can be seen as representing different points on a continuum of creativity, reflecting different stages of civilization.

2. FOLKLORE IN LITERATURE

From another perspective, many analysts follow what has often been called the "lore in lit" approach. This second approach focuses on folklore as a resource for literature, and folklore here may be thought of in a broader sense as equipment for living, as a whole range of traditional or vernacular practices—verbal, material, and customary—that are a part of life. Thus, folklore enters literary works because it is an essential ingredient of lived reality.

Such root assumptions aside, source studies have been undertaken for a number of reasons. Countless papers have culled examples of folklore from written works to add to the record of folklore, most particularly for historical periods for which records of vernacular culture and forms of folklore are lacking. The folklore identified is then carefully cross-referenced to affirm the "traditionality" of the materials by offering parallel examples recorded in the folklorists' reference works: the type and motif indexes (throughout the entries in this volume, the reader will find references by number to types and motifs: these are recurring narrative materials indexed in various reference works of which the most frequently used, and cited, are those developed by Antti Aarne and Stith Thompson).

Practitioners of the historic-geographic method use such printed versions or records of oral materials in part to provide an historical benchmark, as an aid in dating the time of origin of a particular example of oral art. Other scholars have used the literary record as ethnography, a way to reconstruct a larger cultural environment as well as the traditional forms there embedded, as a source for information about context. These approaches are folklore centered. By contrast, other folklorists and literary scholars have sought oral sources for some literary works in order to understand the process whereby literatures are made: where, for example, do writers get their materials? The early British literary folklorists Francis Douce, James Orchard Halliwell-Phillipps, and Charles Cuthbert Southey, for example, sought to answer the question with reference to William Shakespeare: where did he get the beliefs, customs, and narratives he used in his drama? (See Dorson 1968, chapter 3.) Bruce Rosenberg (1991) suggests that this approach may reveal an "author's learning, working methods, relation to contemporaries, nature and extent of originality, and artistic intention."

Many scholars have focused on understanding more about the cultural environment in which literary artists have lived, assuming that writers build on the surroundings of which they are a part: W. F. Bryan and Germaine Dempster's *Sources and Analogues of Chaucer's Canterbury Tales* (1941) includes numerous suggestions, from both written and oral sources. Presumably Chaucer would have heard or read these sources and thus incorporated known and often shared cultural resources into his masterful written works. Additionally, Chaucer's treatment of character and his development of literary situations include the use of other cultural practices—the pilgrimage, festive customs, the practice of oral insult, dialect, and various oral styles—and in depicting the exchange of stories, Chaucer deftly gives storytellers tales to tell that reflect the tastes of those who belong to particular classes (Lindahl 1987).

At their most sophisticated, such source studies consider folklore as a resource on a number of levels—content, of course, but also style and technique, form and structure, context and historical milieu (Dundes 1964). When exact sources can be found, they open the way for studies of individual artistry. Robert Burns, Scotland's national poet, used a number of aspects of the traditional culture of which he was a part. His use of a legend as the basis for one of his masterpieces—"Tam o' Shanter"—enables the critic to suggest ways Burns added to the oral legends that undoubtedly circulated in his environment (Brown 1984).

Other scholars have taken another approach and criticized the literary "users" for straying too far away from the originals, a view that clearly places a higher value on the oral versions.

Attention has also been given to the ways folklore is used in literary works, the function of folklore—be it background, employed to create verisimilitude, or centrally and integrally used as part of the core theme. There have been attempts, building on specific studies, to codify the uses to which writers have put folklore, to delineate the functions folklore has served in literary works; clearly, folklore may motivate plot in literature as in life (Grobman 1979). Yet the study of individual authors reveals far greater subtlety and variety than such codified systems allow; in fact, the study of each author's involvement in and appropriation or incorporation of folklore into his or her work seems to demand recognition of the specific way any given writer is a part of a particular time, place, and experience.

Some students of folklore and literature have been primarily concerned with the ways in which folklore (variously defined) can aid the reader in understanding the work of literature. Perhaps the most extraordinary folklore and literature study from this perspective, and thereby a model, was made by Mikhail Bakhtin on François Rabelais: Bakhtin contends that to understand Rabelais, one has to understand his world, the tensions that existed between classes, the value placed on laughter, the entire polyglot cultural climate, and the way folklore was used to reveal those aspects. Rabelais described a world in flux, focusing on people's voices, the diversity of carnival behavior; he used these elements, according to Bakhtin, to reveal values and central issues of the real environment, depicted fictively. Thus, Bakhtin reconstructs what Rabelais's readers would have known and reveals the people's perspective, in fact a counterhegemonic view to that known historically as "official culture." That other world is permeated with folk culture, and to understand the work of literature, one must know that world.

Although practitioners of the "folklore as source" approach define folklore variously, all implicitly seem to share the assumption that folklore—genres, structures, styles, milieu—is a rich cultural resource that is always already available to creative writers (and artists of all sorts), whether drawn from oral observation or from written record. Yet folklore and literature are, at base, qualitatively different. Folklore, especially when seen as verbal art, is immediate when performed in a face-to-face situation; literature, on the other hand, is a mediated and commodified form. Ferdinand Saussure's distinction between *langue* and *parole* puts folklore under the former and literature under the latter.

Langue, of which folklore is a part, is community based, oral, and collective; literature, belonging to *parole*, is individual, a written permanent record. Continuing the distinction, Susan Stewart would say that folklore belongs to sense, to culture, while literature belongs to another level, to nonsense, which always refers to "sense" but does so in a different frame, with its own discursive rules. In brief, folklore and literature are related but different.

3. FOLKLORE AND LITERATURE AS PARALLEL FORMS OF ART

Other scholars have taken a third approach, seeing both folklore and literature as parallel modes of art, as communication, as performance. Similar theoretical and methodological approaches can thus be used in studying both kinds of communication. People interested in style, poetics, and the nature of narrative have looked for the parallel ways in which oral and written literatures tell stories: Vladimir Propp's ideas about the structure of the Russian fairy tale have been applied to written literary works, suggesting that certain patterns and structures are widely shared; similarly, the ideas of Axel Olrik and Max Lüthi have been employed.

Folklorists Linda Degh and Andrew Vazsonyi's analysis of the dialectics of the legend identified a conversational mode that seems to have been recognized by authors and transposed into literary works. The legend in context is more than a single-stranded narrative: various individuals participate, polyphonically, in the story creation, providing a multiplicity of voices offering now one perspective, now another. In "Young Goodman Brown," Nathaniel Hawthorne would seem to have used this strategy to embed alternate interpretations within the narrative: the text presents and indeed voices alternate possibilities, much as participants in the telling of legends offer theirs: "This, of course, must have been an ocular deception"; "Either the sudden gleams of light flashing over the obscure field bedazzled Goodman Brown, or he recognized a score or more of church members of Salem famous for their especial sanctity"; or "Had Goodman Brown fallen asleep in the forest and only dreamed a wild dream of a witch meeting?" Other interpreters have recognized parallel themes, the "problem" in abstract, in written and oral works.

Approaches focusing on reader/audience reception have added readers and listeners to the field of study, seeing them as involved in responsive processes influenced by elements within the written text or oral performance, which call forth response. Still other critics have suggested that there are classics in both oral and written literature, stressing the fact that verbal art is a form of art worthy of study in its own right (Coffin

1964). And, in fact, one of the ways to ensure that verbal art is as valued as written art has been to develop appropriate means of transcribing and often translating oral performances onto the written page—a practice called ethnopoetics—in order to preserve in frozen texts a greater sense of the art of live performance.

The process of moving the oral performance into written form has been eloquently illustrated in the works of folklorists Dell Hymes and Barre Toelken. Interestingly, this kind of approach was earlier developed by the poet Charles Olson in his projective verse, his personal campaign to carry the orality of a reading of poetry into writing—to force subsequent performances, whether oral or written, to reflect the poet's original intention. These kinds of studies implicitly suggest that folklore and literature as related and parallel communicative media are equally artistic. This approach returns to the idea of folklore as oral literature, as verbal art; but without the evolutionary premise.

Through time, various cultural and political movements have stimulated concern for folklore-literary relationships, most particularly romanticism and the recurring sentiments of nationalism. Romantics consciously sought a return to the old: ostensibly a collection of oral literature, Bishop Thomas Percy's *Reliques of Ancient English Poetry* (1765) became a source book for poets, offering examples of style, form, and content to counteract newer kinds of literature that were judged to be alienating and divorced from the natural and privileged forms. National enthusiasms have stimulated movements for literatures that reflect and thus affirm a national entity because they are in the vernacular, providing a literary-cultural mandate for the nation-state. Such interests have over and over again stimulated the collecting of folklore, most particularly oral, artistic forms—tales and songs—in a national language to justify the parameters of the nation-state and to form the basis for a national literature, much as Percy's work had provided precedents and models.

The approach taken in the former Soviet Union was to conflate folklore and literature and to encourage gifted performers to create new materials, affirming a particular ideology. Colonial movements have sometimes suppressed native literatures—written and oral—and replaced them with exogenous literatures in foreign languages. Postcolonial literatures may offer interesting responses to historical factors, yielding rich and diverse blurred genres, works of varied stylistic qualities, and even appropriating the colonial language. The fascinating work of Amos Tutuola, *The Palm-Wine Drinkard* (1952), paratactically links multiple tales and motifs to form a coherent narrative and thus offers a lively example of postcolonial literature.

Written literature's various appropriations of folklore, however defined, play a part in the ongoing process of traditionalizing: through use, kinds of transformation, materials are repeated, taken from one context to another, and affirmed as valuable. Sometimes these appropriations are negatively viewed as violating the integrity of the originals, and they are labeled *folklorism* or *fakelore*. Such negative terms, however, fly in the face of real cultural processes by which human beings constantly reuse, even recontextualize, available cultural resources—in both life and art. Literary authors and their uses of folklore can be seen as providing another link in the chain of transmission, which might originally have been oral. At its best—for example, in the work of Bakhtin—we realize Rabelais's great artistry because he built on the traditions of the world in which he lived: his ability to transmute, to recontextualize, to resituate lived reality in his works of fiction enabled him to produce extraordinary depictions that reconfigured his world in such a way as to make critical statements about cultural levels and cultural processes, hegemonic and counterhegemonic positions. And yet, for all its brilliance, Bakhtin's analysis is reductive, limiting folklore and festival to mostly parodic forms, and thus unwittingly illustrating that no folklore and literature study to date is complete or fully realized (Lindahl 1996). Past studies enrich our knowledge; future studies may more fully unlock the secrets that tie folklore and literature together.

Mary Ellen Brown

BIBLIOGRAPHY

Aarne, Antti, and Stith Thompson. *The Types of the Folktale: A Classification and Bibliography*. 2d rev. ed. Folklore Fellows Communications, no. 184. Helsinki: Academia Scientiarum Fennica, 1964.

Abrahams, Roger. "Folklore and Literature as Performance." *Journal of the Folklore Institute* 9 (1972): 75–94.

———. "Introductory Remarks to a Rhetorical Theory of Folklore." *Journal of American Folklore* 81 (1968): 143–158.

Baer, Florence E. *Folklore and Literature of the British Isles: An Annotated Bibliography (1890–1980)*. New York: Garland, 1986.

Bakhtin, Mikhail. *Rabelais and His World*. Trans. Helene Iswolsky. Cambridge, Mass.: M.I.T. Press, 1968.

Bauman, Richard, and Charles Briggs. "Poetics and Performance as Critical Perspectives on Language and Social Life." *Annual Review of Anthropology* 19 (1990): 59–88.

Brown, Mary Ellen. *Burns and Tradition*. London: Macmillan; Urbana: University of Illinois Press, 1984.

Brown, Mary Ellen (Lewis). "The Study of Folklore in Literature: An Expanded View." *Southern Folklore Quarterly* 40 (1976): 343–351.

Bryan, W. F., and Germaine Dempster, eds. *Sources and Analogues of Chaucer's Canterbury Tales*. Chicago: University of Chicago Press, 1941.

Chadwick, H. Munro, and N. Kershaw Chadwick. *The Growth of Literature*. 3 vols. Cambridge: Cambridge University Press, 1968.

Coffin, Tristram P. "Another Sunset, Another Kiss." *Southern Folklore Quarterly* 38 (1964): 95–102.

Degh, Linda, and Andrew Vazsonyi. "The Crack on the Red Goblet, or Truth and Modern Legend." In *Folklore in the Modern World*, ed. Richard M. Dorson, pp. 253–272. The Hague: Mouton, 1978.

Dolby (Stahl), Sandra. *Literary Folkloristics and the Personal Narrative*. Bloomington: Indiana University Press, 1989.

Dorson, Richard M. *The British Folklorists*. Chicago: University of Chicago Press, 1968.

———. "The Identification of Folklore in American Literature." *Journal of American Folklore* 70 (1957): 1–8.

Dundes, Allan. "The Study of Folklore in Literature and Culture." *Journal of American Folklore* 78 (1965): 136–142.

———. "Texture, Text, and Context." *Southern Folklore Quarterly* 28 (1964): 251–265.

Foley, John Miles. *Oral-Formulaic Theory and Research: An Introduction and Annotated Bibliography*. New York: Garland, 1985.

Georges, Robert, and Michael Owen Jones. *Folkloristics: An Introduction*. Bloomington: Indiana University Press, 1995: Introduction.

Grobman, Neil. "A Schema for the Study of the Sources and Literary Simulations of Folklore Phenomena." *Southern Folklore Quarterly* 43 (1979): 17–37.

Hawthorne, Nathaniel. *Young Goodman Brown and Other Tales*. Ed. and intro. Brian Harding. New York: Oxford University Press, 1987.

Hoffman, Daniel G. *Form and Fable in American Fiction*. New York: Oxford University Press, 1961.

Hurston, Zora Neale. *Novels and Stories*. New York: Library of America, 1995.

Hymes, Dell. "Folklore's Nature and the Sun's Myth." *Journal of American Folklore* 88 (1975): 345–369.

Jones, Steven Swann. *Folklore and Literature in the United States: An Annotated Bibliography of Studies of Folklore in American Literature*. New York: Garland, 1984.

Lindahl, Carl. "Bakhtin's Carnival Laughter and the Cajun Country Mardi Gras." *Folklore* 107 (1996): 57–70.

———. *Earnest Games: Folkloric Patterns in the Canterbury Tales*. Bloomington: Indiana University Press, 1987.

Lord, Albert. *The Singer of Tales*. New York: Atheneum, 1965.

Luthi, Max. *Once upon a Time: On the Nature of Fairy Tales*. Trans. Lee Chadeqyne and Paul Gottwald, intro. Francis Lee Utley. New York: F. Ungar, 1970.

Motherwell, William. MS Robertson 28 (1210). Glasgow University Library.

Olrik, Axel. "Epic Laws of Folklore." In *The Study of Folklore*, ed. Allan Dundes. Englewood Cliffs, N.J.: Prentice-Hall, 1965.

Olson, Charles. "Projective Verse." In *Selected Writings of Charles Olson*, ed. and intro. Robert Creeley, pp. 15–26. New York: New Directions, 1966.

Ong, Walter. "Oral Residue in Tudor Prose Style." *Publications of the Modern Language Association of America* 80 (1965): 145–154.

———. *The Presence of the Word: Some Prolegomena for Cultural and Religious History*. New Haven, Conn.: Yale University Press, 1967.

Propp, Vladimir. *Morphology of the Folktale*. Trans. Lawrence Scott. Bloomington: Indiana University Press, 1968 (1958).

Rabelais, François. *The Complete Works of François Rabelais*. Trans. Donald M. Frame. Berkeley: University of California Press, 1991.

Rosenberg, Bruce. *Folklore and Literature: Rival Siblings*. Knoxville: University of Tennessee Press, 1991.

Scott, Sir Walter. *The Heart of Midlothian*. Ed. Claire Lamont. New York: Oxford University Press, 1982.

Stewart, Susan. *Nonsense: Aspects of Intertextuality in Folklore and Literature*. Baltimore: Johns Hopkins University Press, 1979.

Thompson, Stith. *Motif Index of Folk Literature*. 6 vols. Rev. ed. Bloomington: Indiana University Press, 1955–1958.

Toelken, Barre. "The 'Pretty Language' of Yellowman: Genre, Mode, and Texture in Navaho Coyote Narratives." In *Folklore Genres*, ed. Dan Ben Amos, pp. 145–170. Austin: University of Texas Press, 1976.

Tutuola, Amos. *The Palm-Wine Drinkard*. New York: Grove Press, 1994 (1952).

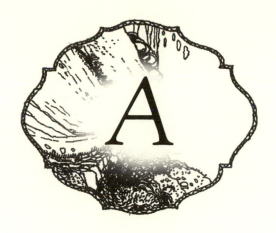

Aarne, Antti (1867–1925)

The name of the Finnish folklorist and folktale researcher Antti Aarne is known everywhere in the world because of the type-index of folktales he compiled in 1910. The basic materials of the catalog were the great Finnish folktale collections, but Aarne also used the Grimm brothers' publications and the collections of Svend Grundtvig in Denmark. Working in collaboration with Aarne were his teacher Kaarle Krohn from Finland, Johannes Bolte from Germany, Axel Olrik from Denmark, and Carl von Sydow from Sweden. In 1911, Aarne published a catalog of Finnish folktale variants arranged according to the new system. In the type-index, the folktales are divided into four main categories—animal tales, ordinary tales, jokes and anecdotes, and formula tales—and each folktale type is given its own number. Stith Thompson, an American, later expanded the catalog twice, each time revising it to include a broader range of material.

Aarne also compiled type- and variant-catalogs of Finnish etiological legends and imitations of nature sounds. Following his own type-system, he analyzed the tales of five great folktale collections and published a catalog of them. He also made a catalog of Estonian collections, including the legends. Legends were likewise included in Aarne's amplified listing of Finnish collections in 1920. Thus, Aarne was a pioneer in the cataloging of legends, although his catalogs, built upon too meager a corpus, have not received as much international attention as his folktale index.

As a scholar, Aarne made known the so-called historic-geographic method developed by his teacher Kaarle Krohn by publishing *Leitfaden der vergleichenden Märchenforschung* (1913), which was the first theoretical presentation of the method. In that textbook,

Aarne defined his own standpoint concerning some basic problems of folktale study, such as the origin and distribution of folktales, and gave practical advice concerning collecting and arranging materials.

In his own research, Aarne followed the historic-geographic method rigorously. Almost all of his studies are monographs on single folktale types. Aarne's conclusions concerning, for example, age, original form, or wanderings of tales seem limited in the eyes of modern researchers, yet his monographs give us significant insight into the destiny and development of the individual types.

Pirkko-Liisa Rausmaa

See also Historic-Geographic Method; Krohn, Leopold Kaarle; Sydow, Carl Wilhelm von; Tale-Type; Thompson, Stith

✳✳✳✳✳✳✳✳✳✳✳✳✳✳✳✳✳

References

Aarne, Antti. *Finnische Märchenvarianten: Verzeichnis der bis 1908 gesammelten Aufzeichnungen*. Hamina, Finland: Academia Scientiarum Fennica, 1911.

———. *Leitfaden der vergleichenden Märchenforschung*. Folklore Fellows Communication no. 113. Hamina, Finland: Academia Scientiarum Fennica, 1913.

———. *Der Mann aus dem Paradiese in der Literatur und in Volksmunde*. Folklore Fellows Communication no. 22. Hamina, Finland: Academia Scientiarum Fennica, 1915.

———. *Verzeichnis der Märchentypen*. Folklore Fellows Communication no. 3. Helsinki: Academia Scientiarum Fennica, 1910.

ACHEBE, CHINUA (1930–)

An African writer born in Ogidi, southeastern Nigeria, Chinua Achebe was the son of an Igbo Christian convert who taught in the Church Mission Society. Achebe graduated from University College in Ibadan, Nigeria, in 1953 and then studied in London in 1956. For several years, he worked for the Nigerian Broadcasting Corporation before turning his attention to teaching and writing. Known mostly for his novels, Achebe has also published collections of poems, essays, children's stories, and short stories.

Achebe's 1958 novel *Things Fall Apart* and subsequent novels like *Arrow of God* (1964) and *Anthills of the Savannah* (1987) have caught the attention of outsiders for the insider's view they offer of

Igbo life and culture, both past and present, in transition, in contact with colonial forces, and as part of a struggling independent country. The novels provide a panoramic view of material and verbal art within a fictive context: foodways and rituals; festivals like the Feast of the Pumpkin Leaves and the Feast of the New Yam; beliefs and seasonal patterns; and examples of code switching, costume, oratory, riddles, legends, folktales, and proverbs. On the one hand, the examples of traditional culture illustrate the richness of the Igbo folklore, and on the other, they are deeply embedded in the fictive world Achebe creates by serving not only as the milieu for the events but also as mechanisms for character development and plot motivation.

The ethnographic detail of the novels has stimulated studies of his use of several genres, most particularly proverbs, which, Achebe says, "enable the speaker to give universal status to a special and particular incident and they are used to soften the harshness of words and make them more palatable. They are called in Igbo 'the palm oil with which words are eaten'" (Achebe 1964, p. viii). Metaphorically intense, the proverbs almost demand recognition even without their cultural context: "The fly that has no one to advise it follows the corpse into the grave"; "A disease that has never been seen before cannot be cured with everyday herbs"; "The man who brings ant-infested faggots into his hut should not grumble when lizards begin to pay him a visit."

Achebe's fictive depiction of Igbo history and culture combats any contrary notions that Africa had no culture before contact: "African peoples did not hear of culture for the first time from Europeans; ... their societies were not mindless but frequently had a philosophy of great depth and value and beauty, ... they had poetry and, above all, they had dignity. It is this dignity that many African peoples all but lost in the colonial period, and it is this that they must now regain. The writer's duty is to help them regain it by showing them in human terms what happened to them, what they lost" (Achebe 1964, p. 157). Himself both a bearer of the cultural tradition and a recorder of it, Achebe consciously sees himself as a storyteller—one with memory of the past—but also as a controversial voice calling on his people to regain their culture. The storyteller is a recorder but also a threat, calling attention to dysfunctional, destructive patterns of behavior because of traditions denied. Achebe then is an activist and through his novels and other literary forms deals with what he perceives to be very real cultural issues: the abuse of power and the evils and legacy of colonialism, which denied African reality and did not prepare Africans for life after colonialism.

His primary audience is African, those whose stories he tells. And through the shared culture he fictively preserves—like the richly embedded proverbs—he tells a story that calls attention to things that have gone wrong, things that need to be changed. The role of the storyteller, his role, is to educate or reeducate, to nudge, to cajole—both to reveal problem areas he perceives and to call attention to the redemptive power of aspects of the traditional culture and its worldview. Folklore in Achebe's fictive works serves a very powerful role: as a reminder of identity, as a call to identity, and as a basis for a revitalized nation. Achebe takes art very seriously, both his own craft as a writer and the art of the Igbo.

Mary Ellen Brown

See also Festival; *Märchen*; Proverbs

✳✳✳✳✳✳✳✳✳✳✳✳✳✳✳✳✳

References

Achebe, Chinua. "Foreword." In *A Selection of African Prose*, vol. 1, comp. Wilfred Howell Whiteley. Oxford: Clarendon Press, 1964.

———. "The Role of the Writer in a New Nation." *Nigeria Magazine* 81 (1964): 157–160.

Lewis, Mary Ellen B. "Beyond Content in the Analysis of Folklore in Literature: Chinua Achebe's *Arrow of God*." *Research in African Literatures* 7 (1976): 44–52.

Lindfors, Bernth. *Folklore in Nigerian Literature*. New York: Africana, 1973.

Shelton, Austin J. "The 'Palm-Oil' of Language Proverbs in Chinua Achebe's Novels." *Modern Language Quarterly* 30 (1969): 86–111.

Aesop's fables

Aesop's fables are brief narratives, usually featuring animals (and/or inanimate objects) as actors, attributed to one Aesop, himself a legendary figure, who lived perhaps as early as the sixth century B.C.E. Seemingly told to point out the follies and weaknesses of people, many versions have a punch line or moral in the narrative that is explicitly formulated at the end: "A hungry fox saw some grapes hanging from a vine in a tree and, although he was eager to reach them, was unable to do so. As he went away, he said to himself, 'They're sour grapes.' So it is with men, too. Some who can't do what they want because of their own inability blame it on circumstances." This situation-incident-result pattern recurs frequently in the little sketches, or fables, which were first referred to in the eighth century B.C.E. by the Greek poet Hesiod as stories teaching a lesson.

Similar materials appear in Sumerian cuneiform and in the Indian Hitopadesa and *Panchatantra* and are known in China—perhaps adapted from India by Buddhists for religious purposes—and Japan, but the materials generally referred to as Aesop's fables, written down in the fourth century B.C.E., were ascribed to Aesop in the fifth century B.C.E. by Aristophanes, Plato, and Aristotle. The identity of Aesop himself is murky: there are several theories, and some commentators question his historicity altogether, suggesting that the name Aesop was invented for stories dealing with and centering on beasts with a moral of greater import than the brief narrative attached; these commentators suggest that the fables themselves reflect the Greek absorption with self-examination, seeing the self as pointedly revealed in animal behavior.

Nonetheless, there are accounts of Aesop's life. Supposedly born a slave with a rather grotesque body—dwarfish, with a pot-belly, bandy legs, and short arms—he was said to have been dumb as well until the goddess Isis gave him the power of speech in return for kindnesses he showed a priestess. Thereafter, his wit and ingenuity enabled him to outwit others and solve problems that puzzled even his philosopher/owner, Xanthus, who freed him in return for his perspicacity. Sometime later, Aesop effectively persuaded the Lydian king Croesus not to attack the Greek island of Samos—reputed to have been Aesop's own place of origin—and returned home a hero. He raised a shrine to his patronesses, the Muses and Mnemosyne, alas slighting Apollo, who later punished Aesop in Delphi, where he died.

The materials, recorded in various literary forms, have had—and continue to have—a rich and varied life. Recorded in Latin by the Roman fabulist Phaedrus in the first century C.E., the fables were then imbued with satire and invective. Later Romans used them to practice their oratory. Rhymed versions replaced the prose of the Greek, and through the years there were countless reworkings by such personages as the twelfth-century French poet Marie de France, the fifteenth-century Scottish poet Robert Henryson, and the seventeenth-century French poet Jean de La Fontaine, which suggests the opacity of the skeletal materials and their susceptibility to multiple retellings with their own meanings and functions: La Fontaine, for example, used them to satirize the French court and the bourgeoisie.

Animals as characters who behave in generic human fashion offer scope for continuing use, and the narrative materials have been re-presented and embedded in different historical epochs to point out and identify particular human failings. In a general way, too, the fables of Aesop have achieved a paradigmatic, allusive significance: references to the hare and the tortoise, the boy who cried wolf, or the goose that laid the golden egg are immediately recognized by most people who have ever been introduced to the sagacity and wisdom of this kind of fluid material. Both literary and individual allusions to Aesop's fables keep the material alive.

Mary Ellen Brown

See also Children's Literature; *Fabliau; Panchatantra*

✳✳✳✳✳✳✳✳✳✳✳✳✳✳✳✳✳✳

References

Daly, Lloyd William, ed. *Aesop without Morals: The Famous Fables and a Life of Aesop.* New York: T. Yoseloff, 1961.

Smith, M. Ellwood. "Aesop, a Decayed Celebrity." *Publications of the Modern Language Association* 46 (1931): 225–236.

Thompson, Stith. *The Folktale.* New York: Holt, Rinehart and Winston, 1946.

Akhmatova, Anna (1889–1966)

Anna Akhmatova is numbered among the half-dozen or so truly outstanding poets of the twentieth century, a century that has included one of the great ages of Russian poetry. Two of the Russian poets are women—Akhmatova and Marina Tsvestaeva—and both draw on the unusually rich and comparatively well-preserved Russian folk tradition. In Akhmatova's case, there are easily recognizable connections with a wide range of folk genres—the woman's lyric song in particular, but also cradle songs, songs for the road, table songs, *chastushki*, the folktale, the Pushkinian literary version of the folktale, the lament, the incantation, and so on. The relation to the folk source may be quite close or really quite distant. She sometimes borrows more or less liberally from the tradition but transmutes the material in her own particular way. Indeed, the folk reference may be very slight, although the interpretation of the entire poem may hinge on it—as can be seen in one of the poems cited below.

There is a distinct resonance in theme between the first six volumes of Akhmatova's poetry, which established her reputation, and the traditional content of the *pesenka* ("lyric song"), especially the woman's love song. The perception of love in both instances is as something predominantly sad, star-crossed, ill-fated, tragic. Marriage is a trap; the husband is unloved, often cruel; the beloved abandons—or is taken away from—the woman. All this is part of the thematics called *zhenskaia dolia* ("a woman's lot"). The *pesenka* covers a wide range of themes—planting, spinning, calendrical, special occasion songs, etc.—but it is the love songs that are the most numerous and of particular interest with regard to Anna Akhmatova. In general, she keeps her thematic range deliberately narrow—mostly love themes and folk themes that make up a part of a matrix of references to Russian cultural and historical sources that include Russian orthodoxy, Kievan and Muscovite Russia, Old Russia assumptions, Russia's great historical cities, the way of life on the estate, and "the old patriarchal way of life."

The following example derives its color from that matrix; moreover, one would be hard put to interpret it without reference to the traditional folk song:

> Ever Since Agrafena-Kupal'nitsa's Day,
> He's kept my raspberry-colored kerchief.
> He is quiet, and rejoices like King David.
> In his frosty cell, the walls are white,
> And no one talks with him.
> I will go and stand on the threshold,
> And say, "Give me back my kerchief."

The theme of abandonment after seduction is clear only in relation to the women's folk lyric. St. Agrafena's (Agrippina's) Day in the Eastern Church calendar is the day before the Feast of St. John the Baptist (called by the folk Ivan or Vanka Kupalo, whence the "Kupal'nitsa" attached to St. Agrippina's name). Thus, the time is the Eve of St. John, or Midsummer's Eve, and the association is with solstice rites and seduction. The raspberry-colored kerchief is a compounded symbol of virginity: the berry, of course, and the kerchief here replaces the red ribbon woven into the plait—it is removed, and the hair is let loose. Now it is winter: the lover is distant, haughty, cold—and inaccessible, as the white walls of a monk's cell suggest (here, the adjective "white" is in the form of a false archaism that the folk-song tradition has preserved). The poem's pathos lies in the abandoned girl's plea for what she has lost.

A more obvious example is the following poem, which Akhmatova constructs against the background of typical songs. She borrows the color, images, and symbols but characteristically ignores the rigidly fixed rules of the genre. She calls this poem simply *pesenka* ("lyric folk song"), but the patterns are not followed, or only partly so.

> At sunrise,
> I sing of love;
> On my knees in the kitchen garden
> I'm pulling pigweed.
> I pull it up and throw it aside—
> May it forgive me.
> I see a barefoot girl
> Weeping at the wattle fence.
> Frightful to me are the voices of woe
> Because of their ringing wails;
> Stronger and stronger is the warm smell
> Of the dead pigweed.
> A stone instead of bread
> Will be my cruel reward.
> Above me is only the sky
> And with me your voice.

The association with the "green garden/vineyard" of the folk lyric is clear, as is the suggestion of the metaphorical parallelism of the drying plant and the shriveling heart—but the directness of the last stanza and the whole construction of the poem are unlike the folk song. Rather, the person of the poem conveys her grief by reference to the weeping girl and the folk-song conventions.

The folk song, and in general oral literature, are not the only sources in the folk tradition that Akhmatova uses. An important category of images in her poetry, one that is connected with the Old Russia thematic matrix, has to do with peasant superstition and with the peculiar phenomenon of *dvoeverie* ("double belief"), that is, belief in both religion and superstition. Although references to the spirit world exist in the Western literary tradition (especially in later, longer works), more typical, and certainly statistically so, are references to specifically Russian folk beliefs. Fortune-telling, amulets, curses from crumbling books, minor devils, sorcery, ghosts, talismans, prophecy, dowsing, good luck charms, palmistry, clairvoyance, spells, witchcraft, *ruskali*, and house sprites all lend a very special cachet to Akhmatova's brief, spare lyrics. It should be said that compilations out of context such as this one can be misleading: Akhmatova uses such images carefully and not too frequently. Nevertheless, they can be effective in invoking the folk culture with a richness of association that serves the characteristically laconic poet well.

Sam Driver

See also Folktale; *Rusalka*; Russian Folk Lyric Song; Women

✳✳✳✳✳✳✳✳✳✳✳✳✳✳✳✳✳✳

References

Akhmatova, Anna. *My Half Century: Selected Prose*. Ed. Ronald Meyer. Ann Arbor, Mich.: Ardis, 1992.

Amert, Susan. *In a Shattered Mirror: The Later Poetry of Anna Akhmatova*. Palo Alto: Stanford University Press, 1992.

Driver, Sam. *Anna Akhmatova*. New York: Twayne Publishers, 1972.

Ketchian, Sonia. *The Poetry of Anna Akhmatova: A Conquest of Space and Time*. Munich: Sagner, 1986.

Reeder, Roberta. *Anna Akhmatova, Poet and Prophet*. New York: St. Martin's Press, 1994.

ANAYA, RUDOLFO ALFONSO (1937–)

Born in Pastura, a small village on the high plains of eastern New Mexico, Anaya has become a highly regarded Chicano novelist and short-story writer. His awards include fellowships from the National Endowment for the Arts and the W. K. Kellogg Foundation as well as an invitation to read at the White House in a Salute to American Poets and Writers. He is currently professor of English and creative writing at the University of New Mexico.

A devoted folklorist of the indigenous cultures of Mexico and New Mexico, Anaya is recognized as a narrator because of his trilogy *Bless Me, Ultima* (1972); *Heart of Aztlán* (1976); and *Tortuga* (1979), novels that draw heavily on his childhood on the plains.

He comments: "It's a harsh environment. I remember most that sense of landscape which is bleak, empty, desolate, across which the wind blows and makes music" (Bruce-Novoa 1980, p. 184). This allure of primal natural forces is visible in characters at various stages of their spiritual development; they find in earth-related beliefs a symbolic understanding of the human psyche.

In *Bless Me, Ultima,* Anaya demonstrates his interest in ritualistic narrations as characters engage in folk religious practices that increase their own knowledge of the inner self. This is the case of the protagonist Antonio Márez, a young man who inadvertently develops his own rite of manhood, aided by an old *curandera* ("herb healer"). The process is lengthy and painful. Anaya presents it through surrealist descriptions of rural Chicano life, transcending time and place by connecting contemporary Chicano culture to its historical Spanish and Native American roots.

Heart of Aztlán follows the vicissitudes of a rural family that sells its land and moves to Barelas, a Chicano ghetto in Albuquerque, New Mexico. Anaya's political commentary on the Chicanos' underprivileged condition is clear, as he appropriates the mythological concept of Aztlán, the Chicano prototype of a paradise. For the Chicano activist of the 1960s, utopian Aztlán is the southwestern territory lost to the United States in the 1848 Treaty of Guadalupe Hidalgo. In *Heart of Aztlán*, it takes on a new dimension. Although Aztlán is physically and symbolically represented by rural locales, in obvious opposition to the urban and Americanized milieu, characters survive city life aided by their memories of the old life. When the experiential recollection is lost or nonexistent, as in the case of the city-born generation, an elder shaman provides a bridge to their collective memory.

The mythic journey associated with a rite of passage is also *Tortuga's* major thematic approach. The story places Tortuga, a 16-year-old mountain boy, in a city hospital where he undergoes treatment for his paralysis, which includes a body cast that makes him resemble a turtle, the reason for his nickname. His uprooting from his natural element creates psychological disruptions that endanger his recuperation. Fortunately, a deaf patient mysteriously communicates with Tortuga and helps him to recover.

Anaya explores indigenous Mexican lore by placing Chicano characters in contact with ancient philosophical thoughts that give them the strength to survive the harsh environment of urban life in the United States. The shamanistic characters are necessary connectors to ancient values of earth-based practices, and they are constant reminders of the human relationship to nature in the face of the impersonality of technological advances.

Rafael Ocasio

See also Latino and Chicano Folklore and Literature; Ritual

✳✳✳✳✳✳✳✳✳✳✳✳✳✳✳✳✳

References

Bruce-Novoa, Juan. "Rudolfo A. Anaya." In *Chicago Authors: Inquiry by Interview*, pp. 182–202. Austin: University of Texas Press, 1980.

Johnson, David, and David Apodaca. "Myth and the Writer: A Conversation with Rudolfo Anaya." *New America* 3:3 (1979): 76–85.

Martínez, Julio A., and Francisco A. Lomelí, eds. "Anaya, Rudolfo Alfonso." In *Chicano Literature: A Reference Guide*, pp. 34–51. Westport, Conn.: Greenwood Press, 1985.

Mitchell, Carol. "Rudolfo Anaya's *Bless Me, Ultima*: Folk Culture in Literature." *Critique* 22:1 (1980): 55–64.

ANDERSEN, HANS CHRISTIAN (1805–1875)

An accomplished writer in several genres, Hans Christian Andersen's fame today rests almost completely on his fairy tales, many of which have been translated into over 100 languages and are among the most often anthologized and retold stories for children.

Born in Odense, Denmark, the only child of a poor shoemaker and his wife, Andersen later fabricated a seemingly happy childhood. He had little formal schooling, but his father often read to him from such works as Jean de La Fontaine's fables, *The Arabian Nights*, and the dramas of the Danish playwright Holberg. From his mother, Andersen heard many folktales that he later transformed using his vivid imagination.

Despite suggestions that he should learn a trade, Andersen pursued a literary career, first as an actor and a playwright and later as a poet and novelist. His international fame was secured in 1835 when he published *Fairy Tales Told for Children*. He eventually published 156 stories between 1835 and 1872, and of that number, Andersen claimed that only 9 were retellings of tales he had heard as a child: "The Tinder Box," "Little Klaus," "The Princess and the Pea," "The Traveling Companion," "The Wild Swans," "The Garden of Eden,"

"The Swineherd," "Simple Simon," and "What Father Does Is Always Right." The rest were his own invention, although some can be identified as having sources in other works: "The Emperor's New Clothes" derives from an old Spanish story; "The Rose Elf," from an old Italian folk song; "The Flying Trunk" obviously borrows its main motif from *The Arabian Nights*; and "The Naughty Boy" is loosely based on a short poem by the Greek classical poet Anacreon. In a letter to a friend in 1843, Andersen noted that the first stories he wrote were "mostly old ones I had heard as a child and that I usually retold and recreated in my own fashion [in oral storytelling sessions]" (Grønbech 1980, p. 91).

While there is little evidence that Andersen enjoyed telling stories to children, his early training in the theater may have enabled him to dramatize his tales vividly, including appropriate language and gestures. Whatever its origins, he was able to develop a distinctive narrative voice and format for his written tales.

Andersen's genius lies in his successful blending of the genre of oral folktale with the literary conventions of his day—appealing, as he did so, to two audience levels: children, to whom the language and the settings were suited, and educated adults, to whom both the literary stylistic conventions and the underlying messages were aimed.

Andersen's fairy tales have often suffered at the hands of his many retellers. The original Danish stories are hard to translate since Andersen used a colloquial style replete with Danish idioms and untranslatable puns. Sometimes deplored for a maudlin sentimentality that is as much the fault of his Victorian rewriters as it is inherent in the originals, Hans Christian Andersen is nevertheless perennially popular. He is generally credited with opening the doorway to the explosion of fairy tale literature that occurred in the latter half of the nineteenth century.

Martha Hixon

See also Fable; *Märchen*; Performance

✳✳✳✳✳✳✳✳✳✳✳✳✳✳✳✳✳

References

Andersen, Hans Christian. *Hans Christian Andersen: The Complete Fairy Tales and Stories*. Ed. Erik Christian Haugaard. Garden City, N.Y.: Doubleday, 1974.

Bresdorf, Elias. *Hans Christian Andersen: The Story of His Life and Work*. New York: Noonday, 1975.

Grønbech, Bo. *Hans Christian Andersen*. Twayne World Authors Series. Boston: G. K. Hall, 1980.

ANDERSON, WALTER (1885–1962)

Walter Anderson was one of the greatest practitioners and advocates of the historic-geographic method of folklore study. He studied classical philology in Kazan, Tatarstan, where he subsequently became an instructor of Western European literature. Between World War I and World War II, he taught at the University of Tartu in Estonia; later, he was a visiting professor at the University of Kiel in Germany until his retirement in 1953. Early in his career, he traveled extensively to meet distinguished European folklore scholars. He wrote about many genres of folklore as well as about folklore theory.

Anderson's doctoral dissertation was expanded into the well-regarded work, *Kaiser und Abt* [Emperor and abbot (1923)]. Its subject, a tightly knit tale with three characters, three wisdom questions, and characteristic deception, was ideally suited to the motif analysis that a historic-geographic study requires. In this work, Anderson introduced several theoretical ideas. The most controversial was the law of self-correction, the idea that a tale maintains its established form because narrators hear the same story several times, often from different sources. Those who have heard more than one form of a tale can choose the elements they prefer. This explains how, for example, in a text of "Emperor and Abbot" the characters may have come from one source and the wisdom questions from another so that it is impossible to draw neat stemmas showing the derivation of each variant.

Anderson believed that the law of self-correction explained the extraordinary stability of folktales, and he formulated and carried out classroom experiments to prove this point. In all of the experiments, however, the narrative deteriorated. Thus, these experiments could not possibly show what circumstances are necessary for the *successful* transmission of a folktale.

Another of his innovations was the notion of the special redaction, a derived form of a tale that has been important for the tale's dissemination and which may coexist with older forms of the tale. This observation led to the concept of the *normalform*, a form of a tale that was typical and influential but not, in all likelihood, original.

Anderson's ideas regarding folktale stability were forged in opposition to those of folklorist Albert Wesselski, who maintained that narrative traditions were disseminated through written versions and that oral tradition was not an important factor. It is unfortunate that both of these formidable scholars were so cantankerous, because the notoriety of the conflict between them has obscured the fact that both men believed that the dissemination of traditional narratives is a central problem of literary and cultural history. Decades after Anderson's death, a division between scholars who believe that literary sources are sufficient for characterizing the nature of early folktales and others who insist that the modern oral tradition provides important evidence for this subject is still apparent.

Christine Goldberg

See also Historic-Geographic Method; Motif

✻✻✻✻✻✻✻✻✻✻✻✻✻✻✻✻✻

References

Dégh, Linda, and Andrew Vázsonyi. "The Hypothesis of Multi-Conduit Transmission in Folklore." In *Folklore Performance and Communication*, ed. Dan Ben-Amos and Kenneth S. Goldstein, pp. 207–252. The Hague: Mouton, 1975.

Glade, Dieter. "Zum Anderson'schen Gesetz der Selbstberichtigung." *Fabula* 8 (1966): 224–236.

Hoppál, Mihály. "Narration and Memory." *Fabula* 22 (1981): 281–289.

Levin, Isidor. "Walter Anderson." *Deutsches Jahrbuch für Volkskunde* 9 (1963): 293–311.

Ranke, Kurt. "Walter Anderson (1885–1962)." *Fabula* 5:3 (1962): (pages unnumbered, follows p. 183).

ANGELOU, MAYA (1928–)

An American autobiographer, poet, dramatist, and performer, Maya Angelou is regarded as one of the foremost voices of African-American literature. In addition to five volumes of autobiography, Angelou's work includes seven volumes of poetry and a number of plays, screenplays, television scripts, and recordings. The strength of Angelou's most powerful work lies in her skillful use of folk idiom to articulate an African-American woman's struggle for liberation and belonging.

The first of Angelou's five-volume autobiographical series, *I Know Why the Caged Bird Sings* (1969), describes her childhood and adolescence in Stamps, Arkansas, and, briefly, in California. In this work, Angelou evokes the folk culture of the rural South and contrasts that culture with city life in urban black enclaves in St. Louis in the 1930s and Oakland and San Francisco in the early 1940s.

African-American poet Maya Angelou's work often builds on oral folk tradition.

Although her eloquent treatment of the customs, stories, and linguistic rhythms of the rural, black southern community of her youth is the most richly folkloric element of this work, and in fact of any of her subsequent work, later sections of the volume also effectively convey the cadences of languages and the stream of events of the lives of black city folk.

In the four subsequent volumes, Angelou's personal odyssey continues: coping with young motherhood on the social fringes of black society in Los Angeles (*Gather Together in My Name* [1974]); struggling with the demands of the white world in San Francisco and performing in Europe (*Singin' and Swingin' and Gettin' Merry Like Christmas*); working as a singer, dancer, and civil rights activist in New York City (*Heart of a Woman* [1981]); and, finally, exploring her African roots in Ghana (*All God's Children Need Traveling Shoes* [1986]).

Critics who highly praised her first volume have generally been less enthusiastic about the subsequent ones, complaining in particular that her descriptions of relationships with men, including a brief excursion into prostitution, lack self-reflection and fail to generate reader empathy. But Angelou's mode of storytelling reflects a kind of unsparing, clear-eyed examination that, at the same time, refuses judgment. This self-acceptance and absence of confessional self-criticism are characteristic of literature in the slave narrative tradition—a literature of survival and self-assertion in the face of efforts to suppress, silence, and represent.

A more valid criticism notes the diminishing vigor and resonance of folk idiom in each succeeding autobiographical installment. By the last volume, the retelling of an African-American folktale as Angelou's contribution in a tense, multinational exchange of stories in Berlin seems flat and contrived: the scene is uncomfortably close to a parody of urban black teenagers in the United States playing "the dozens," a form of ritual insult.

Angelou's dozen volumes of poetry (one of which, *On the Pulse of Morning* [1993], contains the text of her reading at the 1993 presidential inauguration) are enormously popular, but they, too, have received mixed reviews. Some critics dismiss their strongly rhythmic phrasing and persistent rhyme as banal, but these elements reflect the roots of Angelou's work in a highly oral African-American folk tradition. Her best poems are performance-oriented: "Times-Square-Shoeshine-Composition" and "The Calling of Names" (*Just Give Me a Cool Drink of Water 'Fore I Diiie*), for example, might be spoken aloud, or shouted, to powerful effect. In her most effective work, Angelou can be an exhorter in the tradition of Sojourner Truth.

Taken as a whole, Angelou's diverse body of written work and performance enlarges a personal narrative to encompass the rich and complex experience of African America.

Joanne Pope Melish

See also Folktale; Storytelling

✳✳✳✳✳✳✳✳✳✳✳✳✳✳✳✳✳

References

Angelou, Maya. *The Complete Collected Poems of Maya Angelou*. New York: Random House, 1994.

Essick, Kathy Mae. "The Poetry of Maya Angelou: A Study of the Blues Matrix as Force and Code." Ph.D. dissertation, Indiana University, 1994.

Estes-Hicks, Onita. "The Way We Were: Precious Memories of the Black Segregated South." *African-American Review* 27 (1993): 9–18.

McPherson, Dolly A. *Order out of Chaos: The Autobiographical Works of Maya Angelou*. New York: Peter Lang, 1990.

ANZALDÚA, GLORIA (1942–)

Chicana lesbian, woman of color, essayist, novelist, and poet, Gloria Anzaldúa (along with Cherríe Moraga) published *This Bridge Called My Back: Writings by Radical Women of Color* (1981), a collection of essays and testimonies that criticize the middle-class and racist underpinnings of the women's movement in the United States.

In *Borderlands/La Frontera: The New Mestiza Writes* (1987),

Anzaldúa posits "the borderlands" as a new space from which to understand the in-between position of Mexican Americans and other minorities. The text itself is a generic hybrid: part U.S., Mexican, and borderland folklore, myth, and revisionist history; part autobiography; part collection of poems and compilation of border corridos. It is a bilingual work made readable for monolingual English speakers because Anzaldúa translates the Spanish she uses. *Borderlands* has played a crucial role in the understanding of the Latino experience in the United States, among the general public and the academic community as well, initiating the inclusion of Latino literature into the literary canon.

Anzaldúa's latest work to date, *Making Face, Making Soul: Haciendo Caras; Creative and Critical Perspectives by Women of Color,* is, like *This Bridge Called My Back,* a compilation of the testimonial, critical, and fictional writings of women of color. Anzaldúa has also written a bilingual children's book, *Friends from the Other Side/Amigos del Otro Lado* (1993).

Silvia Spitta

See also Moraga, Cherríe

✳✳✳✳✳✳✳✳✳✳✳✳✳✳✳✳✳

References

Calderón, Héctor, and José David Salvidar, eds. *Criticism in the Borderlands: Studies of Chicano Literature, Culture, and Ideology.* Durham, N.C.: Duke University Press, 1991.

Saldívar, José David. *The Dialectics of Our America: Genealogy, Cultural Critique, and Literary History.* Durham, N.C.: Duke University Press, 1991.

Spitta, Silvia. *Between Two Waters: Narratives of Transculturation in Latin America.* Houston: Rice University Press, 1993.

Apuleius (c. 125–180 c.e.)

Apuleius, a second-century author and philosopher, is best known for writing the *Metamorphoses*, or the *Golden Ass* as the work is more commonly called. Apuleius was born in the mid-120s C.E. in Madaura, a Roman colony in Africa, and studied at Carthage, Athens, and Rome. There are many gaps in what is known about his life, and his own works are the primary source of information about him. Through his writings, as Elizabeth Haight points out, he appears in multiple guises—as novelist, lawyer, philosopher—and adapts styles appropriate to those different roles. According to his own description, he studied a variety of subjects including philosophy, literature, dialectic, rhetoric, poetry, geometry, and music. He became so famous as a writer and lecturer that he was honored at Carthage with a public statue. The date and place of his death are unknown.

Apuleius's *Apologia* is one of the key sources of information about his life. In this work, Apuleius defends himself at a trial in Sabrata, the exact date of which is unknown. At the trial, Apuleius successfully fends off charges of being immoral, of having won his elderly wife, Pudentilla, by sorcery, and of marrying her in order to obtain her money. In the course of his defense, he declares that he has learned many religious mysteries, rites, and ceremonies out of religious fervor and a desire to seek truth. The mysteries Apuleius refers to probably provide the basis for his account of religious experience and rites described in the *Metamorphoses*. Many scholars believe that Apuleius's *Metamorphoses* is at least partially autobiographical, especially in the description of religious experience that is such a striking feature of the novel.

Apuleius's *Metamorphoses* is not only a crucial source of information about the mystery religions in the ancient Greek and Roman worlds but also of great importance for the history of literature and folklore because it is the literary source for one of the most beautiful stories of all time, the tale of Eros and Psyche. Although there is no literary evidence of this tale prior to Apuleius's novel, many artistic representations of Eros and Psyche date back to at least the fourth century B.C.E. Of special interest to scholars is the relationship of the Eros and Psyche tale, the centerpiece of Apuleius's novel, to the narrative about Lucius that frames the whole. Current scholars observe many links between the tale of Psyche and Lucius's story, and while there is some debate on the extent to which the Eros and Psyche tale relates to Lucius, there is general agreement that the tale serves to characterize, on a mythical level, Lucius's transformations during the course of the novel. Psyche's curiosity, trials, search for the god Eros, and deification all seem to parallel Lucius's curiosity, wanderings as an ass, and ritual divinization in the cult of Isis. In this regard, Apuleius's *Metamorphoses* provides a remarkable example of how folklore can reinforce and deepen the meaning of a literary work.

James Gollnick

See also *Golden Ass;* Myth

✳✳✳✳✳✳✳✳✳✳✳✳✳✳✳✳✳

References

Gollnick, James. *Love and the Soul: Psychological Interpretations of the Eros and Psyche Myth.* Waterloo, Ont.: Wilfrid Laurier University Press, 1992.

Haight, Elizabeth. *Apuleius and His Influence.* New York: Cooper Square Publishers, 1963.

Norwood, Frances. "The Magic Pilgrimage of Apuleius." *Phoenix* 10 (1956): 1–12.

Tatum, James. *Apuleius and the Golden Ass.* Ithaca, N.Y.: Cornell University Press, 1979.

Walsh, P. G. *Apuleius: The Golden Ass.* New York: Oxford University Press, 1994.

ARCHETYPE

Archetype is a term that is variously used in theories of folklore and literature. Since the literal meaning is "original form," the term can refer to historical, ritual, or psychological concepts. For adherents of the historic-geographic school of folklore methodology, archetype refers to the original text of a tale-type that was created in a particular place and time. This single beginning (monogenesis) generates multiple variants as the tale is told over and over again and transmitted over time and through many cultures until it appears to be universal or at least widespread. The aim of folklore research, according to this school of thought, should be to track down the history of every variant of a given narrative type in order to reconstruct a hypothetical ur-form, the original tale or the archetype.

The archetype of a mythic text may have a historical basis, as was suggested around 300 B.C.E. by the Macedonian Greek rational philosopher Euhemerus. Gods and goddesses were real people about whom mundane archetypal narratives were told and gradually exaggerated during the course of multiple retellings until they emerged in tradition as the fantastical accounts we now know as myths. In *The Hero: A Study in Tradition, Myth, and Drama* (1936), Lord Raglan offered a different perspective on the emergence of the heroic pattern. In his view, the actual history of a heroic personage becomes irrelevant and possible historical reconstruction becomes impossible over time as life-cycle rituals surrounding birth, initiation, and death create an archetypal "monomyth," a formula that dominates all heroic literature.

Although the myth-ritual concept had some impact on narrative scholarship, the psychological basis of archetype, particularly as expounded by Carl Jung, has been the most influential for literary theory. A colleague of Jung, Otto Rank, wrote *The Myth of the Birth of the Hero* (1914), which postulates a psychological basis for much the same formula that Lord Raglan later ascribed to ritual. For Jung, the hero monomyth was only one of several archetypes manifested in dreams and delusions as well as in folklore. His archetypes could be more generalized symbols—such as the sun, the self, and animus/anima—or somewhat more specific characters—such as earth mother, wise old man, and divine child. Jung postulated that the basic images of dreams and myths, these archetypes of human imagination, emerged from a collective unconscious that is inherited like genetic traits are inherited.

For some literary critics, the Jungian notion of archetype inspired an examination of literary traditions as inherently informed by myth, ritual, and folklore, and literary critic Northrop Frye saw the search for archetypes in literature as a kind of literary anthropology. Interpretation of complex works can become more coherent when seen through simpler, more primitive, more universal formulas. Mythologists such as Joseph Campbell have made extensive use of Jung's archetypes to speak of universal meanings for myths.

Even though Jung and his disciples frequently invoke folklore in discussing archetypes, folklorists have often found Jungian theories too abstract, almost mystical, and without basis in cultural contexts. Still, some literature theorists continue to find Jung's psychological theories and Campbell's application of archetype attractive constructs toward a unified theory of literature.

Kenneth A. Thigpen

See also Campbell, Joseph; Heroic Pattern; Jung, Carl Gustav; Myth; Rank, Otto; Ritual; Tale-Type

✳✳✳✳✳✳✳✳✳✳✳✳✳✳✳✳✳

References

Campbell, Joseph. *The Hero with a Thousand Faces*. New York: Meridian, 1956.

Drake, Carlos C. "Jung and His Critics." *Journal of American Folklore* 80 (1967): 321–333.

———. "Jungian Psychology and Its Use in Folklore." *Journal of American Folklore* 82 (1969): 122–131.

Jung, Carl G. *The Archetype and the Collective Unconscious*. Bollingen Series. Princeton, N.J.: Princeton University Press, 1959.

Jung, Carl G., Maria-Louise von Franz, et al. *Man and His Symbols*. New York: Dell, 1968.

Kirk, G. S. *Myth: Its Meaning and Function in Ancient and Other Cultures*. Berkeley: University of California Press, 1970.

Raglan, Lord. *The Hero: A Study in Tradition, Myth, and Drama*. London: Methuen, 1936.

Thompson, Stith. *The Folktale*. New York: Holt, Rinehart and Winston, 1946.

ARENAS, REINALDO (1942–1990)

A novelist, short-story writer, and playwright, Reinaldo Arenas became Cuba's most outspoken counterrevolutionary activist and its leading representative of the neobaroque, an experimental literary aesthetic in Latin America. Born in Holguín, Cuba, a rural eastern town, after the revolution, Arenas traveled to Havana in 1962 to start a literary career. The themes of his first short stories, published in 1965, drew upon his peasant background—natural life in mystical communication with higher spiritual forces—but in his portrayal of country life, grim poverty and desolation prevail. Boys and young adult males find themselves oppressed by the harsh environment of an oppressive society.

Such memories of childhood inspired Arenas's first novel, *Celestino antes del alba* [Before the dawn], winner of a literary prize in 1964. Government institutions criticized the novel's lack of political commitment; Arenas responded that his work was both autobiographical and imaginative, which is itself a kind of reality. *Celestino* initiated a trend in Cuban literature: fantastic descriptions of natural occurrences by means of complex, baroque linguistic constructions. Arenas's interest in folklore is evident in his imitation of Cuban rural speech patterns and in his detailed descriptions of the Cuban countryside.

Arenas's commitment to folklore appears again in *El mundo alucinante* [A hallucinated world], a novel smuggled into France and published in French in 1968. In a Mexican setting, Arenas fictionalizes the life of Servando Teresa de Mier (1773–1827), a Dominican friar who in 1794 publicly questioned the divine appearance of Mexico's patron saint, the Virgin of Guadalupe; Arenas suggested that this figure had existed in regional indigenous cults as a mother-earth goddess. This novel also was the first to show Arenas's interest in homosexual themes.

Cuban publishers censored Arenas's novels because of their homosexual characters, forcing the author to smuggle his manuscripts out of Cuba. Such was the case with *El palacio de las blanquísmas mofetas* [The palace of the whitest skunks (1990)]. In this continuation of *Celestino*, a peasant child struggles with his sexual orientation in an environment that violently rejects the homosexual. This repudiation is emphasized in *El central* [The central], written in 1970 when Arenas worked at a sugarcane mill. A poetic novel, *El central* shows a parallel between the experiences of modern Cuban homosexuals and those of colonial African slaves—both became social outcasts.

In *El central*, Arenas's attraction to history and folklore is evident in his carefully researched slave trade data: the material includes documents like those by Bartolomé de las Casas (1474–1566), the Dominican friar who advocated use of African slaves in order to protect Caribbean Indians. Further commitment to history is clear in *Arturo, la estrella más brillante* [Arturo, the most brilliant star (1984)], which is set in a fictional labor camp inspired by Cuban revolutionary penal institutions created between 1964 and 1968 to indoctrinate homosexuals accused of "improper conduct" or violations of the laws against immorality. *Arturo* presents the world of a transvestite who refuses to obey revolutionary patterns of behavior and continues his underground cross-dressing.

Exiled to the United States in 1980, Arenas became an anti-Castro spokesperson and a gay activist, and his writing continued to describe male characters of solitary disposition who struggled for societal acceptance. This is the case in *El portero* [The doorman (1989)], which was inspired by his cross-cultural experiences in New York City. Arenas committed suicide on December 7, 1990, to avoid death by AIDS, shortly after finishing *Antes que anochezca* (1992), an autobiographical account of the underground homosexual world in revolutionary Cuba.

Rafael Ocasio

See also Dialect; Latino and Chicano Folklore and Literature

✳✳✳✳✳✳✳✳✳✳✳✳✳✳✳✳✳✳

References

Foster, David William. *Gay and Lesbian Themes in Latin American Writing*. Austin: University of Texas Press, 1991.

Ocasio, Rafael, and Fiona Doloughan. "Literary Offspring: The Figure of the Child in Marcel Proust and Reinaldo Arenas." *Romance Quarterly* 41:2 (Spring 1994): 111–118.

Soto, Francisco. *Reinaldo Arenas: The Pentagonía*. Gainesville: University of Florida Press, 1994.

ARGUEDAS, JOSÉ MARÍA (1911–1969)

The Peruvian novelist, Quechua poet, translator, editor, compiler of Andean myths, ethnographer, professor of regional cultures at the University of San Marcos in Lima, professor of Quechua at the Universidad Nacional Agraria, and director of numerous institutes of Peruvian folklore, José María Arguedas devoted his ethnographic and novelistic writings to Andean cultures. In a speech "I am not acculturated" (*Yo no soy un aculturado*), Arguedas explained that the motivation for all his literary, ethnographic, and personal efforts was the desire to embody the life of the Andes as well as that of the cities, of Quechua and Spanish, of Andean agrarian communism and Western Marxism, of "animism" and Christianity. He attempted to expand the concept of "national," which had until then excluded all but a small, literate minority, to include "all the races" (*todas las sangres*) and all the heterogeneous cultures, languages, races, and bodies into that impossibility called "Peru."

As an ethnographer, Arguedas adopted the Cuban anthropologist Fernando Ortiz's theory of transculturation and argued that cultural influences do not flow unidirectionally from colonizers to colonized. New, vital, and viable configurations have arisen in Latin America out of the clash of cultures and colonial and neocolonial violence. The focus of Arguedas's ethnographic studies shifted from an early emphasis on peasants living in small, rural, and isolated Andean villages to the ever-more-complex mestizo cultures arising in the urban centers of the coast. His most important ethnographic works are *Cuentos mágico-realistas y canciones de fiestas tradicionales; Folklore del valle del Mantaro, provincias de Jauja y Concepción; Las comunidades de España y del Perú; Evolución de las comunidades indígenas; El arte popular religioso y la cultura mestiza; Formación de una cultura nacional indoamericana* (1981); and *Señores e indios: Acerca de la cultura quechua*. Arguedas also compiled, edited, transcribed, and translated Quechua stories, poems, and myths: *Canto kechwa; Mitos, leyendas y cuentos peruanos; Poesía quechua;* and Francisco de Avila's *Dioses y hombres de Huarochirí* (1975).

As a novelist, Arguedas attempted to reproduce the transculturations in the Andean and mestizo communities he studied as an ethnographer. He used the style of the nineteenth-century European realist novel to write about a world exterior to that genre, and in the process of appropriating the novel to write about an oral, Andean culture, he altered the form of the novel in fundamental ways. The language of Arguedas's novels is fiction—both Quechua and Spanish—and the structure of his novels is mythical and musical. His narrators and characters are all ambiguous, split, bilingual, and bicultural beings who operate according to two different—and at times mutually exclusive—cultural explanatory systems.

Arguedas's career as a novelist began with the publication of a collection of stories, *Agua,* in 1935. In *Agua,* he depicted the life of a small and isolated Andean village dominated by the confrontation between despotic white landowners and Indian serfs. This early Manichaean scheme gave way to an increasingly complex view of Peru in his later works: *Yawar fiesta* (1987); the stories in *Diamantes y pedernales* (1974), *Los ríos profundos* (1957), *El sexto* (1979), *Todas las sangres* (1970), *Amor mundo;* and the unfinished novel *El zorro de arriba y el zorro de Abajo* (1987). Arguedas also wrote Quechua poetry, including *Túpac Amaru Kamaq Taytanchisman/A nuestro Padre creador Túpac Amaru, Temblar/Katatay,* and his reflections on his teaching career have been compiled in *Nosotros los maestros.*

Silvia Spitta

See also Myth

✳✳✳✳✳✳✳✳✳✳✳✳✳✳✳✳✳✳

References

Columbus, Claudette Kemper. *Mythological Consciousness and the Future: José María Arguedas.* New York: Peter Lang, 1986.

Higgins, James. *A History of Peruvian Literature.* Liverpool: Francis Cairns, 1987.

Klaren, Sara Castro. *The Fictional World of José María Arguedas.* Ann Arbor, Mich.: Xerox University Microfilms, 1975.

Spitta, Silvia. *Between Two Waters: Narratives of Transculturation in Latin America.* Austin: University of Texas, 1993.

ARNIM, ACHIM VON (1781–1831)

Achim von Arnim was a German author and member of the Heidelberg romantic circle, which included among others the Grimm brothers and Arnim's collaborator and later brother-in-law, Clemens Brentano. Born into Prussian aristocracy and an ardent Prussian patriot throughout his life, Arnim studied law, mathematics, and physics at the universities of Halle and Göttingen before meeting Brentano in 1801 and deciding to pursue literary interests. Although Arnim produced several minor novels, dramas, and volumes of novellas, he is perhaps best known for his imaginative adaptation of folk narrative material, particularly folk songs.

Arnim's enthusiasm for collecting folk songs grew out of his travels in England and Scotland where he became acquainted with Sir Walter Scott's *Minstrelsy of the Scottish Border* (1802). Both Arnim and Brentano were inspired by Johann Gottfried Herder, and in 1804 they began work on a collection devoted to folk songs in the German language. *Des knaben Wunderhorn* [The boy's magic horn], a three-volume collection of songs and poems drawn from print sources as well as compositions of their own and lesser-known German poets of the early nineteenth century, was published between 1805 and 1808. It contains more than 700 ballads, folk songs, and poems, including poetic adaptations of German legends such as "The Pied Piper of Hamelin" and "The Lore Lay." Whereas Herder's collection *Stimmen der Völker in Liedern* [Voices of the peoples in song (1807)] reflected a uniquely international perspective and a universal appreciation of the "national spirit" of folk songs from many parts of the world, Arnim and—to a lesser extent—Brentano were interested in creating a new golden age of German literature based on the rediscovery of folk literature.

Scholars have tended to overemphasize the differences in the editorial policies and practices of the two collaborators. Brentano is generally credited with possessing the greater literary talent and more systematic mind. Unfortunately, his goal of including a systematic treatment of regional variation in folk songs was not realized. Arnim's epilogue, "On Folksongs," which was included in the first volume without Brentano's knowledge, outlines with romantic and naturalistic metaphors similar to Wilhelm Grimm's prefaces to the *Kinder- und Hausmärchen* [Children's and household tales (1850)]. Arnim's hope was that the collection would contribute to a political-national reawakening of Germany. What Arnim and Brentano shared was the tendency to appropriate motifs, themes, and plots from traditional literature for their own creations, as evidenced in Arnim's poem, "Getrennte Liebe" [Divided love], which drew its motif of two young lovers divided by a river from the traditional ballad "Two King's Children."

Mary Beth Stein

See also Ballad; Brentano, Clemens; Grimm, Jacob and Wilhelm; Herder, Johann Gottfried; Nationalism; Scott, Sir Walter

✵✵✵✵✵✵✵✵✵✵✵✵✵✵✵✵✵

References

Hoermann, Roland. *Achim von Arnim*. Boston: Twayne Publishers, 1984.

Migge, Walther, ed. *Achim von Arnim: Samtliche Romane und Arzahlungen*. Munich: Carl Hanser Verlag, 1962–1965.

Willoughby, L. A. *The Romantic Movement in Germany*. New York: Russell and Russell, 1966.

Arthur, King

King Arthur (probably sixth century C.E.) is a legendary British king represented by medieval romancers as the paragon of chivalry. In Great Britain, he is often the hero of popular and local legend. A capable British leader with a similar name probably did exist in the fifth or sixth century, but there is little evidence of this possibility. Gildas, a monastic historian (c. 540), tells of a successful but unnamed war hero who may have been Arthur. Gildas's record, along with such works as the Welsh *Mabinogion* (c. eleventh century) and Geoffrey of Monmouth's fabricated *History of the Kings of Britain* (c. 1136), provided the background for medieval romances such as the French *Le Morte d'Arthur* [The death of King Arthur (c. 1230–1235)]. These romances presented Arthur as the champion of chivalrous knighthood and courtly love.

Whatever the veracity of Arthur's historical existence, there can be no doubt as to his significance as a folk hero and literary figure. Sir Thomas Malory's *Le Morte d'Arthur* (1485) did much to standardize and establish Arthur's own story, and most modern writers who make use of Arthurian themes base their works on Malory's. In brief, Arthur is the son of Uther Pendragon, king of Britain, and Igraine, the wife of the duke of Cornwall. Because Arthur is conceived out of wedlock, he is raised not in the king's household, but anonymously. Ignorant of his parentage, Arthur proves his right to the throne through his ability to draw a magical sword from the stone and anvil where it has been trapped by the magician, Merlin. The faithlessness of Arthur's wife, Guinevere, ultimately causes the downfall of his kingdom, and Arthur begins his quest for the Holy Grail, sending his knights in search of the cup that Christ drank from at the Last Supper in the hope that the cup's holiness will restore prosperity to his land. In local British tradition, particularly that of Wales and Cornwall, Arthur will return one day to aid his country in its time of direst need. According to many local legends he waits for this hour in the company of a host of sleeping knights in a variety of caves and hollow hills throughout Britain.

King Arthur is remarkable in that his character has been developed in both popular tradition and in high literature. The folk characterization of the figure differs from that of the literary one: the Arthur of popular tradition is both more human and more godlike. The Arthur of the folk is apt to make mistakes or to fly into rages, unlike his staid and just literary counterpart; similarly, the folk Arthur may have supernatural powers that are rarely credited to him in literature. Whatever the interpretation of his character, Arthur is never represented alone but is always in the company of a full retinue consisting of consort (Guinevere), favorite (Bedwyr, or Lancelot), treacherous sister (Morgan), treacherous nephew or son (Mordred), wizard and adviser (Merlin), and any number of loyal knights. The popular variations on Arthur's story tell of his own exploits, while the more literary representations tend to focus on those of his knights and the downfall of his kingdom. But Arthurian literature nearly always ends with the promise, borrowed directly from folk tradition, that Arthur will rise again in spirit if not in body as England's "past and future king."

Elizabeth E. Wein

See also Arthurian Tradition; Legend

✳✳✳✳✳✳✳✳✳✳✳✳✳✳✳✳

References

Alcock, Leslie. *Arthur's Britain: History and Archaeology, AD 367–634*. Harmondsworth, Eng.: Penguin, 1971.

Geoffrey of Monmouth. *The History of the Kings of Britain*. Trans. Lewis Thorpe. Harmondsworth, Eng.: Penguin, 1966.

Gildas. *The Ruin of Britain and Other Works*. Ed. and trans. Michael Winterbottom. London and Chichester: Phillimore, 1978.

Jones, Gwyn, and Thomas Jones, trans. *The Mabinogion*. London: Dent; New York: Dutton, 1949.

Malory, Sir Thomas. *Le Morte d'Arthur*. Ed. Norma Lorre Goodrich. New York: Washington Square Press, 1966.

ARTHURIAN TRADITION

The Arthurian tradition, often referred to as "the matter of Britain," can be said to represent the entire canon of literature and popular belief surrounding the legendary British King Arthur and his retainers. Tales of King Arthur and his court originated in obscure British history and were refined in medieval French romances as representing the perfection of chivalry. The characterization of Arthur and his followers, though rooted in Celtic tradition that was neither Christian nor at heart "chivalrous," nevertheless gathered to itself themes from both of those aspects. The association of Arthur with the Holy Grail is an obvious example. Jessie Weston's work *From Ritual to Romance* (1920) is one attempt to connect the Arthurian grail tradition back to its possible pre-Christian roots.

The pre-Raphaelite movement of the Victorian era, spearheaded by William Morris, made use of Arthurian motifs not only in literature but in popular art as well. Tapestries, paintings, stained-glass windows, and other useful items were given Arthurian themes in order to inspire and delight their users. This movement was based on the notions that the age of Arthur had been exemplary and that nineteenth-century England was in need of a return to the values and ideals extant at that lost time.

The appeal of Arthur was so deep-rooted that various legends and beliefs associated with the tradition were kept alive without any connection to literature. It is said that more places in Britain are named for Arthur than for any other single character except the devil himself; local legends often claim that Arthur was responsible for causing the placement or existence of a particular rock or mound or pool, and Arthur's knights are supposed to lie sleeping beneath a number of hills in Britain. The belief that Arthur would one day return to lead his people to victory was so pervasive that Edward I diplomatically gave Arthur's "remains" a ceremonial interment in 1278, partly to prove to the recently conquered Welsh that Arthur was in fact dead.

In the late twentieth century, renewed interest in Arthurian literature has made use of many aspects of the tradition. "The master

King Arthur and his knights of the round table epitomized courtly love and chivalry.

of Britain" is now manifested in such popular forms as the comic book, film, and musical comedy. The old longing for the golden age represented by Camelot, Arthur's capital, is evidenced by the "medieval" fairs and festivals that are now common throughout Great Britain and the United States. Similarly, the mystery associated with Merlin, Arthur's adviser and magician, has been incorporated into current beliefs and folk practices. The places associated with the Arthurian tradition, particularly Glastonbury (which has Christian as well as magical associations), have become the focus for gatherings and ritual events; the annual Glastonbury festival is attended by thousands of people from all over Britain.

Certain aspects of the Arthurian legend have taken on a literary or folk significance of their own. Modern Arthurian tradition draws upon the available literature perhaps more than was once true, as its devotees are more likely to be able to read than were their predecessors. Presently, the ideals represented by this tradition continue to play an important role in the lives of many people.

Elizabeth E. Wein

See also Arthur, King; Camelot; Legend; Ritual

✳✳✳✳✳✳✳✳✳✳✳✳✳✳✳✳✳

References

Ashe, Geoffrey, ed. *The Quest for Arthur's Britain*. London: Granada, 1971.

Chrétien de Troyes. *Arthurian Romances*. Trans. William W. Kibler. London: Penguin, 1991.

Weston, Jessie L. *From Ritual to Romance*. Gloucester, Mass.: Peter Smith, 1983.

ASTURIAS, MIGUEL ANGEL (1899–1974)

The poet, novelist, and translator Miguel Angel Asturias was born in the capital of Guatemala, Guatemala City. At the age of four he moved to his grandparents' farm in the rural town of Salamá, where his father felt they would be safe from the wrath of the dictator, Estrada Cabrera. Asturias often spoke of the years he spent with the inhabitants of Salamá, remembering in particular the stories he loved to hear from his mother and nanny. As a young man, Asturias lived in Paris from 1923 to 1933 while he studied with Professor Georges Raynaud, a scholar who had translated into French the *Popol Vuh*, popularly referred to as the "bible" of the Quiché Maya. This text, by anonymous writers who referred to themselves simply as "we," was written in Quiché using the Spanish alphabet and was first translated into Spanish in 1703 by Father Francisco Ximémez. In 1927, Asturias translated Raynaud's French version of this rendition of Quiché myth, legend, and cosmogony into Spanish.

During his stay in Paris, Asturias was influenced by and participated in the surrealist movement. Surrealism's fascination with dreams, myth, and magic blended felicitously with Asturias's memories of childhood stories and with the Mayan beliefs and worldview reflected in the ancient texts he had studied and translated. He once said that magic was like a second language, a complementary language with which to penetrate the universe that surrounds us.

Spanish colonial cities often were built upon the ruins of indigenous cities. The original buildings were destroyed, but the indigenous peoples of Guatemala have survived and resisted assimilation. The persistent and enduring presence in Guatemala of stories about their origin, their relation to nature, and their gods are generally interpreted as magic, dream, or fantasy by the Western-influenced observer. Asturias was openly proud of his mestizo, or mixed-race, heritage and believed that the old myths and legends of the Maya form the basis of, and continue to exist in, the collective unconscious of the Guatemalan people. This belief, combined with his preference for the surrealist-inspired automatic writing (a technique of clearing oneself of all distractions to open a channel to the unconscious so that it pours forth onto the page), affected his work in a profound and holistic fashion.

In Asturias's poetry and novels, there is not a meshing of influences or an imposition of the past on the present but a truly original expression that seems to grow from a pretextual integration of Mayan and Spanish belief systems and narrative expressions of it. In his poetry as well as in his prose, the rhythm of the language reflects the particular musicality of the *Popol Vuh*, a text endowed with a dignity of mission: to preserve and pass on the secrets and lessons of the ancestors regarding the creation of the earth and sky, the gods' attempts to create the right human being, and the sacred genealogy of gods and rulers who gave form and soul to the Mayan race.

In his writing, Asturias has approached this "folklore" with respect and wonder; it in turn served him as a gateway to a profusion of expressive possibilities. To his credit, he did not forget the contemporary context of the indigenous communities of Guatemala. He has been lauded by some critics for creating indigenous characters and themes with sensitivity, intuition, and poetry, yet he has also been criticized for portraying the indigenous through their mythical past rather than through the harsh reality of their present situation.

In fact, in many of his works the social and mythical/magical are fused so completely as to be inextricable. Even in his *Legends of Guatemala* (1932) there is a blending of the popular and legendary with harsh social and political realities. In "Legend of the Tatuana," for example, a shaman who is also an almond tree loses his soul to Xibalbá, or the underworld. His soul comes into the possession of the merchant of priceless jewels, who refuses to return it to its owner, exchanging it instead for the most beautiful slave. When the shaman and the most beautiful slave finally meet, they no sooner recognize each other as soul mates than they are arrested and imprisoned for witchcraft by the civil authorities of Spanish colonial rule. The legend is thus retold in the context of Spanish oppression by the indigenous population, thereby actualizing the magical, or endowing the "real" with a magical quality. Asturias, in fact, is often identified as one of the first practitioners of the narrative style now known as *magical realism,* a term that for many people has come to epitomize contemporary Latin American literature.

In *Men of Maize* (1972) the problem of the corn farmers who destroy the land in their lust for profit is constructed through the lens of ancient myths and ancestor reverence. The fundamental Mayan belief in their oneness with nature finds expression in a variety of ways in this novel. The title alludes to the story in the *Popol Vuh* that tells how the gods created humans from corn. Since corn is a sacred substance, indeed the very flesh of the Maya, it follows that one should not trade in it for profit. People are described as corn, such as looking like tamales dressed in clothes or an old woman looking like a handful of cornsilk wrapped in black rags. Those who forsake the land or desecrate it by exploiting it for profit receive their just rewards: they die penniless or are murdered in revenge by the faithful who adhere to the ancestors' ways.

Corn has a special significance to the Maya as is shown in their creation story. According to the *Popol Vuh,* the gods attempt several times to create humans, fail in their experiments with clay and wood, and finally use corn to produce beings who will praise them in words—and thus sustain them and keep them alive. The Maya also believe in the *gran lengua,* the voice or spokesperson of the tribe. Asturias on several occasions announced that he saw himself as just that—the voice of his tribe.

Janet N. Gold

See also Latino and Chicano Folklore and Literature; Legend; Myth

✳✳✳✳✳✳✳✳✳✳✳✳✳✳✳✳✳

References

Asturias, Miguel Angel. *Leyendas de Guatemala.* Buenos Aires: Editorial Pleamar, 1948.

———. *Men of Maize.* Trans. Gerald Martin. New York: Delacorte Press, 1972.

———. *The Mirror of Lida Sal: Tales Based on Mayan Myths and Guatemalan Legends.* Trans. Gilbert Alter-Gilbert. Pittsburgh: Latin American Literary Review Press, 1997.

———. *The President.* Trans. Frances Partridge. New York: Atheneum, 1969.

Callan, Richard. *Miguel Angel Asturias.* New York: Twayne Publishers, 1970.

ATWOOD, MARGARET (1939–)

A prolific writer of poetry, fiction, and nonfiction, the Canadian-born Margaret Atwood is perhaps best known for her analysis of Canadian literature, *Survival* (1972), and her fiction, including *The Edible Woman* (1969), *Surfacing* (1972), *Bluebeard's Egg* (1983), *The Handmaid's Tale* (1985), and *Cat's Eye* (1988). Her most notable poetry collections are *The Circle Game* (1967), which won the prestigious Governor General's Award for 1966; *The Journals of Susanna Moodie* (1970); and *Power Politics* (1971). Educated at the University of Toronto and Radcliffe College, Atwood has taught in numerous universities and has received numerous awards and honors.

Atwood "embeds" elements of folktales, monster tales, märchen, fantasy, quest, and romance formulas in both her poetry and her fiction. As George Woodcock (1983) noted, all of Atwood's work concerns itself not merely with survival but with metamorphoses. From the transforming cake-woman in *The Edible Woman* to the shamanism and Amerindian creation pictographs of ghostly submersion-surfacing images in *Surfacing* to the wondrous and frightening egg in *Bluebeard's Egg*, Atwood's work emphasizes change that is also linked to continuity and community.

Continuity with earlier oral literary traditions is found in her processes of tale telling, in its quality of orality, and in its speech-act performance. Barbara Godard (1986) points out Atwood's use of "never-ending" stories in *Bluebeard's Egg*, for example, in which "images of growth and process" dominate the text. In "Unearthing Suite," the narrative begins with its end as the parents tell the riddling story of their demise, which turns out to be their beginning in the text. Atwood's narrative, presented mimetically in this tale as in others, allows us to "hear" the parents as we "watch" their performance of the story and their daughter's reaction to it. As readers, we are thus drawn into the loop of such narratives; indeed, Atwood's brilliance as a writer, herself a teller of tales, rests in her ability to shape stories so that we recognize not only her characters' generational ties, with their inevitable—and often magical—changes, but our own ties with the broader community of humankind as well.

Josie Campbell

See also *Märchen*; Orality

✳✳✳✳✳✳✳✳✳✳✳✳✳✳✳✳✳

References

Atwood, Margaret. "Canadian Monsters: Some Aspects of the Supernatural in Canadian Fiction." In *The Canadian Imagination*, ed. David Staines, pp. 97–122. Cambridge: Harvard University Press, 1977.

Godard, Barbara. "Tales within Tales: Margaret Atwood's Folk Narratives." *Canadian Literature* 109 (Summer 1986): 55–84.

Woodcock, George. "Metamorphosis and Survival: Notes on the Recent Poetry of Margaret Atwood." In *Margaret Atwood: Language, Text, and System*, ed. Sherrill E. Grace and Lorraine Weir, pp. 125–142. Vancouver: University of British Columbia Press, 1983.

AUCASSIN AND NICOLETTE

As the only medieval European *cante fable* extant, *Aucassin and Nicolette* stands as a generic model for folklorists' use of that term for an oral narrative that alternates spoken prose and sung verse. Love conquers all in this thirteenth-century tale in Old French, for Aucassin and Nicolette overcome a series of obstacles to their union. However, without Nicolette's enterprising wit and without his father's money, Aucassin would have proven a sorry hero indeed.

Preserved in a single manuscript in the Picard dialect (Paris B.N. fr. 2168), *Aucassin and Nicolette* differs substantially from any comparable work of either learned Latin or popular vernacular verbal art: nowhere else do sung passages advance the plot. Thirteenth-century Latin education commonly included *Consolation of Philosophy* by Boethius (480–524? C.E.), which alternates prose and verse. It is a treatise not a story, however, and each *cantus* ("song") reiterates or develops the philosophical concept just explicated in prose. In Old French vernacular literature, superficial resemblances to *Aucassin and Nicolette* appear in verse narratives and transitional drama, as characters may burst into song in order to convey a state of mind or relate a previous occurrence. But only in this sole medieval cante fable do verse and prose sequentially generate the story line.

Like the prose sections of *Aucassin and Nicolette*, the songs are presented by a third-person narrator who relates characters' thoughts and actions along with conversations, monologues, and even songs within the songs. The technique seems self-consciously innovative, insofar as the anonymous author draws attention to the distinction between song and prose. While seeking Nicolette, for example, Aucassin overhears shepherds singing her praises. They refuse to repeat their song but, upon payment of ten sous, agree to speak about meeting her.

Unique in form, *Aucassin and Nicolette* also stands alone in that no comparable work contains explicit instructions for oral performance of prose. Each song, its melody notated on staff lines, is followed by "Now they say and recount and relate." Each prose section then concludes, "Now it is sung." At the close of the work, after assurance that the lovers will live happily ever after, the author names the genre and predicts the dilemma of present-day medievalists: *No cante-fable prent fin / N'en sai plus dire* ("Our song-story ends / I know no more to say").

Scholars can always find something to say, but because *Aucassin and Nicolette* thwarts expectations for high seriousness in literature, it has long appealed to a more popular than academic audience. The first modernization of the Old French text appeared in 1752, and translations into other languages followed, including one in 1887 by Andrew Lang. It was not until the 1960s, however, that literary scholars agreed upon a way to analyze the work's playful attitude toward love, war, questing, parental guidance, and masculine prowess. *Aucassin and Nicolette* seems to function as parody, as an intentional hodgepodge of genres that may also be mocking specific works no longer extant. Armed with that possibility, scholars are now struggling to reconstruct a medieval audience's understanding of the work in which the indomitable Saracen slave girl triumphs over prohibitions and distances that separate her from the lovesick, ineffectual, upper-class European heir to his father's lands.

Although preserved in writing, *Aucassin and Nicolette* contains evidence that members of an unofficial oral culture in thirteenth-century Picardy challenged the official values of religious and secular authorities. For example, when Aucassin's father forbids marriage upon pain of eternal damnation, the son declares preference for a hell full of jongleurs and fun-loving ladies to a paradise of old priests and beggars. Thus, there is potential for using the ideas of Mikhail Bakhtin to understand actions and attitudes. The text itself incorporates traditional folkloric materials, besides offering data for diachronic performance analysis. The lovers escape from prisons and pirates, encounter helpful strangers and hideous churls, and in many other adventures enact standard folktale motifs—most often, however, with a reversal of standard male/female roles. In addition, the author refers to folkloric rituals and customs, notably *couvade*, in the topsy-turvy land of Torelore, where the king lies in childbed while the queen wages war by tossing foodstuffs into a ford.

Despite such richness, folklorists have so far neglected the work. A responsible interdisciplinary study of *Aucassin and Nicolette* could create a fresh understanding of oral and lost literary traditions in thirteenth-century France and in other places and eras as well—perhaps even in Torelore, once upon a time.

Betsy Bowden

See also Bakhtin, Mikhail Mikhailovitch; *Cante Fable*; Lang, Andrew; Motif; Performance

✳✳✳✳✳✳✳✳✳✳✳✳✳✳✳✳✳

References

"Aucassin and Nicolette (*Aucassin et Nicolette*)." In *The Pilgrimage of Charlemagne / Aucassin and Nicolette*, ed. Anne Elizabeth Cobby; introd. and trans. Glyn S. Burgess, pp. 91–183. New York: Garland, 1988.

Hunt, Tony. "Precursors and Progenitors of *Aucassin et Nicolette*." *Studies in Philology* 74 (1977): 1–19.

Martin, June Hall. *Love's Fools: Aucassin, Troilus, Calisto, and the Parody of the Courtly Lover*. London: Tamesis Books, 1972.

Sargent-Baur, Barbara Nelson, and Robert Francis Cook. *Aucassin et Nicolette: A Critical Bibliography*. London: Grant and Cutler, 1981.

AZADOVSKII, MARK KONSTANTINOVICH
(1888–1954)

The Russian folklorist, literary scholar, and ethnographer Mark Konstantinovich Azadovskii completed his studies in history and philology at St. Petersburg University in 1913. He went on to teach at the universities of Tomsk, Irkutsk, and Leningrad, where he also served as director of the Folklore Sector at the Institute of Ethnography and initiated the periodical publication *Soviet Folklore* (*Sovietsk'ii fol'klor*). His expeditions along the Amur and Lena Rivers (1913–1915) and in the Tunka Valley (1925, 1927) yielded materials of fundamental importance in the study of traditional Siberian cultures. While at the University of Irkutsk, he initiated and edited the journal of regional culture, *Living Siberian Antiquities* (*Sibirskaia zhivaia* starina). His 1924 handbook, *Conversations about the Collection of Oral Folk Art Pertaining to Siberia* (*Besedy sobiratelia o sobranii pamiatnikov ustnogo narodnogo tvorchestva, primanitel'no k Sibiri*), instructed a subsequent generation of Russian folklorists.

Azadovskii's published compilations of folktales told by N. O. Vinokurova and F. I. Aksametov were groundbreaking attempts at studying the entire repertoires of individual narrators; another book containing tales told over a span of 13 years by E. I. Sorokovikov demonstrates the value of repeated recordings in the study of the changes that occur over time in a narrator's tales. In *The Russian Folktale: Selected Masters* (*Russkaia skazka: Izbrannye mastera* [1932]), Azadovskii reiterated the ideas that set him and most other contemporary Russian folklorists apart from the methods and theories prevailing elsewhere in the world: "The folktale preserves deep traces of individual experience and the personal feelings of the narrator. Experiences, contemplations, occupation—all of these factors exert a deep influence on the text of a story he is telling. . . . Storytellers are in no way simple transmitters" (1932, pp. 26, 33). To illustrate the point, Azadovskii included at the end of the collection the texts of a single tale plot as told by six different narrators.

Azadovskii became internationally known when he published in 1926 a brief, German-language summary of Russian narrator studies and a case study of N. O. Vinokurova's storytelling in the prestigious series Folklore Fellows Communications. The article had a lasting impact on folktale scholars in Germany, Hungary, the United States, and elsewhere: a collection of folktales may no longer be considered to be complete until it gives consideration to the personalities and artistic creativity of the individuals who narrate the texts.

Azadovskii's research on the interrelations between oral and written traditions has remained largely unknown outside the Russian-speaking parts of the world. In "Narration and the Book" (*"Skazitel'stvo I kniga"*), Azadovskii proved that popular books had influenced many folktales that earlier folklorists had imagined to be the product of pure oral tradition. In the same article, he examined the biographies of folktale narrators to disprove the generally accepted notion that literacy had a detrimental effect on folk narration; to the contrary, he found that literacy was not uncommon among the most gifted narrators and that it often stimulated creativity and provided a new source of subject matter. Azadovskii also studied influences traveling in the opposite direction, from oral traditions to written literature. Throughout his career, he published numerous studies of "folklorism" (the transplanting of traditional culture into new contexts, literary or otherwise) in the works of Pushkin, Turgenev, Lermontov, Korolenko, and many others.

Azadovskii's major contribution to folkloristics, and to the study of Russian culture in general, is his *History of Russian Folkloristics* (*Istoriia russkoi fol'kloristiki*), published posthumously in two volumes. Unlike most previous surveys, which limited themselves to the narrow field of scholarly folkloristics, Azadovskii's work is a broad synthesis of his many years of research on folklore, Russian literature, and the history of Russian thought.

Guntis Smidchens

See also Folklorism; *Märchen*; Storytelling; Tradition

✳✳✳✳✳✳✳✳✳✳✳✳✳✳✳✳✳

References

Azadovskii, Mark K. *Literatura I fol'klor: Ocherki I etiudy* [Literature and folklore: Essays and sketches]. Leningrad: Gosudarstvennoe izdatel'stvo "Khudozhestvennaia literatura," 1938.

———. *A Siberian Tale Teller*. Trans. James R. Dow. Center for Intercultural Studies in Folklore and Ethnomusicology Monograph Series no. 2. Austin: University of Texas Press, 1974 (1926).

Ber, N. S. *Bibliografiia M. K. Azadovskogo, 1913–1943* [Bibliography of M. K. Azadovskii, 1913–1943]. Irkutsk: n.p., 1944.

Vinogradov, V. V., et al., eds. "Pamiati M. K. Azadovskogo: Nekrolog; Khronologichsekii spisok pechatnykh rabot M. K. Azadovskogo za 1944–1956 gg" [In memory of M. K. Azadovskii: Obituary; Chronological list of published works by M. K. Azadovskii, 1944–1956]. *Literaturnoe nasledstvo* 60 (1956): 641–646.

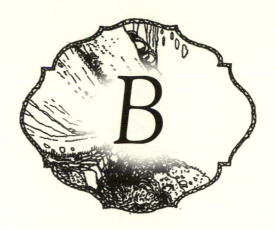

Baba Iaga (also baba yaga)

The Russian witch Baba Iaga, or Baba Yaga, appears primarily in folktales and in written literature. She is ugly, old, and thin; sometimes she is distinguished by a bony leg. Baba Iaga lives in the middle of the forest in a hut that stands on a chicken's leg and can thus rotate, always facing away from human intruders. When an intruder, such as a folktale hero, manages to enter the hut, Baba Iaga always detects him by his smell. She flies through the air, riding in a mortar that she propels with the pestle. Sometimes she flies in an iron kettle, sweeping her tracks up with a broom. She is an ogress and eats human flesh, especially the flesh of children, though she can also be kind, granting "the water of life," flying horses, or magical objects such as a comb that turns into a forest, a handkerchief that turns into a desert, and a mirror that becomes a lake. The more helpful Baba Iaga sometimes appears in triplicate as three sisters who test the hero and then provide information or magic objects to aid him in his quest.

Baba Iaga, like the *rusalka*, a female supernatural being found among the eastern Slavs, may well be a remnant of prehistoric goddess worship, in which case the *rusalka* would be the young manifestation of this deity and Baba Iaga the old one. Baba Iaga has many cosmic features. In various folktales she possesses "the water of life" and "the water of death." She commands three horsemen—one white, one red, and one black—who are morning, noon, and night, respectively. She controls a flame that is both inextinguishable and burns the unrighteous to a crisp.

It should be remembered that the Baba Iaga version of the witch is quite genre-specific. There was widespread belief in witchcraft among the Russians, Ukrainians, and Belarussians, and narratives about witches appeared in memorate, fabulate, and legend form. Witches lived in virtually every village and city district, either in the past or in the present. They could be male or female. They were not necessarily evil or destructive and were sought out as healers, advisers, veterinarians, and agricultural consultants. Evil was attributed to them only when something went wrong, such as when the crops failed or when there was illness. If there was any distinction among them, it was between born witches and learned witches. Born witches were good; learned witches had the potential to be evil. The terms for witches include *ved'ma* (Ukrainian, *vid'ma*) with the possible male counterpart of a *ved'mak*; *znakhar'* ("man"), *znakhar'sha* ("woman"), *charodei* ("man"), *charodeika* ("woman"). The terms *ved'ma* and *znakhar'* both contain roots meaning "knowledge," and the witches are likely a remnant of the *volkhvy*, pagan priests who officiated at agrarian cycle rites and promoted crop fertility.

The witch appears in a number of literary works, such as Nikolay Vasilyevich Gogol's collection of short stories called *Evenings on a Farm near Dikanka* (1831 [Part 1], 1832 [Part 2]). Probably the most famous literary witch is Margarita of Bulgakov's novel *Master and Margarita* (1966). Although Margarita is a witch and controls demons, she is young, beautiful, and kind. She not only serves as the master's muse but redeems him with her love.

Natalie Kononenko

See also *Rusalka;* Witchcraft

✸✸✸✸✸✸✸✸✸✸✸✸✸✸✸✸

References

Ivanits, L. *Russian Folk Belief.* New York: M. E. Sharpe, 1989.

The Magic Egg and Other Ukrainian Stories. Retold by Barbara Suwyn, ed. Natalie Kononenko. Englewood, Colo.: Libraries Unlimited, 1997.

Pomerantseva, E. V. *Mifologicheskie personazhi v russkom fol'klore.* Moscow: Nauka, 1975.

Zguta, R. *Russian Minstrels: A History of the Skomorokhi.* Philadelphia: University of Pennsylvania Press, 1978.

BAKHTIN, MIKHAIL MIKHAILOVITCH (1895–1975)

A rebellious member of the Russian formalist critical school, Mikhail Mikhailovitch Bakhtin wrote or collaborated on *Freudianism, a*

Marxist Critique (1927, signed by V. N. Volosinov), *The Formal Method in Literary Scholarship* (1928, signed by P. N. Medvedev), and *Marxism and the Philosophy of Language* (1929, also signed by V. N. Volosinov). In his own name he published *Problems of Dostoevsky's Poetics* (1929). Exiled under Stalin, Bakhtin subsequently wrote a dissertation, published on his return to Russia as *Rabelais and His World* (1965). Obscurity and illness persisted until younger scholars began to pay attention to his Dostoevsky and Rabelais books (his other canonical authors were Goethe, Gogol, and Pushkin).

Since his death, Bakhtin has gained enormous prominence for his concepts of dialogism and polyphony in fiction. The special excellence of the novel genre, Bakhtin asserted, is that it synchronizes diverse consciousness in diverse languages and registers. It does not harmonize them into "monologism"; its reality is polyglot. Because literature derives this "heteroglossia" from the multilingualism of peasants, literature depends on the speech practices of the folk. Thus, of all twentieth-century critics, Bakhtin most effectively illustrated the dependence of literature on folklore.

In *Rabelais and His World*, Bakhtin demonstrates this dependence. Marketplace language, images of food and banqueting, and (most important) grotesque images of the lower body—all creations of the folk—give François Rabelais's work its special character as political protest. Oversimplifying somewhat, Bakhtin's work attributes antiabsolutist and antiwar attitudes to an ill-defined "folk." Evidently he was writing anti-Stalinist allegory, and against such repressive monologism, he seems to say, there was but one weapon, folk laughter. Vernaculars, dialects, and scatology can restore a sense of reality. Proclaiming the gift of folklore to literature, Bakhtin says that the carnival-grotesque functions in Rabelais "to consecrate inventive freedom, to permit the combination of a variety of different elements and their rapprochement, to liberate from the prevailing point of view of the world, from conventions and established truths, from clichés, from all that is humdrum and universally accepted" (*Rabelais and His World*).

Bakhtin's concepts of carnival time as a distinct alternative and of heteroglossia as the simultaneous play of voices have strongly influenced criticism (Julia Kristeva was the transmitter of these concepts) and folklore studies. In contrast to the mythmaking of a Northrop Frye, a Bakhtinian reading of the central sections of *A Midsummer Night's Dream*, *As You Like It*, or *Twelfth Night* sees them as carnival times in which social roles are reversed. When the world is reordered, creative possibilities for an alternative culture are released. Prince Hal in *1 Henry IV* temporarily leads a carnivalesque life of irresponsibility, over which the clown Falstaff has been crowned king. Carnival time is as real a time as its alternative. Bakhtin thus parallels anthropologist Victor Turner's research into liminality. As to heteroglossia, folklore offers the finest data available for observing the multiplicity of social voices. Parodic verbal forms and the imitation of one performance in another allow an original and its parody to sound simultaneously. Folk speech and music of creolized societies in the Caribbean and Africa continually mix languages, styles, and traditions.

Lee Haring

See also Gogol, Nikolay Vasilyevich; Rabelais, François

✳✳✳✳✳✳✳✳✳✳✳✳✳✳✳✳✳

References

Bakhtin, Mikhail Mikhailovitch. *Problems of Dostoevsky's Poetics*. Ed. and trans. Caryl Emerson; introd. Wayne C. Booth. 1963 (1929). Theory and History of Literature, vol. 8. Minneapolis: University of Minnesota Press, 1984.

————. *Rabelais and His World*. Trans. Helene Iswolsky. Cambridge: Massachusetts Institute of Technology Press, 1968.

Medvedev, P. N./Bakhtin, M. M. *The Formal Method in Literary Scholarship: A Critical Introduction to Sociological Poetics*. Trans. Albert J. Wehrle. Goucher College Series. Baltimore: Johns Hopkins University Press, 1978 (1928).

Volosinov, V. N. *Freudianism, a Marxist Critique*. Trans. I. R. Titunik, ed. Neal H. Bruss. New York: Academic Press, 1976.

————. *Marxism and the Philosophy of Language*. Trans. Ladislav Matejka and I. R. Titunik. New York: Seminar, 1973 (1930).

Balkan folklore and literature

Folklore has played a central role in the formation and development of Balkan national literatures. Oral tradition—one of the few treasures that survived centuries of foreign (primarily Ottoman) domination—served as a means of discourse in the creation of national identities, especially during the nineteenth century. As an expression of struggle against foreign influence, that tradition provided the source from which virtually all modern literature developed.

With the exception of the Dalmatian renaissance in Croatia and the early modern Cretan poetry of Greece, national literatures in the Balkans did not develop until the nineteenth century. The romantic nationalism that swept through Eastern Europe at that time promoted interest in folklore and resulted in the widespread collecting and publishing of oral literature. Folklore affected primarily the romantic (poetic) and realist (prose) trends, and national literatures in the Balkans followed more or less parallel patterns of development. Narrative poetry—often akin to the oral epic—typically was the first genre to emerge. Lyric poetry, drawing from the style, language, and content of the oral lyric, followed. Village realist prose became widespread in the latter part of the nineteenth century: the idealization of village life and presentation of folklore were hallmarks of this style. New concerns emerged in peasant realism in the early twentieth century; for instance, the darker sides of village life were often explored.

The first broad stage of literary development in the Balkans was characterized by long narrative poems that were reminiscent of the oral epic. Modern Greek poetry developed after 1453, mainly on Crete. The epico-lyric poem *Erotokritos* by Vitzentzos Kornaros, though closely related to Western poetry, was notably influenced by Cretan folk songs and is considered the greatest poem of early modern Greece. The first evidence of folklore in southern Slavic literature can be found in sixteenth-century Croatian poetry—namely, several folk songs in the long narrative poem *Fishing and Fishermen's Talk* by the Dalmatian Petar Hektorovič (1487–1572). In 1756, the Croat Andrija Kačić-Miošić (1704–1760) published *A Pleasing Account about the Slavs*, a history of the southern Slavs written in the decasyllabic meter of oral epic.

In Serbia, the folklorist and linguistic reformer Vuk Karadžlć (1787–1864) published the first of many collections of oral poetry in 1814. Vuk's contributions were instrumental in the evolution of Serbo-Croatian literature as they inspired generations of writers. The Montenegrin Petar Petrović Njegoš (1813–1851) is considered the greatest nineteenth-century Serbian poet. His dramatic poem in oral epic meter, *The Mountain Wreath*, describes the conflict between Montenegrins and Turks and provides ethnographic details and examples of oral genres such as the lament. Nineteenth-century literature in Croatia was dominated by the Illyrian movement, which fostered interest in folklore and sought a revival of the Dalmatian renaissance. Ivan Mažuranić (1814–1890) was the first major poet of this movement. His narrative poem *The Death of Smail Aga Čengić* mirrors the southern Slavic epic in its depiction of the struggles between Cross and Crescent, that is, Christian and Muslim, and is rendered in epic meter.

The earliest writers of the Bulgarian revival were romantic revolutionaries who wrote poetry to promote national independence; often they were also folklorists. Georgi Rakovski (1821–1867) collected many folk songs and published an index of Bulgarian ethnography and folklore in 1859. His narrative poem *Woodland Traveler*—a statement on Bulgarian independence—features *haiduti* ("social outlaws") who were frequent subjects of Balkan folk poetry.

In nineteenth-century Greece, there was a redirection of poetic theme and language, and both folklore and the vernacular became important concerns in literature. Dionysios Solomos (1798–1857) was an influential poet in this school. Jeronim De Rada (1814–1903)—one of the greatest nineteenth-century Albanian writers—collected oral poetry and later, influenced especially by the epic, wrote narrative poems based on Albanian oral tradition and history.

The writers who created modern Romanian literature during the nineteenth century also typically turned to folklore. In the Romanian principalities, Anton Pann (1797–1854) was among the first to collect oral genres; his own narrative poetry reflects folktale and proverb. Vasile Alecsandri (1819–1890), a poet who incorporated folklore into his own works, played a major role in the development of Romanian national literature. His collections of oral poetry (the first of which was *Folk Poetry—Ballads* deeply inspired other nineteenth-century writers, much as Vuk's had in Serbia.

The second broad stage in the development of Balkan literature was distinguished by lyric poetry, which was greatly influenced by folk song. The foremost romantic poets in Croatia—Stanko Vraz (1810–1851) and Petar Preradović (1818–1872)—turned to oral lyric and ballad in their poetry. The outstanding Serbian lyric poet Branko Radičević (1824–1853) also drew from the style of oral verse in his writing. Jovan Jovanović-Zmaj (1833–1904)—an influential Serbian author of the late nineteenth century—adopted the language of folk poetry in his lyrics. In Bulgaria, Petko Slaveikov (1827–1895) collected thousands of folk songs and proverbs, and his own lyric poetry mirrors *haidutin* songs and folk legend. Khristo Botev (1848–1876), a zealous nationalist and the greatest lyric poet of the Bulgarian revival—also found inspiration in oral poetry. He wrote in the style of the folk song in much of his verse as an expression of Bulgarian national identity.

In Romanian literature, Mihail Eminescu (1850–1889) is regarded as the greatest nineteenth-century poet. He combined Western literary technique with oral tradition, such as in his stylized folktale in verse, "Hyperion." The poetry of Gheorghe Coşbuc (1866–1918) is imbued with rustic themes and style. Many of his works are idyllic presentations of folklore, drawn from his native Transylvanian village. The prominent Albanian lyric poet Naim Frashëri (1846–1900) also turned to folklore as inspiration in much of his verse.

In the late nineteenth century, Balkan writers began to embrace the genres of short stories and novels. Village realist prose, which turned to folklore and idealized rural life, was among the first prose genres to flourish. In Bulgaria, the village prose of Lyuben Karavelov (1834–1879) includes ethnographic detail and folk language. Karavelov also published a massive work in 1861 that documented Bulgarian folklife. Ivan Vazov (1850–1921) was the most outstanding Bulgarian writer of the postliberation period (after 1878). His novel *Under the Yoke* is a literary monograph of rural life and customs. Yordan Yovkov (1880–1937), best known for *Legends of Stara Planina*, colorfully evoked the rustic world of his childhood village.

The Romanian Ion Creangă (1837–1889) focused on the Moldavian village of his youth in his prose. In addition to literary folktales, his greatest contribution was *Memories from Childhood*, which is filled with folklore and rustic humor. Ioan Slavici (1848–1925) was among the founders of the Romanian short story and novel, and his fiction treats his native rural Transylvania and its folklife in peasant realist style, such as in *Mara*. Liviu Rebreanu (1885–1944), well known for his psychological prose, displayed Transylvanian village life and its customs in realistic terms, for example, in *Ion*.

In Serbia, Milovan Glišić (1847–1908) and Laza Lazarević (1851–1890) wrote nostalgically about the Serbian *zadruga* ("rural extended family") and its folklore. Later, Borisav Stanković (1876–1927) critically portrayed Serbian peasant life in his fiction, such as in *The Tainted Blood*. Ivo Andrić (1892–1975)—the greatest novelist of Serbo-Croatian literature—turned to the traditional Bosnian world of town and village for his many short stories and novels. In *The Bridge on the Drina*, a Nobel Prize–winning work that chronicles three and a half centuries in the life of his native Višegrad, Andrić masterfully depicts the vibrant customs, beliefs, and folklore of the multiethnic Bosnian world.

Critical scholarship on Balkan oral traditions developed during the twentieth century. Most prominent was the publication in 1960 of Albert B. Lord's *Singer of Tales*, a seminal work that explains oral composition in Serbo-Croatian epic. Based on extensive fieldwork in Yugoslavia, it revolutionized oral literary scholarship and has generated countless other studies of orality and literature.

Despite the indisputable role of folklore in the early development of Balkan literature, folklore has gradually lost its pivotal influence in the literature of the twentieth century. Western literary trends—especially modernism—became more pronounced, particularly in the decades before communist rule. During the communist period, urbanization, industrialization, and socialist ideology radically altered society and culture while socialist realism dominated in the arts. Later, literary postmodernism began to emerge. The collapse of communism throughout the Balkans (1989) and the Yugoslav civil war (1991–1995) engendered passionate nationalist sentiments that embrace folklore as a powerful resource for their expression. Although folklore now no longer serves the purposes of earlier times by aiding in the creation of national identities and literatures in primary agrarian societies, it continues to provide a deep and resonant means for the cultural perpetuation of nationalist ideologies.

Margaret Hiebert Beissinger

See also Ballad; Epic; Folktale; Nationalism; Proverbs; Style

✳✳✳✳✳✳✳✳✳✳✳✳✳✳✳✳✳

References

Andrić, Ivo. *The Bridge on the Drina*. Trans. Lovett F. Edwards. Chicago: University of Chicago Press, 1977.

Beissinger, Margaret H. *The Art of the Lăutar: The Epic Tradition of Romania*. New York: Garland, 1991.

Bynum, David E., ed. and trans. *Serbo-Croatian Heroic Poems*. New York: Garland, 1993.

Lord, Albert B. *The Singer of Tales*. Cambridge: Harvard University Press, 1960.

Njegoš, Petar Petrović. *The Mountain Wreath*. Trans. Vasa D. Mihailovich. Irvine, Calif.: C. Schlacks, Jr., 1986.

Parry, Milman, col., Albert B. Lord, and David E. Bynum, eds. and trans. *Serbocroatian Heroic Songs*. Vols. 1–4, 6, 14. Cambridge: Harvard University Press, 1953–1980.

BALLAD

Defined minimally as a stanzaic narrative poem or song, the ballad was one of the earliest forms of material to interest folklorists. Their interest was exclusively in those exemplars that were orally transmitted, that reflected a small homogeneous community, that used recurrent phrases/lines denominated "commonplaces," that focused mostly on the tragic familial and love relations, and that told the story without analysis or interpretative embellishment—songs/poems with such names as "The Twa Sisters," "Sir Patrick Spens," or "Lord Randal." Called by Gordon Hall Gerould (1932) "the ballad of tradition," they were referred to by Francis James Child as "popular," and the latter's 1882–1898 five-volume work, *The English and Scottish Popular Ballads*, provides 305 examples, in multiple versions, of just the kind of ballad he meant, a type whose day had passed.

Cognates, or similar forms, of the English ballad are found elsewhere, especially in Europe, where the Scandinavian versions, most particularly those included in *Danmarks gamle Folkeviser [Denmark's Old Folksongs*, published between 1853 and 1976], begun by Child's adviser and correspondent Svend Grundtvig, provide near parallels to some of the so-called Child ballads (after Francis James Child, their editor). Grundtvig's earliest materials are medieval; few of the Child texts are that old, most having been recorded in the eighteenth and nineteenth centuries.

Scholars have been interested in and concerned about the origin of the ballad form as well as individual items. Early enthusiasts placed the ballad far back in time, near the origins of language and poetry. The assumption was that the contemporary examples contained echoes of this early kind of literature, which contained a simpler, purer, more natural expression. Thus, from time to time, writers of poetry have been attracted to the ballad as a model, using lines and phrases, typical rhyme schemes and verse patterns (the so-called ballad stanza: abcb, 4343 stress pattern), or otherwise building on stylistic traits, such as the use of the supernatural.

Nationalists and romanticists both have been attracted to the ballad for ideological reasons. It was perhaps something similar that led to William Wordsworth and Samuel Taylor Coleridge's 1798 *Lyrical Ballads*, which references the ballad as a conceptual model even though the individually authored poems seem far removed from the oral progenitors and may well have owed more to the thriving broadside press.

Broadside ballads were published texts, often sold in the streets and rural enclaves by chapmen who sometimes both sold and sang their wares. The broadside texts—classically on a sheet of paper with the words, a reference to the appropriate tune, and a woodcut chosen to embellish the otherwise utilitarian page—had many origins. Some were versions of orally circulating materials, and some were written by known and not-so-known authors, frequently for financial gain, offering more modern accounts; this latter type may well have been the precursor to the newspaper.

The designation of ballad is an academic one: few singers of songs make such a generic distinction. The songs collected orally are seldom as complete as the versions published in the eighteenth and nineteenth centuries, versions that had clearly undergone collation and sometimes extensive rewriting by would-be poet-enthusiasts including Bishop Thomas Percy, Sir Walter Scott, and Robert Burns. Those texts silently call into question scholarly distinctions between the "popular" and the "literary" ballad. Widely recognized, though literarily somewhat denigrated, the ballad as appropriated and reappropriated by literary artists has been little studied, even when the resulting poems have been works of recognized beauty.

Mary Ellen Brown

See also Burns, Robert; Chapbook; Child, Francis James; *Corrido*; Literary Ballad; Nationalism; Percy, Thomas; *Romancero*; Romanticism; Scott, Sir Walter

✳✳✳✳✳✳✳✳✳✳✳✳✳✳✳✳✳

References

Buchan, David. *The Ballad and the Folk*. London: Routledge and Kegan Paul, 1972.

Child, Francis James. *The English and Scottish Popular Ballads*. 5 vols. Boston: Houghton, Mifflin, 1882–1898.

Gerould, Gordon Hall. *The Ballad of Tradition*. Oxford: Clarendon Press, 1932.

Grundtvig, Svend. *Danmarks gamle Folkeviser*, 12 vol. Ed. Erik Dahl. Copenhagen: Universitets-Jubilæets Danske Samfund, 1853–1976.

Basile, Giambattista (1575–1632)

A soldier, public official, poet, and author of short stories, Giambattista Basile became fascinated with the local culture of the Neapolitan area. He engaged in serious study of the local folklore, customs, music, and dialect, including the collecting of folktales. The fruit of this work is his *Lo cunto de li cunti* [The story of stories], which appeared in 1634. Also called the *Pentamerone*, it is written in Neapolitan dialect. Ten women tell 50 stories over five days to a prince and princess. At the end of this time, the real princess reappears, tells her own story last, and ousts the false princess.

The formula of telling stories in a setting separate from the everyday, and the division of the stories into five days of 10 stories each, shows a debt to Boccaccio's *Decameron*. Among the tales are "Puss-in-Boots," "Rapunzel," "Snow White and Rose Red," "Cinderella," and "Beauty and the Beast." The *Pentamerone* was one source for Jacob and Wilhelm Grimm, and found its way into the Italian commedia dell'arte through the works of the dramatist Carlo Gozzi.

Basile's collection of folktales has been analyzed by märchen scholars interested in the way magic and reality appear in the form of the folktale and märchen and the way the real world is represented in a form designed to represent the magical world. Through the märchen, the characters in *Lo cunto de li cunti* use wit and witlessness to respond to and contest the structures of power and class. Since the märchen also has to do with illustrating the way adolescents come to terms with growing up and with sexuality, the depiction of romantic love in the tales has also been studied.

When the psychological approach is used to compare Basile's collection with Perrault's and the Grimm brothers' work, one finds that certain patterns of relationships are depicted and contrasted in märchen. In particular, the difference between the closeness of a young brother and sister or such relatives is opposed to the closeness of the bride and groom; the experience of sexual desire in these relationships is addressed through didactic fantasy.

John Cash

See also Boccaccio, Giovanni; Cinderella; *Commedia dell'arte*; *Decameron*; Folktale; Grimm, Jacob and Wilhelm; *Märchen*; Perrault, Charles

✳✳✳✳✳✳✳✳✳✳✳✳✳✳✳✳✳✳

References

Basile, Giambattista. *The Pentamerone of Giambattista Basile*. Trans. from the Italian of Benedetto Croce and ed. by N. M. Penzer. London: John Lane the Bodley Head, 1932.

Broggini, Barbara. *Lo cunto de li cunti von Giambattista Basile: Ein Ständepoet in Streit mit der Plebs, Fortuna, und der höfischen Korruption*. Frankfurt am Main: Peter Lang, 1990.

McGlathery, James M. *Fairy Tale Romance: The Grimms, Basile, and Perrault.* Urbana: University of Illinois Press, 1991.

BÉDIER, JOSEPH (1864–1938)

A prominent literary medievalist, Joseph Bédier cast overt scorn upon "folk-loristes moins familiarisés avec le moyen âge" (folklorists not familiar with the middle ages) and helped motivate the methodological transition from the cross-cultural, diachronic search for folklore origins (i.e., the historic-geographic method) to the attempted reconstruction of each specific item's significance within its precise sociohistorical context. In retrospect, Bédier appears to have been molded by his own social context, notably by nationalism. His major studies deprecate possible Indian, Celtic, and German influences on the medieval French fabliau, romance, and epic, respectively. For his milieu, though, from his influential position at the Collège de France (1903–1936), Bédier identified genuine deficiencies in previous scholarship and gave guidance toward alternative approaches.

After Bédier succeeded his mentor Gaston Paris in the prestigious professorship of medieval French language and literature at the Collège de France, he helped prepare a bibliography of 1,197 scholarly publications by Gaston Paris, who had almost single-handedly established Old French vernacular literature as a valid field of academic inquiry. As early as 1893, Bédier had respectfully disagreed with assumptions in his mentor's 103 publications on folklore. In Bédier's doctoral dissertation, he declared that polygenesis alone accounts for any resemblances between the Old French fabliaux and stories collected earlier in India. He also documented other directions for investigation, so that scholars had to continue to define their own positions relative to his on the origins, function, social-class appeal, and other questions relevant to the fabliau.

Early in his career, while focusing on Tristan and Isolde, Bédier also laid out lines of inquiry still pursued in studies of medieval Arthurian narratives. Despite names and incidental details from Celtic tradition, he argued, the romances' essential theme of tragic adulterous love was French in origin and spirit. Thereafter, Bédier turned to *Les Légendes épiques* [The epic legends], published in four volumes (1908–1913), and proved their independence from medieval

Germanic narratives and from nineteenth-century German scholarship. According to his analysis, an individual French author composed all of *La Chanson de Roland* (Song of Roland) in about 1100. Here again, Bédier articulated problems that medievalists and folklorists continue to confront: individual vs. cumulative authorship, international vs. regional significance, and so on.

Bédier favored the individual French scribe as well as the individual French author. He argued for "best-text" editing of works that survive in several manuscripts—that is, for transcribing one carefully selected manuscript. Bédier denounced the method dominant then and now, which was developed by German scholars, whereby an editor compares manuscripts in order to publish a reconstructed text resembling the author's supposed original. Although literary medievalists remain unconverted, no folklorist today would analyze some scholar's amalgam as if it were a valid text. Folklorists regard each oral verbal artist as Bédier did each medieval scribe, as the creator of a version aesthetically satisfying to its intended audience.

Besides attacking German scholarship, Bédier published pamphlets on German war crimes. In 1921 he was elected to the Académie Française, but his later scholarship breaks little new ground.

Bédier's students and colleagues recall a man as scrupulous in personal affairs as in scholarship. He seldom wrote letters, for example, lest he let slip an infelicitous phrase. Bédier would never have allowed analogues of fabliaux to be uttered in the presence of his wife and three children; nor would he ever have invited Tristan and Isolde into his home.

Betsy Bowden

See also Epic; *Fabliau;* Historic-Geographic Method; Monogenesis; Romance; *Song of Roland*

✳✳✳✳✳✳✳✳✳✳✳✳✳✳✳

References

Charle, Christophe, and Eva Telkès. *Les professeurs du Collège de France: Dictionnaire biographique (1901–1939)*. Paris: Éditions du CNRS, 1988.

Corbellari, Alain. "Joseph Bédier, Philologist and Writer." In *Medievalism and the Modernist Temper,* ed. R. Howard Bloch and Stephen G. Nichols, pp. 269–285. Baltimore: Johns Hopkins University Press, 1996.

Gérard-Zai, Marie-Claire. "Joseph Bédier." In *Menschen und Werke: Hundert Jahre wissenschaftliche Forschung an der Universität Freiburg Schweiz / Les Hommes et les œuvres de l'université: Cent ans de recherche scientifique à l'Université de Fribourg Suisse,* pp. 115–117. Fribourg: Éditions Universitaires, 1991.

Lot, Ferdinand. *Joseph Bédier (1864–1938)*. Paris: Droz, 1939.

Nykrog, Per. "A Warrior Scholar at the Collège de France: Joseph Bédier." In *Medievalism and the Modernist Temper*, ed. R. Howard Bloch and Stephen G. Nichols, pp. 286–307. Baltimore: Johns Hopkins University Press, 1996.

Vinaver, Eugène. *A la recherche d'une poétique médiévale*. Paris: Nizet, 1970.

BELIEF

Belief is the a priori or on-faith acceptance of the validity of a hypothetical relationship set. Belief implies that phenomena hypothesized to be related and/or the nature of the relationships posited to exist between them either have not been, cannot be, or need not be verified scientifically. To believe that it will rain if there's a ring around the moon or that a dead person can't be at peace in the grave as long as survivors mourn excessively is to regard such notions as being rooted in conventional wisdom. Such beliefs are valid because of the trustworthiness of the individuals from whom they are learned and because of personal experiences that exemplify and reinforce them.

Believing is panhuman and, as far as we know, unique to Homo sapiens. It is the basis for and essential for the perpetuation of all religions. Beliefs associated with recognized faiths are usually designated as *sacred* and judged to be more lofty and defensible than those dubbed *profane*. This qualitative distinction manifests itself linguistically in the widespread tendency to identify the former simply as beliefs and the latter as folk beliefs, popular beliefs, or superstitions. But the notion that a person can be cured miraculously from a fatal, medically untreatable disease is a belief whether the miracle worker is conceived to be a beneficent omnipotent deity or a tribal medicine man.

Historically, folklorists have focused on beliefs they judge to be either profane or quasi-sacred (i.e., seemingly associated with institutionalized religions but not sanctioned by their leaders or codified dogma). Some of these profane beliefs give traditional meanings of particular signs (e.g., a shooting star, a howling dog, or a ringing in one's ears portends a death). Others specify actions one should take or avoid (e.g., hang a horseshoe over your front door, carry a rabbit's foot, or eat black-eyed peas on New Year's Day to ensure good luck;

don't walk under a ladder, cross your legs on Sunday, or sweep the floor before sunrise or you'll have bad luck).

Fiction writers often utilize beliefs to exemplify or imply the worldviews and behaviors of their characters. Mark Twain portrays Huck Finn and Jim as both victims and exploiters of beliefs in supernatural phenomena and natural portents. Witchcraft beliefs define and dictate the behavior of Nathaniel Hawthorne's Young Goodman Brown. Shakespeare's plays are populated with a host of supernatural beings, and one must understand the belief in the existence of those beings if one is to comprehend and appreciate the plays. Characterizations in literary works of what individuals believe mirror the central part that belief plays in the lives of all human beings.

Robert A. Georges

See also Hawthorne, Nathaniel; Shakespeare, William; Twain, Mark

✳✳✳✳✳✳✳✳✳✳✳✳✳✳✳✳✳

References

Dundes, Alan. "The Structure of Superstition." In Alan Dundes, ed., *Analytic Essays in Folklore*, pp. 88–94. The Hague: Mouton, 1975.

Hand, Wayland D., ed. *Popular Beliefs and Superstitions from North Carolina*. Frank C. Brown Collection of North Carolina Folklore, vols. 6–7. Durham, N.C.: Duke University Press, 1961–1964.

Jones, Michael Owen. "Folk Beliefs: Knowledge and Action." *Southern Folklore Quarterly* 31 (1967): 304–309.

Ketner, Kenneth L. "Superstitious Pigeons, Hydrophobia, and Conventional Wisdom." *Western Folklore* 30 (1971): 1–17.

*B*EOWULF

Beowulf, the earliest English epic and one of the earliest English poems, is a frothy concoction of history, myth, and legend. Hygelac's raid into Francia occurred around the year 520, and Hrothgar built Heorot at what is now the Danish village of Leire, near Roskilde. But much occurred between the datable historical events on the Continent in the early sixth century, the composition of the poem in a Christian Anglican court in the early eighth century, and the unique manuscript of about 1100, which preserves the poem in an English dialect different from the one in which it was composed.

The action of the poem may be briefly described as follows. After

v.

Strǣt wæs stān fāh stīg wīsode gumum
ætgædere gūðbyrne scan heard
hond locen hring iren scir song in searo
wum þa hie to sele furðum in hyra gry
re geatwum gangan cwomon setton
sǣ meþe side scyldas rondas regn hearde
wið þæs recedes weal bugon þa to bence
byrnan hringdon guð searo gumena
garas stodon sæ manna searo samod
ætgædere æsc holt ufan græg wæs
þin heat wæpnum gewurþad þa ðær
wlonc hæleð oret mecgas æfter hæle
þum frægn hwanon ferigeað ge fætte
scyldas grǣge syrcan ⁊ grim helmas
here sceafta heap ic eom hroð gares
ar ⁊ ombiht ne seah ic elþeodige þus
manige men modiglicran wenic þ.gefor
wlenco nalles forwræc sīðum ac for hige

A page from the manuscript of Beowulf in the British Museum.

Hrothgar extends his political control over neighboring tribes, he builds a great meadhall called Heorot to epitomize his triumphs. The celebratory joys of the meadhall arouse the envy of the outcast monster Grendel, who attacks in the middle of the night, devours Hrothgar's warriors, and pollutes the seat of government. After 10 years of such desecration, Beowulf hears of the monster's depredations, crosses the sea to Hrothgar's kingdom, and offers to rid the hall of the demon. Beowulf defeats Grendel in hand-to-hand combat, but Grendel's mother avenges her dead son in an unexpected night attack. Beowulf defeats Grendel's mother in her hall beneath the sea and returns to triumph and reward in Heorot.

Beowulf returns to his own country to report his exploits to his king, Hygelac. When Hygelac dies, Beowulf rules for 50 peaceful years until a slave steals a goblet from the hoard of a dragon who takes vengeance by burning Beowulf's own meadhall and terrorizing the kingdom. Aided by the one faithful warrior, Wiglaf, who remains when Beowulf's other retainers flee, Beowulf eventually destroys the dragon but loses his life in doing so.

Early readers saw Beowulf's struggle with Grendel and his mother as a nature myth of a divine deliverer who saved the people from the personified powers of the stormy North Sea in early spring (or the pestilential swamp, or the terror of the winter night), and they saw the fight with the dragon as the lord's defeat by the onslaught of winter. More modern readers recognize in the poem a wonder tale of giant killing and dragon slaying popular among all the peoples of Europe. Both *Beowulf* and the Icelandic *Grettis saga* derive from a common original story of a monster who invades a dwelling and renders it uninhabitable until the hero arrives to defeat him. Since the name Beowulf means "bee-foe" (i.e., "bear") in many northern European languages, the core tale, or narrative kernel, may have contained some elements of the widely spread "Bear's Son," "Doughty Hans," or "The Hand and the Cradle" type of folktale (which emphasizes the ursine characteristics of the hero, especially his skill in wrestling) joined to a dragon-slayer tale (AT 300). Therefore, because the poem seems composed of two or three imperfectly connected lays (the struggles with ogres and a dragon) and the hero's adventures seem violently inserted among the historic names and exploits of early Danish and kings, *Beowulf* represents the confluence of a popular folktale with the heroic poetry of an aristocratic class.

Jerome Mandel

See also Epic; Tale-Type

✳✳✳✳✳✳✳✳✳✳✳✳✳✳✳✳✳✳

References

Bjork, Robert E., and John Niles, eds. *Beowulf Handbook*. Lincoln: University of Nebraska Press, 1997.

Clark, George. *Beowulf*. Boston: Twayne Publishers, 1990.

Fulk, R. D., ed. *Interpretations of Beowulf: A Critical Anthology*. Bloomington: Indiana University Press, 1991.

Hasenfratz, Robert J. *Beowulf Scholarship: An Annotated Bibliography, 1979–1990*. New York: Garland, 1993.

Klaeber, Fr., ed. *Beowulf and the Fight at Tinnsburg*. 3d ed. Boston: D. C. Heath, 1950.

Stitt, Michael J. *Beowulf and Bear's Son: Epic, Saga, and Fairytale in Northern Germanic Tradition*. New York: Garland, 1992.

Text in the original Old English and in an older translation, together with bibliography, and information about Anglo-Saxon life, history, language, and culture are available at <http://www.georgetown.edu/labyrinth>.

BIBLE

The Bible, meaning the Hebrew Bible, the sacred writings of Judaism and Christianity, and the New Testament—the sacred writings of Christianity—is a document that was largely created and developed in oral tradition. The Hebrew scriptures were transcribed between the sixth and fifth centuries B.C.E., and the Christian writings were transcribed in the early centuries of the common era.

Biblical literary critics, typified by the work of the German theologian Julius Wellhausen (1844–1918), have sought to discover the documentary sources used in the composition of the Hebrew Bible, and because of such work and the growing popularity of comparative methods and the associated ideas of cultural evolution, biblical scholars began to search for the antecedents of the Bible. Survival elements of more "primitive" times are thought to be evident in the Bible, and according to this thinking, folklore not only preceded the Hebrew Bible but actually evolved into the Bible. Form criticism developed in this context, and practitioners such as Herman Gunkel looked behind the texts to identify narrative elements or literary forms and to explore their context.

The goal of form criticism is to describe the character and significance of the situation in which biblical accounts developed. Gunkel, in *Das Märchen im Alten Testament* [Folktales in the Old Testament (1921)] attempted to isolate biblical narratives into separate literary units that, he argued, existed independently in recitation and in song long before they were written down in their biblical format; furthermore, he believed these narratives bore evidence of their origin. To discover or understand the context of formulation and recitation and to evaluate the original community and cultural settings of practitioners and believers, Gunkel separated these early folkloric elements by utilizing theories of European narrative formulation and transmission. Scholars such as J. G. Frazer and Lord Raglan have maintained that certain genres of literature—poetry, song, and drama—rose directly from the verbalization of religious myth and ritual. Others, including Susan Niditch, have addressed the role of recurrent themes and motifs in the Bible such as archetypes like "trickster" or the "child god." Alan Dundes, Lord Raglan, and Otto Rank have studied the lives of Moses and Jesus in relation to the characteristics of the traditional hero tale.

Biblical literary study continues with redaction criticism, which includes the last stages of editing the scriptures, structural study, analysis of biblical narratives, and biblical history. Additionally, scholars have examined character motifs and themes that have often been incorporated into nonbiblical works, including medieval mystery plays; the works of Dante, John Milton, Thomas Mann, William Faulkner, and Herman Melville; as well as contemporary writers who incorporate biblical themes into the plotlines, characterizations, and tone of their works.

Amanda Carson Banks

See also Archetype; Frazer, James George; Gunkel, Herman; Ritual

✳✳✳✳✳✳✳✳✳✳✳✳✳✳✳✳✳✳

References

Barton, J. *Reading the Old Testament: Method in Biblical Study.* Philadelphia: Westminster, 1984.

Gunkel, Herman. *Folktales in the Old Testament.* Trans. Michael D. Ritter. Sheffield, Eng.: Almond, 1987.

———. *The Psalms: A Form Criticism Introduction.* Trans. Thomas M. Horner. Philadelphia: Fortress, 1967.

Hayes, J. H. *An Introduction to Old Testament Study.* Nashville: Abingdon, 1979.

Niditch, Susan. *Folklore and the Hebrew Bible.* Minneapolis: Fortress, 1993.

BIERCE, AMBROSE GWINNETT (1842–1913?)

An American fiction writer, journalist, and critic, Ambrose Gwinnett Bierce made frequent use of folklore in his short stories. In addition, he manipulated cultural expectations of folk genres in his humorous collections of fables, poetry, and lexicography. In accordance with his famously bitter and misanthropic character, Bierce attacked folklore in his *Devil's Dictionary* (1906), a collection of humorous, sarcastic definitions:

> Mythology, *n*. The body of a primitive people's beliefs concerning its origin, early history, heroes, deities and so forth, as distinguished from the true accounts which it invents later.
>
> Fable, *n*. A brief lie intended to illustrate some important truth.

In those two entries, Bierce displayed a familiarity with folklore and harshly criticizes its nature, sneering at it as a medium for personal or collective gain. In his collection entitled *Fantastic Fables*, he manipulated the traditional form and contents of the genre. Traditional characters of fables such as dogs, lions, queens, soldiers, and birds inhabit the realm of Bierce's fables and interact freely with his own population, which includes doctors, lawyers, art critics, and "an inoffensive person." Bierce delivered characteristically scathing attacks on American civilization and, through his appropriation of this folk genre, packaged them in a way that is accessible and appealing to a very wide audience, in his day and now.

Bierce also applied the structure and contents of legend to many of his short stories. Stories in *In the Midst of Life* (*Collected Works*, vol. 2), influenced in large measure by his experiences as an officer in the Federal Army during the Civil War, and *Can Such Things Be?* (*Collected Works*, vol. 3) bear the markings of traditional oral legend and belief narrative. Most of these short stories are brief and episodic, have specific local or regional settings, and involve an element of belief regarding extraordinary events. "Present at a Hanging" (*Collected Works*, vol. 3), for example, is the story of a ghostly sighting not unlike contemporary urban legends that describe vanishing hitchhikers or other mysterious disappearances. Bierce's primary character and witness in this ghost story, a Christian minister, validates the legend through the peerless character and authority of his office, and the tale's conclusion lends itself more to a supernatural interpretation than to an explanation based on conventional circumstance. "Present at a Hanging," like most of Bierce's ghost stories, contains numerous motifs and beliefs listed in major folklore indexes.

Described as mean-spirited, imperious, and "the wickedest man in San Francisco" by his contemporaries and biographers, Bierce was nevertheless a celebrity in the city in which he did the majority of his writing. With a flair for the dramatic and almost certainly aware of the irony of the act, Bierce orchestrated his own disappearance in 1913. To this day, rumor and speculation dominate most of the discussions about his fate. In death, Bierce has himself become the subject of belief and legend—an appropriate afterlife for a man whose deep dissatisfaction with people led him to exploit folk narrative in his own writings.

Christopher Antonsen

See also Fable; Legend; Myth

✳✳✳✳✳✳✳✳✳✳✳✳✳✳✳✳✳

References

Bierce, Ambrose Gwinnett. *The Collected Works of Ambrose Bierce.* 12 vols. San Francisco: Neale Publishing Company, 1909–1912.

McWilliams, Carey. *Ambrose Bierce: A Biography.* New York: Archon Books, 1967.

Saunders, Richard. *Ambrose Bierce: The Making of a Misanthrope.* San Francisco: Chronicle Books, 1985.

*B*ILDUNGSROMAN

Sometimes translated into English as "apprenticeship" or "education," *Bildung* implies both cultivation and acculturation and refers indirectly to the *Bildungsreise* ("finishing voyage") taken by many privileged nineteenth-century youths after completing their studies and before settling into adult roles. Coined by Karl von Morgenstern in 1803, and later reinvented and popularized in Wilhelm Dilthey's biography of Friederich Schleiermacher, bildungsroman originally referred to a genre of German romantic novel typified by Goethe's *Wilhelm Meister's Apprenticeship* (1796). Christoph Martin Wieland's 1767 *Geschichte des Agathon* is also considered an early prototype.

Perhaps because early authors of the bildungsroman neither used the term nor defined their work as a single type, definitions and examples of the genre vary broadly. For some literary historians, the bildungsroman remains a phenomenon specific to its original era and/or place. Other critics identify most character development or plot resolution as thematic parallels to the type of development portrayed in the bildungsroman, and thus apply the term to modern literature, including nonfiction, films, poetry, and even modern fairy tales. Most scholars, however, limit the genre to works whose primarily German authors were influenced by the bildungsroman tradition and whose plots, structures, and philosophical resolutions parallel those of the earlier bildungsroman. Commonly cited postromantic examples include: Adalbert Stifter's *Der Nachsommer* [Indian summer (1857)], Gottfried Keller's *Der grüne Heinrich* [Green Henry (1880)], Thomas Mann's *Der Zauberberg* [The magic mountain (1924)], Hermann Hesse's *Das Glasperlenspiel* [The glass bead game (1943)], and more recent works by Peter Handke and Ulrich Plenzdorf.

In the traditional bildungsroman, a youth who is dissatisfied with his origins and the society in which he is expected to take a prefigured role leaves the familiar for individual goals and ideals. Destinations may be spiritual or geographic and have included alternative political and religious systems, theater, the big city, local or foreign countrysides, and even schizophrenic hallucinations. Experience brings the protagonist to the realization that he is ill-suited to the new life, and he returns home with, as Georg Hegel complained, "the rough spots knocked off of him ... and becomes a philistine just like all the others" (translation in Hardin 1991, p. 50). Other commentators have considered this resolution exemplary, crediting new wisdom or maturity for the youth's return.

As a genre defined largely by its concern with articulating the ambiguous relations of role to identity, society to the individual, fate to free will and self-creation, integrity to both psychic conflict and social mobility, and self to "other," the bildungsroman has remained relevant to modern culture and identity for the nearly 200 years since it first became popular. Because of the genre's biographical or autobiographical style (usually diaristic or confessional), it has reinforced a teleological model of identity in Western fiction and nonfiction, including many ethnographic accounts of interaction with cultural "others."

As "bourgeois epic," the originally democratizing bildungsroman is sometimes considered exclusive today. Implicit in most models of the genre are fixed social divisions, a nostalgic and exoticized image of social otherness, an image of *Bildung* as a finite process, and the implication that a relational model of identity is an immature phase. Many recent scholars have pointed out that these and other factors have excluded women and minority protagonists and thus denied them *Bildung* and the developed identity it implies. Others, such as Doris Lessing, who explicitly described her *Children of Violence* (1952–1969) series as a bildungsroman, suggest that concepts and expression move apace. And one of the genre's greatest problems, the ability to capture and evoke ambiguity, has always been one of its greatest strengths.

Clover Williams

See also Heroic Pattern

✳✳✳✳✳✳✳✳✳✳✳✳✳✳✳✳✳

References

Hardin, James, ed. *Reflection and Action: Essays on the Bildungsroman*. Columbia: University of South Carolina Press, 1991.

Kontje, Todd. *Private Lives in the Public Sphere: The German Bildungsroman as Metafiction*. University Park: Pennsylvania State University Press, 1992.

Labovitz, Esther K. *The Myth of the Heroine: The Female Bildungsroman in the Twentieth Century: Dorothy Richardson, Simone de Beauvoir, Doris Lessing, Christa Wolf*. New York: Peter Lang Verlag, 1986.

BLUES

"The blues" is a folk-song and musical genre reflecting the African-American cultural experience. A musical form with distinct features, harmonic progression, lyrical content, and performance style, the blues have also been influential in the shaping of African-American literature.

Blues most often conform to or vary somewhat from a basic 12-bar, AAB pattern. Lyrics typically contain several stanzas, each one comprising 12 measures of 4/4 time. The first line is usually repeated by the second, and the stanza ends with the third line, which often rhymes with the first two; however, each of the three lines may only take a few measures to sing, allowing two measures for an instrumental "response" to the vocal line. The most common harmonic sequence in these musical phrases is: tonic (I), subdominant (IV), and dominant (V) chords. The scale of most blues is based on "blue" notes, which are played slightly lower or flatter than they normally would be in a scale. Such notes include both major and minor thirds, major and minor sevenths, and perfect and flatted fifths.

Themes deal with problems in the everyday secular world, particularly relationships between men and women, an area of life on which the blues performer comments but finds no resolution. As David Evans (1982) points out, perhaps such a topic is common in blues lyrics because of the day-to-day uncertainty of relationships as well as the dancing and partying contexts in which the bluesman usually performs. Unemployment, ill health, alcohol and drugs, gambling, crime and prison, and tragedy are also subjects a performer might address. Lyrics employ culturally specific images and metaphors, such as comparing the object of one's desire to a horse or to a "handyman"; a distinctive vocabulary, such as "rider" referring to "woman" and "diddy-wah-diddy" referring to an ideal community or place; and traditional themes and subject matters mentioned above.

The blues as a distinct form emerged at least by the 1890s as a body of music African Americans performed not only for entertainment but also to commiserate with others about their frustrations and problems in everyday life. In a natural context, a bluesman would draw upon his knowledge of the blues tradition: he might extemporaneously compose on the spot, not by coming up with new stanzas or ideas, but by combining stanzas in a unique way.

A part of the African-American oral tradition, the blues are meant to be heard rather than read, yet much African-American literature is rooted in the blues, such as the poetry of Langston Hughes, who utilized a classic blues structure. The blues have also been central in shaping black literary traditions as defined by such twentieth-century writers as Ralph Ellison, Zora Neale Hurston, Alice Walker, Arthur Flowers, and Gloria Naylor.

Not only is the blues a central tradition in American music, but its poetry incorporates many aspects of black expressive culture. James Weldon Johnson viewed the blues in the 1930s as a wonderful repository of folk poetry, one that the poet Sterling Brown celebrated in his writings as well and that Langston Hughes perpetuated in his 1958 edition of *The Book of Negro Folklore*. Having first heard the blues in Kansas City in 1911 at the age of nine, Hughes embraced the classic blues singers of the 1920s and recognized the traditional mood associated with the blues, despondency. However, when sung, the blues also made people laugh; therefore, blues was a transforming agent to Hughes, something that brought pleasure out of unpleasurable emotions.

Hughes felt that the blues as an expressive form was vital to the poetic movement in the United States in the 1920s, which emphasized that poetry should attempt to capture experiences with just a few visual and auditory images. He demonstrated his own use of the blues in such poems as "The Weary Blues," which describes a blues performance, and "Young Gal's Blues," which focuses on a young friend's sudden death that reminds the protagonist of her own mortality. In these and other poems, Hughes underscored a common theme that testifies to the universal appeal of the blues: bad things must happen; hard luck is going to take place.

Among late-twentieth-century writers who employ the blues and blues themes is Arthur Flowers, who wrote *Another Good Loving Blues* (1993). "I am *griot*," says the narrator in the opening lines, identifying himself as an active bearer of an oral African-American literary tradition. The *griot*, or storyteller, has the power to give people immortality, to transcend mutability, to transform reality in order to create one's own reality—a "true lie."

Gloria Naylor is another of a growing number of African-American novelists who infuses her art with blues themes and techniques. Naylor's main narrator of *Bailey's Cafe* (1992) is a bluesman who claims, "There's a whole set to be played here if you want to stick around and listen to the music."

Such trends in literature, particularly African-American literature, testify to the blues as a vital part of black expressive culture and identity. Nowhere does this prospect seem more evident than in Houston A. Baker, Jr.'s poststructural analysis of African-American literature in which he argues that the blues should be viewed as a network, the "enabling *script* in which Afro-American cultural discourse is inscribed."

Richard Allen Burns

See also Ellison, Ralph; Hurston, Zora Neale; Johnson, James Weldon; Oral-Formulaic Composition and Theory; Poststructuralism; Storytelling

✳✳✳✳✳✳✳✳✳✳✳✳✳✳✳✳✳

References

Baker, Houston A., Jr. *Blues, Ideology, and Afro-American Literature: A Vernacular Theory*. Chicago: University of Chicago Press, 1984.

Evans, David. *Big Road Blues: Tradition and Creativity in the Folk Blues*. Berkeley: University of California Press, 1982.

Flowers, Arthur. *Another Good Loving Blues*. New York: Viking, 1993.

Hughes, Langston, and Arne Bontemps. *The Book of Negro Folklore*. New York: Dodd, Mead, 1958.

Naylor, Gloria. *Bailey's Cafe*. London: Heinemann, 1992.

Titon, Jeff Todd. *Downhome Blues Lyrics: An Anthology from the Post–World War II Era*. Chicago: University of Chicago Press, 1990 (1981).

BOCCACCIO, GIOVANNI (1313–1375)

The Italian poet, scholar, and author of the *Decameron,* Giovanni Boccaccio was the illegitimate son of a merchant. He was brought up in his father's family and learned commerce in Naples where he was introduced to admirers of Petrarch, with whom he would become close friends. He claimed, like Petrarch and Dante, that while in Naples he actually met the woman whom he exalted in idealized love, Fiammetta. With the bankruptcy of his family in 1340, Boccaccio moved to Florence; he faced financial difficulties for the rest of his life.

Boccaccio's early work—imaginative, creative, and written in the vernacular—makes use of a number of traditional tales. His many sources included classical authors such as Ovid, the Provençal poets William of Poitou and Guilhem de Cabestanh, the churchman Peter Abelard, and recent or contemporary authors like Dante and Petrarch as well as current oral tradition and local folklore. Among his early works are *La caccia di Diana* [Diana's hunt (1340)] and *Teseida* (1340–1341), based on classical themes, and *Filostrato* (1338), a retelling of the legend of Troilus and Cressida. The principal work of his years in Florence is the *Decameron* (1348–1355), for which he is best known today. At once medieval and modern, its stories provided inspiration for Geoffrey Chaucer as well as for Giambattista Basile, Hans Sachs, Gianfrancesco Straparola, William Shakespeare, and many other European authors.

By the early 1350s, Boccaccio had come under the influence of Petrarch and the ideals of Renaissance humanism, and his later works (excepting the misogynistic *Il Corbaccio* [1354–1364] and his notes on the life of Dante) are very different from his early ones. His early works were considered entertainment and were addressed to an audience of women, but his later works were meant for educated men. They show the influence of classical writers such as Varro, Martial, Apuleius, Seneca, Ovid, and especially Tacitus. These works are scholarly rather than imaginative in character and were written in Latin instead of Italian. Among them are *De claris mulieribus* [Concerning famous women (1360–1374)], *De casibus virorum illustrium* [On the fates of famous men (1355–1374)], and *De genealogia deorum gentilium* [On the genealogy of the gods and the gentiles (1350–1374)]. The last work is a compendium of stories of the classical gods, goddesses, and heroic figures—not so much a collection of allegories as an encyclopedia of mythology. These three were his best known and most respected works during his lifetime. Boccaccio was also instrumental in the translation of Homer's poems from Greek to Latin, which marks the beginning of Greek studies by the humanists.

Scholars have preferred Boccaccio's early work, paying special attention to the assessment of this body of work in relation to the development of the novella as a literary form. Folklore scholars have assisted by determining the origin and provenance of tale-types and motifs and by examining Boccaccio's role in the transmission of these tales to later authors. Drawing on theories concerning the relationship between literary and oral traditions, more recent scholarship has examined the process of tale transmission and transformation under the influence of social change, the appropriation of folk material by the new bourgeoisie, the emergence of new literary forms, and the relationship of text to orality in the determination of the historical circumstances of a tale's generation.

John Cash

See also Apuleius; Chaucer, Geoffrey; *Decameron*; Homer; Motif; Shakespeare, William; Tale-Type

✳✳✳✳✳✳✳✳✳✳✳✳✳✳✳✳✳✳

References

Bergin, Thomas G. *Boccaccio*. New York: Viking Press, 1981.

Bruni, Francesco. *Boccaccio: L'Invenzione della letteratura mezzana*. Bologna: Il Mulino, 1990.

Cassell, Anthony K. *The Corbaccio*, 2d rev. ed. Binghampton, NY: *Medieval and Renaissance Texts and Studies*, 1993.

Neuschäfer, Hans-Jorg. *Boccaccio und der Beginn der Novelle: Strukturen der Kurzerzählung auf der Schwelle zwischen Mittelalter und Neuzeit*. Munich: Wilhelm Fink Verlag, 1969.

Rotunda, D. P. *Motif-Index of the Italian Novella in Prose*. Bloomington: Indiana University, 1941.

Serafini-Sauli, Judith Powers. *Giovanni Boccaccio*. Boston: Twayne Publishers, 1982.

BOTKIN, BENJAMIN A. (1901–1975)

Benjamin A. Botkin, a folklorist now remembered mainly for his highly successful folklore "treasuries," or anthologies, taken from folk tradition and printed sources, was also an early advocate of applied folklore and multicultural studies. Born in 1901, his youth was spent in and around Boston. He earned a B.A. at Harvard in 1920 and took an M.A. in English at Columbia in 1921, writing a thesis on a Manx poet. Ten years later, in 1931, Botkin received his Ph.D. from the University of Nebraska with a thesis on play-party songs that was published in 1937 as *The American Play-Party Song*, his first book. Before completing his doctorate, Botkin founded and edited the regional annual *Folk-Say*, which was published from 1929 to 1932. The annual took its title from a term Botkin coined in 1928 to describe freely circulating historical and literary material, mostly oral.

In 1937, Botkin went to Washington, D.C., to do research at the Library of Congress and remained there for eight years. He spent the years 1938–1941 as national folklore editor for the Works Progress Administration (WPA) and as chief editor of the Writers' Unit of the Library of Congress Project; in 1942, he became head of the library's Archive of Folk Song. In 1945, after the great success of his book *A Treasury of American Folklore* (1944), he resigned from the Library of Congress and moved to New York to devote himself full time to writing. Over the next 30 years he turned out a large number of books; at the time of his death he was planning a book on American social myths and symbols, which was supposed to be a summation of his ideas and life's work.

Of Botkin's several publications, a few deserve special mention. His study of play-party songs is still a valuable comparative reference dealing with a once-popular folk tradition. *Lay My Burden Down*, (1945), a book based on WPA interviews with ex-slaves, is a pioneering work in oral history. His several "treasuries" of folklore gained much favorable publicity for folklore, making the topic accessible and enjoyable for people who would not otherwise have picked up a book on the topic. Some of these compilations dealt with occupational and urban lore, aspects of traditional lore that at the time had received little attention from folklorists. The whole series is marred, however, by the mixing of traditional and nontraditional materials with no real distinctions made between them. If one considers Botkin's concept of folklore and his ultimate goal, it is not surprising that he took such an approach, for he subscribed to the anthropological view that folklore is merely part of the study of culture rather than an independent field having value in its own right. Therefore, he primarily thought of traditional lore as material that is useful in achieving some goal beyond that of folklore scholarship—in his case, to document the soul of America.

W. K. McNeil

See also Oral History; Tradition

✳✳✳✳✳✳✳✳✳✳✳✳✳✳✳✳✳

References

Botkin, B. A. *The American Play-Party Song.* New York: Frederick Ungar, 1963 (1937).

———. *Lay My Burden Down: A Folk History of Slavery.* Chicago: University of Chicago Press, 1945.

———. *A Treasury of American Folklore: Stories, Ballads, and Traditions of the People.* New York: Crown, 1944.

Hirsch, Jerrold. "Folklore in the Making: B. A. Botkin." *Journal of American Folklore* 100 (1987): 3–38.

Widner, Ronna Lee. "Lore for the Folk: Benjamin A. Botkin and the Development of Folklore Scholarship in America." *New York Folklore* 12 (1986): 1–22.

BRENTANO, CLEMENS (1778–1842)

Clemens Brentano was a German romantic author of poems, novellas, and fairy tales. Together with Achim von Arnim, he published *Des knaben Wunderhorn* (1805–1808), the first collection of German folk songs. European legends and folktales were the inspiration for much of Brentano's poetry and prose, and as with many of the romantic writers, Brentano's interest in oral tradition grew out of a desire to reproduce the style of folk songs in his own poetry. Contained in *Des knaben Wunderhorn* are many of his own creations, including "The Lore Lay," his rendition of the legend of a young woman seated atop a cliff overlooking the Rhine whose appearance and voice caused sailors to crash onto the rocks below.

The Rhine was also the setting for many of Brentano's fairy tales. *Fairy Tales of the Rhine* was written in 1812–1813 but was published posthumously with other tales in 1846–1847 by Guido Görres, another member of the Heidelberg circle and author of *The German*

Folk Books, under the title *The Fairy Tales of Clemens Brentano*. In the frame story of the Rhine fairy tales, Brentano mixed and matched motifs from the legends of the Pied Piper of Hamelin and the Lore Lay, to name a few of the more recognizable sources, with stylistic brilliance and yet with a disturbing disregard for the integrity of individual legend traditions. Brentano's Italian heritage and familiarity with Giambattista Basile were also reflected in his collection of Italian fairy tales.

Ironically, Brentano's greatest contribution to the study of the fairy tale lies in his carelessness in leaving behind a manuscript of early folktale notations sent to him by Jacob Grimm. The discovery of the Ölenberg manuscript (after the Ölenberg monastery in Alsace) in the early twentieth century has been attributed the status of an ur-text for *Kinder- und Hausmärchen* [Children's and household tales (1850)], offering subsequent generations of scholars invaluable insights into the editorial practices of Jacob and Wilhelm Grimm.

Mary Beth Stein

See also Arnim, Achim von; Basile, Giambattista; Fairy Tale; Grimm, Jacob and Wilhelm; Legend; Motif

✳✳✳✳✳✳✳✳✳✳✳✳✳✳✳✳✳

References

Fetzer, John. *Clemens Brentano*. Boston: Twayne Publishers, 1981.

———. *Romantic Orpheus: Profiles of Clemens Brentano*. Berkeley and Los Angeles: University of California Press, 1974.

Hanak, Miroslav. "Brentano's Manifestation of the Romantic Ethos: Sublimation of Meaning into Music and Legend." In *A Guide to Romantic Poetry in Germany*, ed. Miroslav Hanak. New York and Bern: Peter Lang, 1987, pp. 123–141.

Briggs, KATHARINE (1898–1980)

Born 1898 and educated at Oxford, Katharine Briggs was for many years an active member of the English Folk-Lore Society, and after her death, the society established a lecture series in her name. Briggs was a prolific writer whose specialty was the study of fairy lore, though she also published important works on witchcraft and folk narrative.

Briggs's collection of English folk narrative, *Folktales of England*

(1965), done with the storyteller Ruth Tongue, is an excellent short collection and is partially based on fieldwork. Briggs was, however, primarily a literary and archive-oriented folklorist. Her edition of *A Dictionary of British Folktales in the English Language*, 4 vols. (1970)—which like her *Folktales of England* contains legends as well as folktales—is essential for the study of the English language folk narrative in Great Britain and largely contains stories collected in the nineteenth and early twentieth centuries. Thus, although the work is often well annotated in terms of motifs and tale-types and parallels, it reflects older British traditions rather than current ones.

Her work on fairy lore and witchcraft also emphasizes the older traditions. Briggs's two books on early modern folk belief, *The Anatomy of Puck: An Examination of Fairy Beliefs among Shakespeare's Contemporaries and Successors* (1959), a study of fairy beliefs, and *Pale Hecate's Team* (1962), a study of witchcraft, remain useful for their use of literary sources. But, as Keith Thomas notes in his *Religion and the Decline of Magic* (1971), Briggs is not "much concerned with their social function" (p. 606). This lack of analytical interest is characteristic of all of her work, which, in fact, tends toward the popular survey. The best of her work is *The Vanishing People: Fairy Lore and Legends* (1978), a survey based largely on English materials, but with comparisons to other fairy traditions, and *An Encyclopedia of Fairies, Hobgoblins, Brownies, Bogies, and other Supernatural Creatures* (1976). The *Encyclopedia* is one of those rare works that is at once useful to the scholar as a reference work and accessible to a popular audience. In it, Briggs gives, in dictionary form, a survey of fairy beliefs and brief entries on scholars and writers who have written about the fairies.

Even though recent work on fairy lore—especially Barbara Rieti's *Strange Terrain: The Fairy World in Newfoundland* (1991); Peter Narváez, ed., *The Good People: New Fairy Lore Essays* (1991); and the special issue of *Béaloideas* (also in 1991) titled *The Fairy Hill Is on Fire!*—has largely superseded Briggs's work on the fairies, her works do retain value for their assemblage of disparate sources and for their accessibility.

David E. Gay

See also Belief; Folktale; Motif; Tale-Type; Witchcraft

✳✳✳✳✳✳✳✳✳✳✳✳✳✳✳✳✳✳

References

Briggs, Katharine. *The Anatomy of Puck: An Examination of Fairy Beliefs among*

Shakespeare's Contemporaries and Successors. London: Routledge and Kegan Paul, 1959.

Narváez, Peter, ed. *The Good People: New Fairylore Essays*. New York: Garland, 1991.

Rieti, Barbara. *Strange Terrain: The Fairy World in Newfoundland*. St. John's: Institute of Social and Economic Research, Memorial University of Newfoundland, 1991.

Thomas, Keith. *Religion and the Decline of Magic*. New York: Scribner, 1971.

Bulosan, Carlos (1911–1956)

The Asian-American poet, novelist, and labor journalist Carlos Bulosan was born into a peasant family in the town of Binalonan, Pangasinan Province, in the Philippines in 1911. Although the Bulosan family faced increasingly difficult circumstances and were forced to sell off much of their land to finance the emigration of Carlos's three older brothers to the United States, Carlos received a formal education in the Philippines that included two years of secondary school, during which time he wrote for the school newspaper. In 1930, he joined his brothers and tens of thousands of other young Filipino men by emigrating to the United States and working in the fields and canneries on the West Coast.

After his arrival in the United States, Bulosan worked for a time as an agricultural and a fish cannery worker, but his frail health would not permit long-term physical exertion. He became a writer and publicist for the United Cannery, Agricultural, Packing and Allied Workers of America (UCAPAWA), one of the few unions that was interested in organizing farmworkers and would accept Filipinos as members. Bulosan's commitment to the struggle for social justice would be the central theme of his literary career.

It was Bulosan's poetry—anthologized in Helen Hoyt's collection of California poets, *244 Contemporaries*, and published in *Lyric, Poetry*, and other magazines—that first brought him literary acclaim in the 1930s. In the 1940s, he published numerous short stories and essays in the *Arizona Quarterly, Commonwealth Times, New Yorker, Harpers*, and *Saturday Evening Post*.

In 1944, Harcourt, Brace published Bulosan's *The Laughter of My Father,* a collection of short stories about peasant life in the Philippines, many of which were based on Filipino folktales. His autobiographical novel and best known work, *America Is in the*

Heart (1946), is a personalized account of the struggle of thousands of Filipino laborers for dignity in the face of brutal hardships in both the colonized Philippines and in the United States. The physical poverty and spiritual strength of peasant life in the Philippines were both something to escape from and a potential source of strength for Bulosan. His account of peasant life and his retelling of a Philippine folktale in the beginning of the collection is completely unsentimental.

Although the stories retold in *The Laughter of My Father* were for the most part humorous, it would be a mistake to miss the irony in them and to label Bulosan, as one critic did, a "pure comic spirit." Responding in an essay, "I Am Not a Laughing Man," published in *Writer* in 1946 and reprinted in *On Becoming Filipino* (1995), Bulosan revealed that the motive force behind his writing was anger, not humor (p. 138). In writing *America Is in the Heart*, Bulosan found that Filipino folklore, ignored by Filipino writers up to that time, was "a new treasure" to be "integrated in our struggle for liberty." In his essay "How My Stories Were Written," published after his death, an ancient Filipino storyteller, Apo Lacay, engages in an imaginary dialogue that reveals Bulosan's intention to demonstrate the ways in which the peasants' laughter is an expression of wisdom and is deployed as a form of resistance in the everyday lives of the poor and oppressed.

In the late 1940s, Bulosan came under attack by the right wing both in the United States and in the Philippines for his openly acknowledged enthusiasm for proletarianism. Although his career as a writer was severely curtailed, Bulosan continued to write, and in the years before his death, he turned his attention to the struggle in the Philippines. His collection of Filipino folktales was published posthumously with the title *The Philippines Is in the Heart* (1975), and *Power to the People*, a novel about the communist Hukbalahap movement, was published in Canada in 1977.

Robert Lee

See also Folktale

✳✳✳✳✳✳✳✳✳✳✳✳✳✳✳✳✳✳

References

Bulosan, Carlos. *The Laughter of My Father*. New York: Harcourt, Brace, 1943.
———. *The Philippines Is in the Heart*. Intro. E. San Juan, Jr. Quezon City: New Day Publishers, 1978.
San Juan, Jr., E. *If You Want to Know What We Are*. Albuquerque: West End Press, 1983.

————. *Reading the West/Writing the East: Studies in Comparative Literature and Culture*. New York: Peter Lang, 1992.

San Juan, Jr., E., ed. *Bulosan: An Introduction with Selections*. Manila: National Bookstore, 1983.

————. *On Becoming Filipino: Selected Writings of Carlos Bulosan*. Philadelphia: Temple University Press, 1995.

BUNRAKU

The puppet theater of Japan, *bunraku*, combines the manipulation of puppets, the strumming of a single three-stringed musical instrument, *shamisen*, and a chanter who speaks the parts of all the puppets. Founded in the late sixteenth century, *bunraku* achieved its greatest fame and popularity between the late seventeenth and mid-eighteenth centuries with the appearance of the great chanter Takemoto Gidayū (1651–1714) and Japan's greatest playwright, Chikamatsu Monzaemon (1653–1724).

The larger puppets used in *bunraku* are manipulated by three men. The main puppeteer controls the head and right arm, the second controls the left hand, and the third controls the feet. During the performance, the main puppeteer wears very formal dress while the other two are dressed in black with hoods covering their faces. It is said this convention developed from both the ego of the early main puppeteers, who wanted to be recognized for their art, and the desire of the audience to see their faces.

During the period of greatest development and popularity, that is, the seventeenth and eighteenth centuries, *bunraku* and *kabuki* were locked in a fierce competition with each other. Some playwrights, like Chikamatsu, wrote for both kinds of theater. By 1705, however, Chikamatsu began writing exclusively for *bunraku*, and it was at this time that he became famous for his *shinjūmono* ("love suicide plays"). These plays, based as they were on actual events, became instant hits and were so popular that the government periodically banned their performance since they seemed to glorify people who chose death together rather than an unhappy life fulfilling their appointed roles. These plays displayed the classic conflict of a Confucian-based society between *giri* ("duty") and *ninjo* ("human feelings/emotions").

The most popular *bunraku* play was written by three playwrights

A bunraku (*puppet theater*) *performance in Kyushu, Japan, 1993.*

soon after Chikamatsu's death. This play, *Kanadehon Chūshingura*, which consists of 11 acts, is based on the true story of 47 *ronin* ("masterless samurai") who plotted for two years (1701–1703) to slay an evil government official who had insulted their master. In an attempt to avenge this insult, their master had attacked the official and, as a result, was forced to commit *seppuku* ("ritual disembowelment"). After two years of meticulous and secret planning, the *ronin* attacked, captured, and beheaded the official and triumphantly marched through the streets of Edo (Tokyo) carrying the severed head to the grave of their master. Months later, the government ordered all 47 *ronin* to disembowel themselves to atone for the crime of carrying out their vendetta. When these events occurred, they created a sensation in the capital, and the play, which also created a sensation, has been one of the mainstays of *bunraku* and *kabuki* through the years. Although based on historical fact, many of the episodes and characters, as in most historical *bunraku* plays, have taken on larger-than-life qualities. The play's themes of duty, honor, and loyalty and the ability of the *ronin* to sacrifice personal happiness and family for those ideals have struck a cord with many Japanese for over 250 years.

Richard W. Anderson

See also *Kabuki; Opera di Pupi*

✳✳✳✳✳✳✳✳✳✳✳✳✳✳✳✳✳

References

Brandon, James R., ed. *Chūshingura: Studies in Kabuki and the Puppet Theater.* Honolulu: University of Hawaii Press, 1982.

Gerstle, Andrew C. *Circles of Fantasy: Convention in the Plays of Chikamatsu.* Cambridge, Mass.: Council on East Asian Studies, 1986.

Keene, Donald. *Bunraku: The Art of the Japanese Puppet Theatre.* Tokyo: Kodansha, 1965.

Keene, Donald, trans. *The Battles of Coxinga.* London: Taylor Foreign Press, 1951.

———. *Chūshingura: The Treasury of the Loyal Retainers.* New York: Columbia University Press, 1971.

———. *Major Plays of Chikamatsu.* New York: Columbia University Press, 1961.

Ortolani, Benito. *The Japanese Theatre: From Shamanistic Ritual to Contemporary Pluralism.* Princeton, N.J.: Princeton University Press, 1995.

BUNYAN, PAUL

Dismissed in the 1950s by folklorist Richard Dorson as "fakelore" and a "pseudo folk hero of twentieth-century mass culture," the giant lumberjack hero, Paul Bunyan, nevertheless continues to be associated in the popular imagination with the best known heroes of American folklore. The first printed reference to Paul Bunyan is probably a 1910 newspaper article by James McGillivray, but the broad popularization started with an advertising booklet written by one W. B. Laughead for a lumber company in 1914. By the 1920s, there were two books and numerous articles in national magazines about Paul Bunyan, and in subsequent years, children's literature became the major vehicle for disseminating Paul Bunyan stories. Continued interest in him is manifest in the many local festivals, wood carvings, regional dramas, and log-rolling and wood-chopping contests named for Paul Bunyan.

One of the popularizers of Paul Bunyan was the folklorist Benjamin A. Botkin, who saw him as both tall tale and legendary hero for lumberjacks. Botkin was aware of the print influences on the tradition but preferred to emphasize Paul Bunyan as a distinctly American folk hero. Bunyan then became a contested figure in the scholarly argument between Benjamin Botkin and Richard Dorson over folklore versus fakelore, with Botkin promoting Paul Bunyan in his treasuries of national, regional, and occupational folklore and Dorson debunking Bunyan in his scholarly articles and books.

There have been some orally told Paul Bunyan tales collected by folklorists and others, but there does not seem to be a strong oral tradition of Bunyan lore. That fact does not mean that Paul Bunyan is not worthy of study; Dorson recognized Paul Bunyan's cultural importance as a symbol of American economic power even as he dismissed him as fakelore. A more fruitful and less judgmental approach, as Alan Dundes (1985) has pointed out, would be to consider Paul Bunyan as an "invented tradition," part of a cultural process that European folklorists call *folklorismus*, the commercialization of folklore. Folklorists should study the Paul Bunyan stories that are sometimes told in the small-group context of loggers' camps while recognizing how the local occupational tradition interacts with the larger context of the national media. Also of interest to folklorists should be the local Paul Bunyan festivals and how an invented tradition becomes accepted as part of community behavior and identity, often with tourism as a contributing factor.

The images of Paul Bunyan that are familiar to most Americans are of a giant lumberjack standing next to his giant blue ox, Babe, after having dug out the Grand Canyon or created some other tremendous topographical feature. The specific stories can be found in a wide range of popular literature from chamber-of-commerce brochures to comic books and children's stories, but there are only a few direct references to Paul Bunyan in the American literary canon. Robert Frost wrote a poem about "Paul's Wife," Louis Untermeyer rendered some of the tales in poetic form, and W. H. Auden wrote an operetta, *Paul Bunyan*, with Benjamin Britten. A greater influence on American literature is an indirect one: the way Paul Bunyan has become part of American consciousness as the elemental American occupational hero—powerful, determined, good-natured, able to perform impossible tasks—the embodiment of American optimism and achievement.

Patrick B. Mullen

See also Botkin, Benjamin A.; Dorson, Richard M.; Fakelore; Folklorism; Legend; Tall Tale

✱✱✱✱✱✱✱✱✱✱✱✱✱✱✱✱✱

References

Botkin, Benjamin A. A *Treasury of American Folklore*. New York: Crown,
1944.
Dorson, Richard M. *American Folklore*. Chicago: University of Chicago Press,
1959.
Dundes, Alan. "Nationalistic Inferiority Complexes and the Fabrication of
Fakelore: A Reconsideration of Ossian, the *Kinder- und Hausmärchen*, the
Kalevala, and Paul Bunyan." *Journal of Folklore Research* 22 (1985): 5–18.
Hoffman, Daniel G. *Paul Bunyan, Last of the Frontier Demigods*. Philadelphia:
University of Pennsylvania Press, 1952.

Burns, Robert (1759–1796)

The Scottish poet Robert Burns incorporated a variety of folkloric
traditions into his own work, a largely unconscious practice that in
part earned him the appellation "national poet of Scotland." The
son of a gardener and tenant farmer, Burns learned agricultural practices at firsthand and absorbed from the agrarian milieu a range of
cultural beliefs and customs. Together with his more formal education and an innate interest in and awareness of larger social issues,
this societal context provided Burns with the material—both concrete and abstract—for many of his finest creative works.

At least on the surface, Burns depicted things that seemed
uniquely Scottish in both poetry and song, evidenced in the so-
called Kilmarnock edition of *Poems, Chiefly in the Scottish Dialect*
(1786), which received notice from the literary arbiters of the day
who had turned their attention to artistic evidence of a distinctly
Scottish culture. "The Cottar's Saturday Night" describes a farming
family in repose and depicts family worship; "Holy Willie's Prayer"
mocks the false piety of a religious zealot; "The Jolly Beggars" depicts
a rousing musical gathering of the down-and-out of society. In part,
these poems describe the traditional way of life as essential background against which or within which Burns could offer his own particular point of view/commentary whether idealizing the cottar's life
or pointing out the shortcomings of certain behavior, like that of
Holy Willie.

Burns's many and rich uses of folklore constitute on occasion ethnographic description, what has been called by literary analysts "manners painting," as in "Halloween," a marvelous poem, complete with footnotes, that explains beliefs and practices. Elsewhere, as in his masterpiece "Tam o' Shanter," Burns retells then-current legends, presenting them in a believable context that poetically reproduces the dialectics of the legend: the multiple responses typically exhibited whenever potentially and/or hypothetically believable oral narratives are shared.

First and last, Burns was a consummate writer of songs, and he almost always had a particular tune, often a traditional one, in mind. Some of his songs were completely his own; others were inspired by or based on traditional materials; still others were undoubtedly transcriptions of songs he had heard or learned orally. In fact, Burns was one of the first serious students of the Scottish folk song and actively, if informally, collected them, particularly for James Johnson's *The Scots Musical Museum* (1787–1803). So close to tradition are some of his own songs, whether original or edited, that it is almost impossible to know for sure whether or not a lyric—such as the one beginning "O my Luve's like a red, red rose"—is indeed his.

As a man, Burns seems to have risen above, or at least out of, his peasant and artisanal roots, by reputation if not in reality—something no doubt many people would like to do. He gained a near-heroic status in his own time and certainly afterward: a legendary tradition grew up focusing on his poetic capabilities, his impromptu compositions, his success rate at seduction, and his kindnesses to people less fortunate than himself. In fact, he has become over time a symbol for Scotland. His birthday is celebrated yearly around January 25 in a calendar custom, most typically called the Burns Night Supper, which features speeches recalling the legendary traditions, performances of his poems and songs, and the sharing of Scottish food and drink.

As a poet and songwriter, Burns drew from the cultural tradition that he inherited, making the customs, beliefs, songs, and tunes—orally current and lived—a part of his permanent literary work. Without conscious plan or design, he gave back to that ongoing cultural tradition by creating songs that have become a part of the traditional fund of songs but more especially by becoming the central figure in a legendary and calendrical tradition that, like his creative works, continues to have literary and cultural relevance today.

Mary Ellen Brown

See also Legend; Scottish Literature

✳✳✳✳✳✳✳✳✳✳✳✳✳✳✳✳✳

References

Brown, Mary Ellen. *Burns and Tradition*. London: Macmillan, 1984.

————. "Robert Burns (1759–1796)." In *Dictionary of Literary Biography: Eighteenth-Century British Poets*, vol. 109, 2d series, ed. John Sitter. Detroit: Gale Research, 1991, pp. 33–53.

Crawford, Thomas. *Burns: A Study of the Poems & Songs*. Edinburgh: Oliver and Boyd, 1960.

Kinsley, James, ed. *The Poems and Songs of Robert Burns*. 3 vols. Oxford: Clarendon Press, 1968.

Bylinas

Bylinas (Russian, *byliny*) are Russian songs recorded mainly in the eighteenth and nineteenth centuries but going back to older periods. The oldest bylinas were probably composed in the eleventh century. As a genre, bylinas are hard to distinguish from so-called historical songs about such figures as Ivan the Terrible and Peter I. The best known bylinas center around Grand Duke Vladimir and his *bogatyrí* ("retinue") "heroes": Iliá Múromets, Dobrynia Nikítich, and Alésha Popóvnich. Although Vladimir died in 1015 and the Mongol ruler Batu Khan invaded Russia in 1236–1242, bylinas of the Kiev cycle depict the victories of Vladimir's *bogatyrí* over the Mongols. Unlike his ancient Greek and Western European counterparts, the Russian epic hero usually returns home in triumph and is ready for new exploits. Vladimir himself does little and is often portrayed as a despot and coward.

Some bylinas resemble novellas and popular farces; others are close to fairy tales and draw on mythological plots. The supernaturally strong Sviatogór, for example, fails to pick up a bag that contains the weight of the whole earth; later he gets into a coffin and the lid closes shut. Volkh is born to a woman and a snake and can take the shape of different animals. Sadkó spends time as the guest of the underwater king, Iliá Múromets's first opponent is a rapacious bird, and Pótyk marries a swan maiden. Many episodes in bylinas are based on such international motifs as the male Cinderella, the husband at his wife's wedding, heroic wooing, and a duel between father and son. Vladimir's retainers are not the only protagonists in Russian bylinas.

Sadkó is a Novgorod merchant, Vasílii Busláevich instigates the Novgorod rabble, and Mikúla Selianínovich is a peasant who skillfully puts an aristocrat to shame. Some of the recorded texts reach 1,000 lines, but the average bylina is much shorter.

The chronology of individual bylinas, their historicity, and their dependence on foreign models, as well as the circumstances under which they arose, are matters of debate. Bylinas became popular among Russian intellectuals when A. F. Iakubóvich published a collection in 1804 of 26 songs dictated or recorded by Kirsha Danilov. Since then, hundreds of texts have been collected. It is not known in what social stratum bylinas originated. The hypothesis that many of them were composed by courtly singers, later became the property of jugglers (tumblers), and finally reached the peasants has been attacked chiefly on ideological grounds as belittling the creative powers of common people.

In the North of Russia, bylinas are chanted by only one person. In some other regions, two or three singers participate, and among the Cossacks, bylinas are performed in chorus. A few bylinas are among the staples of children's literature in present-day Russia. Very popular are Rimsky-Korsakov's opera *Sadko* (1867) and Anton Arensky's fantasy for piano and orchestra, "Phantasia on the Themes from Riabinin" (1899). Bylina tunes have been used by a number of composers, including Mussorgsky in the opera *Boris Godunov* (1869).

Anatoly Liberman

See also Ballad; Motif; Russian Ballad

✳✳✳✳✳✳✳✳✳✳✳✳✳✳✳✳✳

References

Propp, Vladimir. *Theory and History of Folklore*. Trans. Ariadna Y. Martin and Richard P. Martin, ed. with intro. and notes by Anatoly Liberman. Minneapolis: University of Minnesota Press, 1984.

Sokolov, Y. M. *Russian Folklore*. Trans. Catherine R. Smith. New York: Macmillan, 1950. Reprinted, with intro. and biblio., by Felix J. Oinas. Hatboro, Pa.: Folklore Associates, 1966.

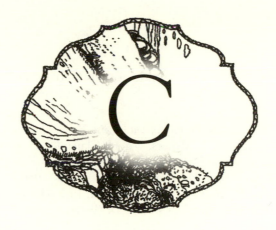

CAEDMON (SEVENTH CENTURY C.E.)

Caedmon is the first English poet of whom we have a written record. Bede's *Ecclesiastical History of England* describes Caedmon as an unlearned man who was unable to compose, memorize, or recite poetry. In social settings where others shared poetry, he would slip out of the room before his turn to perform. Then, one night, as he slept in a cowshed, he received a vision in which he was commanded to sing of the world's creation. Upon waking, Caedmon could not only remember the poem he had sung in his dream but had also developed an amazing memory and the ability to convert passages of scripture into poetry overnight.

Bede's account of Caedmon's poetic conversion is of special interest because it provides a glimpse of the social context in which Old English poetry was shared. The poems were evidently accompanied on a harp, which was passed around the banquet hall, and each guest was apparently expected to contribute a piece.

Bede provides readers with a Latin translation of Caedmon's poem of creation, usually called "Caedmon's Hymn." The Old English original must have also enjoyed wide popularity, for the nine-line poem is preserved in various dialects in 21 manuscripts from the Middle Ages. Like most Anglo-Saxon verse, "Caedmon's Hymn" reflects oral-formulaic composition, the creation of a new poem from existing formulas or phrases.

Because Bede reports that Caedmon went on to compose other religious poems, nineteenth-century scholars attributed to Caedmon all the biblical poems from the Junius Manuscript of Old English poetry. Subsequent scholars, however, have rejected any attribution of extant Old English poems to Caedmon except for his famous hymn.

David Sprunger

See also Oral-Formulaic Composition and Theory; Orality

****

References
Bede. *Bede's Ecclesiastical History of the English People*. Ed. and trans. Bertram Colgrave and R. A. B. Mynors. Oxford: Clarendon Press, 1969.
Greenfield, Stanley, and Daniel Calder. *A New Critical History of Old English Literature*. New York: New York University Press, 1986.
Magoun, Francis P. "Bede's Story of Caedman [*sic*]: The Case History of an A-S Oral Singer." *Speculum* 30 (1955): 49–63.

CALVINO, ITALO (1923–1985)

Born to Italian parents in Cuba, the writer Italo Calvino grew up in San Remo in northwestern Italy on the Ligurian Sea, participated in World War II as a partisan, and lived his adult life first in Turin and then in Paris and Rome. Influenced by Edgar Allan Poe, Immanuel Kant, Robert Louis Stevenson, Giacomo Leopardi, and Franz Kafka among others, Calvino's writings range from journalism and neorealism to experimental fictions, philosophical meditations, and essays about literature. The Italian writer Cesare Pavese was the first to note a fairy tale tone in Calvino's 1947 *Il sentiero dei nidi di ragno* [The path to the nest of the spiders, trans. 1976], a seemingly neorealistic novel that tells the experience of World War II in northern Italy from a child's perspective. As Calvino himself remarked much later, this affinity with the märchen or folk and fairy tale marked his writing throughout and contributed to his strength as a storyteller as well as to his highly self-reflective style.

In 1956, Calvino published *Fiabe italiane* [Italian folktales, trans. 1980], the result of a two-year journey into the realm of tales from various regions of Italy as found in library manuscripts and books. In this popular collection, his scholarly understanding of and appreciation for folklore's law of endless repetition and variation successfully blended with his own storyteller's desire to invent. He selected and translated tales from a number of Italian dialects and also admittedly "enriched" the tales by editing them to foreground what he considered to be the Italian folktale's foremost stylistic qualities—the "joyous logic" of its transformations, the precision of its rhythms and metaphors, its light but intense focus on love, and its encyclopedic representation of life's necessities and extravagances.

His introduction to the volume, a landmark discussion of the Italian folktale, was posthumously collected in *Sulla fiaba* [On/about the fairy tale]. Later essays on Giambattista Basile, Jacob and Wilhelm Grimm, Charles Perrault, Giuseppe Pitrè, and Paul Radin's collection of African tales (also included in *Sulla fiaba*) continued to display Calvino's interest in the märchen's structure and style, in particular its mapping of history and culture through metaphors that ring marvelously true to everyday experiences, that is, folk and fairy tales as an inventory of human destiny.

Calvino's *Il visconte dimezzato* [1952; The cloven viscount, trans. 1977], *Il barone rampante* [1957; The baron in the trees, trans. 1977], and *Il cavaliere inesistente* [1959; The nonexistent knight, trans. 1977] each enact the stylistic connection with the märchen by relying on a single image to develop a story of human interest. Just as the image of a girl emerging from a split fruit is at the center of Basile's "*I tre cedri*" [The three oranges (1634–1636)], at the core of Calvino's narratives lies a powerful image: a man cut in two whose halves live on—one all evil, the other all good; the boy who climbs on a tree and never sets foot on earth again while continuing to be an active part of his community; the ideal knight with no body at all whose perfectly white armor is sustained by willpower. Later fictions like *Le cosmicomiche* [1965; Cosmicomics, trans. 1970] and *Il castello dei destini incrociati* [1973; The castle of crossed destinies, trans. 1981] self-consciously explore the idea of narrative, both folk and literary, as a combinatorial game, analogous to chess and shaped but not limited by a scientific rigor. Calvino's essay "Cibernetica e fantasmi" ["Cybernetics and ghosts"] (in *Gli usi della letteratura* 1980; The uses of literature, trans. 1982) best articulates his understanding of folk and literary narrative as it emphasizes the potential for discovery in repetition and questions the association of literature with extraordinary originality.

Although some critics feel that Calvino's later narrative experiments with science and philosophy seemed to indicate that the wonder tale was an exhausted source of imagination, in *Six Memos for the Next Millennium* (1988), the Charles Eliot Norton lectures he was preparing to deliver at Harvard University when he died, Calvino promoted lightness, quickness, exactitude, visibility, multiplicity, and consistency as values for the literature of the future, and once again he recognized the prominence in the märchen and in the modern literature of what he called the "party of the Crystal." Calvino's structurally based understanding of the continuity between folklore and literature and the way his own works of fiction reproduce and defy that very structure in producing a new "myth" have inspired folklorists, literary critics, and writers.

Cristina Bacchilega

See also Fairy Tale; Grimm, Jacob and Wilhelm; Märchen; Perrault, Charles

✳✳✳✳✳✳✳✳✳✳✳✳✳✳✳✳✳✳

References

Bacchilega, Cristina. "Calvino's Journey: Modern Transformations of Folktale, Story, and Myth." Journal of Folklore Research 26:2 (1989): 81–98.

———. "The Fruit of the Womb: Creative Uses of a Naturalizing Tradition in Folktales." In Creativity and Tradition in Folklore, ed. Simon Bronner, pp. 153–166. Logan: Utah State University Press, 1992.

Bronzini, Giovanni Battista. "From the Grimms to Calvino: Folktales in the Year Two Thousand." In Storytelling in Contemporary Societies, trans. Chiara Simeone, ed. Lutz Röhrich and Sabine Wiener-Piepho. Tübingen: Gunter Narr Verlag, 1990.

Calligaris, Contardo. Italo Calvino. Milan: Mursia, 1973.

Calvino, Italo. Sulla fiaba. Ed. Mario Lavagetto. Turin: Einaudi, 1988.

Cannon, JoAnn. Italo Calvino: Writer and Critic. Ravenna: Longo, 1981.

Frigessi, Delia, ed. Inchiesta sulle fate: Italo Calvino e la fiaba. Bergamo: Pierluigi Lubrina Editore, 1988.

Weiss, Beno. Understanding Calvino. Columbia: University of South Carolina Press, 1993.

CAMELOT

Camelot was the stronghold and capital of King Arthur, the legendary hero of Britain; however, the city is more the invention of medieval French romance than of British folk tradition. In medieval literature, Camelot represented the center of all chivalry and learning, and as such it has in modern times come to be used as the symbol of an ideal place and age. Rarely described as fortified or even under siege, Camelot also symbolizes the golden age that was associated with the reign of Arthur.

Like any golden age, part of the enchanting allure of the concept of Camelot was that it existed no longer and was irreplaceable, a lost ideal. Many variations of the story assume and explain the fall of

Camelot as much as they actually describe the splendor of the presumed golden age itself. Much of the interest and tragedy of the perfect city lies in its demise and in the fact that the demise is brought about by inner treachery: Camelot is doomed by deceit and corruption at its heart, by trusted members of the king's retinue, rather than by war or pestilence or any other outside force.

The probable site of the historic Camelot, the stronghold held by the sixth-century British leader who may have been Arthur, is Cadbury Castle in South Cadbury, Somerset; both William Caxton, the printer of Sir Thomas Malory's *Le Morte d'Arthur* (1485), and John Leland (1542) spoke of the Cadbury country folk as being convinced that Arthur had once resided in their locale. Cadbury Castle is an Iron Age hill fort that was reinforced and given a new structure by a chieftain at some point during the sixth century. Excavations in the 1960s uncovered the foundations of a cruciform church, indicating the presence of a Christian settlement, while the remains of what appears to be a foundation sacrifice at one of the corners of the church eloquently testify to the continuing existence at that time of native pagan beliefs. The excavations also uncovered objects of fine and imported design, suggesting that whoever inhabited the site was not merely wealthy but also in contact with other areas of the world at a time when Britain seems otherwise to have been isolated from foreign cultures.

Modern literary representations of Camelot vary from the Victorian notion of an age of chivalry set in a gleaming city, as illustrated in the works of Alfred, Lord Tennyson, to the twentieth-century picture presented by Rosemary Sutcliff of Camelot as a coarsely real stronghold held by a calculating chieftain. However, it is the notion of the lost golden age that prevails in popular tradition. An example of the pervasiveness of Camelot's charm is the connection made in the United States between Camelot and the presidency of John F. Kennedy, for both are considered to be times of idealism tragically cut short. The concept of Camelot, though finite in its duration, represents peace and home; it is immobile, immutable, unassailed. The benevolent king rules justly and prescribes just rules; knights set forth from its portals and bring home booty of wealth and tales of adventure without ever tainting the place with the action that occurred beyond its walls.

Elizabeth E. Wein

See also Arthur, King; Arthurian Tradition

✻✻✻✻✻✻✻✻✻✻✻✻✻✻✻✻✻

References

Alcock, Leslie. *Arthur's Britain: History and Archaeology AD 367–634*. Harmondsworth, Eng.: Penguin, 1971.

Ashe, Geoffrey, ed. *A Guidebook to Arthurian Britain*. Wellingborough, Eng.: Aquarian Press, 1983.

———. *The Quest for Arthur's Britain*. London: Granada, 1971.

Sutcliff, Rosemary. *Sword at Sunset*. London: Hodder and Stoughton, 1963.

Tennyson, Alfred. *Selections from the Poems of Tennyson, with Parts of the Idylls of the King*. Chicago, Atlanta, and New York: Scott, Foresman, 1904.

CAMPBELL, JOSEPH (1904–1987)

Comparative mythologist, author, and educator Joseph Campbell was born in New York City. He credited his early fascination with mythology to his childhood trips to the American Museum of Natural History and to performances of Buffalo Bill's Wild West Show, which performed annually at Madison Square Garden. Campbell pursued this fascination throughout his adult life, reading widely and writing about the commonalities he found within mythic diversity. For example, on the strength of his Columbia University M.A. thesis on Sir Thomas Malory's fifteenth-century prose romance *Le Morte d'Arthur* [The death of King Arthur (c. 1230–1235)], Campbell won a Proudfit Fellowship to the University of Paris for 1927–1928. There his encounters with the paintings of Pablo Picasso and Henri Matisse and with James Joyce's novel *Ulysses* (1922), among other works, began to formalize his sense of them as modern equivalents of shamanic vision quests. The next year, on a fellowship renewal, Campbell moved to the University of Munich where he studied the novels of the German author Thomas Mann (e.g., *The Magic Mountain* [1924]), the holy books of Indian Sanskrit, and the published writings of psychoanalysts Sigmund Freud and, most significantly, Carl Jung. Deeply impressed in particular by Jung's universalizing concepts of archetype and "mythos," Campbell returned to the United States where he began to keep interpretative journals of his own dreams while, at the same time, investigating Sir James Frazer's massive 13-volume comparative study of religion and mythology, *The Golden Bough* (1890–1915). Accepting a position in 1934 at Sarah Lawrence College where he remained a popular teacher of comparative literature until his academic retirement in 1972, Campbell met the noted German Indologist Heinrich Zimmer, Jr., who, like Jung, had a marked effect on Campbell's thinking. Zimmer, Campbell later explained, was the first man he had known who spoke "about myths as though they had messages that were valid for life, not just interesting things for scholars to fool around with" (Campbell, *The Power of Myth*, p. 10).

Having already examined a striking variety of narratives focusing on the call to the adventure quest of self-meaning, in 1949 Campbell published the monograph for which he became most widely known, *The Hero with a Thousand Faces*, which he originally envisioned as bearing the title "On How to Read a Myth." Arguing that all hero myths are basically the same and thus exemplars of a single "monomyth," Campbell detailed the recurrent motifs of the hero myth as a type of "wisdom story." Specifically, on his journey, the hero encounters entities that represent hitherto unrecognized facets of his own unconscious energies. His responsibility is to negotiate these encounters successfully along his Road of Trials, facing such adventures as the descent into the belly of the whale, the meeting with the Goddess, and the encounter with the shadow. Finally, the hero attains a trophy (such as a treasure) that, upon his return to everyday life, he offers to his community as a life-transforming boon, one that symbolizes the knowledge about self-identity that he has learned.

Throughout his writings, Campbell described four general functions of myth, which are fulfilled to differing degrees in different eras. Myth functions (1) to instill a sense of wonder and curiosity about the mysteries of the universe; (2) to provide symbolic images for explaining the world; (3) to maintain the social order by justifying its practices and institutions, and (4) to harmonize the individual with society, the cosmos, and him/herself. Campbell explored these functions most far-reachingly in his synthesis of world mythology, *The Masks of God*, which appeared in four volumes: *Primitive Mythology* (1959), *Oriental Mythology* (1962), *Occidental Mythology* (1964), and *Creative Mythology* (1968). In the latter volume, Campbell called for positive attention to "living mythologies," those based in the visions and values of the current day. Examples of works setting forth living mythologies, in Campbell's opinion, are the plays of

William Shakespeare and the novels of Miguel de Cervantes (e.g., *Don Quixote de la Mancha* [1605, 1615]) and the paintings of Paul Cézanne and Paul Klee. In contrast to esoteric ancient myth or to otherworld-focused religious myth, such secular mythologies can advise people in their own everyday pursuit of "earthly, human, and humane purposes, and support [them] in their spiritual tasks, not by a supernatural grace ... but by the *natural* grace of individual endowment and the worldly virtue of loyalty in love" (Campbell, *Creative Mythology*, p. 476).

According to Campbell, myth also offers the inspiration and comfort of familiarity—the knowledge that someone else (the myth's hero) has already gone through psychological/spiritual adventures analogous to those encountered by the myth's hearer/reader. Campbell's argument that such bridges of familiarity *should be* built has represented a core element in the widespread popularity of his writings. Campbell was catapulted into national awareness as a result of his televised conversations with journalist Bill Moyers, entitled *The Power of Myth*, which appeared in six one-hour segments during 1988. These conversations were taped at filmmaker George Lucas's Skywalker Ranch. And, indeed, prior to the airing of *The Power of Myth*, Campbell's monomyth had already had a marked impact on many Americans through Lucas's translation of many of its motifs into his rite of passage *Star Wars* movie trilogy: *Star Wars* (1977), *The Empire Strikes Back* (1980), and *Return of the Jedi* (1983). During his 1985 speech to the National Arts Club, as a footnote to his acknowledgment of Campbell's influence, Lucas explained that, in *The Empire Strikes Back*, the Muppet character of Yoda was intended to represent Campbell himself. While Campbell was generally indifferent to movies and television, in his conversations with Moyers he did ratify science fiction as an important "mythogenetic zone," a place out of which mythic material is spawned.

Throughout much of the twentieth century, Campbell's successful revitalizing of popular interest in mythology has affected the personal lives of many individuals and has influenced as well the construction of a variety of popular culture art forms.

Danielle M. Roemer

See also Archetype; Cervantes (Saavedra), Miguel de; Frazer, James George; Freud, Sigmund; *The Golden Bough*; Jung, Carl Gustav; Motif; Myth; Shakespeare, William

✳✳✳✳✳✳✳✳✳✳✳✳✳✳✳✳✳

References

"Campbell, Joseph." 1984 *Current Biography Yearbook*, ed. Charles Moritz, pp. 57–61. New York: H.W. Wilson, 1984.

Flowers, Betty Sue, ed. *Joseph Campbell: The Power of Myth, with Bill Moyers.* New York: Doubleday, 1988.

Golden, Kenneth L., ed. *Uses of Comparative Mythology: Essays on the Work of Joseph Campbell.* New York: Garland, 1992.

Segal, Robert A. *Joseph Campbell: An Introduction.* New York: Garland, 1987.

CANTE FABLE

A *cante fable* is a prose narrative interspersed with brief rhymes or sung verses. These rhyming stanzas, or couplets, advance the plot and heighten the story's dramatic intensity. A mode of narration as much as a distinct narrative genre, tales told as cante fables range from neck riddles, jokes, anecdotes, and ballads to fairy tales. Some cante fables are acted as short plays.

The idea of mingling verse and prose is ancient and widespread. It appears in satires attributed to Menippus (c. 280 B.C.E.) (Reinhard 1926, p. 160); in oriental tale collections, for example, *Panchantantra* and *The Arabian Nights*; and in medieval European literature, such as *Aucassin et Nicolette*, and is a favored technique in African storytelling. In European and North American fairy tales, intercalated songs or rhymes add to the magical effect. Communication between human and supernatural characters is often achieved through the special channel of sung or recited verse. Giants, witches, and other ogres may speak in rhyme, as may the supernatural helpers of the young heroes and heroines. Threats ("Fee, fi, fo, fum"), warnings ("Be bold, be bold, but not too bold"), revelations ("My mother slew me, my father ate me"), and petitions to oracles ("Mirror, mirror on the wall") are set in verse or song for emphasis, memorability, and delight.

In the Anglo-American tradition, a particular set of jocular tales using the cante fable form play upon the themes of adultery and anticlericalism. In "The Parson's Sheep" (AT 1735A), the boy bribed by the parson to reveal the sheep stealer's name turns the tables by singing to the congregation how he saw the priest cavorting with a woman (Halpert and Widdowson 1996, pp. 867–874).

Such comic reversals, emphasized by the verses on which the story turns, suggest the dramatic possibilities inherent in the form. One of the best known cante fables, "Old Hildebrand" (AT 1360C), in which a cuckolded husband is hidden in a sack and carried home to observe his wife's dalliance with a clergyman, has a long theatrical as well as narrative history. Charles Read Baskervill identifies it as one of many farce jigs performed as afterpieces to longer stage plays in the Elizabethan era (Baskervill 1965, pp. 310–311). Herbert Halpert and J. D. A. Widdowson found that on the Great Northern Peninsula of Newfoundland, "Little Dicky Melburn" (AT 1360C) has, within living memory, been acted as a skit at Christmas concerts.

The satiric potential of the cante fable is also evident in anecdotes that center on local characters and wits who are said to have improvised comic mock graces before meals or coined impromptu but cutting epitaphs. Sometimes, however, the rhyme is all that is remembered, the surrounding story having been discarded by narrators (Halpert 1941, p. 193). Neck riddles may be given in this abbreviated form, reduced to the rhymed riddle text without the surrounding story that tells how someone had once been obliged to pose this riddle to save his or her life. The verse component in cante fables is never as extensive as in formula tales. In full form, the cante fable depends on the contrast between prose and verse; each is necessary to complete the other.

Martin Lovelace

See also *Aucassin and Nicolette*; Formula Tale, *Panchatantra*

✴✴✴✴✴✴✴✴✴✴✴✴✴✴✴✴✴✴

References

Baskervill, Charles Read. *The Elizabethan Jig and Related Song Drama*. New York: Dover, 1965 (1929).

Halpert, Herbert. "The Cante Fable in Decay." *Southern Folklore Quarterly* 5:3 (1941): 191–200.

Halpert, Herbert, and J. D. A. Widdowson. *Folktales of Newfoundland*. New York: Garland, 1996.

Ives, Edward D. "Larry Gorman and the Cante Fable." *New England Quarterly* 32 (1959): 226–237.

Reinhard, John R. "The Literary Background of the *Chantefable*." *Speculum* 1 (1926): 157–169.

CANTERBURY TALES

Generally judged one of the greatest poems of the English Middle Ages, Geoffrey Chaucer's *Canterbury Tales* (c. 1387–1400) portrays a group of fourteenth-century English travelers engaged in a storytelling contest. Begun when the poet was an established literary and public figure, and left incomplete at his death, this poem is a major departure from Chaucer's earlier work. The poet abandoned the courtly settings portrayed in his previous poetry and focused on one of the most popular pastimes in fourteenth-century England, a pilgrimage to Canterbury Cathedral, the shrine of England's most revered saint, Thomas Becket.

Pilgrimage was a popular context of medieval storytelling, and Chaucer's rendering of the pilgrimage proved so compelling for some scholars that they judged the poem a realistic account of an actual oral entertainment. John Manly and others attempted to identify real-life counterparts for Chaucer's pilgrims and achieved reasonable success in establishing that Herry Bailly, host of Chaucer's pilgrim band, and Bailly's Tabard Inn, from which the pilgrims depart, are both documented in historical records.

Nowhere is the breadth of Chaucer's knowledge of both elite and folk artistry more apparent than in the *Canterbury Tales*, as the work depicts the members of a mixed social group—ranging from a knight to a plowman—exchanging tales as they ride together toward Canterbury. The tales borrow from the most revered international literary figures of the time—including Boccaccio, Dante, and Petrarch—as well as from several popular English forms, including the tail-rhyme romance ("Sir Thopas") and the Breton lay ("Franklin's Tale"). As Francis Lee Utley (1965) pointed out, nearly all of the tales possess extensive analogues in modern oral tradition. If folktales were defined exclusively by content, the *Canterbury Tales* would rank among the greatest of early folktale collections.

A close look at the *Canterbury Tales* reveals, however, that its narratives are no more, or less, folktales than are most late-medieval literary productions. The poem represents a range of entertainment at least as broad as the diverse society of storytellers assembled by Chaucer: the "Knight's Tale" (borrowed from Boccaccio's *Teseida*) and the "Squire's Tale" (a pastiche of "oriental" romance motifs) reflect the tastes of contemporary gentility. A group of pious romances, including the "Clerk's Tale" (a close reworking of Petrarch's "Tale of Griselda"), reflect the more sober tastes of upper-class patrons. Yet

❡ The tale of the chanons yeman

❡ And begynneth the tale

With this chanon I duellyd vij yere.
And of his siena am I neuer the nere
All that I had I haue lost ther by
And god woot so haue mo than I
There as I was wont to be right fressh & gay
Of clothynge and of other good aray
Now may I were an hose vp on myn hed
And where my colour was both fressh & rede
Now it is wan and of a ledyn hewe
Who so it vseth sore shal he rewe
And of my swynk y blent is myn eye
Lo suche auauntage it is to multiplye
That slydyng siena hath made me so bare
That I haue no good where that euer I fare
And yet I am endetted so sore therby,
Of gold that I borowed trewly

A page from the second edition of Geoffrey Chaucer's Canterbury Tales *printed by William Caxton.*

Chaucer is equally adept in portraying both the literary and oral styles of nonnoble England. The Reeve speaks in the regional dialect of Norfolk (a performance that has been labeled the earliest example of dialect writing in English); the Parson mocks the "ruf, ram, ruf" style of Midlands' alliterative poetry.

More suggestive than the tales themselves is the context into which the poet sets them. Unlike most medieval European frame tales, whose bracketing narratives often serve merely as an excuse for authors to present a series of unrelated stories, the narratives in the *Canterbury Tales* are extensions of the concerns and social standings of the storytellers. The tales are told as part of a storytelling contest that is similar in structure to actual, documented fourteenth-century entertainments. In addition to providing the General Prologue, which describes the occupation and personal quirks of each pilgrim, the poet supplied links that set most of the tales in specific contexts. The tales of the Miller and the Reeve, for example, are not only masterful comic poems but also pointed thrusts in a verbal duel between the two tellers, a duel that brings into play the traditional rivalry between reeves and millers, aspects of social criticism, personal slurs, and oral techniques of indirect insult. Adhering closely to the folklorist's premise that the meaning of a tale is inseparable from its function in context, the *Canterbury Tales* presents not only a rich sampler of the types of narrative popular in its time but also a vivid, extended lesson in why, how, and for whom such tales might be told.

The *Canterbury Tales* has many affinities with fifteenth-century popular poetry. After Chaucer's death, his poem was imitated by merchant-class and popular authors; this fact, and the number and distribution of manuscripts of the poem, as well as the fact that it was the first major English poem to be printed in England (by William Caxton in 1478), demonstrate the degree to which Chaucer had earned the status of a truly popular poet by the end of the fifteenth century.

The anonymous "Tale of Beryn" (c. 1410), in which the pilgrims arrive at Canterbury Cathedral, provides a conclusion for the *Canterbury Tales*. Such romances as *The Sultan of Babylon* (c. 1450) freely borrow from the language of the *Canterbury Tales*, and comic poems such as "The Wedding of Sir Gawain and Dame Ragnell" proliferated in the fifteenth century; these anonymous works bear some stylistic resemblance to Chaucer's playful verse. Some critics maintain that the fifteenth-century poems are examples of *gesunkenes Kulturgut* [sunken cultural items], a process in which elite forms "trickle down" to the lower classes. At least as plausible, however, is the possibility that Chaucer's work was popular with the lower classes precisely because he employed the popular idioms of his own time, and did so with such talent that his poems were, in essence, popular poetry, imbued with folk values from the beginning. As late as the sixteenth century, the anonymous *Complaynt of Scotlande* states that Scottish shepherds *told* the Canterbury tales, which suggests that many of Chaucer's poems grew from, immediately reentered, and long survived as part of living British storytelling traditions.

Carl Lindahl

See also Chaucer, Geoffrey; Frame Tale; Romance

****

References

Bowden, Betsy. *Chaucer Aloud: The Varieties of Textual Interpretation*. Philadelphia: University of Pennsylvania Press, 1987.

Bryan, W. F., and Germaine Dempster, eds. *Sources and Analogues of Chaucer's Canterbury Tales*. Chicago: University of Chicago Press, 1941.

Justice, Steven. *Writing and Rebellion: England in 1381*. Berkeley: University of California Press, 1994.

Lindahl, Carl. *Earnest Games: Folkloric Patterns in the Canterbury Tales*. Bloomington: Indiana University Press, 1987.

Manly, John M. *Some New Light on Chaucer*. New York: Holt, 1926.

Utley, Francis Lee. "Some Implications of Chaucer's Folktales." *Laographia* 22 (1965): 598–599.

Cardenal, Ernesto (1925–)

Ernesto Cardenal, one of Central America's best known poets, incorporates aspects of traditional culture and folklore into his socially committed writing. Born in 1925 in Granada, Nicaragua, Cardenal has evolved through various stages in his life and in his writing. Although first and foremost a poet, he is also a sculptor, a Catholic priest, a Sandinista, and a visionary. As a priest who espoused liberation theology, he founded, on an island in Lake Nicaragua in 1965, the Solentiname commune, an experiment in creating a small-scale ideal Christian society. On Sundays, instead of delivering a sermon, Cardenal discussed with his community—local farming and fishing families—the meaning of the Gospels. He was so moved by the insights of these seemingly simple people that he began to record the weekly conversations and collected them in *El evangelio en Solentiname* [The gospel in Solentiname]. He believes that the Gospel or "good news" was written for them and for people like them and that their response to it reflects the clarity and profundity of the original message.

He also seeks to merge the poetic and profound with the super-ficial/quotidian—indeed, to eliminate the boundaries separating high and popular culture—in his numerous experiments with what has come to be recognized as his unique poetic style, which he calls *exteriorismo*, a direct, unadorned poetry composed of what he calls the elements of real life. Through the use of a collage technique that often creates the effect of a cinematographic montage of images, Cardenal retells history, narrates political events, gives lessons in economy and indigenous cultures, ponders the injustices of capital-ism, and expresses his love for the people and his hatred of dictator-ships. He insists that nothing lies outside the realm of the poetic and freely incorporates proper names, statistical data, fragments of let-ters, information from local newspapers, and passages quoted directly from historical chronicles. In accordance with his stated goals of clarity and accessibility, his language is unpretentious, conversa-tional, and often colloquial. Topics as diverse as the big-bang theory of the creation of the universe and the price of bras in Managua find their way into his poetic reconstructions of reality.

Cardenal's commitment to the democratic notion of poetry for the people and by the people was put into practice while he was Nicaraguan minister of culture from 1979 to 1985. During that time, he was instrumental in establishing workshops in which writing poetry based on the principles and techniques of *exteriorismo* was taught to farmers, factory workers, and soldiers, many of whom had only recently achieved literacy. Examples of the poetry that came out of these workshops were collected in *Poesía de la nueva Nicaragua* (1983).

Cardenal's poetry is permeated with the duality of love and anger. His passion for justice for the oppressed and exploited peoples of Latin America is often expressed in an open and biting icono-clasm that shatters the oppressor's elitism, whether it be through an attack on the conquerors and dictators and capitalists who live off the people's labor or by rewriting the history of Latin America to give primacy and authority to indigenous and popular myths and leg-ends of gods and heroes such as the Aztec god Quetzalcoatl and the Nicaraguan revolutionary hero Augusto César Sandino. In his poetry as well as in his life's work, Ernesto Cardenal has elevated the "folk" and diminished the pretensions of the "literary."

Janet N. Gold

See also Latino and Chicano Folklore and Literature; Legend; Myth

✳✳✳✳✳✳✳✳✳✳✳✳✳✳✳✳✳

References

Cardenal, Ernesto. *Apocalypse and Other Poems*. Ed. Robert Pring-Mill and Donald D. Walsh, trans. Thomas Merton et al. New York: New Directions, 1977.

———. *The Gospel in Solentiname*. Trans. Donald D. Walsh. Maryknoll, N.Y.: Orbis, 1976.

———. *Homage to the American Indians*. Trans. Monique and Carlos Altschul. Baltimore: Johns Hopkins University Press, 1973.

Jiménez, Mayra, ed. *Poesía en la nueva Nicaragua*. Mexico City: Siglo Veintiuno, 1983.

Smith, Janet Lynne. *An Annotated Bibliography of and about Ernesto Cardenal*. Tempe: Arizona State University, 1979.

CARIBBEAN FOLKLORE AND LITERATURE

Folklore in the multiethnic, multilingual, multicultural Caribbean is particularly lively and diverse, which goes far to explain its influence on the explosive development of Caribbean literature during the last half century. The culmination was when Derek Walcott of St. Lucia won the Nobel Prize.

A veritable laboratory for the study of the interrelationships between folklore, literature, language, and culture, the Caribbean, culturally speaking, includes some 36 political-geographical entities, not only the large Spanish-speaking island states of Cuba, the Dominican Republic, and Puerto Rico; Creole-speaking Haiti; and the French *départements* of Guadeloupe, Martinique, and French Guiana but also the recently independent ex-British and ex-Dutch island nations plus the remaining colonial island outposts in the volcanic chain of the Lesser Antilles. Thus, the Caribbean of folklore ranges from Bermuda in the North Atlantic to Belize in Central America to Guyana and Suriname in northeastern South America.

For all their diversity in geology, language, ancestry, and political structure, these areas share a similar history of rapid aboriginal depopulation after colonial contact; the introduction of African slaves; one-crop plantation economies; and the subsequent immigration of Europeans, Chinese, Javanese, Venezuelans, and especially East Indians. Today, the majority of Caribbean inhabitants claim more than one ancestry, and even those who are unmixed are surprisingly well informed about the cultures/religions/cuisines/folklore of their neighbors with whom they have spent their lives.

Aboriginal myths are still told in Belize, the Guianas, and among the handful of Caribs still living in Dominica, while African (particularly Yoruba) religious myths, beliefs, and practices—often syncretized with Christian and known as Santeria or Vodun (Macumba and Candomble in Brazil)—are spreading rapidly throughout the Americas. In *African Folktales in the New World* (1992), William Bascom brilliantly documents 14 probably African tales that are widely told around the Caribbean, answering Richard Dorson's (1975) contention, based on the Eurocentric type- and motif indexes of folk literatures, that most tales told by Africans in the New World are of European origin. Of course, considering the longtime presence in the Caribbean of numerous Europeans, Asians, and aboriginal Americans, as well as Africans and every possible admixture thereof, it would be surprising indeed if Caribbean narrative or performance artists of whatever ancestry did not pick up the folkloric riches available all around them.

Even so, the widespread tales about the victory of clever animal and human underdog heroes, such as the spider trickster, Ananse, of the Asante people of Ghana, are a truly remarkable achievement, not only in cultural preservation, but also as psychological support during the long and painful years of enslavement. Similarly witty riddles, wise proverbs, and a wealth of multi-entendre songs such as Trinidad calypsos come out of the African tradition, and even against stiff competition from the international media, seem to be as persistent, subtle, and viable as ever.

Daniel J. Crowley

See also Motif; Proverbs; Tale-Type; Trickster

✳✳✳✳✳✳✳✳✳✳✳✳✳✳✳✳✳✳

References

Bascom, William. *African Folktales in the New World.* Bloomington: Indiana University Press, 1992.

Crowley, Daniel J. *African Folklore in the New World.* Austin: University of Texas Press, 1977.

Dorson, Richard. "African and Afro-American Folklore: A Reply to Bascom and Other Misguided Critics." *Journal of American Folklore* 88 (1975): 151–164.

CARTER, ANGELA (1940–1992)

The British novelist and short-story writer Angela Carter was noted for her distinctive and often shocking blend of surreal fantasy, Gothic elements, dark humor, and sex and violence. She used these elements to examine gender roles in modern society, to reveal how men and women relate to and interact with one another.

Carter broke new ground in many ways, one of which was her retelling of traditional fairy tales. In the ten stories in *The Bloody Chamber* (1979), Carter recast such tales as "Bluebeard," "Beauty and the Beast," "Sleeping Beauty," and "Little Red Riding Hood" in order to explore themes of female sexuality and the often thin line between human nature and animal nature. For example, one of Carter's retellings of "Beauty and the Beast" in this collection ends with beauty and an untransformed beast living "happily ever after" while her retelling of "Little Red Riding Hood" ends with Red Riding Hood taming the wolf.

Carter was also not afraid to explore the latent appeal that sex and violence have for most people, as her nonfiction study of pornography, *The Sadeian Woman* (1979), indicates. This theme runs throughout her retelling of fairy tales. Several of the stories also examine mother-daughter relationships: in the title story from *The Bloody Chamber*, for example, which retells the Bluebeard story, the young bride's mother replaces the brothers of the traditional story to save the overly curious bride from death. This mother, who is the only purely heroic figure in all of the stories in this collection, is alerted by motherly intuition to her daughter's impending danger and, in a characteristically Carteresque lushly dramatic scene, comes riding to the rescue on horseback, sword in hand, like an avenging angel. Although not considered a mainstream feminist writer, Carter was deeply concerned with the question of what it means to be female, and all of her fairy tale works focus on this question in various ways.

Carter also edited several collections of traditional folktales, including two for children—*The Fairy Tales of Charles Perrault* (1977) and *Sleeping Beauty and Other Favorite Fairy Tales* (1984), for which she won the Kate Greenaway Medal—and two for adults—*The Virago Book of Fairy Tales* (1990), published in the United States as *The Old Wives' Fairy Tale Book*, and *The Second Virago Book of Fairy Tales*, published posthumously in 1993. The adult collections include international tales that center on women protagonists, sometimes clever and resourceful ones and sometimes silly or cruel ones, in order, as Carter says in her introduction to the first collection, "to demonstrate the extraordinary richness and diversity of responses to the same common predicament—being alive—and the richness and diversity with which femininity, in practice, is represented in 'unofficial' culture: its strategies, its plots, its hard work."

Martha Hixon

See also Fairy Tale; Folktale; *Märchen*

****

References

Carter, Angela. *The Bloody Chamber.* New York: Harper and Row, 1979.

Carter, Angela, ed. *The Old Wives' Fairy Tale Book.* Pantheon Fairy Tale and Folklore Library. New York: Pantheon, 1990. Published in Great Britain as *The Virago Book of Fairy Tales.* London: Virago, 1990.

———. *The Second Virago Book of Fairy Tales.* Intro. Marina Warner. London: Virago, 1993.

Duncker, Patricia. "Re-Imagining the Fairy Tales: Angela Carter's Bloody Chambers." *Literature and History* 10:1 (Spring 1984): 3–14.

CARVAJAL, MARIA ISABEL (1888–1949)

Maria Isabel Carvajal, who used the pseudonym Carmen Lyra, was an educator, a writer of short stories, and one of the founding members of the Costa Rican Communist Party. In her work, folklore is intimately tied up with memory, childhood, and sweet nostalgia for a simple, moral way of life. Lyra worked as a teacher most of her life and was devoted to her students and to introducing into Costa Rica some of the progressive reforms she had studied in Europe. It is not surprising, then, that her first fictional works were either written for children or have children as their main characters.

Her most popular book for the child reader, *Los cuentos de mi tía Panchita* [The stories of my aunt Panchita (1920)], which continues to be read and loved by Costa Rican children, has two different kinds of stories: retellings of favorite European fairy tales, such as Cinderella and Snow White, and others that she remembered hearing as a child, some of which she later stumbled upon again, but always from someone's lips, she claimed, not from a book. All of the stories, whatever their origin or inspiration, are written with a distinctively

Costa Rican flavor, beginning with her description of Aunt Panchita, an archetypal repository of stories, a white-haired old woman
who bakes mouth-watering confections of orange and coconut and
rolls her own cigarettes between stories. She is beloved by her family but criticized for filling her grandchildren's heads with tales of
witches and fairies, tales her uncle Pedro, a professor of logic and
ethics, calls trashy and silly. Panchita's language is peppered with
Costa Rican colloquialisms and familiar forms of address, her characters eat typical Central American foods, and the landscape is that
of her country.

Carmen Lyra favored the traditional märchen of the youngest
son gaining the father's throne because he is generous and kind
while his two older brothers' fates reflect their mean-spirited selfish-
ness and the type of märchen in which gentle and self-sacrificing
young girls end up marrying princes. Unfazed by the non–Costa
Rican origin of many of these tales, Lyra recognized their power to
satisfy children's longings for moral narratives with clear rewards and
punishments. She reflected the strong Catholic influence predominant in Costa Rica when she claimed that every little girl's dream is
to be as beautiful and long-suffering as Cinderella, to weep as soul-
fully as she did; for Cinderella, not unlike the Virgin Mary, heads
every girl's calendar of saints. Her own childhood love of such stories convinced her that fairy tale characters can be more real and
beloved than some actual people, and indeed she created endearing
characters that are beloved by the young at heart and the innocent
of spirit. Her familiarity with Joel Chandler Harris's Uncle Remus
inspired the creation of Tío Conejo ("Uncle Rabbit") and Tío Coyote ("Uncle Coyote").

In her stories, many of them published in the respected Costa
Rican journal *Repertorio Americano*, the predominant themes are
memory and the innate goodness of people, so often oppressed by
other people who are tempted by wealth or false prestige. Objects and
places are replete with memories. In "Mi calle" [My street], for example, a stroll down memory lane, she passes the house where two old
women lived when she was a child. She recalls in particular the one
who let her open her armoire and her box of memories and also let her
look at her books, her photographs, her dried flowers. They seemed
then full of mystery and enchantment, like the stories she read. She
envies the children playing in the street, chanting the same rhymes
she and her friends sang years ago. She wonders if some of her old
friends might be the mothers who now call their children in from play.

In "Los caminos" [The roads], she remembers again the peaceful past, the simple pleasure of walking country roads and hearing the women singing as they do their wash in the brook. But she sees that things have changed: the brook has been rerouted to irrigate a field, the meadow where a rustic cottage stood now contains a pretentious house inhabited by a fat-bellied merchant and his family, and she realizes the fleeting and delicate nature of childhood joy, wonder, and innocence.

Social commentary appears particularly in her collection of stories titled *Bananos y hombres* [Bananas and men (1931)], in which the total absence of anything "folkloric" is her harshest indictment of the United Fruit Company, barely disguised as "the United Banana Company." There are children in these stories, but no comforting laps in which to snuggle and hear stories, no shady chayote tree with low wooden benches or a mossy well to provide cool drinks of water on hot summer afternoons, no smells of tobacco cured with fig leaves or honey to create nostalgic childhood memories. In *Bananos y hombres*, the Costa Rican workers have been stripped of history, tales, customs, legends, and rituals, except those rituals that are degrading habits or addictions that are compulsions brought on by dehumanization—the result of profit-motive practices of a foreign company operating on Costa Rican soil.

Janet N. Gold

See also Fairy Tale; Latino and Chicano Folklore and Literature; Legend; Myth; Uncle Remus

✳✳✳✳✳✳✳✳✳✳✳✳✳✳✳✳✳

References

Carvajal, María Isabel. *Los cuentos de mi tía Panchita*. San José, Costa Rica: Editorial Española, 1936
———. *Relatos escogidos de Carmen Lyra*. San José, Costa Rica: Editorial Costa Rica, 1977.

CATHER, WILLA (1873–1947)

A writer and chronicler of immigrant experiences, Willa Cather was born in Virginia but spent what she referred to as her formative years in Nebraska. She graduated from the University of Nebraska at Lincoln at 22 (in 1895), but her education as a writer had begun earlier, during her childhood in and around Red Cloud, Nebraska. There she met European immigrants who were homesteading near her family's farm, and in a 1913 interview, Cather said, "I have never found any intellectual excitement any more intense than I used to feel when I spent a morning with one of those old [immigrant] women at her baking or butter making" and that "the old women somehow managed to tell me a great many stories about the old country . . . I always felt as if every word they said to me counted for twenty" (Bohlke 1986, p. 10). The immigrant women fed Cather's appetite for stories, a hunger so intense it led a local shopkeeper to dub her the "young curiosity shop" (Robinson 1983, p. 20), and fueled her admiration for pioneers of all sorts. In her works, Cather combines her admiration with her extensive knowledge of folk narratives; she uses legends, märchen, myths, and personal experience narratives to define her characters, to emphasize the extraordinary qualities of seemingly ordinary lives, and to provide structural support for her thematic concerns.

In *O Pioneers!* (1913)—Cather's second novel and her first to receive critical acclaim—crazy Ivar tells Alexandra, his employer and protector, about Peter Kralik, who swallowed a snake while drinking out of a creek. After doing so, Kralik could eat only what the snake liked and drank alcohol in order to quiet it. According to Ivar, although Kralik was sane and a good worker, "they locked him up [in the asylum] for being different in his stomach." Ivar's story is a variant of the familiar bosom serpent legend, told by Ivar in order to explain his own situation more fully. Ivar fears that he, too, will be confined in the asylum at Hastings, Nebraska, because the neighbors are uncomfortable with his eccentric ways.

Likewise, in *My Ántonia* (1918) as the Russian immigrant Pavel lies dying, he recalls the time he and his brother Peter led a doomed wedding party from one Ukranian village to another. The sledges carrying the wedding party and their guests were pursued by wolves; to save himself and Peter, Pavel threw the bride and groom to the wolves. Afterward, the brothers were shunned by everyone, and misfortune followed them everywhere. Though it is difficult to trace any direct connection between Pavel's story and traditional Russian folk narratives, similarities exist between his account and traditional stories. Still, the wolf story clearly defines Pavel's and Peter's characters. While other immigrant characters learn to adapt to the needs of the frontier without forgetting their heritage or becoming obsessed by it,

Pavel and Peter are unable to make creative use of a past that haunts, rather than helps, them.

For Cather, folk narratives not only elucidate issues of characterization and theme but also provide an empathetic, expressive structure for her novels. Particularly in her later novels, Cather makes great use of both story and the storytelling situation. In her last novel, *Sapphira and the Slave Girl*, several characters tell the story of the slave girl Nancy, a story that is based on a personal experience narrative Cather heard as a child. The effect created by Cather's multiple narrators is one of confusion: each seems to be telling the truth, yet each has reasons for wishing to tell the story in a specific way, which is exactly Cather's point. The truth is always filtered through the imprecise prism of human experience. In *Shadows on the Rock*, emphasis is put not so much on the tellers of tales, as on the audiences that hear them. Cecile, Jaques, and especially Euclid are deeply affected by the stories they hear, stories that assist them in their metamorphosis from being French immigrants to being French-Canadians.

Cather's extensive use of folk narratives and her careful attention to the situations in which they are told serve as testament to her belief in the power of stories. Indeed, the narratives inset in her novels often provide the most compelling, lasting images associated with her works.

Debbie A. Hanson

See also Legend; *Märchen*; Personal Experience Story

✳✳✳✳✳✳✳✳✳✳✳✳✳✳✳✳✳✳

References

Bohlke, L. Brant, ed. *Willa Cather in Person: Interviews, Speeches, and Letters*. Lincoln: University of Nebraska Press, 1986.

Cather, Willa. *My Ántonia*. Boston: Houghton, Mifflin, 1918.

———. *O Pioneers!* Boston: Houghton, Mifflin, 1913.

Robinson, Phyllis C. *Willa Cather: A Personal Memoir*. New York: Doubleday, 1983.

CELTIC LITERATURE

There are six modern Celtic languages: the "Q-Celtic," "Goidelic," or "Gaelic" subfamily consists of Irish, Scottish Gaelic (often called just "Gaelic"), and Manx (spoken on the Isle of Man in the Irish

Sea); the "P-Celtic," "Brittonic," or "Brythonic" subfamily includes Welsh, Breton, and Cornish. There are no living native speakers of Manx or Cornish, but there are attempts to revive those languages. Different varieties of Celtic were also spoken on the European continent in ancient times (including Eastern Europe, Gaul, northern Italy, and Spain) although only a little inscriptional evidence remains.

In Britain and France, the Celtic languages are associated with minority ethnic groups. Governmental and social pressures in these countries (as in Ireland before independence) have frequently restricted the use of the Celtic languages, so the maintenance and revival of these languages have often been associated with social and political nationalism. Literature from these areas has also been written in varieties of the dominant language (English, French) and in Latin.

The earliest surviving Celtic literature dates from the early Middle Ages and consists of poetry and tales in Old Irish and poetry in Old Welsh. Very little of the histories and tales in prose and verse that were told by the professional classes of poets and storytellers is extant, although the survivals suggest a shared set of stories and compositional techniques. Each tradition has its own rules, but in very broad terms, Celtic poetry may be described as being composed according to rules of syllable count, accent, interline linking, and special rhyming conventions.

This early literature—among the earliest in Western Europe—offers evidence of a Celtic "heroic" culture in which the poets were both seers and preservers of aristocratic social values. Professional poets of several ranks (along with legal specialists and harpers) were members of the recognized and formalized social order. Traditional genres included genealogies, political poetry, eulogies, heroic elegies, sagas or tales, requests and thanks, laments, admonitions (often gnomic), and satirical, religious, and nature poetry. The poets were also known for retaliating against insult ("satire") or conducting invective-filled disputations (e.g., "flyting" in Scottish verse), and there were bardic contests on many topics. These themes remained important as long as the traditional social order endured and were revived whenever there was a conscious desire to return to that order. Later poetic themes include love, nature, exile, longing for home, and social protest. Christian religious poetry, plays, and prose make up the bulk of extant literature in middle-late medieval and early modern Breton, Cornish, and Manx, although a handful of early dictionaries and some secular songs and tales, including a few fables, folk songs, and bits of folklore, have also survived.

The Celts have contributed to general European culture and literature at several periods. In the early Middle Ages, Irish monks founded monasteries in Scotland, Italy, Germany, Switzerland, and France; therefore much of the earliest Old Irish material is from Continental manuscripts. Irish scholars were also important at Carolingian courts. The Arthurian tales of the Middle Ages began among the Celts, and the rhyme of early Welsh verse may have influenced European poetry.

In the eighteenth century, the Ossianic poems by the Scotsman James Macpherson (which were ostensibly translations from early Scottish Gaelic but were, in fact, adaptations) presented a view of Scotland and an attitude toward local customs that spread throughout Europe and were taken up by the romantics. The eighteenth- and nineteenth-century "Celtomania" in Great Britain and Europe viewed the Celts as having a mystical connection with nature and reflected a nostalgia for the lost heroic past. The "Celtic twilight" in British and Irish literature of the late nineteenth and early twentieth centuries continued to present elements of this view of the Celts—for example, their otherworldliness and close relationship to the world of magic, fairies, and other supernatural beings—as does much modern fantasy literature and much of the modern nonscholarly fascination with things Celtic. Conversely, extremely negative stereotypes of the overdeferential, often drunken, fighting Irishman or the dour, miserly Scot or the overly legalistic Welsh lawyer have also persisted, in spite of their offensiveness.

Although Edward Lhuyd stands as an isolated predecessor, modern Celtic studies really began in the nineteenth and early twentieth centuries. Folk material was collected, editions of old texts were prepared, grammars and philological works were written, national libraries and museums were opened, and scholarly journals were begun. In addition, national and pan-Celtic language and culture organizations and celebrations as well as Celtic-language magazines were founded at this time in all the Celtic areas, and the individual languages and literatures were strongly linked with separate expressions of a modern form of nationalism, which have persisted.

Pamela S. Morgan

See also Arthurian Tradition; Macpherson, James; Ossian; Scottish Literature; Welsh Literature

****
References

Chadwick, Nora. *The Celts*. Harmondsworth, Eng.: Penguin, 1970.

Chapman, Malcolm. *The Celts: The Construction of a Myth*. New York: St. Martin's Press, 1992.

Jackson, Kenneth. *A Celtic Miscellany*. Rev. ed. Harmondsworth, Eng.: Penguin, 1971.

MacCana, Proinsias. *Celtic Mythology*. Feltham, Eng.: Hamlyn, 1970.

Powell, T. G. E. *The Celts*. Rev. ed. New York: Thames and Hudson, 1980.

Price, Glanville. *The Languages of Britain*. London and Baltimore: Edward Arnold, 1984.

Rees, Alwyn, and Brinley Rees. *Celtic Heritage: Ancient Tradition in Ireland and Wales*. London: Thames and Hudson, 1961.

CERVANTES, LORNA DEE (1954–)

A native of San Francisco and a graduate of San Jose State University, Lorna Dee Cervantes is among the most acclaimed of the contemporary female Mexican-American poets. Like Bernice Zamora, Ana Castillo, Marcela Christine Lucero-Trujillo, Carmen Tafolla, and other Chicana poets of the 1970s, Cervantes's creative impulse initially drew sustenance from both the civil rights (especially *La Raza*) and the women's movements. Yet she is of the second generation of Chicano writers who came of age in the mid-1970s when Chicano literature turned to questions of style rather than a dogged politicism, when women writers were more readily accepted as cultural spokespeople, and a community of artists existed who would nurture young talented people like Cervantes.

The poem, "Beneath the Shadow of the Freeway," written when Cervantes was only 23, won her quick respect from critics and peers alike. The poem's structural skill, quiet blend of feminist and ethnic consciousness, and symbolic and lyrical eloquence would become her stylistic signature. In 1978, the National Endowment for the Arts awarded her a Creative Writing Fellowship, and she has subsequently received many grants from state, federal, and community arts councils. Her first collection of poetry, *Emplumada*, won the 1982 American Book Award.

Cervantes emphasizes the Native American folk dimension to her Mexican-American heritage in her choice of birds as a recurrent poetic image. In the words of the critic Juan Bruce-Novoa, through an "interlingual play on words," Cervantes "blends [birds] into the image of her art in the metaphor of the pen ... —pluma in Spanish means pen and feather, so to be emplumada is to be feathered like a bird or Indian, or to be armed with a pen like a writer" (Bruce-Novoa 1990, p. 2579). The postmodern folkways of urban Mexican-American women are also central to Cervantes's work. By recording the female oral tradition, Cervantes preserves the knowledge of older generations of women and adjusts it to the dilemmas of contemporary women.

In 1976, Cervantes founded *Mango,* a literary magazine devoted to Chicano arts. She served as managing editor until 1980 when, owing to financial pressures, *Mango* folded. In 1990, she founded and began codirecting *Red Dirt,* a literary journal devoted to cross-cultural, international poetry. Another book of poems, *Genocide: Poems on Love and Hunger,* appeared in 1991.

Krista Comer

See also Latino and Chicano Folklore and Literature

✳✳✳✳✳✳✳✳✳✳✳✳✳✳✳✳✳

References

Bruce-Novoa, Juan. "Biographical Essay on Lorna Dee Cervantes." In *The Heath Anthology of American Literature,* vol. 2, ed. Paul Lauter et al., p. 2579. Lexington, Mass.: D. C. Heath, 1990.

Fulton, Len, ed. *The International Directory of Little Magazines & Small Presses.* Paradise, Calif.: Dustbooks, 1992.

Sánchez, Maria Ester. *Contemporary Chicana Poetry: A Critical Approach to an Emerging Literature.* Berkeley: University of California Press, 1985.

CERVANTES (SAAVEDRA), MIGUEL DE (1547–1616)

Spain's foremost writer, Miguel de Cervantes Saavedra, composed a wide range of literary works: plays, interludes, poetry, a pastoral novel, and short and long prose fiction. His most famous book, *Don Quixote,* published in two parts in 1605 and 1615, parodies chivalric literature through its self-conscious narrative and the hilarious exploits of an idealistic knight and his down-to-earth squire, Sancho Panza. Its perceptive commentary on all human desires, dreams, and limitations makes it the first modern novel.

Cervantes's writings make extensive and adroit use of folklore, mining the rich Spanish oral tradition for ballads, folktales, and jokes. In *Don Quixote*, the reworkings of anonymous oral poems (*romances*) on Carolingian themes contribute to the novel's parody of chivalric behavior. They also establish a common ground of popular beliefs among different social classes: the knight first reveals his altered state to a surprised innkeeper by singing modified fragments of a well-known ballad (I.2). Although Sancho Panza's recitations of long strings of proverbs have supplied scholars with a lasting source of folk sayings, Don Quixote's speech accounts for many popular expressions as well. In their humorous aphorisms, both protagonists invoke commonsensical folk wisdom, which frequently serves to counter the knight's idealized worldview.

The figure of Sancho Panza embodies the Western archetype of the rustic (whose literary origins, however, have also been documented). His victimization by the practical jokes played on him, his misapprehension of abstract concepts, and his identification with his donkey all point to the character's profound roots in the comic tradition of the fool. Another index is Sancho's given name, traceable to proverbs that stress either craftiness ("A wise silence is called Sancho") or animal-like qualities ("Pig, pork, or Sancho, they're all the same"). The carnivalesque meaning of the name Sancho Panza as "holy belly" affiliates the character with the greed and gluttony that is often ascribed in folklore to Spanish villagers. Names gleaned from proverbs endow their characters with burlesque characteristics: following numerous sayings, the name of a peasant girl, Aldonza, resonates with promiscuity and moral laxness ("There's no shame to Aldonza").

Cervantes's other exemplary novels also utilize subject matter taken from oral tradition: *El licenciado vidriera* [The glass licentiate (1613)] includes apothegms collected from oral sources, and *El coloquio de los perros* exploits folk belief in witches and talking animals. Based on oral legends about the Inquisition, the novel relies on the popular conception of witches as being capable of flying, of transforming children into animals, and of taking part in demonic rituals.

Spain's strong oral culture is further evinced in Cervantes's many allusions to storytelling and by his incorporation of folktales and jokes into his main narratives. In *Don Quixote*, Sancho's "never-ending story" conforms to Thompson motif Z11 while his and his wife's arguments over the imaginary island are motif J2060. Traditional stories, such as the legend of Pedro de Urdemalas, give form to several of his plays. The interlude *El retablo de las maravillas* [The wonder show (1615)] brings together both cultured and popular traditions in its retelling of the story of an object made visible only to a certain public, similar to Hans Christian Andersen's "The Emperor's New Clothes," and corresponding to motif K445. Such folktales as the old man cuckolded by his young bride are at the core of the interlude *El celoso extremes* [The jealous extremaduran (1613)].

Cervantes's narratives are populated with an ample array of folk types: innkeepers, widows, students, peasants, shoemakers, and tailors, among others, all contribute their traditional brand of humor to the written text. Ironically, by seamlessly assimilating the oral tradition in his literary production, Cervantes preserved a number of folktales, jokes, and proverbs for posterity by providing their only documented source.

Anne J. Cruz

See also Andersen, Hans Christian; Archetype; Ballad; Belief; Folktale; Legend; Proverbs; Storytelling

✳✳✳✳✳✳✳✳✳✳✳✳✳✳✳✳✳✳

References
Chevalier, Maxime. *Folklore y literatura: El cuento oral en el Siglo de Oro.* Barcelona: Editorial Crítica, 1978.
———. "Huellas del cuento folklórico en *El Quijote.*" In *Cervantes: Su obra y su mundo: Actas del Primer Congreso Intenacional sobre Cervantes,* ed. M. Criado de Val, pp. 881–893. Madrid: Edi-6, 1981.
———. *Tipos cómicos y folklore (siglos XVI–XVII).* Madrid, Edi–6, 1982.
Joly, Monique. "Aspectos del refrán en Mateo Alemán y Cervantes." *Nueva Revista de Filología Hispánica,* 20 (1971): 95–106.
Molho, Maurice. *Cervantes: Raíces folklóricas.* Madrid: Gredos, 1976.

CHAPBOOK

Chapbook is the word used since the early nineteenth century to designate any small unbound book that formerly was sold on the streets and at markets and fairs by peddlers who obtained their wares from urban printshops. The name was formed on the model of "chapman," meaning merchant (Old English, *ceapmann* or *cypeman*). Most chapbooks, sometimes called "penny histories," measured about 3.5 inches by 5.5 inches in dimension and consisted of 24 pages with

The Tragicall Hiſtory
of the Life and Death
of *Doctor Fauſtus.*

Written by *Ch. Marklin.*

LONDON,
Printed for *Iohn Wright,* and are to be ſold at his ſhop
without Newgate, at the ſ: ... the
Bib' 1656.

*The cover of a seventeenth-century chapbook depicts the legend of Doctor Faustus, who was thought to
have made a pact with the devil.*

woodcuts. Some were somewhat larger or smaller and had 8, 16, or 32 pages. The chapbook trade flourished in Europe from the early seventeenth century to the late nineteenth century, by which time it had been displaced by journals, newspapers, and other forms of print.

In Britain, chapbooks cost anywhere from a penny to sixpence. The British trade was stimulated by seventeenth-century licensing acts that prohibited the establishment of printing presses except in London, Oxford, or Cambridge, thereby limiting the sale of books in the provinces to those peddled by chapmen. With sundry household articles for sale as well as broadsides and chapbooks, chapmen were essential agents in the flow of commerce between urban and rural areas, and their activities helped to promote a common culture. Chapbook sales in North America, though never as brisk as those in Britain, were active during the period 1725–1825. Many chapbooks were imported although some were of native manufacture. Similar books are still sold on the streets in other parts of the world.

Most individual chapbooks were of anonymous authorship, and some were severely condensed versions of well-known works such as the Bible, Shakespeare's plays, *Robinson Crusoe*, and *Gulliver's Travels*. Favorite items included fairy tales (e.g., "The History of Jack the Giant Killer" or "Sleeping Beauty"), legendary romances (e.g., "The History of Guy of Warwick"), sensational tales of magic and enchantment (e.g., "The Tragical History of Dr. Faustus"), and rhymes of Robin Hood. Also popular were jestbooks, almanacs, recipe books, books of cures, and books of onomastic interpretation as well as tales of giants, prodigies, miracles, witchcraft, pirates, and highwaymen. Some books told of crimes, executions, and other contemporary events. Others, such as collections of nursery rhymes, were aimed at young adults or children. In part to counteract the frequent frivolity and sensationalism of street literature, religious societies distributed large numbers of chapbooks on moral subjects.

For folklorists and social historians, chapbooks are important as an index of popular taste in former times. They introduce one to the colorful mental world of writers of few literary pretensions and of readers with only limited education. Chapbooks reveal much about sexual mores, popular religious beliefs, and attitudes toward childhood, past history, patriotism, crime, and punishment. The distribution of chapbooks provides information on the extent of literacy among the general public in different times and places. Chapbooks also illustrate the complex interplay of print culture and oral culture, for some of these chapbooks may represent the residue of long-standing oral traditions while the substance of others may have entered oral tradition through being read aloud.

Today, though facsimiles are available, most original chapbooks must be consulted in the special collections of major libraries, including the Pepys Library of Magdelene College (Cambridge), the Bodleian Library, the British Library, the National Library of Scotland, Harvard College Library, and the New York Public Library.

John Niles

See also Bible; Fairy Tale; Robin Hood; Romance; Shakespeare, William

✳✳✳✳✳✳✳✳✳✳✳✳✳✳✳✳✳✳

References

Neuburg, Victor. *The Penny Histories*. London: Oxford University Press, 1968.

———. *Popular Literature: A History and Guide*. Harmondsworth, Eng.: Penguin, 1977.

Spufford, Margaret. *Small Books and Pleasant Histories: Popular Fiction and Its Readership in Seventeenth-Century England*. London: Methuen, 1981.

Watt, Tessa. *Cheap Print and Popular Piety, 1550–1640*. Cambridge: Cambridge University Press, 1991.

CHARLEMAGNE (782–814)

Also known as Charles the Great (Carolus Magnus), King of the Franks, Charlemagne was crowned emperor in 800, marking a western revival of this Roman title. He conquered and ruled much of what is today France, Germany, and Italy and thoroughly reorganized Christian ecclesiastical and political structures in Western Europe, in part by mandating tithing to support an extensive parish network.

Few specifics are known about the daily life or personality of this historical personage. In the centuries following his death, however, Charlemagne became one of the most popular figures in many different versions and types of Western European literary materials. He remains as well a central figure in standard interpretations of the history of the eighth and early ninth centuries.

Accounts of Charlemagne's campaigns against the Islamic Umayyads of the Iberian Peninsula provide the background for the *Chanson de Roland* (Song of Roland), an epic poem detailing the exploits of Charlemagne and his lieutenants. Professional minstrels specializing in recounting from memory stories of heroes like Charlemagne popularized a literary genre known now as chansons de geste ("songs of heroes"). These chansons seem to have been especially popular from the tenth through the thirteenth centuries.

Versions of the stories were told across Western Europe and were incorporated into local storytelling traditions. Written evidence shows that stories about Charlemagne were recounted as early as the thirteenth century in Scandinavia, where they became known collectively as the *Karlusmagnussaga*. A thirteenth-century Iberian ballad testifies to Charlemagne's popularity in southwestern Europe. There are similar examples from Provence and the Italian peninsula. A French version of the *Chanson de Roland* was translated into German shortly after Charlemagne's canonization in 1165 in an attempt by one set of claimants to the imperial throne to connect themselves to the earlier legendary ruler of the Franks. This example underlines one of the ways in which the image of Charlemagne has been used over the centuries since his death.

The various Charlemagne epics, songs, chronicles, poems, sagas, ballads, histories, and romances that were popular in Western Europe have been the subject of intense academic debate. Much of the debate centers about issues crucial to the interpretation of folklore: were these stories anonymous echoes of a historical event passed down through the ages in oral tradition, or were they individual literary creations with their origins in documentary sources?

In the nineteenth century, romantic writers repopularized the genre of the medieval romance (the first printed version of the *Chanson de Roland* appeared in 1837). In this period, Charlemagne was also seen as an important figure in the development of both the modern state of France and the modern vision of Germany put forward by the apologists for one of central Europe's ruling houses, the Hohenzollerns of Prussia. Charlemagne, who has been incorporated into central medieval narratives of chivalry, religious virtue, and heroism, has now become firmly entrenched in the modern epic of European state formation.

Joseph F. Patrouch

See also Ballad; Epic; Romance; *Song of Roland*

✳✳✳✳✳✳✳✳✳✳✳✳✳✳✳✳✳

References

de Mandach, André. *Naissance et développement de la chanson de geste en Europe.* 5 vols. Geneva: Droz, 1961–1987.

Duggan, Joseph J. *A Guide to Studies on the Chanson de Roland*. London: Grant and Cutler, 1976.

Early English Text Society. *The English Charlemagne Romances*. 7 vols. London: Oxford University Press, 1966.

Farrier, Susan E. *The Medieval Charlemagne Legend: An Annotated Bibliography*. New York: Garland, 1992.

Halphen, Louis. *Charlemagne and the Carolingian Empire*. New York: North-Holland Publishing Company, 1977.

CHAUCER, GEOFFREY (1344?–1400)

The most famous author of the English Middle Ages, Geoffrey Chaucer composed many poems documenting noble festive customs and also wrote the *Canterbury Tales*, a collection of stories in verse and prose that reveals much about popular culture and storytelling. Nearly 500 records signed by or mentioning Chaucer make his the best documented life of any English medieval poet, but it is noteworthy that none of these records mentions Chaucer's poetry. To the official world, Chaucer was known first as the page of Countess Elizabeth, wife of the English prince Lionel of Antwerp (1357); then as a prisoner of war during Edward III's campaign against the French (1359–1360); and later as a member of the royal household (1367), ambassador for Edward III and Richard II (1366–1370, 1372–1373, 1377, 1378), controller of the London customs (1374–1386), justice of the peace (1385–1390), member of Parliament (1386), clerk of the works (1389–1391), and deputy forester (1391). Compared to the contemporary French royal court, the English court rewarded its poets informally; whatever their opinion of his poetry, Chaucer's patrons viewed him, formally, as a statesman and public official.

Nevertheless, Chaucer's richly documented life allows us to situate him in a world of noble and festive pageantry. As clerk of the works, he directed the building of the stands for the Smithfield tournament of 1390, and we can reasonably assume that Chaucer's poetry reflects a similar world in which members of a wealthy merchant class (Chaucer himself was the son of a rich London merchant) provided artistic backdrops for aristocratic ritual. A suggestive record dated April 23, 1374 (St. George's Day, a court holiday celebrating England's patron saint when little official business was conducted), granted Chaucer a gallon of wine a day for life; many scholars believe this to have been the reward for a festive poem.

Most of Chaucer's early surviving poems were occasional pieces: *The Book of the Duchess* (c. 1368–1372) is apparently an elegy in honor of Blanche, the wife of John of Gaunt. *The Parliament of Fowls* and *The Complaint of Mars* (c. 1385) are the earliest surviving English poems to mention St. Valentine's Day: they allude to the customary belief that birds choose their mates on this day while sketching a picture of refined play during which men and women engaged in elaborate courtship rituals. *The Legend of Good Women* (c. 1387) alludes to two companies of people named Flowers and Leafs, each celebrating the particular virtues of the parts of the plant for which they are named. Reading Chaucer's poems in tandem with such anonymous contemporary works as *The Flower and the Leaf* and *The Assembly of Ladies,* we see that his art adorned the pastimes of a noble "folk" who used elaborate, conventionalized, metaphorical nature games as part of their holiday celebrations. Real-life festive poetic performances, such as the London Pui and the Parisian *Cour amoureuse* (founded on St. Valentine's Day in 1400), engaged noble- and merchant-class men in song competitions; some of Chaucer's poems may well have been written for similar occasions.

The development of Chaucer's poetic and public careers shows that he lived in a time of transition during which the merchant and noble classes grew closer together. Unlike his contemporary, John Gower—who composed in Latin, French, and English—Chaucer is the earliest known court poet to have written exclusively in English, the language of the great majority, which became during his lifetime the official language of Parliament. His commitment to the common tongue of England signifies the breadth of his association with his audiences, and after his death he was hailed by many poets as the man who "taught" English how to become a respectable poetic language. During and after Chaucer's life, knights, princes, and merchants often met together in London households to exchange verses, which indicates the growth of a poetic movement well beyond the confines of the royal court.

Chaucer's allusions to traditional customs make him an important source for medieval English folk culture. In addition to documenting noble pastimes, his poetry is rife with accurate references to urban and village rituals and lifestyles. The "Cook's Tale" refers to a prisoner "led with revel to Newgate," thus documenting the ceremonial punishment of criminals in fourteenth-century London. In the "Miller's Tale," John the Carpenter performs a ritual to protect his home from evil spirits. The Miller himself is described as a champion wrestler who is also adept at breaking doors with his head, a pastime since recorded at many village fairs. The Wife of Bath refers to the Dunmowe Flitch, a slab of bacon awarded to couples who survive a year and a day of wedded life without repenting their marriage; this is a reference to a village tradition also mentioned by Chaucer's contemporary, William Langland, in *Piers Plowman* and later documented in many other sources. Such allusions affirm not only that Chaucer was well acquainted with the folk cultures of artisans and villagers but also that his upper-class audience shared his knowledge. Although a highly stratified society, Chaucer's England was a place in which the highest and lowest social groups had a great mutual familiarity.

Carl Lindahl

See also *Canterbury Tales*

✳✳✳✳✳✳✳✳✳✳✳✳✳✳✳✳✳✳

References

Green, Richard Firth. *Poets and Princepleasers: Literature and the English Court in the Late Middle Ages*. Toronto: University of Toronto Press, 1981.

Knight, Stephen. *Geoffrey Chaucer*. Oxford: Basil Blackwell, 1986.

Lindahl, Carl. "The Festive Form of the *Canterbury Tales*." *English Literary History* 52 (1985): 531–574.

Patterson, Lee. *Chaucer and the Subject of History*. Madison: University of Wisconsin Press, 1991.

Quinn, William A. *Chaucer's Rehersynges: The Performability of the Legend of Good Women*. Washington, D.C.: Catholic University of America Press, 1994.

Strohm, Paul. *Social Chaucer*. Cambridge: Harvard University Press, 1989.

CHESNUTT, CHARLES WADDELL (1858–1932)

A mulatto educator, law practitioner, lecturer, and author, Charles Waddell Chesnutt's early short fiction reveals an extensive and intellectually sophisticated appropriation of antebellum and late-nineteenth-century, Reconstruction-era, African-American rural folk tradition from the environs of Cape Fear River in North Carolina. Fourteen short stories, written between 1885 and 1905, feature Uncle Julius McAdoo, a shrewd ex-slave storyteller employed in grape cultivation on a Tidewater plantation newly obtained during the Reconstruction era by John and Annie, husband-and-wife whites from the North. Chesnutt presents Uncle Julius telling stories in vernacular dialect, a commonplace white literary convention of the time. Uncle Julius emerges as part entertainer, part sage, himself a mulatto and akin to (though not to be taken as) the author—both character and author prone to providing selected accounts that use rhetorical storytelling strategies for didactic intents.

Chesnutt's renowned first book, *The Conjure Woman* (1899), brings together seven such accounts, each inspired by and derivatively modeled upon the then-contemporary precedents of white southern authors Joel Chandler Harris and George Washington Cable and notably encouraged by the prominent American literary critic William Dean Howells. The Uncle Julius stories single out injustices and victimization and exemplify Chesnutt's inclination to use complexities of both metaphor and irony in behalf of a recurrent theme: actual or perceived circumstances potentially open to transformation.

Chesnutt resided from ages 8 to 25 in Fayetteville, North Carolina (Patesville in his fiction). In 1880, in his personal journal, he considered collecting black folk hymns and spirituals that "might be acceptable, if only as a curiosity, to people, literary people, at the North." The author's exposure to regional folklife tradition also included black vernacular folk speech, ex-slave-narrated folk history, and social protest tales like John and Old Marster trickster tales. Although all of the Uncle Julius stories indicate an indebtedness to such heritage, *The Conjure Woman* established Chesnutt's reputation for integrating folklore into fiction.

In *The Conjure Woman*, he successfully combined actual, creatively imagined, and reconstructed slavery circumstances with African-derived folk beliefs and the practice of conjuration "goopher." "Goopher," probably from the Bantu verb *kufwa*, refers to powerful magico-occult intercession by knowledgeable specialists into natural world and human social sphere conditions of being. Conjure practitioners offer services for intervention when real or perceived ailments intrude upon well-being and contentment. In *The Conjure Woman*, Uncle Julius tells stories that single out Aun' Peggy, a free black woman traditionally skilled in conjure, and a male counterpart, Unk' Jube. Overall, the fictive characters' employment of conjuration works toward establishing well-being across race, class, and gender lines. Chesnutt himself hoped to promote moral and social humanitarian reforms across constructed white and black categorizations and barriers in the United States.

Robert D. Bethke

See also Belief; Dialect; Harris, Joel Chandler

✻✻✻✻✻✻✻✻✻✻✻✻✻✻✻✻✻✻

References

Bone, Robert. *Down Home: A History of Afro-American Short Fiction from Its Beginnings to the Harlem Renaissance*. New York: G. P. Putnam's Sons, 1975, pp. 74–105.

Chesnutt, Charles W. *The Conjure Woman and Other Conjure Tales*. Ed. and intro. Richard H. Brodhead. Durham, N.C., and London: Duke University Press, 1993.

———. *The Journals of Charles W. Chesnutt*. Ed. Righard H. Brodhead. Durham, N.C., and London: Duke University Press, 1993, p. 121.

———. *The Short Fiction of Charles W. Chesnutt*. Ed. and intro. Sylvia Lyons Render. Washington, D.C.: Howard University Press, 1981.

———. "Superstitions and Folklore of the South." *Modern Culture* 13 (1901): 231–235.

Hemenway, Robert. "The Functions of Folklore in Charles Chesnutt's *The Conjure Woman*." *Journal of the Folklore Institute* 13 (1976): 283–309.

CHICAGO FOLKLORE SOCIETY

For several years in the late nineteenth century, the Chicago Folklore Society was a rival of the American Folklore Society, and the two organizations were divided over the question of whether or not the study of traditional lore properly belonged to the field of anthropology or literature. The Chicago Folklore Society espoused the literary view while the American Folklore Society championed the anthropological course. Fletcher S. Bassett (1847–1893), a retired U.S. Navy lieutenant, established the Chicago organization in December 1891. Although his health had forced him into early retirement from the navy in 1882, Bassett published a book, *Legends and Superstitions of the Sea and of Sailors in All Lands and at All Times*, in 1885. The work is a pastiche, and the material was culled uncritically from many books, some of which were not first-rate volumes, so the book is less useful than one might expect from someone with as much maritime experience as Bassett. His reputation justly rests not on his publications, but on his organizational abilities.

The Chicago Folklore Society's inaugural meeting was held December 12, 1891, at the Woman's Club Rooms in the Chicago Art Institute, and members of the new organization identified their interest in collecting, preserving, analyzing, and otherwise making traditional literature of the United States—west of the Alleghenies in particular—available. This concept of folklore meant that it had value aside from what it revealed about the larger human universe and placed the new society in opposition to W. W. Newell, the major force in the American Folklore Society, who saw folklore as being inextricably bound to culture and thus most appropriately regarded as part of the science of anthropology.

Having freed folklore from culture, Bassett formulated a concept of traditional literature as a unified, coherent body of material to which the tools of literary analysis could be applied. In other words, folklore required its own distinct methodology and therefore should be separate from general examinations of human nature and solely concerned with the scrutiny of the material itself. His ultimate goal was to display folklore in an engaging, literary manner and, to further this aim, he established the journal *The Folk-Lorist* (published (1892–1893) to oppose the publication of the *Journal of American Folklore*. He also produced *The Folklore Manual* in 1892 to instruct interested parties in how to collect folklore.

The Chicago Folklore Society's greatest success was the International Folk-lore Congress of 1893, which brought together folklore scholars from around the world. Unfortunately, it taxed Bassett's already frail health, and he died on October 19, 1893. With him, the Chicago Folklore Society for all practical purposes also died. It lingered on for a few more years, but no one came forward to replace Bassett. The society's membership consisted mainly of socialites like Mrs. Potter Palmer or literary figures such as Eugene Field. A wide variety of interests were represented, but no one was willing to devote full attention to the society. Bassett's organizational abilities notwithstanding, his main failing was that he was too dominant to leave a real successor. Only nonresident members, who were too far removed from the base of operations to be helpful, had the necessary interests and abilities to keep the organization functioning.

W. K. McNeil

See also International Society for Folk Narrative Research; Modern Language Association of America (MLA)

✼✼✼✼✼✼✼✼✼✼✼✼✼✼✼✼✼

References

Bassett, Fletcher S. *The Folk-Lore Manual*. Darby, Pa.: Norwood Editions, 1973.

———. *Legends and Superstitions of the Sea and of Sailors in All Lands and at All Times*. Detroit: Singing Tree Press, 1971.

The Folk-Lorist. Philadelphia: Norwood Editions, 1973.

McNeil, W. K. "The Chicago Folklore Society and the International Folklore Congress of 1893." *Midwestern Journal of Language and Folklore* (1985).

CHILD, FRANCIS JAMES (1825–1896)

A philologist and teacher at Harvard University, Francis James Child was the editor of *The English and Scottish Popular Ballads*, a monumental collection of 305 traditional ballads in the English language that was issued in 5 volumes (in 10 parts) between 1882 and 1898. The ballads thus canonized are internationally referred to as "the Child ballads" or simply as "Child 1" to "Child 305."

Born in Boston, Child lived in that part of New England almost all his life. He entered Harvard University in the class of 1846 and upon graduation, commenced a lifelong service to that institution, appointed first as tutor and then in August 1851, after a short leave of study in Germany, as the Boylston Professor of Rhetoric and Oratory. He held that position for 25 years, teaching English composition, hearing student recitations, and marking a great quantity of written work. In 1876 a new chair was established, and Child became Harvard's first professor of English. Henceforth, his teaching was more in line with his real interests and expertise, for he had already established himself as an authority on early English literature, especially on ballads, Anglo-Saxon, Chaucer, and Shakespeare.

His first publication, in 1848, was a collection of sixteenth-century dramas (*Four Old Plays*), and that work was followed in 1852 by a reissue of *An Elementary English Grammar*. Also in 1852, he accepted the general editorship of the American reprints of *The British Poets*, and he eventually saw 130 volumes, with alterations and additions, through the press and prepared a highly acclaimed 5-volume edition of Edmund Spenser for the series that was published in 1855. His first ballad collection, *English and Scottish Ballads* in 8 volumes (1857–1859), formed part of this series of reprints and was meant to illustrate the narrative poetry of unknown British poets. Out of this grew the main work of his life, an exhaustive, critical edition of "the genuine ballads of the English speaking people."

Inspired and encouraged by the works of Thomas Percy, William Motherwell, and Svend Grundtvig, as well as the German scholars J. G. Herder and Jacob Grimm, Child made ballad poetry his lifelong concern, taking upon himself the role of "editor of English ballads" within the wider context of collecting and preserving the genuine poetry of all peoples. Although the outbreak of the U.S. Civil War and the care of his growing family (he had married in 1860) delayed his work, the publication of his monumental ballad collection finally began in 1882.

Child's intention was "to include every obtainable version of every extant English or Scottish ballad, with the fullest possible discussion of related songs or stories in the popular literature of all nations." In order to achieve this goal, he established a solid textual foundation by conducting a thorough investigation into the available material from the oral tradition and manuscript sources and surveyed the whole field of international ballads by enlisting the cooperation of scholars from all over the world. Endless collation of texts and manuscripts followed, and 305 individual ballads were eventually printed with introductory, historical, and critical notes as well as references to variants in up to 30 other languages. Given Child's industry, judgment, and accuracy, it is small wonder that *The English and Scottish Popular Ballads* became the standard reference point for all subsequent work in the field of traditional balladry.

The criticism the *English and Scottish Popular Ballads* has attracted is less concerned with what the collection contains than with what it does not contain—like the music to the ballad texts or contextual information or indeed even an outline of selection criteria. It has been a matter of much debate that Child saw his collecting efforts as gleanings: the main harvest had long been over, he argued, since the conditions for the creation and survival of the popular ballad had long gone. The folk ballads and maybe the broadsides lived on, but the true popular ballads, those that made up the earliest literary records of humanity, had been regularly displaced and almost extinguished by the appearance of the poetry of art. The broadsides and folk ballads were such products of art—be it of a low kind—and thus, they had no right to a place in a ballad collection of the people.

If his work on ballads secured him lasting fame, Child will also be remembered for his pioneering work on Geoffrey Chaucer and John Gower—a thorough investigation into the poets' language and versification led Child to discover the silent final *e*. As a recognition of Child's work, F. J. Furnivall founded the Chaucer Society and the Ballad Society in England. Child's name is also associated with the American Dialect Society and the American Folklore Society; he served the latter as its first president from 1888 to 1889. Honorary degrees were conferred upon him by the University of Göttingen in Germany (1854), Harvard (1884), and Columbia (1887). He was also made a fellow of the American Academy.

Sigrid Rieuwerts

See also Chaucer, Geoffrey; Grimm, Jacob and Wilhelm; Herder, Johann Gottfried; Percy, Thomas

****

References

Cheesman, Tom, and Sigrid Rieuwerts, eds. *Ballads into Books: The Legacies of F. J. Child*. Bern: Peter Lang, 1997.

Child, Francis James. "Ballad Poetry." In *Universal Cyclopaedia and Atlas*, ed. Rossiter Johnson, rev. and enl. Charles K. Adams, vol. 1, p. 464. 12 vols. New York: Appleton, 1902. Reprinted in *Journal of Folklore Research* 31 (1994): 214–222.

————. *The English and Scottish Popular Ballads*. 5 vols. Boston: Houghton, Mifflin, 1882–1898.

Hustvedt, Sigurd B. *Ballad Books and Ballad Men*. Cambridge: Harvard University Press, 1930.

Rieuwerts, Sigrid. "The Folk-Ballad: The Illegitimate Child of the Popular Ballad." *Journal of Folklore Research* 33:3 (1996): 221–226.

————. " 'The Genuine Ballads of the People': F. J. Child and the Ballad Cause." *Journal of Folklore Research* 31 (1994): 1–34.

CHILDREN'S LITERATURE

Before the advent of printed literature, oral tales offered entertainment and instruction to children. The Grimm brothers' collection of folktales bore the title *Kinder- und Hausmärchen* [Children's and household tales (1850)], showing the importance of children as a primary audience. Although oral stories for children have circulated for many centuries, the first book written especially for children was John Newbery's *A Little Pretty Pocket Book*. This volume contained fables, games, and a letter to Jack the giant-killer. In the seventeenth and eighteenth centuries, chapbooks provided a means for the dissemination of favorite stories, including many folktales.

After a rapid growth of the children's book industry in the twentieth century, there has been a resurgence of interest in oral folktales, partly because of the popularity of audio- and videocassette renditions. Of the many collections of folktales intended for children, some include thorough documentation and a careful transcription of oral texts. Two especially good collections of North American folktales for children are Richard Chase's *Grandfather Tales* (1948) and Virginia Hamilton's *The People Could Fly: American Black Folktales* (1985). Charles J. Finger's collection of South American folktales, *Tales from Silver Lands*, won the Newbery Medal for excellence in children's literature in 1924.

Since the latter half of the nineteenth century, folklore and fantasy literature for children have been closely connected. The first British fantasy novel, Lewis Carroll's *Alice in Wonderland*, contains riddles, games, and customs. Alice herself is like a folktale heroine, initially unpromising but increasingly clever in her handling of rationally inexplicable events. George MacDonald's *At the Back of the North Wind* also features an unlikely hero and a personified North Wind who helps him. In *Five Children and It* by E. Nesbit, a wonderful sand-fairy transforms the lives of some adventurous but otherwise unremarkable children, and many other fantasy novels develop the theme of sudden confrontation between magic and everyday life.

More recent fantasy novels have built upon myths, tales, and customs integral to a particular culture area. Lloyd Alexander's *Prydain Chronicles*, including *Taran Wanderer*, take their inspiration from the medieval Welsh work. Similarly, in Susan Cooper's *The Dark Is Rising* and other books, Celtic myths and customs create suspenseful situations. In both J. R. R. Tolkien's *The Hobbit* and C. S. Lewis's *Chronicles of Narnia*, one can see the influence of Greek, Roman, and Norse mythology as well as of European folktales.

Folklore has also exerted a considerable influence on nineteenth- and twentieth-century realistic fiction for children. One of the earliest realistic novels, Louisa May Alcott's *Little Women*, gives a detailed portrait of the March family, including customs, games, and stories. Mark Twain's *Tom Sawyer* contains many folk beliefs, games, and cures, including some especially dramatic wart cures. In Frances Hodgson Burnett's *The Secret Garden*, the author places a strong emphasis on magic and ritual as well as on nursery rhymes. From the mid-twentieth century on, realistic fiction for children has burgeoned, with frequent mentions of folk games, pastimes, customs, and beliefs. Among authors of such books are Eleanor Estes (*The Moffats*) and Beverly Cleary (*Henry Huggins* and *Ramona Quimby, Age Eight*, among others). Judy Blume, author of such best-selling novels as *Are You There God? It's Me, Margaret*, has been particularly successful in including folklore in her books. Children may recognize elements of their own lives in such realistic novels, or they may even learn about some kinds of folklore for the first time through reading. Thus, there is a substantial symbiotic relationship between children's folklore and realistic literature.

Elizabeth Tucker

See also Chapbook; Folktale; Grimm, Jacob and Wilhelm; Myth; Tolkien, J. R. R.; Twain, Mark

✹✹✹✹✹✹✹✹✹✹✹✹✹✹✹✹✹

References

Cameron, Eleanor. *The Green and Burning Tree: On the Writing and Enjoyment of Children's Books*. Boston: Little, Brown, 1969.

Chase, Richard. *Grandfather Tales*. Boston: Houghton Mifflin, 1948.

Finger, Charles J. *Tales from Silver Lands*. New York: Doubleday, 1924.

Hamilton, Virginia. *The People Could Fly: American Black Folktales*. New York: Knopf, 1985.

Meigs, Cornelia, et al. *A Critical History of Children's Literature*. New York: Macmillan, 1953.

CHIN, FRANK (1940–)

The Asian-American playwright, essayist, and novelist Frank Chin was born February 25, 1940, in Berkeley, California, the son of Frank Chew and Lilac Yoke Quan Chin. He graduated from high school in Oakland, California, and attended the University of California at Berkeley and Iowa State University. During this time, Chin worked intermittently as a clerk for the Western Pacific Railroad. After he received a bachelor of arts degree from the University of California at Santa Barbara in 1965, Chin became the first Chinese-American brakeman on the Southern Pacific Railroad, a job he held for three years.

In 1971, Frank Chin was the first Asian American to have a play produced on the New York stage when his *Chickencoop Chinaman* was produced by Joseph Papp at the Public Theater. That work and *Year of the Dragon* established Chin as a major voice in Asian-American theater. Since that time, Chin's essays, lectures, short stories, and anthology projects have played a significant role in shaping the contours of Asian-American literature.

Chin's project, explicated in the introductions to his two anthologies, *Aiiieeeee! An Anthology of Asian-American Writers* (1975) and *The Big Aiiieeeee! An Anthology of Chinese-American and Japanese-American Literature* (c. 1991), has been to expose and combat racist stereotypes that, in his view, have emasculated Asian-American culture. His principal strategy has been to recover an Asian-American literary tradition. At the heart of this immigrant tradition—which, he argues, has been obliterated by Christian missionaries and their Chinese converts—is an authentic non-Christian heroic tradition.

For Chin, this authentic culture is embodied in Kwan Kung, the Chinese god of war and literature. Based on the historical figure Kwan Yu of the Three Kingdoms period at the end of the Han dynasty (about the second century C.E.), Kwan Kung has become a universally popular hero, representing loyalty, daring, and courage. In the millennia since the Han dynasty, Kwan Kung has undergone a lengthy apotheosis, including deification in the Buddhist, Daoist, and popular Confucian traditions. Not the least significant has been his adoption as the patron saint of overseas Chinese communities; no fewer than 18 temples have been erected in his honor in nineteenth- and early-twentieth-century California. Kwan Kung's heroics continued to be heard and read in various versions of stories from the *Romance of the Three Kingdoms* (c. 1522) to Cantonese opera and contemporary popular comic books. For Chin, Kwan Kung is embodied in the spirit of the Chinese-American pioneer who shaped nineteenth- and early-twentieth-century Chinatowns and the tongs and still shape the imaginative universe of 12-year-old Chinese-American boys growing up in Chinatowns.

Kwan Kung has made his presence felt principally in Frank Chin's critical writings, especially in his essay "This Is Not an Autobiography" in *Genre* and his introduction to *The Big Aiiieeeee!* In these essays, Chin has been extremely critical of other Asian-American writers, most notably Maxine Hong Kingston and David Henry Hwang, whom he accuses of appealing to and perpetuating racist stereotypes of the Chinese in the United States by rewriting and distorting Chinese folklore in their work. Chin's *Donald Duk: A Novel* (1991) is a bildungsroman in which Kwan Kung and other figures from the Chinese heroic tradition provide the spiritual guidance for a young boy growing up in San Francisco's Chinatown.

Robert Lee

See also *Bildungsroman*; Kingston, Maxine Hong

****

References

Chin, Frank. *The Chickencoop Chinaman and The Year of the Dragon: Two Plays*. Intro. Dorothy Ritsuko McDonald. Seattle: University of Washington Press, c. 1981.

———. *Donald Duk: A Novel*. Minneapolis: Coffee House Press, 1991.

Chin, Frank, et al., eds. *Aiiieeeee!: An Anthology of Asian-American Writers*. Garden City, N.Y.: Anchor Press, 1975.

———. *The Big Aiiieeeee!: An Anthology of Chinese-American and Japanese-American Literature*. New York: Penguin, c. 1991.

CHINESE OPERA

Chinese opera consists of a dramatic musical performance of songs and traditional stories that derive from both folk and literary sources. The combination of historical legends, traditional romances, and folk songs in the operas has evolved in varying forms to appeal to audiences of all social classes since at least the Ming dynasty (1368–1644). The various forms are an indication of the flexibility of a traditional drama that can rework almost any story into stock roles distinguishing people according to age, sex, and status. Practically every local or provincial area and ethnic group of traditional China has cultivated its own form of opera, sung in the provincial dialect with versions of stories featuring their own favorite heroes. Some forms took on classical status as the roles and singing became more stylized and were supported by the courts or officials. *K'un Ch'u* [Songs of K'un Mountain] and the Peking Opera are commonly recognized as the classical forms of Chinese opera.

Until the Ching-Hsi, known as the Peking Opera, took over in popularity during the Ch'ing dynasty (1644–1912), *K'un Ch'u*, which was developed by literati during the Ming dynasty, was considered the classical form of drama noted for its refined singing of lyrical arias. It contrasted greatly with the more acrobatic *Tsa Chu* ("variety theater"). Although stories from legend provided the background to some of the scenes performed in the *K'un Ch'u*, the styles of singing the songs became more important than the stories. With the advent of the Peking Opera, local forms of rhythm and instrumentation styles—namely, the *hsi-p'i ch'iang* (Western singing style;

A Chinese opera singer at the Beijing Opera wears an elaborate costume depicting a character from an ancient Chinese legend.

derived from the *Ch'in-ch'iang* of the east-central province of Hubei) and the *erh-huang ch'iang* (of ching, or painted face, roles; probably derived from Jiangxi music)—were effectively combined to form the basis of a new operatic form.

The troupes, which had also added stylized acrobatics to the singing styles, gained in popularity, especially during the reign of Emperor Hung-li (1735–1796), who periodically traveled south and enjoyed the performances of the troupes in cities such as Yangzhou. Troupes from Anhui with actors from Jiangxi were invited to Peking and gradually became established there. The court itself established training centers for young boys, and all facets of performance and costume became more refined. The professional actors, trained in the court-supported troupes, soon made this once-local form famous throughout China; cyclically, the acting and singing techniques, as well as the costuming and facial painting refinements of the Peking Opera, began to influence the local dialect troupes throughout China.

In Ch'ing dynasty court opera, men played all roles including those of the women. One of the most famous of the *tan* ("female lead") actors was Mei Lan-Fan. In the Peking Opera today, however, as in the local or folk forms, troupes are made up of both men and women, often members of the same family. In some regions, such as Taiwan, there is a tradition of women playing male roles.

Performance of the stories was learned as part of the singing role so that play scripts were not necessary, and considerable stylistic variation as well as dialogue improvisation could be made by more creative performers. Since the audience concentrated on the style of singing and was familiar with the traditional story, the whole story was usually not presented in the Peking Opera as it was in the local operas. However, folk sources for many of the stories are confirmed, such as that of the popular legend of the White Snake. Folklore motifs are retained sometimes even tacitly, as in the symbols painted on the faces of legendary figures in the *ching* roles or in kinesic representations of the transformations of animal spirits, such as Sun Wu-Kung, the monkey. Since the 1970s, there has been considerable innovation in the opera schools, and new plays are written with stories coming from widely diverse literary sources. New productions based on Hu Yao-heng's reworking of Shakespeare plots and Hwang Mei-shu's postmodernist staging of *King Lear*, for instance, have been recently performed.

Patricia Haseltine

See also *Ch'uan-ch'i*; Legend; Taiwanese Opera

✳✳✳✳✳✳✳✳✳✳✳✳✳✳✳✳✳✳

References

Hwang, Mei-shu. "A Brief Introduction to Peking Opera." *Tamkang Review* 12:3 (1982): 315–329.

Mackerras, Colin P. *The Rise of the Peking Opera 1770–1870: Social Aspects of the Theatre in Manchu China*. Oxford: Clarendon Press, 1972.

Scott, A. C. *The Classical Theatre of China*. London, 1957.

———. *Traditional Chinese Plays*. 3 vols. Madison: University of Wisconsin Press, 1967–1975.

Wichmann, Elizabeth. "Tradition and Innovation in Contemporary Beijing Opera Performance." *Drama Review* 34:1 (1990): 146–178.

CH'UAN-CH'I

The *ch'uan-ch'i* ("legendary tale") is a Chinese traditional literary tale that retains the main distinguishing characteristics of the belief legend. Probably derived from the *chih-kuai* ("supernatural tales") known since the Six Dynasties period (220–589), the *ch'uan-ch'i* developed as a separate genre during the T'ang (618–907) and Sung (960–1279) dynasties, alongside the longer vernacular fiction (*hua-pen*), or literary renditions of the tales of professional storytellers. The short narratives of the *ch'uan-ch'i* genre range from slightly romanticized versions of folktales or legends to stories that show little trace of oral tradition.

The stories are simple narratives with a single plot and only a few characters. Like the belief legends, they begin with an appeal to credibility through the identification of a known place and the names of actual persons. The telling of an encounter with the supernatural is usually in the third person but sometimes in the first, as in personal experience stories. Concrete evidence attesting to the truth of the story is also given. The formulaic closing may contain a brief moral comment on the actions of the characters and on how good is rewarded and evil punished. Yet the tone of the written form of these legends can also be somewhat humorous.

During the literarily diverse Ming period (1368–1644), *ch'uan-ch'i* were written for the variety drama (*tsa-chu*) by some playwrights, and folktale and legend motifs in this genre were also transmitted to the plots of the dramas. New forms of drama evolved so that the original 4 (or later 5) acts became a sequence of up to 11 scenic-length acts that fit the narrative episodes of the stories. In these plays, traditional values of the tales were emphasized by the Confucian writers so that religious, moral, and ethical values could be spread.

Patricia Haseltine

See also Belief; Legend; Personal Experience Story

✿✿✿✿✿✿✿✿✿✿✿✿✿✿✿✿✿

References

Kan, T. H. "The Rise of T'ang Ch'uan-ch'i and Its Narrative Art." Ph.D. dissertation, Cornell University, 1979.

Ma, Y. W., and Joseph S. M. Lau, eds. *Traditional Chinese Stories, Themes, and Variations*. New York: Columbia University Press, 1978.

Yim, Sarah. *"Ch'uan-ch'i."* In *The Indiana Companion to Traditional Chinese Literature*, ed. and comp. William H. Nienhauser, Jr., pp. 356–359. Bloomington: Indiana University Press, 1986.

CINDERELLA

The Cinderella story tells of a little orphan girl (the ash girl, or cinder girl) who, with the aid of an animal or her dead mother, appears at a dance, festival, or, in some versions, at church disguised as a lady of society and catches the eye of a prince who, after discovering her identity by the ring or slipper test, marries her. Arguably, this is the best known folktale in the world, as it is found in almost every country; it is listed in the type index as AT 510/510A. Some scholars believe the folktale originated in the Orient, but it is impossible to prove that fact; all that can really be said with confidence is that the earliest known text dates from the ninth century in China. In Europe and the United States, the version printed by Charles Perrault in *Histoires ou contes du temps passe* [Histories of past times; better known as *Mother Goose* (1697)] has been highly influential. He is responsible for the glass slipper and the witching hour of midnight motifs.

The tale has received considerable attention from writers representing a broad range of disciplines. The earliest of these publications was by a folklorist, Marian Roalfe Cox, whose 1893 work was the first detailed study of a folktale ever made. Even though it was written over 100 years ago, it is still a useful work. In 1951, 58 years after Cox's study was issued, the Swedish folklorist Anna Birgitta Rooth published her doctoral dissertation, *The Cinderella Cycle*, which is still the most comprehensive study of the tale. Both Cox and Rooth were interested in finding the oldest form of the narrative, which would thereby aid in determining its likely origins and in sorting out the complex of different, but related, forms of the Cinderella tale. Other approaches to analyzing the tale include that of French folklorist

Emile Nourry, who saw remains of ancient rituals in the story; the Irish philosopher Aarland Usser examined the tale as an allegory with heavy Christian overtones; and Bruno Bettelheim presented a psychoanalytic interpretation in *The Uses of Enchantment*.

The tale has, of course, been spread not just by oral tradition but by various forms of mass culture ranging from Italian composer Gioacchino Antonio Rossini's 1817 opera *La cenerentola* to versions printed in numerous children's books, but few of these presentations have had the long-term influence of the 1949 Walt Disney feature-length cartoon, *Cinderella*. There was also a 1961 Russian film with the same title, but it achieved nowhere near the popularity of the Disney version. One indication of the Cinderella tale's popularity is that it is often parodied, in both folk tradition and popular culture. The actor Jerry Lewis changed the protagonist from a woman to a man in his 1961 film *Cinderfella*, and country comic Archie Campbell recorded and frequently performed a vaudeville routine called "Rindercella."

W. K. McNeil

See also Disney, Walter Elias; Folktale; Perrault, Charles

✱✱✱✱✱✱✱✱✱✱✱✱✱✱✱✱✱

References

Bettelheim, Bruno. *The Uses of Enchantment: The Meaning and Importance of Fairy Tales*. New York: Vintage Books, 1977.

Cox, Marian Roalfe. *Cinderella: Three Hundred and Forty-Five Variants of Cinderella, Catskin, and Cap o' Rushes, Abstracted and Tabulated, with a Discussion of Medieval Analogues and Notes*. London: David Nutt, 1893.

Dundes, Alan. *Cinderella: A Casebook*. New York: Garland, 1982.

Rooth, Anna Birgitta. *The Cinderella Cycle*. Lund, Sweden: C. W. K. Gleerup, 1951.

Ting, Nai-Tung. *The Cinderella Cycle in China and Indo-China*. Helsinki: Academia Scientarium Fennica, 1974.

CISNEROS, SANDRA (1954–)

Born in Chicago to a Mexican father and Mexican-American mother, and the only sister to six brothers, Sandra Cisneros is the darling of contemporary Chicana writers, beloved by readers, critics, and audiences. Commercially successful and sought after as a speaker, Cisneros is also widely regarded as being among the most sophisticated and technically accomplished of Mexican-American writers. Her first novel, *House on Mango Street* (1984), a stunning display of linguistic innovation, won the 1985 American Book Award from the Before Columbus Foundation.

House on Mango Street contributes to a turning point in narratives about Chicana life and marks a move away from poetry as the prevalent mode of Chicana artistic expression. As the coming-of-age story of a young Mexican-American female artist, the story itself is relatively new. But the way Cisneros tells the story—her blend of the poetic/metaphoric language of "high culture"—is the real evidence of Cisneros's talent. In her hands, the language of the folk is literature, and the category of literature itself is redefined away from its historical association with Western civilization's elite.

Cisneros's second prose work, *Woman Hollering Creek and Other Stories* (1991), develops and extends the linguistic innovation of the first novel. With a perfect ear for regional dialect, Cisneros captures the various nuanced speech patterns and group sensibilities of South Texas Chicanas. Moreover, many Mexican-American legends are rewritten with a distinctly feminist slant. A case in point is the title story. Woman Hollering Creek is a river over which the protagonists repeatedly cross, often fleeing the threat of male violence. The image of cries or hollering at a creekside is probably most readily associated with the well-known Mexican legend of "La Llorona" [Weeping woman], the mourning, lakeside mother whose children have been stolen by European invaders. If the women of Cisneros's story confront the archetypal fate of women as victims each time they pass over the noisy creek, they nevertheless do not cry out with the voice of a victim. Instead they "holler" and howl in a joyous and powerful demonstration of their unwillingness to be defined by archetypal images of femininity. Neither those images nor their current violent male partners will control their psyches or daily lives.

Cisneros's publications also include *My Wicked, Wicked Ways* (1987), a collection of poetry. She has received two National Endowment for the Arts Fellowships for poetry and fiction and has served as a poet-in-the-schools and visiting writer at many colleges. As she puts it in the biographical notes to more than one of her books, "She is nobody's wife and nobody's mother."

Krista Comer

See also Latino and Chicano Folklore and Literature; Legend; La Llorona

✼✼✼✼✼✼✼✼✼✼✼✼✼✼✼✼

References

Herrera-Sobek, María, and Helena María Viramontes. *Chicana Creativity and Criticism: Charting New Frontiers in American Literature*. Houston: Arte Público, 1988.

Salvidar, Ramón. *Chicano Narrative: The Dialectics of Difference*. Madison: University of Wisconsin Press, 1990.

COFER, JUDITH ORTIZ (1952–)

Puerto Rican literature in the United States, traditionally associated with New York City, is led by young voices that are independent of the so-called Nuyorican literary school, and Judith Ortiz Cofer is one representative of those young voices. A poet by preference, she has also written short fiction, a novel, and literary criticism published in mainstream journals. She has received distinguished prizes. *Peregrina*, a chapbook, was awarded first place at the Riverstone International Poetry Competition in 1985. In 1987, she won a Bread Loaf Writers' Conference Fellowship in poetry, and in the same year, she was one of the poets selected to do a reading tour of Georgia on the Georgia poetry circuit. Her first novel, *The Line of the Sun*, also the first novel published by the University of Georgia Press, was nominated for a Pulitzer Prize in 1990. Her poetry has appeared in anthologies such as *Puerto Rican Writers at Home in the USA* and *The Heath Anthology of Modern American Literature*. Currently, Cofer teaches creative writing at the University of Georgia.

Born in Hormigueros, Puerto Rico, Judith Ortiz Cofer was two years old when she arrived in Paterson, New Jersey, because her father, who had enlisted in the U.S. Navy, was stationed in Brooklyn, New York. When Judith's father was assigned to a cargo fleet that spent up to six months in Europe, his family regularly spent those months with relatives in Hormigueros. Those periods in Puerto Rico and her life in a multifamily dwelling in a Puerto Rican barrio in New Jersey are themes of Cofer's work.

In content and language, Cofer departs from traditions of the Nuyoricans (Puerto Ricans living in New York), who insist upon photographic reproduction of continental Puerto Rican life. Cofer often explores the Puerto Rican psyche through symbols that, although recognizably Puerto Rican, have been dismissed as merely folkloric. Whether dealing with Puerto Rican themes or with Puerto-Rican-in-the-United-States popular culture, she writes exclusively in conventional American English and avoids the English and Spanish code-switching that is popularly known as "Spanglish."

Cofer has insisted that Puerto Rican oral traditions and storytelling have played a major part in her work. Her short narratives, or "creative nonfiction," are clear echoes of *cuentos*, the family gossip stories, legends, and myths that she heard as a child from her grandmother. Both folkloric narrations and *exempla*, her grandmother's stories were educational, and they addressed women's issues. For example, *Silent Dancing* develops feminine narrations dominated by strong female characters who explore their inner self in a restrictive, male-dominated society.

In *The Line of the Sun*, Cofer rethinks symbols of Puerto Rican identity transplanted onto patterns of American ethnicity. This novel of strong sociohistorical dimensions pictures the transition of a Puerto Rican family to New Jersey from Salud, a fictional Puerto Rican rural town. The narrator is an adolescent, first-generation American, Marisol, who examines issues of national identity as she looks at Puerto Rican life through the experiences of her relatives both in Puerto Rico and in New Jersey. Of particular interest to folklorists are the parallels that the author draws with the development of African religions into Caribbean *Santería*.

Judith Ortiz Cofer is representative of a new direction in contemporary American literature. Her independence from the Nuyorican school illustrates her postmodernist interest in ethnic literary representation, and her work develops from semantic and linguistic experimentation, from a reevaluation of postcolonial Puerto Rican and American history, and from the understanding of ethnic relations in an openly subversive literary process. This exploration of Puerto Rican identity—including popular traditions—is part of contemporary American society, multiracial and multicultural, in continuous renovation and definition.

Rafael Ocasio

See also Legend; Storytelling; Women

✳✳✳✳✳✳✳✳✳✳✳✳✳✳✳✳✳✳

References

Kanellos, Nicolás. "Cofer, Judith Ortiz." In *Bibliographical Dictionary of Hispanic Literature in the United States: The Literature of Puerto Ricans, Cuban Amer-*

icans, and Other Hispanic Writers, pp. 60–63. New York: Greenwood Press, 1989.

Ocasio, Rafael. "Puerto Rican Literature in Georgia? Interview with Judith Ortiz Cofer." Kenyon Review 14:4 (1992): 43–50.

Ryan, Bryan, ed. "Cofer, Judith Ortiz." In Hispanic Writers, pp. 140–141. Detroit: Gale Research Group, 1991.

COMMEDIA DELL'ARTE

Commedia dell'arte ("comedy of art") was a popular theatrical genre based on improvisation and stock characters. Originating in sixteenth-century Italy, it had spread throughout Europe by the eighteenth century. Never completely dying out, it has undergone a revival in the twentieth century in Europe and the United States. Its popularity across cultural and linguistic boundaries derives from its form, its content, and its venue. Taken together, these factors create a powerful, multivocal way of commenting on themes of enduring appeal in performances brimming with vitality and humor.

The characters of the commedia dell'arte were caricatures of familiar types representing young and old, urban and rural, sophisticated and rustic, rich and poor, and native and foreigner. These types were divided into high and low characters. The former included lovers who were young and attractive and whose speech was the cultivated, courtly dialect of Tuscany. Low characters included clowns (zanni) and their female counterparts, the maids; two old men (Pantalone and the doctor); and the captain, a swaggering and slightly ridiculous coward. In the earliest form, characters were also associated with particular regions of northern Italy and, in one instance, with Italy's enemy, Greece. Regional dialects marked these associations.

Harlequin, Brighella, Pierrot (Pedrolino), and Pulcinella are all low, masked clowns. In Italian, the generic term is zanni, and in early scenes, this term may have been used rather than a specific clown name. Harlequin and Brighella were first and second zanni, respectively. Both were from Bergamo, a town considered by Venetians to be rustic and crude. Harlequin was the more crude of the two—always hungry, always nosy, always getting into trouble, and always vexing his master. His costume was made up of multicolored patches and a wooden sword or bat hung at his side (the original slapstick). He wore a black half-mask with bushy eyebrows and mustache, carbuncles, and

The commedia dell'arte, *a theatrical form that originated in sixteenth-century Italy, often caricatured romantic social conventions and has had a lasting influence on comedy and acting into the twentieth century.*

a snub nose, above which he wore a felt hat with a rabbit's tail. Brighella, though also from Bergamo, was the smarter of the two, and often guided the action of the play. He was unscrupulous, conniving, and cynical.

Pierrot, or Pedrolino as he was known in Italy, was the sad clown who could never do anything right. Forever falling in love with high characters and serving maids, he was never successful in courting. His costume consisted of a loose-fitting white smock and a black skullcap, and he had a white face. Originally, the white face was a mask. Pulcinella, a character from Naples, was also a *zanni*. He was a glutton; was sometimes dull-witted, sometimes cunning; and frequently beat others and was beaten. His costume included a white smock, belted at the waist; a tall, conical white hat; and a half-mask with a wrinkled forehead and a hooked nose. He spoke in a Neapolitan dialect.

The two old men characters, both masked, were Pantalone and the Doctor. The former was modeled on the Venetian merchant: he spoke in Venetian dialect and was avaricious, lascivious, harsh with his daughter or ward, and often foolish. He wore red woolen tights and tunic, slippers with upturned toes, and a black cape. His half-mask had a long nose, bushy eyebrows, and pointed beard. His friend the Doctor (sometimes a professor) was from Bologna and represented a pedant. He, too, was always looking for a romantic adventure but succeeded only in being the butt of jokes. He dressed entirely in black academic robes. The Captain, always a foreigner, initially was a Greek and only later became a Spaniard. His speech, whether in Greek or Spanish, was full of braggadocio, but his actions were cowardly.

Commedia dell'arte plots were standard, revolving around the romantic love of the young high characters, declared in act 1, thwarted in act 2, thrown into confusion by a night scene, and resolved in act 3. The old men were the primary opponents of young love, and the servants were its promoters and rescuers. And although social conventions may have been mocked by the *zanni* during the course of the play, they were always upheld in the denouement.

Lazzi, or bits of mimed, comic action, were the mainstay of the *zanni*. Some were quite well known—the *lazzi* of the letter, the *lazzi* of suicide, the *lazzi* of the night scene—and particular players were known for their interpretations of them. The familiarity of the *lazzi* and the standard plots let players improvise, bringing freshness by performance rather than by script.

Originally, the commedia dell'arte was produced by groups of young amateurs, the *compagnie della calza* ("companions of the stocking"), for example. Then troupes became part of the household of dukes, princes, and kings and performed for those courts. During this period, troupes traveled throughout Europe, even to Poland and Bavaria. It was only in the early eighteenth century that the commedia dell'arte was performed in established theaters for paying audiences. Whatever its venue, the commedia dell'arte was and is extremely appealing because of its lively, witty commentary on the society of the day.

Anya Peterson Royce

See also Genre; Performance

✳✳✳✳✳✳✳✳✳✳✳✳✳✳✳✳

References

Duchartre, Pierre-Louis. *La Commedia dell'arte et ses enfants*. Paris: Editions d'Art et Industrie, 1955.

Heck, Thomas. *Commedia dell'arte: A Guide to the Primary and Secondary Literature*. New York: Garland, 1988.

Lea, Kathleen M. *Italian Popular Comedy: A Study in the Commedia dell'arte, 1560–1620, with Special Reference to the English Stage.* Oxford: Clarendon Press, 1934.

Royce, Anya. "The Venetian Commedia: Actors and Masques in the Development of the Commedia dell'arte." *Theatre Survey* 30 (1986): 45–57.

Scott, Virginia. *The Commedia dell'arte in Paris, 1644–1697.* Charlottesville: University Press of Virginia, 1990.

COMPARATIVE METHOD

Although Giuseppe Cocchiara (1971, p. 29) saw the beginning of the comparative method in folklore in the notion of the "noble savage" that emerged among Europeans after the "discovery" of the New World, a thorough history of the method would have to begin with the contributions of such writers from classical antiquity as Hesiod, Herodotus, Pausanias, Strabo, and Tacitus. One should also survey the work of European humanists as well as works by British antiquarians. It is virtually impossible for the historian of folklore and literature to write its history, for as Alan Dundes pointed out, "Many if not most academic disciplines are comparative in nature and scope" (1986, p. 125).

For the study of both folklore and literature, the beginnings of the scholarly fascination with the comparative method began in the eighteenth century when Sir William Jones (1746–1786) addressed the Asiatic Society in London in 1785. Jones, a pioneer Orientalist who had lived in India and knew 13 languages well and 28 moderately well, made the following modest observation that helped reshape the scholarly world:

> The Sanskrit language, whatever may be its antiquity, is of wonderful structure: more perfect than Greek, more copious than Latin, and more exquisitely refined than either, yet bearing to both of them a stronger affinity, both in the roots of verbs and in the forms of grammar, than could have been produced by accident: so strong that no philologer could examine all three without believing them to have sprung from some common source that perhaps no longer exists. There is a similar reason, though not quite so forcible, for supposing that

both Gothic and Celtic, though blended with a different idiom, had the same origin with the Sanskrit. (Feldman and Richardson 1972, p. 268)

Not only did Jones correctly recognize the relationships, he drew the correct inferences from his observations: the linguistic relationships were true cognates that sprang from a common source that no longer existed. Jones recognized that Sanskrit was just another of many cognate languages and not a common source. Thus, he planted the seed of comparative Indo-European studies. Subsequently, the ideas of folk and nature poetry that had been advanced by Johann Gottfried Herder (1744–1803) would be combined with the notion of a great Indo-European ancestor culture (Ward 1981). This union formed the basis for ideas upon which much of German romanticism was founded, especially the works of the brothers Grimm (Jacob, 1785–1863; Wilhelm, 1786–1859).

The Grimm brothers and their compatriots soon became enraptured with the knowledge that this language family had, in the distant past, sprung from a single language spoken by the members of a single nation. They furthermore delighted in the notion that the nation still lived but was scattered across the continents of Europe and Asia. The original language had not died but lived on in the now separate languages of a score of related nations.

The term Jacob and Wilhelm Grimm used for the lost language and the nation of its speakers was Indo-Germanic, which appears at first glance to reflect a strong degree of ethnocentric nationalism on the part of its users. Indeed, the term later acquired such a sense, but in the beginning it was simply intended as a geographic designation. The language family in question was distributed from the peoples of India to the Germanic speakers of Iceland, hence Indo-Germanic.

Because the comparative method of the historical reconstruction of Indo-European had been in part developed by the Grimms, it was inevitable that the brothers and their followers would also apply it to the emerging field of folklore: the idea had been signaled by Herder, who saw culture as an organic whole, with roots in the past, and who insisted that each nation had its own character and its own identity. Picking up on this theme, the Grimms were convinced that surely the German nation might well have roots in the past that were more unspoiled, more genuine, and more in tune with the laws of nature than was true for the present. This premise was devolutionary in the extreme.

Whether the field is language, folklore, customs, law, or literature, the comparative method is indispensable for reconstructing that which is no longer extant in a culture. Wilhelm Grimm, in trying to explain how it came about that countless variants of individual tale-types existed through time and space, correctly proffered in his "commentaries" to the *Kinder- und Hausmärchen* [Children's and household tales] published in volume three of the 1850 edition (cited from Ward 1981, pp. 362–366) three possible explanations: First, separate and independent invention in many places at different times (today folklorists speak of "polygenesis"; these assumptions dominated the works of the "cultural evolutionists"; see Lang 1884). Second, the unique creation by an individual and then the transmission of the artifact by borrowings through wide ranges of time and space (today called "monogenesis," and diffusion that characterized the comparative method of folk-narrative research known as "the historic-geographic method"; see Krohn 1971).

Third, in the case of the märchen, Wilhelm had another explanation. He used the daring poetic metaphors so common in the age of romanticism and likened the extant variants to the "tiny pieces of a shattered gem that lie scattered on the ground, overgrown by grass and flowers and that can only be discovered by the most sharp-sighted eyes" (Ward 1981, p. 365). The implication is that the original gem is lost forever, but the imaginative scholar can gain a glimmering of how splendid it must have been in its original form. Originally, the splendor of the gem came from its religious/mythical essence. "The farther back we go, the more this mythic element intrudes; indeed, it appears to have constituted the sole content of the earliest poetry" (Ward 1981, p. 365). Wilhelm then concluded his observations with the inference that he was referring to the religion and myths of the Indo-Germanic nation.

Regardless of which explanation the scholar preferred, the comparative restoration of the lost artifacts became the dominant method of scores of academic disciplines. The construct that the comparatist was compelled to use was that of the stemma, or family tree. The new comparative study was destined to become the foundation for a whole complex of new scholarly disciplines—historical linguistics, history of literature, text criticism and editing, Germanic philology, Germanic antiquities, and above all, comparative folklore and mythology.

After Jacob Grimm published his *Deutsche Grammatik* (1819–1825), editors were provided with an apparatus that permitted them to reconstruct the development of the German language (and dialects) up to and through the Middle Ages; they were no longer working in the dark in their attempt to reconstruct, with a degree of accuracy, the lost texts. Especially influential on the emerging field of comparative folklore was the method employed by scholars of literature. When they were confronted by a manuscript tradition of many variant texts of a work for which the original text was lost, they set up the hypothetical stemma of the major branches with the goal of re-creating the lost original. The rigorous method that text critics devised for their historical reconstructions provided the model of stemma reconstruction that later informed the historic-geographic method of folk narrative research for almost 100 years.

Today, textual critics are aware that the task was virtually a hopeless one, and they now publish, in lieu of critical reconstructions, a diplomatic text of a single manuscript together with an apparatus of the variant readings from all the extant manuscripts and editions. There is a lesson for folklorists in this failure. If the textual critics, when working with a limited, and often complete, number of extant manuscripts, are unable to reconstruct a missing original text—the main problem lies in the defective construct of the stemma as an analytical tool—think how much more difficult and indeed how impossible it must be to reconstruct the archetype of a tale-type based on the faulty data of the stemma of the oral variants of the type. As a number of narrative scholars have shown, collections of oral variants can only be based on chance, and the notion that one can assemble a reliable database for setting up a stemma is illusory (Apo 1986).

Nonetheless, folklore scholars will always be dependent on the comparative method for their analyses if for no other reason than each and every type of folk narrative, proverb, song, etc., is defined by its being the sum of all its variants that exist in tradition.

Donald Ward

See also Grimm, Jacob and Wilhelm; Herder, Johann Gottfried; Historic-Geographic Method; Nationalism; Romanticism

✹✹✹✹✹✹✹✹✹✹✹✹✹✹

References

Apo, Satu. "Questions Arising in the Comparative Study of Magic Tales." *Journal of Folktale Research* 23 (1986): 177–186.

Cochiara, Giuseppe. *The History of Folklore in Europe.* Trans. J. McDaniel. Philadelphia: Institute for the Study of Human Issues, 1971 (1953).

Dundes, Alan. "The Anthropologist and the Comparative Method in Folklore." *Journal of Folklore Research* 23 (1986): 125–146.

Feldman, Burton, and Robert Richardson, eds. *The Rise of Modern Mythology 1860–1860*. Bloomington and London: Indiana University Press, 1972.

Krohn, Kaarle. *Die folkloristische Arbeitsmethode*. Oslo: Institutet for Sammellignende Kulturforskning, 1926. Trans. by Roger Welsch as *Folklore Methodology*. Austin: University of Texas Press, 1971.

Lang, Andrew. "The Method of Folklore." In *Custom and Myth*. Ed. Andrew Lang. London: Longmans, Green, 1884.

Ward, Donald. "Epilogue." In *The German Legends of the Brothers Grimm*, vol. 2, pp. 341–384. 2 vols. Philadelphia: Institute for the Study of Human Issues, 1981.

Weber-Kellermann, Ingeborg, and Andreas Bimmer. *Einführung in die volkskunde/europäische Ethnologie*. Stuttgart: Metzler Verlag, 1985.

COOPER, JAMES FENIMORE (1789–1851)

James Fenimore Cooper's use of native materials in his fiction led naturally to the introduction of vernacular characters, their language and traits, and the popular lore associated with them. Early in his career, the native types that Constance Rourke identified in *American Humor* appeared: the Yankee peddler, Harvey Birch, in *The Spy*; the comic black, Agamemnon, in *The Pioneers*; and the exuberant backwoodsman, a rather tame version of which appears as Paul Hover in *The Prairie*. Each kind of fiction Cooper wrote, moreover, led to the introduction of folk material.

In his frontier novels, Cooper created a variety of vernacular characters, most notably Leatherstocking, who derives in part at least from the legend of Daniel Boone. But there are also others who have their roots in popular lore: the professional woodcutter, Billy Kirby, in *The Pioneers*, who delights in chopping trees; bee hunters, both Paul Hover in *The Prairie* and Ben Boden in *The Oak Openings*, whose trade Cooper explains in detail; amoral frontiersmen, Hurry Harry and Tom Hutter in *The Deerslayer*, who scalp for bounty money; and lawless squatters, Ishmael Bush in *The Prairie* and Aaron Thousandacres in *The Chainbearer*, who embody the fears that many Americans had of what the white man might become on the frontier.

In addition, there are the Indians, who fall into two groups: evil ones, like the Huron Magua in *The Last of the Mohicans*, who reflect the popular view of the bloodthirsty savage that was well known from captivity narratives, and noble ones, like the Mohicans Chingachgook and Uncas, whose tribe, the Lenni Lenape, or Delaware, had been displaced—betrayed, Cooper believed, by both the whites and the Iroquois whom they had trusted. In his portrayal of the Delaware, Cooper drew on the writings of the Moravian missionary John Heckewelder, who accepted the tribal account of history.

In his maritime novels, Cooper also introduced much vernacular material. The inventor of the sea tale, Cooper included in these novels a large amount of nautical knowledge about the seaman's life and work, and in Long Tom Coffin, the old salt in *The Pilot*, he created the first of a long line of sailors whose language and attitudes Cooper presents in detail. Thus, these novels illustrate the readiness of seamen to believe in the appearance of ghosts and specters and that it is bad luck to sail on a Friday or to sing in a gale.

Throughout Cooper's fiction, the New Englander is a recurring vernacular character. Often included for comedy in the early novels, as Elnathan Todd in *The Pioneers* or David Gamut in *The Last of the Mohicans*, the Yankee becomes a source for social criticism in the later works. In these novels, stable social values are embodied in the New York characters, either Dutch, like Guert Ten Eyck, or English, like Corny Littlepage, in *Satanstoe*. The threat to that social order is embodied in the New Englanders, like Jason Newcome in the same novel, who are represented as being hypocritical, self-seeking, law-honest (those who get away with unscrupulous acts by staying just inside the law), leveling democrats. Such character types served Cooper well. In the conflict between New Yorker and Yankee, he found the means to present the fundamental issue faced, he believed, by contemporary American society: the challenge to the republic that is posed by an unrestrained democracy.

Donald A. Ringe

See also Legend; Rourke, Constance Mayfield

✳✳✳✳✳✳✳✳✳✳✳✳✳✳✳✳✳

References

Walker, Warren S. "Cooper's Fictional Use of the Oral Tradition." In *James Fenimore Cooper: His Country and His Art*, ed. George A. Test, pp. 24–39. Oneonta: State University of New York College at Oneonta, 1981.

———. "Elements of Folk Culture in Cooper's Novels." In *James Fenimore Cooper, a Re-Appraisal*, ed. Mary E. Cunningham, pp. 457–467. Cooperstown: New York State Historical Association, 1954.

———. *James Fenimore Cooper: An Introduction and Interpretation*. New York: Barnes and Noble, 1962.

CORRIDO

A *corrido* is a ballad form derived from the Spanish *romance* and has been cultivated most prominently in Mexico and among Mexican Americans in the United States. It is stanzaic, composed most often of 8-syllable lines—or in one regional variant, *la bola suriana* (the southern bola, a poetic form), in sequences of 8- and 12-syllable lines—and displays either assonance or consonantal end-rhyme on the even-numbered lines.

Corridos typically begin and end with a reference to the performance occasion. The opening line is often *Voy a cantar un corrido* ("I will sing a corrido"), and the *despedida*, or farewell, may start with *Ya me voy a despedir* ("Now I will say farewell"). In the intervening stanzas, the corrido poet tells a story, usually interpolating one or several episodes of reported speech and often contributing some commentary on the narrated events. Although the narrative passages are remarkable for their effective renderings of the plots, it is the episodes of reported speech—which display the hero's defiant eloquence or his acceptance of impending death—that often function as the emotional core of the corrido. Not all corridos are about desperate situations, for there are love-struck corridos, personal laments, and anthems to a singer's hometown, but the corrido achieves its most powerful expression in the *corrido trágico* ("the tragic corrido"), which centers on episodes of mortal conflict.

Corridos may be performed in both public and private settings, and though men constitute their primary constituency, women are often involved as singers or as audience members. At social gatherings in private homes, a guitar may pass from hand to hand as people take turns performing corridos from the national corpus or from the local stock. In cantinas and restaurants, professional musicians arrive and perform corridos on request, in ensembles ranging from a single musician or duet or trio to a mariachi group. In general, the makeup of the larger ensembles reflects the musical styles of the region, though it is almost obligatory to include at least one guitar. Corrido melodies fall into a series of families, from which new tunes can be generated with minimal alterations. The melodies are straightforward and devoid of complex harmonic progressions and, with the exception of the Costa Chica region in the Mexican states of Guerrero and Oaxaca, are invariably set in major keys.

The custom of printing and selling broadside sheets with corrido texts and companion engravings, once a prominent means of distributing traditional and newly composed corridos, lives on in the cheap chapbooks with corrido texts that are available in the popular markets. Well-known corrido plots have formed the basis for cinematic productions, sometimes featuring the most popular musicians and actors of the day.

Historically, the corrido emerged from a general substratum of Spanish-American narrative song to become the balladry of the Mexican people. The word *corrido* apparently derived from the term *romance corrido,* which signified a sung popular ballad, and corridos are found intermittently in several of the Spanish-American republics. But it is in Mexico, toward the end of the nineteenth century and most conspicuously during the first several decades of the twentieth, that this ballad form arose as a chronicle of local and regional history experienced by the common man and woman. In particular, the tumultuous years of the Mexican revolution (1910–1930) provide the grist for ballad poets, and the corridos of that period are revered in Mexico as a composite epic of the revolution. Corridos were produced as broadside ballads in Mexico City by publishing houses such as the one founded in 1880 by Antonio Vanegas Arroyo, for which the acclaimed illustrator José Guadalupe Posada (1852–1913) provided classic woodblock designs, but the authentic ballads of the revolution were composed by close observers of the fray, often by poets and musicians who traveled with the warring factions.

An earlier generation of corrido scholars, notably Vicente T. Mendoza and Américo Paredes, described a historical trajectory running from the initial rise of the genre in the latter part of the nineteenth century to its peak during the years of the revolution—and they predicted its demise in postrevolutionary Mexico. This scheme has some truth to it in regard to the presence of the corrido as a national passion that infects virtually every region of Mexico to a greater or lesser extent. However, assertions of the corrido's decline have proved to be somewhat hasty in view of the persistence of isolated pockets where the corrido has continued to flourish as a living ballad tradition and its current revival in the northern zones of Mexico in response to the narcotics trade. In the coastal settlements of Guerrero and Oaxaca, and along the northern frontier, the corrido never really entered into a period of decline, and these regions are joined today by a large swath to the north (including transborder populations in the United States) where the *narco corrido,* the corrido about episodes in the drug war, is a vital expressive and commercial force.

The corrido is essentially an oral form, but it has at times served as a model and an inspiration for literary expression. Especially during the grip of a populist and nationalist fervor in the latter phases of the revolution, Mexico's artists and writers incorporated forms of popular expression into their artistic output. Muralists such as Diego Rivera, José Clemente Orozco, and David Alfaro Siqueiros adapted popular themes and visual motifs; composers such as Carlos Chávez wrote symphonic and choral pieces they sometimes called corridos; and writers composed poems with corrido-like elements and in some cases literary corridos. This nationalistic movement stressed the grounding of Mexican art in a true Mexican idiom to be found in popular forms of expression such as the corrido. This movement began in the early 1920s with encouragement of the passionate minister of education, José Vasconcelos, and has remained a conspicuous artistic influence in Mexico.

John H. McDowell

See also Ballad; Nationalism; *Romancero*

✳✳✳✳✳✳✳✳✳✳✳✳✳✳✳✳✳

References

McDowell, John. "Folklore as Commemorative Discourse." *Journal of American Folklore* 105 (1992): 403–423.

Mendoza, Vicente T. *El corrido mexicano: Antología, introducción, y notas*. Mexico City: Fondo de Cultura Económico, 1954.

Paredes, Américo. *A Texas-Mexican Cancionero: Folksongs of the Lower Border*. Urbana: University of Illinois Press, 1976.

———. *"With His Pistol in His Hand": A Border Ballad and Its Hero*. Austin: University of Texas Press, 1958.

Serrano Martínez, Celedonio. *La bola suriana: Un espécimen del corrido mexicano*. Chilpancingo, Mexico: Gobierno del Estado de Guerrero, 1989.

Simmons, Merle. *The Mexican Corrido as a Source for Interpretive Study of Modern Mexico*. Bloomington: Indiana University Press, 1957.

COSQUIN, EMMANUEL (1841–1919)

A folklorist who initially studied law, Emmanuel Cosquin became a journalist who wrote for various French periodical publications. His long-standing interest in folklore was expressed both in folktale collecting and in comparative scholarship. He corresponded with Jacob

Grimm in Germany and was particularly interested in the work of Theodor Benfey. At the end of the nineteenth century, Cosquin participated in international debates regarding the sources and nature of folklore, and his major folklore works were reprinted as books: the annotated collection *Les contes populaires de Lorraine*, 2 vols. (1886) and two posthumous books of articles, *Les contes indiens et l'Occident* and *Études folkloriques* (both 1922).

Cosquin, with the help of his sisters, began collecting the 84 tales published in *Les contes populaires de Lorraine* in the 1860s. The tales all come from one French village, Montiers-sur-Saulx, and many were told by one young woman. Cosquin had a relatively high standard of accuracy: variant versions are given for several of the tales, and when he occasionally found his notes inadequate to present a text in full, he gave it only in summary. The annotations, which conveniently follow each tale, summarize variants from many countries and even now give a reasonably good overview of many of those tale-types. Unfortunately, references to these notes are not given in Antti Aarne and Stith Thompson's (1964) *The Types of the Folktale* (which does not even include all of these tale-types). References can be found in Johannes Bolte and Georg Polívka's *Anmerkungen zu den Kinder- und Hausmärchen der Brüder Grimm* and, perhaps more easily, in Paul Delarue and Marie Louise Tenèze's *Le conte populaire français* (1955–).

The two collections of Cosquin's folklore articles are likewise interesting and authoritative. Most of the articles start from a "theme" (usually a folktale motif or episode) and then trace that theme in different tales and traditions. Thus, one essay deals with the image of blood on snow; another, the motif of pins that cause sleep; and another, the notion that a mother's breasts flow with milk when her lost child is restored to her. References to the articles in these books are listed at the appropriate places in Stith Thompson's *Motif Index of Folk Literature* (1955–1958).

Cosquin is usually remembered, when he is remembered at all, as a "disciple" of Theodor Benfey, who argued repeatedly that European folktales came originally from India. No one now believes that such a thing could be true, so Cosquin is left unread. That is unfortunate because, regardless of the paths by which the folktales were disseminated, Cosquin's work shows that motifs, episodes, and larger configurations were known throughout wide areas. It also shows, through the summaries of variants, what is the same and what is different in the tales in which those components occur. Thus, as so often happens in folklore scholarship, the assemblage of evidence remains valuable past the time when the pet theory that provoked it is deemed worthy of debate.

Christine Goldberg

See also Grimm, Jacob and Wilhelm; Motif; Tale-Type; Theme; Thompson, Stith

✳✳✳✳✳✳✳✳✳✳✳✳✳✳✳✳✳✳

References

Bolt, Johannes, and Georg Polivka. *Anmerkungen zu den Kinder- und Hausmärchen der Brüder Grimm*. 5 vols. Leipzig: Dieterich, 1913–1932.

Delarue, Paul, and Marie Louise Tenèze. *Le Conte populaire francais*. 3 vols. Paris: Erasme, 1957; G.-P.

Saintyves, Pierre. "L'Oeuvre d' Emmanuel Cosquin." *Revue anthropologique* 33 (1923): 180–184.

Tenèze, Marie-Louise. "Cosquin, Emmanuel." *Enzyklopädie des Märchens* 3 (1981): 157–160.

CROCE, GIULIO CESARE (1550–1609)

Giulio Cesare Croce, or Giulio dalla Lira (because he was always accompanied by the violin), was a prolific Bolognese street singer (*cantastorie*) who drew heavily on oral traditions and is best known for *Bertoldo* and *Bertoldino* (1606). Born during the period of Carnival in 1550 to a very poor but "honest" family of blacksmiths, his work is marked by the carnivalesque. When orphaned at age seven, a paternal uncle, also a blacksmith, sent him to be schooled by a "pedant." Croce's true vocation, it was soon discovered, was as a *poeta campestre* ("rustic poet") and *cantastorie*. After his complete conversion to poetry (after reading Ariosto and Ovid), the pen and the bellows "did constant battle" as Croce alternated between smithing and street performance, between rural and city life, entertaining landowners and commoners alike.

As a widower with seven children (and another seven by his second wife), he was constantly forced back to the blacksmith's shop to make ends meet. Thus, his poetry was born out of a battle with hunger, and hunger is frequently the theme of his work. That work, between 300 and 500 major and minor works in Italian and in Bolognese, includes dialogues, songs, jokes, riddles, sad or humorous letters, *contrasti* between lovers, laments of the poor, and a vast number of comedies in pamphlet form or printed on *ventarole* (in the form of printed "fans") that sold for a penny in the public piazza. Croce's fertile and capricious imagination and his genius for linguistic mimesis prompted one eminent critic to call Croce's richness of expression and lively lexicon *barocco contadino* ("peasant baroque").

Croce's style derives from a "poetics of the natural" (*poetica del naturale*), that is, an openness toward all linguistic codes and registers in a faithful mirroring of social reality and a predilection for the "plain and clear" rather than the lofty and sublime. Although affirming that human dignity and honor are present in all levels of society and that even a poor man can commune with the muses (as he himself does) or can give lessons at court (see *Bertoldo*), Croce nonetheless made no overt social protest or demand for improving the conditions of the poor and marginalized. The themes he wove into his works were drawn heavily from topoi ("topics") that are well known in the oral tradition—such as the ship of fools (*La barca dei rovinati* or *La gabbia dei matti*), topsy-turvy land (*Il mondo alla rovescia*), land of Cockaigne or plenty (*paese di Cuccagna*)—and reflect a conventional peasant's and poor man's worldview, however much verve and humor may have gone into their performance.

Le sottilissime astuzie di Bertoldo (based on the *Dialogus Salomonis et Marcolphi*, a medieval legend figuring prominently in a *disputa* involving heresy) and its sequel, *Le piacevoli e ridicolose simplicità di Bertoldino*, are Croce's best known works. In *Bertoldo*, Croce changed the protagonist of the *Dialogus* into a "rough and monstrous peasant but with a quick, astute, and subtle intelligence" and gave him a wise wife (Marcolfa) and later a foolish son, Bertoldino.

Bertoldo, a peasant jester at the fairy tale–like court of Alboin, King of the Lombards, is an antihero. He is quick to spew forth proverbial wisdom, to solve riddles ingeniously, to engage in verbal games of double entendre and reverse speech, to play practical jokes, and to perform visual gags in the commedia dell'arte tradition. Although he is irreverent and rude, a straight-talker who takes the king to task for his foolishness, his kindness, his sympathy for women, and his indulgence of courtiers, ultimately Bertoldo is a great defender of the social order and, consequently, of the crown. Indeed, once he accepts the king's offer to live at court as his counselor (and thus oversteps class limits), Bertoldo falls ill and dies because the court doctors would not have him eat beets and beans— foods proper to a peasant's "physical" constitution (i.e., social condition). In the end, Bertoldo's irreverence, rather than being subversive, fits within the matrix of the carnivalesque as permissible temporary inversion.

While Bertoldo celebrates the wisdom and dignity of the poor, Bertoldino, in a dialectic of opposites, is the quintessential fool. One represents the positive defense of the *villano* ("peasant") while the other represents the most negative satire. In *Bertoldo* and *Bertoldino*, two legendary cycles meet: Bertoldo derives from the eastern Salomonic-Marcolfian saga, and Bertoldino draws from local, Emilian oral tradition. A sequel written by Adriano Banchieri (1567–1634) added a foolish grandson to the triumvirate: *Bertoldo, Bertoldino* (1606), *e Cacasenno* (exact date unknown).

Bertoldo and *Bertoldino* were lost to view for two centuries, but after they were rediscovered at the end of the eighteenth century, the Bertoldo character became hugely successful, was taken over by the theater, and underwent many remakings, not only in Italy but throughout Europe.

Luisa Del Giudice

See also Legend; *Paese di Cuccagna*; Proverbs

✳✳✳✳✳✳✳✳✳✳✳✳✳✳✳✳✳✳

References

Camporesi, Piero. *La maschera di Bertoldo: Giulio Cesare Croce e la letteratura carnevalesca.* Turin: Einaudi, 1976.

Croce, Franco. "Giulio Cesare Croce e la realtà popolare." In *La Rassegna della letteratura italiana*, VII, LXXIII, 1969, nn. 2–3, p. 186.

Croce, Giulio Cesare. *Le sottilissime astuzie di Bertoldo, le piacevoli e ridicolose simplicità di Bertoldino.* Ed. Piero Camporesi. Turin: Einaudi, 1978. English translation by Palmer Di Giulio, *Bertoldo.* New York: Vantage, 1958.

Doglio, Maria Luisa. "Giulio Cesare Croce." In *Dizionario critico della letteratura italiana*, s.v., vol. 1, pp. 648–650. Turin: UTET, 1974.

Guerrini, Olindo. *La vita e le opere di Giulio Cesare Croce.* Bologna: Zanichelli, 1879. Reprinted Bologna: Forni, 1969.

Cuchulain

Cuchulain (Cu Chulainn, Cuchulainn, Cuchulinn, Cuchullin) is the hero of the Ulster cycle of Old Irish tales, which relates the exploits of the warriors—known as the Order of the Red Branch—serving King Conchobar of Ulster. By many accounts the son of

Lugh, god of light, Cuchulain's extraordinary beauty, courage, and accomplishments made him the foremost champion of Ulster's heroic age.

Cuchulain begins his heroic deeds while still a child. He earns his name, meaning "the hound of Culann," by killing a ferocious guard dog, while Cuchulain is unarmed, and promising to take the animal's place. He takes arms at seven years of age, thereby claiming a destiny foreseen by the king's druid; in doing so, he chooses for himself undying fame and an early death. Cuchulain prevails in many contests to secure preeminence among the heroes of the Red Branch and overcomes many dangers to win his wife, Emer. In wooing Emer, Cuchulain seeks instructions from the warrior woman Scathach, from whom he receives his spear, *gae bolga*. During his training, he defeats Scathach's rival, Aife, in combat, and fathers her son, Conlai.

Cuchulain's greatest fame comes in defending Ulster in a devastating war with Connaught, as told in the *Tain bo Cuailnge* [The cattle rain of Cuailnge], an eighth-century epic. Connaught, ruled by Queen Maev and defended in large part by a band of exiled Ulstermen, invades Ulster when King Conchobar's warriors are incapacitated by a curse. Cuchulain single-handedly holds Maev's forces at bay until the men of the Red Branch recover. He slows the army by meeting a series of Connaught's champions in single combat, finally killing his best friend, Ferdia.

Cuchulain later meets a similar test of duty: an unknown warrior lands on Ulster's coast, refuses to identify himself, and defeats several defenders. Cuchulain fights the stranger, only to discover that his opponent is his only son, Conlai. Nevertheless, Cuchulain kills Conlai, then casts his son's body at Conchobar's feet.

At age 27, Cuchulain falls victim of superior odds, satirists' taunts, and broken vows. His many enemies unite under Maev to invade Ulster again while the Red Branch is helpless. On his way to meet them, Cuchulain encounters three old women roasting a dog and is thereby forced to break one of his two long-standing vows: never to eat dog meat and never to pass a cooking fire without sharing in the meal. Later, in battle, Cuchulain is tricked three times into letting his *gae bolga* fall into his enemies' hands, and they use it against him, finally inflicting a mortal wound. Cuchulain ties himself to a stone pillar so that he may die standing; his foes, unsure of his strength, do not dare approach him until a raven begins to pick at his body.

In battle, Cuchulain becomes physically distorted, a "hero's light" shines from his forehead, and he cannot distinguish between friends and enemies. By some accounts, he is marked by seven fingers on each hand, seven toes on each foot, and seven pupils in each eye.

The bulk of the Ulster cycle was recorded before the twelfth century, yet tales of Cuchulain continued in the oral tradition into the twentieth century. Lady Augusta Gregory's *Cuchulain of Muirthemne* (1902) is a translation of Irish manuscripts, mostly medieval ones. Cuchulain's deeds also inspired a series of plays by William Butler Yeats, including *On Baile's Strand* (1906), *The Green Helmet* (1910), and *At the Hawk's Well* (1917).

Lorraine Walsh

See also Celtic Literature; Gregory, Lady Isabella Augusta; Yeats, William Butler

✳✳✳✳✳✳✳✳✳✳✳✳✳✳✳✳✳

References

Gregory, Lady Augusta. *Cuchulain of Muirthemne*. Gerards Cross, Eng.: Colin Smyth, 1902.

Hull, Eleanor. *Cuchulain, the Hound of Ulster*. London: George G. Harrap, 1909.

Nutt, Alfred. *Cuchulainn, the Irish Achilles*. Popular Studies in Mythology and Romance, no. 8. London: David Nutt, 1900.

O'Grady, Standish. *The History of Ireland*. New York: Lemma, 1970 (1878–1880).

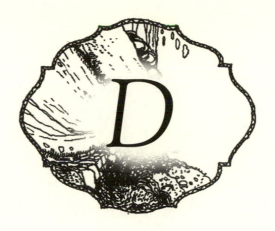

DECAMERON

Decameron refers to a collection of 100 stories written by Giovanni Boccaccio between 1348 and 1353; it is the author's best known work and is one of the monuments of Italian literature. Escaping Florence when it was ravaged by the plague of 1348, seven women and three men find refuge at an idyllic country estate where they arrange to tell stories to pass the time. The stories exhibit a tension between the effectiveness of spiritual guidance and the ability of the individual to use wit and resourcefulness in the resolution of problems.

The sources of these tales, and their subsequent transmission orally and in literature, have provided a rich vein for scholarship. Boccaccio drew upon classical works, the Provençal poets William of Poitou and Guilhem de Cabestanh, the *Legenda Aurea* of Jacobus de Voragine, and Boccaccio's compatriots Dante and Petrarch. In addition, he made use of material from current Italian oral tradition concerning magic, superstitions, ghosts and their exorcism, and the efficacy of prayer. His stories became sources for Geoffrey Chaucer, Hans Sachs, Juan de Timoneda, William Shakespeare, and many other European authors.

Boccaccio's formula of presenting stories told by storytellers in a setting removed from the everyday has roots in *A Thousand and One Nights* and provides the framework for the later collections of Gian Francesco Straparola and Giambattista Basile. Scholars have examined the appearance of motifs such as the eaten heart (*Decameron* Book IV, Sections 1 and 9; Thompson Q478.1) and the pot of basil (*Decameron* IV, 5) and the tale-type patient Griselda (*Decameron* X, 10; AT 887) as to their origins and use in *Decameron*

A fifteenth-century illustration of Boccaccio's "narrators" of the Decameron *(1348–1353), women and men who escaped the plague-ridden city of Florence to a country estate.*

and have considered the treatment of these sources in light of the relationship between oral and literary forms.

Decameron reveals Boccaccio as a pioneer in the development of the novella. In the course of the study of the origins of this narrative form, *Decameron* has been compared to its predecessors in connection with its organization as a storytelling session, its difference from other forms such as the märchen, its rhetorical style, and the internal paradoxes accompanying the replacement of divine aid by human agency in confronting reality. The turning of the tables through wit and the role of deception, intended sometimes as critique, sometimes as comic farce, marks a new way the marvelous or fantastical is conveyed in the tales. This change in method suggests a change in the values of the audience and a change in form. Good and evil are no longer diametrically opposed, as in the folktale, but are problematized in the novella as vice and virtue, which may be affected by human agency. *Decameron* was popular with the emerging mercantile and middle classes.

Decameron appears at the midpoint of Boccaccio's literary development, straddling his imaginative and his scholarly periods. At the same time, through the tension between divine agency and human agency, it stands with one foot in the medieval world and the other in the modern world.

John Cash

See also Basile, Giambattista; Boccaccio, Giovanni; Chaucer, Geoffrey; Folktale; *Märchen;* Shakespeare, William; Storytelling; Straparola, Gian Francesco; *The Thousand and One Nights*

✳✳✳✳✳✳✳✳✳✳✳✳✳✳✳✳✳

References

Almansi, Guido. *The Writer as Liar: Narrative Techniques in the Decameron.* Boston: Routledge and Kegan Paul, 1975.

Bettridge, William Edwin, and Francis Lee Utley. "New Light on the Origin of the Griselda Story." *Texas Studies in Literature and Language* 13 (1971): 153–208.

Boccaccio, Giovanni. *The Decameron.* Trans. Mark Musa and Peter Bondanella. New York: W. W. Norton, 1982.

Falassi, Alessandro. "Il Boccaccio e il folklore di Cerraldo." In *Boccaccio: Secoli di vita. Atti del Congresso Internazionale: Boccaccio, 1975, Universita di California Los Angeles 17–19 ottobre 1975,* ed. Marga Cottino-Jones and Edward F. Tuttle, pp. 265–292. Ravenna: Longo, 1977.

Giardini, Maria Pia. *Tradizioni popolari nel Decameron.* Florence: Leo S. Olschki Editore, 1965.

DELARGY, JAMES HAMILTON (1899–1980)

As an assistant to Professor Douglas Hyde, the first president of the Republic of Ireland, the young James Delargy (Séamus Ó Duilearga) traveled the Gaeltacht, or Gaelic-speaking areas of the Republic, to collect Gaelic legends and stories. Later, as a lecturer and professor of folklore at University College, Dublin, Delargy was involved in the establishment of the Folklore Society of Ireland (An Cumann le Béaloideas Éireann), becoming cofounder and editor of its journal, *Béaloideas,* in 1927. Known as the Irish Folklore Institute from 1930 to 1935, the society became the Irish Folklore Commission in 1935, and Delargy became director of the organization. In an editorial in the first edition of *Béaloideas*, Delargy recognized the dwindling opportunity for collecting indigenous folklore in Ireland. Political difficulties, especially during the years 1916–1921, had resulted in the destruction of much Gaelic material and even among the few storytellers remaining, vast numbers of tales had been forgotten. Aware of the need for a collection schema, Delargy offered six points, or reminders, for collectors. It was, however, Delargy's colleague, Seán Ó Súilleabháin (Sean O'Sullivan), who designed the collection system for the new commission.

In 1934, Delargy assisted filmmaker Robert Flaherty in producing *Oiche Sheanchais* [Storytelling Night], the first Irish-language sound film, but the focus of his efforts was to preserve Irish culture by collecting folktales. The Irish Folklore Commission was given a grant of £3,200, through the support of President Eamon De Valera, to collect Gaelic tales, catalog, and preserve them. Aided by Seán Ó Súilleabháin, Caoimhìn Ó Danachar, and Máire MacNeill, Delargy directed a team of volunteers who collected tales and their variants as well as local lore of all types.

The stories are most authentic in the original Gaelic, and Delargy, like Douglas Hyde, was convinced that the preservation of Gaelic stories must proceed hand in hand with the preservation of the Gaelic language. Delargy himself had learned Gaelic as a teenager. Intrigued by the stories he heard even as a child (he cites his first haircut as the occasion of hearing his first Irish tale), he determined to learn the language of the tale tellers, and on travels with his aunt he soon learned about regional variations in spoken Irish. Simultaneously, he began recording tales he heard and taking photographs of the storytellers.

For a brief period Delargy was a novice with the Vincentian Fathers, but then he entered University College where he came under the guidance of Osborn Bergin, professor of Old Irish. Receiving an M.A. in Celtic studies in 1923, Delargy followed Bergin's advice and traveled to Ballinskelligs in County Kerry in southwestern Ireland to continue a lifetime of folklore collecting, having acquired a scholarly background not only in Celtic languages, but also in German, French, Swedish, and Icelandic.

In his landmark 1945 Sir John Rhys lecture, "The Gaelic Storyteller," Delargy describes the rich cultural heritage kept by the *shenachies,* or *scéalaithe,* the talented purveyors of song and story in every community who took seriously the art of storytelling and their responsibility for handing down the tales to later generations. The *shenachies* were often farmers or fishermen whose repertoire might run into hundreds of tales. Among the numerous storytellers with whom Delargy was acquainted were Sean Ó Conaill, a Kerry Irish speaker whose tales are recorded in Delargy's *Leabhar Sheáin Í Chonaill* (1948), and Peig Sayers of Dúnchaoin, one of the few noted woman storytellers, of whom Delargy and Robin Flowers wrote in *Seanchas Sayers of Tiar* (1956).

Sylvia McLaurin

See also Celtic Literature; Folktale; MacNeill, Máire; Ó Súilleabháin Seán; Storytelling

✶✶✶✶✶✶✶✶✶✶✶✶✶✶✶✶✶

References

Delargy, James Hamilton. "The Gaelic Story-teller, with Some Notes on Gaelic Folk-Tales." *Proceedings of the British Academy* 31 (1945): 177–221.

McCann, Jack. "Two Members Remembered." *Glynns* 9 (1981): 62–63.

Ó Duilearga, Séamus. "Introduction" to Seán Ó Súilleabháin, A *Handbook of Irish Folklore*. Detroit: Singing Tree Press, 1970.

Whitaker, T. K. "James Hamilton Delargy, 1899–1980." *Folk-Life: Journal of Ethnological Studies* (Cardiff, Wales) 20 (1982): 101–106.

DIALECT

A dialect is a configuration of words and their pronunciations, forms, and combinations common to people who share a geographical or sociocultural identity. A dialect is distinguishable from a hypothetical standard or learned way of speaking a given language and representing it in writing.

Dialects are most often identified according to the parts of a country in which they are spoken. Early scholars differentiated among four Middle English dialects (inferred from documents written between 1150 and 1500) on the basis of geography, identifying them as northern, east Midlands, west Midlands, and southern. Pioneering work on American dialects was similarly regional in orientation. Researchers distinguished among northern, midland, and southern speech areas along the Atlantic seaboard of the United States and also designated subdivisions of each geographically (e.g., the Delaware Valley, Susquehanna Valley, upper Potomac and Shenandoah Valleys, upper Ohio Valley, northern West Virginia, southern West Virginia, and western North and South Carolina subdialect areas of midland speech).

Early-twentieth-century surveys of American dialects indicated noteworthy contrasts among these areas in pronunciation (the absence of the postvocalic *r* in such words as *barn* and *father* in most of the North and the upper South); lexicon (*snap beans* in the South, *green beans* in the Midlands); word forms (*dove* as the past tense of *dive* in the North, *drinkt* as the past tense of *drink* in the southern Midlands and the South); and word combinations (quarter *till* the hour in the Midlands, *hadn't ought* in the North).

Aware that linguistic variety is not limited to regional speech, as a majority of dialect studies worldwide state or imply, some scholars have posited that dialect is also definable on the basis of the speakers' educational level, social class, and racial or ethnic identification. Designations such as substandard English, Black English (or Ebonics), and Spanglish imply a sociocultural rather than a regional basis for the existence of some contrasting but comprehensible alternative varieties of a given language. Conceptualizing dialect broadly to include other kinds of speech besides provincialisms suggests that all speakers of all languages are, or have the potential to be, multidialectal and capable of switching from one dialect to another as the participants in, and purpose and nature of, interactions dictate or warrant.

Collectors who record folklore from, and creative writers who interact with, dialect speakers often try to reproduce their speech orthographically. Vance Randolph coauthored with George P. Wilson a book-length compendium of phonological approximations of dialect speech examples he documented over time while living in the Ozarks. In two seminal essays, Richard M. Dorson presents a selection of dialect stories he recorded from French, Italian, and Finnish immigrants in Michigan's Upper Peninsula and a set of Jewish dialect tales he elicited from colleagues and friends. Throughout his career, the journalist and writer Joel Chandler Harris represented in alternative ways the speech of African Americans whose tales and talk served as the basis for his eight Uncle Remus books. Mark Twain's familiarity with speech differences and his ability to capture them in writing enabled him to create a stylistically classic novel in which Huck Finn and Jim relate to and communicate with each other while speaking different dialects of a common language.

Robert A. Georges

See also Dorson, Richard M.; Harris, Joel Chandler; Twain, Mark; Uncle Remus

✳✳✳✳✳✳✳✳✳✳✳✳✳✳✳✳✳✳

References

Dorson, Richard M. "Dialect Stories of the Upper Peninsula." *Journal of American Folklore* 61 (1948): 113–150.

———. "Jewish-American Dialect Stories on Tape." In *Studies in Biblical and Jewish Folklore*, ed. Raphael Patai, Francis Lee Utley, and Dov Noy, pp. 111–174. Bloomington: Indiana University Press, 1960.

Harris, Joel Chandler. *The Complete Tales of Uncle Remus*. Comp. Richard Chase. Boston: Houghton, Mifflin, 1955 (1880, 1881, 1892, 1903, 1906, 1910, 1918, and 1948).

Randolph, Vance, and George P. Wilson. *Down in the Holler: A Gallery of Ozark Folk Speech*. Norman: University of Oklahoma Press, 1979 (1953).

Twain, Mark. *The Adventures of Huckleberry Finn*. New York: Chas. L. Webster and Company, 1885.

DICKENS, CHARLES (1812–1870)

Charles John Huffam Dickens, considered by many people to be the greatest English novelist of his own or any other era, was born in Portsmouth, England, February 7, 1812, and died in his home, Gad's Hill Place, June 9, 1870. His own early life, which was mostly unhappy, inspired much of his fiction, in particular the early chapters of *David Copperfield* (1850). Dickens's father, John, a clerk in the navy pay office, was constantly in debt and was even thrown into debtors' prison in 1824, where he remained for 14 months. The same year, Charles was sent to work in a blacking factory. Although neither of these experiences was enjoyable, the failure of his parents to provide him with an education pained the youth even more. He compensated for this shortcoming by working hard, a characteristic that proved useful for one who would later become a prolific novelist.

He held various jobs, including office boy in a law firm, county reporter, and reporter for the *Morning Chronicle* of debates in Parliament in 1835. During these years, he also contributed articles to the *Monthly Magazine*, the *Evening Chronicle*, and other publications; the articles appeared in book form as *Sketches by 'Boz', Illustrative of Every-Day Life and Every-Day People* (1836–1837). This volume

The character of Uriah Heep from Dickens's novel David Copperfield (1850).

gained the author much attention and led to requests from publishers for other works.

During the remainder of his life, Dickens turned out a large number of books of very high quality. Many of his volumes indicted the society of his era, especially its mistreatment of children and the poor. He was very skillful at creating characters representing a broad range of emotions, utilizing various details, such as gestures, expressions, speech patterns, and other elements of folklore, to bring them to life. Perhaps his own fascination with many types of folklore led him to include such material in his writings. He did not just use items of lore he knew from experience, he also made specific attempts to collect material to be used in his novels. For example, he sought out slang terms to be used in *Hard Times* (1854) from various friends.

Proverbs are the genre of folklore most often associated with Dickens, in large part because of *The Posthumous Papers of the Pickwick Club* (1837), in which a character, Samuel Weller, frequently adds a phrase or clause that casts a traditional saying in a new light. Dickens used these sayings to make comments of an ironic, detached, and often humorous sort on sociopolitical issues of the day. Although Dickens did not invent this usage, the extensive number of examples in the same novel has led scholars to designate them "wellerisms." His popularization of this subgenre of proverbs proved useful in stimulating a large number of wellerism collections, but it has obscured the fact that Dickens used many other types of proverbs as well. They serve a variety of purposes in his novels, including characterization, humor, punning, metaphorization, dramatization, and leitmotivs, that is, they are regularly used with specific characters as their identifying phrase.

Because of the popularity of *A Christmas Carol* (1843), ghostlore is the second aspect of folklore most often associated with Dickens. Ghosts appear elsewhere in his fiction, for example, in "The Signalman," but this lore, as well as the numerous folk beliefs and items of folk speech found throughout his published works, has been little studied.

W. K. McNeil

See also Belief; Ghosts; Proverbs

✳✳✳✳✳✳✳✳✳✳✳✳✳✳✳✳✳✳

References

Ackroyd, Peter. *Dickens*. New York: HarperCollins, 1990.
Brook, G. L. *The Language of Dickens*. London: Andre Deutsch, 1970.

Bryan, George B., and Wolfgang Mieder. *The Proverbial Charles Dickens: An Index to Proverbs in the Works of Charles Dickens*. New York: Peter Lang, 1997.

Mieder, Wolfgang, and George B. Bryan. *Proverbs in World Literature: A Bibliography*. New York: Peter Lang, 1996.

Mieder, Wolfgang, George B. Bryan, and Stewart A. Kingsbury. *A Dictionary of Wellerisms*. New York: Oxford University Press, 1994.

DISNEY, WALTER ELIAS (1901–1966)

An American director and producer of animated and live-action films for children and adults, Walter Elias Disney began his career in Kansas City, Missouri, and moved to southern California in the 1920s during the early days of the Hollywood film industry. Disney and his filmmakers drew on folktales almost from the beginning of his film career. Some of his first cartoons in Kansas City humorously adapted popular stories like "Goldie Locks and the Three Bears," "The Four Musicians of Bremen," "Jack and the Beanstalk," "Cinderella," "Puss in Boots," and "Little Red Riding Hood." Later cartoons produced in his California studios included "The Three Little Pigs" and "Mickey and the Beanstalk," with Mickey Mouse portraying Jack in this popular folktale. Disney himself was not an active animator but focused his talents on producing and directing the films created by Walt Disney Productions. Walt's brother Roy was his financial expert.

Disney was particularly noted for his full-length animated fairy tales based on stories from popular German and French tales. The first of these films, *Snow White and the Seven Dwarfs* (1937) from the Grimm collection, was an unexpected success that set the pattern for his future feature-length cartoons. The literary fairy tales of Charles Perrault and his imitators inspired *Cinderella* (1950) and *Sleeping Beauty* (1959). Disney favored popular stories that portrayed passive heroines, but he encouraged his writers and animators to make them more interesting than their literary counterparts. The influence of these early films is still seen in recent releases like *Beauty and the Beast* (1991), *The Little Mermaid*, and *Aladdin*, all made decades after Disney's death in 1966.

In *Song of the South*, Disney used live action and animation to adapt some of the Uncle Remus stories of the nineteenth-century writer Joel Chandler Harris, who created his own literary versions of the African-American trickster tales of Brer (Brother) Rabbit.

In all of his movies, Disney and his filmmakers reworked plots, characters, and motivations from the original stories. They often trivialized the stories by adding appealing animals and engaging inanimate objects as secondary characters, some of whom managed to upstage the main characters. Protagonists and villains were often exaggerated almost into parody, and romantic aspects were greatly highlighted. The Disney films alter the balance of the fairy tales from which they derive, but audiences continue to find these films attractive and entertaining. Walt Disney, like Charles Perrault, the Grimm brothers, Hans Christian Andersen, and other folktale adapters, was an effective storyteller in his own medium.

Kay Stone

See also Andersen, Hans Christian; Folktale Adaptations; Grimm, Jacob and Wilhelm; Harris, Joel Chandler

✳✳✳✳✳✳✳✳✳✳✳✳✳✳✳✳✳

References

Finch, Christopher. *The Art of Walt Disney*. New York: Harry N. Abrams, 1975.

Shickel, Richard. *The Disney Version*. New York: Avon, 1968.

Stone, Kay. "Fairy Tales for Adults: Walt Disney's Americanization of the Märchen." In *Folklore on Two Continents: Essays in Honor of Linda Degh*, ed. Nikolai Burlakoff and Carl Lindahl, pp. 40–48. Bloomington, Ind.: Trickster Press, 1980.

DORSON, RICHARD M. (1916–1981)

As a folklore teacher, mentor, scholar, editor, and administrator, Richard M. Dorson's major contribution was promoting folklore as a serious academic discipline in the United States, though he also contributed significantly to folk narrative research and to historical approaches in folklore studies. Trained in the history of American civilization at Harvard University, Dorson succeeded Stith Thompson as chair of the folklore program at Indiana University in 1957 after teaching at Harvard (1943–1944) and Michigan State University (1944–1957). Dorson insisted that a folklorist should be broadly trained in comparative studies but should know at least one culture in depth. Accordingly, most of his fieldwork and many of his publications were in his area of specialty, American folklore, though he also published in international folklore studies, notably books he wrote or edited on Japanese, African, and British folklore.

Dorson first wrote about folklore and literature in his published doctoral dissertation, *Jonathan Draws the Long Bow* (1946), in which he devoted a chapter to seven "literary folklorists," but his major contribution to folklore and literary relations was an article, "The Identification of Folklore in American Literature," published in 1957. In that article, he argued that many studies of folklore and literary relations have a fuzzy concept of folklore, fail to prove the presence of oral traditions in literature, or say nothing meaningful about folklore influences on literature. He insisted that a clear relationship of literature and folklore be established by providing three kinds of evidence. First, the critic should demonstrate that an author had direct contact with oral traditions with *biographical evidence*. Second, from the literary work itself, the critic should show that the author had firsthand knowledge of folklore with *internal evidence*, such as faithful descriptions of the context and performance of folklore. Third, the critic should prove the traditional quality of the alleged folklore with *corroborative evidence* by citing folklore indexes and field collections. He realized that it is not always possible, and not always necessary, to provide all three kinds of evidence.

About 15 years later in "Africa and the Folklorist" (1972), Dorson admitted a fourth consideration, "intermediary literary influences." He acknowledged that "writers sensitive to oral folklore may also be kindled by their reading of legends, as was Hawthorne, who profited both from his direct recording of New England traditions in the nineteenth century and from perusing seventeenth-century versions in Cotton Mather's *Magnalia Christi Americana*." Dorson's admission that an author may be influenced by literary uses of folklore as well as by oral traditions pleased some of his critics, who had accused him of being a purist in his methodology; however, it failed to satisfy others, who felt that he was overly concerned with identification and documentation of particular folklore genres in regional writers and had nothing to say about interpretation or literary value, especially in the works of major authors.

Dorson, however, did not consider identification an end in itself but, rather, a place to begin. As he clearly stressed in the last sentence of "The Identification of Folklore in American Literature," "Once we can prove that authors have directly dipped into the flowing streams of folk tradition, we are then in a position to discuss whether or not this folklore contributes to a given literary work in an important way." Thus, for Dorson, the critic's job does not end with documentation. After identifying folklore in literature, the critic must turn to another critical approach for interpretation.

Ronald L. Baker

See also Fakelore; Thompson, Stith

✻✻✻✻✻✻✻✻✻✻✻✻✻✻✻✻✻✻

References

Carpenter, Inta. "Selected Publications of Richard M. Dorson." In Linda Dégh, Henry Glassie, and Felix Oinas, ed., *Folklore Today: A Festschrift for Richard M. Dorson*, pp. 525–537. Bloomington: Indiana University Press, 1976.

Dorson, Richard M. "Africa and the Folklorist." In *African Folklore*, ed. Richard M. Dorson, pp. 3–67. Garden City, N.Y.: Anchor Books, 1972.

———. "Folklore in American Literature: A Postscript." *Journal of American Folklore* 71 (1958): 157–159.

———. "The Identification of Folklore in American Literature." *Journal of American Folklore* 70 (1957): 1–8.

———. *Jonathan Draws the Long Bow*. Cambridge: Harvard University Press, 1946.

Georges, Robert A., ed. *Richard M. Dorson's Views and Works*. Special issue of *Journal of Folklore Research* 26 (1989).

Dracula

The name "Dracula" refers to several overlapping figures. Historically, he is Vlad Tepes, the fifteenth-century Romanian prince whose cruelty inspired legends throughout much of Europe, even during his own lifetime. The vampire in Bram Stoker's 1897 novel, *Dracula*, was modeled in part on this historical figure, though Stoker had other inspirations as well. Finally, cinema and other popular culture genres have used Stoker's fictional Dracula as the basis for a wide range of variations, helping to make the name and its film portrayal synonymous with "vampire" in the popular imagination.

Vlad Tepes ("the impaler") was born around 1428, one of six children born to Vlad Dracul ("dragon," or "devil"), then prince of Wallachia. The nickname "Dracula" ("son of Dracul") was first used by the people of Wallachia and later adopted by Tepes during his own reigns (1448, 1456–1462, 1476). His reigns were during a period that was especially bloody—marked by strife within and between local principalities and by an intricate struggle for religious and political power involving Poland and the Ottoman, Hungarian, and Holy Roman Empires. Most historical and folkloric accounts emphasize Dracula's cruelty: according to one history, he impaled 25,000 Turkish civilians on a single occasion and burned down several of his own villages on suspicion of treachery. Texts in several languages, including German, Latin, Greek, and Czech, echo this tone.

Other traditions present him as a Solomon-like arbiter. One Romanian epic poem tells of his having fooled Turkish pursuers by shoeing his horses backward. The soldiers who helped in this escape were granted possession of the surrounding mountains, and villagers in the region still cite this legend in property claims. Romanian historians in recent periods of marked nationalism have reenvisioned Dracula as a national and religious hero. They stress that under Dracula's leadership, Wallachia remained the only state on the Balkan peninsula not transformed into a Turkish pashalik.

Despite Vlad Tepes's legendary cruelty, there is no record associating him with vampirism. This and other elements were inspired by another legendary Slavic noble, the Transylvanian countess Elizabeth Bathory, who, except for gender, more closely fits the description of the literary Dracula than does Tepes. The countess tortured and killed at least 600 girls and used their blood as an elixir of youth. She was famous for biting victims on the breast and neck, and Stoker's sources also identify her with werewolves.

Stoker's was one of several nineteenth-century works patterned after Dr. John Polidori's 1819 novella (sometimes attributed to Lord Byron), "The Vampyre," about a vampire who seduces and kills a friend's sister. *Dracula* was first presented unsuccessfully on the stage in the spring of 1897 and then adapted into a novel. Despite tepid reviews, the novel has sold steadily since its publication. But Dracula's real popularity came, as Stoker had anticipated, through performance.

The German expressionist director F. W. Murnau's unauthorized 1922 film adaptation, *Nosferatu, Eine Symphonie des Grauens* [A symphony of horror] (starring Max Schreck in the title role), and the 1927 hit London stage production (with a "nurse in attendance at all performances") helped to make Dracula a familiar motif of many popular culture genres. Historical, folkloric, literary, and cinematographic figures combine to make up the modern Dracula, satirized on

Sesame Street by "the count" and a breakfast cereal named "Count Chocula." For adults, Dracula societies maintain research libraries and archives; and the novels of the twentieth-century American writer Anne Rice have made vampires familiar throughout the world.

Clover Williams

See also Legend; Stoker, Bram

****

References

McNally, Raymond T., and Radu Florescu. *In Search of Dracula*. New York: Warner Books, 1972.

Skal, David J. *Hollywood Gothic: The Tangled Web of* Dracula *from Novel to Stage to Screen*. New York: W. W. Norton, 1990.

Treptow, Kurt W., ed. *Dracula: Essays on the Life and Times of Vlad Tepes*. East European Monographs no. 323. New York: Columbia University Press, 1991.

THE DRAGON SLAYER

The Dragon Slayer (Type 300) and the related tale *The Two Brothers* (Type 303) are among the oldest and most widespread of all traditional European folktales. The first story was so central in the European folktale tradition that the Aarne-Thompson type-index listed it first in the category of "Ordinary Folktales." The basic story of *The Two Brothers* contains all of *The Dragon Slayer* within it, so the two cannot be considered separately. In the simpler story of *The Dragon Slayer*, a young man slays a many-headed dragon and rescues a young woman but is then betrayed by another man who claims the victory; the hero later shows the dragon's tongues as proof of his valor and claims his just reward. In the longer tale of *The Two Brothers*, the first brother slays the dragon and marries the princess but is then captured by a witch from whom his twin brother rescues him. The story is unusual in showing the brothers as compatible rather than competitive.

Motifs found in *The Dragon Slayer* and *The Two Brothers* appear in many other basic folktales. For example, the hero is often a common peasant youth who has little to recommend him except a good heart and simple courage; the dragon is an archetypal guardian of

The dragon slayer is one of the oldest and most widespread tale-types in European folklore.

dark realms and a predator who demands ritual human sacrifice; helpful animals (often extraordinary dogs or horses) aid the protagonists and hinder antagonists; a false hero claims the reward; the princess awaits a rescuer and gives the hero advice and objects needed to slay the monster.

The theme of a hero slaying a dragon to free humanity of its evil power is also found in written literature: in the early Greek myth of Perseus and Andromeda, in various medieval legends of St. George, and the Old English epic *Beowulf*. Modern examples of dragon encounters are found in Richard Wagner's operatic *Ring* cycle (*The Ring of the Nibelung*, 1876), J. R. R. Tolkien's modern fantasy *The Hobbit*, and in Ann McCaffrey's multivolume *Dragon Rider* series—the last unusual in that it portrays dragons positively. Dragons also lurk in a number of modern films.

There are more than 1,000 collected oral variants of the two closely allied tales from modern Europe; one index that lists tales published in contemporary North American and European anthologies cites 79 variant texts of *The Dragon Slayer* and another 51 texts of *The Two Brothers*. The number and variety of these stories indicate a long oral history.

A mere summary of basic tale-types does not do justice to the rich variety of individual texts from contemporary collections. For example, in a modern French folktale the hero is a young man "all crippled and hunched," armed with only an enchanted white stick. In a Mexican tale a farmer's son slays a seven-headed dragon, while in a variant from Spain a fisherman's son does so. A Scottish story depicts the dragon as a cruel wizard called "the Draglin Hogney," and he is defeated by the hero, his horse, his dog, and his hawk.

Kay Stone

See also Motif; Tale-Type; Tolkien, J. R. R.

****

References

Briggs, Katharine. A *Dictionary of British Folktales in the English Language*. 2 vols. London: Routledge and Kegan Paul, 1971–1977.

Luthi, Max. *The European Folktale: Form and Nature*. Trans. John D. Niles. Philadelphia: Institute for the Study of Human Issues, 1982.

Thompson, Stith. *The Folktale*. New York: Holt, Rinehart and Winston, 1946.

Dumy

Dumy (singular, *duma*) are the folk heroic epics of Ukraine. They tell about the lives and the struggles of the Cossacks, a special military cadre. *Dumy* are usually divided into three cycles: the Turko-Tatar cycle, which tells of events that occurred in the fourteenth to seventeenth centuries; the Khmel'nyts'kyi cycle, which is based on the Cossack rebellion of the second half of the seventeenth century, and the so-called *dumy* about everyday life, which tell about family life rather than battle and cannot be connected to any specific historical period. *Dumy* have an elegiac tone and have been compared to laments. Many deal with the deaths of protagonists and some, especially the ones that describe the horrors of Turkish captivity, are actually called laments.

In form, *dumy* resemble other Slavic heroic epics although they differ from the epics of the Russians and the Balkan Slavs more than those two poetries differ from each other. Ukrainian epic songs are relatively short, averaging 100–300 lines, though some may be as long as 500–600 lines. Line length is quite variable, ranging from 3 to 16 syllables, with 13 syllables the most common line length. One of the most distinctive formal features of a *duma* is its "tirade" rhyme pattern (variable number of lines that all rhyme verbally). *Dumy* are essentially stychic (line-by-line composition, not rhyming), like other Slavic epic poetries, but large sections have end-rhyme. These sections are of uneven length and most closely resemble the *laisse* structure of the French chansons de geste ("songs of heroes").

Dumy were performed by professional, blind, mendicant minstrels called *kobzari* and *lirnyky*. Up until the Stalin era, *kobzari* and *lirnyky* had to be blind, and they had to be members of guilds called *hurty* or *bratstva* ("brotherhoods"). The guilds were all church affiliated, and the repertory of the minstrels included religious songs, psalms, and historical, satirical, and lyric songs as well as *dumy*. Although we do not know what the original *dumy* were like, the church affiliation of their performers probably had a significant effect on both their form and their content. The content is fairly heavily moralizing, emphasizing respect for the church and for parents, especially the mother. As for form, the *rechitatyv* ("recitative") of the *dumy* bears a resemblance to ecclesiastical chant.

The first collection of *dumy* was published in 1819 by Tsertelev, and the fullest collection to date was published by Kateryna Hrushevs'ka (1927–1931). After *dumy* came to public attention in the nineteenth century, they acquired great nationalistic significance. They were considered the epitome of Ukrainian folk literary creativity, and they and the Cossacks who are their heroes were held to be emblematic of the Ukraine's struggles for independence. Various scholars have tried to formulate the history of the Ukraine based on *dumy*, sometimes adding other historical songs, sometimes themselves creating new *dumy* where no folk material existed. Thus, the problem of the authenticity of certain texts has existed for quite some time.

It is precisely because *dumy* have been so closely bound with Ukrainian nationalism and Ukrainian identity that they and the *kobzari* and *lirnyky* were subjected to Russian and later Soviet repression, the most notorious event being the execution of Ukrainian minstrels in 1939. For similar reasons, Ukrainian writers have titled works that were meant to be particularly serious or to have particular nationalistic significance *dumy*, and, since the breakup of the Soviet Union, a number of new *dumy* have appeared on topics such as the Chernobyl disaster.

Natalie Kononenko

See also Epic; *Kobzari*

✳✳✳✳✳✳✳✳✳✳✳✳✳✳✳

References

Hrushevs'ka, Kateryna. *Ukraiins'ki narodni dumy.* 2 vols. Kiev and Kharkiv: Derzhavne Vydavynstvo, 1927–1931.

Kirdan, Boris P. *Ukrainskie narodyne dumy.* Moscow: Nauka, 1972.

Kononenko, Natalie. *Ukrainian Minstrels: And the Blind Shall Sing.* Armonk, N.Y.: M. E. Sharpe, 1997.

Luckyi, G., ed. *Ukrainian Dumy.* Cambridge and Toronto: Harvard Ukrainian Research Institute/Canadian Institute of Ukrainian Studies, 1979.

Dylan, Bob (1941–)

As the first singer-songwriter ever to be nominated for the Nobel Prize in Literature (1997), Bob Dylan differs from others of his generation in that his performance art yields prolific data for current methodological concerns in both of the academic fields of folklore and literature. Dylan regularly performs his own songs, creating versions with quite different oral effects. Folklorists have access to multiple recorded versions, of known origin, that are fully documented for purposes of comparison. Literary scholars must confront radical implications for textual analysis. Dylan purposely gives different meanings in performance to the same artistic unit of his own creation. To what extent, therefore, do words on paper acquire multiple meanings as each reader imagines them performed?

Born Robert Zimmerman in Hibbing, Minnesota, Dylan had no intention whatsoever of supplying grist for scholarly mills. By 1960 he had dropped out of the University of Minnesota; he would return to academia only for an honorary doctorate in music from Princeton University (June 1970). Instead, inspired by the lifestyle and songs of Woody Guthrie, Dylan relocated in New York City where he began to play in small clubs and met other topical songwriters who were being encouraged by Sis Cunningham and Gordon Friesen via *Broadside* magazine.

Dylan performed and recorded traditional folk songs for his first album, *Bob Dylan* (March 1962), and occasionally later (*Self Portrait* [June 1970] and *Good as I Been to You* [November 1992]). Primarily, he performs his own songs. During his early career he was able to create—words and music both—at a stunning pace. Only three months passed between the recording sessions for *Freewheelin' Bob Dylan* (May 1963) and *The Times They Are A-Changin'* (January 1964), and his most thematically unified album, *John Wesley Harding* (December 1967), was conceived and executed in a matter of weeks. The albums recorded in his early years are still the most acclaimed: the love and antilove songs on *Another Side of Bob Dylan* (August 1964), the electric-blues influence on *Bringing It All Back Home* (March 1965), the intricately developed road imagery of *Highway 61 Revisited* (August 1965), the Nashville jamming on *Blonde on Blonde* (May 1966), and the mellow vocals on *Nashville Skyline* (April 1969).

During his first decade of recording, Dylan insisted on playing "live in the studio," as he put it. He eschewed production gimmicks, maintained near-total artistic control, and sometimes released the first take of a song. Subsequent to *Blood on the Tracks* (January 1975), his albums include more experiments with studio technology and far fewer compelling songs. In concert performances two decades afterward, Dylan nearly always chose pre-1976 songs for oral re-creation, as if to prove that artistic excellence in verbal art precisely means an enduring potential for variation in performance.

Betsy Bowden

See also Performance

✻✻✻✻✻✻✻✻✻✻✻✻✻✻✻✻✻

References

Bowden, Betsy. *Performed Literature: Words and Music by Bob Dylan*. Bloomington: Indiana University Press, 1982. Rev. ed. forthcoming from Borgo Press, San Bernardino, Calif.

Heylin, Clinton. *Bob Dylan: The Recording Sessions, 1960–1994*. New York: St. Martin's Press, 1995.

McGregor, Craig, ed. *Bob Dylan: A Retrospective*. New York: Da Capo, 1990 (1972).

Thomson, Elizabeth, and David Gutman, eds. *The Dylan Companion: A Collection of Essential Writing about Bob Dylan*. New York: Delta, 1990.

Wissolik, Richard D., ed. *Bob Dylan, American Poet and Singer: An Annotated Bibliography and Study Guide of Sources and Background Materials, 1961–1991*. Greensburg, Pa.: Eadmer, 1991.

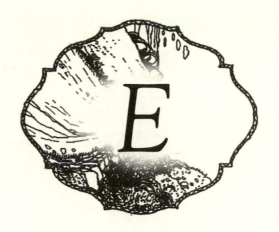

Edda, Poetic

The name *Poetic Edda* (sometimes "Sæmund's Edda" and "Elder Edda") is applied to an anthology of poems and connecting prose passages found in an Icelandic manuscript written about 1270. The manuscript, Codex Regius or Gml. kgl. saml. 2365 4to (once housed in the Royal Library in Copenhagen, now returned to Iceland), was based on a collection of pamphlets dating from the first three or four decades of the thirteenth century, but most of the approximately 29 poems must be much older—some from the ninth and tenth centuries, others as late as the late twelfth. As anonymous oral poems, survivals of a flourishing oral literature, they elude the dating methods of written literatures. A second, but very fragmentary, Icelandic manuscript from a few decades later contains parts of some of the poems in a different order, confirming the impression that the Codex Regius was carefully assembled as a unified book.

The mysterious term *Edda* was taken from the *Prose Edda*, which had as one source a collection similar to the *Poetic Edda*. The word *Edda* itself seems to be the same as its homonym meaning "great-grandmother." The stylistic concept Eddic is further applied to a variety of similar poems preserved in other Icelandic manuscripts. The ancient oral literature collected in the *Poetic Edda* comprises three general modes of folklore-related verbal art: myths, heroic legends, and wisdom or lore (partly gnomic, sentential, and proverbial, partly esoteric religious knowledge). All three modes represent traditional, not invented, material.

The narrative myths concern exploits of the pre-Christian Norse gods—Thor, Odin, Loki, Freyr, Baldr, and others. The literary peak of the mythological poems is arguably the manuscript's first, "The Sybil's Prophecy" (tenth century?), in which a seeress recounts the

173

The Poetic Edda collected poems narrating the exploits of pre-Christian Norse gods such as Thor as well as popular thirteenth-century wisdom and lore.

origin and fated end of the universe. After this overview come 10 more mythological poems, apparently grouped according to the gods who play major roles, ending with minor supernatural characters such as the wise dwarf of "The Lay of Alvís" and the nearly human elf of "The Lay of Völund." The 18 heroic poems are arranged in the supposed chronological order of events in the lives of nondivine heroes, such as Sigurd, and figures ultimately derived from distant Continental legend, such as Atli (Attila), Gunnar (Gunther), and Jörmunrek (Ermanarich).

The oldest of the heroic poems (including "The Lay of Atli" and "The Lay of Hamdir") seem to belong to the tenth century; "The Lay of Völund," generally viewed as more heroic than mythological despite its penultimate placement in the mythological group, may be from the ninth century. Other of the poems, especially an elegiac group with female protagonists (e.g., "First Lay of Gudrun"), are thought to date appreciably later, after the conversion of Iceland to Christianity in 1000 and belonging, perhaps, to the twelfth century.

Nonnarrative lore is scattered among poems in both the mythic and heroic sections of the manuscript, but the chief collection is in "The Words of the High One," that is, Odin. This is a complex assemblage of very old and younger life wisdom and sayings together with cryptic narrative passages. Several mythic poems (e.g., "The Lay of Skírnir") display a dramatic quality that led to the belief that they had been associated with ritual, but it is very difficult to connect any of this traditional poetry with real life except hypothetically.

The four meters used in Eddic poetry are based on the language's stress accent and alliteration and are thus closely related to Old English poetry; at least one, "old lore meter," is part of the common Germanic heritage. Influences from skaldic verse, a type of poetry developed only in Scandinavia, are perceptible in poems such as "The First Lay of Helgi Hunding's-Slayer." Eddic poetry has been studied outside Iceland since the eighteenth century; perhaps the high point of its modern reception is Richard Wagner's adaptations in *The Ring of the Nibelung*.

Joseph Harris

See also *Edda, Prose;* Legend; Myth; Proverbs; Ritual

References

Hallberg, Peter. "Eddic Poetry." In *Medieval Scandinavia: An Encyclopedia*, ed. Phillip Pulsiano et al., pp. 149–152. New York and London: Garland, 1993.

Harris, Joseph. "Eddic Poetry." In *Dictionary of the Middle Ages*, ed. Joseph R. Strayer, vol. 4, pp. 385–392. New York: Scribner, 1984.

———. "Eddic Poetry." In *Old Norse–Icelandic Literature: A Critical Guide*, ed. Carol J. Clover and John Lindow, pp. 68–156. Islandica 45. Ithaca and London: Cornell University Press, 1985.

Kristjánsson, Jónas. *Eddas and Sagas: Iceland's Medieval Literature*. Trans. Peter Foote. Reykjavík: Hið íslenska bókmenntafélag, 1988.

EDDA, PROSE

Also called "Snorra Edda" and "the Younger Edda," the *Prose Edda* is a treatise on poetics and mythology written about 1223 by an Icelandic magnate, Snorri Sturluson (1178/9–1241). Snorri was a wealthy member of the leading Icelandic family of the thirteenth century and a major player in the savage civil conflict of "the Sturlung age." He was also the most important named author of the Nordic Middle Ages. The attribution of the *Prose Edda* to Snorri, resting on a note in one of its four major medieval manuscripts and on scattered later medieval references, is regarded as secure; the same note in the Uppsala manuscript (c. 1300) is the source also of the work's title, *Edda*, a largely opaque name perhaps meaning "great-grandmother," perhaps "poetics." The manuscript genealogy is especially difficult, but the Uppsala manuscript may be an authorial draft while the other early manuscripts may have been variously augmented by later hands.

The *Prose Edda* comprises four sections: "Prologue," "Gylfaginning" ("the beguiling of Gylfi"), "Skáldskaparmál" ("poetic diction"), and "Háttartal" ("list of meters"). They are generally thought to have been written in reverse order, starting about 1220 when Snorri returned from a visit to the rulers of Norway, the young king Haakon IV and his regent. "*Háttartal*" is based on Snorri's own 102-stanza encomium to those rulers, illustrating different meters and accompanied by a prose commentary, which is chiefly on metrical issues. The longest of the parts, "*Skáldskaparmál*," centers on a discussion of kennings (poetic periphrases traditional in early Germanic verse, e.g., "the steed of the waves" for "ship") and *heiti* ("poetic synonyms"). To explain them, Snorri often introduces narratives of myths and heroic legends, and the section begins with a dramatic dialogue based on Norse myth, a framing device that is dropped after a few pages.

In *"Gylfaginning,"* such a dramatic framework is fully carried through: a Swedish king, Gylfi, is imposed upon by a tribe of magicians as they tell him versions of the myths and claim to be the gods themselves. The "Prologue" (its attribution to Snorri is disputed) puts the whole understanding of the heathen gods and ancient times into a learned Christian, chiefly euhemeristic, perspective, according to which the heathen gods are men of old who came to be worshiped when humans forgot the real God. This viewpoint is more or less in keeping with Snorri's statement of purpose (in a passage in *"Skáldskaparmál"*): the *Prose Edda* is an attempt to revive the ancient art of skaldic poetry, but its Christian users are not to believe the myths that the art depended on except in the distanced way provided by Snorri's frame.

The *Prose Edda*'s theory of paganism is not, however, perfectly reconcilable with Snorri's other major statement on and account of the heathen gods, *"Ynglinga saga,"* the first saga in his history of the Norwegian kings, *Heimskringla.* Thus *"Gylfaginning"* and *"Skáldskaparmál"* relate versions of traditional beliefs and such famous narratives as Ragnarök, the death of Baldr, the punishment of Loki, the Völsung-Nibelung tragedy, and the giant-killing exploits of Thor. But the *Prose Edda* is the product of a writing culture—to a large extent an offshoot of Continental learned mythography and rhetorical treatises. It is a very sophisticated literary creation, which, however, draws on ancient oral tales and traditional Eddic verse—elements of folklore. The *Prose Edda* also draws on, and incidentally performs a great service by preserving, skaldic poetry, which flourished as the preeminent "literary" art in the oral milieu of preconversion (c. 1000) Iceland and Norway and continued down to Snorri's time and beyond.

Joseph Harris

See also Belief; *Edda, Poetic*; Legend; Myth

✳✳✳✳✳✳✳✳✳✳✳✳✳✳✳✳✳

References

Faulkes, Anthony. "Snorra Edda." In *Medieval Scandinavia: An Encyclopedia*, ed. Phillip Pulsiano et al., pp. 600–602. New York and London: Garland, 1993.

Faulkes, Anthony, trans. *Snorri Sturluson, Edda.* London: Dent; Rutland, Vt.: Tuttle, 1987.

Kristjánsson, Jónas. *Eddas and Sagas: Iceland's Medieval Literature.* Trans. Peter Foote. Reykjavík: Hið íslenska bókmenntafélag, 1988.

Lindow, John. "Mythology and Mythography." In *Old Norse–Icelandic Literature:*

A *Critical Guide*, ed. Carol J. Clover and John Lindow, pp. 21–67. Islandica 45. Ithaca and London: Cornell University Press, 1985.

———. "Snorra Edda." In *Dictionary of the Middle Ages*, ed. Joseph R. Strayer, vol. 11, pp. 352–358. New York: Scribner, 1988.

EINFACHE FORMEN

Although the term *einfache Formen* ("simple forms") has been used in many fields, in the study of folklore and literature it refers exclusively to a remarkable study of narrative genres by the Dutch literary scholar André Jolles (1874–1946). Jolles's work is very much a product of its time, a period when scholars of many fields were concerned with matters of form in human culture.

Following the notion of "nature poetry" championed by Jacob Grimm, Jolles conceived of the simple genres as emerging by automatic generative modes produced by the same forces that generate language. He differentiated them sharply from complex literary genres ("art poetry," concocted consciously by professional authors).

Jolles's most impressive contribution is the delineation of the psychological and mental processes that permit the automatic emergence of simple genres. A key concept in Jolles's scheme is *Geistesbeschäftigung* ("dominant mental concern," hereafter referred to as DMC). Each of Jolles's nine simple genres comes into being under the forces exerted by its own specific DMC. The very building blocks of these genres are the narrative motifs, but Jolles eschews this term as being too neutral and too passive and uses *Sprachgebärden* ("linguistic gestures") instead—that is, language acts that contribute the narrative matter as well as providing the vehicle that permits the structuring force of language to produce generic forms of narrative. One can envision the process by imagining a large sheet of paper filled with a formless heap of metal filings (only some of which are magnetic). When one passes a magnet (a specific DMC) under the sheet, the magnetic filings (i.e., the targeted linguistic gestures) form structured patterns. The important concept here is that of the "targeted" gestures, for Jolles insists that only very specific *Sprachgebärden* can be charged by the given DMC: "Elements that are identical or similar unite with their own kind [being] transformed by the charged field so they are curled and twirled, pulled and shoved, and pressed together into new forms" (Jolles 1929, p. 265).

1. *Legende* ("saints' legend") is the first of the nine simple genres examined by Jolles, probably because it is best suited to illustrate his generative theory. Jolles used the Latin term *imitatio* to designate the DMC that sets the generative process for the saints' legend in motion. After the DMC charges the field, specific "linguistic gestures" are selected and structured into the generic form. These linguistic structures foreground the torment suffered by the early Christian martyrs. Saint George, for example, was martyred by a spinning disk whose circumference was equipped with sharp blades that sliced him to shreds in a most cruel but efficient manner. The language that describes this apparatus and its mutilation is more than powerful visual imagery. Indeed, as Jolles made clear, it is a scene that is virtually impossible for most people to visualize. As a "linguistic gesture," however, it conveys the meaning of the martyrdom suffered by all early Christians as it combines with related speech acts to demonstrate the willingness of the martyrs to accept torment and death rather than renounce their religious faith.

Jolles believed the DMC of *imitatio* continued to play an important role in the centuries after the persecution of the early Christians, especially in the Middle Ages. It dominated the lives of worshipers in many a village church and especially in pilgrimage chapels where one could see in the 14 stations of the cross the Passion of Christ. The pious pilgrim, in stopping at each, was guided by the spirit of *imitatio*, forcing identification with the derision, flagellation, and all the torments that culminated in the Crucifixion. Jolles understood correctly that the experience was more than a mere reminder of the accounts in the Gospels, it was a complete immersion into the very body of Christ.

It is advantageous to recognize that Jolles's DMCs truly dominated only during specific times and places in history. When one acknowledges this point, one can recognize in Jolles's scheme that both sociocultural factors and innate structuring principles combine to produce the simple genres. They are not exclusively the product of sociocultural contexts nor exclusively innate structural forces in the human mind. They are both.

2. *Sage* ("legend" and "saga"). Jolles's examination of this simple genre is the least satisfactory of the nine he undertakes. However, he identified the DMCs as *Familie*, *Stamm*, and *Blutsverwandschaft* ("family," "clan," and "bloodlines").

3. *Mythe* ("the mythical"). This designation is Jolles's own neologism, and by it he meant not just the myth as narrative, but a whole

range of religious behaviors. Jolles observed three stages in the generative process of the mythical: the mythical in the form of a narrative, and thus a philological artifact; the conceptualization and theory of the mythical in the daily context of life in human society; and the process of "mythologizing" as a dynamic flowing state that transforms reality into myths.

4. and 5. Although the next two of the nine simple genres, *Rätsel* ("riddle") and *Spruch* ("proverb"), both qualify as simple forms, Jolles's examination of them has not made a lasting contribution to the understanding of either. He identified the DMC for the riddle as "knowledge and the act of testing it." The riddling process, Jolles argued, is oriented toward the secrets of the world, expressed as enigmatic questions that often make use of the ambivalence of language (Jolles 1929, pp. 127–130). For the proverb, the underlying DMC is the notion that all knowledge comes from experience. When proverbs are invoked, people attempt to summarize human experience by looking back in time with a feeling of resignation.

6. *Kasus* can only be paraphrased as "a case to be weighed and judged" and can also include narratives involving criminal and civil law codes. Jolles insisted that a description of a broken norm told in juridical language is not a simple form; it becomes one only when the component parts are "linguistic gestures" that come under the influence of the appropriate DMC, which in this case is *Sich die Welt als ein nach Normen beurteilbares und wertbares* ("Conceiving the world according to the norms that are capable of being weighed and evaluated") (Jolles 1929, p. 179).

Although it is evident that Jolles has again delineated a narrative genre that few trained folklorists will recognize, his analysis of the *Kasus*—that is, a narrative form that weighs "cases" on the scales of the law and further evaluates them according to their underlying norms—is an astute observation that merits the scrutiny of folklore scholars.

7. *Memorabile* ("memorabilia"). Memorabilia means essentially memorable events, but as a designation for a narrative genre, it means more than that. It means that individuals will choose from everyday events those that are especially memorable and tell and retell them in narrative form to express the essential meanings they embody (Jolles 1929, p. 216; Petzoldt 1986, pp. 5–6). As such, memorabilia include the stories that folklorists know as "contemporary legends" or "urban legends," but they also include the sensationalized accounts that we know from so-called vulgar ballads as well as

such blues ballads as "Frankie and Johnny." The force that generates this form is the DMC of making *Das Tatsächliche konkret* ("the genuinely concrete"), that is, "shaping a presumed actual occurrence into something concrete" (Jolles 1929, p. 216). It is especially remarkable that Jolles recognized in 1929 that even though these stories have been well known for centuries, they are especially suited for the contemporary world.

8. *Märchen* ("magic tale"). Although the German word *Märchen* is often used to describe the totality of popular narratives, Jolles uses it exclusively as "magic tale." Jolles sees the DMC for this genre in a popular attitude that he calls *Die naive Moral* ("the naive moral"). This attitude poses the question, Would it not be great if the world were really like it should be, where all evil is punished, where all the objects and creatures and all magic and wonder exist for the sole purpose of achieving love, fortune, fame, and happiness? The magic tale thus describes the world not as it is, but as it should be.

There have been many attacks upon Jolles's analysis of the magic tale; many scholars object to calling this complex and artistic narrative genre "a simple form" while others believe the main weakness lies in the notion of the "naive moral," which they believe misses the essence of the genre (summarized in Petzoldt 1986, pp. 7–10, and Lüthi 1982, pp. 89–92).

9. *Der Witz* ("the joke"). Jolles's analysis of this simple form, from his designation of *Die Auflösung der Spannung durch den Komik* ("the suspension of tension by the comical") as the genre's DMC to his analysis of meanings, is generally disappointing. Even though his observation that the joke is a form that is manifested in diverse ways, depending on the values of the group and the spirit and style of the times, is valid enough (Jolles 1929, p. 248), that one observation cannot rescue this chapter from oblivion. Petzoldt is essentially correct when he notes that Jolles's analysis of the joke is hardly mentioned in contemporary research on jokes and joke-telling (Petzoldt 1986, p. 7).

In summary, it can be said that most European scholars acknowledge that Jolles wrote an ingenious yet highly flawed work. However, because the work has never been translated into English, it is almost totally ignored by American folklorists. The one German scholar who has dealt extensively with Jolles is Kurt Ranke, and although he rejects some of Jolles's specific arguments, he nevertheless has adopted and modified the main thrust of Jolles's theory of the production of a limited number of his simple genres—namely, folktale, legend, myth, and Schwank.

> We must regard the *Einfache Formen* of folk-literature as genuine forms. They are indeed archetypal forms of human expression that spring from dreams, emotions and cognitive processes. . . . All these *Einfache Formen*, then, originate in basic needs of the human soul and are therefore forms indicated by necessity. They are, in fact, the ontological archetypes of the various genres. (translation in Nicolaisen 1989, p. 119)

Donald Ward

See also Grimm, Jacob and Wilhelm; Legend; *Märchen*; Motif; Myth; Proverbs; Ranke, Kurt; Riddle; Urban Legends

✳✳✳✳✳✳✳✳✳✳✳✳✳✳✳✳✳✳

References

Bausinger, Hermann. "Einfache Formen." *Enzyklopädie des Märchens* 3 (1981): 124–126.

———. *Formen der Volkspoesie*, 2d ed. Berlin: Erich Schmidt, 1980.

Berendsohn, Walter. "Einfache Formen." *Handwörterbuch des Märchens* 1 (1930): 484–498.

Jolles, André. *Einfache Formen: Legende/Sage/Mythe/Rätsel/Spruch/Kasus/Memorabile/Märchen/Witz*. Halle: Max Niemeyer, 1929.

Lüthi, Max. *The European Folktale: Form and Nature*. Trans. John D. Niles. Philadelphia: Institute for the Study of Human Issues, 1982.

Nicolaisen, W. F. H. "Kurt Ranke and Einfache Formen." *Folklore* 100 (1989): 113–119.

Petzoldt, Leander. "Einfache Formen." *Reallexikon der germanischen Altertumskunde*, 2. neubearbeitete und stark erweiterte Ausgabe 7 (1986): 2–11.

Ranke, Kurt. *Die Welt der Einfachen Formen: Studien zur Motiv- und Quellenkunde*. Berlin and New York: De Gruyter, 1978.

ELLISON, RALPH (1914–1994)

An African-American writer and critic who was born in Oklahoma City, Oklahoma, Ralph Ellison's major works are the novel *Invisible Man* (1952); two collections of essays, *Shadow and Act* (1964) and *Going to the Territory* (1986); and two posthumously published volumes, *The Collected Essays of Ralph Ellison* (1995) and *Flying Home and Other Stories* (1996). His published short stories include "Flying Home," "King of the Bingo Game," "In a Strange Country," and "And

Hickman Arrives." Ellison attended Tuskegee Institute on a music scholarship, and his great interest in blues and jazz music influenced his fiction. He structured his fiction on African-American conversational lore and oral traditions, and he incorporated folklore thematically.

Ellison used Oklahoma frontier folklore in his early Buster and Riley stories (1940–1943), which deal with the adventures of two young boys. "Flying Home" (1944) makes thematic use of the Icarus myth as well as the African-American legend of the flying Africans, people who escaped slavery by flying away. The story also uses the well-known African-American folktale that is sometimes called "The Flying Fool." In that tale, a black man goes to heaven and is given angel's wings, but he flies too recklessly and is put out of heaven. In Ellison's "Flying Home," the tale is told by an old black man to a young black pilot-in-training whose plane has crashed in a field after hitting a buzzard. There is also black revivalist preaching as part of a hallucination dream sequence in the story and another tale about two buzzards rising from a dead carcass.

Many of Ellison's essays discuss the importance of jazz and blues in African-American culture and the complex relationship of folklore to African-American literature. In "Change the Joke and Slip the Yoke," Ellison seems to minimize the connection between the African-American trickster and literary art. Many scholars, however, read his fiction as a brilliant integration of the two. This theory is particularly evident in the Trueblood episode of *Invisible Man*. Trueblood is a sharecropper, blues singer, and gifted folk storyteller who manifests characteristics of the African-American trickster. His duality, ambivalence, and narrative strategy enable him to survive his breaking of the incest taboo and, indeed, to evoke admiration. Blues also serves as a mediating, integrative force.

Ellison's use of jazz and blues as structural devices in *Invisible Man* contributes to a fluidity of style and a vernacular of expression, sometimes called "playing around the note" in music. This quality is similar to the African-American oral tradition of "playing the dozens," "signifying," or "rapping," as each involves indirection and duality. Ellison incorporated the kind of improvisation that was typical of African-American music and speech. He also used names and renaming traditions: Rinehart is a name from the blues tradition, but in *Invisible Man*, Rinehart personifies chaos, a master of disguise and thus a prototypical trickster figure. Peter Wheatstraw, the trickster-jiver who makes reference to Brer Bear and Brer Rabbit, is also representative of black folk tradition and the blues.

The "Battle Royal" episode in *Invisible Man* is usually regarded as an initiation ritual or a rite of passage. It is also a ritual to preserve racial castes in the U.S. South. The episode develops the dualities and ambiguities that recur in the novel, beginning with the call-and-response sermon, "Blackness of Blackness," in the dream sequence in the Prologue. There is also the quest theme and search for identity throughout the novel.

"And Hickman Arrives" (1960) is an excerpt from Ellison's long-awaited novel about a folk preacher/evangelist. Seven other Hickman stories have been published, including "Juneteenth" (1965). *Going to the Territory* continues Ellison's discussions on the interconnections between African-American folklore and fiction.

At the time of his death, Ellison left a novel in progress and several unpublished short stories. John F. Callahan, Ellison's literary executor, edited the two posthumously published works and is editing the novel for publication. *The Collected Essays of Ralph Ellison* brings together the entire texts of Ellison's published nonfiction as well as his previously unpublished speeches and writings. *Flying Home and Other Stories* is a collection of 13 stories written by Ellison between 1937 and 1954. Six were not published during Ellison's lifetime.

Marcia Gaudet

See also Legend; Myth; Ritual; Sermon

✳✳✳✳✳✳✳✳✳✳✳✳✳✳✳✳✳

References

Baker, Houston A., Jr. "To Move without Moving: An Analysis of Creativity and Commerce in Ralph Ellison's Trueblood Episode." *Publications of the Modern Language Association* 98 (1983): 828–845.

Busby, Mark. *Ralph Ellison*. Boston: Twayne Publishers, 1991.

Callahan, John F. "Introduction." In Ralph Ellison, *Flying Home and Other Stories*, pp. ix–xxxviii. New York: Random House, 1996.

O'Meally, Robert G. *The Craft of Ralph Ellison*. Cambridge: Harvard University Press, 1980.

Ostendorf, Berndt. "Ralph Waldo Ellison: Anthropology, Modernism, and Jazz." In *New Essays on Invisible Man*, ed. Robert O'Meally, pp. 95–121. Cambridge and New York: Cambridge University Press, 1988.

Parr, Susan Resneck, and Pancho Savery, eds. *Approaches to Teaching Invisible Man*. New York: Modern Language Association, 1989.

EPIC

An epic is a narrative, either orally performed or textual, that describes the exploits of one or more heroic characters, often from a national perspective, in a distinct, identifiable poetic style. Heroic characters are usually of great physical and/or mental prowess, of royal or at least noble descent, and capable of extraordinary deeds beyond the ability of ordinary humans. Epic narratives generally portray conflicts on a grand scale and may also be defined by patterns such as quest, return home, or escape from peril. The themes of epics range from topics associated with mythology and folktale to historical features and events. Invocations to a higher power for inspiration and poetic assurances for the authenticity of the narrative often help to define the epic genre. Epics from regions such as China, Mongolia, and Turkic-speaking Central Asia can reach prodigious length, running to 100,000 lines and more, but examples from other traditions, especially western ones, are much shorter. The term *epic* is ultimately derived from the ancient Greek word *epos*, meaning an utterance, statement, or other unit of speech.

The epic narrative has its beginnings in oral poetry composed by preliterate bards in a performance setting. During performance, the oral poet composes by speaking a special language of typical scenes and formulaic phrases. Typical scenes include descriptions of a hero arming for or waging battle, banquets, journeys, and other recurrent actions. Primary oral epics are thereby performed for each occasion; the poet draws from a traditional reservoir of poetic material, making adjustments to fit the particular demands of the given audience and occasion.

The earliest surviving examples of epic narrative are *Gilgamesh* (c. 2000 B.C.E.) from the Middle East, the *Iliad* and *Odyssey* (c. 750 B.C.E.) from Greece, and the *Mahabharata* (c. 200 B.C.E.) from India. Replete with the typical scenes and formulaic phrases that characterize oral poetry, these works apparently circulated for centuries in primary oral versions and were later transferred to the written medium, in which form they have survived to the present.

In the West, the advent of literacy transformed the epic into a written genre. Virgil's *Aeneid* (first century B.C.E.), which spawned other Roman textual epics such as Lucan's *Pharsalia* (first century C.E.) and Statius's *Thebaid* (first century C.E.), is the most famous example from antiquity. The epic narrative continued to flourish during the medieval period with long heroic poems such as the

Anglo-Saxon *Beowulf* (eighth century C.E.), the Old French *Song of Roland* (eleventh century C.E.), and the medieval Spanish *Poema de Mio Cid* (thirteenth century C.E.). The tradition of writing epic poetry continued in the West well after the medieval period, most prominently with John Milton's *Paradise Lost* and Edmund Spenser's *Faerie Queene*.

Oral epic poetry survives in many parts of the modern world. In Africa, the *Mwindo Epic* is still performed in Zaire, and traditional *griots* ("poets") orally compose the *Epic of Son-Jara* in many countries of West Africa. The *Geser Epic*, numbering as many as 100,000 lines, can be heard on the steppes of Mongolia; other living oral epics include the Arabic *Bani Hilal* and the *Candaini* from India.

Anastasios Daskalopoulos

See also *Beowulf*; Hindu Epics; Performance; *Song of Roland*

✳✳✳✳✳✳✳✳✳✳✳✳✳✳✳✳✳✳

References

Bowra, Cecil M. *Heroic Poetry*. London: St. Martin's Press, 1966 (rpt).

Foley, John Miles. *Immanent Art: From Structure to Meaning in Traditional Oral Epic*. Bloomington: Indiana University Press, 1991.

———. *Traditional Oral Epic: The Odyssey, Beowulf, and the Serbo-Croatian Return Song*. Berkeley: University of California Press, 1990.

Jackson-Laufer, Guida. *Encyclopedia of Traditional Epics*. Santa Barbara, Calif.: ABC-CLIO, 1994.

Oinas, Felix. *Heroic Epic and Saga: An Introduction and Handbook to the World's Great Folk Epics*. Bloomington: Indiana University Press, 1978.

Okpewho, Isidore. *The Epic in Africa: Toward a Poetics of the Oral Performance*. New York: Columbia University Press, 1979.

ERDRICH, LOUISE (1954–)

The Native American novelist and poet Louise Erdrich refers to herself as a "storyteller," and orality is significant throughout her work. Like many successful Native-American writers today, she is of mixed blood (German and Chippewa or Ojibwa). In her attempt to evoke her Native American roots, but also as a member of contemporary American society, she combines and crosses genres, cultures, and themes in her writing, which earns acclaim as being among the most original American literature of its generation. Erdrich's rich body of work offers opportunities to increase the reader's understanding of the world, Native American and European American, traditional and contemporary.

Most of Erdrich's stories revolve around a fictional community set on or near the Turtle Mountain Reservation in North Dakota, similar to the place where she grew up. Erdrich's best and fullest representation of contemporary reservation life remains her first published novel, *Love Medicine* (1984). *The Beet Queen* (1986), *The Bingo Palace* (1994), and *Tales of Burning Love* (1996) also focus on this community (of both natives and nonnatives) in the present. Erdrich traces the past of some of the North Dakota families in *Tracks* (1988), her most "traditionally" Native American novel in terms of narrative elements, events, and characters.

Erdrich's return to the same community in many novels connects her to a growing tradition among Native American authors who emphasize place and nature. Erdrich uses place to bind, determine, and define her characters. Places like the reservation, the town, particular houses, a cave, a lake, a section of woods, a store, or a convent beckon, hold, and shape her characters. In her poetic stories of Potchikoo, for instance, Josie is literally a wooden cigar-store Indian until the trickster-like Potchikoo throws her into a lake. The water animates her as she drifts across, and life returns to her fully when she reaches the wooded side opposite the city (Potchikoo and Josie's story can be found in the poetry collections *Jacklight* [1984] and *Baptism of Desire* [1989]). Erdrich emphasizes and describes the natural world often and especially well in some of her poetry and *The Blue Jay's Dance* (1995).

The communities in Erdrich's works are replete with recurring, remarkable characters. One of the most powerful of the families whose lives are followed through several generations in five novels is the Nanapush family. Their name links them to the traditional Chippewa trickster Nanabozho. In *Tracks*, Nanapush is a key figure with irrepressible, trickster-like irreverence and humor. His descendants in *Love Medicine* (and the other North Dakota novels), such as Lipsha Nanapush, carry on his powerful medicine and trickster nature, undiluted by their modern circumstances. In trying to create "love medicine," Lipsha substitutes a frozen supermarket turkey heart for the required wild goose heart. He taints the ritual further by stealing Catholic holy water to bless the heart. As is the case with many tricksters, Lipsha is a would-be hero who unwittingly creates a medicine with deadly consequences, but the whole incident is not without humor. For good or bad, the medicine and the character remain powerful. Religion, in its traditional tribal and Catholic forms, and more often in syncretic form like this ritual, often figures prominently in Erdrich's work.

In all of her work, Erdrich weaves together numerous stories, voices, and perspectives. Often the various viewpoints, characters, and the stories they tell challenge the reader to decipher plot, relationships, dialogue, symbols, meaning, and reality. Erdrich has explained her remarkable, multivocal style, comparable to the styles of William Faulkner and magical realists, as an attempt to represent the collective perspective she believes is typical of traditional Native American culture. She credits her awareness of a collective, multicultural world and her sensitivity to orality to her family, as she credits her former husband, Michael Dorris (who was also part Native American and a writer), with being essential to every word of most of her writing. Erdrich and Dorris described their process of team writing in many interviews, but only *The Crown of Columbus* (1991) bears both of their names as authors.

Mary Magoulick

See also Faulkner, William; Ritual; Storytelling; Trickster

✳✳✳✳✳✳✳✳✳✳✳✳✳✳✳✳✳

References

Chavkin, Allan, and Nancy Feyl Chavkin, eds. *Conversations with Louise Erdrich and Michael Dorris*. Jackson: University Press of Mississippi, 1993.

Erdrich, Louise. *Baptism of Desire*. New York: Harper and Row, 1989.

———. *The Beet Queen*. New York: Holt, 1986.

———. *The Bingo Palace*. New York: HarperCollins, 1994.

———. *The Bluejay's Dance*. New York: HarperCollins, 1995.

———. *Jacklight*. New York: Holt, 1984.

———. *Love Medicine*. New York: Holt, 1984.

———. *Tales of Burning Love*. New York: HarperCollins, 1996.

Erdrich, Louise, and Michael Dorris. *The Crown of Columbus*. New York: HarperCollins, 1991.

ESPADA, MARTÍN (1957–)

Born in the Brownsville section of Brooklyn, New York, Martín Espada represents the newest generation of continental Puerto Rican poets committed to social and political activism. He received a B.A. from the University of Wisconsin and a degree in law from Northeastern University. He has been awarded fellowships from the National Endowment for the Arts and a Massachusetts Artists' Foundation Fellowship in Poetry.

Espada exemplifies the changes in contemporary Latino literature. Like an increasing number of Hispanics, he is university educated and trained in community work. His legal background and his firsthand knowledge of Hispanic communities enable him to record contemporary barrio life in *The Immigrant Iceboy's Bolero*, his first book of poetry. The inspiration for his poetry is the plight of the Latino immigrant, which is underlined by two common themes, racism and institutional violence. His strong imagery is reflected in five photographs by his father, Frank Espada, a professional photographer whose work documents multiple facets of Latino barrios.

Martín Espada has also written on Puerto Rican literature and popular culture in the United States. In an essay, "Culture and Independence in Puerto Rico" (1991), he equates Puerto Rican artists with the community's "popular memory" or "popular voice," which differs from official colonial history. His poetic activism is clearly expressed in his words: "By remembering insurrection, we can reawaken the potential for insurrection in ourselves, we can see clearly again the need for insurrection" (Espada 1991, pp. 87–95). In fact, it can be argued that Espada's close treatment of Puerto Rican folklore becomes a political statement as it constructs his definition of Puerto Rican identity.

Trumpets from the Islands of Their Eviction considers the history of Puerto Rican immigration to the continental United States and provides the "popular voice" for Latino barrios and projects. Memories of Puerto Rico become the emotional support against urban malaise. Of particular importance to folklorists is Caribbean music, its rhythms and songs, especially the *salsa*, which Espada's essay "Documentaries and Declamadores" presents as a product of New York and, therefore, an important element in the barrio's popular culture. *Salsa* music also acquires a strong political content since it represents the voice of Latinos living in underdeveloped barrios.

National recognition of Martín Espada's poetic craft came with *Rebellion Is the Circle of a Lover's Hands*, which won the 1989 Paterson Poetry Prize and became the first book to be awarded the Pen/Revson Foundation Fellowship for Poetry. It came out in an English-Spanish bilingual edition, cotranslated by Espada. On its acknowledgment page, he explained that he had written the book "in an effort to communicate with the people of Latin America who are the inspiration for many of these poems." Espada's training in history is visible in his continued exploration of the long oppression of Puerto Rican leftists in poems inspired by political movements against American control over the island. One poem recalls the Ponce Massacre of 1936, a demonstration organized by the Nationalist Party in Puerto Rico that ended in tragedy when military forces attacked the activists. The poem resulted from a conversation between Espada and Clemente Soto Vélez, a Puerto Rican poet in New York; half a century after the massacre, Soto described his participation in the event, for which he was imprisoned.

Espada has become Puerto Rico's most outspoken independence advocate in the United States. His poetry, in keeping with his own cause of Latino equality, proudly joins in the Latin American tradition of social commitment on the part of the arts and politics.

Rafael Ocasio

See also Soto, Pedro Juan

✱✱✱✱✱✱✱✱✱✱✱✱✱✱✱✱✱

References

Espada, Martin. "Culture and Independence in Puerto Rico." In *Being America: Essays on Art, Literature, and Identity from Latin America*, ed. Rachel Weiss and Alan West, pp. 87–95. New York: White Plains, 1991.

Gunderson, Elizabeth. "An Interview with Martín Espada." *Poets and Writers* 23:2 (March 1995): (no page number).

Pérez-Erdelyi, Mireya. "With Martín Espada." *Americas Review* 15:2 (Summer 1987): 77–85.

Vélez, Diana L. "Dancing to the Music of an 'Other' Voice: Martín Espada." In *Trumpets from the Islands of their Eviction*, pp. 69–89. Tempe, Ariz.: Bilingual Press/Editorial Bilingüe, 1987.

ETHNOPOETICS

Ethnopoetics studies the creative expression of non-Western and marginal cultures through translation, performance, and criticism. The poet and translator Jerome Rothenberg, who coined the term *ethnopoetics* in the late 1960s, says that it refers "to a redefinition of poetry in terms of cultural specifics, with an emphasis on those alternative traditions to which the West gave names like 'pagan,' 'gentile,' 'tribal,' 'oral,' and 'ethnic'" (Rothenberg & Rothenberg 1983, pp. xi–xiv). Although much of the work of ethnopoetics has been concerned with oral poetry and recovering its vibrant performance features in print and performance, the range of poetries studied is quite broad and includes dance, oral narratives, "wordless songs and mantras," "pictographs and hieroglyphs, aboriginal forms of visual and concrete poetry, sand paintings and earth mappings, gestural and sign languages, counting systems and numerologies, divinational signs made by man or read (as a poetics of natural forms) in the tracks of animals or of stars through the sky" (Rothenberg and Rothenberg 1983, pp. xi–xiv). In their anthology *Symposium of the Whole: A Range of Discourse Toward an Ethnopoetics* (1983), Jerome and Diane Rothenberg trace the concept of ethnopoetics from earlier thinkers such as Giambattista Vico, Johann Gottfried Herder, William Blake, Henry David Thoreau, and Tristan Tzara to recent writers such as Charles Olson, Mircea Eliade, Gary Snyder, and Imamu Amiri Baraka.

Since most people who encounter the artistic expression of other cultures do so through literature, ethnopoetics has been centrally concerned with issues of aesthetics and translation, not only from one language to another, but from performance to print. In the early 1970s, the anthropologist Dennis Tedlock published two influential works that demonstrated how typographic techniques borrowed from American free-verse poets could be used to approximate the sounds and silences of performers such as traditional Zuni storytellers. Representing slight pauses with line breaks and longer pauses with a dot between strophes, or larger spaces between strophes, Tedlock tries to represent the original contrasts in line length. Using small type for softly spoken words, large type for midlevel volume, and capitals for loud passages, he strives to record vocal dynamics. He represents the three half-tone interval of Zuni chants with split lines, slightly raising or lowering the words in a line according to the rise and fall of the voice. A final technique, italicized comments, is used to describe special voice qualities and metanarrative or nonverbal elements, such as gestures, laughter, or sighs.

Influenced by Tedlock, Dell Hymes, and David P. McAllester, Jerome Rothenberg coined the term *total translation* in 1969 for "translation (of oral poetry in particular) that takes into account any or all elements of the original beyond the words" (Rothenberg 1972, p. xxiii). He and Tedlock launched the journal *Alcheringa: Ethnopoetics* (in publication throughout most of the 1970s) to provide "a ground for experiments in the translation of tribal/oral poetry and a forum for the discussion of the problems and possibilities of translation from widely divergent languages and cultures" (*Alcheringa* 2).

The emphasis on a fuller and more sensitive translation of oral and nonverbal features into print has been a major contribution of ethnopoetics to both folklore and literature. Scholars such as Dell Hymes, Richard Dauenhauer, and Barre Toelken have retranslated Native American texts in an effort to discover and present more of the original performance style in print. Although transcribing performance features has become standard practice among ethnographers of Native American traditions, ethnographers of the European-American tradition are increasingly adopting the practice. William Bernard McCarthy, in *Jack in Two Worlds* (1994), utilizes an ethnopoetic methodology synthesized in Elizabeth Fine's *The Folklore Text: From Performance to Print* (1984) to present the performances of ten different tellers of Jack tales. Through ethnopoetics, readers are better able to appreciate the aesthetics of the narrative traditions of different cultures.

Elizabeth C. Fine

See also Herder, Johann Gottfried; Performance

✳✳✳✳✳✳✳✳✳✳✳✳✳✳✳✳✳

References

Fine, Elizabeth. *The Folklore Text: From Performance to Print.* Bloomington: Indiana University Press, 1994 (1984).

McCarthy, William Bernard, ed. *Jack in Two Worlds.* Chapel Hill: University of North Carolina Press, 1994.

Rothenberg, Jerome, and Diane Rothenberg, eds. *Symposium of the Whole: A Range of Discourse Toward an Ethnopoetics.* Berkeley: University of California Press, 1983.

Tedlock, Dennis. *Finding the Center: Narrative Poetry of the Zuni Indians.* New York: Dial Press, 1972.

Evil eye

The evil eye is a human glance or look believed by many individuals to bring about the death, injury, or misfortune of people and animals and/or the destruction or damage of inanimate objects. Assumed by some people to be deliberate and by others involuntary,

Egyptian painting of "evil eye," a universal symbol of malevolence, but most prevalent in the folklore of Mediterranean countries.

an individual's ability to affect adversely the status or well-being of other persons or things through a look or glance has been documented and feared since the beginning of recorded history. It is mentioned in the Bible and Koran and in Hinduism's sacred books and is characterized in Sumerian and Irish myths. Folklorist Alan Dundes (1992) enumerates European treatises published from the Renaissance through the nineteenth century that provide anecdotal evidence of evil-eye beliefs and speculate about their origins. Reports of individuals' experiences with the evil eye come from around the world, but belief in the evil eye is most pervasive in the Indo-European- and Semitic-speaking worlds and is most persistent in countries bordering the Mediterranean Sea.

Famous people as well as common folk are thought capable of casting the evil eye. According to Edward S. Gifford, Jr., Pope Pius IX (1792–1878) was widely believed to be able to do so—for example, there is the story of a baby who fell from its nurse's arms through an open window to the pavement below and was killed just as the pope was driving by on a Roman street. The composer Jacques Offenbach (1819–1880) was similarly thought to have had the power to cast an evil eye on others (perhaps because his eyes had a noticeable glitter) and was ridiculed for it. A University of Rome physics professor and colleague of Enrico Fermi was reputed to possess the evil eye and to have been responsible for the loss of 300 passengers on the *Principessa Mafalda*, an Italian ship that sank as he looked on.

The fear of receiving the evil eye makes believers take action. Precautionary measures include wearing protective colors (blue, for instance) or amulets (often with painted or carved eyes on them); spitting (usually three times) toward the source or victim of the evil eye; uttering secret prayers or incantations; and making hand gestures such as the *manus obscenus* (thrusting the thumb between the first and second fingers of a closed fist) or *mano cornuta* (extending the small and fourth fingers while holding down the second and third with the thumb). Numerous culture-specific rituals (enumerated and described in works by Frederick Thomas Elworthy, Gifford, and Dundes) enable people to determine for certain that one has received the evil eye, identify the guilty party, and sometimes cure or counteract the damage done to the afflicted.

Passing references and allusions to the evil eye are found throughout literature, including works by Francis Bacon, William Shakespeare, and Edward Bulwer-Lytton. In one of his novels, Ignazio Silone uses belief in the evil eye to account for Italian peasants' fatalistic worldview. Anthony Mancini makes it the focal point of a detective story.

Robert A. Georges

See also Belief; Bible; Myth; Shakespeare, William

✻✻✻✻✻✻✻✻✻✻✻✻✻✻✻✻✻

References

Dundes, Alan, ed. *The Evil Eye: A Casebook*. Madison: University of Wisconsin Press, 1992 (1981).

Elworthy, Frederick Thomas. *The Evil Eye: The Origins and Practices of Superstition*. New York: Julian Press, 1958 (1895).

Gifford, Edward S., Jr. *The Evil Eye: Studies in the Folklore of Vision*. New York: Macmillan, 1958.

Mancini, Anthony. *Minnie Santangelo and the Evil Eye*. New York: Fawcett Crest Books, 1977.

Silone, Ignazio. *Bread and Wine*. Trans. Harvey Fergusson II. New York: New American Library, 1963 (1936).

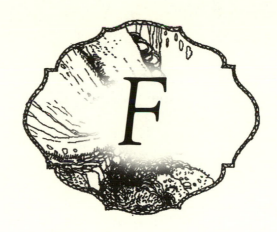

F ABLE

A fable is a brief, single episode—oral or written—that, because it employs speaking animals, plants, and inanimate objects as well as humans as characters, is said to illustrate metaphorically and satirize the conduct of human beings (e.g., "The fly sat upon the axle-tree of the chariot-wheel and said, What a dust do I raise?"). Around the first century C.E., written versions of earlier and orally transmitted Aesopian fables began to acquire a concluding proverbial moral (or epimythium), which was intended to clarify the story's instructional message. Centuries later, in 1740, the Swiss fable theorist Johann Jacob Breitinger, reflecting on this didactic intent, defined the fable as "instructive wonder." Although Aesopian (i.e., traditional) fables contain more humans as characters than animals, people in the twentieth century have tended to associate the latter with the name of Aesop.

Over time, the animal fables' portrayal of their dramatis personae has prompted the stereotyping of certain character traits: for example, the cunning fox, the silly goose, and the faithful dog. Likewise, pithy references to specific fable plots have developed into familiar proverbial phrases such as "sour grapes," "the lion's share," and "crocodile tears." Although in theory the fable is a distinct genre, in practice it is occasionally rendered in terms of other generic forms: for instance, as märchen (e.g., "Little Red Riding Hood"), etiological narrative (e.g., why the fox does not eat grapes), limerick (e.g., "The wolf wanted Lamb for his dinner. / Said he, 'You once wrong'd me, you sinner! / If it was not quite you, / 'Twas your grandmother Ewe: / So you must be had for my dinner.'"), and, widespread in modern-day conversation, fable-joke (e.g., "Two men are being chased by a bear when, in flight, one tries to put on his running shoes. When asked by the second friend 'Why?' the first replies, 'I don't have to outrun the bear. All I have to do is outrun you!'"). In addition, fabular motifs are widespread across folk art forms. The complex of interrelationships among a fabular story, its components, and its versions is referred to as that fable's "open-ended set."

Fables are one of the oldest types of story. Written versions of oral animal fables date to 3000 B.C.E. in Sumerian "wisdom literature," and traditional Indian fables, found in the *Panchatantra* and spread throughout the Middle East and Europe as well as India, were generally attributed to the Brahman philosopher Bidpai, the legendary Indian counterpart of the Greek Aesop. In Europe, the oral fables of Aesop, who was reputed to have lived in the 500s B.C.E., were introduced to Rome as written literature by the Roman fabulist Phaedrus (early first century C.E.), who translated them into Latin verse. Later written Latin translations were attributed to the legendary figure Romulus. A prose version of one Romulus collection served as the (possibly indirect) source for the verse fables of the French poet Marie de France. Writing in England during the reign of either the Norman king Henry II (1154–1189) or Richard I (1189–1199), Marie was perhaps the first European to translate Aesop into the vernacular.

In the centuries prior to Marie, fable collections had served primarily as reference handbooks for orators, sermonizers, and others who wanted to employ fables as rhetorical devices. Toward the end of the twelfth century, fables began to be put to two new purposes: as art to be appreciated for its own sake and as sociopolitical satire. As to the first of these purposes: in the opinion of many, the poetic fable reached its high point in France, particularly in the fables of Jean de La Fontaine. His 12 books of fables, *Fables choisies mises en vers* [Selected fables versified], which were published between 1668 and 1694, in part contain adaptations of the Aesopian tradition and emphasize entertainment over didacticism. His books were one of the publishing successes of the seventeenth century, and his fables continue to be acclaimed today for their topical variety, tantalizing ambiguities, multileveled framing, and comic ridicule of human vanities.

Also toward the end of the twelfth century, fabulists began turning the traditionally general lessons of fables to the more specific purposes of social commentary and satire. In this vein, they tended to associate predatory-animal characters (e.g., the lion or the wolf) with stereotypically oppressive social institutions, classes or roles (e.g., the courts, the monarchy, the rich man), and nonpredatory animals (e.g., the lamb) with less powerful social groups. Thus, Odo of Cheriton (d. c. 1246) populated his fables with characters such as spider bishops, frog priests, and dog officials who exploited those in their charge any way they could. The Jewish fabulist Berechiah Ben Natronai (writing in the late 1100s/early 1200s) used animal fables to comment with sympathetic sadness on the plight of the poor.

Later, during England's Augustan age (c. 1700–1750), various literary authors, who typically worked in genres other than fable, contributed to the political activism thread of the then-current "Aesop craze." Among them were John Dryden, whose much maligned poetic animal fable *The Hind and the Panther* (1687) argued for increased tolerance of Roman Catholics, and Samuel Richardson, in whose novel *Pamela* (1740) the working-class heroine co-opts Aesopian fables from her dead mistress's library. Fifty years later in Russia, a similar but more intense political unrest gave rise to the agitational fable: for instance, in 1803, the Decembrist activist Denis Davydov circulated his Aesopian-based fable "The Head and the [Lower] Limbs," which called, metaphorically, for the renegade limbs (i.e., revolutionaries led by military officers) to revolt against and smash the hegemonic head (i.e., the monarchy as then constituted). Whether in explicit or implicit reference, such fables acknowledged Aesop as a model fabulist in that he had gained his freedom from slavery through his telling of fables.

Other social applications of the fable in Augustan England derived from its traditionally didactic intent. In addition to their use in classrooms to teach Latin, French, and English, fables appeared in the burgeoning children's literature of the time. For example, Anna Barbauld's *Evenings at Home* (1792) tried to instill moral values in its child readers by describing rebellious and selfish small animals who were usually punished (sometimes with death) for their transgressions. Also in vogue from the 1740s through the 1770s were fable collections designed to instruct young women in moral and social behavior. For instance, in Edward Moore's verse *Fables for the Female Sex* (1744), one illustration shows a satyr holding up a mirror to a woman; the caption reads, "Truth under Fiction I impart / To weed out Folly from the Heart." Challenging the perspective of patriarchal adherents such as Moore, however, were a few Augustan women fabulists. Among them was the playwright, poet, and romance writer Aphra Behn, who served as the fabulist for the illustrator Francis Barlow's well-received *Æsop's Fables with his Life* (1687). In that work, Behn feminized a number of traditional fables, sometimes in bawdy style: in one, a female ape begs in vain for a fox's tail to "vaile [veil]" her "bum."

Except for the emerging area of children's literature, popular, artistic, sociopolitical, and critical interest in the fable declined in the nineteenth century. The attention—whether serious or dilettantish—that had been increasingly lavished upon fable had run its course by the end of the 1700s. In addition, the reading public was becoming more sophisticated, and its interests increasingly shifted from fable to more complex genres such as the novel and, later, the short story.

Nonetheless, some literary fable-telling has continued through the twentieth century. One well-respected fabulist is James Thurber, whose *Fables for Our Time* (1939) and *Further Fables for Our Time* (1956) have never gone out of print. These collections contain what Pack Carnes (1992) has termed "anti-fables"—that is, parodies of Aesopic form that conclude with parody morals. For example, in "The Little Girl and the Wolf," when the girl realizes that it is the wolf and not the grandmother in the bed, she immediately takes "an automatic out of her basket and [shoots] the wolf dead. Moral: It is not as easy to fool little girls nowadays as it used to be." Other of Thurber's parody morals include: "It is better to have loafed and lost than never to have loafed at all," "A word to the wise is *not* sufficient if it doesn't make sense" (italics in the original), and "There is no safety in numbers or in anything else." The last functions as a meta-moral in that it sums up the overall didactic purpose of Thurber's fables: to remind (i.e., to instruct) readers that traditional wisdom cannot be trusted in the modern age. Other modern fabulists of note include Ambrose Bierce, *Fantastic Fables: Æsopus Emendatus* (1899); William Saroyan, *Fables* (1941); George Orwell, *Animal Farm* (1945); Jean Anouilh, *Fables* (1962); Robert Zimler, *Aesop Up-to-Date* (1964); Hoshi Shin'ichi, *Mirai Isoppu* [The future Aesop] (1971); and Arnold Lobel, *Fables* (1980).

Across their three-and-a-half-millennia history, fables have been used to serve a handful of functions: to teach, persuade, entertain, satirize, and challenge. Even today, at the turn of the twenty-first century, the fable remains one of the most versatile of oral and literary genres.

Danielle M. Roemer

See also Aesop's Fables; Bierce, Ambrose Gwinnett; Children's Literature; *Märchen; Motif; Panchatantra;* Proverbs; *Romance of Reynard*

✳✳✳✳✳✳✳✳✳✳✳✳✳✳✳✳✳

References

Carnes, Pack. *Fable Scholarship: An Annotated Bibliography*. New York: Garland, 1985.

———. "The Fable and the Anti-Fable: The Modern Faces of Aesop." *Bestia: Yearbook of the International Beast Fable Society* 4 (1992): 5–33.

Carnes, Pack, ed. *Proverbia in Fabula: Essays on the Relationship of the Proverb and the Fable*. Bern and New York: Peter Lang, 1988.

Lewis, Jayne Elizabeth. *The English Fable: Aesop and Literary Culture, 1651–1740*. Cambridge: Cambridge University Press, 1996.

Noel, Thomas. *Theories of the Fable in the Eighteenth Century*. New York: Columbia University Press, 1975.

Patterson, Annabel. *Fables of Power: Aesopian Writing and Political History*. Durham, N.C.: Duke University Press, 1991.

F*ABLIAU*

Traditionally defined by Joseph Bédier as "humorous stories in verse," medieval *fabliaux* are most popularly known for their scurrilous subject matter and graphic sexual accounts. In fact, more than simply "dirty tales," the fabliaux, most of which were recorded from the twelfth to the fourteenth centuries, are important keys to understanding the social reality of the Middle Ages. The notion of three traditional estates of society—peasants, clergy, and knights—provided an ideal for the medieval social structure. Historical evidence indicates that, in reality, these traditional estates were continually challenged as newly rich peasants bought into the aristocracy and as poor nobles lost wealth and status. The structure of the fabliau reflects such societal mobility.

A fabliau typically begins by establishing that its characters are socially transient (such as rich peasants or poor knights), and the narratives are concerned with the comic situations that result from changing social roles. For example, in the prototypical fabliau *D'Aloul, a vilein riche* [D'Aloul, a rich villain] D'Aloul uses his wealth to buy a bride, the daughter of an impoverished knight. Despite this socially profitable marriage, the *vilein* is unable to rise above his lowly birthright. Rather, he finds himself the victim of an elaborate trick devised by his wife: she cuckolds him in their marriage bed. As

D'Aloul illustrates, fabliaux are frequently structured around elaborate tricks that reveal the true social status of the dupe. These tricks often involve such themes as cuckoldry, castration, and thievery.

The fabliau employs folk motifs (such as "the weeping bitch" [K1351], "the talking vagina" [D1610.6.1], and "the foolish wishes" [J2071]) and reworks the traditional elements to create a genre that is primarily concerned with changing social roles. Fabliau motifs are evident in other types of medieval literature, such as the exemplum, lyric, beast epic, Latin comedy, and fable. Etymologically, the relationship between fabliau and fable is especially obvious, for the word *fabliau* is a diminutive of *fable*, meaning "fiction." Unlike the fable, the fabliau is not a moralistic genre. Although many fabliaux include morals, fabliau morals are loosely or not at all connected to the story line and probably function as devices that signal closure.

The fabliau also shares characteristics with the romance. Courtly themes and courtly language, reserved for the elite in the romance, are made accessible to all levels of society in the fabliau and become a source of irony. Courtly details are interspersed with realistic, quotidian passages, and passages of courtly love are set beside bawdy and direct sexual language to show the changing implications of the language of romance in a changing social environment.

Because of the oral nature of the fabliau and because multiple versions of many fabliaux are extant, an exact historical chronology is impossible. However, one can with some degree of accuracy develop a general understanding of the historical evolution of the genre. Most scholars accept as the corpus of fabliaux the nineteenth-century collection by Anatole de Montaiglon and Gaston Raynaud (1872–1890), although a number of additional works might now be added to the 155 in their six volumes. Although fabliaux are evident in a number of manuscripts and fragments, Nico van den Boogard (1985) identifies four major collections: ms. Paris BNf.fr 837; ms. Berne, Bibliotheque de la Bourg 354; ms. Berlin Hamilton 257; and ms. Paris BNf.fr 19.152. In collaboration with Willem Noomen, Boogard is working on a collection (to be entitled *Nouveau recueil complet des fabliaux*) that will contain authoritative versions of the 58 fabliaux in ms. Paris BNf.fr 837.

In addition to the Old French tales, fabliaux and fabliau-like works are found in German and Spanish literature. The fabliau tradition also existed in England, as evidenced by 12 extant Anglo-Norman fabliaux, a handful of English tales such as *Dame Siriz* and *A Penniworth of Witte*, and Chaucer's fabliaux in *The Canterbury*

Tales (including the tales of the Miller, Reeve, Cooke, Friar, Summoner, Merchant, and Shipman). The importance of the fabliau to folklore and literature studies is far-reaching, for the fabliau tradition continued into the late Middle Ages and early Renaissance. As the fabliau changed shape and merged with preexisting literary forms, it developed into the "churl's tale" of the late Middle Ages and influenced the novelle and the jest of the Renaissance. In fact, the attention to character and realistic details of the fabliau could be seen as precursors of modern fiction.

Carol Jamison

See also Bédier, Joseph; Chaucer, Geoffrey; Fable; Motif; Romance

✳✳✳✳✳✳✳✳✳✳✳✳✳✳✳✳✳✳

References

Bédier, Joseph. *Les Fabliaux*. 6th ed. Paris: Champion, 1893.

Bloch, R. Howard. *The Scandal of the Fabliaux*. Chicago: University of Chicago Press, 1986.

Boogard, Nico van den. *Autour de 1300: Etudes de philologie et de littérature médiévales*. Amsterdam: Rodopi, 1985.

Cooke, Thomas Darlington. *The Old French and Chaucerian Fabliaux: A Study of Their Comic Climax*. Columbia: University of Missouri Press, 1978.

Montaiglon, Anatole de, and Gaston Raynaud, eds. *Recueil général et complet des fabliaux des XIIIe et XIVe siècles*. 6 vols. Paris: Librarie des Bibliophiles, 1872–1890.

Muscatine, Charles. *The Old French Fabliaux*. New Haven: Yale University Press, 1986.

Fairy tale

A fairy tale is "a long, fictitious narrative with a human main character; the narrative includes fantasy and it is told as a means of passing the time, as entertainment" (Apo 1995, p. 16). Fairy tales are episodic: the main character is separated from, or otherwise in trouble with, his or her family. He or she encounters severe or supernatural challenges and difficulties until, finally, all ends happily. Within this framework are set one or more extraordinary, usually magical, motifs, such as a character's ability to assume another shape, to come back from the dead, or to summon supernatural aid. Some fairy tales involve a quest for a spouse or for a magic object, some tell of a confrontation with an ogre or an evil human adversary, and some integrate magical motifs into a humorous story. Typically, the tale is set apart from everyday speech with formulas such as "Once upon a time" and "They lived happily ever after."

Fairy tales are of interest to scholars, artists, readers, narrators, and audiences of both adults and children because they contain many thought-provoking layers, including ancient superstitions, archetypal fears, contemporary folk beliefs, exquisite symbolism, heartfelt wishes, and social commentary. Some of the transformations in myths and in shamanic rituals are very similar to some of the magical motifs in fairy tales. For many purposes, a fairy tale ought to be studied in connection with mythological, legendary, or sung traditions when its motifs are present in those other genres.

The long-standing debate concerning the age and origin of fairy tales is fueled both by differences of definition and by scholarly disagreement about the amount of oral tradition that lies behind the early literary representations of fairy tale motifs and structures. Magical transformations appear in the ancient Egyptian tale of the two brothers (Anup and Bata). The Greek story of Jason and Medea includes two episodes ("Son-in-law Tasks" and "Flights from the Ogre") of AT 313, "The Girl as Helper in the Hero's Flight." Apuleius's "Cupid and Psyche" places mythological characters in a fairy tale plot (AT 425B). Several *lais* ("metrical romances") of the French poet Marie de France (late twelfth century) include fairy tale plots and motifs, and some other medieval romances do so as well.

By the sixteenth century, there is considerable evidence of a significant oral tradition of fictional complex tales with magical motifs in Italy and France. Gian Francesco Straparola's *Pleasant Nights* (1550–1553) includes, among other tales, 20 fairy tales attributed fictitiously to guests at a villa party. Giambattista Basile's *Pentamerone* (1634) contains 50 familiar tales set in a frame that is a version of AT 437, "The Needle Prince." In the late seventeenth and eighteenth centuries, the French literary vogue for *Contes des feés* (this phrase is the source of the English "fairy tale") prompted the importation of oriental tales including Antoine Galland's translation of *The Thousand and One Nights* (1704). The fairy tales were disseminated in inexpensive chapbooks.

Because the fairy tale is such a cosmopolitan genre, national and language-based histories cannot do it full justice. Oral tradition has long provided material for literary fairy tales, and the dynamics of oral transmission have affected the fairy tale's artistic construction.

Thus, investigations of fairy tales should often properly include both literary and oral material.

Christine Goldberg

See also Apuleius; Belief; Legend; *Märchen*; Myth; Ritual; Romance; *The Thousand and One Nights*

✳✳✳✳✳✳✳✳✳✳✳✳✳✳✳✳✳

References
Apo, Satu. *The Narrative World of Finnish Fairy Tales*. Folklore Fellows Communication no. 256. Helsinki: Academia Scientiarum Fennica, 1995.
Lüthi, Max. *The Fairytale as Art Form and Portrait of Man*. Bloomington: Indiana University Press, 1984.
McGlathery, James M. *Fairy Tale Romance: The Grimms, Basile, and Perrault*. Urbana and Chicago: University of Illinois Press, 1991.
Röhrich, Lutz. *Folktales and Reality*. Bloomington: Indiana University Press, 1991.
Storer, Mary Elizabeth. *La Mode des contes des feés (1685–1700)*. Paris: Honoré Champion, 1928.

FAKELORE

Fakelore is a term coined by Richard M. Dorson in 1950 in an article in the *American Mercury* in which he attacked the popularization, commercialization, and distortion of traditional materials passed off as authentic folklore. In *American Folklore* (1959), Dorson says that "fakelore falsifies the raw data of folklore by invention, selection, fabrication, and similar refining processes ... for capitalistic gain [or totalitarian conquest]. The end result is a conception of the folk as quaint, eccentric, whimsical, droll, primeval" (p. 4). There are two kinds of fakelore: folklore material that has been so extensively reworked that it no longer resembles authentic folklore and outright fabrication of materials passed off as authentic folklore. So-called folktales in anthologies of children's literature and collections like Richard Chase's *The Jack Tales* (1943), also primarily for children, are examples of folklore materials that have been extensively reworked, and synthetic hero tales about Paul Bunyan, Pecos Bill, Febold Feboldson, Old Stormalong, and Joe Magarac are examples of fabricated material that has been passed off as authentic folklore. Also labeled fakelore by Dorson are "scrapbooks of Americana," like

Benjamin A. Botkin's *Treasury of American Folklore* (1944) and his subsequent regional treasuries. In fact, Dorson wrote that "it was directly as a consequence of these treasuries and their influence that I publicized the word *fakelore*" (Dorson 1971, p. 5).

Dorson, always the champion of academic folklorists and the enemy of popularizers, coined the term *fakelore* when the study of folklore was just beginning its struggle for academic legitimacy and there was, as he said, "a shortage of trained folklorists and oversupply of amateurs" (Dorson 1976, p. 16). Although at the time most of the few trained folklorists readily accepted Dorson's neologism, generally the term was met with recrimination by the so-called amateurs—that is, by people not formally trained in folklore studies. Today, even trained folklorists—believing the term *fakelore* to be pejorative and apparently still trying to placate some hard feelings stirred by the controversy surrounding the introduction of the term—have rejected Dorson's coinage in favor of more neutral terms like *folklorismus*, *poplore*, and *folklure* to describe the commercialization and popularization of folklore, the melding of folk culture and popular culture, and mass-culture creations passed off as folklore.

There is, of course, a symbiotic relationship among folk culture, popular (or mass) culture, and formal culture. Recognizing that the three cultures constantly nourish one another, Dorson's intention was to distinguish clearly among them. He argued that there was a legitimate literary use of folklore but that the products of creative writers who were influenced by folklore should be called literature and should not be passed off as folklore. Likewise, heroes created for and circulated by the mass media properly are mass-culture heroes and should not be passed off as folk heroes. Dorson examined some of the mass-culture heroes, notably Paul Bunyan, in a section of a chapter in *American Folklore*, and he showed how "literary folktales bind together folk and culture [formal] literature in a significant relationship" in a chapter of *Jonathan Draws the Long Bow* (1946, p. 199).

Dorson's error was in vociferously blacklisting works he considered fakelore and in his scathing attacks on authors he considered fakelorists. As Alan Dundes has noted: "It is far better to accept the fact that fakelore may be an integral element of culture just as folklore is. Rather than reject fakelore on the a priori grounds that it is impure or bastardized folklore, let us study it as folklorists, using the tools of folklorists" (Dundes 1959, p. 3).

Ronald L. Baker

See also Botkin, Benjamin A.; Bunyan, Paul; Dorson, Richard M.; Folklorism

✳✳✳✳✳✳✳✳✳✳✳✳✳✳✳✳✳

References

Bluestein, Gene. *Poplore*. Amherst: University of Massachusetts Press, 1994.

Dorson, Richard M. *American Folklore*. Chicago: University of Chicago Press, 1959.

———. "Fakelore." In *American Folklore and the Historian*, ed. Richard M. Dorson, pp. 3–14. Chicago: University of Chicago Press, 1971.

———. "Folklore and Fake Lore." *American Mercury* (1950): 335–343.

———. *Folklore and Fakelore: Essays toward a Discipline of Folk Studies*. Cambridge: Harvard University Press, 1976.

———. *Jonathan Draws the Long Bow*. Cambridge: Harvard University Press, 1946.

Dundes, Alan. *Folklore Matters*. Knoxville: University of Tennessee Press, 1989.

FAULKNER, WILLIAM (1897–1962)

Considered by many people to be the greatest American novelist of the twentieth century, William Faulkner is best known for his Yoknapatawpha saga, a cycle of 14 novels and many short stories dealing with the life, culture, and history of a fictional town (Jefferson) and county (Yoknapatawpha) based on Oxford, Mississippi, and Lafayette County where Faulkner lived for most of his life. Faulkner's fictions are a rich source of information about the culture of the Deep South, particularly relations between whites and blacks, one of Faulkner's central themes.

Faulkner is also noted for his representation of the oral culture of his region. His novels abound in oral narratives and in brilliantly realized versions of many different oral genres such as the legend, the tall tale, the folk sermon, and the humorous anecdote. His work is also replete with incidents that represent important forms and rituals of oral encounter: bartering and trading, swapping stories, the hunt, and many other aspects of southern small-town and rural folklife.

Faulkner's powerful critique of southern racism, a central component of such major novels as *Light in August* (1932), *Absalom, Absalom!* (1936), *Go Down, Moses* (1942), and *Intruder in the Dust* (1948), remains one of the most complex portrayals of the racist myths, stereotypes, and social patterns that have dominated American society since the beginning of African slavery. Faulkner's characters, both black and white, effectively delineate the folkways of racism, showing how the obsession with race dominates every aspect of society and how the overriding fear of miscegenation—ironic in a culture where the sexual exploitation of black slaves by their white owners was a major cultural practice—resulted in an undercurrent of violence that is likely to break out in crisis situations like murder and lynching.

The dark side of Faulkner's portrayal of the southern heritage is to some extent balanced by his richly appreciative celebration of some of the strengths of traditional southern folk culture in works like *The Hamlet* (1940) and *The Reivers* (1962). In these and other novels, Faulkner's remarkable gifts as a humorist come to the surface in wonderful renditions of the traditional southwestern tall tale, a folk resource also exploited by earlier southern writers like George Washington Harris and Thomas Bangs Thorpe as well as Mark Twain. In *The Hamlet*, for example, Faulkner's tall tales of horse-trading and buried treasure are classic examples of the genre, while the great story of Flem Snopes and his wild spotted horses ranks with the greatest of literary folktales. Even in more tragic fictions like *As I Lay Dying* (1930) and *Light in August* (1932), the feel of folk legend and oral narrative is always strongly present.

Like many modern novelists, Faulkner made extensive use of mythical parallels, both classical and biblical, in his fiction. These parallels, such as his use of the biblical story of King David and his son Absalom in *Absalom, Absalom!* or of the Odyssean epic journey in *As I Lay Dying*, help to explain the universal significance of his stories in spite of the intense locality and particularity of people and places that characterize his fiction.

John Cawelti

See also Bible; *Odyssey*; Sermon; Tall Tale; Twain, Mark

✽✽✽✽✽✽✽✽✽✽✽✽✽✽✽✽✽

References

Blotner, Joseph. *Faulkner: A Biography*. New York: Random House, 1984.

Brooks, Cleanth. *William Faulkner: The Yoknapatawpha Country*. New Haven: Yale University Press, 1963.

Hoffman, Daniel. *Faulkner's Country Matters: Folklore and Fable in Yoknapatawpha*. Baton Rouge: Louisiana State University Press, 1989.

Williamson, Joel. *William Faulkner and Southern History*. New York: Oxford University Press, 1993.

FAUST LEGEND

One Georg (Latin, Johannes) Faust, a historical figure from Swabia (Germany), became the central character in a German popular printed legend by Johann Spies entitled *Die Historia von Dr. Johann Fausten* (1587). The historical Faust is thought to have been an itinerant soothsayer or perhaps a doctor. Soon after the publication of the legend in Germany, it was translated into English, and Christopher Marlowe produced a modified English version, *The Tragical Story of Dr. Faustus* (1589–1592). The central element in the literary handlings of Faust is his pact with the devil. Marlowe, for example, portrayed Faust as a prideful man in pursuit of learning and other forms of earthly satisfaction.

The Faust legend is one of the most used story themes in modern European literature. It has also been repeatedly employed since its conception in popular dramas and various other types of performance. The contents of at least two multivolume bibliographies of Faust themes in European literature attest to the legend's popularity. Writers such as Johann Wolfgang von Goethe, Thomas Mann, Jean-Paul Sartre, and Somerset Maugham have written important works of fiction based in some way on this legend. The German philosopher of history Oswald Spengler (1880–1936) has gone so far as to describe modern European civilization as "Faustian" with its prideful search after knowledge and individual satisfaction, whatever the cost.

The Faust legend reflects traditions in European folktales, popular religious beliefs, and elite attitudes toward literacy, science, and the supernatural. It seems clear that attributes associated with Faust, for example, were elsewhere associated with famous philosophers such as Albertus Magnus (1193–1280) and Paracelsus (1493–1541). Faust was portrayed by Spies as a man in the tradition of the great early modern Hermetist philosophers and alchemists and their search for the "philosopher's stone" and the chemical foundations of the physical world.

Various aspects of the legend reflect popular conceptions of demons and the devil as well. Legends collected in Austria (where, incidentally, there is supposedly a small castle near the Danube once inhabited by Dr. Faust) focus on pacts with the devil and tricks played on him by local inhabitants. The motif of a bargain with the devil has been identified by the folklore scholar Stith Thompson in various kinds of folk literature. The Faust story can also be seen, however, to be part of the folklore traditions of stories about "absurd wishes" or "foolish bargains" (motifs J2070–79, J2080–89).

Some of the details of the Faust legend reflect the early modern central European context of its initial publication. Living in a society riven with confessional strife engendered by the Protestant and Catholic reformations, some thinkers sought to find a unifying philosophy in science. Spies and Marlowe can be seen as questioning this modern enterprise, likening it instead to a search for unknowables, a search that is possible only at the cost of one's soul.

Witchcraft trials, which periodically took place (sometimes on a massive scale) during this period, also contributed to the image of the devil as an individual with whom it is possible to make a pact. In modern, Western Christian thought, an image of the devil was developed to balance the image of Christ. The devil is seen as the ruler of this world while Christ rules in the next. Faust, then, can be seen as tied to earthly pursuits specific to the devil's realm.

The legend's tremendous appeal to the literate elite of Europe since the sixteenth century, an appeal documented by the scores of literary productions relating to its themes, is at least partially attributable to the persistence of the dualistic perceptual framework.

Joseph F. Patrouch

See also Goethe, Johann Wolfgang von; Legend; Satan; Witchcraft

✳✳✳✳✳✳✳✳✳✳✳✳✳✳✳✳✳✳

References

Henning, Hans. *Faust-Bibliographie*. 5 vols. Berlin: Aufbau Verlag, 1966–1976.

More, Robert Pattison, and Philip Mason Palmer. *The Sources of the Faust Tradition*. New York: Haskell House, 1965 (1935).

Smeed, John William. *Faust in Literature*. New York: Oxford University Press, 1975.

*F*ENG-SHEN YEN-I

The *Feng-shen yen-i* [Investiture of the gods] is a Chinese episodic novel of the Ming dynasty (1368–1644) based on myth and historical legend. Written in verse and prose and containing 100 chapters, it has been attributed to the writer Hsu Chung-lin (d. c. 1566). The term *folk epic* is used by Liu Wu Chi to describe this special genre of novel of which there are several other examples; namely, the *Travels* to the West (*Hsi-you chi* [c. 1592]), *The Romance of the Three Kingdoms* (*San-kuo chih* [c. 1522]), and the *Water Margin* (*Shui-hu chuan* [early sixteenth century]). It is a characteristic of this genre that episodes of the story probably circulated in the repertoires of professional storytellers before being composed into published texts. The written text of the *Feng-shen yen-i* combines several major traditional story cycles and imaginatively elaborates upon a variety of mythological and folk motifs as well as tale-types. Popular dramatic versions of some episodes have been circulating for centuries.

The frame of the work is the historical legend concerning events leading to the fall of the Shang dynasty and the founding of the Chou dynasty (1000–200 B.C.E.) in ancient China. In the legend, the emperor of the Shang insults the goddess Nu-Wa, who in various myths is the creator of mankind. Her anger instigates a chain of fantastic events that bring about the downfall of the Shang. A new concubine in the court becomes possessed by a 1,000-year-old fox spirit and leads the emperor into extravagance and waste, which is symbolized at its epitome by the building of a fabulous tower. A major turning point in the novel is when the faithful retainer Chiang Tze-ya turns against the Shang ruler to serve the forces of the Chou. Chiang is a Taoist prophet and a fortune-teller with magical power who marshals hosts of magical creatures and transformed animal spirits to combat the forces of the emperor.

The motifs of transformation flight, obstacle flight, and transformation combat in the work are often associated with AT types 325, "The Magician and his Pupil"; 313A, "The Girl as Helper in the Hero's Flight"; and 314, "The Horse as Helper in the Hero's Flight." In an early folklore study of the historic-geographic distribution of magic flight motifs, Antti Aarne came to the conclusion that variants of the obstacle flight, in which common objects are transformed into such hindrances as a forest, a mountain, or a body of water to prevent an ogre's gaining on the hero, were of Asian origin and probably preceded variants of the types that substituted the actual transformations of the hero in escape. In the Chinese *Feng-shen yen-i*, the Taoist concept of the five basic elements and their relations are used to explain the transformations, especially those of the character Yang Hsien. These five elements are earth, fire, water, metal, and wood, which in the traditional Chinese worldview produce and conquer one another in a natural cyclic order. In the folk teleology underlying the novel, the order of dynastic change can also be explained by this cyclic concept.

Besides the episodes involving transformation flight and combat, the episodes that tell of the child-god No-cha's unusual birth and exploits also contain folk motifs, namely, his wielding of various magic objects and his magical rebirth. The concept of investiture or canonization of the gods in the work is related to Taoist deification of worldly heroes. Gods and goddesses of the Taoist pantheon could thus acquire veneration. Some episodes in the novel derive from Buddhist Indian sources, such as the battle of bodhisattvas with three heads and six hands. Since it was only in later times that Buddhism entered China, in this novel—as in other arts of the Ming dynasty—Buddhism is combined with Chinese folk Taoism and popular belief.

Patricia L. Haseltine

See also Aarne, Antti; Chinese Opera; Legend; Motif; Myth; Taiwanese Opera

****

References

Aarne, Antti. "Die magische Flucht." Folklore Fellows Communication no. 92. Helsinki: Academia Scientiarum Fennica, 1930.

Chang, K. C. *Art, Myth, and Ritual*. Cambridge: Harvard University Press, 1983.

Grube, Wilhelm, and Herbert Mueller, trans. *Die Metamorphosen der Goetter*. Leiden: E. J. Brill, 1912.

Liu, Wu-Chi. "The Novel as Folk Epic." In *An Introduction to Chinese Literature*, ed. Wu-chi Liu, pp. 195–212. Bloomington: Indiana University Press, 1966.

Owen, Stephen. "Ne-zha and His Father." In *An Anthology of Chinese Literature*, ed. and trans. Stephen Owen, pp. 771–806. New York: W. W. Norton, 1996. (A translation into English of three episodes of the novel)

Wan, Pin Pin. "Investiture of the Gods (Fengshen Yanyi): Sources, Narrative Structure, and Mythical Significance." Ph.D. dissertation, University of Washington, 1987.

FESTIVAL

An ancient form, a festival occurs annually on a date that marks the seasons, commemorates a religious or historical event, or celebrates an occasion the community has invested with value, such as a homecoming or reunion. The festival provides continuity, but it also fosters and captures change in social and political relations.

Festivals have long provided an important setting for the display of many types of traditional culture.

Festival and literature are beautifully wed when an author re-creates a celebration rich in symbolism and places the characters in that liminal space/time in which the tentative and the possible are transformed into the potent and the powerful. The performance of clowns; the beating of drums; encounters with animals; an excess of food, drink, and noise; cross-dressing and gender switching—all represent the dynamics of festival.

Writers from Aristophanes (*The Thesmophoriazusae*) to William Shakespeare (*A Midsummer Night's Dream*), Angela Carter (*Nights at the Circus*), to Chinua Achebe (*Arrow of God*) and José María Arguedas (*Yawar fiesta*) have recognized the power of festival and the principles of symbolic communication: juxtaposition and hyperbole, inversion and reversal, intensification and condensation, excess and repetition. Enacted in masks, dramas, beauty contests, dances, feasts, rituals, and competitions, these principles lead ultimately to transformations that resolve the conflicts and contradictions the characters experience.

Authors utilize two closely related strategies for invoking the power of festival. In the first, the writer integrates the action of the work with a specific festival performance. Writers who employ the second strategy draw symbols, events, and principles of symbolic communication from the inventory of festival behaviors but the dramatic action does not parallel a specific festival performance. A brilliant example of the latter is Angela Carter's *Nights at the Circus* (1984), a novel whose main character, Fevver, is a woman born with wings. Creating a character that is possible only in the world of liminality, where separate categories can be combined, the author moves this woman-bird into increasingly liminal spaces—from a theater in London to a circus that tours Russia—and finishes up the journey and the novel in Siberia where the characters encounter a shaman.

Larry McMurtry's *Horseman Pass By* (the movie title is *Hud*) utilizes the first strategy. The author builds the action around a rodeo, the festival of cowboy/cattle people, and features the bull as the symbol of male virility. Facing the contradiction inherent in American ideology between inheritance and the self-made man, McMurtry's male characters include a rancher grandfather, a profligate stepson, and an adolescent grandson whose father is dead. The female characters are peripheral to the problem. The cattle develop hoof-and-mouth disease and must be shot, which creates a crisis. The rodeo (a three-day event) begins, and the plot moves toward resolution. At the rodeo, Lonnie, the grandson, learns that Hud has seized the opportunity to take over the ranch and another man's wife. Also at the rodeo, Lonnie's best friend enters the bull-riding event, is injured by the bull, and is immediately hospitalized. Returning to the ranch, Lonnie watches as Hud shoots the grandfather, who wanders on hands and knees under the night sky, having become sick like his cattle. Grandpa, the old bull, is then removed from the scene, and Hud, a young and virile bull, assumes his position. Lonnie, remembering his friend in the hospital, says good-bye to the ranch and hitches a ride out of town with a trucker, leaving Hud to enjoy the spoils of his victory and his new status as the dominant bull. The contradiction between the ideology of the self-made man, who acquires his land and cattle by any means, and that of generational continuity represented by inheritance and the presence of a female has been resolved, leaving discontinuity in the wake of death and chaos.

The incorporation of festival into a literary work permits the author to entertain, inspire, and even disturb the reader by creating a heightened consciousness that guides the reader much as the sound track of a movie or the orchestra of the opera interprets the plot for the audience, revealing the cultural contradictions and announcing the symbolic transformations.

Beverly J. Stoeltje

See also Achebe, Chinua; Carter, Angela; Ritual

✻✻✻✻✻✻✻✻✻✻✻✻✻✻✻✻✻

References

Babcock, Barbara A., ed. *The Reversible World: Symbolic Inversion in Art and Society.* Ithaca, N.Y.: Cornell University Press, 1978.

Cohen, Colleen B., Richard Wilk, and Beverly Stoeltje, eds. *Beauty Queens on the Global Stage: Gender, Contests, and Power.* New York: Routledge, 1996.

Falassi, Alessandro, ed. *Time Out of Time: Essays on the Festival.* Albuquerque: University of New Mexico Press, 1987.

FOLK ETYMOLOGY

Etymology is a recognized, intellectual pursuit within linguistics that seeks for the source and history of words as well as studying the changes in their forms and meanings. Practitioners of the discipline who take the meaning of the term seriously are dismissive of the efforts of untrained but enthusiastic amateurs, describing their work as being of no value and of dealing in popular fallacies. On the other hand, if, as has sometimes been claimed, thinking about and tracing the origins of words is the oldest form of thinking about language, the result of this human preoccupation with words should perhaps not be so easily discarded by those who wish to make etymology exclusively the preserve of academe. After all, the history of certain words would have been very different if the history had not been influenced by what has come to be known as *folk etymology* (German, *Volksetymologie*).

Some relevant English examples are *bridegroom* (Old English *brȳdguma*), through association with the word *groom*; *admiral* (Old French *amiral*, from Arabic *amir*, "commander," as in *Ameer, Emir*), perhaps reinforced through association with *admirable* or *admire*; *sirloin* (Old French *surloigne*, containing the preposition *sur*, "over, above"), under the influence of the English *sir*; *sovereign* (French *souverain*), through connection with *reign; sparrow grass* (common in the seventeenth and eighteenth centuries for *asparagus*); or *sweetheart* (older *sweetard*). One of the most curious instances is possibly *meerschaum pipe* (from the German *Meerschaumpfeife*, a translation of the French *pipe d'écume de mer*, which is a reinterpretation of *Pipe de Kummer*, containing the name of the maker).

As can be seen from these examples, this kind of reshaping of a word—in spelling, pronunciation, or both—occurs most frequently in borrowings from other languages and in English words in which a component has become obsolete (*guma* in *bridegroom*, *-ard* in *sweetheart*). Through association with similar-sounding though etymologically unrelated words, secondary reinterpretation turns a semantically opaque word or element into something seemingly meaningful and therefore usable. This process may obscure the true etymology but explain its modern form.

In contrast to the scientific or academic pursuit of the origins of words, this process has been called *popular* or *folk* etymology, in keeping with the old-fashioned equating of the folk with the uneducated, although many of the so-called folk-etymological explanations can be traced to learned or pseudo-learned speculations. In this respect, folklorists fully support those linguists who prefer the term *associative etymology*, focusing on the process rather than on the cultural register involved.

Even more than in the reinterpretation of words, associative or analogical reshaping takes place in the development of names, particularly place-names, since those names, as the result of their own semantic opacity, tend to be passed on from one language to another with ease. In Scotland, for instance, the place-name *Primrose* in Fife represents an older Celtic *pren rhos* ("tree promontory").

What makes both words and names in this category interesting to the folklorist is the fact that quite frequently stories, however rudimentary, have become attached to them; for instance, the spelling *sirloin* is sometimes given the explanation that an English king knighted the joint. Many of these explanatory stories tend to be highly contrived and not very plausible. The best known example in the United States is probably *Sheboygan*, Wisconsin, which is supposed to have been named when, on the birth of yet another son, a chief was heard to complain, "She boy again." Similarly, in what is now *Owego*, New York, the Native Americans who were expelled from their homes by raids are said to have exclaimed, "Oh we go!" There are many other such stories, many of them humorous, that might well be classified under the heading "local legend" and therefore come into the domain of the folklorist.

The Grimm brothers included in their collection of German *Sagen* several of these etiological narratives concerned with place-names that, on the surface, almost cry out for folk-etymological interpretation: for example, numbers 106, Liebenbach ("stream of love"); 112, Arendsee ("Lake Arend"); 113, Ossenberg ("ox mountain"); 142, Jungfrausprung ("maiden's leap"); and others. Authors of art literature appear to find such folk etymologies particularly attractive; for instance, Archie Hind's novel about Glasgow, *The Dear Green Place* (1966), which reflects the prevailing popular etymology combining elements of the Celtic origins of the name ("green hollow") with components of the legends of St. Mungo, the patron saint of Glasgow.

The fact that the strategies of looking for the "true word" and of providing an etymology through the process of analogical association are occasionally not easily distinguished is demonstrated by the name of an old coaching inn in London, the Elephant and Castle. A linguist took this name to be a folk-etymological reinterpretation of *enfant de Castile,* but that attribution has turned out to be a legend itself. In actuality, the modern name describes the crest of the Cutlers' Company, which depicts an elephant with a howdah in the form of a small castle on its back, an old motif in England.

W. F. H. Nicolaisen

See also Legend

✳✳✳✳✳✳✳✳✳✳✳✳✳✳✳✳✳✳

References

Cox, Barrie. *English Inn and Tavern Names.* Nottingham: Centre for English Name Studies, 1994.

Nicolaisen, W. F. H. "Semantic Causes of Structural Changes in Place Names." *NORNA-rapporter* 34 (1987): 9–19.

———. "Some Humorous Folk-Etymological Narratives." *New York Folklore* 3 (1977): 1–13.

Ross, A. S. C. *Etymology.* London: André Deutsch, 1958.

Schmitt, Rüdiger. *Etymologie.* Darmstadt: Wissenschaftliche Buchgesellschaft, 1977.

Ward, Donald, ed. and trans. *The German Legends of the Brothers Grimm.* 2 vols. Philadelphia: Institute for the Study of Human Issues, 1981.

FOLK RELIGION

Don Yoder defines folk religion as "views and practices of religion that exist among the people apart from and alongside the strictly theological and liturgical forms of the official religion" (Yoder 1974, pp. 2–15). As folk religion exists between official religion and traditional folk culture, it exists in relation to and in tension with organized religions.

Folk religion has as an area of study two roots: The first is described by the German term *religiöse Volkskunde*, which Yoder defines as the religious dimension of folk culture or the folk-cultural dimension of religion. Scholarly interest, however, long preceded the coining of the term, as German folk-cultural scholarship included folk religion in the concept of *Volkskunde*, or folk-cultural scholarship, and early study addressed pilgrimage, hagiography, and religious calendar customs. The second root of the study of folk religion is the anthropological study of syncretism between different forms of religion. It is here that the discussion of the active/creative and passive/survivalist elements of religion began as well as the observation and study of the tension between folk and official levels of religion in a complex society. Folk religion, therefore, includes those aspects that are often unsanctioned or not canonized by an official religion but are practiced as part of the religious experience.

The tension between folk and official religions, as well as survival elements of earlier beliefs and practices, can be seen in the veneration of holy wells in Cornwall and in parts of England, Scotland, and Ireland. Although ostensibly Christian in nature, elements of earlier Celtic practices and beliefs are maintained, as in the leaving of votive offerings and the rituals associated with well visitation and worship. Integrally connected to group membership, such folk beliefs and practices interpret and give meaning to the dogma and ritual of official religion within the daily lives of practitioners and believers.

Folk religious elements have appeared throughout the ages in narratives, tales, novels, plays, and other forms of media, in part because belief is so intrinsic to the human experience. The quest for the Holy Grail in the Arthurian cycle; the works of John Milton, of Thomas Mann, and Umberto Eco's *Foucault's Pendulum*; films like *The Wicker Man*; plays like Brian Friel's *Dancing at Lughnasa*; and contemporary novels of the apocalypse like Neil Gaiman's *Good Omens* are but examples of the literary use of selected aspects of folk religion.

The association between folk religion and literature, however, includes more than the selected use of character and motif. The concept and study of the practice of folk religion have been essential to the study of the Bible and other ancient religious texts. For example, theories of folklore and folk religion, as well as folk literature, were crucial to the work of Herman Gunkel in his efforts to reconstruct the social and cultural milieu and the form and manner of recitation of the oral narrative that preceded the transcription of the Hebrew Bible. This attempt to isolate the *Sitz im Leben* ("situation of life") of the Pentateuch proved formative in the historical study of prose narrative and literary study. Likewise, the study of folk religion has proved significant in the study of ritual and mythology.

Amanda Carson Banks

See also Bible; Frazer, James George; Gunkel, Herman; Ritual; Witchcraft

✳✳✳✳✳✳✳✳✳✳✳✳✳✳✳✳✳

References

Bennett, Gillian. *Traditions of Belief: Women and the Supernatural*. New York: Penguin, 1987.

Farmer, David H. *The Oxford Dictionary of Saints*. Oxford: Clarendon Press, 1978.

Frazer, James George. *The Golden Bough: A Study in Magic and Religion*. 2d ed. London: Macmillan, 1900.

Lawless, Elaine J. *Handmaidens of the Lord: Pentecostal Women Preachers and Traditional Religion*. Philadelphia: University of Pennsylvania Press, 1988.

Yoder, Don. "Toward a Definition of Folk Religion." *Western Folklore* 33 (1974): 2–15.

Folklorism

The sociological term *folklorism*, a translation of the German *Folklorismus*, was introduced into folklore studies by Hans Moser in 1962. It first comprised (1) performance of traditionally and functionally determined elements of folk culture outside that culture's local or class community, (2) playful imitation of folk motifs in another social stratum, and (3) the purposeful invention and creation of "folk-like" elements outside any tradition. Later Moser added the notion of *Rücklauf* ("flowing back"), which means the spread among nonscholars ("the folk") of obsolescent interpretations of folklore by scholars. The supposedly pure Elizabethan speech of southern mountain folk in the United States has been put into the consciousness of local people by *Rücklauf*.

If folklore is separate from nonfolklore, then folklorism is the name for the movement from one to the other. It entails shifts in setting, audience, and genre. *The Old Wives Tale* (1592), a comedy by George Peele, nostalgically dramatizes traditional narratives for a London theater audience: the setting for folktale performance changes from hearth to stage, the audience enlarges, and a script and actors replace solo narration. Ben Jonson's *Bartholomew Fair* (1614), by contrast, is folklorism without nostalgia. The play puts a popular festival onstage, and shaped by the events of the fair, the action lasts for a single, specific day—August 24. Thus, Jonson used the pseudo-Aristotelian unities (time, place, and action) to frame a public event into a theatrical representation. In American literature, "The Celebrated Jumping Frog of Calaveras County" (1865) is an oral tale that Mark Twain put into print as a short story. He thus removed it from its local or class community and enlarged its audience. He transformed its genre from oral anecdote to written story, and by framing the frog anecdote with a larger story, Twain also depicted for a reading audience the oral style of a folk narrator. Because Jonson and Twain are canonical writers, their versions of folklorism are often interpreted as a move from lower to higher strata of culture.

The movement from folklore to nonfolklore may be named *folklorization*. American poetry anthologies contain a quatrain by Gelett Burgess (1866–1951):

> I never saw a Purple Cow,
> I never hope to see one;
> But I can tell you, anyhow,
> I'd rather see than be one!

Informants have asserted that they learned the verses orally from their parents before Burgess was born. The verses have been folklorized.

Is folklorism equivalent to inauthenticity? The hope persists that a folklorist will finally declare why the Scottish ballad "Sir Patrick Spens" is authentic and literary imitations of it are not. But when Samuel Taylor Coleridge is the imitator, or when the most anthologized text of the ballad turns out to have been much altered by "nonfolk" editors, authentication becomes problematic. Because they are an inevitable part of the constant recontextualizing of cultural products, both folklorism and folklorization are dynamic, unceasing cultural processes.

Ramifications of folklorism are documented in an anthology by James R. Dow and Hannjost Lixfeld (1986) and a critique of the Festival of American Folklife by Robert Cantwell (1993).

Lee Haring

See also Fakelore; Twain, Mark

✳✳✳✳✳✳✳✳✳✳✳✳✳✳✳✳✳

References

Bendix, Regina. "Folklorism: The Challenge of a Concept." *International Folklore Review* 6 (1988): 5–15.

Cantwell, Robert. *Ethnomimesis: Folklife and the Representation of Culture*. Chapel Hill: University of North Carolina Press, 1993.

Dow, James R., and Hannjost Lixfeld, eds. and trans. *German Volkskunde: A Decade of Theoretical Confrontation, Debate, and Reorientation (1967–1977)*. Folklore Studies in Translation. Bloomington: Indiana University Press, 1986.

FOLKTALE

A folktale is a traditional fictional narrative told primarily for entertainment. "Traditional" means "handed on," and a folktale is manifested in different texts (called variants) of the same story. As a genre, folktale is distinct from myth, epic, legend, and ballad. However, when a story that is mythic or legendary in one context is fictional in another, or when the same story is traditionally conveyed both in prose and in verse, it is often advantageous for the researcher to cross genre boundaries.

Folktales are classified as simple when they relate to a single incident and as complex when they are composed of a series of episodes. In Antii Aarne and Stith Thompson's classification of folktales in *The Types of the Folktale* (1964), simple tales include animal tales (in which animals are the main characters and act similarly to humans) and humorous anecdotes. Complex tales include fairy tales and romantic tales (called novelle; these have no magical motifs). Tales about confrontations with ogres may consist either of a single episode or of several episodes joined together. There are also complex humorous tales, in which two (or more) episodes are strung together or in which a frame story surrounds one or more inset episodes. Simple tales vary only in their detail motifs; variants of complex tales can differ from each other both in details and in composition. Many scholars used to assume that a record of a part of a tale implied the existence of the whole tale; now, an awareness of structure can help to distinguish between an entire complex tale and one or more of its parts.

The telling of tales for entertainment is very old. Fictional tales that are probably traditional appear in some of the earliest written records from ancient Sumeria and Egypt. In ancient Greece, Homer's *Odyssey* and Herodotus's *History* contain episodes that have been subsequently found as tales in oral tradition, and Asian literature also contains ancient examples of folktales.

When stories are learned and performed orally, this affects both their style and their structure. The characters speak and act rather than think. Long tales are episodic: they are composed of scenes (developed through action or dialogue) linked together by comparatively dry passages. Repetition of speech or of action adds both length and suspense. A tale, or a particular form of a tale, that is very popular is usually also well balanced and aesthetically pleasing. When parts of two tales are joined together, inconsistencies (of motivation, of logistics, etc.) sometimes develop.

Although people in all cultures tell stories, there are evident regional preferences for different forms of tales. However, some folktales, and many more components of folktales such as motifs and episodes, are popular across several continents.

Christine Goldberg

See also Fairy Tale; Homer; *Märchen*; Motif; *Odyssey*; Tale-Type

✳✳✳✳✳✳✳✳✳✳✳✳✳✳✳✳✳✳

References

Aarne, Antii, and Stith Thompson. *The Types of the Folktale: A Classification and Bibliography.* Folklore Fellows Communication no. 184. Helsinki: Academia Scientiarum Fennica, 1964.

Dorson, Richard M., ed. *Folktales Told around the World.* Chicago: University of Chicago Press, 1975.

Fabula: Zeitschrift für Erzählforschung. Berlin and New York: Walter De Gruyter, 1957– .

Ranke, Kurt, et al., eds. *Enzyklopädie des Märchens.* Berlin: Walter De Gruyter, 1977– .

Thompson, Stith. *The Folktale.* New York: Dryden Press, 1946.

FOLKTALE ADAPTATIONS

Folktale adaptations from oral tradition to other forms of expression, notably print and film, have been made for more than three centuries. The people who are the most consistently associated with folktale adaptations are Charles Perrault in the seventeenth century, the Grimm brothers and Hans Christian Andersen in the nineteenth century, and Walt Disney in the twentieth century.

When Charles Perrault rewrote eight French folktales in 1697, he began a pattern of adapting oral material to other media. The success of his modest collection inspired literary imitations by his contemporaries, notably Mmes. Marie d'Aulnoy, Gabrille-Suzanne de Villeneuve, and Marie Leprince de Beaumont. The stories in these compilations were intended to amuse the French court, and they were generally more sentimental and more elaborately stylistic than the oral tales. They were not necessarily intended for children.

In 1812, Wilhelm and Jacob Grimm, searching for a romanticized Teutonic past, published the first edition of their German folktale collection. They claimed to have taken all of their stories from "the very lips of the folk," but in fact they copied down outlines of stories and rewrote them to suit their view of proper folktale style. They combined various stories and added, altered, or omitted elements that did not meet their standards. Cruel mothers, for example, were often changed to stepmothers. Some of the tales—"Snow White," for example—were rewritten for each new edition of the tales from 1812 through the 1850s. Adults were the initial readers of the Grimm tales, though their collections soon came to be regarded as children's reading. The tales were translated and spread throughout Europe and eventually throughout the world, inspiring collectors in other countries to gather and adapt their own tales.

Hans Christian Andersen began writing his own stories in the 1820s. The earliest tales were very loosely based on a few Danish folktales he remembered from his own childhood; others shared folktale-like motifs (magical objects, characters, and situations). They were all, however, his original creations. Some of his more popular stories—like "The Ugly Duckling," "The Little Mermaid," and "The Red Shoes"—became so well known that they are popularly assumed to be authentic folktales, but his stories are generally more self-consciously sentimental or melodramatic than are traditional tales.

In the twentieth century, Walt Disney Productions released several animated films based on those popularized by Perrault and his imitators (*Cinderella, Sleeping Beauty, Beauty and the Beast*), the Grimm brothers (*Snow White and the Seven Dwarfs*), and Andersen (*The Little Mermaid*). One film (*Aladdin*) came from the classic literary collection *The Arabian Nights*. Disney also produced humorous versions of *The Three Little Pigs* and *Jack and the Beanstalk*. All of the films featured stylistic elements that came to characterize "the Disney version": exaggerated terror tempered by preciousness or humor, an emphasis on the sentimental and romantic, an abundance of charming animals and inanimate objects.

Folktales have also inspired adaptations by composers of operas and ballets, writers of short stories and novels, poets like Anne Sexton, and creators of popular jokes and cartoons. All of these genres still rely heavily on the most popular stories of Perrault, the brothers Grimm, and Andersen.

In recent decades, popular collections have been readapted for oral performance. Early in the twentieth century, professional storytellers began retelling printed folktales to young listeners in schools and libraries across North America. Generally the stories were retold word-for-word as they appeared in print, though library tellers had specific training in oral techniques to make their storytelling more compelling. Professional storytelling began to expand beyond schools and libraries in the 1970s, spreading to adult listeners in formal and informal settings. By the 1990s, informal storytelling groups, concerts, and annual story festivals were widespread. Adaptations by amateur and professional performers range from unadorned storytelling to full-scale theatrical pieces. Tellers still draw on Perrault, Grimm, and Andersen, but many have expanded their repertoires to include adapted folktales from around the world.

Kay Stone

See also Andersen, Hans Christian; Disney, Walter Elias; Grimm, Jacob and Wilhelm; Perrault, Charles; Storytelling

✳✳✳✳✳✳✳✳✳✳✳✳✳✳✳✳✳✳

References

Dégh, Linda. *American Folklore in the Mass Media.* Bloomington: Indiana University Press, 1994.

Mieder, Wolfgang. *Disenchantments: An Anthology of Modern Fairy Tale Poetry.* Hanover, N.H.: University Press of New England, 1985.

Sexton, Anne. *Transformations.* Boston: Houghton Mifflin, 1971.

Stone, Kay. "Burning Brightly: New Light on an Old Tale." In *Feminist Messages: Coding in Women's Folk Culture,* ed. Joan Radner, pp. 289–305. Urbana: University of Illinois Press, 1993.

FOOL IN CHRIST

Iurodivyi Khrista radi, or simply, *iurodivyi* (variously translated as "fool in Christ," "holy fool," "blessed fool"), was a unique character in the social life of Muscovy and, later, of Imperial Russia. He was usually a wandering holy man whose behavior combined Christian and shamanic features. It was believed that he (occasionally, she) pretended to be mad for humility's sake and that he was exceptionally pious and clairvoyant. Many fools in Christ wore a variety of metal objects on their bodies, a custom traceable to the Buriat shamans who sometimes wore as much as 30 pounds of iron, including iron headgear. The state of high nervous tension in which most fools in Christ lived is also traceable to shamanic customs.

Among the thousands of fools in Christ, a few have been canonized, but most have been looked upon critically by the authorities of the Russian Orthodox Church. The same was not true of the general population, including some clergy, who believed that fools in Christ knew the short road to the supernatural. Both village and manor revered their *iurodivyi,* as is shown in Leo Tolstoy's book *Childhood* (1852). The most famous of the Russian churches, the Cathedral of Basil the Blessed on Red Square, is named after a sixteenth-century *iurodivyi*.

Under Alexander I (1801–1825), social life in St. Petersburg abounded in "seances" centered around fools in Christ who were invited to prophesy. Some of the invitees were clearly demented; others were perhaps clever cheaters trying to make a living. The most famous of these seances were held in a salon run by a noblewoman, E. F. Tatarinova, who was eventually sentenced to imprisonment in a convent for her inordinate devotion to what sober churchmen considered to be a remnant of paganism. Among Moscow's holy fools in the mid-nineteenth century, the most famous was Ivan Koreisha, who lived in a mental hospital but attracted throngs of visitors of all social classes. Similar, though less famous, fools in Christ crowded the Russian provinces. The custom of holy fools persisted, not only among the Russian Orthodox, but also among the schismatic Old Believers, as evidenced by P. I. Melnikov-Pecherskii's novel *Na gorakh* [In the highlands]. Grigory Rasputin was perhaps the last famous *iurodivyi* of Imperial Russia.

Those fools in Christ who have been canonized by the Russian Orthodox Church usually date back to the Kievan period and were declared saints, not for their early exploits as *iurodivyi,* but for their later achievements. For instance, Kiriil of Beloozero and Avraamii of Smolensk were fools in Christ in their youth but later settled into a less spectacular monkish existence, and they were recognized for their work on behalf of their monasteries.

Russian literature amply reflects the social phenomenon of fools in Christ. The Old Russian and Ruthenian *Chronicles* record the names of many of them. Aleksandr Pushkin's *Boris Godunov* introduces a fool in Christ playing a superpatriotic role, as does Nicolay Zagoskin's *Yurii Mikoslavsky*. Leo Tolstoy, Nikolay Nekrasov, Nikolay Mikhaylovsky, Dmitry Merezhkovsky, and many others portrayed fools in Christ in their novels, stories, poems, and plays. Interestingly, Fyodor Dostoyevsky, whose attitude to Russian social customs was often uncritical, did not idealize fools in Christ in his novels but presented them as mentally retarded individuals.

It can be argued that the phenomenon of "foolishness in Christ," with its dual roots in St. Paul's famous admonition and in the shamanic habits of the Turkic tribes who have inhabited a good portion of the territory called Russia, has had a major influence on Russian social customs and that the habits and behavior of certain Russian revolutionaries, such as Sergey Nechayev and Peter Tkachev, reflected the high esteem accorded to the holy fools of Old Russia. The drawing of parallels between social customs and political behavior is, however, a risky venture, and the methodology of doing so is yet to be worked out.

Ewa M. Thompson

See also Pre-Soviet Prose and Folklore in Russia

****

References

Moszyński, Kazimierz. *Kultura ludowa Słowian* [Folk culture of the Slavs]. 3 vols. Warsaw: Ksiażka i Wiedza, 1968.

Pope, R. W. F. "Fools and Folly in Old Russia." *Slavic Review* 39 (1980): 476–481.

Thompson, Ewa M. *Understanding Russia: The Holy Fool in Russian Culture*. Lanham, N.Y., and London: University Press of America, 1987.

FORMULA TALE

Formula tales are distinguished from other folk narrative genres by their specific structure. For this reason, they did not meet the criteria for Antti Aarne's first (German) compilation of *Märchentypen* [The types of the folktale (1910)], which was largely based on the categorization of narrative substance such as aspects of actors, action, and the means by which actors, both protagonists and antagonists, are able to influence the outcome of an action. Formula tales, as a separate though small category, appeared for the first time in Stith Thompson's revised (English) edition of Aarne's index (1928), in which they are given high numbers (AT 2000–2340) in the system; these are more fully detailed in the second revised edition (1964). Concomitantly, motifs commonly found in formula tales were assigned numbers under the last letter of the alphabet (Z0–Z99) in Thompson's *Motif Index of Folk Literature* (1955–1958). If their severe structural patterning is ignored, many of the formula tales might be appropriately classified according to other criteria that are more frequently applied in the *Tale Type Index,* like "animal tales" or "numskull stories." The codification of formula tales owes much to Archer Taylor.

Since the chief characteristics of formula tales are repetition (sometimes incremental) and cumulation, their largest subcategory consists of "cumulative tales," in which a series of repetitive units are linked by the device of the "chain," as, for instance, "chains based on numbers of objects" (AT 2000–2013), "chains involving contractions or extremes" (AT 2014), "chains involving a wedding" (AT 2019–2020), "chains involving death" (AT 2021–2024), "chains involving the eating of an object" (AT 2025–2029), "chains of accidents" (AT 2042), etc. Other significant subcategories are the "catch tales" (AT 2200–2205), the "unfinished tales" (AT 2250–2299), and the "endless tales" (AT 2300). The internal chaining of events plays such an important role in the concept of formula tales that these are often termed "chain tales" (German, *Kettenmärchen*). In the limited secondary literature on the formula tale, the so-called clock tale (German, *Ringerzählung*) has received particular attention; in this subgenre, with its clocklike sequential movement, the ultimate responsibility for a crime comes back to rest with the original accuser.

Some of the best known formula tales in the English language are, with numerous variants, "Good News and Bad News from the Wedding" (AT 2014A), "The Cow That Wouldn't Stand Still" (AT

2016), "The Flea and the Louse" (AT 2022), "The Fleeing Pancake" or "The Wee Bannock" (AT 2025), "The Old Woman and Her Pig" (AT 2030), "Henny Penny" (AT 2033), "The House That Jack Built" (AT 2035), and "Who Blowed up the Church House" (AT 2300).

Closely related to the formula tale are the equally well-loved, often humorous, and sometimes bawdy cumulative songs like "The Woman Who Swallowed a Fly," "There's a Hole in Your Bucket, Dear Lisa," "The Derby Ram," "The Herrin's the King of the Sea," and the carol "The Twelve Days of Christmas." In fact, some of these stories are traditionally known in both spoken and sung versions.

Although they have been given quite successful literary or art treatment at times, both formula tales and cumulative songs are at their most enjoyable and effective when they have been lifted off the page into performance, involving the audience when appropriate. Their continuing popularity can undoubtedly be, at least partially, ascribed to such actual or mental audience participation.

W. F. H. Nicolaisen

See also Motif; Performance; Tale-Type; Taylor, Archer; Thompson, Stith

❋❋❋❋❋❋❋❋❋❋❋❋❋❋❋❋❋

References

Haavio, Martti. *Kettenmärchenstudien I*. Folklore Fellows Communications no. 88. Helsinki: Academia Scientiarum Fennica, 1929.

———. *Kettenmärchenstudien II*. Folklore Fellows Communications no. 99. Helsinki: Academia Scientiarum Fennica, 1932.

Leach, Maria, ed. *Funk and Wagnalls Standard Dictionary of Folklore, Mythology, and Legend*. New York: Funk and Wagnalls, 1972. See especially pp. 207–208, 268–269, and 412.

Taylor, Archer. "A Classification of Formula Tales." *Journal of American Folklore* 46 (1933): 77–88.

Thompson, Stith. *The Folktale*. New York: Holt, Rinehart and Winston, 1946, pp. 229–234.

FORREST, LEON (1937–)

Leon Forrest is an African-American novelist and essayist whose novels present a complex portrait of African-American life and culture. Taken together, his novels constitute the "Forest County series," being set in a mythical county of that name based on the African-American section of Chicago.

The series of four novels offers a rich representation of African-American folk culture in the urban North and provides insight into the evolution of this culture from that of the rural South and from the African cultures the slaves brought with them. Forrest's novels are notable for their use of oral folk genres such as the sermon, legend, and tall tale as well as elements of folk music and jazz. These aspects of folk culture pervade both style and structure in his work. In addition, Forrest's novels make extensive use of mythic archetypes in the manner of many modern novels, linking the patterns of African and Greek mythology to his epic presentations of contemporary African-American culture. He has been particularly influenced by three major literary figures: James Joyce, William Faulkner, and Ralph Ellison.

Forrest's novels also garner attention for their portrayal of the interplay between different streams of African-American culture. Several of his novels represent the confluence in the northern city of the sophisticated Catholic culture of Creole New Orleans and the vigorous Protestant culture of rural Mississippi. Because of this interplay of cultures, his novels are often very dense in style and sometimes difficult to interpret. However, the very complexity and richness of his understanding of urban folk culture make this intensity of style both necessary and valuable.

Like most African-American authors, Forrest's central theme is the predicament of African Americans in white America and the impact of deracination, racism, and exploitation on their culture. However, unlike writers who emphasize the tragedy of slavery and racism, Forrest's emphasis is on the way in which African Americans have created a meaningful and vital folk culture in spite of the obstructions to cultural creativity that their historical situation has created. Forrest is particularly interested in what he calls *reinvention*, the ways a people, continually cut off from their cultural heritage by historical oppression, manage to improvise and re-create an authentic culture from the materials available to them. African Americans, for example, created a new and vital kind of religion from the materials of southern Protestantism infused with attenuated memories of diverse African rituals. This emphasis on cultural rejuvenation gives Forrest's novels a particularly vibrant quality.

The novels are very different in subject and structure. *There Is a Tree More Ancient Than Eden* explores the dialectic between individual experience and historical and cultural memory in shaping the consciousness of a young African-American male. This is the most experimental of Forrest's works in structure. *The Bloodworth Orphans* is a family saga that makes use of the mythical archetypes of orphaning, estrangement, and sacrifice to analyze the tragic deracination of African Americans. *Two Wings to Veil My Face* is a story of slave times and of the complex relationships of dependence and revolt, hate and love between masters and slaves that have left such an ambiguous cultural heritage for African Americans in the twentieth century. Finally, *Divine Days* is a work of epic dimensions that portrays a gifted young African American's quest for a way to assimilate and reinvent the many conflicting voices he encounters in the urban African-American world of the later twentieth century.

Some of Forrest's nonfiction work also relates to folklore study. In particular, his essays on Billie Holiday and Elijah Muhammad are notable for their insight into important aspects of African-American culture.

John Cawelti

See also Archetype; Ellison, Ralph; Faulkner, William; Legend; Tall Tale

✳✳✳✳✳✳✳✳✳✳✳✳✳✳✳✳✳

References

Byerman, Keith. *Fingering the Jagged Grain: Tradition and Form in Recent Black Fiction*. Athens: University of Georgia Press, 1985.

Cawelti, John G., ed. *Leon Forrest: Introductions and Interpretations*. Bowling Green, Ohio: Bowling Green State University Popular Press, 1997.

Forrest, Leon. "In the Light of the Likeness—Transformed." *Contemporary Authors Autobiography Series* vol. 7. Detroit: Gale Research, 1988.

FRAME TALE

A frame tale is a fictional narrative surrounding other shorter tales and depicts a series of stories whose narrators are characters in the frame. Although frame tales vary in length and complexity, they all provide a context for reading, listening to, and interpreting their interior tales. A frame tale derives its meaning primarily from what it contains and cannot stand independent of the tales enclosed within it. The interpolated tales, taken from both folk and literary traditions, can appear independently, however, or in a different frame with a different connotation.

Frame tales have also been called "boxing tales," or "stories within stories." The genre appears to have been an Eastern invention; it most probably originated in India where it can be traced back at least three millennia. By the tenth century, it had reached the Near East and, by the twelfth, Europe. The frame tale reached the height of its popularity in Europe in the fourteenth century and had faded in most areas by the early Renaissance.

Some of the best known and most studied frame tales are the Sanskrit *Panchatantra*, the Persian *Tuti-Nameh*, the Arabic *Alf Layla wa-Layla* (*The Thousand Nights and a Night*); *Kalila wa-Dimna*, an Arabic version of the *Panchatantra*; the many versions of the *Book of Sindibad* and *Seven Sages of Rome*; Petrus Alfonsi's *Disciplina clericalis*; Juan Manuel's *Conde Lucanor*; Giovanni Boccaccio's *Decameron*; Marguerite de Navarre's *Heptameron*; John Gower's *Confessio Amantis*; and Geoffrey Chaucer's *Canterbury Tales*. Certain wisdom books or "mirrors for princes" may also be included in a broad definition of the frame tale.

Most of the earlier frame tales are of anonymous authorship and most likely descend from an oral storytelling tradition. Later texts, particularly those in the European tradition, have named authors but still draw heavily on both oral traditions and earlier literary texts. Different frame tales may have interpolated tales in common. For example, tales that are in Boccaccio's or Chaucer's works may have appeared earlier in *The Thousand Nights and a Night* or the *Seven Sages of Rome*. Stories in common among frame tales have led some people to draw conclusions about medieval authors reading earlier texts. Frame tales in both oral and written form could transmit tales across linguistic and cultural boundaries; however, which frame tale a particular author might have read or heard is difficult to determine.

The frame tale depicts the oral storytelling tradition and works as a bridge between oral and literate narrative. Framed collections, for example, present traditional tales to a literate audience and cover a spectrum from primarily diverting to primarily didactic. An audience is written into the frame tale, which allows an author or a compiler to guide the readers' interpretation. Different frame tales thereby contain different narrator/audience dynamics. Some have a sole narrator of the interpolated tales, reminiscent of the storytelling style of teachers and parents; others have several narrators, thus leading to an agonistic environment characteristic of public story-telling. A frame tale is thus a self-reflexive form, a story about story-telling in all its variety.

Bonnie D. Irwin

See also Boccaccio, Giovanni; Chaucer, Geoffrey; *Decameron*; *Panchatantra*; *The Thousand and One Nights*

✻✻✻✻✻✻✻✻✻✻✻✻✻✻✻✻✻✻

References

Belcher, Stephen. "Framed Tales in the Oral Tradition: An Exploration." *Fabula* 35 (1994): 1–19.

Clements, Robert J., and Joseph Gibaldi. *Anatomy of the Novella: The European Tale Collection from Boccaccio to Cervantes*. New York: New York University Press, 1977.

Irwin, Bonnie D. "What's in a Frame?: The Medieval Textualization of Traditional Storytelling." *Oral Tradition* 10 (1995): 27–53.

Pinnault, David. *Story-Telling Techniques in the Arabian Nights*. Leiden: E. J. Brill, 1992.

Potter, Joy Hambuechen. *Five Frames for the* Decameron: *Communication and Social Systems in the* Cornice. Princeton, N.J.: Princeton University Press, 1982.

Frazer, James George (1854–1941)

Born in Glasgow, Sir James George Frazer was educated there and at Trinity College, Cambridge, where he for many years held a fellowship. His best known work is *The Golden Bough* (1890), which was enormously influential in British and American literature in the early years of the twentieth century. Frazer, however, also wrote widely on mythology, religion, and classics and left a legacy of great importance in those fields.

Frazer edited several Greek and Latin works that remain essential for the study of classical mythology and religion. The first of these was his great edition and commentary of Pausanias's *Description of Greece* (1897). The *Description* describes many of the sites of Greek cults and their beliefs and customs, and Frazer, coming to it after the first edition of his *The Golden Bough*, used comparisons to the customs and beliefs of a variety of the world's peoples—modern, medieval, and ancient—to explain those of the Greeks. In addition, Frazer made a research journey to Greece to visit the sites, making him, contrary to what is commonly believed, one of the few Victorian anthropologists to have actually done fieldwork.

His edition of Ovid's *Fasti* (1931), an account of the Roman holidays, is another fundamental edition of an important work on classical mythology and religion in which Frazer draws extensively from anthropology and folklore for his commentary, as he does in his Loeb Classical Library edition of Appollodorus's *The Library* (1921). Frazer was one of the first to draw extensively on modern anthropology and folklore to illuminate classical texts—a particularly striking innovation in the very conservative world of classical studies of his time, though, as Robert Ackerman notes, Frazer's innovations "must have irritated a large part of his traditionally minded audience" (Ackerman 1987, p. 129).

Frazer wrote on an enormous variety of topics in addition to his classical work, resulting in important studies like *Folklore in the Old Testament* (1919), *Totemism* (1887), and his study of superstition, *Psyche's Task* (1909). The influence of Frazer's work, especially in the early years of the twentieth century, was widespread in ethnography and literature. Among those influenced were the Cambridge ritualists Bronislaw Malinowski and Joseph Campbell as well as W. B. Yeats, T. S. Eliot, and many other writers. But, even though Frazer had a great influence on the fields of folklore, anthropology, and classical studies, this influence is usually forgotten or minimized today. That situation is unfortunate, for although his work often seems to lose itself in its endless examples, it still repays reading for its literary power and for its insights into magic, religion, and mythology.

David E. Gay

See also *The Golden Bough*; Myth

✳✳✳✳✳✳✳✳✳✳✳✳✳✳✳✳✳✳

References

Ackerman, Robert. *J. G. Frazer: His Life and Work*. Cambridge: Cambridge University Press, 1987.

Frazer, Sir James George. *The New Golden Bough*. Ed. Theodor H. Gaster. New York: Criterion, 1959.

FREUD, SIGMUND (1856–1939)

Sigmund Freud, a Viennese physician, created psychoanalysis and has since become a modern culture hero. The classical psychoanalytic method for interpreting myths, which treats the tales as though they were dreams, was attributed by Freud to Karl Abraham. Freud corroborated Abraham's theory by demonstrating the reciprocal influences of dreams and tales. An essay, "Dreams in Folklore," which Freud wrote in 1911 with the collaboration of the classicist David Ernst Oppenheim, was published posthumously in 1958. Freud published "The Occurrence in Dreams of Material from Fairy Tales" in 1913, and he subsequently used Abraham's method both in passing and in several essays: "The Theme of the Three Caskets" (1913), "A Mythological Parallel to a Visual Obsession" (1916), "The Acquisition and Control of Fire" (1932), and "Medusa's Head" (1940).

Freud also used a second method for interpreting myths. Building on Ludwig Feuerbach's claim that "theology is really anthropology," Freud maintained that "a large part of the mythological view of the world, which extends a long way into the most modern religions, *is nothing but psychology projected into the external world*" (Freud 1960, p. 258). Freud's procedure, which translated "metaphysics into metapsychology," led him to treat the classical Greek legend of Oedipus as a projection of the complex of unconscious fantasies characteristic of boys from age four to five and a half years. Similarly, Freud suggested that the capacity to seek delayed gratification, the developmental acquisition of which is first consolidated upon the resolution of the Oedipus complex, was the basis for the doctrine of reward in the afterlife.

Freud also saw confirmation of the theory that all people are unconsciously bisexual in Aristophanes's myth (in Plato's *Symposium*) that human beings were originally eight-limbed, two-headed, double-torsoed, bisexual creatures but were anciently divided into two halves that have sought their reunion ever since. In similar fashion, Freud's extension of the concept of sexuality was inspired by a demythicizing of Jewish mysticism while German romanticism furnished the metaphysical conceptions that Freud reworked as the theory of the unconscious and the dualistic conflict model of the psychical apparatus. Following the introduction of Abraham's method, Freud's technique of translating mythological tales into psychical complexes was abandoned by Freudians. The procedure was adopted, however, by Carl G. Jung and has since been perpetuated by the Jungian tradition.

Dan Merkur

See also Jung, Carl Gustav; Oedipus

✳✳✳✳✳✳✳✳✳✳✳✳✳✳✳✳✳

References

Bakan, David. *Sigmund Freud and the Jewish Mystical Tradition*. Princeton, N.J.: D. Van Nostrand Company, 1958.

Freud, Sigmund. "The Psychopathology of Everyday Life." In *The Complete Psychological Works of Sigmund Freud*, vol. 6, ed. James Strachey, pp. 1–279. London: Hogarth Press, 1960.

Merkur, Dan. "Mythology into Metapsychology: Freud's Misappropriation of Romanticism." *Psychoanalytic Study of Society* 18 (1993): 345–360.

GAINES, ERNEST J. (1933–)

Born in Oscar, Louisiana, the African-American novelist, short-story writer, and user of folklore Ernest J. Gaines portrays African-American culture in rural southern Louisiana and its interactions with the Creole and Cajun cultures. Gaines's fiction, which is typically set in the ex-slave quarters of plantations, incorporates the forms of African-American oral tradition and storytelling as well as influences from the blues and jazz traditions. Folk culture, customs, beliefs, and speech are integral parts of his writing. Gaines, who has to date published six novels and a collection of short stories, is best known for the novel *The Autobiography of Miss Jane Pittman* (1971).

Gaines is particularly good at rendering speech patterns: he credits black oral tradition and blues singing as great influences on his style, particularly his use of indirection, repetition, and understatement. In addition, Gaines was inspired by Lightnin' Hopkins's blues song, "Mr. Tim Moore's Farm," to write the novel *Of Love and Dust* (1967). The narrator, Jim Kelly, is a guitar player, and the blues tradition influences his performance, both as musician and as storyteller. Marcus, the protagonist, has been compared to Stagolee, the bad man of black folklore.

The narrative voice in Gaines's fiction is often based on folk memory of the past. Gaines uses the slave narrative form in *The Autobiography of Miss Jane Pittman*, a novel framed as a life story told by a 108-year-old ex-slave and recorded by a black history teacher during the civil rights movement of the 1960s. Gaines has referred to this novel as a "folk autobiography." It presents memory of the past that is typical of ex-slave narratives and includes such things as emancipation celebrations and naming ceremonies. It also includes such folk practices and beliefs as jumping over the broom as a marriage ceremony and advice from a hoodoo woman, said to have been a rival of Marie Laveau in New Orleans. Miss Jane's admiration for Huey Long and her explanation of his death reflect folk belief and oral tradition in Louisiana.

The influence of oral storytelling is evident in Gaines's fiction, particularly in his use of first-person narrators and forms from oral tradition. The novel *A Gathering of Old Men* (1983) and "Just Like a Tree," a story in *Bloodline* (1968), use multiple first-person narrators to create the effect of communal oral storytelling, each narrator telling part of the story until the story line is picked up by the next narrator. The title "Just Like a Tree" is from a Negro spiritual: "Just like a tree standing side the water / I shall not be moved." In addition, Gaines incorporates folk forms and motifs in the other *Bloodline* stories. In "Three Men," his character, Munford, tells a tall tale about a preacher who tried to emasculate him in his cradle ("This preacher going 'Mumbo-jumbo, mumbo-jumbo,' but all the time he's low'ing his mouth toward my little privates"). In "The Sky Is Gray," a faith healer or *traiteur* (Monsieur Bayonne) tries to heal a toothache, and in "A Long Day in November," a hoodoo lady gives advice to a young husband who is estranged from his wife.

Gaines often uses southern Louisiana foodways in his fiction. Foods such as gumbo, red beans with rice, baked sweet potatoes, clabber, and pralines, as well as rituals of food preparation, help to situate the cultural context of his works. In *A Lesson before Dying* (1993), foodways are also important thematically, both as symbols of love and caring and as sources of power and control.

Marcia Gaudet

See also Storytelling

****

References

Babb, Valerie Melissa. *Ernest Gaines*. Boston: Twayne Publishers, 1991.

Estes, David C., ed. *Critical Reflections on the Fiction of Ernest J. Gaines*. Athens: University of Georgia Press, 1994.

Gaudet, Marcia, and Carl Wooton. *Porch Talk with Ernest Gaines: Conversations on the Writer's Craft*. Baton Rouge: Louisiana State University Press, 1990.

Rowell, Charles, ed. *Ernest Gaines*. Special Issue of *Callaloo*. 1 (1978).

García Márquez, Gabriel (1926–)

A world-renowned Latin-American author from Aracataca, Colombia, Gabriel García Márquez is best known for the magical realism in his Nobel Prize–winning novel, *One Hundred Years of Solitude* (1967). The magical realism undergirding his literary universé is in turn permeated with numerous folklore genres, which unites García Márquez with numerous world-class authors, such as Miguel de Cervantes and William Shakespeare, who have cleverly woven folklore items into their literary works. The Latin-American writer and his works clearly exemplify the close relationship between folklore and literature and the manner in which literary geniuses avail themselves of oral traditions to fashion works of art that achieve international recognition.

The term *magical realism* may be defined as an artistic literary style through which the real and the nonreal coexist in harmony. It is a style that erases the borders separating reality from the magical, the supernatural, the fantastic, the nonreal. In García Márquez's books, the world inhabited by the characters is phantasmagoric, but at the same time, it has a solid infrastructure of historical reality. The people are real although they may possess uncanny traits, such as the ability to communicate with the dead. The dead, on the other hand, are able to transgress the laws of nature and return to the world of the living. The living are endowed with extraordinary powers: foretelling the future, unimaginable physical and sexual prowess, the ability to levitate, and so forth.

In García Márquez's representation of a small Latin-American town, the fictive village of Macondo, folklore is a basic ingredient in the construction of the place. Analysis of the author's works provides insight into how folkloric material plays an important role in the construction of his novels and short stories. For example, folklore is used (1) as a source of humor, (2) as a source of fantastic elements and in the construction of fantastic scenes, (3) as structural and thematic sources for the construction of circular time, (4) as linguistic structural models—that is, the structure of the folktale, the legend, etc., is used to configure short stories or scenes in his novels—and (5) as purveyors of culture.

For humorous purposes, proverbs, exaggerations, and comparisons are excellent one-liners to produce comical effects. Folk remedies, likewise, play an important role in the development of humor. The folk remedies appearing in *One Hundred Years of Solitude* are particularly funny to the contemporary reader who is versed in present scientific medical techniques. For example, when the recurrently migrating gypsies arrive, they bring with them all kinds of pseudoscientific apparatus that apparently serves to cure different maladies.

The fantastic, surrealistic, phantasmagoric episode is another trademark of García Márquez's writings, and folklore is again employed to enhance and develop this particular aspect of his work. The author's use of folkloric material for the purpose of producing the fantastic and the extraordinary in his short stories and novels is characterized by two different techniques. One of his favorite techniques is to take a folk motif from oral tradition and develop it into a literary work of art. In the second instance, the Colombian author intersperses folk motifs throughout the literary work. He does this not by just sprinkling the motifs without a preconceived plan, but with a carefully laid-out structure in which the folk items are an integral part of the literary infrastructure—for example, to construct the circular nature of time.

Some of the fantastic motifs García Márquez has utilized for plot development include supernatural beings such as revenants, death, the devil, a ghost ship, the wandering Jew, angels, and poltergeists. In addition, he uses folkloric motifs that appear in fairy tales or folktales for the purpose of producing the extraordinary, the marvelous, the fantastic: some of these include "Deluge" (A1010); "Paradise Lost Because of Forbidden Fruit" (A1331.1); "Loss of Sight from Breaking Taboo" (C943); "Murdered Person Cannot Rest in Grave" (E414); "Ghost Visible to One Person Alone" (E421.1.1); and "Brother-Sister Incest" (T415).

García Márquez learned the oral traditions that were extant in the Latin-American world when he was a child growing up with his grandparents in Aracataca. The folklore learned in his formative years was never forgotten and became an integral part of his imaginary world.

María Herrera-Sobek

See also Cervantes (Saavedra), Miguel de; Fairy Tale; Folktale; Legend; Motif; Proverbs; Shakespeare, William; Supernatural; The Wandering Jew

✳✳✳✳✳✳✳✳✳✳✳✳✳✳✳✳✳

References

García Márquez, Gabriel. *Collected Novellas.* New York: HarperCollins, 1990.
———. *Collected Stories.* New York: Harper and Row, 1984.

————. *The General in His Labyrinth*. Trans. Edith Grossman. New York: Random House, 1990.

————. *Innocent Erendira and Other Stories*. Trans. Gregory Rabassa. New York: Harper and Row, 1978.

————. *No One Writes to the Colonel and Other Stories*. Trans. J. J. Bernstein. New York: Harper and Row, 1968.

————. *Of Love and Other Demons*. Trans. Edith Grossman. New York: Random House, 1995.

————. *One Hundred Years of Solitude*. Trans. Gregory Rabassa. New York: Avon Books, 1970.

Mendoza, Plinio Apuleyo. *The Fragrance of Guava: In Conversation with Gabriel García Márquez*. Trans. Ann Wright. London: Verso, 1983.

GARRO, ELENA (1920–1998)

The Mexican writer Elena Garro's extensive narrative and dramatic works consistently interweave the popular culture of rural Mexico with the international literary trends of the twentieth century. A cursory review of her life to date sheds some light on this blend of influences. The daughter of a Spanish father and Mexican mother, Garro was born in Puebla and spent the majority of her childhood in the provincial Mexican town of Iguala. Although this upbringing facilitated her understanding of more rural belief systems, Garro later became quite well acquainted with a more urban, cosmopolitan culture when she studied humanities and dance in Mexico City and when she traveled and lived abroad extensively while married to Octavio Paz from 1937 to 1959. Since 1971, she has lived in the United States, Spain, and France, where she currently resides.

An avid reader of the Spanish classics, Garro has claimed that her interest in the literary fantastic was piqued by such writers as Miguel de Cervantes and Lopez de Vega rather than by any surrealistic influence (a movement with which she is, nonetheless, intimately acquainted). Many readers, however, see the influence of indigenous Mexican culture as a key to the magical realist strain in her work, that is, the blurring of boundaries between reality and fantasy and the acceptance of supernatural events. The various threads of both European and Mexican culture are woven together in her work in ways that continue to elicit rich and varied readings. Critical attention to her work increased in the 1990s.

This blending of the worlds of rural Mexico with more European or international trends is quite apparent in the themes that emerge time and again in Garro's creative work. Perhaps the most immediately obvious aspect of her narrative and dramatic corpus that bears the distinct imprint of Mexican folklore is her particular use of circular time and repetition. Garro explained in one interview that she sees the temporality of Mexican culture as a combination of the Western sense of time brought by the Spaniards and the view of time in the pre-Columbian Mexico of the Aztecs and the Maya.

Time and the related themes of repetition, memory, rebirth, and transformation are especially prevalent in two of her most important novels, *Los recuerdos del porvenir* (1963) and *La casa junto al río*. The former is a collective chronicle of the violence and oppression occasioned by the occupation of Ixtepec by enemy forces after the Mexican revolution. In the text, past and present mythically coexist as events are portrayed as continuously repeating themselves. In *La casa junto al río*, circular or mythic time is also central. This story recounts the quest of a female protagonist who returns to Spain in search of her family's history. Once again, the presence of the past in the present is a predominant theme, and the story ends with the protagonist's death portrayed as a mythical return to a center, the *casa* ("house") of the title of the novel and the symbolic goal of the protagonist's quest.

Folk traditions of rural Mexico play an integral role in many of Garro's plays and short stories as well. For example, in her short story "Perfecto Luna" from the collection *La semana de colores*, the protagonist is killed by a dead man, reflecting popular Mexican beliefs about the continued existence of the dead among the living. Her one-act play "Los perros?" published in *Un hogar sólido* takes place during a popular religious festival and represents the mythical possibilities of a pilgrimage to the mountain as an escape from the drudgery, poverty, and violence faced by a mother and her young daughter. This imagery of a marvelous escape that remains out of reach contrasts sharply with the dramatization of the abduction and rape of the girl, a repetition of the fate suffered years before by her broken and disempowered mother.

Garro's use of the popular beliefs and traditions of rural Mexicans stretches beyond mere regionalism to question rationalistic ideas about the nature of reality and of the passage of time and to critique the power structures dominant in Mexican society. Indeed, Garro frequently presents the plight of the indigenous peoples in her works, often delineating the conflict in Mexican culture between metropolitan and rural belief systems. Several readers point to Garro's three-act play, *La dama boba,* as a brilliant dramatization of this dichotomy.

Mary Beth Tierney-Tello

See also Belief; Legend; Myth

✳✳✳✳✳✳✳✳✳✳✳✳✳✳✳✳✳✳

References

Franco, Jean. *Plotting Women: Gender and Representation in Mexico.* New York: Columbia University Press, 1989.

Larson, Catherine. "Recollection of Plays to Come: Time in the Theatre of Elena Garro." *Latin American Theatre Review* 22:2 (Spring 1989): 5–17.

Stoll, Anita. *A Different Reality: Essays on the Works of Elena Garro.* Lewisburg, Pa.: Bucknell University Press, 1990.

GAWAIN AND THE GREEN KNIGHT, SIR

Sir Gawain and the Green Knight is the title given by modern editors to an English narrative poem of the fourteenth century. The poem exists in only one manuscript, which contains three other works, apparently by the same author. *Sir Gawain* is written in the style of the alliterative revival, a literary movement of the late fourteenth century in the north and west of England. This style is characterized by a return to some of the values of Old English poetry, including the use of a regular pattern of stresses and of alliteration, as well as the vocabulary of the northwestern Midlands dialect, which is rich in Anglo-Saxon words. In this respect, *Sir Gawain* and its companion poems in the manuscript contrast sharply with the other best known contemporary works, those by Geoffrey Chaucer and other London poets who were heavily influenced by Continental and Anglo-Norman tastes.

Unlike most products of the alliterative revival, *Sir Gawain and the Green Knight* is in large part an adventure story and an Arthurian romance; it is thought by many people to be the finest such romance written in English, and it is certainly the most cohesive. In 2,531 lines, the poem tells the story of a feast, a quest, and several tests of courage, honor, and ethics—all inextricably bound together by intricacies of plot.

The story can be summarized as follows: A bright green warrior on an armored green horse enters King Arthur's hall on Christmas Day and challenges the knights to a test, an exchange of blows. Gawain accepts the challenge and severs the green man's head. The headless body then picks up the head, which tells Gawain to meet his opponent at the green chapel in a year's time to receive his return blow.

Nearly a year later, after arduous travel, Gawain stumbles across a castle inhabited by the household of one Sir Bertilak. Bertilak makes Gawain welcome as a guest and proposes a game to occupy them for the three days until Gawain is to keep his appointment. Each day Bertilak is to go hunting, and when he returns, he and Gawain are to exchange all that they have won during the day.

Each day, Bertilak's hunting, described with the poet's characteristic vigor, parallels another hunt taking place in his castle: his wife is attempting to seduce Gawain. Gawain accepts nothing from the wife but chaste kisses, which he dutifully returns to Bertilak at day's end. On the final day, however, the lady offers Gawain a magic garter that she claims will protect him from the Green Knight's blow. Gawain accepts the gift and conceals it from Bertilak.

When the time for Gawain's appointment comes, he proceeds to the chapel. Three times the Green Knight brings an ax down upon Gawain's neck. The first two do not touch him; the third nicks his neck. The Green Knight bids Gawain to rise and reveals that he is none other than Bertilak and that the whole affair has been an elaborate test of Gawain's courage and character. The two harmless blows are for Gawain's honest days, the nick is for his peccadillo of concealing the garter.

The plot has been traditionally seen as a fusion of two well-known romance elements, that of the head-cutting test and that of the exchange of winnings. The origins of these elements have been sought and found in medieval Irish sagas. The temptation theme has also been seen (by the Arthurian scholar Roger S. Loomis) as a contribution of Celtic high literature, in this case, of Welsh saga.

For many scholars, the question of narrative source ends there, and folklore sources are not considered. Others, however, have regarded folklore as a possibly rich source of narrative elements. George Lyman Kittredge, in the first full-length study of the poem, devoted 50 pages to discussing the folklore and literature analogues of the beheading alone, and gave similar attention to the other major motifs. More recently, Claude Luttrel (1988) recognized an overall similarity of plot between the romance and the folktale known in the Aarne-Thompson index as AT313, or "the tasks." A single version of this type collected in Ireland by Jeremiah Curtin provides possible analogues for most of the major plot elements—the game opening, the agreement to an appointment a year from the first meeting, the long and arduous quest, the sexual temptation, the magically protective object, and the ultimate triumph of the hero— as well as such minor motifs as the unruly appearance of the stranger and the green color of his home and person.

The use of tale-type 313 leaves the head-cutting unexplained, and that is one of the most distinctive features of the poem. A possible source has been offered by Frederick Jonassen (1986), namely, the folk dramas of England, the mummer's play and the sword dance. Many of the most vivid descriptive elements of the poem have parallels in the folk dramas, including the head-cutting itself, the hunts of Bertilak, and a pentangle that is lovingly inscribed on Gawain's shield. The location of the poem at a Christmas feast makes a connection with these plays natural, since they are traditionally seasonal and performed during the Christmas period. In addition, it has been suggested that Arthur's court perceives the intrusion of the Green Knight as a mumming, certainly evidence, if true, that the poet was aware of the similarities between his poem and the folk dramas.

Ultimately, an impartial scholar interested in the sources of narrative elements in *Sir Gawain and the Green Knight* should consider both folklore and the antecedent literature. The great genius of the Sir Gawain poet lay partly in his ability to synthesize a seemingly seamless plot from elements gathered from widely scattered sources. There is no reason to suppose, as some scholars have done, that folklore material could not have been among those sources, and there is ample evidence that it was. We may hope that among the great volume of unannotated, unexplored folklore materials in European archives, more discoveries will be made to shed light on this remarkable poem.

Stephen Winick

See also Arthur, King; Folktale; Kittredge, George Lyman; Tale-Type

✱✱✱✱✱✱✱✱✱✱✱✱✱✱✱✱✱✱

References

Brewer, Elisabeth. *From Cuchulainn to Gawain*. Cambridge, Eng.: D. S. Brewer, 1973.

Cawley, A. C., and J. J. Anderson, eds. *Pearl, Cleanness, Patience, Sir Gawain and the Green Knight*. London: J. M. Dent and Sons, 1976.

Jonassen, Frederick B. "Elements from the Traditional Drama of England in Sir Gawain and the Green Knight." *Viator: Medieval and Renaissance Studies* 17 (1986): 221–254.

Loomis, Roger S. *Wales and the Arthurian Legend.* Cardiff: University of Wales, 1956.

Luttrell, Claude. "The Folk-Tale Element in Sir Gawain and the Green Knight." *Studies in Philology* 77 (1980): 105–127.

Moorman, Charles, ed. *The Works of the* Gawain-*Poet.* Jackson: University Press of Mississippi, 1977.

GAY, JOHN (1685–1732)

The English poet and dramatist John Gay was born in the Devonshire trading town of Barnstaple in southwestern England and orphaned at the age of ten. He was educated in the local grammar school and went to London apprenticed to a draper in 1704. By 1707, he was part of the London literary circle of the poet and playwright Aaron Hill, also from Barnstaple. With others, Gay collaborated on Hill's *The British Apollo,* a "question and answer" journal catering to a middle-class readership. Facetious in tone, *The British Apollo* contained a plethora of popularly held beliefs, customs, rhymes, and so on. Its ironic yet exuberant presentation of quotidian popular materials typifies Gay's ongoing use of folklore.

Gay's early works show the features of his style and sensibility that made him a writer who was innovative in literary history and important to the history of folklore: recurring popular themes and motifs; such traditional materials as proverbs, riddles, customs, and beliefs; incorporation in his dramas of songs that imitated popular styles and circulated independently on broadsides; and a burlesque method that linked cultural expression to social class. By 1713, Gay's published works included poems, pamphlets, and plays.

The Wife of Bath, a comedy of 1713, borrowed from ballads, is laden with proverbs and hinges upon the courtship custom of the "dumb supper." In 1714, Gay published *The Shepherd's Week,* a collection of six mock-pastoral poems whose shepherds and milkmaids are notably unidealized English rustics, recognizable by their expression of traditional custom, lore, and belief. Despite its topical literary satire, *The Shepherd's Week* captured a large popular audience and continued to be reprinted through the century. Gay's *The What d'Ye*

Call It of 1715, a genre-confounding farce, similarly takes up the circumstances, themes, and stylistic elements of folk mumming plays: servants in a manor house, military recruitment, bastard babies, rhymed couplets, and interjected songs. Despite its burlesque foolery, the play satirizes the social structure of the English squierarchy from the vantage point of the servant mummers. *The What d'Ye Call It* remained popular through the eighteenth century.

By 1714, Gay was associated with satirists Alexander Pope and Jonathan Swift and sought aristocratic patronage to stabilize his finances. However, the political climate shifted with the succession of George I to the throne, and Gay's ties to the out-of-favor Tory Party worked against his hopes for a court appointment. Significant works of this period are *Trivia* (1717), a mock-georgic poem that tutors its reader in the art of walking the streets of London and includes a wealth of facetiously invoked mythological and traditional lore, and the operatic masque, *Acis and Galatea* (c. 1718), written in collaboration with the composer George Frederic Handel. The latter work refers to the English stage and street songs in its portrayal of the Cyclops Polyphemus of the mythical story.

Gay's use of street ballads marks his most notable contribution to folklore and literature, *The Beggar's Opera* of 1728. A satiric-comic drama laced with songs set to popular ballad tunes, *The Beggar's Opera* was the first so-called ballad opera. A critique of the prime minister, Robert Walpole, the play nevertheless long outlived its political context and was staged continuously well into the nineteenth century. Gay wrote two other ballad operas immediately after *The Beggar's Opera*, a sequel entitled *Polly* (1729), which was suppressed by the government, and *Achilles*, produced posthumously in 1733. Gay's ballad operas, together with the nearly 200 imitations of the 1730s and 1740s, are an invaluable collection of printed tunes for popular ballads and dances of the seventeenth and eighteenth centuries. This interest in ballads marks a stage in the preoccupation with popular songs that would develop into a ballad revival in the mid-eighteenth century.

Toward the end of his life, Gay wrote animal fables modeled on those of the seventeenth-century French poet Jean de La Fontaine and such classical writers as the first-century Roman writer Phaedrus. Gay's first collection of fables was published in 1727, and an unfinished second collection appeared posthumously in 1738. These fables rely upon traditional characterizations, beliefs, and motifs—fairy changelings, witches and their cats, ill-betiding ravens, and so on. Gay's fables were enormously popular at all social levels into the nineteenth century.

Gay's works contain materials from and references to the folk culture of his time. Moreover, in his use of these materials—songs, sayings, customs, beliefs—Gay defined the social and cultural identities that shaped the study of popular materials, especially the ballad, in the generation that followed him. The popularity of his works through the eighteenth century and the persistence of his songs attest to Gay's adeptness in tapping the traditions of his era. At least one song, "Sweet William's Farewell to Black-eyed Susan," continues in the oral traditions of our own day.

Dianne Dugaw

See also Ballad; Fable; Motif

✳✳✳✳✳✳✳✳✳✳✳✳✳✳✳✳✳

References

Burgess, C. F., ed. *The Letters of John Gay.* Oxford: Clarendon Press, 1966.

Dearing, Vinton, ed. *John Gay, Poetry and Prose.* 2 vols. Oxford: Clarendon Press, 1974.

Dugaw, Dianne. "Folklore and John Gay's Satire." *Studies in English Literature 1500–1900* 31 (1991): 515–533.

Fuller, John, ed. *John Gay, Dramatic Works.* 2 vols. Oxford: Clarendon Press, 1983.

Lewis, Peter, and Nigel Wood, eds. *John Gay and the Scriblerians.* London: Vision Press; New York: St. Martin's Press, 1988.

Nokes, David. *John Gay: A Profession of Friendship.* Oxford: Oxford University Press, 1995.

Rubsamen, Walter, ed. *The Ballad Opera.* 28 vols. New York: Garland, 1974.

Winton, Calhoun. *John Gay and the London Theatre.* Lexington: University Press of Kentucky, 1993.

GENJI, TALE OF

The *Tale of Genji* (*Genji Monogatari*), written in the early eleventh century, is considered to be one of the greatest masterpieces of Japanese literature and the earliest great novel in world literature. The work is attributed to Murasaki Shikibu, a court lady who would have been both witness to and participant in many events similar to episodes related in the novel.

A "modern" Genji (a dandy from a nineteenth-century parody of the Tale of Genji) *with his pets.*

The story covers three-quarters of a century and focuses primarily on the life and loves of Genji, who is often referred to as "the shining prince." Genji, the son of an emperor and his favorite wife, cannot become emperor owing to certain complications. This denial of the right to succeed and his high birth give Genji the freedom to indulge in a life of pleasure unfettered by the demands of court protocol.

The *Tale of Genji* has had a tremendous impact on other genres of Japanese literature, drama, and the arts. Episodes from the novel have been adapted and retold in the *nō* (*noh*) drama, *kabuki* drama, modern cinema, and on television. Use of material from the *Tale of Genji* has been so pervasive that Edward Seidensticker, the great modern translator of the *Tale of Genji* into English, once claimed in a lecture that the work was one of the greatest pieces of folklore in Japan. He went on to explain that what he meant by the remark was that the vast majority of Japanese had never read the *Tale of Genji*, and indeed could not read it in the original language, but they still had an intimate knowledge of many of the scenes in the story. This knowledge was obtained through various conduits, but usually not from the original source.

Interest in the *Tale of Genji* lies not only in its value as literature but also in its value as a reference for customs and folk beliefs current among the aristocracy in the Heian period (794–1185) of Japanese history. For example, one of the most famous examples of *ikiryō*, spirits of the living who leave their bodies and attack others, seeking revenge, appears in the work. One of Genji's lovers, Rokujō, becomes extremely jealous and then enraged when Genji's ardor toward her cools. On one occasion when Genji is with a new lover, Rokujō's spirit appears in the night and scolds him; in the morning, the lover Yūgao is found dead. Later, at the installation ceremonies for a high priestess at a Shinto shrine, Rokujō's retainers and those of Aoi, Genji's wife, clash. In the ensuing confusion, Rokujō's carriage is damaged. Angered by this insult, Rokujō's spirit later reappears, possesses the pregnant Aoi, and despite the incantations of powerful Buddhist priests, causes her death. In the *nō* adaptation of this episode, the outcome is changed: the priests are successful, the spirit is driven out, and Aoi's life is saved.

The *Tale of Genji* also illustrates the very important Buddhist teaching of *mujō* ("evanescence," "change"). *Mujō* is a fundamental Buddhist idea that the only constant in this world is change, and during the Heian period there was a very strong feeling of decline associated with change. Buddhism taught that there would be three periods after the death of the Buddha, with each successive period representing a decline from the previous one. The third and last period, which began around the time the *Tale of Genji* was written, was the period of the *mappō*, when it was impossible for humans to become enlightened through their own efforts. Murasaki illustrated this feeling of decline in numerous ways, most notably in her depiction of the characters who take center stage in the novel after Genji's death as smaller people with less physical charm who possess only average mental and artistic abilities.

Richard W. Anderson

See also Belief; *Kabuki*; *Nō* (*Noh*)

✳✳✳✳✳✳✳✳✳✳✳✳✳✳✳✳✳✳

References

Bargen, Doris G. *A Woman's Weapon: Spirit Possession in "The Tale of Genji."* Honolulu: University of Hawaii Press, 1997.

Field, Norma. *The Splendor of Longing in the Tale of Genji.* Princeton, N.J.: Princeton University Press, 1987.

Morris, Ivan. *The World of the Shining Prince: Court Life in Ancient Japan.* New York: Kodansha International, 1994 (1964).

Seidensticker, Edward G., trans. *The Tale of Genji.* New York: Knopf, 1982.

Shirane, Haruo. *The Bridge of Dreams: A Poetics of the Tale of Genji.* Stanford, Calif.: Stanford University Press, 1987.

Waley, Arthur, trans. *The Tale of Genji.* New York: Random House, 1960.

Genre

Genre is an analytical concept that refers to a conventionalized kind, form, or category of discourse. Terms such as lyric, epic, drama, narrative, comedy, or tragedy, for example, describe broad genres of literary expression; terms such as short story, novel, folktale, joke, insult, and ballad identify more narrowly constituted genres of literature. By analogy, the concept of genre is used to refer to any conventionalized category or type of human creative activity. In this sense, it is possible to talk, for example, about genres of music, belief, or architecture.

Genre classification has long served as an important organizing principle in the study of both folklore and literature, and it has been used as a primary method of identifying folklore forms used in written literature. Yet genres have been conceptualized in a number of different ways. Genres have traditionally been understood as typological categories into which items of folklore and literature can be classified for analysis. A great deal of effort has therefore been directed toward defining genres in a way that captures their essence and clearly distinguishes one genre from another. Genre distinctions draw on a wide range of criteria such as communicative intent, structure, form, content, use, function, reception, and truth value. For example, science fiction or horror novels can be distinguished from other narrative genres in terms of content. Legends and folktales are frequently distinguished in terms of perceived truth value—legends are believed to be true (or minimally to engage issues of belief) while folktales are understood to be fictional accounts.

Some theorists claim universality for genre categories by attributing their origins to facets of human cognition or human nature. These theorists consequently argue that genre study can yield insight not only into artistic dimensions of literature, but also into differing worldviews, intellectual orientations, fields of knowledge, psychological energies, and so on. Structuralist approaches to genre definition, for example, hope to understand the universal principles that inform the underlying similarities and differences in genre distinctions found in cultures throughout the world.

Despite the apparent universality of some genres of literary expression, however, cross-cultural research suggests that conceptualizations of genres as fixed, typological categories are oversimplified. Although all communities use genres to organize their oral and written discourse in meaningful and interpretable ways, these genres, and the criteria on which the genres are based, are culturally specific. Further, neither culturally situated nor analytical genre systems achieve a comprehensive categorization of all discourse. Some works of literature, for example, defy classification because they blur generic boundaries or because they coexist in several genres simultaneously. In order to account for this variability and flexibility, theories of genre must address the relationships among different genres, the change and development of genres over time, and the role of creativity and agency in genre use.

Recent conceptions of genre, consequently, downplay genre as category and emphasize the role of genre in communication. One such perspective, for example, argues that genres are best understood as locally and historically derived orienting frameworks for the production and interpretation of discourse. In this sense, genres are used because they are recognized and understood within local systems of meaning and communication. These frameworks, however, are not fixed but are emergent associations evoked through intertextual relationship with past discourse. As such, generic associations may be used strategically or adapted, transformed, or blended into new forms that carry interpretable meaning. For example, tall tales effectively play on the conventional expectations of personal narratives, the expectation that the events being related are actual experiences. Similarly, advertising jingles frequently make use of conventions normally associated with proverbs and thereby lend a sense of credibility, memorability, and traditional sanction to a product. Alternately, new genres may emerge out of social interaction as they become useful conventions—as can be argued for some forms of electronically mediated communication on the Internet.

Donald Braid

See also Ballad; Belief; Folktale; Legend; Personal Experience Story; Proverbs; Structuralism; Tall Tale

✳✳✳✳✳✳✳✳✳✳✳✳✳✳✳✳✳

References

Bakhtin, M. M. "The Problem of Speech Genres." In *Speech Genres and Other Late Essays,* trans. Vern W. McGee, ed. Caryl Emerson and Michael Holquist, pp. 60–102. Austin: University of Texas Press, 1986.

Ben-Amos, Dan, ed. *Folklore Genres.* Austin: University of Texas Press, 1976.

Briggs, Charles L., and Richard Bauman. "Genre, Intertextuality, and Social Power." *Journal of Linguistic Anthropology* 2 (1992): 131–172.

Hernandi, Paul. *Beyond Genre: New Directions in Literary Classification.* Ithaca, N.Y.: Cornell University Press, 1972.

GESTA ROMANORUM

The *Gesta Romanorum* [Deeds of the Romans] is a compilation of stories written in the first half of the fourteenth century, each one concluding with an allegorical moral. It was popular throughout Europe into the eighteenth century. Although the texts are not Roman in origin or content, each tale is ostensibly set in the reign of some often-fictitious Roman emperor. The allegorical morals suggest that the stories were compiled for use in monasteries, probably as illustrations for sermons.

An example of the *Gesta Romanorum*'s typical storytelling method is seen in the tale of the Emperor Alexander and the poisonous princess. The Queen of the North raises her beautiful daughter on a diet of poison and sends her as a bride for Alexander. Alexander is overjoyed, but his tutor Aristotle warns that to touch her is death. Instead, a condemned prisoner is placed alone with the princess, and when he kisses her, he dies. Alexander thanks Aristotle and returns the girl to her mother. The story's afterword explains that Alexander is the Christian believer; the poisonous woman is luxury and gluttony, "which feed men with delicacies, that are poison to the soul"; Aristotle is reason, "which reproves and opposes the union that would undo the soul"; the condemned prisoner is anyone who embraces sin, "by whose deadly touch is he spiritually destroyed."

Gesta Romanorum comprises a total of 283 stories although no single edition contains all of them. The tales have a range of origins, and there are analogues in Herodotus, Aesop, Aristotle, Plutarch, Cicero, Ovid, Seneca, Lucan, the Bible, Josephus, Ambrose, Augustine, the Vitae Patrum, and Bede as well as oriental and Middle Eastern folklore. Each source has, however, been blended with details of daily British and European life. Emphasis in the stories is on plot and marvels, and there is much use of magical folk belief, necromancers, and dragons.

Gesta Romanorum provided material for many subsequent authors. Among the tales, one finds analogues with the romance of Guy of Warrick, Thomas Hoccleve's tale of Darius, Geoffrey Chaucer's and John Gower's stories of Constance, Gower's retelling of the story of Appolonius of Tyre, Horace Walpole's Mysterious Mother (1768). William Shakespeare apparently drew several items from the Gesta Romanorum (probably the 1595 edition), including the test of the three caskets, which is included in The Merchant of Venice, the Appolonius tale in the plot of Pericles, and the story of Theodosius and his daughters in King Lear.

Because of variants in the number and order of tales and because of the vast combinations of printed and manuscript editions, the genesis of the work is not known. Scholars speculate that the first Gesta Romanorum was written in Latin in England and was carried to the Continent, where it flourished in Germany. From the German-Latin versions evolved what scholars call the "vulgate text," an expanded collection of tales. Versions of Gesta Romanorum are found in Latin, English, German, French, Dutch, Polish, and Russian.

Gesta Romanorum's long publishing history suggests that the reading public greatly enjoyed these tales with their combination of adventure and piety. Gesta Romanorum was first translated into English during the reign of Henry V (1387–1422). Around 1510–

1515, the printer Wynkyn de Worde published an English translation of 43 of the stories. This translation proved so popular that it was reprinted from six to eight times before 1557. Richard Robinson revised de Worde's edition, and his work went through seven editions between 1577 and 1602. Additional compilations of *Gesta Romanorum* (an estimated 25 editions) circulated into the eighteenth century, including a chapbook edition for children.

David Sprunger

See also Chaucer, Geoffrey; Shakespeare, William

****

References

The Early English Versions of the Gesta Romanorum. Ed. Sidney Herrtage. Early English Text Society no. 33. London: Oxford University Press, 1962 (1897).

Gesta Romanorum: A Record on Ancient Histories Newly Perused by Richard Robinson. Facsimile of 1595 edition with intro. John Weld. Delmar, N.Y.: Scholars' Facsimiles and Reprints, 1973 (1595).

Gesta Romanorum, or Entertaining Moral Tales. Trans. and ed. Charles Swan and Wynnard Hooper. New York: Dover, 1959.

GHOSTS

Ghosts are disembodied spirits, and they generally are thought to refer to the human soul after death although there are also animal ghosts. The words *revenant*, *wraith*, *specter*, *apparition*, and *spirit* are all used to describe essentially the same phenomenon. Returning dead are thought to come back in several forms. They may return in the same body they had while alive, they may appear in spectral form, or they may be invisible and known only by their deeds, noise, or mischief.

Belief in the dead returning in unearthly form dates back to the beginnings of human history; some of the earliest written records—cuneiform clay tablets—contain legends about apparitions that even then were quite ancient. Classics of ancient literature, such as the *Epic of Gilgamesh*, the *Odyssey*, and the *Aeneid*, contain accounts of ghosts, and they have maintained a presence in literature ever since. Until the early nineteenth century, literary ghost stories were little more than slightly embellished accounts of reported ghostly sightings;

in the 1820s, such narratives matured into a distinct literary form, with Sir Walter Scott's "Wandering Willie's Tale" (1824) being the genre's first masterpiece.

When thinking about ghosts, many people envision an old abandoned house with loose, banging shutters and doors that seem to be closed by an unseen hand. Houses are the favorite hangout of ghosts, but they also frequently appear in various other places, including battlefields, mines, highways, boats, graveyards, gallows, and wells. Usually tied to a specific place, some wraiths carry their haunting farther afield. Generally they move about by horseback or automobile rather than by supernatural means. This activity has a lengthy tradition throughout much of Europe, where stories about traveling ghosts were reported at least as early as the 1660s.

Most ghosts return for a specific reason: to reveal the whereabouts of hidden treasure, to complete business left unfinished at the time of death, to find some forgotten possession, to protest their own unjust execution, because the ghost committed suicide, or because it has a restless soul. Most ghosts are harmless to anyone with a clear conscience, but some are malicious and return to torture their victims eternally. Ghosts of dead lovers or husbands or wives return to haunt their unfaithful sweetheart or spouse; parents come back to make life unpleasant for their children; a dead person returns to slay a wicked man or woman, to take revenge on the one who murdered, injured, or cheated him or her in life, or to punish someone mistreating a relative of the spirit or who has disturbed the dead person's grave or stolen part of its corpse. Most ghosts have specific motivations for their return.

There are, of course, numerous ghost legends, the most popular ghost narrative in the Western world being the vanishing hitchhiker. Versions of this tale tell the story of a driver picking up a hitchhiker on a lonely highway; the mysterious passenger then vanishes seemingly into thin air when the driver arrives at the presumed destination. This legend can be traced back well over a century and has inspired a number of movies and at least two popular songs.

W. K. McNeil

See also Legend; *Odyssey*; Scott, Sir Walter

✳✳✳✳✳✳✳✳✳✳✳✳✳✳✳✳✳✳

References

Briggs, Katharine. *British Folktales*. New York: Pantheon Books, 1977.

Brunvand, Jan Harold. *The Vanishing Hitchhiker: American Urban Legends and Their Meanings*. New York: W. W. Norton, 1981.

Haining, Peter. *A Dictionary of Ghosts*. New York: Dorset Press, 1993.

McNeil, W. K. *Ghost Stories from the American South*. Little Rock, Ark.: August House, 1985.

Montell, William Lynwood. *Ghosts along the Cumberland*. Knoxville: University of Tennessee Press, 1975.

GIL'FERDING, ALEKSANDR FEDOROVICH (1831–1872)

Aleksandr Fedorovich Gil'ferding was a nineteenth-century Russian scholar of Slavic linguistics and history. His writings on language, history, and folklore reflect the Slavophile (pan-Slavic) ideas that were popular in his day; among them are his master's thesis at Moscow University, "On the Relationship of the Slavic Language to Related Languages" and books such as *The History of the Baltic Slavs* (1854) and numerous publications about the Serbs, Bulgarians, Poles, and other Slavic peoples. While he was serving as Russian consul in Bosnia, Gil'ferding published an account of his travels, *Bosnia, Herzegovina, and Old Serbia* (1859), which is still of interest today because of its ethnographic descriptions of several Slavic cultures.

In modern folkloristics, Gil'ferding is noted for his work on the traditional Russian epic songs, the *byliny*. Two aspects of his research are recognized as innovations in the history of folklore research: his emphasis on the study of living oral tradition and the attention that he paid to the individual singers of epic songs. Through his detailed literary and biographical analyses of folksingers, Gil'ferding recognized that these artists were equal to the great poets of written literature.

In Russia, a sensation had been caused by P. N. Rybnikov (1831–1885), who in 1860 had discovered a thriving tradition of epic songs in the Olonets district in the northwestern part of Russia. Previous fragmentary *byliny* publications by Kirsha Danilov and Piotr Vasil'evich Kireevskii had indicated that the oral Russian epic tradition was dead and that Russian epic poetry could be continued only in written literature. Rybnikov's 224 song texts proved that oral epic was very much alive and that it could be found in relatively close proximity to St. Petersburg. In 1871, Gil'ferding, excited by the prospects of meeting living "rhapsodists" (he called them *rapsody* to emphasize a connection between the Russian singers and those of southern Slavs in the Balkan regions), retraced the footsteps of Rybnikov.

Gil'ferding discovered many new singers, but he also visited persons encountered by his predecessor. Mark Azadovskii called this expedition one of the greatest events in the history of Russian folklore research, pointing out that Gil'ferding was the first folklorist ever to return to previously studied narrators in order to observe how their songs changed over time.

Gil'ferding has also been credited with being the first folklorist to demonstrate the ties between folklore texts and the lives and personalities of the individual singers who perform those texts. In his collection *Onega Byliny*, published posthumously in 1873, Gil'ferding organized the songs he had collected, not by their content, as was customary, but by their performers. He included the biographies of the singers, showing how the individual creative personality produces unique folklore texts. Thus, Gil'ferding founded the field of narrator research; subsequent Russian folklorists have applied his approach to folk laments and folktales.

Despite the fact that *Onega Byliny* was republished twice during the Stalinist period, Gil'ferding himself was attacked at that time as a "Slavophile" and a precursor of "formalism." A biography, possibly written by Mark Konstantinovich Azadovskii or Anna Mikhailovna Astakhova, that was to have introduced the third edition (1938–1940) was never published, and the fourth edition (1949–1951) included a strongly worded negative critique of Gil'ferding.

Guntis Smidchens

See also Azadovskii, Mark Konstantinovich; Bylinas; Epic

✳✳✳✳✳✳✳✳✳✳✳✳✳✳✳✳✳✳✳

References

Gil'ferding, Aleksandr Fedorovich. *Onezhskiia byliny, zapisannye A. F. Gil'ferdingom letom 1871. g.* [*Onega Byliny*, recorded by A. F. Gil'ferding in the summer of 1871]. St. Petersburg: Tip. Imp. Akademii nauk, 1873.

Phillips, James C. "Gil'ferding, Aleksandr Fedorovich." In *Modern Encyclopedia of Russian and Soviet Literatures*, vol. 8, ed. Harry B. Weber, pp. 160–162. Gulf Breeze, Fla: Academic International Press, 1987.

GOETHE, JOHANN WOLFGANG VON (1749–1832)

Germany's most renowned classicist, Johann Wolfgang von Goethe, is primarily known as a writer who used the prosody, motifs, and

Goethe recorded folk poetry and songs and was most intrigued by the legend of Faust, upon which he based his renowned play.

images of ancient Greece, but he excelled in almost all literary genres. It is also apparent that he frequently drew on German folk sources for his writings. In the tenth chapter of his autobiography, *Dichtung und Wahrheit* [Poetry and truth (1811)], he documents quite clearly the influence that German folklore had on his early writings. As a young student in Strasbourg, he states that it was his acquaintance with Johann Gottfried Herder that "was to have the weightiest consequences" for his early literary development, and it was indeed Herder who pointed him toward such "folk poets" as Homer, Shakespeare, and Ossian. Goethe was particularly drawn to the songs of the third-century Celtic bard Ossian and even included translations in his epistolary novel *Sorrows of Young Werther* (1774). Only later did Goethe learn that these verses had been, in fact, created and published by James Macpherson from 1760 to 1763.

It was also Herder who urged the young Goethe to go out into the countryside in search of folk poetry, and Goethe eagerly followed the suggestion, making repeated trips into the surrounding German and Alsatian regions. His early collection of poems, the *Sesenheimer Lieder* [Sesenheim poems (1775)], considered by many scholars to be among his best lyric poetry, draws on traditions and images that he acquired during frequent visits to the household of a young Alsatian girl, Frederika Brion, with whom he was infatuated. Goethe describes local costumes, folk songs, storytelling sessions, and German folk dances, called *Allemandes,* in the Alsace. In contrast to Herder, who drew most of his folk songs from printed sources, Goethe recorded local ballads for which his sister later provided the musical notation. Goethe also tells of composing lyrics to familiar melodies, and in these early years he wrote ballads based on local legends. Two of the best known from this early period are the *Fischer* [Fisher (1779)] and the *Erlkönig* [The alder king (1782)]. The former tells of a fisherman who is drawn to his death by a water spirit, and the latter is the story of an elf king who steals a child from his father while the two are riding horseback through the woods. Both are euphemistic presentations of death as supernatural forces that are believed but not understood.

In his autobiography, Goethe also reveals that he concealed certain of his interests from Herder, specifically mentioning the play *Götz von Berlichingen* (1773) and his growing interest in Faust. In local legends, there were stories of the crude but well-meaning knight Götz as well as the sixteenth-century pseudoscientist Faust. It was the latter that would consume Goethe for most of his life and finally result in the work for which he is renowned in world literature. It is not clear just when Goethe first became acquainted with the Faust theme, but there were numerous sources from which he might have drawn. He saw puppet plays as a child in Frankfurt, the well-known *Kasperltheater* ("Punch and Judy theater"), but he does not mention Faust in these connections; he knew of the Faust *Volksbuch* ("chapbook") that had been sold at fairs at least since 1587, and as a student in Leipzig, he saw paintings of the legendary figure on the walls of a favorite student wine cellar, the Auerbachs Hof.

When Goethe began to write his play, however, he incorporated few of the traditional characteristics of Faust that presented him as a charlatan and a magician. Instead, Goethe created a new figure who reflected more completely Goethe's own intellectual and emotional struggles. The most significant addition to the play was the Gretchen affair, an episode reflecting current urban legends that grew up around the public execution in 1772 of a young unwed mother, Susanna Margaretha Brandt, who had murdered her own child. Throughout Goethe's masterpiece, there are numerous elements taken directly from German folk traditions, such as student drinking songs and the witches in the *Walpurgisnacht* [Walpurgis night] scene. The central concept of the pact with the devil is a well-known tale-type and motif in folk literature (AT 1170–1199—"A Man Sells His Soul to the Devil"; *M210—"Bargain with the Devil"; *M211—"Man Sells Soul to the Devil").

Throughout his works, there is much evidence of Goethe's extensive knowledge of traditional folk motifs. In his ballads, for example, many of which he wrote when he and Johann Christoph Friedrich Schiller challenged each other to a *Balladenjahr* ("ballad year") in 1797, he includes many motifs in the *Schatzgräber* [Treasure seeker] from treasure lore: a blood oath, a pact with the devil, a magic circle, and conjuration. In Goethe's *Getreuer Ekhard* [Faithful Ekhard (1815)] there is the "wild hoard" in Thuringia and the legend of the constantly filled beer mug. The *Braut von Korinth* [Bride of Corinth (1797)] includes a vampire legend, a revenant (one who returns after death), and a wedding of the dead. Goethe also recorded local folk customs and practices, beliefs, and superstitions. There is, for example, a detailed description of a local festival based on a well-known saint's legend, the St. Rochus festival in Bingen, which Goethe attended in 1814. St. Rochus is the patron saint of people afflicted with the plague. Proverbial expressions and traditional local wisdom are also recorded by Goethe as part of his description of this festival.

James R. Dow

See also Ballad; Herder, Johann Gottfried; Homer; Legend; Macpherson, James; Ossian; Schiller, Johann Christoph Friedrich; Shakespeare, William

✳✳✳✳✳✳✳✳✳✳✳✳✳✳✳✳✳

References

Friedenthal, Richard. *Goethe: His Life and Times*. Cleveland and New York: World Publishing Company, 1963.

Goethe, Johann Wolfgang von. *Aus meinem Leben: Dichtung und Wahrheit*. Hamburger Ausgabe, vols. 9–10. Hamburg: Christian Wegner Verlag, 1959.

Heffner, R-M. S., Helumt Rehder, and W. F. Twaddell, eds. *Faust*, vols. 1–2. Madison: University of Wisconsin Press, 1975.

Röhrich, Lutz. "Volkskunde und Literatur." In *Reallexikon der deutschen Literaturgeschichte, Band 4*, begründet von Paul Merker und Wolfgang Stammler, pp. 742–761. Berlin and New York: Walter De Gruyter, 1982.

GOGOL, NIKOLAY VASILYEVICH (1809–1852)

One of Russia's greatest and most enigmatic nineteenth-century comedy and prose writers, Nikolay Vasilyevich Gogol is regarded in his homeland as second in literary importance only to Aleksandr Pushkin. Gogol was born in Great Sorochintsy in the Mirgorod district of the Ukraine, the setting for his immensely successful first collection of stories, *Evenings on a Farm near Dikanka* (1832). That collection and a subsequent one, *Mirgorod* (1835), constituted a series of tales in a Ukrainian setting.

Richly descriptive of local color and expressing the pathos of heroism and supernatural terror stemming from native folk beliefs and legends, the tales are also filled with examples of the coarse humor, banality, silliness, and sheer stupidity that permeated provincial life. Peopled by Cossacks, gypsies, clerics, and local folk buying and selling pretzels, kerchiefs, bushels of wheat, and all kinds of wares at country fairs as well as bolting their food and choking on their dumplings, this world was also inhabited by drowned maidens, witches, devils, and other folk creatures. The tales in *Evenings* and *Mirgorod* present a grotesque gallery of creatures and characters with radish-shaped heads, distended bellies, magnetic eyes—all inextricably bound to their land and simultaneously coarsely prosaic, enchanted, and mystical. Although surely more a product of Gogol's mind and his taste for the carnivalesque than a potpourri of "slice-of-life episodes" strung together by the narrator of the *Evenings*, the series was received in St. Petersburg as a perfect reflection of Ukrainian folk life and ensured Gogol's reputation as a major prose writer.

This recognition was further reinforced when Gogol changed the locale of his stories to the urban setting of St. Petersburg. He initiated a new and perhaps his most accomplished cycle of stories united by a common city setting—the so-called Petersburg tales. This new cycle began with the publication of a book entitled *Arabesques* (1835), which was received as a shapeless miscellany of essays on art and literature combined with examples of prose fiction. The term *arabesques* was not used by Gogol accidentally, since the concept it denoted allowed his now "sophisticated" narrator to reach broadly into such disciplines as painting, architecture, design, music, and folk dance; address each as an individual topic; and yet relate it to his "fiction" in *Arabesques*. The pattern of interlacing disparate elements allowed Gogol to break free from the prescribed forms of his day, to mix fiction with art criticism freely, and to allow parts of the represented world protrude or "grow beyond" its confines. Images of plants reaching into the heavens, breaking the simple geometry of buildings; of moonlight unable to be contained by the frame of a window—these are but a fraction of the arabesque imaging with which the author bombarded his readers.

As in his Ukrainian tales, Gogol was still interested in the common folk in *Arabesques*, but the urban people existed in a world devoid of the relative security provided by the folk milieu. Instead of the mystical creatures of the fields and forests, the terror of the city came from within oneself or was provided by material objects that took on lives independent of their owners. In this urban world, Gogol's new characters—such as poor artists, petty officials, barbers, clerks, and scribes—their vision blurred by fogs, see prostitutes turn into ideal females, poodles turn into runaway clerks, other dogs writing letters, and portraits "stepping out" of their frames—some of them even imagine themselves to be the kings of Spain.

In a story related to the cycle, "The Nose," an arabesque framing device is employed throughout the story and so are the fogs in those places where the narrative takes an abrupt shift. Although this story, if superficially viewed, does not offer to its readers much more than an anecdote in which the protagonist's nose finally finds its proper place on its owner's face, the work as a whole represents the emergence of a crisis in Gogol's worldview. The discrepancy between the real and imagined worlds became so patent, so insistent, for Gogol at this time that he could no longer accept the neoromantic imagery that contemplated an ideal world, particularly as imagined in his *Arabesques*. At the same time, he was extremely loath to give it up and accept the real world. A tension developed in his imagery between the two worlds, which he had formerly seen as separate, the ideal and the real: they ceased to interact and began to merge and fuse. An alternate, new world arose from these polarities: a mixed-up world in which the motivation of the fantastic and the real became the same—a world of the absurd. It is for these reasons that in "The Nose," the separated nose independently achieved a rank higher than its noseless owner.

Similarly, in the last story of Gogol's Petersburg cycle, "The Overcoat," a ghost in the fantastic ending of the story was just as intent on stealing coats as thieves were in the world occupied by the poor protagonist. Thus, the stories of the Petersburg cycle were united by criteria other than those posited in Gogol's early provincial tales and should be viewed as being among the first precursors of the fiction that is characteristic of such writers as Franz Kafka or Jorge Luis Borges.

But Gogol was, of course, more than only a prose tale writer. His first major play, *The Inspector General,* appeared in 1836, and it brought him instant recognition as a playwright. Gogol's spirited satire of corruption and stupidity in the provincial administration was not only a huge success but also led to vehement attacks on Gogol by the reactionary press. In order to escape the controversy, Gogol went abroad to Germany and Italy, where he lived for most of the next 12 years, returning to Russia for brief periods only.

Nevertheless, Gogol's fame grew in Russia until the year 1842, which marked the high point of his career and saw the publication of his *Dead Souls,* a narrative of epic proportions again concerned with aspects of provincial life. An exhilarating flight of fantasy, written in the traditions of the picaresque, and a blend of satire with visions of the absurdity and triviality of the human condition, Gogol's first Russian "epopoeia" (epic poetry) in prose sealed forever his destiny as Russia's greatest writer of the period.

After 1842, however, Gogol turned more and more to religious contemplation, and his creativity seemed to desert him. His only complete work of the last decade of his life was *Selected Passages from the Correspondence with Friends* (1847), a miscellany of essays on morality, religion, citizenship, literature, and art, which was welcomed by a few and denounced by many as a hypocritical book. Unnoticed to this day as a literary work, the book was an ingenious revival of the classical and gothic "dialogues of the dead"—a genre that demanded commentary on the moral side of human existence. Again, perhaps entrapped by his techniques of reaching out beyond frames, Gogol attempted to break through the final barrier separating the living from the dead (in the Prologue to the book he mentions that he was "almost dead"). In this case, however, just as with his *Arabesques,* the technique was not understood by his readers as a literary device, which prompted inadequate commentaries in both instances.

Gogol's anguish as a result of his isolation from his former friends, combined with his strict observance of the practices of Russian Orthodox Lent, resulted in his premature death in 1852. His death functioned as a grim reminder of the dangers stemming from the removal of the limits that normally separate our physical world from its metaphysical hypostasis—dangers that Gogol consistently ignored in his life and in his art.

A. *Levitsky*

See also Legend; Pre-Soviet Prose and Folklore in Russia

✳✳✳✳✳✳✳✳✳✳✳✳✳✳✳✳✳✳

References

Erlich, V. *Gogol*. New Haven: Yale University Press, 1969.

Fanger, D. *The Creation of Nikolai Gogol*. Cambridge, Mass.: Belknap Press, 1979.

Maguire, Robert A., ed. *Gogol from the Twentieth Century: Eleven Essays*. Princeton, N.J.: Princeton University Press, 1974.

Nabakov, V. *Nikolai Gogol*. Norfolk: New Directions, 1944.

GOLDEN ASS

A prose romance in 11 books written by Apuleius of Madaura (c. 125–180 C.E.), the *Golden Ass* (*Asinus Aureus*) was originally entitled *Metamorphoses* and was based on a now-lost Greek romance of the same title. A Greek version (*Lucius, or The Ass*) of the latter survives and is falsely ascribed to Lucian. The lost Greek original is known only from the brief summary given by the ninth-century Byzantine patriarch Photius.

Apuleius's romance is presented as the fictionalized autobiography of the narrator Lucius, who, like Faust, disregards repeated warnings against meddling in magic and witchcraft and comes to grief. In the third book of the romance, Lucius is accidentally turned into a donkey and undergoes a series of painful adventures in the service of various owners, just like the rogue-heroes of early European picaresque romances. Lucius's adventures culminate in the eleventh book when, through the intervention of the goddess Isis, he is transformed back into his human shape and becomes a priest of the goddess. There is no trace of this conclusion in the surviving Greek version, and it is generally agreed that this ending is the work of Apuleius himself.

In structure, the *Golden Ass* represents one of the oldest forms of storytelling: a central framing narrative into which are inserted various shorter narratives. The best known and longest of the tales interpolated in the *Golden Ass* is "Cupid and Psyche," which is dovetailed into the fourth (chap. 28) and sixth (chap. 24) books. This fairy tale recapitulates Lucius's adventures in the framing tale and prefigures the happy resolution in the eleventh book. Psyche is assigned difficult tasks to complete for Venus (probably a witch in the original folktale), performs them successfully with the help of supernatural agencies, marries Cupid, and lives happily ever after in Olympus. Apuleius's version of this tale is the earliest extant written version and was adapted by Apuleius to suit its literary context in the *Golden Ass*. It is impossible to determine whether the Roman writer derived the tale from an oral or a literary source. There is no trace of it in the surviving Greek version.

The frame tale of the romance in many respects resembles the modern migratory legend known to folklorists as "Following the Witch" (ML 3045 in Christiansen [1958]). According to this legend, a young man visits a witch and is accidentally transformed into a beast of burden while the witch flies off to attend a Sabbath. In some versions of the legend, the hero regains his human form by eating lilies, or roses (as in Apuleius), while attending a religious procession as part of a Corpus Christi festival. The earliest written versions of this modern legend appeared in Western Europe during the "witch craze" of the sixteenth and seventeenth centuries, shortly after the publication of the first vernacular translations of the *Golden Ass*. Versions of the legend are also widespread in the Americas, particularly in Spanish-speaking areas stretching from Colorado and New Mexico to Peru and Chile, and an oral version is current in Quechua-speaking areas of the Andes. It seems likely that the Spanish versions of the legend in the Americas derive ultimately from López de Cortegana's translation of the *Golden Ass*, which was first published in 1525 and has been reprinted many times since.

Alex Scobie

See also Apuleius; Frame Tale; Romance

✳✳✳✳✳✳✳✳✳✳✳✳✳✳✳✳✳✳

References

Christiansen, R. T. *The Migratory Legends*. Helsinki: Folklore Fellows Communication no. 175. Helsinki: Academia Scientiarum Fennica, 1958.

Scobie, Alex. *Apuleius and Folklore: Toward a History of ML 3045, AaTh 567, 449A*. London: Folklore Society, 1983.

Swahn, Jan Ojvind. *The Tale of Cupid and Psyche*. Lund, Sweden: C. W. K. Gleerup, 1975.

Tatum, James. *Apuleius and the Golden Ass*. Ithaca, N.Y.: Cornell University Press, 1979.

THE GOLDEN BOUGH

Sir James George Frazer's work *The Golden Bough* is one of the great nineteenth-century works of comparative anthropology. First appearing as a 2-volume work in 1890, it was revised into a 3-volume version in 1900, and appeared in a 12-volume edition between 1906 and 1915. The work is ostensibly an explanation of the priesthood of Nemi and the rites and customs surrounding it. Frazer's interest was captured by the facts that the priesthood could be held only by a runaway slave, that it centered on a sacred tree, and that by breaking a branch of the sacred tree another runaway could challenge the priest to single combat and, if successful, take over the priesthood. For Frazer the two key questions were, as Robert Fraser notes, "Whoever had heard of a kingship confined to slaves and runaways?" and "What kind of kingdom was it that could be focused on a tree?" (Frazer 1994, pp. xvii–xix). To answer these questions, the author turned to broadly based comparisons, believing

> that by an application of the comparative method . . . I can make it probable that the priest represented in his person the god of the grove . . . and that his slaughter was regarded as the death of the god. . . . This raises the question of the meaning of a widespread custom of killing men and animals regarded as divine. . . . The resemblance of many of the savage customs and ideas to fundamental doctrines of Christianity is striking. But I make no reference to this parallelism, leaving my readers to draw their own conclusions, one way or the other. (Letter of November 8, 1889, to George Macmillan; cited in Ackerman 1987, p. 95)

Through using the comparative method, Frazer hoped to illuminate not only the seemingly odd priesthood at Nemi, but also a whole manner of thinking that was part of the intellectual and psychological history of mankind.

The Golden Bough was the first anthropological work to have a profound impact on literature. Of particular influence were Frazer's discussions of the dying God and his use of primitive parallels to Christianity to explain the meanings of Christian beliefs and rites, especially the meaning of the story of the Crucifixion. The latter, though well developed and presented in Frazer's work, was for Frazer's time quite controversial and original, and its influence can be seen in a number of writers of the early twentieth century, such as W. B. Yeats, D. H. Lawrence, Wyndham Lewis, and T. S. Eliot. Although often ignored, it has influenced modern anthropology and folklore as well, providing terms and concepts for the study of magic and ritual.

David E. Gay

See also Comparative Method; Frazer, James George; Ritual

✳✳✳✳✳✳✳✳✳✳✳✳✳✳✳✳✳✳

References

Ackerman, Robert. *J. G. Frazer: His Life and Work.* Cambridge: Cambridge University Press, 1987.

Frazer, James George. *The Golden Bough.* Abridged, with intro. and notes by Robert Fraser. Oxford: Oxford University Press, 1994.

———. *The Golden Bough: A Study in Comparative Religion.* London: Macmillan, 1980.

GREECE, ANCIENT

The study of folklore in Greek literature presents two definitional problems at the outset. The first is how to identify folklore in a literary setting, given our limited access to ancient Greek popular tradition. The strategy customarily applied is a comparative one, the gathering of narrative parallels from folk traditions known elsewhere. In the event—as is most common—that our evidence for these parallels is relatively late, it must then be determined whether these later analogues really constitute evidence for an underlying folk tradition that goes back to, and provides material for, the Greek text under investigation or whether they are merely derived from that text.

The second problem concerns the relationship between folklore and the mythic tradition upon which much of Greek literature is based. Many definitions of folklore would seem to include at least some mythic narratives, yet traditionally the two have been treated separately. Various factors have been suggested as the basis for a distinction: myth is primarily about gods; it is more serious, dealing in timeless truths of cosmic significance; people believe myths to be true in a way they do not in the case of folktales. It is worth noting that the Greeks themselves seem to have made no such distinction: Aristotle used the term *mythos* to refer to the plots of epic and drama, but also to what we today would characterize as folk beliefs rather than myths. Perhaps it is best to say that traditional folk narratives and motifs became attached to the characters of myth and legend, and thereby gained entry into Greek literature.

Greek participation in the cross-cultural diffusion of popular tales at least as early as the first recorded Greek literature can be illustrated by the so-called Potiphar's wife tale, the virtuous man who rejects the (variously illicit) amorous advances of a woman and is then falsely accused by her of sexual misconduct (AT 2111). The same story also appears in the book of Genesis, chapter 39, as part of a complex of Joseph stories; and an Egyptian version is recorded in the "Tale of Two Brothers," whose oldest preserved text is dated to around 1200 B.C.E. In Greek literature, we find it first in the *Iliad*, attached to the character of Bellerophon, but it is best known as the story of Hippolytus and his stepmother Phaedra, made famous in Euripides' *Hippolytus*. Although not conclusive, it is noteworthy that the Joseph story takes place in Egypt and the Bellerophon story partly in Asia Minor.

A general program for the study of folklore in Greek literature would consist first of the identification of folk elements in Greek texts and then the analysis of their use and adaptation to further the thematic and ethical interests of the text. Such a program can be particularly fruitful when applied to the genres of hymn, epic, and tragic poetry, in which popular narrative is attached to divine figures as well as to the human heroes of epic and tragedy.

The tension, inherent in Greek thought and art, between idealism and humanism is especially salient in Greek thinking about the gods: they are near, yet far; they are like us, yet not like us. The tension provides for an ambivalent role for folklore in divine narrative, a creative tension between the humanizing effect of popular narrative, and the theological demands of superhuman power or knowledge. This duality characterizes the longer Homeric hymns and can be seen with particular clarity in Hesiod's *Theogony*, which is basically a hymn to Zeus. The career of Zeus consists of a sequence of folkloric elements: the unsuccessful attempt to destroy the fateful child (AT 5301); the youngest brother who succeeds where older siblings are at a loss (AT 1242); the outwitting of the cannibalistic ogre, his father Kronos (AT G11.2); the need for magic helpers, "the hundredhanders" (AT N810); and the employment of magic weapons, the thunderbolts supplied by the Cyclopes (AT D1080). The *Theogony* can be read as an attempt to reconcile these popular narrative elements with the seemingly irreconcilable ideal of an omnipotent and omniscient deity.

In the Greek epic tradition, the physical and mental excellence united in Zeus is divided in accordance with an ideology that incorporates it in two antithetical types, Achilles and Odysseus, each of whom is idealized in one of the Homeric poems. The ethos of the Achilles type means it is not particularly amenable to the absorption of folk elements; the Odysseus type on the other hand is more amenable to such absorption than any other figure in Greek literature. Both the nature of the hero and the episodic structure of the *Odyssey* invite the incorporation of numerous folktales, all skillfully adapted to the larger narrative and thematic context of the poem, which could reasonably be called a folk epic. Comparative studies of such figures as Circe and Calypso, the lotus-eaters, the sirens, and Polyphemus have identified analogues from numerous folk traditions, and literary analysis of their use in the *Odyssey* makes it clear that the poet expects and exploits an audience familiar with these story types.

Fifth-century Athenian tragedy questions everything it touches, and its treatment of the characters and events of popular tales is no exception. The qualities that so obviously rendered the Odysseus of the *Odyssey* an ideal folk hero appear highly ambiguous on the Athenian stage: his wily cleverness and genius for self-preservation are here seen as amoral calculation and self-interested sophistry, particularly in Sophocles' *Philoctetes* and a number of plays by Euripides. The tale of Oedipus provides the subject for some of the most famous Greek speculation about the human condition. Very much in the manner of the biblical Job, Euripides' *Alcestis* probes the moral and ethical dimensions of a seemingly simple tale of virtue rewarded (AT T211.1). For the best illustration we might return to the tale of Potiphar's wife as Euripides employs it in *Hippolytus:* the innocent youth and lustful women are here transformed into avatars of the awesome and uncontrollable power of Artemis and Aphrodite, human characters fatally involved in an ambiguous nexus of divine action and inner compulsion. They have become paradigms, like many of their tragic peers, of the inexpressible confluence of forces that determine individual destiny.

Robert Mondi

See also Belief; Epic; Folktale; Homer; *Iliad*; Legend; Myth; *Odyssey*; Oedipus; Polyphemus; Siren

❋❋❋❋❋❋❋❋❋❋❋❋❋❋

References

Mondi, Robert. "Tradition and Innovation in the Hesiodic Titanomachy." *Transactions of the American Philological Association* 116 (1986): 25–48.

Page, Denys. *Folktales in Homer's Odyssey*. Cambridge: Harvard University Press, 1973.

Yohannan, John D. *Joseph and Potiphar's Wife in World Literature*. New York: McClelland and Stewart, 1968.

The Green Man, an archetype symbolizing the unity of human beings with the natural world, can be found throughout European folklore.

GREEN MAN

A representation of a human head with leaves and vines, the green man—an architectural and artistic image—is a composite figure depicting the union of humanity and the natural world. As an archetype, the green man is the vegetation god, the personification and continuation of the spirit of the earth, the creative powers of nature, the unity of humanity with nature, the tree of life. Along with the trickster and the three-in-one goddess, the green man is one of the primary archetypes that Carl Jung and other analysts believe are universal and representative of the collective unconscious.

A significant architectural design in the Gothic period, the representation became known as "the green man" because of a 1939 article, "The

Green Man in Church Architecture." In this study, Lady Raglan pointed out the resemblance between the architecture motif and the appearance in many folk dramas and rituals of a leaf-covered figure known variously as the green man, Jack in the green, Robin of the wood, and the king of May, a central figure in May Day celebrations throughout northern and central Europe. It is believed that this figure derives from a proto-Dionysus and/or the horned god of old Europe. In Celtic Europe, the god was called Esus, the god of spring, and sometimes Cernunnos, the god of forests and the underworld, in which manifestation he appears horned. As a relic of old European tree worship, the folk motif is also associated with the Swiss Whitsuntide basket, the Hanoverian leaf king, the Slovenian green George, and the Yorkshire Jenny Greenteeth.

In both oral and written literature, this motif or archetype has been prevalent for centuries in association with the legend of the holy rood, in which a tree grows from a seed planted in the mouth of Adam's skull. In the contemporary period, with the interest in the environment and the reaction to and alienation from nature, this archetype has experienced new popularity. The role of the human head merged with nature is found in children's stories such as Susan Cooper's *The Greenwitch* as well as in the novels of Kingsley Amis, Storm Jameson, Henry Treece, and Andrew Young.

Amanda Carson Banks

See also Archetype; Jung, Carl Gustav; Trickster

✱✱✱✱✱✱✱✱✱✱✱✱✱✱✱✱✱

References

Anderson, William. *Green Man: The Archetype of Our Oneness with the Earth.* San Francisco: Harper, 1990.

Day, Martin S. *The Many Meanings of Myth.* New York: University Presses of America, 1984.

Jung, Carl Gustav. *The Archetypes and the Collective Unconscious.* 2d ed. Trans. R. F. C. Hull. London: Routledge and Kegan Paul, 1968.

———. *Four Archetypes: Mother, Rebirth, Spirit, Trickster.* Trans. R. F. C. Hull. Princeton, N.J.: Princeton University Press, 1969.

Raglan, Lady. "The Green Man in Church Architecture." *Folklore* 50:1 (1939): 45–47.

GREGORY, LADY ISABELLA AUGUSTA (1852–1932)

The Irish writer, folklore collector, founder of the Abbey Theatre, and active promoter of the arts in Ireland, Lady Isabella Augusta Gregory (née Persse), played an important role in the Irish literary renaissance. In 1880, she married Sir William Gregory, a member of Parliament 35 years her senior, and she began her literary career in earnest after Sir William's death in 1892 by editing his autobiography.

Inspired by the work of the Gaelic League, particularly that of Douglas Hyde and William Butler Yeats, Lady Gregory volunteered to collect and translate the Old Irish heroic cycles found in medieval manuscripts. In *Cuchulain of Muirthemne* (1902), she consolidated tales from the Ulster cycle into a unified narrative, working primarily from manuscripts ranging in date from the eleventh to the nineteenth centuries. This was the first appearance of her "Kiltartan" dialect, an English translation that preserves Irish syntax. She continued to use the dialect throughout her career. *Gods and Fighting Men* (1904) recounts the deeds of a variety of other legendary figures. Lady Gregory also collected folklore in her native Galway and published her findings in Kiltartan editions like *Poets and Dreamers* (1903) and *Visions and Beliefs in the West of Ireland* (1920). *Cuchulain of Muirthemne* raised interest in Irish culture abroad, particularly in the United States; in Ireland, her successful use of dialect fueled the movement toward developing a uniquely Irish art rooted in the common people.

In 1899, Lady Gregory and Yeats founded the Irish Literary Theatre in order to produce innovative, noncommercial Irish drama. Supported by Lady Gregory's fund-raising and organizational efforts, the project was eventually subsidized and offered a permanent theater, opening as the Abbey Theatre in 1904. As one of three directors, with Yeats and John Millington Synge, Lady Gregory devoted herself to the theater's ambitious goals, sometimes in opposition to popular tastes and government censors. She defended Synge's *The Playboy of the Western World* when the theater opened the play to riots in Dublin in 1907 and insisted on continued performances despite violent public outrage, even a death threat, during a tour of the United States in 1911. In 1909, she supported George Bernard Shaw's censored *The Showing up of Blanco Posnet* and produced the play, though threatened with losing the theater's license.

Lady Gregory wrote almost 40 plays based on Irish folkways,

including comedies, like *Spreading the News* (1904), *The Rising of the Moon* (1907), and *The Workhouse Ward* (1908); folk histories, like *Grania* (1911); and tragedies, like *The Gaol Gate* (1906). She also translated works by Jean-Baptiste Molière and Douglas Hyde into Kiltartanese, advised Yeats on most of his play writing, and encouraged many young Irish playwrights, notably Sean O'Casey.

Lady Gregory dedicated much of her later career to a prolonged and ultimately fruitless battle for the Dublin National Gallery on behalf of her nephew, the art collector Sir Hugh Lane who was killed when the *Lusitania* sank in 1915. Lane's well-known intention of leaving 39 French Impressionist paintings to the National Gallery was thwarted by his own will, which at the time of his unexpected death bequeathed the paintings to the National Gallery of England. Lady Gregory lobbied tirelessly for many years to persuade England to donate the collection to Dublin. She began to keep a journal at this time, which was later published as *Lady Gregory's Journals 1916–1930* (1946), and wrote *Hugh Lane's Life and Achievement* (1921).

Lorraine Walsh

See also Cuchulain; Synge, John Millington; Yeats, William Butler

✳✳✳✳✳✳✳✳✳✳✳✳✳✳✳✳✳✳✳

References

Adams, Hazard. *Lady Gregory*. Lewisburg, Ohio: Bucknell University Press, 1973.

Coxhead, Elizabeth. *Lady Gregory, a Literary Portrait*. 2d ed. London: Secker and Warburg, 1966.

Kopper, Edward A., Jr. *Lady Isabella Persse Gregory*. Boston: Twayne Publishers, 1976.

GRIEVE, CHRISTOPHER MURRAY (1892–1978)

Christopher Murray Grieve (pseudonym, Hugh MacDiarmid) was a Scottish poet, critic, and essayist whose views on Scottish national identity and the Scottish language and its use in poetry have proved seminal in the development of Scottish literature in the twentieth century. Born in Langholm, close to the border between England and Scotland, in an area noted for the independent character of its natives, Grieve trained as a teacher but took up journalism as a profession until his war service (1915–1919) with the Royal Army

Medical Corps. In the 1920s, he combined journalism with politics and polemics as a local councillor and as a founder of both the Scottish Centre of PEN (the campaigning organization for poets, playwrights, essayists, editors, and novelists) and the National Party of Scotland.

Grieve edited and contributed to a number of literary periodicals and in 1922 began to write as Hugh MacDiarmid, the pseudonym being associated with his most challenging ideas: "From the beginning I took as my motto—and I have adhered to it all through my literary work—Thomas Hardy's declaration: 'Literature is the written expression of revolt against accepted things'" (MacDiarmid 1994, p. 232).

In poetry, he advocated the use of "synthetic Scots," vernacular Scots reinvigorated by the use of vocabulary drawn from earlier periods, particularly that of the medieval makars (poets) such as Robert Henryson and William Dunbar. Grieve subscribed to the view that "Scotland still had something to say to the imagination of mankind, something that she alone among the nations can say, and can say only in her native tongue" (MacDiarmid 1995, p. 262). His most influential work, *A Drunk Man Looks at the Thistle*, appeared in 1926 and "broke on a startled and incredulous Scotland with all the shock of a childbirth in a church" (MacDiarmid 1953, p. xiii). This "gallimaufry in braid Scots verse" set out to prove that Scots could not only be used for lyric and emotional expressiveness but also for treating all kinds of subjects and specifically in investigating the Scottish character and nation, the thistle of the title.

Grieve went on to produce further large-scale, highly allusive works drawing on contemporary writing and ideas, but many readers find the most satisfaction in his early lyrics, in which he is closest to the bold imagery and simplicity of older forms, particularly the traditional ballad, despite the fact that he eschewed the use of the ballad form itself as being overworked in mainstream literary tradition. Some lyrics, like "Empty Vessel" ("I met ayont the cairney / A lass wi' tousie hair") deliberately echo traditional songs like "Jenny Nettles."

Inspired by James Joyce and T. S. Eliot, but also aware of the "volume and quality of Scottish Folk Song, which is undeniably one of the finest in the world" (MacDiarmid 1995, p. 105), Grieve sought to build directly on this rootstock to develop an authentic and distinctive Scottish voice with the confidence to address the most important philosophical, aesthetic, and political issues.

Elaine Petrie

See also Ballad; Joyce, James; Scottish Literature

✳✳✳✳✳✳✳✳✳✳✳✳✳✳✳✳

References

Bold, Alan, ed. *The Letters of Hugh MacDiarmid*. London: Hamish Hamilton, 1984.

Buthlay, Kenneth. *Hugh MacDiarmid*. Edinburgh: Scottish Academic Press, 1982.

MacDiarmid, Hugh. *The Complete Poems of Hugh MacDiarmid*. 2 vols. Ed. Michael Grieve and A. R. Aitken. Middlesex, Eng.: Penguin, 1985.

———. *Contemporary Scottish Studies*. Ed. Alan Riach. Manchester, Eng.: Carcanet with Mid Northumberland Arts Group, 1995.

———. *A Drunk Man Looks at the Thistle*. Intro. David Daiches. Glasgow: Caledonian Press, 1953.

———. *Lucky Poet: A Self Study in Literature and Political Ideas*. Manchester, Eng.: Carcanet with Mid Northumberland Arts Group, 1994.

GRIMM, JACOB (1785–1863) AND WILHELM (1786–1859)

The brothers Jacob Grimm and Wilhelm Grimm were German scholars whose wide-ranging works in linguistics, law, literature, folklore, and mythology had a pioneering influence worldwide. The Grimm brothers' important collections—such as their *German Dictionary* (1854) and Jacob's *Deutsche Mythologie* [German mythology (1835)] and *Deutsche Altertümer* [Ancient German Law (1828)]—provided models for scholars who wanted to undertake historical studies of language and culture, and their *German Legends* and *Kinder- und Hausmärchen* [Children's and household tales (1812–1815)] helped legitimize the scholarly study of texts outside the literary canon. Although the Grimm brothers were not the first to study folklore, their collections contained methodological statements and scholarly notes that served as authoritative models for scholars who sought to collect, edit, and study the oral traditions of folk culture. In addition to their scholarly importance for folklore studies, these collections, especially the fairy tales, had a much broader popular reception as literary texts for both children and adults.

The brothers Grimm became interested in Old Germanic literature and folk traditions while they were students at Marburg University in Germany. While there, they began gathering traditional texts for the writer Clemens Brentano, who published in collaboration with Achim von Arnim a collection of older literary and traditional

Witches were common characters in the Grimm brothers' famous fairy tale collections, which captured the imagination of generations of children worldwide.

folk songs in *Des knaben Wunderhorn* (1805–1808). As poets, Brentano and Arnim were less interested in remaining literally faithful to tradition than they were in using their own imaginations to re-create the songs for print. Unsympathetic to this treatment of the folk texts, the Grimms distinguished between natural poetry (*Naturpoesie*) and

275

literary poetry (*Kunstpoesie*). Natural poetry they held to be the unreflective, spontaneous creation of the collective folk, who exist in harmony with nature. Literary poetry, which they identified with Brentano's work, was the literate, self-conscious creation of writers striving for individual artistic effect. In the Grimms' view, folk texts represented the very origin of poetry and were not at all inferior to literary works of art. Consequently, in theory the Grimms did not think folklore needed to be artistically transformed to be culturally valuable.

Although the Grimms intended to preserve the essence of natural poetry in their folklore collections, the texts they transmitted are really much more complicated phenomena. For example, their scholarly notes make it clear that many of the stories in their fairy tale collection did not come directly from the oral tradition but from published, literary sources. Other tales emanated not from storytellers belonging to the Grimms' idealized folk, but from highly literate, middle-class, and aristocratic informants belonging to the Grimms' own circle of friends and family. Because these tales have been filtered through a literary consciousness, they must be disqualified as natural poetry or oral folklore.

The Grimms did not actually claim that the texts they published were verbatim transcriptions of oral narratives, and they admitted to tinkering with variants and making stylistic improvements. Each of 17 different editions of Grimms' fairy tales published between 1812 and 1858 reveals the editorial interventions of Wilhelm Grimm. Whether these interventions actually restored the tales' natural authenticity, as the Grimm brothers and some other scholars have claimed, is questionable. Generally, the editorial emendations reveal Wilhelm's ongoing attempt to create a fairy tale style that reflected his own generic ideal.

Some scholars point out that not only did this aesthetic ideal motivate Wilhelm's editing but the Grimms' social and moral values, which corresponded to those of Germany's nineteenth-century middle-class culture, also had an effect. There is evidence, too, that early criticism of the fairy tale collection and its reception as a work of children's literature influenced Wilhelm's editing of content, style, and theme. Although Wilhelm Grimm might have seen himself as just one in a long chain of storytellers, this long-term process of collecting and editing tales for publication so they would meet not only the Grimms' personal expectations but also the aesthetic, moral, and educational expectations of both their scholarly and public audiences makes the tales something other than the spontaneous oral creations of an unreflective folk.

It is not too obvious, then, to state that the Grimms created a book of folklore that lies somewhere between folklore and literature, between the oral folktale (*Volksmärchen*) and the literary folktale (*Kunstmärchen*). Unique in nature, the classical fairy tale they created often goes by the designation "book tale" (*Buchmärchen*) or "Grimm genre" (*Gattung Grimm*), and it deserves the attention of both folklorists and literary scholars. However, because Grimm brothers' fairy tales seemed to belong primarily to folklore and children's literature, literary scholars long neglected them, despite their literary characteristics.

Whatever their status as literature, the Grimms' fairy tales and legends have long been used in literature. Creative writers, especially in Western culture, have adapted the stories in virtually every genre for diverse purposes. The countless examples range from Anne Sexton's lyric poetry adaptations in *Transformations* (1971) and Günter Grass's novel *Der Butt* [The flounder (1977)] to Erika Mann's anti-Nazi cabaret sketches and Tankred Dorst's radical modern drama *Herr Korbes*. Authors as diverse as Theodor Adorno, Margaret Atwood, Donald Barthelme, Angela Carter, Robert Coover, Roald Dahl, Randall Jarrell, Tanith Lee, Friedrich Nietzsche, Thomas Pynchon, Peter Straub, Martin Walser, Eudora Welty, and Jane Yolen have responded to the Grimms' tales by rewriting them or incorporating them into their own works. The adaptations may be serious, humorous, satirical, parodistic, philosophical, or subversive.

In Germany, the Grimms' tales have been the object of frequent adaptation and revision by a host of writers, especially those with a social or political orientation who wish to subvert the Grimms' cultural values with anti–fairy tales or reclaim the stories' utopian vision. Because of the fairy tale's role in the education and socialization of children, authors of children's literature regularly produce fairy tale adaptations that variously confirm, question, or directly challenge the value of the Grimms' stories.

Ironically, the Grimm genre has become such a literary institution that the published form has influenced not only writers but also oral narrators, whose idea of oral narrative depends on the Grimms' "book tale." Authors and storytellers frequently describe the profound influence the Grimms' collection had on them as children and how the stories confirmed their belief in the power of language. In each case, creative artists respond and react to the Grimms' stories because, spanning folklore and literature, they serve as fundamental narratives of Western culture that shape the way we see the world.

Donald Haase

See also Arnim, Achim von; Brentano, Clemens; *Märchen*

✳✳✳✳✳✳✳✳✳✳✳✳✳✳✳✳✳✳

References

Haase, Donald, ed. *The Reception of Grimms' Fairy Tales: Responses, Reactions, Revisions*. Detroit: Wayne State University Press, 1993.

McGlathery, James M., ed. *The Brothers Grimm and Folktale*. Urbana: University of Illinois Press, 1988.

Zipes, Jack. *The Brothers Grimm: From Enchanted Forests to the Modern World*. New York: Routledge, 1988.

GUNKEL, HERMAN (1862–1932)

The German biblical and Hebrew narrative scholar Herman Gunkel combined analysis of traditions, customs, and beliefs with the classification of literature and the search for historical origins, bringing the insights of folklore and historical and literary criticism to bear on the study of Hebrew narrative. He sought to reconstruct the original community and cultural setting of ancient Israel and, thus, the context from which the Hebrew Bible arose.

To develop a history of ancient Israel, Gunkel analyzed the various types of literary compositions in the Hebrew Bible. He argued that literary history could show how the literature had grown out of the people by isolating the form, process, and environment of the origin of the narratives using folktale analysis, breaking the material down into types and motifs. Gunkel felt that not only were motifs incorporated in the Hebrew Bible but that various narratives of the Hebrew Bible had existed in oral tradition long before being written down in their present narrative form. The goal of the scholar, in this light, was to explain the origin and nature of the writings as products of the human experience. This methodology opened the way for the use of secular literary and historical analysis in biblical studies.

Gunkel's particular approach was predicated on the theory that genres were constituted by their (1) linguistic form, vocabulary, and grammar; (2) thoughts and moods; and (3) connections with life.

Every literary unit had a specific mood, a language of expression, and a setting of life and was tied to a specific aspect of life. By study and analysis, the use to which each particular type of literature had been destined could be determined. Gunkel named this concept *Sitz im Leben* ("situation of life"), which designated the social interaction and context in which these Hebrew Bible narratives had evolved. The written forms of these narratives provided "clues" to the oral forms from which they had originated.

Gunkel reduced these narratives to separate literary units, which, he argued, existed independently in recitation and in song long before they were written down in the Hebrew Bible. By taking the analysis of the narratives a step back and comparing the form and process with contemporary work on oral tradition, Gunkel perceived that the narratives of the Hebrews had lost their earlier poetic quality when they became frozen in written accounts. In oral tradition, narrators would pause between individual stories; when they became incorporated into a text, these performed pauses were lost, and individual stories appeared in close association with other narratives with which they previously might have had no relation. Gunkel became sure that even the arrangement and grouping of the various "sagas" had been accomplished at the oral stage.

Although Gunkel's work was clearly formative to the study of the Hebrew Bible, as well as other ancient literature, and many of his conclusions and theories still have value, some of his conclusions have been called into question. Much of his work has been dismissed because of his insistence on the role of oral tradition in the transmission of the Hebrew Bible and his reliance on anthropological and historical theories of the nineteenth century. Yet his suggestion of the oral composition of the Hebrew Bible and his assertion that within the Hebrew Bible there are narratives which were transmitted orally over long periods, and that these narratives contain motifs familiar in many parts of the world, have continued to be relevant in biblical studies.

Amanda Carson Banks

See also Bible; Motif; Orality; Tale-Type

✳✳✳✳✳✳✳✳✳✳✳✳✳✳✳✳✳✳

References

Coats, George W. *Saga, Legend, Tale, Novella, Fable.* Sheffield, Eng.: JSOT Press, 1985.

Gunkel, Herman. *Folktales in the Old Testament.* Trans. Michael D. Ritter. Sheffield, Eng.: Almond, 1987.

———. *Legends of Genesis, the Bible, Saga, and History.* Trans. W. H. Carruth. New York: Schocken Books, 1964.

Koch, Klaus. *The Growth of the Biblical Tradition, the Form-Critical Method.* Trans. S. M. Cupitt. New York: Scribner, 1969.

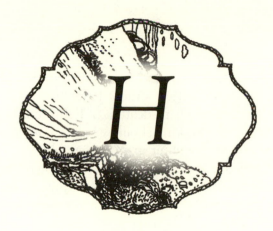

Hamlet

The story of Hamlet has inspired literary treatment by many writers from the Middle Ages, when it circulated as an oral legend, to the present day. Of these authors, the most notable are Saxo Grammaticus, whose *Gesta Danorum* [History of the Danes] contains the earliest account of the life of Hamlet, and William Shakespeare, whose *Tragicall Historie of Hamlet, Prince of Denmarke*, ranks among the best known dramas in world literature. Shakespeare's story rests upon Saxo's, with one or two intermediaries. The Hamlet story appeared in Danish and Icelandic oral tradition up to the seventeenth century, but some time after that, it disappeared as a living oral tradition. The literary treatment that most closely reflects the old Danish legend is that given by Saxo in his *Gesta Danorum*.

According to Saxo, two brothers, Ørvendil and Fengi, jointly ruled the Danish peninsula of Jutland. Ørvendil's successes made Fengi so envious that he murdered his brother and married his widow, Geruth. Fearing for his own life, Amleth, the young son of Ørvendil and Geruth, feigned madness so that Fengi might spare him in the belief that Amleth was incompetent to avenge his father. Amleth spent his time sitting at the hearth fashioning wooden crooks, whose purpose no one could fathom, and in all ways behaved and spoke like a fool, though a clever and witty one. Some observers suspected that he was more cunning than mad, so the youth was tested by being confronted with a beautiful woman in a secluded place in order that the king's men might observe whether he would respond normally to sexual pleasures; he did so, but only after eluding his observers. Since the test was inconclusive, one of the king's friends hid himself in Geruth's bedroom in order to overhear what Amleth would say to his mother in private, but Amleth slew the eavesdropper.

Now very suspicious, Amleth's uncle dispatched him to Britain with two escorts who carried a runic letter instructing the British monarch to put the youth to death. Amleth secretly changed the message to read that the king should execute Amleth's two escorts and give Amleth his daughter in marriage, which he did. Amleth returned to Denmark just as men were celebrating his funeral, and to increase their merriment he acted the fool, joining the servers and plying Fengi's men with drink. When the men fell drunkenly asleep in the hall, Amleth cut down the hangings from the walls, bound the men together in them using his old wooden crooks, and set fire to the hall. Finally he went to Fengi's bedroom and slew the king. The next day, Amleth was acclaimed king by the people. He had other adventures, eventually fell in battle, and was buried in Jutland.

In 1570, a Frenchman, François de Belleforest, retold Saxo's life of Amleth in a collection of tragic stories, *Histoires tragiques*, and by 1589 there seems to have been a play, inspired by Belleforest's Amleth, on the London stage. This early play was probably purchased by Shakespeare's company, the Chamberlain's Men, and the bard reworked it for that company around 1600. Accordingly, Shakespeare's *Hamlet* appears to be a revision of an early English dramatic treatment of a French retelling (Belleforest) of a Latin literary treatment (Saxo) of a Danish legend.

Important differences between Saxo's and Shakespeare's treatments include a shift of setting from the old North to a generic Renaissance court, a change from a pagan to a Christian ethos, and a shift of emphasis from action to character. There are several significant innovations in the plot: the hero's uncle now murders his own brother secretly rather than openly, which makes the reason for Hamlet's decision to play the fool more problematic than Amleth's, and the revenge scene concludes with the hero's tragic death rather than with his triumph.

William Hansen

See also Legend; Orality; Shakespeare, William

✳✳✳✳✳✳✳✳✳✳✳✳✳✳✳✳✳✳

References

Gollancz, Israel, ed. and trans. *Hamlet in Iceland: Being the Icelandic Romantic Ambáles Saga, with Extracts from Five Ambáles Rímur and Other Illustrative Texts, for the Most Part Now First Printed, and an Introductory Essay*. London: David Nutt, 1898.

Hansen, William F. *Saxo Grammaticus and the Life of Hamlet: A Translation, History, and Commentary*. Lincoln and London: University of Nebraska Press, 1983.

Olrik, Jørgen, and Hans Ræder, eds. *Saxonis Gesta Danorum*. 2 vols. Copenhagen: Munksgaard, 1931–1957.

HAND, WAYLAND D. (1907–1986)

Wayland D. Hand was the most productive American scholar of folk belief in the twentieth century. His academic degrees were in German: an M.A. from the University of Utah in 1934 and a Ph.D. from the University of Chicago, where he studied with Archer Taylor, in 1936. His dissertation was on "The Schnaderhüpf: An Alpine Folk Lyric." From 1937 until his retirement in 1974, he taught in the German Department at the University of California, Los Angeles (UCLA). He helped found the California Folklore Society in 1942 (editing its journal from 1954 to 1966) and the Center for the Study of Comparative Mythology and Folklore at UCLA in 1961. In 1957 and 1958, he was president of the American Folklore Society.

Hand won the Giuseppe Pitré Folklore Prize, the first American to do so, for his *Popular Beliefs and Superstitions of the Frank C. Brown Collection of North Carolina Folklore* (2 vols., 1961–1964). More than 8,000 beliefs are enumerated in the work, and, for each, an annotation that includes previously published American examples and references to European sources is provided. This comprehensive collection is useful for documenting examples of traditional beliefs that are incorporated in works of American literature. Additional material and cross-references later brought the number of items in Hand's archive of American popular beliefs to well over a million. Hand also took charge of two other collections of folk beliefs: Newbell Niles Puckett's for Ohio (36,209 numbered items published in three volumes in 1981) and Arthur S. Cannon's for Utah (1984). Hand urged collectors to gather folk beliefs from all the different states, which he intended to incorporate into a cooperative analytic work that would be an encyclopedia of American popular beliefs and superstitions.

Hand sorted beliefs into categories—with such themes as the human body, the life cycle, domestic activities, farming, communication, and weather—and arranged the items in each according to their expected results. Even slight variations were usually treated as separate items. This system of organization has been adopted by numerous other archives and publications in Europe as well as in the United States.

Hand also arranged material for a catalog of American legends. He intended this to be a contribution to an international legend classification, a project that he attempted to organize through the International Society for Folk Narrative Research. However, there was growing resistance to the idea that legends could or should be classified, and neither the American nor the international catalog has been published.

Hand was impressed by how many folk beliefs pertain to health and disease, and he created a separate archive for traditional medicine. He organized a conference on this subject in 1973, the papers of which are published in *American Folk Medicine* (1976). Hand's own medical articles are reprinted in *Magical Medicine* (1980).

In addition to these specialties, Hand's bibliography of more than 150 items ranges from fieldwork (both purposeful and serendipitous) to studies of folktale and legend motifs. In his medical works and elsewhere, he paid attention to the symbolism of peculiar practices and beliefs and such superstitious notions as *couvade*, the evil eye, and the use of parts of corpses.

Christine Goldberg

See also Belief; International Society for Folk Narrative Research; Legend; Taylor, Archer

✳✳✳✳✳✳✳✳✳✳✳✳✳✳✳✳✳✳

References

Cattermole-Tally, Frances. "From Proverb to Belief and Superstition: An Encyclopedic Vision." *Western Folklore* 48 (1989): 3–14.

Hand, Wayland D. *American Folk Legend: A Symposium*. Berkeley, Los Angeles, and London: University of California Press, 1971.

Sobel, Eli, D. K. Wilgus, and Donald Ward. "Wayland D. Hand." In *University of California in Memoriam*, pp. 121–122. Berkeley: University of California Press, 1986.

HARDY, THOMAS (1840–1928)

Thomas Hardy, novelist and poet, created in "Wessex" one of the most credible "regions of the imagination" in English literature (Keith 1988). The apparent real Wessex—rural southern England of the 1840s—owes much to Hardy's interest in folklore and care to describe it accurately: Hardy assured the folklorist Edward Clodd that he had not invented any of the folklore in his novels. This claim to authenticity extends to dialect terms, beliefs, customs, dramas, songs, narratives, and folklife in the sense of the occupations and ways of life that define a vernacular region.

Hardy was born into a family of storytellers and village musicians: his mother was his source for many supernatural legends, and his father, a mason, played both church and secular music. As a youth, Hardy played the fiddle at village weddings, christenings, and house parties, alone or with his father and uncle. Yet, like several of his fictional characters, Hardy as a young man found himself between worlds as his work as an architect, his marriage, and at last his literary recognition enabled him to climb into elite society. His major novels (*The Woodlanders* [1887], *Far from the Madding Crowd* [1874], *The Return of the Native* [1878], *The Mayor of Casterbridge* [1886], *Tess of the d'Urbervilles* [1891]) all involve conflict between older communitarian values in Wessex and intruding representatives of modernity and capitalism. *Jude the Obscure* (1895), Hardy's last novel, shows Wessex destroyed by these forces. The railway reached Dorchester, Hardy's hometown, during his boyhood, and although it opened markets for dairy produce in London, it also brought music-hall songs, which, in Hardy's opinion, "slew at a stroke" the traditional ballads. The train took him to London, but it changed the country; as an ironist, he saw these contradictions.

Despite the convincing texture Hardy gives to Wessex, he was not a realist. He took notes on strange stories he was told and described his theory for literary fiction in terms of oral storytelling: "a story *must be worth the telling*" (Hardy 1965, p. 362). His oral storytelling background comes out in his novels in his doubling of the main narrative by traditional tales that bear upon it, as in *Tess* where dairyman Crick's legend of the bull that knelt when the Nativity hymn was played and Clare's comment on that legend establish the strain of idealistic medievalism in Clare that dooms his relationship with Tess.

The most direct transposition of local legend into literary form occurs in Hardy's short-story collections—*Wessex Tales* (1888), *Life's Little Ironies* (1894)—most notably in "The Superstitious Man's Story," with its motif of the soul leaving the body as a moth. This idea recurs in Hardy's poem "Something Tapped," which only gives up its meaning to a reader who is aware of the tradition. It is in the poems, especially those involving ghosts, that Hardy draws unselfconsciously closest to folk tradition, so that stories of fateful and supernatural encounters heard from his family in Dorset become as influential as reading in classical and modern literature for his thought and literary creation.

Martin Lovelace

See also Ballad; Belief; Dialect; Legend; Storytelling

✳✳✳✳✳✳✳✳✳✳✳✳✳✳✳✳✳✳

References

Firor, Ruth A. *Folkways in Thomas Hardy*. New York: Barnes, 1962 (1931).

Hardy, Florence Emily. *The Life of Thomas Hardy*. New York: St. Martin's Press, 1965.

Keith, W. J. *Regions of the Imagination: The Development of British Rural Fiction*. Toronto: University of Toronto Press, 1988.

Preston, Cathy Lynn. "'The Tying of the Garter': Representations of the Female Rural Laborer in 17th-, 18th-, and 19th-Century English Bawdy Songs." *Journal of American Folklore* 105 (1992): 315–341.

Purdy, R. L., and Michael Millgate, eds. *The Collected Letters of Thomas Hardy*. 7 vols. Oxford: Clarendon Press, 1978–1988.

HARLEM RENAISSANCE

The Harlem Renaissance was one of the richest eras in African-American literature in terms of its complex interplay of folklore and literature. Known also as the New Negro movement, the Harlem Renaissance spanned the years of the "roaring" 1920s, America's "jazz age." This was the time when Ma Rainey, Bessie Smith, Sippie Wallace, and other women were crying the blues. It was also the era when the exploits of Marcus Garvey and Joe Louis would ensure their place in future ballads and bad-man songs.

Nurturing the renewed emphasis in an oral tradition, the African-American writers sought to celebrate an African past and a New World experience shaped by slavery and struggle. In "The Negro Artist and the Racial Mountain" (1926), Langston Hughes advocated a black aesthetic steeped proudly in its indigenous forms and voices. A writer of blues poetry, Hughes ignored divisions of "high" and "low" art, creating instead the communal voices of characters such as Madame and Jesse B. Simple, whose speech and philosophies challenge notions of literacy and genre purity. Hughes's poems fuse jazz, blues, spirituals, work songs, and bebop lyrics with strong statements about heritage, resiliency, and America's democratic experiment. Many people consider his Simple stories oral epics.

Trained by the anthropologist Franz Boas and an Eatonville, Florida, community that relished folktales, toasts, songs, and proverbs, Zora Neale Hurston was the most noted folklorist of the Renaissance. Her collection of lore, *Mules and Men* (1935), remains a major source book for African-American writers, and her novel *Their Eyes Were Watching God* (1937) is an ingenuous blend of the way folklore and literature can inform and perform within each other. In this novel, Hurston makes narrative use of playing the dozens, signifying, and mule and buzzard animal tales.

In addition to Hughes and Hurston, many other Harlem Renaissance writers experimented with the interlocking possibilities of folklore and literature. Jean Toomer conceived of *Cane* (1923) as a "swan song" to a folk tradition, and in using a call-and-response framework, *Cane* lyrically bridges folk traditions with modern impulses. *The Blacker the Berry* (1929) is Wallace Thurman's narrative commentary on the ways folklore has been used to denigrate self-esteem. His work's protagonist, Emma Lou, is as surely a victim of the historical folk proverbs that ridicule dark-skinned black women as Jessie Fauset's Angela Murray in *Plum Bun* (1928) is a beneficiary of such lore. In her autobiography, *Dust Tracks on a Road* (1942), Zora Neale Hurston notes that dark-skinned women are often the butt of folk jokes.

James Weldon Johnson's sermonic poetry stands as a tribute to the verbal dexterity of black preachers. His classic folk sermon, "The Creation" (1927), pictures God performing his creative work "like a mammy bending over her baby." Equally engaging and far-reaching in their influences are Sterling Brown's poetic reworkings of gospel and blues traditions.

As an era, the Harlem Renaissance set the pace for future African-American writers in developing the folkloric underpinnings of African-American culture and literature. Paul Lawrence Dunbar's and Zora Neale Hurston's early attempts at folk speech eventually reach the smoothness of Celie's language in Alice Walker's *The Color Purple*. Hughes's and Toomer's early innovations with spoken and written forms set the stage for the complex ways in which works such as Ralph Ellison's *Invisible Man* and Toni Morrison's *Song of Solomon* enshrine the voice and vision of the oral tradition. The Harlem Renaissance is distinctive for its dual emphases on oral and written traditions, and the era provided a blueprint for the intricate relationship that African-American literature and African-inflected oral traditions would continue to revive and revise.

Valerie Lee

See also Ballad; Ellison, Ralph; Epic; Folktale; Hurston, Zora Neale; Johnson, James Weldon; Morrison, Toni; Proverbs; Sermon; Walker, Alice

✳✳✳✳✳✳✳✳✳✳✳✳✳✳✳✳✳

References
Baker, Houston A., Jr. *Modernism and the Harlem Renaissance*. Chicago: University of Chicago Press, 1987.

Hill, Patricia Liggins, gen. ed. *Call and Response: The Riverside Anthology of the African American Literary Tradition*. Boston: Houghton Mifflin, 1998.

Huggins, Nathan Irvin. *Voices from the Harlem Renaissance*. New York: Oxford University Press, 1995.

Hurston, Zora Neale. *Mules and Men*. Philadelphia: J. B. Lippincott, 1935.

Jones, Gayl. *Liberating Voices: Oral Tradition in African American Literature*. Cambridge: Harvard University Press, 1991.

HARRIS, JOEL CHANDLER (1848–1908)

A newspaperman and novelist, Joel Chandler Harris is particularly remembered for his treatment of Georgia dialect, his skill with humor, and his knowledge and use of folklore. He is often referred to as the first novelist of American folklore, for although several earlier authors used American folklore in their writings, Harris was the first to focus on folklore throughout his life's work.

Harris's first book-length collection of short stories, *Uncle Remus: His Songs and His Sayings*, was published in 1880 and began what was to be eventually an eight-volume set of works that used African-American oral narratives. This series included the works *Nights with Uncle Remus*; *On the Plantation: Uncle Remus and His Friends*; *The Tar-Baby and Other Rhymes of Uncle Remus, Told by Uncle Remus*; *Uncle Remus and Brer Rabbit*; and two posthumous volumes, *Uncle Remus and the Little Boy* and *Uncle Remus Returns*.

Born and raised in Georgia, Harris left school at the age of 12 to learn the printing trade at Turnwold Plantation, where he helped to produce the local weekly newspaper. He also acquired much of his knowledge of African-American folklore at this time, spending hours listening to the slaves' narratives. Many of these tales were used in his Uncle Remus writings; others that were used were solicited from friends and acquaintances who were asked for oral narratives they recalled hearing in similar situations. From these oral sources, Harris collected examples of myths, folktales (especially trickster tales), supernatural legends, and supernatural folktales.

Further reflecting the time Harris spent in the slaves' quarters, the Uncle Remus tales unfold around the structure of a young boy visiting an older African American to hear oral narratives. Structuring his writings and characterization around regional folklore and personal experience, Harris created humorous scenes of everyday life for readers of all ages, utilizing folklore without knowing that it was a subject of academic interest.

Correspondence from the academic community following the fourth edition of *Uncle Remus: His Songs and Sayings* spurred Harris to explore the theories of folklorists. Harris's explorations in and beliefs about the field were incorporated into his turn-of-the-century writings. In his work *Tales of the Home Folks in Peace and War*, he included a story that commented on folklore theory. "The Late Mr. Watkins of Georgia: His Relation to Oriental Folklore" communicates Harris's cynicism about anyone's ability to trace either the origin or migration route of tales from one culture to another. Such public commentary echoes elements of Harris's personal correspondence as it emphasizes his interest in the Georgia region and in the humorous performance of a tale, be that performance oral or written. Harris's opinion that folklore performance is more important than intellectual folklore pursuits was publicly acknowledged by Harris in *Wally Wanderoon and His Story-Telling Machine*, in which he parodies the study of folklore, ultimately implying that a story's value arises from its ethical and humanistic themes.

Harris's final years were filled primarily with work centering around his two most famous characters, Uncle Remus and Billy Sanders. Billy Sanders first appeared in a serialized story for the *Saturday Evening Post* in June 1900. From that time through 1907, this young man often appeared in Harris's newspaper writing, revealing his humorous exploits as a private during the U.S. Civil War. In 1906, Harris took on a new project, becoming managing editor of *Uncle Remus' Magazine*, and in 1908, the magazine became *Uncle Remus' the Home Magazine* after a merger with Indianapolis's *Home*

Magazine. This merger placed Uncle Remus solidly in the popular press market and possibly helped the character continue to live after its creator's death.

Rachel Gholson

See also Legend; Trickster

✳✳✳✳✳✳✳✳✳✳✳✳✳✳✳✳✳

References

Binkley, R. Bruce, Jr. *Joel Chandler Harris*. Athens: University of Georgia Press, 1987.

Brookes, Stella Brewer. *Joel Chandler Harris, Folklorist*. Athens: University of Georgia Press, 1950.

HAWTHORNE, NATHANIEL (1804–1864)

An American fiction writer whose work often incorporates folklore, Nathaniel Hawthorne was born in Salem, Massachusetts. He spent most of his early life there, leaving in 1821 to enter Bowdoin College in Brunswick, Maine, but returning in 1825 to pursue his ambition of becoming a professional writer. During the next 25 years, Hawthorne wrote one romance, *Fanshawe: A Tale* (1828), and enough stories to fill two substantial volumes, *Twice-Told Tales* (1837) and *Mosses from an Old Manse* (1846), but the professional and commercial success he sought did not come until the 1850s and after, when he published *The Scarlet Letter* (1850), *The House of the Seven Gables* (1851), *The Blithedale Romance* (1852), and *The Marble Faun* (1860).

Evident throughout Hawthorne's tales and romances is his fascination with folklore in its varied aesthetic, cultural, and psychological dimensions. Linked by family heritage and place of birth to the earliest settlers of New England and to the witchcraft trials at which his ancestor John Hathorne served as a chief prosecutor, Hawthorne was especially drawn to what has been called the "folk supernaturalism" that was pervasive in every aspect of Puritan life. The devil and his minions materialize in the dark wood bordering Salem village in "Young Goodman Brown"; the Puritan belief in divine providence is shared by the fictional Bostonians of *The Scarlet Letter* who witness and ascribe various meanings to a meteor shower the night

Nathaniel Hawthorne is particularly well known for his portrayals of folk supernaturalism concerning witchcraft in his native Salem, Massachusetts.

of Dimmesdale's secret vigil in the town square; and countless other wonders of the Puritan world find literary expression as well, notably in the legends associated with the ghostly visitations of Matthew Maule and his curse on the House of Pyncheon.

As these and other works attest, Hawthorne was familiar not only with the forms of folk expression but also with the processes of oral transmission and the dynamics of story-telling events. The title of his first collection of stories— *Twice Told Tales*—is itself indicative of the connections he saw between his literary narratives and oral expressive genres, and he makes the con-nection explicit in a subgroup of stories entitled "Legends of the Province House" by relating each of the four tales through a narrator who retells a story attributed to another individual who "professed to have received it at one or two removes from an eye-witness."

Those stories, like Zenobia's legend of Theodore and the veiled lady in *The Blithedale Romance* and Tomaso's legend of Monte Beni in *The Marble Faun*, are clearly imaginative simulations rather than retellings of authentic oral narratives, but usually the boundaries between genres are less definite and the relationships between oral and written sources are more problematic. In *The Marble Faun*, for example, the sight of blood trickling from the nostrils of a murdered Capuchin monk reminds one of the observers of the "old supersti-tion" that "blood flowing from a dead body" signals that the mur-derer is nearby. There is no way to determine, however, whether Hawthorne learned of the belief in Italy or in America, through the oral tradition or from one of the many accounts of such phenomena in Gothic romances, Puritan histories, or other published works he is known to have read.

Whatever its sources, folklore exerted a powerful influence on

Hawthorne's fiction, manifesting itself in ways that resist easy generalizations. Sometimes he built an entire story around a single folk motif, as in "Egotism; or, The Bosom Serpent." More often, he combined disparate folkloric elements within the same narrative frame, as in "My Kinsman, Major Molineux," which begins with a series of comic "skylarking" events and ends with a violent ceremony suggestive of ancient scapegoat rituals. But always Hawthorne sought to create, by all the means available to him, what he described in "The Custom House" introduction to *The Scarlet Letter* as "a neutral territory, somewhere between the real world and fairy-land, where the Actual and the Imaginary may meet, and each imbue itself with the nature of the other."

James W. Kirkland

See also Legend; Motif; Ritual; Storytelling

✳✳✳✳✳✳✳✳✳✳✳✳✳✳✳✳✳✳

References

Barnes, Daniel R. "'Physical Fact' and Folklore; Hawthorne's 'Egotism; or The Bosom Serpent.'" *American Literature* 43 (1971): 117–121.

Daly, Robert. "Liminality and Fiction in Cooper, Hawthorne, Cather, and Fitzgerald." In *Victor Turner and the Construction of Cultural Criticism: Between Literature and Anthropology*, ed. Kathleen M. Ashley, pp. 70–85. Bloomington: Indiana University Press, 1990.

Hoffman, Daniel G. *Form and Fable in American Fiction*. New York: Oxford University Press, 1961.

Thorpe, Coleman W. "The Oral Story Teller in Hawthorne's Novels." *Studies in Short Fiction* 16 (1979): 205–214.

Winslow, David J. "Hawthorne's Folklore and the Folklorists' Hawthorne: A Reexamination." *Southern Folklore Quarterly* 34 (1970): 34–52.

HECATE

Hecate, whose name can also appear as Ecate, Echate, Hecat, and Heccat, was the ancient Greek goddess of the dead. She may have been the daughter of Perseus and Asteria, as well as the mother of Circe, and possibly also the mother of Medea; she is the ancient goddess of magic, and as such she is often associated with witchcraft. The goddess was probably of Thracian or Hellenic origin, or the name may have come from an Egyptian midwife-goddess called

Heqit, Heket, or Hekat. The Greek Hecate was identified with both Artemis and Persephone. She was a witness to the rape of Persephone and assisted Demeter in locating her lost daughter. Because of Hecate's traditional three-way association with other goddesses, she is a deity of triple aspect: byways and crossroads, particularly three-way intersections, were sacred to her. The term *Hecate supper* for any kind of cheap and solid food derives its name from the ancient practice of leaving offerings to the goddess at crossroads dedicated to her.

Because of her triple aspect, Hecate is often associated with many other goddesses of a similar nature. The triple goddess—the white goddess of Robert Graves's eponymous and epic volume (1948)—appears in a number of guises throughout Eastern and Western civilizations. The goddess represents womanhood in its three clearly delineated stages: maid, matron, and crone, or, less poetically, virgin, mother, and old woman. In some of her aspects, the goddess also represents creator, preserver, and destroyer. In Greek mythology, she has many guises: the Fates, the Graeae, the Gorgons, the Furies, and the Graces are all aspects of Hecate. In Norse mythology, she appears as the three Norns, who—like the Greek Fates—spin, weave, and unravel the cloth of human destiny. In Irish legend, she is the Morrigan (a tripartite war goddess and prophetess) although she takes other guises in Ireland, including that of Brigit, the pagan goddess turned Christian saint. In Arthurian legend, she appears variously as Arthur's three sisters—Morgan, Morgause, and Elaine—or as his three wives, all named Guinevere. Tripartite or mother goddesses, representative of fertility (the original Hecate was a goddess of plenty), also appear in Roman, Celto-Germanic, and Slavic mythology.

The three aspects of womanhood can never be far from human consciousness, and Hecate as a triple goddess often makes her way into literature. She is there in William Shakespeare's *Macbeth* as the famed three witches, and Shakespeare mentions Hecate by name in three other plays. The Norse Norns appear in Richard Wagner's *Ring of the Nibelung*. In the twentieth century, perhaps because of a concentration on the emerging freedom, right, and prominence of the female sex, literature in English has taken the image of Hecate to heart and exploited it. From Robert Graves's fascination with what he calls "the antique story ... of the all-powerful Threefold Goddess" who is worshiped "from the British Isles to the Caucasus" (Graves 1948, p. 24) to the appearance of the three changeable witches in modern children's books such as *The Black Cauldron*

(Lloyd Alexander), *A Wrinkle in Time* (Madeleine L'Engle), and *The Moon of Gomrath* (Alan Garner), whimsical or frightening interpretations of this deity abound in modern stories. Strange and subtle variations appear in modern adult literature as well, in such myriad works as *The Mists of Avalon* (Marion Zimmer Bradley) and *The Natural* (Bernard Malamud). Nor is popular culture free of Hecate's influence: she appears in comic books (notably, Neil Gaiman's *Sandman* series) and in films (Peter Greenaway's *Drowning by Numbers*).

As a triple goddess, Hecate is also something of a cult figure in New Age religion, possibly because of her resurgence in modern fantasy and in popular culture, which has helped to place "the goddess" (as she is familiarly and worshipfully called) in the consciousness of the general public. This mythic and eternal figure continues to wield a profound influence on the human psyche.

Elizabeth E. Wein

See also Arthurian Tradition; Myth

✳✳✳✳✳✳✳✳✳✳✳✳✳✳✳✳✳

References

Graves, Robert. *The White Goddess: A Historical Grammar of Poetic Myth*. New York: Farrar, Straus and Giroux, 1948.

Green, Miranda J. *Dictionary of Celtic Myth and Legend*. London: Thames and Hudson, 1992.

Grimal, Pierre. *The Penguin Dictionary of Classical Mythology*. London: Penguin, 1990.

Walker, Barbara G. *The Woman's Encyclopedia of Myths and Secrets*. New York: HarperCollins, 1983.

Heike, Tale of the

Tale of the Heike (*Heike monogatari*) is the greatest war tale (*gunki monogatari*) from Japan's medieval period (1185–1568). It recounts the events of an approximately 25-year period from 1160 to 1185, focusing initially on the power and glory of the Taira family (also known as the Heike) and then telling of their eventual decline and ultimate destruction at the hands of their sworn enemies, the Minamoto family (also known as the Genji). Although the *Heike* contains many legends and epiclike tales, it is based essentially on historical fact.

The tale can be divided into three parts. The first part focuses on Taira no Kiyomori, the overbearing ruthless leader of the Taira, and his hatred of the Minamoto. It is his evil nature that, through the working of Buddhist karmic retribution, leads to the eventual destruction of his descendants. The second and third parts of the tale focus on Minamoto no Yoshinaka and, after his death, Minamoto no Yoshitsune. Yoshitsune, one of Japan's greatest tacticians and warriors, is also one of its most tragic heroes. His successes, which are vividly depicted in the *Heike*, lead to mistrust and deceit in his relations with his elder brother, Yoritomo, and eventually lead to Yoshitsune's being hunted down and killed. This latter part of his life is also depicted in other war tales.

Helen McCullough (1988) points out that the *Heike* contains numerous formulaic epic themes, for example, the dressing of the hero, self-naming before individual combat, competition to be first, and inspection and identification of prisoners or heads taken in battle. McCullough also mentions the emphasis in the tale on visual effects, action-stopping devices similar to those in the Song of Roland, the use of omens to create suspense, linguistic repetition, and the use of similar imagery in similar contexts.

The appearance of these formulas and techniques can be explained, according to Kenneth Butler (1966, 1969), by the textual evolution of the *Heike*. Butler and other scholars now feel that the original text, which was compiled using various sources, was written early in the thirteenth century. By mid-century, two traditions for the dissemination of the tale had appeared: a written text for reading alone and a text used by oral chanters, usually blind entertainers, who accompanied themselves with a lutelike instrument called a *biwa*. There are, therefore, numerous extant texts of the *Heike*, but today, the most widely studied version is one dictated by the master *Heike* performer Akashi Kakuichi around 1371.

The *Heike* has had a tremendous impact on Japanese literature and the arts. For example, in the classical *nō* theater, there are five categories of plays that appear in a fixed order during a formal presentation. The second category of plays, whose main protagonist is always the ghost of a dead warrior, is usually referred to as *shura-nō*. Of the sixteen *shura-nō* that are still extant in the repertoire of different schools of *nō*, only one of them has a main character who was not a member of either the Heike or the Genji.

Richard W. Anderson

See also Epic; Legend; *Nō (Noh)*; *Song of Roland*

✳✳✳✳✳✳✳✳✳✳✳✳✳✳✳✳✳

References

Butler, Kenneth D. "The Heike Monogatari and the Japanese Warrior Epic." *Harvard Journal of Asiatic Studies* 29 (1969): 93–108.

———. "The Textual Evolution of the Heike Monogatari." *Harvard Journal of Asiatic Studies* 26 (1966): 5–51.

McCullough, Helen Craig. *The Tale of the Heike.* Stanford, Calif.: Stanford University Press, 1988.

Morris, Ivan. *The Nobility of Failure: Tragic Heroes in the History of Japan.* New York: New American Library, 1975.

Shimazaki, Chifumi. *Warrior Ghost Plays from the Japanese Noh Theater: Parallel Translations with Running Commentary.* Ithaca, N.Y.: Cornell University East Asia Program, 1993.

HENRY, JOHN

John Henry is an African-American folk hero whose steel-driving contest with a steam-driven drill is celebrated in ballad, work song, and legend. Most scholars agree that the story is based on an actual worker who helped build the Big Bend tunnel on the C&O Railroad in West Virginia from 1870 to 1872, although the first ballads of John Henry were not collected until the early twentieth century. The folklore of John Henry has been thoroughly studied by scholars, and the songs have been widely disseminated in popular culture. Folk-song scholar Norm Cohen writes of John Henry in *Long Steel Rail: The Railroad in American Folksong*, "In recent decades no other ballad native to this country has been more widely known or more often recorded, has stimulated more printed commentary, or has inspired more folk and popular literature" (Cohen 1981).

The story exists in many different versions, but the salient features are that a strong black steel driver named John Henry is challenged to a contest with a new steam drill; John Henry wins the contest but dies in the effort. In many versions, his wife or woman is mentioned, and there are either metaphoric or direct sexual references in the story. The work-song versions were sung by African-American railroad workers as a rhythmic accompaniment to the driving of spikes in railroad ties. The ballad versions are sung by both black and white singers, but as a hero figure John Henry is more important in African-American culture.

Two questions dominated the early research on John Henry: Was he a historical figure? and Was he one and the same as another African-American ballad character, John Hardy? The research clearly indicated two separate ballads for John Henry and John Hardy, but the question of origin was more complex and controversial. After extensive research, two scholars, Guy B. Johnson (1929) and Louis W. Chappell (1933), made convincing arguments for the historical origin of the ballad although Chappell accused Johnson of plagiarizing his research. Later, folklorist MacEdward Leach (1966) posited a Jamaican origin for "John Henry."

The popularization of John Henry is parallel to that of Paul Bunyan—books, magazine articles, children's literature, comic strips, animated cartoons, and local festivals helped spread awareness of John Henry throughout the United States—but John Henry has an advantage over Paul Bunyan in one area: the ballad version of his story has been sung by white country singers, black blues singers, and folk revival singers and recorded commercially scores of times by everyone from Burl Ives, Leadbelly, and Harry Belafonte to Johnny Cash, Memphis Slim, and Bill Monroe. The best known literary manifestation of the John Henry narrative is Roark Bradford's novel *John Henry*, which was adapted for the Broadway stage and starred Paul Robeson as John Henry.

Interpretations of the John Henry narrative are as varied as the theoretical models available for analysis. Some scholars see the story mainly in sexual terms and concentrate on the steel-driving metaphor as phallic. Others see John Henry's story in class terms, expressing the fear of workers that their jobs will be taken over by new technology. John Henry is also an occupational hero in that, like other working men in ballad and legend, he must finish the job at all costs. John Henry is above all an African-American culture hero—a dignified, hardworking black man who achieves victory over the white man's machine and who is a powerful expression of black sexuality.

Earlier in the twentieth century, John Henry was probably the best known folk hero among African Americans. The appeal to white audiences may be explained as an inversion of the African-American meaning: the black man who dies without protest in order to finish what is, after all, the white man's business. Most of these interpretations have been made by white scholars without much supporting evidence in the form of interviews with African-American informants. John Henry has become a complex cultural symbol with different meanings in different contexts; no one explanation of his appeal is satisfactory by itself.

Patrick B. Mullen

See also Ballad; Bunyan, Paul; Leach, MacEdward; Legend

✲✲✲✲✲✲✲✲✲✲✲✲✲✲✲✲✲

References

Chappell, Louis W. *John Henry*. Jena, East Germany: Frommannsche, 1933.

Cohen, Norm. *Long Steel Rail: The Railroad in American Folksong*. Champaign: University of Illinois Press, 1981.

Dorson, Richard M. "The Career of 'John Henry.'" *Western Folklore* 24 (1965): 155–163.

Johnson, Guy B. *John Henry*. Chapel Hill: University of North Carolina Press, 1929.

Leach, MacEdward. "John Henry." In *Folklore and Society*, ed. Bruce Jackson, pp. 93–106. Hatboro, Pa.: Folklore Associates, 1966.

Levine, Lawrence W. *Black Culture and Black Consciousness: Afro-American Folk Thought from Slavery to Freedom*. Oxford: Oxford University Press, 1977.

Herder, Johann Gottfried (1744–1803)

The German theologian and philosopher Johann Gottfried Herder was a student in Könighberg University under the influence of Immanuel Kant and Johann Georg Hamann. He was ordained in Riga, Latvia, met Johann Wolfgang von Goethe in Strasbourg in 1771, first served as a court preacher and superintendent in Bückeburg, Germany, and then became a leading churchman in Weimar, where he renewed his friendship with Goethe. Despite claims to the contrary, Herder was not the first to offer a modern notion of *Volkskunde* ("study of the folk")—that claim belongs to Justus Möser—but Herder's influence on the development of the collection and study of folklore, especially the folk song, cannot be exaggerated.

As the presence of Lithuanian, Latvian, and Estonian songs in Herder's collections indicates, he was aware of the existence and significance of "folk poetry" as early as his stay in Riga when he was still in his twenties; at that time, he also experimented with translations of Ossian. Herder's own views as to what constituted a "folk song" were somewhat broader than folklorists today would allow.

In a seminal essay of 1773, entitled "Extract from a Correspondence on Ossian and the Songs of Ancient Peoples," he pled with urgency for the timely collection of folk songs, provincial songs, and peasant songs. "Only who is it," he asks, "who will collect them? Who will care about them? Who will care about the songs of the people? In streets and lanes and fishmarkets? In the untaught rounds of the rural people? About songs that often do not scan and rhyme badly? Who should collect them?" We know that, among others, he encouraged Goethe to collect folk songs in Alsace. Herder's dramatic image—"We are close to the edge of the cliff: another half century, and it will be too late!"—has been echoed by many folklore collectors and archivists ever since, in metaphors of their own.

It is ironic that Herder himself was initially stimulated by James Macpherson's translations of Ossianic poems and by Bishop Percy's *Reliques of Ancient English Poetry* (1765). Herder, in turn, influenced, through the Grimm brothers, people like William Thoms.

Herder's best known folklore-related publication is his *Volkslieder* [Folk songs], the first part of which (1778) contains songs mostly from Germany, Great Britain (including from William Shakespeare), and Scandinavia; the second part (1779) goes further afield. The title under which this collection is best known, *Stimmen der Völker in Liedern* [Voices of the peoples in songs], is not Herder's own but was attached to the work posthumously in 1807 by Johann von Müller in an edition of Herder's works. In that edition, the songs were rearranged according to their geographical origins, whereas, in contrast to his earlier manuscript, *Alte Volkslieder* [Old folk songs] of 1774, Herder's own arrangement of the items included was not according to their ethnic, linguistic, or cultural origin but according to aesthetic criteria. For Herder, particular generic characteristics or anonymity of authorship were not decisive; what mattered were the inner tone and natural simplicity, both of the chosen subjects and of their treatment. His collection, therefore, includes songs that today would not be regarded as belonging to the folk-cultural register.

What Herder looked upon as *volksartig* ("folklike") is "light, simple, grown out of the topics and language of the masses, as well as nature, rich and felt by all." Thus, for Herder, *die Seele des Volks* ("the soul of the people") is the creative source of all poetic revelation, and, in keeping with his idea that the character and customs of peoples are formed by *Volkspoesie* ("literature by and for the people"), the emphasis of his concept of folk shifts from cosmopolitan to national, from *vulgus* to idealized nations, a meaning that is not normally inherent in the English word *folk*. To call his modified concept "nationalistic" would, however, be inappropriate as it would falsely anticipate a later-nineteenth-century attitude. For Herder, "songs are the archives of the people," and he tried to examine and explain the processes that bring about continuity and change in folk poetry.

Herder's acknowledged eminent status in the history of ideas in general and in the intellectual world of Germany in the second half of the eighteenth century in particular does not depend solely on his influential position in the history of folkloristics. Unfortunately, however, his several other important achievements—for example, his innovative thinking on the question of language origins, on the relationship between nature and culture, on a social dimension of history, on theological matters, etc.—cannot be included in this appraisal.

W. F. H. Nicolaisen

See also Goethe, Johann Wolfgang von; Grimm, Jacob and Wilhelm; Macpherson, James; Ossian; Percy, Thomas

✳✳✳✳✳✳✳✳✳✳✳✳✳✳✳✳✳✳

References

Herder, Johann Gottfried. *Reflections on the Philosophy of the History of Mankind*. Chicago: University of Chicago Press, 1968.

———. *The Spirit of Hebrew Poetry*. Trans. James Marsh. 2 vols. Burlington, Vt.: E. Smith, 1833.

MacEachran, Frank. *The Life and Philosophy of Johann Gottfried Herder*. Oxford: Clarendon Press, 1939.

Mayo, Robert S. *Herder and the Beginnings of Comparative Literature*. Chapel Hill: University of North Carolina Press, 1969.

Nevinson, Henry. *A Sketch of Herder and His Times*. London: Chapman and Hall, 1884.

Thoms, William. Letter in *Athenaeum* 982 (1846): 862–863.

Heroic pattern

The heroic pattern is the symbolically interpreted and/or structurally derived pattern of the life and/or actions of hero figures. Various patterns have been suggested. The American comparative mythologist Joseph Campbell (1904–1987) argued that all hero narratives tell essentially the same story—hence, there is but one "monomyth."

Viewed broadly, the monomyth illustrates the three stages of rites of passage: in order, the individual's separation, initiation, and return. On a more detailed level, the monomyth develops specific "key images," including the following: Upon receiving the "call to adventure," the hero leaves his everyday environment and encounters a "guide," or teacher, who provides advice, knowledge, magic implements, etc. The hero proceeds to "the threshold of adventure" (the entryway to a place of power), which is protected by a "threshold guardian." Defeating, conciliating, or succumbing to the guardian, the hero crosses the threshold into the realm of the unknown. Aided by previous gifts from the guide, the hero undergoes a series of trials ("the road of trials"). Following the supreme trial, the hero receives his reward, whether it be union with the "goddess-mother," his recognition by a "father-creator," or his own divinization ("apotheosis"). If authority figures (for example, deities) have sanctioned his efforts, the hero returns to the world under their protection. If they oppose his efforts (as in the case of bride theft or fire theft, for example), the hero is pursued. The hero recrosses the threshold into the everyday world. His reward (the Golden Fleece, the runes of wisdom, spiritual illumination) restores the world. If the hero is a warrior-king (other hero types are the shaman-sage and the martyr-saint), then after his return the hero may rule wisely. However, with time, he may become a tyrant who must be destroyed by a new hero. The hero undergoes his final separation from the world by reconciling himself to death ("the end of the microcosm"). Eventually, the universe itself comes to an end ("the end of the macrocosm"), only to be reborn again in the continuing "cosmogonic cycle."

Influenced by the Freudian interpretation of dreams and the Jungian concept of archetypes, Campbell interpreted the monomyth as the journey of the hero-self, or individual consciousness, toward individuation and growth. At one level, Campbell saw this journey as the hero's confronting and reconciling with symbolically portrayed parental figures. At a more transcendental level, the hero's ultimate reward is union with divine will or the "one presence." Campbell's work is distinguished from that of other scholars in that he illustrated his hero pattern with myths from many different cultures—ancient Egyptian, Indian, European, Native American, Australian aboriginal, Japanese, Middle Eastern, Polynesian—thus suggesting its universality.

The British ritualist Lord Raglan (1885–1964) emphasized the relationship between hero narratives and ancient religious ritual. Influenced by Sir James Frazer's *The Golden Bough* and the motif of the fisher king, Raglan interpreted hero narratives as descriptions of "royal ritual"—what a king should do to secure the prosperity of his subjects. Typically, these duties included the king's sacrificial death so that his people might live.

Raglan identified 22 elements in the "biographical pattern," or life story, of the hero: (1) The hero's mother is a royal virgin; (2) his father is a king and (3) often a near relative of his mother; (4) the circumstances of his conception are unusual; and (5) he is reputed to be the son of a god. (6) At birth, an attempt is made to kill him, but (7) he is spirited away and (8) reared by foster parents in a far country. (9) We are told nothing of his childhood, but (10) on reaching manhood, he returns or goes to his future kingdom. (11) After a victory over the king and/or a giant, dragon, or wild beast, (12) he marries a princess and (13) becomes king. (14) For a time he reigns uneventfully and (15) prescribes laws, but (16) later he loses favor with the gods and/or his subjects and (17) is driven from the throne and city, after which (18) he meets with a mysterious death, (19) often at the top of a hill. (20) His children, if any, do not succeed him. (21) His body is not buried, but nevertheless, (22) he has one or more holy sepulchres.

Because of the commonality of the pattern, Raglan argued, the events it depicts are fiction and cannot be taken as fact; the narratives reflect a recurring perceptual framework. Raglan primarily based his pattern on myths and legends from ancient Greece but also included some from northern Europe and the Old Testament.

The Russian folklorist Vladimir Propp's (1895–1970) contribution to the heroic pattern came by way of his pioneering study of the syntagmatic (chronological) structure of fairy tales. Propp posited a series of "dramatis personae functions" (actions of the characters) that propel the narrative. Each function may be fulfilled positively or negatively. Following an introductory section, the fairy tale illustrates one or the other of two crucial functions: the villain causes harm to someone (for example, he abducts the princess), or someone lacks something (for example, the king is dying and needs "the water of life"). The hero receives the call for help and leaves home. He meets one or more donors (trebling—threefold repetition—is a common motif here) who give him advice or magical implements. The hero arrives at the desired location, struggles with and conquers the villain, or liquidates the previous lack (he might obtain the water of life). The hero is "branded" (or marked) in some way, and as he returns home, he may be pursued and receive aid from helpers. The hero is unrecognized upon his arrival and faces the threat of a false hero (perhaps someone else claims to have slain the dragon). A difficult task is proposed, which only the hero can resolve successfully. The hero is recognized, and the false hero is punished. The hero marries and ascends the throne. Propp based his study on 100 Russian fairy tales. Other scholars have applied his structural method of study to the hero narratives of other cultures, as well as to literary works, which suggests that such narrative structuring may be part of humanity's perceptual framework.

Danielle M. Roemer

See also Campbell, Joseph; Frazer, James George; Propp, Vladimir I.

✽✽✽✽✽✽✽✽✽✽✽✽✽✽✽

References

Campbell, Joseph. *The Hero with a Thousand Faces*. 2d ed. Princeton, N.J.: Princeton University Press, 1968.

Dundes, Alan. "The Hero Pattern and the Life of Jesus." In *Interpreting Folklore*, ed. Alan Dundes, pp. 223–261. Bloomington: Indiana University Press, 1980.

Propp, Vladimir. *Morphology of the Folktale*. 2d rev. ed. Austin: University of Texas Press, 1968 (1928).

Raglan, Lord Fitzroy. *The Hero: A Study in Tradition, Myth, and Drama*. Westport, Conn.: Greenwood Press, 1956 (1936).

HINDU EPICS

As the two great epics of ancient India, the *Mahabharatha* and the *Ramayana* reflect an extraordinary bond between oral and literary traditions. These epics have generated a varied body of folk traditions through communal re-creations of myths, legends, songs, shadow play, and drama in India and later in several Southeast Asian countries. Religious discourses held at temples in rural and urban India are one more form of folk performance that has been inspired by the epics. The written word of the epics has had a lasting impact on the spoken word of the oral traditions, particularly in relation to the perpetuation of Hindu beliefs and practices.

Scholars continue to debate the authorship of the *Mahabharata* and the *Ramayana*, and there is some agreement that a legendary bard named Vyasa compiled a major portion of the 220,000 lines of the former and a robber-chief-turned-holy-man, Valmiki, composed most of the 96,000 lines of the latter. Together, the two epics constitute the largest body of religious literature in the world. The events of the *Mahabharatha* date back to 850 B.C.E.–500 C.E., and the *Ramayana* story is traceable to 400 B.C.E.–200 C.E. The first epic consists of 18 books called "parvans," and the second one has 7 books called "kandas." Valmiki, praised as the *"adi kavi,"* or the "first poet," is believed to have improvised the metric form called the *sloka* as he started reciting the *Ramayana* in a moment of acute grief when he came upon a female heron mourning the loss of her mate killed by a hunter. The *sloka* has a two-line structure in the *Mahabharatha* and a four-line stanzaic form in the *Ramayana*.

Written first in Prakrit and later standardized in Sanskrit, both of the epics flourished in oral circulation among *rishis* ("holy men"), priests, and poets. Textual variations and additions characterized the several thousand manuscripts found in Indo-Aryan languages by 1500 C.E., and the orality of the epics has been a dominant issue among scholars in and outside India. One notable comment made during a 1975 *Ramayana* conference held in New Delhi reiterated the "amazing tenacity of the oral traditions ... which have supported, supplemented, and complemented the traditions of the written word" (Vatsyana 1980, p. 700).

To look just for the story in either of the epics would amount to an oversight of a morality code these epics have generated in the Hindu lifestyle. Cosmology, theogony, statecraft, the science of war, philosophical interludes, legendary history, mythology, fairy tales, and commentary on ethics may all be found here. The main narrative in each of the epics, and the several sets of legends and tales constituting the subplots and the digressions, are widely recognized as stories with a universal appeal.

The *Mahabharatha* is essentially an account of a battle between two sets of brothers, the Pandavas and the Kauravas. Some scholars believe that the Battle of Kurukshetra was fought in north-central India, somewhere near Delhi, and that the historical origins of the battle are traceable to 3100 B.C.E. A sage with the unique gift of being able to survey the whole scene narrates the course of action, "panning" troop movements in all sectors of the battlefield. This narration is by the sage, Sanjaya, who can "zero in and out" of the camps of both armies. Only five Pandava brothers; their common wife, Draupadi; and Krishna the charioteer survive. It is in the better known segment of the epic, the Bhagavad Gita, that Krishna

Krishna, the charioteer in the Mahabharata, later revealed his identity as the god Vishnu in the renowned Bhagavad Gita.

reveals his identity as god Vishnu come down to help the cause of the Pandava brothers. It is in the Gita that we find a philosophic defense of war when it is waged for a right cause.

Ramayana is about Rama's miraculous birth, his appointment as the successor to the throne; his banishment from his father's kingdom; the abduction of his wife, Sita, by the demon Ravana during the exile; and the reunion of Rama and Sita. Like Krishna in the *Mahabharatha*, Hanuman is a resourceful helper in the *Ramayana*. Hanuman is the leader of the army of monkeys that invades the island of Sri Lanka to rescue Sita. Even though he is captured and his tail is set ablaze, Hanuman manages to get free, jump from house to house, and burn down the enemy city. Accounts of Hanuman's exploits match those of Rama's feats in their popular appeal. Sita's chastity, commitment to his brother's cause by Lakshmana as well as the trickery of the demons are all standard subjects of many a tale that has been told and retold. In allegorical terms, the battle between Rama and Ravana is a struggle between good and evil.

The scholar A. K. Ramanujam has pointed out that "repetition, elaboration, and variation" are basic elements of narration in the *Mahabharatha*. The "repetitive phrases, similes, and formulaic descriptions" characterize the storytelling in the epics, just as these features have been found by Western scholars to be the standards of most oral poetry (Ramanujam 1991, p. 419). Sanskrit scholar Barend A. Van Nooten has commented that the folklorist may find in these epics points of comparison for collections of fables in world literature, and that the Hindu epics offer the universal theme of a hero killing a demon that is found in stories around the world. For Indians in particular, a *Mahabharatha* story like that of Savitri's, a legendary heroine who succeeded in reclaiming her husband from the god of death with her display of conjugal devotion, has become a model of righteous conduct. Festivals in honor of Rama are similarly another example of the pervasive influence the epics have had in shaping Indian life.

The epics are in Sanskrit, which means they have not been as easily accessible as the stories have been through oral currency. Even Muslims in India hear the stories of Pandavas and Kauravas and stories of Rama and Sita from schoolteachers and Hindu friends. It would not be incorrect to reaffirm the widespread awareness of the epics in India as treasure houses of didactic narratives and fountains of philosophic expositions.

Mohammed S. Ansari

See also Epic; Fable; Fairy Tale; Legend; Myth; Performance

****

References

Ramanujam, A. K. "Repetition in the *Mahabharatha*." In *Essays on the Mahabharatha*, ed. Arvind Sharma, pp. 401–443. New York: E. J. Brill, 1991.

Van Nooten, Barend A. "The Sanskrit Epics." In *Heroic Epic and Saga: An Introduction to the World's Great Epics*, ed. Felix J. Oinas, pp. 49–75. Bloomington: Indiana University Press, 1978.

Vatsyana, Kapila. "Ramayana in the Arts of Asia." In *The Ramayana Tradition in Asia: Papers Presented at the International Seminar on The Ramayana Tradition in Asia, New Delhi, December 1975*, ed. V. Raghavan, pp. 681–701. Madras: Sahitya Akademi, 1980.

Walker, Benjamin. *The Hindu World: An Encyclopedic Survey of Hinduism*, vol. 2. New York: Frederick A. Praeger, 1968.

Historic-Geographic Method

Also called "the Finnish method" because of its beginnings in Finland during the nineteenth century, the historic-geographic method was an early attempt to apply scientific principles to the study of oral literature. Proponents of this method developed techniques for the comparative analysis of literary history by documenting the diffusion of oral and written narratives from one linguistic region to another, particularly within the Indo-European landmass. Scholars attempted to trace the origins of a particular narrative core, or tale-type, by accumulating every possible text and then documenting the time and place of each variant of a story to determine a hypothetical urform, or original version, for each text analyzed.

The scholarly interest in a new historical-geographical methodology for studying folklore was in part a reaction against the romantic views of folklore promulgated in Europe during much of the nineteenth century. Speculative theories had been proposed to explain the origins and continuity of folklore: survivals, relics either of unevolved savages and peasants or, conversely, of a noble "racial" heritage; automigration from India; degeneration of ancient solar myths. Epic poetry was discovered, rewritten, or made up out of whole cloth to venerate a heroic ancestry.

Scholars during this era faced emerging European nationalism and ethnocentric currents of colonialism. They were also confronted with discoveries of geographers, anthropologists, and archaeologists—exotic discoveries that revealed not only an incredible diversity of human experience but also striking similarities of certain myths, customs, and folktales. One theory forwarded to account for thematic and narrative similarities among diverse peoples was polygenesis, which held that it was possible for the same or similar narratives to have been created independently at different times and places. A more compelling theory for folklorists, however, was that every complex tale was created at a particular place and time (monogenesis) and, through diffusion, was disseminated throughout contiguous lands.

Monogenesis of narrative tradition was the basic assumption of the historical-geographical scholarship that was coming out of Finland by the beginning of the twentieth century. As early as 1884, Julius Krohn (1835–1888) spelled out the essentials of a new methodology, which he used to track down the origins of the Finnish national epic, the *Kalevala*. He argued that before drawing final conclusions, he would arrange and observe various versions of the epic folk songs according to their chronology and topography in order to separate the original components from later additions. His conclusions, published posthumously in 1891, argued that the *Kalevala* songs were not as old as had been previously thought and that much of the narrative substance had been borrowed from neighboring peoples.

Julius Krohn's international perspective and objective methods profoundly challenged the nationalistic assumptions about ethnic origins of European folklore. The brothers Grimm, for example, had argued that German folktales were inherited from the ancient Indo-German (Aryan) mythology and represented a special German ethos. The Grimms were so influential that many folktales that were known to have international counterparts were still referred to by the number assigned in their *Household Tales* (1884). The methodology of Julius Krohn was developed by his son, Kaarle Krohn (1863–1933), and finally published by him in 1926 as *Die folkloristische Arbeitsmethode* [Folklore methodology].

During the 1920s, the historical-geographical school charted the direction for international folktale research. Even before Kaarle Krohn's definitive guide to the method appeared, scholarly monographs were being published that carefully presented variants of a particular tale-type according to chronological and geographical distribution and that suggested a hypothetical time and place for an original archetype. Notable monographs based on the historic-geographic method have been published in Helsinki by the Folklore

Fellows Communications series, including Reidar Christiansen's *The Tale of the Two Travelers, or The Blinded Man* (1916), Walter Anderson's *Kaiser und Abt* [Emperor and abbot (1923)], and Archer Taylor's study of Finnish variants of a tale, *The Black Ox* (1927). Texts culled from written sources dominated oral texts as data and were the only possible bases for indicating a date before which a given tale may have existed. The Austrian scholar Albert Wesselski (1878–1941) even argued with considerable influence that literary versions were significantly more important than oral versions for disseminating any particular tale.

The Finnish folklorist Antti Aarne (1867–1925), who was a student of Kaarle Krohn, compiled an international tale-type catalog in 1910. His index gave numbers to plots, broke them down into smaller narrative units, or motifs, and listed all known international versions of each tale-type. But it was not until 1928 that this index became a compulsory tool for folktale research, when the American folklorist Stith Thompson published a greatly expanded version of the Aarne index in English as *The Types of the Folktale: A Classification and Bibliography*. Also referred to as the Aarne-Thompson index, this monumental work was expanded and republished in 1964; tale-types have subsequently been referred to by AT (Aarne-Thompson) numbers as well as by common titles. Thompson also published the massive *Motif Index of Folk Literature* in six volumes (1932–1936; revised, 1955–1958), carefully interrelating motifs and tale-types in the two parallel indexes. A number of other type- and motif indexes have been published over the years, derived from the work of Aarne and Thompson.

Of all the proponents of the historic-geographic method, Stith Thompson has remained one of the most important in folklore scholarship, even though Thompson's major contributions, the type and motif indexes, did not offer new directions. His student, Warren Roberts, did write an important historic-geographic study, "The Tale of the Kind and the Unkind Girls: A-T 480," with Thompson's guidance. Thompson himself published a single study using the historic-geographic method. In that study, "The Star Husband," an American Indian folktale with many variants collected throughout North America, Thompson drew modest conclusions, finding evidence for the same processes of diffusion suggested by studies of European tales and postulating hypothetical origins for the tale.

The limited conclusions that could be drawn from a method of research that required tremendous time and effort, along with the development of new interests in folklore and literary scholarship, have led to a recent lack of interest among folklorists for using the historic-geographic method. The classic studies already published, the contributions of the method to genre classification, and the index tools developed through application of the method all remain important references for the study of folklore and literature.

Kenneth A. Thigpen

See also Aarne, Antti; Anderson, Walter; Grimm, Jacob and Wilhelm; Krohn, Leopold Kaarle; Monogenesis; Motif; Tale-Type; Taylor, Archer; Thompson, Stith

✳✳✳✳✳✳✳✳✳✳✳✳✳✳✳✳✳✳

References

Aarne, Antti, and Stith Thompson. *The Types of the Folktale: A Classification and Bibliography*. Folklore Fellows Communication 184. Helsinki: Academia Scientiarum Fennica, 1964.

Anderson, Walter. *Kaiser und Abt: Die Geschichte eines Schwankes*. Folklore Fellows Communication 42. Helsinki: Academia Scientiarum Fennica, 1923.

Grimm, Jacob, and Wilhelm Grimm. *Household Tales*. 2 vols. Trans. and ed. Margaret Hunt, intro. Andrew Lang. London, 1884.

Krohn, Kaarle. *Die folkloristische Arbeitsmethode*. Oslo, Norway: The Institute for Comparative Research in Human Culture, 1926. Trans. Roger L. Welsch as *Folklore Methodology*. Austin: University of Texas Press, 1971.

Roberts, Warren. "The Tale of the Kind and the Unkind Girls: Aa-Th and Related Tales." *Fabula*, suppl., series B, no. 1. Berlin: De Gruyter, 1958.

Taylor, Archer. *The Black Ox: A Study in the History of a Folktale*. Folklore Fellows Communications 70. Helsinki: Academia Scientiarum Fennica, 1927.

Thompson, Stith. *The Folktale*. New York: Holt, Rinehart and Winston, 1946.

———. "The Star Husband Tale." In *The Study of Folklore*, ed. Alan Dundes, pp. 414–474. Englewood Cliffs, N.J.: Prentice-Hall, 1965 (1953).

HOGG, JAMES (1770–1835)

James Hogg was born in Ettrick, Selkirk, in the Borders region of Scotland. Beginning at age six, he worked as a herder, having had only six weeks' formal schooling. Understandably then, the indigenous culture of Ettrick was a deep source of subject matter and form for Hogg. His family were skilled tradition-bearers: his mother, Margaret Laidlaw, contributed to Walter Scott's *Minstrelsy of the Scottish*

Border (1802–1803), though Hogg's own reliability as a folklore informant has been questioned. Serving with his employers, the Laidlaws, at Willenslee and Blackhouse, he had access to a wide variety of reading material, including Blind Hary's *The Wallace* (c. 1477) and Allan Ramsay's *The Gentle Shepherd* (1725).

Hogg's first publication, drawing on lyric precedents, was "Mistakes of a Night," published in *Scots Magazine* in 1794. His *The Mountain Bard* (1807) emulates ballad and lyric forms while *The Shepherd's Guide* (1807) is an authoritative treatment of agrarian lifestyles and animal remedies. *The Brownie of Bodsbeck* (1818) subjectively treats Ettrick's religious history and supernatural beliefs, and *The Private Memoirs and Confessions of a Justified Sinner* (1824) innovatively explores extreme Calvinism.

Hogg collected the materials for *Jacobite Relics of Scotland* (1819–1821), a two-volume collection of songs from oral tradition, manuscript collections, and printed sources commissioned by the Highland Society of London. Many of his versions of traditional songs and original compositions, such as "Charlie Is My Darling" and "Birniebouzlel," are sustained in the oral tradition. Like the "plowman poet" Robert Burns (whose *Works* Hogg edited with William Motherwell between 1834 and 1836), James Hogg himself has entered into oral and literary tradition. The Ettrick shepherd, "the boozing buffoon" of the Scottish poet John Wilson's (Christopher North) *Noctes Ambrosianae* (1822–1835), is a persistent stereotype.

After failing in more than one farming scheme, Hogg moved to Edinburgh in 1810 to pursue a literary career. His ventures included the short-lived satirical magazine *The Spy* (1810–1811), and critical success came with *The Queen's Wake* (1813), a poetic cycle utilizing ballad forms.

In 1815, however, he returned to the Borders area and rented a farm from the Duke of Buccleuch; in 1820, he married Margaret Phillips. He continued to be associated with *Blackwood's Edinburgh Magazine*, contributing the controversial "Chaldee Manuscript" and ethnographic "Shepherd's Calendar." He visited Edinburgh periodically and was feted during an 1832 trip to London. The Edinburgh literati, like John Wilson and John Gibson Lockhart, were ambivalent toward Hogg, who described his ambiguous relationship with Sir Walter Scott in *The Domestic Manners and Private Life of Walter Scott*, published in 1834. Hogg parodied literary acquaintances, including Lord Byron and William Wordsworth (who wrote "Extempore Effusion upon the Death of James Hogg" in 1835), in *The Poetic Mirror* (1816).

Victorian editors such as Thomas Thomson bowdlerized Hogg's work: *The Three Perils of Man* (1823), shorn of supernaturalism, became the insipid *Siege of Roxburgh* (1883). Modern editors have been less intrusive. Hogg influenced writers from Robert Louis Stevenson to Muriel Spark; the composers Beethoven and Haydn arranged his songs. Most important, Hogg played a vital role in preserving and recontextualizing the rich tradition of the Borders into a high cultural context.

Valentina Bold

See also Burns, Robert; Scott, Sir Walter; Scottish Literature

❊❊❊❊❊❊❊❊❊❊❊❊❊❊❊❊

References

Garden, Mrs. *Memorials of James Hogg, the Ettrick Shepherd*. London: Gardner, 1885.

Gifford, Douglas. *James Hogg*. Edinburgh: Ramsay Head Press, 1976.

Hughes, Gillian. *Hogg's Verse and Drama: A Chronological Listing*. Stirling, Scot.: James Hogg Society, 1990.

Mack, Douglas. *Hogg's Prose: An Annotated Listing*. Stirling, Scot.: James Hogg Society, 1985.

Strout, Alan Lang. *The Life and Letters of James Hogg, the Ettrick Shepherd*. Lubbock: Texas Tech Press, 1946.

HOMER

An archaic Greek epic poet and, according to ancient tradition, author of the *Iliad*, *Odyssey*, and various other epics and hymns, Homer was probably a legendary figure who served as an anthropomorphization of the Greek epic poetic tradition. Ancient authorities ascribed various dates to this figure, from roughly contemporaneous with the Trojan War (c. 1225 B.C.E.) to 400 years prior to Herodotus (484–425 B.C.E.). Similarly, within a few hundred years of his supposed existence, various regions of Greece, especially Ionia, claimed Homer as a native son. His supposed descendants, the Homeridae, reputedly preserved his compositions into historical times.

One theory holds that under the Peisistratid rulers of Athens, during the sixth century B.C.E., the *Iliad* and the *Odyssey* were transferred to written form. How the transmission of these primary oral epics into writing affected them remains unknown, but subse-

A representation of Homer reciting the Iliad.

quently, the Greeks viewed Homer as a literary genius and his work as the greatest of literary products. Centuries later, the Alexandrian critics arranged both poems into their current organization of 24 books each.

Homer's precise identity has generated much debate among scholars. The critical issues include the presence of varied regional dialects, both early and later forms; apparent irregularities of plot and theme; and anachronisms involving weapons and cultural practices such as burial. Eighteenth-century Homeric scholar Friederich Wolf first raised these questions in 1795 in his *Prolegomena ad Homerum*, posing the modern version of what is now known as "the Homeric question."

The debate about Homeric poetry continued throughout the nineteenth century, dividing critics into two opposing camps. The analysts argued that the *Iliad* and *Odyssey* are too long and varied in dialect, as well as too subject to narrative inconsistencies, to be the composition of any one poet. The unitarians insisted that both epics were composed by a single individual of extraordinary genius.

In the 1930s, Milman Parry, using the living oral tradition found in the former Yugoslavia, conducted research suggesting that an oral tradition of epic composition lay behind the Homeric poems. Parry's evidence consisted of formulaic phraseology and typical scenes in both the southern Slavic tradition and the Homeric texts. Parry and his student and successor Albert Lord showed how the inconsistencies in narration that plague readers do not pose problems for oral audiences who have heard the stories many times before and are familiar with the reality of performance.

It now appears unlikely that a single individual named Homer composed the *Iliad* and *Odyssey* or that originally separate stories were stitched together to form a composite poem. Rather, Homer stands as a symbol of an oral poetic tradition that is many centuries old.

Anastasios Daskalopoulos

See also Epic; *Iliad*; *Odyssey*; Oral-Formulaic Composition and Theory

✽✽✽✽✽✽✽✽✽✽✽✽✽✽✽✽✽✽

References

Edwards, Mark. *Homer: Poet of the Iliad*. Baltimore: Johns Hopkins University Press, 1987.

Foley, John Miles. "Isak and Homer: The Legendary Singer." In *Arethusa*, forthcoming, 1998.

———. *The Theory of Oral Composition*. Bloomington: Indiana University Press, 1988.

Martin, Richard. *The Language of Heroes: Speech and Performance in the* Iliad. Ithaca, N.Y.: Cornell University Press, 1989.

Nagler, Michael N. *Spontaneity and Tradition: A Study in the Oral Art of Homer*. Berkeley: University of California Press, 1974.

Parry, Adam, ed. *The Making of Homeric Verse: The Collected Papers of Milman Parry*. Oxford: Clarendon Press, 1971.

HUGH OF LINCOLN (c. 1247–1255)

Hugh of Lincoln did nothing remarkable in his short life, but in death he became a legend. His body was found in 1255, partly decomposed and apparently the victim of foul play. His death was blamed on the Jews of Lincoln, England, who, it was said, had ritually crucified him in mockery of Christ. The body had miraculously refused to be hidden, however, so the crime was discovered. For this outrage, many of the Jewish inhabitants of Lincoln were imprisoned in the Tower of London, and 18 of them were hanged. Meanwhile the corpse, having performed further miracles, was removed to the Lincoln cathedral and entombed as a saint and martyr. Nineteenth-century English folklorist Joseph Jacobs provided a summary of the case, and an interesting speculative re-creation of events, in an 1893 essay on Hugh.

The case of Hugh of Lincoln was not the first accusation of ritual murder made against the Jews; medieval Europe abounded with them. The tradition was particularly strong in England, and some scholars, including Joseph Jacobs, are of the opinion that it originated there. However, Hugh's story became more widely known than any of the previous ones. There were several political and economic reasons for King Henry III and John de Lexinton, his right-hand man in the affair, to believe in the guilt of the Jews. These, coupled with pure anti-Semitism, led to the king's acceptance of their guilt and the subsequent public and newsworthy nature of the affair. Matthew Paris, the greatest chronicler of medieval England, commented on the case, and there are other accounts in the contemporary annals of several abbeys. This high visibility in turn caused Hugh's story to be remembered for centuries; Geoffrey Chaucer's Prioress tells a version of the ritual murder story in the *Canterbury Tales* and inserts the invocation: "O yonge Hugh of Lyncoln, sleyn also / With cursed Jewes as it is notable," attesting to the fact that the case was still the best remembered English instance of the ritual murder accusation more than a hundred years after its occurrence.

It was principally in popular ballads, however, that the story was immortalized. This process began immediately after the event, for an Anglo-Norman ballad of the thirteenth century has been preserved. In the English language, 18 different versions survived to be written down in the eighteenth and nineteenth centuries, and they were eventually included by the ballad scholar Francis James Child in his collection of ballads. The sources of these versions range from various Scottish manuscripts to a version collected orally from an African-American child in the streets of New York.

One of the most remarkable features of the ballad is the frequent and graphic description of blood and bloodletting. In most versions, the running of Hugh's blood is described; in some, the daughter of the Jew who performs the murder holds a cup or dish with which to collect the blood. This is probably owing to a related tradition known as "the blood libel," the assertion that Jews perform ritual murder in order to collect blood for ritual or magical purposes. Although the blood accusation was not made against the Jews of Lincoln in 1255, they were accused of using Hugh's entrails for augury, a similarly grisly slander. Hugh's case was not the last instance of the blood libel; indeed, this pernicious tale survives even today. Most scholars believe that the accusation has no basis in fact.

Stephen Winick

See also Ballad; *Canterbury Tales*; Chaucer, Geoffrey; Child, Francis James; Legend; Ritual Murder

✹✹✹✹✹✹✹✹✹✹✹✹✹

References

Child, Francis James. *The English and Scottish Popular Ballads*. New York: Dover, 1965 (1882–1898).

Dundes, Alan, ed. *The Blood Libel Legend: A Casebook in Anti-Semitic Folklore*. Madison: University of Wisconsin Press, 1991.

Jacobs, Joseph. "Little St. Hugh of Lincoln." *Transactions of the Jewish Historical Society of England* 1 (1893–1894): 89–135.

Langmuir, Gavin I. "The Knight's Tale of Young Hugh of Lincoln." *Speculum* 47 (1972): 459–482.

HURSTON, ZORA NEALE (1891–1960)

The African-American novelist, anthropologist, folklorist, and dramatist Zora Neale Hurston was born at the close of the nineteenth century in Eatonville, Florida, an all-black community in Orange County near Orlando. Census records establish her birthdate as January 7, 1891, not January 1, 1901, as is usually stated (Hurston herself has variously cited 1898, 1899, 1900, 1901, 1902, 1903, and even 1910 as the year of her birth). Almost inevitably, she was acquainted from childhood with African-American folklife, initiated into its sacred traditions through the Macedonia Baptist Church, where her father preached and learning secular lore in such settings as the porch of Joe Clarke's store, where local men gathered to swap "lies." Befitting the adult Hurston's dual orientations as artist and academician, and her twinned vision of her cultural heritage,

Zora Neale Hurston, foremother to contemporary American writers such as Maya Angelou, Toni Morrison, and Alice Walker, recorded southern African-American folklife.

both of these scenes, but especially the latter, would figure prominently in her two greatest works, *Mules and Men* (1935), a landmark in African-American folklore scholarship, and *Their Eyes Were Watching God* (1937), a piece of "fiction" that rings truer than many anthropological tracts.

In 1915, Hurston left Eatonville to be a maid and wardrobe girl with a traveling theatrical troupe. She eventually graduated from high school in Baltimore, Maryland, and earned an associate degree from Howard University in Washington, D.C. Soon afterward, she moved to New York City, where she became the first black student to attend Barnard College, earning her B.A. in anthropology in 1928. Later, she continued her anthropological studies at Columbia University under Franz Boas, a founding figure in the field and a major influence in Hurston's own life.

Having first experimented with creative writing at Howard University, in New York, Hurston also gravitated to the artistic milieu known as the Harlem Renaissance, befriending such contemporaries as Langston Hughes and Arna Bontemps. During this period, too, she returned to the South to document formally the folklore she had casually experienced in her youth. The results of this intensive collecting were distilled in *Mules and Men*, an account of southern black folklife set mainly in and around Eatonville that is supplemented by a description of New Orleans voodoo previously published in the *Journal of American Folk-Lore* (1931) and sundry of Hurston's other field data from Florida, Alabama, and Louisiana. *Mules and Men* was, however, preceded by Hurston's first novel, *Jonah's Gourd Vine* (1934).

Aided by a pair of Guggenheim Fellowships (1936, 1938), she next conducted fieldwork in Haiti, Jamaica, and Bermuda, gathering the material on West Indian folk beliefs that is included with an account of her travels in *Tell My Horse* (1938). During this period, she was also completing her most celebrated novel, *Their Eyes Were Watching God*. Between 1938 and 1939, she returned to Florida to collect folklore for the Works Progress Administration. She published a third novel of the African-American worldview, *Moses, Man of the Mountain* (1939), and an autobiography, *Dust Tracks on a Road* (1942). Her fourth and final novel, *Seraph on the Suwanee* (1948), completed while collecting folklore in Honduras, portrays working-class southern whites. Over this span of years, she also wrote numerous essays and short stories, worked as a staff writer for Paramount Studios in Hollywood, and taught drama as well as writing for the stage. Her notable achievements in the last area included *Mule Bone: A Negro Comedy in Three Acts*, coauthored with Langston Hughes and published in 1931, and *The Great Day*, which was produced on Broadway in 1932.

Notwithstanding her many accomplishments, *Mules and Men* remains Hurston's masterpiece and one of the earliest and best accounts of African-American folklore from an insider's perspective. Fittingly, the book is also emblematic of Hurston's life and career as a whole, challenging in both its inception and its execution many contemporaneous notions of race, class, and gender and blurring the boundaries among literature, folklore, and anthropology. Even as a native southerner and an African American, Hurston was, as a college-educated African-American woman, by no means guaranteed ready acceptance in the predominantly male performance settings she sought to document among the rural black underclass. That fact renders her intimate portraits of that class's oral traditions all the more remarkable and testifies to her profound empathy for, and rapport with, her subjects. Not that such issues were entirely irrelevant among the intelligentsia that constituted Hurston's audience. Indeed, if her formal education distanced her from her own folk group, the novelistic, highly personal style in which she presented her data contrasted sharply with the more conventional, "scientific" folklore collections of the day, prompting reservations even on the part of Hurston's own mentor, the scholarly and patriarchal Franz Boas, whom she nonetheless coaxed into writing the preface to her book.

The literary vignettes with which Hurston framed her folktales—

"the between-story conversations and business" as she called them—in many ways prefigured the concern of later scholars with the social contexts and interpersonal dynamics of folklore and arguably provided a far more "scientific" depiction of the tradition than the arrangement of mere narrative texts with comparative annotations that was more typical at the time. From the alternative perspective, many of Hurston's ostensibly fictional works derive their profound ethnographic value from this same sensitivity to sociocultural contexts and traditional verbal textures as well as to oral or literary texts. Moreover, while some African-American intellectuals accused Hurston of understating the grim realities of black experience in the pre–civil rights South, or even of perpetuating pejorative or paternalistic images of southern blacks, her own narrative—like many of the folk performances it incorporates—suggests a traditional African-American "masking" technique, deliberately playing to white stereotypes as a cover for more subtle and ironic modes of protest and resistance. In form as in content, then, *Mules and Men*—like so much of Hurston's other work—seems truly to offer outsiders an unparalleled glimpse of the African-American expressive culture from within.

Despite her auspicious early accomplishments, Hurston's later years were characterized mainly by personal and professional hardships. In 1948, she was falsely accused of impairing the morals of a minor. Eventually cleared of the charge, she was nonetheless devastated and left New York for her native Florida. Although she continued to write sporadically, she was at one point reduced to working as a domestic and, later, as a librarian. Suffering a stroke in 1959, Hurston died on January 28, 1960, in the St. Lucie County Welfare Home in Fort Pierce, Florida. Donated funds enabled her to be buried there in an unmarked grave.

Appropriately, if regrettably, Hurston's dual vision of black expression and experience appears also to have affected her posthumous reputation, an imbalance only lately redressed: that is, while folklorists have never wholly lost sight of Zora Neale Hurston's singular contributions to the study of black culture, it is only since the late 1970s that she has been accorded her rightful place in the literary canon of the United States.

John Minton

See also Harlem Renaissance; Performance

References

Gates, Henry Louis, Jr., and K. A. Appiah, eds. *Zora Neale Hurston: Critical Perspectives Past and Present.* New York: Amistad, 1993.

Hemenway, Robert E. *Zora Neale Hurston: A Literary Biography.* Urbana: University of Illinois Press, 1977.

Hyman, Stanley Edgar (1919–1970)

A critic and teacher, Stanley Edgar Hyman was also a pioneer in extending literary criticism by incorporating knowledge from other fields. In addition, he initiated the criticism of criticism that became the next generation's major activity.

In his audacious *The Armed Vision* (1948), Hyman argues that the study of literature cannot be confined to the "merely" artistic. History, biography, psychology, anthropology, and the symbolic action of his colleague Kenneth Burke are all required to do justice to the complexity of great literature. Yet no one school, whether Anglo-American new criticism, psychoanalysis, Marxism, or sociology, should dominate. Although one reading might serve as a "hub" for the others, Hyman asserts that to hierarchize critical methods is invariably reductive. In his complex drama of clashing literary methods, folklore and anthropology are the principal players.

Hyman coupled his training in literature with self-education as a "literary" folklorist by reading E. B. Tylor, J. G. Frazer, and other members of the pre–World War I "Cambridge school." Under their influence, and greatly admiring Jane Ellen Harrison's *Themis* (1912) and Jessie L. Weston's *From Ritual to Romance* (1920), Hyman advocated myth criticism. With a curious blend of skepticism and faith that he found in another critic, Hyman committed himself to Lord Raglan's ritual-to-myth theory, which he intemperately defended against the American anthropological folklorist William Bascom. After that exchange, though Hyman became disaffected with the field of folklore, myth continued to fascinate him. He expounded the ritual theory with the fanaticism of a true believer, hoping it could even be made to apply to his beloved blues. In *The Tangled Bank*, he pioneered the application of literary critical methods to four "nonliterary" writers, Charles Darwin, James George Frazer,

Karl Marx, and Sigmund Freud, anticipating the later critical movement "from work to text."

In an innovative chapter of *The Armed Vision*, Hyman advocates folk criticism by discussing Constance Rourke, the author of *American Humor*. From Rourke, Hyman extracts three key ideas about folklore in literature. First, "A tradition is not in subject but in *form* . . . the secret does not lie in painting a hillbilly building a silo, but in painting *as* a hillbilly builds a silo" (Hyman 1955, p. 118). Second, "The important relationship of art literature to folk literature lies, not in the surface texture of folk speech, but in the archetypal patterns of primitive ritual, the great myths" (a point Hyman wishes Rourke had understood). Third, "American folk tradition is not primarily naturalistic but abstract" (p. 122). Here, as always, while seeming to review one critic's writings, Hyman creates a program for future critics.

In his final book, *Iago: Some Approaches to the Illusion of his Motivation* (1970), Hyman continues to argue that no one approach gives "the" answer to a literary problem. "They are all the answer," says Hyman. Pluralist criticism produces "a richer and more complex understanding of the imaginative work" (Hyman 1970). At this point, folklore and anthropology play only minor roles in Hyman's pluralism. The five critical approaches he applies to Shakespeare's most fascinating villain are drawn from the history of literary forms, Christian myth, Kenneth Burke's symbolic action, psychoanalysis, and history of ideas. In the last approach, ignoring the folklore of ethnic slurs that folklorists were investigating, he shows Iago to be a Jacobean folk stereotype, the wicked Italian.

Lee Haring

See also Frazer, James George; Freud, Sigmund; Myth; Rourke, Constance Mayfield; Shakespeare, William; Weston, Jessie Laidley

✱✱✱✱✱✱✱✱✱✱✱✱✱✱✱✱✱

References

Hyman, Stanley Edgar. *The Armed Vision: A Study in the Methods of Modern Literary Criticism*. New York: Vintage Books, 1955 (1948).

———. *Iago: Some Approaches to the Illusion of His Motivation*. New York: Atheneum, 1970.

———. "Reply to Bascom." *Journal of American Folklore* 71 (1958): 152–155.

Raglan, Lord. *The Hero: A Study in Tradition, Myth, and Drama*. New York: Vintage Books, 1956 (1936).

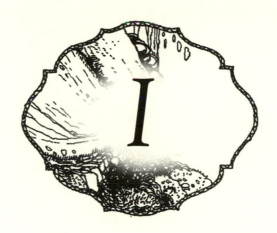

ILIAD

An ancient Greek epic poem, the *Iliad* is ascribed to Homer and drawn from oral tradition. The surviving textual record consists of over 15,000 dactylic hexameter lines and is divided into 24 books, or chapters. The narrative begins in the tenth year of the Trojan War, during which a Greek army (referred to as Achaeans, Argives, and Danaans) led by Agamemnon, king of Mycenae, has been fighting for the return of his brother Menelaus's wife, Helen, who was kidnapped by the Trojan prince Paris. The war has drawn the attention of the gods, and they have chosen sides and assist their favorite heroes, at times even directly participating in the action.

The major Greek heroes at Troy include Menelaus and Agamemnon as well as Achilles, Odysseus, Nestor, Ajax, and Diomedes. The Trojan defenders, led by Hector, son of the Trojan king Priam, include Aeneas, Helenus, Antenor, Sarpedon, and Polydamas. The gods Athena, Poseidon, Hera, and Hephaestus support the Greeks while Apollo, Artemis, Aphrodite, and Ares favor the Trojans. Zeus, upon whose will the outcome of the conflict depends, attempts to remain impartial during the course of the war.

The focus of the narrative rests on the anger, or wrath, of Achilles, which resulted from the capture of Chryseis, a woman held prisoner by Agamemnon (book 1). Apollo imposes a plague on the Greek camp to punish Agamemnon for refusing to restore Chryseis to her father Chryses, a priest of Apollo. While the sickness ravages the Achaean camp, the prophet Calchas declares that the plague can only be eliminated by Chryseis's return. Agamemnon agrees reluctantly, but only if Briseis, the captive and prize of Achilles, is awarded to him as a substitute. In anger, Achilles withdraws from the fighting and prays to his mother, the sea goddess Thetis, to persuade

Zeus to punish the Achaeans and their leaders for Agamemnon's insolence. Zeus pledges that he will grant victory to the Trojans until Agamemnon atones for his affront to Achilles.

After cataloging the forces on both sides (book 2), the Trojans, under the leadership of Hector, drive the Greek army back to the hastily built walls of the camp that Nestor, the aged Achaean counselor, had urged them to fortify (books 3–8). The Achaeans send Odysseus, Aias, and Phoinix to try to appease Achilles' wrath with a large reward (book 9); Achilles refuses the so-called embassy but allows Patroclus, his closest companion, to don his armor as a disguise and to lead out the Greek army against the Trojans, who have nearly succeeded in destroying the Argive ships (books 9–16). Hector, with the aid of Apollo, kills Patroclus (book 16); this is the crucial act that forces Achilles' return to battle. After slaughtering many Trojans, Achilles kills Hector in single combat and drags the body back to his tent (books 16–22). The last two books of the poem consist, respectively, of funeral games for Patroclus and the successful ransom of Hector's corpse by his father, Priam.

A story of violence, divine intrigue, and human emotion, the *Iliad* originated as an oral narrative. After its transmission to written form, the *Iliad* maintained its status as the greatest and most influential work of Greek literature.

Anastasios Daskalopoulos

See also Homer; Oral-Formulaic Composition and Theory

✹✹✹✹✹✹✹✹✹✹✹✹✹✹✹✹✹✹

References

Edwards, Mark W. *Homer, Poet of the* Iliad. Baltimore: Johns Hopkins University Press, 1987.

Griffin, Jasper. *Homer*. New York: Hill and Wang, 1980.

Martin, Richard P. *The Language of Heroes: Speech and Performance in the* Iliad. Ithaca, N.Y.: Cornell University Press, 1989.

Nagler, Michael N. *Spontaneity and Tradition: A Study of the Oral Art of Homer*. Berkeley: University of California Press, 1974.

Schein, Seth L. *The Moral Hero: An Introduction to Homer's* Iliad. Berkeley: University of California Press, 1984.

INTERNATIONAL SOCIETY FOR FOLK NARRATIVE RESEARCH

The International Society for Folk Narrative Research (ISFNR) "is a scientific society whose objectives are to develop scholarly work in the fields of folk narrative research and to stimulate contacts and the exchange of views among its members." During meetings in Kiel, Germany, and Copenhagen, Denmark, in 1959, a committee was given the task of founding an international society: ISFNR was then founded in Paris in 1960 and further developed in Athens in 1964 under the presidency of Professor Kurt Ranke.

The society is directed by a president and six vice-presidents—five of whom represent Africa, Asia, Europe, North America, and South America—and three additional members. The founding president, Kurt Ranke from the universities of Kiel and Göttingen, served until 1974; he has been followed by Lauri Honko, Turku University (1974–1989), and Reimund Kvideland, of the universities of Bergen and Turku (1989–1998). "Any person qualified by his [sic] scholarly work in the field of narrative research may become a member of the Society." By 1966, the society had 632 elected members from 75 countries.

To promote international folk narrative research, the society arranges for an international congress every few years. The 1959 congress was counted as the first, and it was followed by two seminars on legend research in Antwerp in 1962 and Budapest in 1963; the second international congress, in Athens in 1964, was then numbered as the fourth congress. Other congresses have been held in Bucharest (1969), Helsinki (1974), Edinburgh (1979), Bergen (1984), Budapest (1989), Innsbruck (1992), Mysore (1995), and Göttingen (1998). Seminars have been held in Liblice, near Prague (1966), and Beijing (1996).

"Committees to undertake special tasks or to study special problems in the field of folk narrative research may be appointed by the general assembly." The Theoretical Committee was founded in 1974 and chaired by Lutz Röhrich. The activities of the society have resulted in a number of publications. News of the society was first published in the Nordic Institute of Folklore *Newsletter*, sent free of charge to all members of the society, and is currently published in the journal *Fabula*.

Reimund Kvideland

See also Fairy Tale; Folktale; Legend; *Märchen*; Ranke, Kurt

✳✳✳✳✳✳✳✳✳✳✳✳✳✳✳✳✳✳

References

Handoo, J., et al., eds. *Papers 1–6*. Mysore, 1996.

Kvideland, R., and T. Selberg, eds. *Papers of the 8th Congress of ISFNR 1–4+Plenary Papers*. 5 vols. Bergen, 1984–1985.

Megas, G. A., ed. "IV International Congress for Folk-Narrative Research." In *Athens: Lectures and Reports XVI. Laographia* 22 (1965).

Ortutay, G., ed. "Tagung der Sagenkommission der International Society for Folk-Narrative Research . . . 1963." *Acta Ethnographica Academiae Scientiarum Hungaricae* 13 (1964): 1–131.

Peeters, K., ed. Tagung der "International Society for Folk-Narrative Research." In *Antwerp: Bericht und Referate*. Antwerp: Centrum voor Studie en Documentatie, 1963.

Pentikäinen, J., and T. Juurikka, eds. "Folk Narrative Research." *Studia Fennica* 20 (1976).

Petzoldt, L., ed. *Folk Narrative and World View 1–2. zur Europäischen Ethnologie und Folklore*. Suppl. series B, no. 7. Frankfurt am Main: Peter Lang, 1996.

Ranke, Kurt, ed. *Internationaler Kongress der Volkserzählungsforscher in Kiel und Kopenhagen. Fabula*, suppl. series B, no. 2. Berlin: Walter De Gruyter, 1961.

Röhrich, L., and S. Wienker-Piepho, eds. "Storytelling in Contemporary Societies." *ScriptOralia* 22 (1990).

Voigt, V., ed. *Folk Narrative and Cultural Identity 1–2. Artes populares* 16–17 (1995).

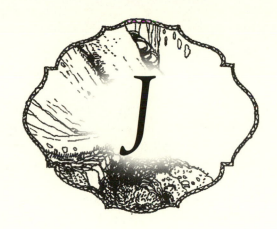

Jackson, Kenneth Hurlstone (1909–1991)

One of the greatest Celtic scholars of all time, Kenneth Hurlstone Jackson acquired and displayed a comprehensive knowledge of matters Celtic and was equally at home in Celtic linguistics, literature, history, archaeology, mythology, and folklore—to all of which he applied his excellent mind and meticulous scholarship.

After obtaining two first-class degrees at Cambridge University in 1932, he did research in Celtic languages at the University College of North Wales, Bangor, and at University College, Dublin, before taking up duties as a fellow of St. John's College and as faculty lecturer in Celtic at Cambridge University. From 1939 to 1949, interrupted only by war service as a "censor," he served as a lecturer, associate professor, and professor in Celtic languages and literature at Harvard University and then returned to Great Britain as professor of Celtic languages, literature, history, and antiquities at the University of Edinburgh, a post he held until his retirement in 1979. In Scotland, he was one of the first prime movers behind the creation of the School of Scottish Studies of the University of Edinburgh and served as president of the Scottish Anthropological and Folklore Society from 1952 to 1960. He was made a fellow of the British Academy in 1957 and received several honorary degrees.

His most influential publication is undoubtedly his monumental *Language and History in Early Britain* (1953). Other major publications include an edition of *Early Welsh Poems* (1973); his account of the evolution of Goedelic languages; his translations from Celtic literature in *A Celtic Miscellany*; *Contributions to the Study of Manx Phonology*; his masterly *Historical Phonology of Breton*; his study of *The Gododdin, the Oldest Scottish Poem*; his commentary on *The Gaelic Notes in the Book of Deer*; and most important for folklorists,

Scéalta ón mBlascaod and *The Oldest Irish Tradition: A Window on the Iron Age*.

In his numerous articles, reviews, and chapters of books, he demonstrated not only that he was a linguistic expert in all the branches of the Celtic languages, both historical and modern, but also that he was at ease in their folklore, with a special emphasis on folk narrative. This interest, kindled early, stayed with him throughout his scholarly life and resulted in such essays as "The International Folktale in Ireland," "Some Fresh Light on the Miracle of the Instantaneous Harvest," "Incremental Repetition in the Early Welsh Englyn," "The Folktale in Gaelic Scotland," and "Some Popular Motifs in Early Welsh Tradition," as well as an edition of folktales and anecdotes from Ireland, Scotland, Wales, Cornwall, and Nova Scotia. Of these, his extensive essay "The Folktale in Gaelic Scotland" is particularly significant, insofar as it highlights both the universality and the regional character of the Gaelic storytelling tradition in Scotland and of the corpus of stories that it has produced. In addition to all his other achievements, Jackson must therefore be regarded as one of the most eminent Celtic folklorists.

W. F. H. Nicolaisen

See also Celtic Literature; Scottish Literature; Storytelling; Welsh Literature

✳✳✳✳✳✳✳✳✳✳✳✳✳✳✳

References

Jackson, Kenneth Hurlstone, ed. *Early Welsh Poems*. Cardiff: University of Wales Press, 1973.

———. *The International Popular Tale and Early Welsh Tradition*. Cardiff: University of Wales Press, 1961.

———. *Language and History in Early Britain*. Edinburgh: Edinburgh University Press, 1953.

JACOBS, JOSEPH (1854–1916)

Both an esteemed folklorist and a noted Judaic scholar, Joseph Jacobs was born to Jewish parents in Sydney, Australia, and studied history, anthropology, and philosophy in England, where he showed early promise as a literary critic. Profoundly influenced by what he saw as a broad and implicit intellectual bias against the Jewish people—demonstrated in the critical reception of George Eliot's *Daniel Deronda* and the general apathy toward the Russian persecution of the Jews shortly thereafter—Jacobs spoke out in a perceptive review of Eliot's novel and then moved to Germany for two years to study Jewish history.

Upon his return to England, Jacobs took up the study of folklore and became one of the early members of the English Folk-Lore Society in 1878. He quickly emerged as one of the most prolific and visible of the Victorian folklore scholars: he edited the society's journal *Folk-Lore* from 1890 to 1900 while producing several critical editions and studies of European and Indian folktales. His most well-known works, however, were his collections of native English and Celtic folktales: *English Fairy Tales* (1890), *Celtic Fairy Tales* (1892), *More English Fairy Tales* (1894), and *More Celtic Fairy Tales* (1894), plus *Indian Fairy Tales* (1892).

Like his contemporary Andrew Lang, Jacobs directed his collections to a juvenile audience. Although the stories he chose were indeed commonly known, Jacobs followed the practice of other literary folklorists of the time by relying primarily on already written versions of the tales, freely adapting them to conform to his own ideas of audience appropriateness and literary art. Because Jacobs's books were written for children, his retellings are in simplified language, without dialect, and are often humorous but lacking the violence and sexual innuendo of the original versions. Although he was roundly condemned for such liberal-handed treatment of his material, he felt he was actually following tradition, since, as he pointed out in his preface to *More English Fairy Tales*, traditional storytellers themselves do the same thing. Unlike Lang, Jacobs did include scholarly introductions and copious endnotes on his sources, complete with "parallels" and "remarks" that are still valuable to the modern folklorist and literary critic.

In his theory of the ultimate origins of folklore, Jacobs sided with the diffusionists, which soon led to his being one of the leading combatants in a celebrated controversy in the English Folk-Lore Society during the 1890s. The controversy was between the survivalists, or the anthropological school of folklore, led by Lang, and the diffusionists, or the migration theory school.

Jacobs never abandoned his calling as a Jewish historian. He published several works concerned with Jewish history and biblical archeology throughout his career, including *The Jewish Year Book*

(1896), and was one of the founders of the Jewish Historical Society of England, serving as its president in 1898. In 1900, he accepted the post of revising editor of the American *Jewish Encyclopedia* and moved to New York City, where he lived and taught until his death.

Martha Hixon

See also Fairy Tale; Lang, Andrew; *Märchen*

✳✳✳✳✳✳✳✳✳✳✳✳✳✳✳✳✳✳

References

Dorson, Richard M. *The British Folklorists: A History.* Chicago: University of Chicago Press, 1968.

Fine, Gary Alan. "Joseph Jacobs: A Sociological Folklorist." *Folklore* 98 (1987): 183–193.

Jacobs, Joseph. *English Fairy Tales.* London: Nutt, 1890; New York: Dover, 1967.

JĀTAKA

Jātakas are stories of the former lives of the Buddha. These tales are included among the works of the early Buddhist canon, or *Tripitaka.* Although the best known collection of jātakas is the fifth-century C.E. *jātakatthavannana* [Elucidation of the meaning of the jātakas], scenes from many of the tales, some even labeled with their titles, are found in southern Indian stone reliefs carved in the second or third century B.C.E. Theravada Buddhist tradition holds that the jātaka stories were originally told by Shakyamuni (the historical Buddha) and later compiled by the great scholar Buddhaghosa. Strong similarities between these tales and folktales from other Indo-European societies have led some scholars to conclude that early monks adapted a wide range of traditional, possibly pre-Buddhist, stories to fit the jātaka form, in much the same way that contemporary religious teachers use apocryphal material to teach important lessons. Because the jātakas incorporate many common tale-types, the early collections have been of particular interest to folklorists studying the historical dimensions of tales.

Most jātakas are structured around five main elements: an introductory story, a prose narrative, a number of stanzas, a short commentary on the stanzas, and a final section of connection and identification. The introductory stories are set in the time of Shakya-

A Gupta cave painting in Ajanta, India, depicts a scene in the Palace of Jātaka.

muni, and in them, the Buddha addresses a problem in the present by telling a story of one of his past incarnations. The prose narrative, which is generally the longest section, presents the general story. The stanzas, or *Gāthās*, are usually interspersed throughout the narrative. They often parallel the action, although they sometimes conflict with it. *Gāthās* may be the lines or songs of particular characters, or they may be spoken by the Buddha to explain parts of the narrative. After a brief commentary on the stanzas, each tale ends with the Buddha essentially revealing the cast of characters, identifying previous incarnations of himself and his followers among the central figures of the story.

Most scholars of Buddhist scriptures, following the lead of Maurice Winternitz, believe that the *Gāthās* are generally older and better preserved than the prose portions of the jātakas. Indeed, some branches of Buddhism have traditionally held that the original canonical form of the jātakas included only the *Gāthās*. These verses were memorized, while the prose narratives were more flexible in form, tailored by individual narrators to fit their own style of performance. Early jātaka collections, in which the tales were translated into Old Singhalese, retained the *Gāthās* in Pāli, the language of the earliest Buddhist scriptures. The relative stability of the poetic sections, together with the presence of many repetitions, stock phrases, and metrical devices, indicates that most of these tales had been transmitted orally in jātaka form before they were set in writing. Although such elements have often been removed from English-language translations for the sake of clarity, quite a few remain in the version edited by E. B. Cowell at the beginning of the twentieth century.

Inclusion in the Buddhist canon has kept one version of the jātaka collection in a relatively stable form for centuries, but the tales continue to be told and reworked in the present. Jātakas are still in oral circulation in many Buddhist cultures, and they have long been popular as the inspiration for dances, songs, sculptures, and paintings. In Europe and the Americas, writers and composers as diverse as Sir Edwin Arnold, Richard Wagner, Gary Snyder, and Laurie Anderson have drawn inspiration from stories of the Buddha's past lives. Authors in the Western countries have primarily used jātakas as the basis for children's literature. Turn-of-the-century collections such as Joseph Jacobs's *Indian Fairy Tales* (1910) and W. H. D. Rouse's *The Giant Crab and Other Tales from Old* (1900) included many jātaka adaptations, and a wave of recent titles such as Judith Ernst's *The Golden Goose King* (1995), Paul Galdone's *The Monkey and the Crocodile* (1987), and Margaret Hodges's *The Golden Deer* (1992) have presented individual jātakas in picture-book form. Through such adaptations, jātakas have continued to provide valuable examples of kindness, compassion, and self-sacrifice for new audiences throughout the world.

Peter G. Harle

See also Children's Literature; Folktale Adaptations; Performance; Tale-Type

✳✳✳✳✳✳✳✳✳✳✳✳✳✳✳✳✳

References

Cummings, Mary. *The Lives of the Buddha in the Art and Literature of Asia.* Michigan Papers on South and Southeast Asia no. 20. Ann Arbor: Center for South and Southeast Asian Studies, University of Michigan, 1982.

Rhys Davids, Caroline A. F. *Stories of the Buddha: Being Selections from the Jātaka.* New York: Dover, 1989 (1929).

JOHN AND OLD MARSTER TALES

A prominent subtype of the African-American trickster tale, John and Old Marster tales, a cycle of humorous narratives, are named for the protagonists, a wily slave usually called "John" and his owner or "Old Marster." More than even the better known animal trickster tales (the famous Brer Rabbit stories), the John tales unmistakably reflect the desperate predicament of enslaved Africans and their descendants in the Old South; indeed, despite their antebellum setting, these stories were documented almost entirely during the period from Reconstruction to the civil rights era, though elderly informants confirmed that the tradition was well established before emancipation.

Incorporating many migratory types and motifs, the cycle also produced a large body of original tales, and, whether because of a selective adaptation of well-traveled trickster and numskull narratives or because of its many indigenous creations, revolved around a few themes of obvious concern to southern blacks during slavery and, later, the days of "Jim Crow." Thus, there are strings of stories concerning the misappropriation or willful destruction of "the marster's" property (theft of food may in fact constitute the cycle's single most popular theme); the avoidance of manual labor or circumvention of the draconian "black codes" (e.g., the harsh restrictions on the movement of blacks, especially at night); and the uses of deceit and deception as means of manipulating, or of ingratiating oneself to, whites as a shield against racially motivated vigilantism and violence, or simply as forms of covert resistance in and of themselves.

However, while some authors have characterized the John tales as relatively simplistic parables—presumably providing black tradition-bearers with a vicarious release through John's inevitable triumph over Old Marster, the archetypal embodiment of white oppression—the folk cycle's overall import seems far more complex and frankly ambiguous. Rather than depicting the inevitable triumph of the oppressed over their oppressors, the tales more precisely evoke a milieu that is incapacitated by ceaseless and pointless exploitation and victimization. Actually, John and Old Marster alternate in the roles of trickster and dupe, deceiver and deceived, victimizer and victim—an impasse that is more consistent both with the self-defeating nature of the southern caste system and with the ambivalent ethos of trickster tales generally. It is worth noting that the foregoing interpretation is equally applicable to the African-American animal tales, which have themselves often been "read" as rather straightforward allegories depicting the ultimate triumph of the "underdog."

Given the prominence of the John tales in African-American folklore, and their many apparent borrowings from international tradition, these tales have, again like the animal trickster stories, also figured prominently in the debate over the relative contributions of Africans and Europeans to the New World black narrative; here, too, however, the cycle defies pat explanations.

The conventional content and controversial context of the John tales are neatly illustrated by an item that Richard M. Dorson (1967) judged the "best known of all the Old Marster stories," the anecdote typically entitled "The Coon in the Box." In the basic story, John has, through stealth and deception, convinced his owner that he possesses extrasensory powers and turns that circumstance to his advantage. His subterfuge backfires, however, when the Old Marster boasts of his slave's abilities to a neighboring plantation owner, who, skeptical of the claims, demands proof. To resolve the matter, the two planters place a raccoon in a box, summon John, and demand that he divine the box's contents. Realizing that he's finally trapped, and that punishment is at hand, John exclaims in exasperation, "Well, Marster, it looks like you've caught the old 'coon' at last"— thereby unwittingly passing the test. The tale turns, of course, on the southern usage of "coon" both as the contraction of "raccoon" and as a pejorative epithet for blacks.

Although folklorists have customarily identified the above anecdote with an Indo-European tale—that is, Type 1641, "Doctor Know-All"—that relationship is by no means clear-cut, since the two stories really share only a single element, the serendipitous pun serving as the conclusion of "The Coon in the Box." Moreover, while the John tale's punch line is thus usually classed with its European parallel (i.e., under motif N688, "What Is in the Dish: 'Poor Crab'"), that comparison arguably obscures the far more significant contrasts between the European and African-American traditions. Even if, as seems likely, the "The Coon in the Box" is in some measure related to the European tradition—at least in this single detail—the John tale just as clearly entails a distinct African-American elaboration of an obvious (and hence, near-universal) plot device that is recast as a racial slur unique to, and emblematic of, the southern milieu.

Significantly, similar colloquial touches or adaptations distinguish most of the John tales, even those whose Old World origins have likewise been taken for granted—for example, the well-known narrative identified as motif B210.2, "Talking Animal or Object Refuses to Talk on Demand; Discoverer Is Unable to Prove His Claims and Is Beaten," a story universally accepted as being of African origin. (It is also revealing that in this tale, which rivals "The Coon in the Box" in popularity, John plays the dupe, suffering a severe, in some instances fatal, beating or even a beheading.) Taken together with the cycle's many indigenous items, such adaptations affirm that whatever their debt to Old World traditions, the John tales primarily reflect the ingenuity and insights of African-American raconteurs and their communities.

Although the John tales and animal trickster stories are almost evenly matched in black oral tradition, in the realm of popular literature, the former are indisputably overshadowed by the animal tales, best known through Joel Chandler Harris's Uncle Remus collections; nonetheless, the John and Old Marster cycle has also been subject to literary treatment. Harris himself included one of the John tales ("On the Plantation: Death and the Negro Man") in *Uncle Remus and His Friends* (1892). However, the most notable retellings come from such African-American authors as J. Mason Brewer, Zora Neale Hurston, and Julius Lester, a circumstance suggesting that, just as literary adaptations of the Brer Rabbit tales were partly influenced by patriarchal white views of black culture, the more overt social commentary of the John tales held a greater attraction for black intellectuals pursuing a quite different agenda. In fact, some of these authors rank among the foremost exponents of the aforementioned "underdog theory," epitomized by Zora Neale Hurston's claim that "Old Massa couldn't get the best of him [John] ... Old John, High John could beat the unbeatable. He was top-superior to the whole mess of sorrow. He could beat it all, and what made it so cool, finish it off with a laugh." Although such categorical statements are hardly supported by the tales' oral tradition, the statements nevertheless represent an important African-American perspective on the John and Old Marster cycle, belonging, however, primarily to a literary, not a folk, lineage.

John Minton

See also Dorson, Richard M.; Harris, Joel Chandler; Hurston, Zora Neale; Motif; Tale-Type; Trickster; Uncle Remus

✳✳✳✳✳✳✳✳✳✳✳✳✳✳✳✳✳

References

Brewer, J. Mason. "John Tales." In *Mexican Border Ballads and Other Lore*, ed. Mody C. Boatright, pp. 81–104. Publications of the Texas Folklore Society no. 21. Austin: Texas Folklore Society, 1946.

Dorson, Richard M. *American Negro Folktales*. Greenwich, Conn.: Fawcett Publications, 1967.

Hurston, Zora Neale. "High John de Conquer." In *Mother Wit from the Laughing Barrel: Readings in the Interpretation of Afro-American Folklore*, ed. Alan Dundes, pp. 541–548. Jackson: University Press of Mississippi, 1990 (1943).

Lester, Julius. *Black Folktales*. New York: Richard W. Baron, 1969.

JOHNSON, JAMES WELDON (1871–1938)

An African-American author, editor, lyricist, educator, diplomat, and civil rights activist, James Williams Johnson was born in Jacksonville, Florida, on June 17, 1871, the second of three children in a comfortably middle-class family. (He changed his middle name to "Weldon" in 1913 because, he felt, it sounded more "literary.") Johnson's father, James Johnson, Sr., was the headwaiter at a local luxury hotel, and his mother, Bahamian-born Helen Louise Dillet Johnson, was Florida's first female black public schoolteacher.

Johnson's own life was marked by a number of similar firsts. Among his many other achievements, he became the principal of the first black public high school in Florida (Jacksonville's Stanton School, originally the grammar school where his mother taught), the founder and publisher of America's first black daily newspaper (the *Daily American*, also in Jacksonville), the first black to be admitted to the Florida bar, and the first black professor at New York University. These distinctions barely suggest the breadth of his accomplishments, however. As an international crusader for racial equality, he was one of the true forbears of the civil rights movement; as a creative artist, he was likewise a true pioneer, serving as a driving force in the artistic movement that came to be known as the Harlem Renaissance and forging, both through his own work and his influence over others, a vital link between African-American folk idioms and formal literary genres.

After attending the primary grades at the Stanton School in

Jacksonville, Johnson entered Atlanta University in 1887 and there completed his secondary and college education. In 1894, he returned to his hometown, and after being appointed as the principal at Stanton, he eventually expanded the school's offerings to include the high school curriculum. During this same period, Johnson began a law practice and founded the *Daily American*. As one portent of his later artistic endeavors, in 1900 he wrote the lyrics for "Lift Every Voice and Sing," which was later adopted as the official song of the National Association for the Advancement of Colored People (NAACP) and dubbed "the black national anthem"; the song's music was provided by his brother, J. Rosamond Johnson, with whom he would frequently collaborate over the years.

Despite his accomplishments, in 1901, Johnson was nearly lynched by a white mob in a Jacksonville park, which prompted him to leave the South for New York City. There, he formed a successful songwriting team—Cole and the Johnson Brothers—with brother J. Rosamond and their friend Bob Cole, and they produced over 200 songs, including such popular standards as "Under the Bamboo Tree," "Ain't That Scandalous," and "Congo Love Song." The partnership ended in 1906 when Johnson was appointed the Roosevelt administration's consul to Venezuela (1906–1909) and, later, Nicaragua (1909–1913).

At the conclusion of his foreign service, he returned to New York—in 1910, he had married Grace Elizabeth Nail, the daughter of a prominent Harlem businessman—and accepted a position as a contributing editor to the black weekly the *New York Age*. In the company of such other luminaries as Irving Berlin and John Philip Sousa, he helped found the American Society of Composers, Authors, and Publishers (ASCAP), and he also became active in the NAACP—quite understandably, he was especially intent on combating the wave of lynching that then racked the South—serving as that organization's chief officer from 1920 to 1930. In addition to the voluminous writings that were related more directly to his social and political activism, Johnson continued throughout this period to produce creative works and, upon resigning as the NAACP's secretary, accepted an appointment as the Adam K. Spence Professor of Creative Literature at Fisk University. In 1934, he was also appointed a visiting fall-term professor at New York University, where he continued to lecture annually until his death in an automobile accident on June 26, 1938.

Although Johnson's family background and personal accomplishments may have distanced him somewhat from black folk culture, he deliberately strove, as both scholar and artist, to close that gap. Indeed, in the preface to his landmark anthology *The Book of American Negro Poetry* (1922), he judged the folk traditions of American blacks "the only things artistic that have yet sprung from American soil and been universally acknowledged as distinctive American products" (Johnson 1931). Certainly he drew liberally on such sources in his own poetry, beginning with *Fifty Years and Other Poems* (1917) and continuing through his final book, *Saint Peter Relates an Incident: Selected Poems* (1935). Perhaps most successful among these experiments was his use of black folk oratory in *God's Trombones: Seven Negro Sermons in Verse* (1927), in which he attempted, as he explained in his autobiography *Along This Way* (1933), to "take the primitive stuff of the old-time Negro sermon and, through art-governed expression, make it into poetry … in a way similar to that in which a composer makes use of a folk theme in writing a major composition" (Johnson 1990).

If Johnson's characterization of his folk sources seems a bit condescending by current standards, within the context of his own day, those comments in fact represented an atypically perceptive critical perspective on the relation of oral and literary modes, actually confirming, moreover, Johnson's belief in the intrinsic value and inherent dignity of black folk tradition. Besides his literary adaptations, Johnson also compiled, with J. Rosamond Johnson, two collections of African-American sacred music, *The Book of American Negro Spirituals* (1925) and *The Second Book of Negro Spirituals* (1926), while his *Black Manhattan* (1930) traced the accomplishments of Harlem blacks from the 1620s to the 1920s, including a generous accounting of their folk traditions.

Johnson's own vita and personal vision for black folklore are also given an intriguing twist in his great work of fiction, *The Autobiography of an Ex-Coloured Man* (1912). Completed during his service abroad and first published anonymously in 1912, *The Autobiography* was reprinted under Johnson's name at the height of the Harlem Renaissance in 1927, signaling a watershed in African-American letters. Initially the source of some confusion, the book's "author" is in reality a fictitious half-caste southerner whose ability to "pass" as white is a mixed blessing. Adrift between cultures, the protagonist experiences an epiphany when, on a trip abroad, he witnesses a classical interpretation of traditional piano ragtime. He resolves there and then to revisit his native South and devote his own life to elevating black folk music to the level of canonical art. Returning home, however, he is unhinged by a brutal lynching and thereafter abandons his cultural heritage and returns to the North to pass permanently into white society. Drawn in part from his creator's own life, the "ex-coloured man" obviously also personified a central dilemma of the early-twentieth-century black intelligentsia. Johnson himself may have similarly wavered, but in the end he chose a much different path.

John Minton

See also Harlem Renaissance; Sermon

✳✳✳✳✳✳✳✳✳✳✳✳✳✳✳✳✳

References
Johnson, James Weldon. *Along This Way: The Autobiography of James Weldon Johnson*. New York: Penguin, 1990 (1933).
———. *The Book of American Negro Poetry*. New York: Harcourt, Brace, 1931 (1922).
———. *God's Trombones: Seven Negro Sermons in Verse*. New York: Viking, 1927.
Wilson, Sondra Kathryn, ed. *The Selected Writings of James Weldon Johnson*. 2 vols. New York: Oxford University Press, 1995.

JOYCE, JAMES (1882–1941)

James Joyce, born in Dublin, Ireland, was a preeminent practitioner of twentieth-century English fiction. Although he left Ireland permanently on June 16, 1904, he was most fortunate to have been born there. For all the faults Joyce depicted in *Dubliners* (1914), he saw Ireland as a great repository of some of the oldest and richest folklore. Ironically, Joyce is the one who put Dublin on the map, a map so intimately accurate that Joyce claimed that were the city destroyed, it could be reconstructed from his works. Each summer, one can see foreigners with maps and guides looking for Joyce's places. In a sense, Joyce involves his readers in the continuing creation of the legend of Dublin. The continual storytelling of the Irish preserves and develops their myths—and Joyce the exile was very Irish.

From his first published book of fiction, *Dubliners*, a linked collection of stories; through *A Portrait of the Artist as a Young Man* (1916), the cinematically episodic story of Stephen Dedalus; and in his most famous novel, *Ulysses* (1922), the story of a middle-aged Jewish advertising salesman named Leopold Bloom, his wife Molly, and his ersatz son, Stephen Dedalus, Joyce used Irish and Greek myth and folklore based in the collective unconscious of all humanity. In his last work, *Finnegans Wake* (1939), Joyce, who was a brilliant linguist, tells a tale so layered that, as he said himself, "no one will ever figure it all out."

Joyce's early bitterness about Ireland and its folklore, which was being avidly collected by such people as Lady Augusta Gregory and W. B. Yeats, was partially responsible for his reference to the first 14 stories in *Dubliners*—from "The Sisters" to "Grace"—as examples of the "moral paralysis" of Dublin. Although these stories have elements of folkloric material, it is the final tale, "The Dead," that is evidence of not only a change in Joyce's attitude toward Ireland, but also his growing awareness of the important place Irish history and folklore would have in his future work.

Joyce's invocation of universal human truths, particularized by individuals, is a hallmark of all his later works. In *A Portrait of the Artist as a Young Man*, a sensitive young man, Stephen Dedalus, moves from infancy to late adolescence and finally leaves Ireland "to forge the uncreated conscience of my race." In this novel, in the famous Christmas dinner scene, Joyce uses the recently dead Irish nationalist leader Charles Stewart Parnell to show how myth and legend are created and how, in Ireland, the two are inextricably linked to politics. Parnell is being made a legend as either a "dead king" (Mr. Dedalus) or a "devil" (Dante Riordan).

In one of Stephen Dedalus's last diary entries in *Portrait*, his mother "prays he will learn what the heart is and what it feels." *Ulysses*—the novel that is so kaleidoscopically rich in its language, its use of myth as a method of organization (inverting Homer's *Odyssey*), and its use of myth as a living, constantly accreting force in human life—shows that Joyce had found his heart. The story of Stephen Dedalus, Leopold Bloom, and Molly Bloom takes place on one day, June 16, 1904. Every possible angle of vision of the characters and on the characters is explored. Leopold Bloom and Stephen wander through Dublin, passing each other several times before they meet at last. Along the way, Joyce employs every conceivable method of storytelling: in the "Oxen of the Sun" section, the very development of the English language becomes a narrative technique. The catalogs of the "Ithaca" section, the transmogrifications of "Circe," as well as all sorts of traditional and popular folklore,

Freudian symbols, and Jungian archetypes, went into making *Ulysses* an exciting novel.

Joyce's final work, *Finnegans Wake*, represents the extreme development of the method of mythical archetypes. It is the ultimate family myth: Earwicker, Shem and Shaun, Issy, and the unforgettable Anna Livia Plurabelle refract and multiply as the narrative flows through Joyce's Dublin. The language itself is full of new words (birthwrong, Scheekspair), and there are puns on multiple linguistic levels (holmsted, gramma's grammar, mascarine, pheline or nuder). The work is so dense that it defeats most readers, and as yet, no writer in English or probably any other language has sought to pursue further the linguistic-archetypal methods of this work. In fact, nearly every word in *Finnegans Wake* can be analyzed to reveal a labyrinth of linguistic and traditional material.

The bitterness of the young Joyce is completely superseded by his characterizations of Leopold Bloom, Molly Bloom, and Anna Livia Plurabelle. Today, on O'Connell Street in Dublin, there is a sculpture representing Anna Livia Plurabelle, and Dubliners, with their own wonderful punning, mythologizing capacity, have named her "the floozie in the jacuzzi." Joyce's works, difficult as they may seem, live on because he so effectively combined literary art with traditional narrative and belief.

Mary Catherine Flannery

See also Archetype; Jung, Carl Gustav; Legend; Myth; *Odyssey*; Storytelling; Yeats, William Butler

✶✶✶✶✶✶✶✶✶✶✶✶✶✶✶✶✶

References

Bowen, Zack, and James Carens, eds. *A Companion to Joyce Studies*. Westport, Conn.: Greenwood Press, 1984.

Ellman, Richard. *James Joyce*. New York: Oxford University Press, 1982.

Staley, Thomas. *An Annotated Critical Bibliography of James Joyce*. New York: St. Martin's Press, 1989.

JUNG, CARL GUSTAV (1875–1961)

A Swiss psychiatrist, Carl Gustav Jung developed analytical psychology as a theory and practice of psychotherapy, a perspective that has influenced the understanding of religion, folklore, mythology, literature, and art. Although Jung was deeply influenced by Sigmund Freud and others early in his career, he was very much an independent and original thinker.

From his earliest years, Jung was intrigued by religious questions. His study of religion included folklore and mythology as part of the history of religion in its widest sense, and he was convinced of the fundamental importance of religion for human meaning and psychological health. Although Jung reflected on theological topics, he was always more interested in people's experience of God than with the theological questions about God's existence or nonexistence.

Jung held that the god-image or god-archetype is an especially important "psychological fact" that can be found everywhere and at all times in history; therefore, it is a significant datum for psychological study. Jung called such universal ideas "archetypes," and he used folklore as well as dreams, mythology, and literature to demonstrate their universality. Jung distinguished between the *archetypes themselves* and *archetypal images*, although he was not always consistent and careful about uniform terminology throughout his extensive writings. For Jung, the archetypes themselves are universal psychic structures, not directly observable but inferable from the uniformity and regularity of certain images and motifs that appear in dreams, visions, folklore, mythology, literature, and art. He believed that archetypes themselves, as psychic structures, are innate. The archetypal images, on the other hand, are not inherited; they vary somewhat across cultures and are directly observable in dreams, fairy tales, mythology, and literature. The archetypes, along with the instincts, make up what Jung called "the collective unconscious," the deep layer of the psyche that transcends and unifies all humanity. In his later works, Jung refers to the collective unconscious as a "universal substrate" in which everything resides.

Jung believed that fairy tales and myths are products of archetypal experiences—that is, people's experiences of the universal images and motifs emerge from the collective unconscious into their field of consciousness—and he sought to understand these underlying experiences in his study of folklore, mythology, and religion. Jung believed that only through comparative studies in these areas could the nature of relatively fixed symbols be evaluated, and he attempted to show the evolutionary stratification of the psyche through such studies. For this purpose, the study of folklore has advantages over the analysis of dreams in that fairy tales enable one to avoid all the details of individual case histories necessary to understanding dream symbols. For Jung, folklore allowed the psyche to tell its own story in which relatively universal symbols were revealed in their "natural setting."

In literature as in folklore, Jung was primarily interested in the effect of certain archetypes and the various ways in which they manifest themselves. Thus, he studied the process by which a work of literature was created rather than the early biographical history of the author. Jung distinguished between those works of art or literature in which the artist is completely in control and those in which a creative complex more or less takes over. When an archetype is at the heart of the creative complex, Jung spoke of a "visionary" work of art. Such works of literature resemble fairy tales and myths in that archetypal images and motifs are prominent.

Jung saw his psychology of the unconscious as a science of the deep forces that give rise to the images, symbols, and ideas of folklore, mythology, and religion. In fact, Jung compared his own method to that of folklorists who investigate certain motifs and figures that appear again and again, though each time in slightly altered disguise. Jung believed that these figures go far back into history and even prehistory. He considered the folkloric and mythological dimensions of life to be of enduring value, not primarily as a matter of historical interest, but as a key to unlocking the workings of the human mind.

Jung's theories of the archetypes and the collective unconscious allow the symbols of folklore and literature to come alive for people in a way that sheds light on the meaning of their present experience. In fact, Jung treated folklore and mythology as a treasure-house of archetypal forms from which to draw parallels and comparisons in his practice of psychotherapy. According to Jung, these symbols and motifs supply the context for those fantastic images that emerge in people's dreams and fantasies and threaten to disorient them. With the help of fairy tales and myths, Jung found that he could clarify the meaning of such images by giving them an appropriate framework and thereby calm the person who was psychologically at sea and in danger of being overwhelmed by such powerful material. In this way, Jung believed that folklore and mythology could help to offset neurosis. Similarly, he held that there is considerable value in telling children fairy tales as a means of channeling unconscious contents into consciousness. Such stories can reassure children that they are not alone in having such dreams or fantasies, which helps to integrate images and ideas that may appear frightening to them.

James Gollnick

343

Jung, Carl Gustav

See also Archetype; Fairy Tale; Freud, Sigmund; Motif; Myth

✳✳✳✳✳✳✳✳✳✳✳✳✳✳✳✳✳✳

References

Jung, Carl Gustav. *The Archetypes and the Collective Unconscious*. Princeton, N.J.: Princeton University Press, 1980.

———. *The Spirit in Man, Art, and Literature*. Princeton, N.J.: Princeton University Press, 1978.

KABUKI

One of the three classical theaters of Japan, *kabuki* traces its origins in the early seventeenth century to female entertainers who performed sensual dances and erotic scenes and practiced prostitution. Because of their notoriety, the government banned all female entertainers from *kabuki* performances in 1629. Their places were taken by young men who continued the performances, and they in turn were banned in 1652. The government then imposed a number of restrictions on the actors (only older men) and performances (e.g., a ban on prostitution) in the hope of presenting a more wholesome form of entertainment. These restrictions led to one of the most famous developments in the Japanese theater, that is, the role of the *onnagata* ("female impersonator").

By the late seventeenth century, *kabuki* was firmly established in the larger cities as one of the most popular forms of entertainment. The basic repertoire consists of *jidaimono* ("historical plays"), *sewamono* ("domestic plays"), and *shosagoto* ("dance and pantomime scenes"). The dramatic action of many of the plays relies on widely known legendary materials and/or folk beliefs.

The *jidaimono* often retold some current event that had occurred among elite samurai families. To disguise the actual characters and events, and thereby avoid government criticism, the story was usually set in the distant past. One of the most famous *jidaimono* is *Kanadehon Chūshingura* [Treasury of loyal retainers], a play based on the two years (1701–1703) of intrigue and plotting by 47 *ronin* ("masterless samurai") to avenge the death of their master. The play is so long and complex that although it is classified as a *jidaimono* play, it also contains acts that are *sewamono* or *shosagoto*.

The *sewamono* plays are similar to the *jidaimono* in that they

Theatergoers bought prints of Kabuki actors, like this 1865 woodblock print of Otani Tomoemon playing a male role and a female role, to commemorate great performances.

reenact some current scandal, but they differ in that the events related occurred among townspeople. Some of the most popular plays in this group, as in *bunraku* ("puppet play"), were the *shinjūmono*, or love suicide, plays. One of the most famous *sewamono* plays is *Sonezaki shinjūmono* [The love suicides at Sonezaki], an adaptation of a *bunraku* play by Chikamatsu Monzaemon (1653–1724).

One of the most famous *shosagoto* is *Kagamijishi* [The lion at the New Year's banquet]. During a New Year's party, a young attendant picks up a lion puppet and begins to dance with it. Eventually, the attendant is possessed by the spirit of the lion and then appears on stage as the lion and performs a very dramatic dance that features the dramatic twirling of the long lion's mane.

Richard W. Anderson

See also *Bunraku*; Performance

✳✳✳✳✳✳✳✳✳✳✳✳✳✳✳✳✳

References

Brandon, James R., trans. *Kabuki: Five Classic Plays*. Cambridge: Harvard University Press, 1975.

Brandon, James R., William P. Malm, and Donald H. Shively. *Studies in Kabuki: Its Acting, Music, and Historical Context*. Honolulu: University of Hawaii Press, 1978.

Gerstle, Andrew C. "Flowers of Edo: Eighteenth-Century Kabuki and Its Patrons." *Asian Theatre Journal* 4:1 (1987): 52–75.

Ortolani, Benito. *The Japanese Theater: From Shamanistic Ritual to Contemporary Pluralism*. Princeton: Princeton University Press, 1995.

Thornbury, Barbara E. *Sukeroku's Double Identity: The Dramatic Structure of Edo Kabuki*. Ann Arbor, Mich.: Center for Japanese Studies, 1982.

*K*ALEVALA

The *Kalevala* (1828–1849), the national epic of Finland, was constructed by Elias Lönnrot from folk poems he collected from the unlettered folk in Karelia, an area comprising eastern Finland and Finnish-speaking regions across the Russian border. The *Kalevala*, written in trochaic tetrameters and relying heavily on parallelism and alliteration, begins with the creation of the world and ends with the coming of Christianity.

The action takes place in a magical, shamanistic world in which heroes fight less with swords than with powerful words, incantations.

The epic recounts the struggle between the heroes of Kalevala and the people of the dark, forbidding land to the north, Pohjola—a struggle often interpreted as the clash between good and evil, light and darkness. The central characters from Kalevala are steadfast old Väinämöinen, who participated in the creation of the world and can charm all nature by playing his kantele (a stringed musical instrument) and by reciting powerful incantations; Ilmarinen, the mighty smithy who helped forge the lids of heaven; and brash Lemminkäinen, mighty warrior and lusty lover of women. In Pohjola they encounter the old hag Louhi and her minions as well as Louhi's beautiful daughter. The struggles between the two regions revolve around the attempts of the Kalevala heroes, one by one, to win the hand of Louhi's daughter and ownership of the Sampo, a magic mill that brings good fortunes to its possessors. Ilmarinen forges the Sampo—a magic object or talisman that brings wealth and good fortune to those who possess it—for the people of Pohjola in exchange for Louhi's daughter. When she is later killed, the Kalevala people raid Pohjola, steal the Sampo, and flee by boat, pursued by Louhi and her forces.

In the battle that follows, the Sampo is lost overboard and broken into pieces, which float to Kalevala and continue to bring prosperity to the land. For the remainder of the epic, Väinämöinen protects his people against vengeful attacks by Louhi. In the final canto, a virgin, Marjatta, eats a berry and conceives a child who is baptized "king of Karelia." Väinämöinen, recognizing that the old pagan order is changing and that he will be replaced by the child, representing Christianity, sails away toward the "land beneath the heavens," saying that he will yet be needed to construct another Sampo and leaving behind his kantele for the delight of his people. The epic's principal subplot tells of the tragic hero Kullervo, a man of high birth who, raised a slave, unwittingly commits incest with his sister and brings destruction to all he touches.

Although purported to be a reflection of ancient Finnish mythology and history, the *Kalevala* can more accurately be considered the literary creation of Elias Lönnrot; although based largely on actual folk poetry, that poetry was reshaped by Lönnrot to reflect the philosophical and nationalistic sentiments current at the beginning of the nineteenth century. In 1809, Finland's 600-year-old ties with Sweden were severed, and Finland became a Russian grand duchy. Lacking the binding ties of a common language (the upper classes spoke Swedish and the common people, Finnish), a national literature, and a recognized history, the Finns were ill-prepared to face the attempted Russification of the country that was inevitable. At the same time, the romantic-nationalistic ideas of the German philosopher Johann Gottfried Herder (1744–1803) were making their way into the country. Herder held that to be true to itself and to survive as an independent entity, a nation must be true to the national spirit reflected in its language and poetry and must base future cultural development on models inherited from the past. In a country like Finland, which possessed no significant literature written in Finnish, the call to a return to national poetry meant a return to the oral poetry that had originated in the past and survived in the present among the common folk in the countryside. It was these sentiments that sent young Finnish scholar-patriots scurrying into the hinterlands to gather the national, or folk, poetry of their country.

Chief among these collectors was Lönnrot, who traveled thousands of miles, largely in Karelia, collecting the many poems he would eventually develop into the *Kalevala*. Lönnrot initially intended to arrange the poems in order "so that what is to be found in different places about Väinämöinen, Ilmarinen, and Lemminkäinen" could be published together (Lönnrot Manuscript Collection). Then, having observed that some of the better singers combined individual poems into larger narrative cycles, desiring to create for the Finns a work comparable to the world's famous epics, and guided in his effort by classical models, Lönnrot began working his materials through several redactions and combined them into a larger epic unity. He mailed the completed work to the Finnish Literature Society for publication on February 28, 1835. In 1849, after further collecting, he brought out a much expanded version of the epic.

Upon its publication, the *Kalevala* was immediately hailed as a unified epic whole, one that had existed in ancient times and whose fragmented parts Lönnrot had restored to their original form. Lönnrot himself never made such a claim, but the romantic notion of a restored epic persisted for several decades among Finnish scholars and well into the twentieth century among the common people. In reality, as we follow Lönnrot's creative efforts through redaction after redaction to the final work, we move ever further away from the poems as they were sung by the people. Most of the lines in the *Kalevala* actually come from the folk poems (well over 90 percent), but few sequences of lines had ever been sung by the people as Lönnrot arranged them.

His method was to take a variant of a narrative poem he liked and fill it out by drawing lines from other poems, sometimes from other variants of the same poem, sometimes from separate narratives, and sometimes even from different kinds of poems—lyrical poems, incantations, wedding songs. Then, because the lines of his poems had been collected from different singers and from different regions, he would normalize the language, smoothing out dialect features. In other words, using lines drawn from the poems almost as one uses words drawn from one's own language, Lönnrot stitched together a poetic narrative that brought his own romantic vision of the past to the awareness of his countrymen and in the process, gave them a priceless possession, a national epic.

Although most of Lönnrot's contemporaries did not understand Finnish well enough to read the *Kalevala*, the work had an almost magical effect in the country. It served, as some said, as Finland's passport into the family of civilized nations, providing evidence that the Finns had had a glorious past separate from that of their foreign rulers, that the Finnish language was capable of serving as the national language, and that the Finns possessed a body of literature which was worthy in its own right and was capable of stimulating future literary development. Rising Finnish self-esteem in the second half of the nineteenth century can be traced directly to the publication of the *Kalevala*.

At the end of the century, that self-esteem would be sorely tested as the long-feared attempt to assimilate Finnish cultural institutions into Russia became a reality. This time, however, the Finns faced these pressures with a sense of national identity and national purpose that could scarcely have been imagined at the beginning of the century. In what has been called the golden age of Finnish art—Jean Sibelius in music, Akseli Gallén-Kallela in painting, Eino Leino in poetry, and scores of lesser lights—Finns turned to the ancient and glorious world they found in the *Kalevala* for artistic inspiration and for the strength to endure present difficulties. They brought the old heroes—Väinämöinen, Ilmarinen, Lemminkäinen—vividly to life, and as a result, the general public may well have developed a picture of the past based more on these artistic interpretations of the epic than on the *Kalevala* itself. Partly as a result of these creations and the sense of national pride engendered by them, what had in reality never existed would eventually come into being—a Finnish Finland.

As the Finns hoped, the *Kalevala* has carried the name of Finland abroad, winning recognition and acclaim. In 1845, the famous German philologist Jacob Grimm lectured on the epic in Berlin, and from that time to the present, the *Kalevala* has captured the attention of foreign scholars and literati. During the 1985 sesquicentennial celebration of the publication of the epic, conferences and festive events were organized not only throughout Finland, but also throughout much of the world, demonstrating a strong international interest in the *Kalevala*. The *Kalevala* has been translated into more languages than any other work of Finnish literature. It is still studied and enjoyed and still inspires artistic productions both at home and abroad, standing as an enduring symbol of Finland itself.

William A. Wilson

See also Epic; Herder, Johann Gottfried; Lönnrot, Elias; Nationalism

❋❋❋❋❋❋❋❋❋❋❋❋❋❋❋

References

DuBois, Thomas. *Finnish Folk Poetry and the Kalevala*. New York: Garland, 1995.

Kuusi, Matti, and Pertti Anttonen. *Kalevalan lipas*. Helsinki: Finnish Literature Society, 1984.

Lönnrot Manuscript Collection. Helskinki: Finnish Literature Society.

Wilson, William A. *Folklore and Nationalism in Modern Finland*. Bloomington: Indiana University Press, 1976.

KING LEAR

Shakespeare's play *King Lear* (1605–1606) is one of the most universally stirring and troubling works in all of literature—"too huge for the stage" the scholar A. C. Bradley once observed. From the moment that King Lear divides his kingdom among his daughters in the first scene, the play spirals into a tangled exploration of some poignant aspects of the human experience, including notions of filial obedience, paternal obligation, political strife, loyalty, and madness. In the end, Lear is rejected by his daughters Goneril and Regan, whose wiles leave their father destitute. Lear finds himself finally in a universe where he can exist only as a "very foolish fond old man" (act IV, scene vii, line 59). Only too late does he understand his own true nature and the true nature of his daughter Cordelia's genuine love.

King Lear takes counsel from the fool, a common device in the folktales upon which Shakespeare drew for his plays.

It is not surprising that Shakespeare's play has some of its primal roots in old folktales. *King Lear*—specifically, the play's famous first scene—is connected to Antti Aarne and Stith Thompson tale-type 923, "Love Like Salt." Full of ceremony, the scene is orchestrated by Lear as an occasion for Goneril, Regan, and Cordelia to proclaim the depth of their love for him. Cordelia's honest, constrained response ("I cannot heave / My heart into my mouth. I love your Majesty / According to my bond, no more nor less" [I, i, 91–93]) echoes the comments of the youngest daughter in the folktale, who claims to love her father like salt. In both cases, what appears at first to be an insultingly understated proclamation of affection proves to be after all an honest, reasoned articulation of heartfelt filial love. *Lear* also draws episodes from the tale "Cap o' Rushes," a subtype of "Cinderella" (AT 510), one of the oldest and most widespread of all folktales. The opening scene of "Cap o' Rushes" has been designated as "King Lear Judgment—Love Like Salt," related to AT 923 by its inclusion of the characteristic love-test.

"Cap o' Rushes" and "Love Like Salt" serve primarily as a skeletal frame for *Lear*'s plot, upon which Shakespeare builds an elaborate drama that is complicated by intricate subplots and character development; however, thematically, the tales underlie the central problems of the play—for instance, the complications of sibling rivalry and unnatural sexual impulses between father and daughter (the type summary of "Cap o' Rushes" [AT 510B] begins: "Present of the father who wants to marry his own daughter"). Thus, in addition to using folktales as models of plot structure, Shakespeare's *King Lear* may have derived thematic issues from them as well.

Charles Greg Kelley

See also Folktale; Shakespeare, William; Tale-Type

✳✳✳✳✳✳✳✳✳✳✳✳✳✳✳✳✳✳

References

Cox, Marian Roalfe. *Cinderella*. London: Publications of the Folk-Lore Society, 1893.

Dundes, Alan. "'To Love My Father All': A Psychoanalytic Study of the Folktale Source of *King Lear*." *Southern Folklore Quarterly* 40 (1976): 353–366.

KINGSTON, MAXINE HONG (1940–)

The Asian-American writer Maxine Hong Kingston was born in Stockton, California, where her father, a scholar trained in the Confucian classics, and her mother, a medical practitioner, ran a laundry. Maxine Hong attended the University of California at Berkeley where she received a B.A. in English in 1962 and a teaching certificate in 1965. Before her emergence as a writer in 1977, Maxine Hong married the actor Earl Kingston and taught high school in California and Hawaii. She continues to teach writing at Berkeley.

Kingston is perhaps best known for *The Woman Warrior: Memoirs of a Childhood among Ghosts* (1976) and its companion volume *China Men* (1980). Although both were published as nonfiction, Kingston freely mixes history, folklore, and fantasy to explore the Chinese experience in the United States. This willingness to cross the boundaries of genre has been the source of considerable critical commentary. Among her most vocal Asian-American critics is the author Frank Chin, who accuses Kingston of rewriting and hence distorting Chinese folktales and ballads, thereby falsifying Chinese-American history.

It is, indeed, Kingston's narrative strategy to rewrite Chinese folktales and ballads so as to empower them to help give meaning to her own experiences and those of her family in the United States. Most notably, she has rewritten the story of Fa Mulan, a heroine of a folk ballad first recorded in the eighth century. Fa Mulan, the woman warrior of the traditional ballad, dons male garb to serve in place of her elderly father as a general in the emperor's army. Kingston's version strips the story of feudal and patriarchal trappings as the author imagines herself battling the forces of racism and sexism.

Storytelling is so central to Kingston's narrative—"I will tell you a story, you must never tell anyone" is the first line of *Woman Warrior*—that the book may be read as a meditation on oral tradition itself. For Kingston, oral tradition is infinitely supple, and thus frustrating to the naive listener. Its prevarications, constantly changing details in the face of a hostile environment, are what enabled the immigrants of her parents' generation to survive, no matter how frustrating, embarrassing, or tragic this oral tradition might seem to their children.

In the novel *Tripmaster Monkey: His Fake Book* (1989), Kingston rewrote the Chinese Buddhist epic *Journey to the West* as a search for Asian-American culture in the 1960s. The chief protagonist of this novel is one Wittman Ah Sing, a radically alienated playwright who is thought by many to resemble Frank Chin. Wittman embodies the character of a monkey with magical powers (Sun Wu-gong in *Journey to the West*). Like the original epic, the novel draws together a wide and diverse set of characters and cultural referents from the "beat poets" who came into prominence in the 1950s and the Chinatown nightclub scene of the 1940s to the 108 outlaw heroes of the

Water Margin—men forced into social banditry by their oppressive and unlawful rulers. It is precisely because of this breadth of cultural range and "quirky" characters that many mainstream reviewers who are not familiar with the primary referent or do not have a knowledge of Asian-American cultural history find the book confusing.

Robert Lee

See also Ballad; Chin, Frank; Epic; Folktale; Genre; Storytelling

✳✳✳✳✳✳✳✳✳✳✳✳✳✳✳✳✳

References

Goellnicht, Donald. "Tang Ao in America, Male Subject Positions in China Men." In *Reading the Literatures of Asian America*, ed. Shirley Geok-lin Lim and Amy Ling, pp. 191–212. Philadelphia: Temple University Press, 1992.

Kingston, Maxine Hong. *China Men*. New York: Knopf, 1980.

——— *Tripmaster Monkey: His Fake Book*. New York: Knopf, 1989.

———. *The Woman Warrior: Memoirs of a Girlhood among Ghosts*. New York: Vintage Books, 1976.

Lin, Patricia. "Clashing Constructs of Reality: Reading Maxine Hong Kingston's *Tripmaster Monkey: His Fake Book* as Indigenous Ethnography." In *Reading the Literatures of Asian America*, ed. Shirley Geok-lin Lim and Amy Ling, pp. 333–348. Philadelphia: Temple University Press, 1992.

KITTREDGE, GEORGE LYMAN (1860–1941)

The teacher and scholar George Lyman Kittredge adopted the German-based methods (comparative and attentive to origins) developed by Francis James Child for the study of English literature and passed them on to future generations of American scholars. Born in Boston, Kittredge was an outstanding student at the Roxbury Latin School and at Harvard College, where, in addition to classics, he studied English with Child. After graduating in 1882, Kittredge traveled to Germany and studied for a short time in Leipzig and in Tübingen. From 1888 until he retired in 1936, he taught at Harvard, becoming a professor of English in 1895 and, in 1917, the first Gurney Professor of English Literature.

After Child's death in 1896, Kittredge inherited his course on ballads and also assumed responsibility for the publication of the last part of *The English and Scottish Popular Ballads* (1882–1898). Jointly with Child's daughter, Helen Child Sargent, Kittredge then edited a one-volume edition (1904), which was widely distributed. Connected with Harvard University Press and holding an editorial position on the *Journal of American Folklore*, he had a direct influence on the publication of ballad scholarship for several decades.

Kittredge is most famous for his Shakespeare course and for his editions of Shakespeare's plays. He attempted to fill in the linguistic and historical background so that students could appreciate the older works of literature as contemporary audiences and readers would have done. In addition, he regularly taught courses in medieval romance, Old Norse, Germanic mythology, and Germanic and Celtic religions. Many of his students became distinguished scholars, including John Lomax (folk songs), Sigurd Bernhard Hustvedt (ballads), Stith Thompson (folktales), Bartlett Jere Whiting (proverbs), Archer Taylor (proverbs), and Francis Lee Utley (folktales and literature). Thus, Child and Kittredge set the direction of folklore scholarship in America for the first three-quarters of the twentieth century. The combination of high scholarly standards and the prestige of Harvard helped to make a place for folklore studies in many university departments of literature.

Kittredge's own folklore work was primarily in two fields, medieval literature and Americana. In his books *Arthur and Gorgalon* (1903) and *A Study of Gawain and the Green Knight* (1916), he took a comparative approach and listed literary and folklore analogues for the most striking motifs. *The Old Farmer and His Almanack* (1904) is a readable compendium of New England local color, including customs, anecdotes, and superstitions. *Witchcraft in Old and New England* (1929) has, in addition to its historical component, extensive comparative notes regarding practices of sympathetic magic.

Christine Goldberg

See also Child, Francis James; Taylor, Archer; Thompson, Stith; Utley, Francis Lee

✳✳✳✳✳✳✳✳✳✳✳✳✳✳✳✳✳✳

References

Birdsall, Esther K. "Some Notes on the Role of George Lyman Kittredge in American Folklore Studies." *Journal of the Folklore Institute* 10 (1973): 57–66.

Hyder, Clyde Kenneth. *George Lyman Kittredge, Teacher and Scholar*. Lawrence: University of Kansas Press, 1962.

Thorpe, James. *A Bibliography of the Writings of George Lyman Kittredge*. Cambridge: Harvard University Press, 1948.

Whiting, Bartlett Jere. "Kittredge, George Lyman." In *Dictionary of American Biography*, suppl. 3, *1941–1945*, pp. 422–424. New York: Charles Scribner's Sons, 1973.

KOBZARI

Kobzari (singular, *kobzar*) were Ukrainian professional, blind, mendicant minstrels. They may have originated as professional musicians who accompanied the Cossack host (armed forces); indeed, there are some seventeenth-century court records referring to such men. All of the direct information about them, collected from the middle of the nineteenth century onward, indicates that they had to be disabled, which, in all known cases, meant that they were blind. They had to belong to church-affiliated guilds called *hurtyi* or *bratstva* ("brotherhoods"). Each had to serve an apprenticeship with a master *kobzar*, which normally lasted 3 years, and each had to undergo an initiation test before being allowed to enter a guild and start performing on their own. In some regions, a *kobzar* had to be a guild member for 10 years and pass a second test before he could qualify as a master and earn the right to have apprentices of his own.

Kobzari performed religious songs, psalms, heroic epics (*dumy*), and historical songs. Some played lyric songs and dance melodies and earned money by performing at weddings. A typical *kobzar* performance, however, is considered a very serious act, akin to a prayer. *Kobzari* would either perform outside monasteries and cathedrals, especially during church holidays, or they would travel the countryside, going from village to village. In a given village, the *kobzar* would enter a household and perform the *zhebranka*, or begging song, at which point the residents could plead inability to pay and the *kobzar* would move on. If he were asked to stay, the hosts could select the songs to be performed, or they could let the minstrel make his own selection. Payment was normally in goods.

Kobzari sang to the accompaniment of a *bandura*, an asymmetrical plucked and strummed lute that has developed a harp to one side. The *bandura* developed out of the *kobza*, which was a more conventional lute—it no longer exists—and the instrument from which the *kobzari* drew their name. The *kobzari* shared their guild affiliation and their repertory with *lirnyky*, who were also blind mendicants. In fact, they were so much a unit with the *kobzari* that some *kobzari* had *lirnyky* apprentices and vice versa. Although *kobzari* and *lirnyky* were one category of musician by the nineteenth century, they must have been distinct at some point. The *lira* from which the *lirnyky* took their name is strikingly dissimilar from the *bandura*. It is a hurdy-gurdy with three strings, a crank-driven wheel that rubs the strings to produce a droning sound, and piano-like keys that strike individual strings to produce a melody. The usual supposition is that the *lirnyky* were always disabled musicians while the *kobzari* were once military musicians who joined the church-affiliated guilds when the Cossacks were disbanded.

Kobzari, like the *dumy* that they sang, have become a symbol of Ukrainian poetry. Taras Shevchenko (1814–1861), perhaps the most beloved of Ukrainian poets, entitled a collection of his work *Kobzar* (1840) and since then, *kobzari* have represented not just folk poetry, but Ukrainian poetry as a whole.

Natalie Kononenko

See also *Dumy*

❊❊❊❊❊❊❊❊❊❊❊❊❊❊❊❊❊

References

Kirdan, B. P., and O. Omel'chenko. *Narodni spivtsi-muzykanty na Ukraiini*. Kiev: Muzychna Ukraiina, 1980.

Kononenko, Natalie. *Ukrainian Minstrels: And the Blind Shall Sing*. Armonk, N.Y.: M. E. Sharpe, 1997.

Lavrov, F. *Kobzari: Narysy z istorii kobzarstva Ukraiiny*. Kiev: Mystetsvo, 1980.

Shtokalko, Zinovii. *A Kobzar Handbook*. Trans. Andrij Hornjatkevych. Edmonton: Canadian Institute of Ukrainian Studies, 1989.

KONJAKU

Konjaku Monogatari [Tales of times now past] is one of the greatest collections of tales in the world. Compiled in Japan in the early twelfth century, it contains 1,039 tales in 28 volumes (3 have been lost). It is uncertain who the compiler was or why he gathered these tales into a single text. A number of scholars have speculated that it was the work of a Buddhist priest and that it was compiled as an act of devotion to help the compiler and his patron(s) achieve rebirth in Buddhist heaven. Alternately, it may have been a collection for use by itinerant priests who traveled around the countryside preaching and telling stories when trying to make converts to Buddhism or collecting donations for the copying of sutras, the making of religious images, or the building or refurbishing of a temple.

The collection can be broken down into three sections: the first 5 volumes contain tales of India, the second 5 volumes focus on China, and the remaining 18 volumes contain tales that take place in Japan. According to W. Michael Kelsey (1982) the tales can be further categorized as either Buddhist or secular, and these two categories can be further divided into history, praise, and didactic tales.

The grouping of the tales is further related to a Buddhist concept usually referred to as "the decline of the law." It was commonly felt in East Asia that there were three stages in the transmission of the Buddhist law after the death of the Buddha. The first state (*shōbō*) was a time when the true teachings of the Buddha could be transmitted and understood. The second stage (*zōbō*) was a time when the true teaching would start to be polluted with false doctrines, making it much more difficult to achieve enlightenment. The third stage (*mappō*) was a period when the teaching would be so corrupted that it would be impossible for anyone, on their own power, to achieve enlightenment. It was commonly thought that the third period had begun around the time the *Konjaku* was compiled. The Indian tales, therefore, represent the first stage of the law, the Chinese tales the second stage, and the Japanese the third and final stage. So not only is the text divided geographically, it also illustrates the historical decline of society.

The *Konjaku* is such a large and important tale collection that, as D. E. Mills (1970) points out, much of the Japanese tale scholarship has focused on the relationship of other collections to the *Konjaku*. The tales are interesting because they do not focus on only elite personages but on people from all social classes, and though Buddhist tales predominate, secular tales are included. The collection is also important because of its influence on modern Japanese literature. A number of modern writers in Japan have turned to tales in the *Konjaku* for inspiration; probably the most famous among them, Akutagawa Ryūnosuke (1892–1927), claimed he was attracted to these tales because of their primitive beauty and freshness. Akutagawa's best known adaptation from a tale in the *Konjaku* is his story entitled "In the Grove," which is the tale of a bandit who persuades a traveler and his wife to follow him into a grove where he ties up the man and rapes his wife. One of Japan's great film directors, Akira

Kurosawa, used Akutagawa's story as the basis for his award-winning film *Rashōmon* (1950).

Richard W. Anderson

See also Folktale

✳✳✳✳✳✳✳✳✳✳✳✳✳✳✳✳✳

References

Kelsey, W. Michael. *Konjaku Monogatari-shū*. Boston: Twayne Publishers, 1982.

Kobayashi, Hiroko. *The Human Comedy of Heian Japan: A Study of the Secular Stories in the Twelfth-Century Collection of Tales, Konjaku Monogatarishū*. Tokyo: Center for East Asian Cultural Studies, 1979.

Mills, D. E. *A Collection of Tales from Uji: A Study and Translation of Uji Shūi Monogatari*. Cambridge: Cambridge University Press, 1970.

Nakamura, Kyoko Motomochi. *Miraculous Stories from the Japanese Buddhist Tradition: The Nihon Ryōiki of the Monk Kyōkai*. Cambridge: Harvard University Press, 1973.

Ury, Marian. *Tales of Times Now Past: Sixty-two Stories from a Medieval Japanese Collection*. Berkeley: University of California Press, 1973.

KROHN, LEOPOLD KAARLE (1863–1933)

A Finnish professor, folklorist, and developer of the geographic-historic method of folklore research, Leopold Kaarle Krohn is best known outside Finland for his contributions to international folktale research. However, he devoted most of his life to the study of the epic poetry that forms the basis for the Finnish national epic, the *Kalevala*.

From the publication of the epic in 1835 until the mid-1870s, Finnish folklore research was characterized by a heady romanticism that viewed the *Kalevala* as a unified whole whose fragmented parts its compiler, Elias Lönnrot, had collected in the Finnish hinterlands and had then restored to their original form. Kaarle Krohn's father, Julius Krohn (1835–1888), strongly influenced by the evolutionary and positivistic thought that was making its way into Finland from the Continent, set folklore study on a more realistic and scientific foundation. Through a close textual analysis of the variants of the *Kalevala* poems, he concluded that because of its composite nature, the epic could not be used as the basis of scientific study, though it would retain its artistic and cultural value. He further concluded that the poems from which the *Kalevala* had been composed had originated in western Finland and had then migrated eastward to Karelia, the area on both sides of the Russo-Finnish border where Lönnrot had collected them. Krohn reached this conclusion by arranging poem variants in geographical order, based on their place of collection, and then charting the migration path taken as each variant had developed out of another. Julius Krohn drowned in 1888, at the height of his scholarly career, before he could fully develop his geographic approach, and his son carried on his work.

Kaarle Krohn passed his matriculation exams in 1880, earned his candidacy degree in 1883 at Helsinki University, and completed his doctorate in 1888. He had already begun folklore study in 1881 when, at the age of 18, he had conducted field research in northern Karelia. From January 1884 to June 1885, he traveled over much of Finland collecting a rich store of Finnish folklore. In his collecting, he focused especially on folktales because he believed they had been passed by in the search for epic songs. His doctoral thesis, *Bär (Wolf) und Fuchs, eine nordische Tiermärchenkette* [Bear (wolf) and fox: A Nordic animal-tale chain (1888)], based on his folktale collecting and employing his father's geographic-historic research method, won Krohn an immediate international reputation, which, in turn, brought him rapid academic advancement. In 1888, he was named docent of Finnish and comparative literature at Helsinki University; in 1889, acting professor of Finnish and Finnish literature; and in 1898, extraordinary personal professor of Finnish and comparative folklore. In 1908, when a permanent chair in Finnish and comparative folklore was established, he became its first occupant.

In all likelihood, had his father not suffered an unfortunate early death, Kaarle Krohn would have continued his folktale studies. Instead, out of loyalty to his father, he turned his attention to Finnish folk poetry, and he also further developed his father's geographic-historic research method (called the historic-geographic method in the United States). This method was based on the simple observation that versions of the same poems from widely scattered communities differed more than did those from neighboring villages, which meant that as poems migrated from place to place, new variants developed out of old ones. To determine the direction of their diffusion, therefore, one has only to study the varying traits of an item as they occurred in geographic order. "Along side local variation," said Krohn, "chronology, of course, must also be taken into account, so the method is actually historical-geographical" (Krohn

1901a, p. 108). This historical development would be of secondary importance, however, because "the collection of folk materials generally is barely older than one hundred years" (Krohn 1909, p. 108). (Later scholars would stress historical forces much more than Krohn did.) Having arranged all of the variants of a particular poem geographically and having studied the progressively changing traits, one could, believed Krohn, chart the poem's path of migration and then, by going back along this path, locate its point of origin and reconstruct its original form.

In 1909, in his installation address on being appointed to the chair in folklore, Krohn sketched out for the first time what by now had become known as the Finnish method of folklore research. In 1911, he published the presentation in German, "Über die finnische folkloristische methode," to reach an international audience, and in 1918, in *Kalevalankysymyksiä* [*Kalevala* questions], he worked the method out in more detail. In 1926, he extended his analysis beyond folk poetry to other forms of folk tradition and published the result as *Die folkloristische Arbeitsmethode, begründet von Julius Krohn und weitergeführt von nordischen Forschern* [Folklore methodology: Formulated by Julius Krohn and expanded by Nordic researchers],which has exerted enormous influence on folklore research in much of the world. Krohn influenced folklore research in other ways as well. In 1907, with his Danish colleague Axel Olrik, he founded Folklore Fellows, an international organization of prominent folklore scholars, and served as editor in chief of the organization's scholarly series, Folklore Fellows Communications.

Paradoxically, Krohn used his research method to arrive at diametrically opposed conclusions. In his monumental *Kalevalan runojen historia* [The history of the *Kalevala* poems] (1903–1910), he argued that Finnish epic poems had originated as poetic germ cells in western Finland and then, as they moved eastward toward Russo-Karelia, had combined to form larger poems and had at last evolved into miniature epics. Therefore, he did not, in the customary manner, bemoan the fact that the epic songs had been collected so late, when they no longer retained their pristine beauty, but instead rejoiced that they had not been collected earlier, before they had reached full poetic development.

In 1918, in *Kalevalankysymyksiä*, inspired, perhaps, by the nationalistic sentiments current in newly independent Finland, Krohn completely reversed himself. He still believed that the poems had migrated from west to east, but now he argued that the poems had originated in the late Iron Age (700–1100) during a warlike period that corresponded to the Scandinavian Viking age. He also now thought that the events described in the poems had derived neither from mythology nor from saints' legends, as he had earlier argued, but from descriptions of actual historical events when Finnish Viking chieftains had walked as free men on free Finnish soil and had, with the sword, won fame and honor for the fatherland. Most important, he argued that as descriptions of actual historical events, the poems had originated as artistic wholes and had then fragmented and deteriorated as they migrated toward Russo-Karelia. Krohn thus became a devolutionist and now used the geographic-historic method, which he and his father had originally used to prove folklore evolution, to demonstrate folklore decay. He developed this changed point of view in full detail in his second magnum opus, *Kalevalastudien* (1924–1928, six volumes).

Considering that these opposing views were developed through the use of the same research method, a cynic might argue that the method makes a good research tool provided one already knows the conclusions before beginning research. A more charitable view would be that Krohn, a thoroughly honest scholar, could not escape the ideological currents of his time and that a single view of folklore change—first evolution, then devolution—obscured his vision and allowed him to see only that which his theory prepared him to see.

In 1932, a year before he died, Krohn returned once more to folklore research, publishing a review of international folktale scholarship based largely on the methodological approach he had developed, *Übersicht über einige Resultate der Märchenforschung* [A review of some results of folktale research]. Most scholars today recognize that folklore does not necessarily improve or decay as it passes through time and space, it merely changes. To the extent that the Finnish method helps us chart those changes and understand the cultural forces that produce them, it may still remain an important tool of folklore research. Whatever the case, it was the geographic-historic method worked out by Julius Krohn and fully developed by his son Kaarle Krohn that gave scientific respectability to subsequent folklore study.

William A. Wilson

See also Epic; Folktale; Historic-Geographic Method; *Kalevala*; Lönnrot, Elias; Nationalism; Romanticism

✻✻✻✻✻✻✻✻✻✻✻✻✻✻✻✻✻

References

Hautala, Jouko. *Finnish Folklore Research 1828–1918*. Helsinki: Finnish Society of Sciences, 1968.

———. "Kaarle Krohn as a Folklorist." *Studia Fennica* 11 (1964): 3–72.

Krohn, Kaarle. "Suomalaisesta kansanrunouden tutkimuksen metodista." *Valvoja* 29 (1909): 103–112.

Wilson, William A. "The Evolutionary Premise in Folklore Theory and the 'Finnish Method.'" *Western Folklore* 35 (1976): 241–249.

KUNSTMÄRCHEN

Kunstmärchen is one of several German terms used in the fields of folklore and literature for which there are no satisfactory equivalents in English, although "literary tale" and "literary fairy tale" are rough equivalents. Even though narrative researchers have not been able to agree on what does or does not constitute a *Kunstmärchen*, the genre can be roughly divided into two basic types: (1) original compositions that share some of the motifs and traits of traditional folktales, such as L. Frank Baum's *The Wonderful Wizard of Oz* (1900), and (2) the literary adaptation of traditional tales by professional authors, represented by Joel Chandler Harris's *Uncle Remus* (see Bickley 1978) and Richard Chase's *The Jack Tales* (1943) and *Grandfather Tales* (1948).

The term *Kunstmärchen* owes its existence to the distinction drawn by the brothers Grimm between *Naturpoesie* ("nature poetry") and *Kunstpoesie* ("art poetry"). The prefix *Natur-* was used by the Grimms to denote narratives that are produced by a natural, organic process by the nation (or *Volk*) when it remains true to its own national soul. Thus, the Grimms saw *Naturpoesie* as the direct expression of the creative impulse of the collective force of the people. *Kunstpoesie*, by contrast, denotes "art" forms that are concocted by individuals who, more often than not, have lost contact with their natural/national roots. This pejorative connotation, however, in no way inhibited such friends and colleagues of the Grimms as Clemens Brentano, Ludwig Tieck (1773–1832), Friedrich De La Mottee Fouque (1777–1843), E. T. A. Hoffmann, and Novalis (Friedrich von Hardenberg, 1772–1801), from creating a large number of *Kunstmärchen*.

Although the origin of the concept has its roots in romantic nationalism, the beginnings of traditional literary tales occurred many centuries earlier in the Orient in such works as *Kalila and Dimna, Seven Wise Masters, 1001 Nights,* and *Somadeva,* for which there was no generic designation. These collections and scores of others were thoroughly investigated by Theodor Benfey, who, in his introduction to his edition of the *Pantschatantra* (1859), was able to demonstrate convincingly how scores of narratives on the Eurasian continuum had existed as both literary and folktales over a period of centuries. More recently, Manfred Grätz (1996) inferred that because all folktales were necessarily the product of individuals, every folktale presupposes the existence of a *Kunstmärchen.* Bengt Holbek, by contrast, argues vehemently that the folktale as a genre has been around for millennia and thrived long before there were *Kunstmärchen* (Holbek 1987, pp. 250–258 and passim).

Also in existence before romanticism were eighteenth-century literary fairy tales by Marie d'Aulnoy and Charles Perrault, among others. The postromantic period was represented by such writers as Hans Christian Andersen in Denmark, Selma Lagerlöf in Sweden, and Oscar Wilde, William Thackeray, and especially Robert Southey ("The Three Bears") in Great Britain.

Kunstmärchen also have enjoyed great popularity in the United States. Among the authors who have produced literary folktales are, other than L. Frank Baum, Washington Irving, Nathaniel Hawthorne, Mark Twain, and James Thurber. Although some narrative scholars insist that *Kunstmärchen* represent a moribund art form (see, e.g., Tismer 1966, p. 2), since the mid-1960s they have appeared in books, magazines, periodicals, films, and videos under the rubric "fantasy literature," where adaptations of myths, fairy tales, legends, and other traditional narratives thrive. Moreover, the German folklorist Sabine Wienker-Piepho (1993) has shown how magic tales are popular in the workshops of many esoteric organizations.

Donald Ward

See also Andersen, Hans Christian; Brentano, Clemens; Fairy Tale; Folktale; Hawthorne, Nathaniel; Motif; Nationalism; Perrault, Charles; Romanticism; *The Thousand and One Nights*; Twain, Mark

✳✳✳✳✳✳✳✳✳✳✳✳✳✳✳✳✳✳

References

Benfey, Theodor. *Pantschatantra.* 2 vols. Leipzig: F. A. Brockhaus, 1859.

Bickley, Bruce. *Joel Chandler Harris. A Reference Guide.* Boston: G. K. Hall, 1978.

Chase, Richard. *Grandfather Tales*. Boston: Houghton, Mifflin, 1948.

———. *The Jack Tales*. Boston: Houghton and Mifflin, 1943.

Grätz, Manfred. "Kunstmärchen." *Enzyklopädie des Märchens* 8 (1996): 612–622.

Holbek, Bengt. *Interpretation of Fairy Tales*. Folklore Fellows Communication no. 239. Helsinki: Academia Scientiarum Fennica, 1987.

Tismer, Jens. *Kunstmärchen*. Stuttgart: Metzler Verlag, 1966.

Wienker-Piepho, Sabine. "Junkfood for the Soul: Magic Storytelling during Esoteric Workshops." *Fabula* 34 (1993): 225–237.

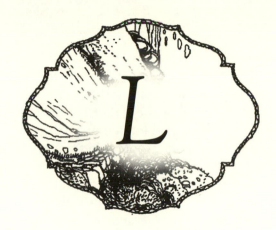

LABOR FOLKLORE AND LITERATURE

Labor folklore consists of an esoteric body of traditions associated with a specific occupation or labor-oriented group (e.g., cowboys, unions) that has been reframed and represented in a literary genre. Elements of oral and customary traditions may be incorporated into literary forms by professional writers, or they may be represented by the workers themselves as a distinct form of literature, usually for an audience of fellow workers or their community.

When the content of labor lore is used by professional writers, it is usually to add color and a sense of authenticity to the artistic work. If one takes the North American timber industry as a representative example, the use of occupational jargon and song is notable in Stewart Edward White's *The Blazed Trail* (1902) and *The Riverman* (1908), as is Ken Kesey's use of the jargon, narrative, and ritual customs of Northwest loggers in his novel *Sometimes a Great Notion* (1964). The figure of Paul Bunyan, a fusion of both logger oral tradition and an advertising campaign, has repeatedly surfaced (fancifully embellished in a style for adults and children) in the literary productions of American writers since 1914, from the poetry of Robert Frost and Carl Sandburg to the playful writings of James Stevens to the operetta *Paul Bunyan* (1941) by Benjamin Britten and W. H. Auden.

Also common is the reshaping of occupational jargon, legends, and customs by workers themselves into literary genres. Although sometimes elegiac, such literature often has strong political and social overtones, especially when used to achieve either a sense of class or occupational solidarity or to state the value of a specific kind of work to modern society. Historically, labor poetry has been among the most powerful literary forms for publicly expressing group sentiment and galvanizing political support. Strengthened in the twentieth century by the concurrent production of socialist poetry and song, particularly the proletarian verse of the Industrial Workers of the World, labor poetry represents a transformation of the sung word to the media of the modern print world, where a poetic message can quickly reach a widely dispersed audience. Such poetry has most commonly been distributed through union and trade journals, but it also appears in local newspapers and privately printed chapbooks that circulate throughout regions and occupations.

Avoiding any pretense of modernist, free-form verse, labor poetry is stylistically and thematically similar to traditional songs, giving aesthetic form to general occupational ideology and experience, and to the radical rhetoric of labor movements. In North America, verse traditions are strongest among men and women of the mining, ranching, and timber industries. Rock and coal miners have used poetry periodically to solidify their base of popular support during strikes. The tradition of written and recited poetry among ranch workers helps reconcile the mythic image of the American cowboy with the realities of their rapidly diminished function. Written poetry among loggers has become increasingly popular as a means of self-reflection and role redefinition, the result of recent environmentalist criticism of their profession.

Robert E. Walls

See also Bunyan, Paul; Chapbook; Henry, John; Legend

❊❊❊❊❊❊❊❊❊❊❊❊❊❊❊❊❊

References

Halker, Clark D. *For Democracy, Workers, and God: Labor Song-Poems and Labor Protest, 1865–95.* Urbana: University of Illinois Press, 1991.

Tannacito, Dan. "Poetry of the Colorado Miners: 1903–1906." *Radical Teacher* 15 (1980): 1–8.

Walls, Robert E. "Logger Poetry and the Expression of Worldview." *Northwest Folklore* 5 (1987): 15–45.

LANG, ANDREW (1844–1912)

As a Scottish scholar and man of letters, Andrew Lang was interested in both classical and modern literature, anthropology, folklore, and history. In the 1870s and 1880s, Lang rose to prominence as a leader of the English Folk-Lore Society and, in 1892, was elected president of the International Folk-Lore Congress held in London. As a folklorist he wrote on a wide range of topics, from Australian customs to variants of Cinderella, and he led the small group of British scholars who came to dominate folktale studies between 1880 and 1900.

Lang's scholarly contributions to folklore began with a series of articles and books disputing Max Müller's philosophy of comparative mythology. Jacob and Wilhelm Grimm in Germany had argued for a devolutionary history of *Volkspoesie* ("folk poetry"), with folklore being the modern remains of an earlier (great) cultural tradition. They pointed to both linguistic changes and folk narratives as evidence of relationships. The language scholar Max Müller went further, arguing for a specific, even degenerative, process whereby a myth mutates into a legend and finally devolves into a tale. He began with Sanskrit names and followed their linguistic mutations as Indo-European cultures developed. Müller argued that narratives grew up to explain names and phrases of uncertain sense.

Lang, on the other hand, argued for an evolutionary development of culture and narrative. He assembled folktales cross-culturally and demonstrated that similar tales existed in (linguistically) unrelated cultures, thus refuting Müller's philological arguments. Lang also argued that traditional märchen are not the detritus of a higher mythology but in fact preceded heroic sagas and myths and are survivals among the folk. Lang was at his best in applying his argument to specific folktales, as he did in extensive introductions to new English translations of the Grimms' *Household Tales* (1884), *Cupid and Psyche* (1887), *Beauty and the Beast* (1887), and Charles Perrault's *Popular Tales* (1888).

Largely unknown are the fairy tale works that Lang himself wrote: *The Princess Nobody* (1884), *The Gold of Fairnilee* (1888), *Prince Prigio* (1889), *Prince Ricardo* (1893), and *Tales of a Fairy Court* (1907). The first two draw on his knowledge of folk narrative conventions as he created his own literary märchen and tale of the fairies. The last three are parodies of the märchen form and some of its conventional elements. *Prince Prigio*, for example, opens with a childless couple (the king and queen of Pantouflia) wishing for a child. They are indeed rewarded with a child. At the christening of their own son, Prince Prigio, the king and queen insult a fairy and generate a "curse." The opening scene and situation are characteristic of traditional märchen.

Although Lang used well-known märchen devices (some of the christening gifts brought to Prince Prigio include seven-league boots, a wishing hat, a magic purse, and a cloak of invisibility) from other specific tales, he began his own narrative with a very appropriate situation (the childless couple and the wish for a baby) in traditional tales. Further, even though the parents are royalty (the king and queen of Pantouflia), Prince Prigio is cursed for his parent's error (as in "Snow White"), and the narrative shows how Prigio deals with that curse.

Lang combined a love for great poetry with a keen sense of history. In addition to having translated both the *Iliad* and the *Odyssey*, he wrote several books on the Homeric epics, defending the notion that one folk poet could indeed have created these works. In his argument he compares the classical Greek tradition of folk poetry to examples from other cultures, including the German *Nibelungenlied*, the French chansons de geste (especially the Song of Roland), the English *Beowulf*, and the Finnish *Kalevala*. Lang wrote on and edited many writers, from William Shakespeare and Alfred, Lord Tennyson to Sir Walter Scott, William Wordsworth, and Robert Burns. He wrote extensively on Scotland and its people, including a four-volume history, several volumes devoted particularly to Mary Stuart and Prince Charles Edward Stuart, and a volume on Scott and the border ballads.

Finally, Lang led folklorists into expanding the study of supernatural events and legends. His *Cock Lane and Common Sense* (1894) and *The Book of Dreams and Ghosts* (1897) applied to contemporary events the methods that anthropologists and historians had previously reserved only for historical accounts.

Because of their enormous and lasting success, his various colored (blue, red, green, yellow, etc.) fairy books—12 volumes of fairy tales translated and compiled from oral and literary sources around the world—are still his most widely known works. This series, prepared as Christmas books for children, constitutes but a small sampling of the over 200 books that Lang wrote or edited during his lifetime.

Eric L. Montenyohl

See also Epic; Grimm, Jacob and Wilhelm; Homer; *Odyssey*; Victorian Fairy Lore

✳✳✳✳✳✳✳✳✳✳✳✳✳✳✳✳✳

References

Dorson, Richard M. *The British Folklorists: A History*. Chicago: University of Chicago Press, 1968.

Green, Roger Lancelyn. *Andrew Lang: A Critical Biography.* Leicester, Eng.: Edmund Ward, 1946.

Montenyohl, Eric L. *Andrew Lang and the Fairy Tale.* Ph.D. dissertation, Folklore Institute, Indiana University, 1986.

Latino and Chicano Folklore and Literature

"Latino(a)" is currently the term most acceptable for ethnic Americans whose ancestors spoke Spanish; "Chicano(a)," for Mexican Americans. These terms are hotly debated. For instance, "Hispanic," the U.S. Census term, contains overtones of white aristocrats tracing their "pure" blood back to Spain, exploiting the Indian and mestizo (mixed Indian and Spanish) majorities. "Chicano," once a slang term for Mexican, is now accepted by many Mexican Americans in a positive way; others think it too closely identified with the Chicano militancy of the 1960s and 1970s. Some scholars prefer "La Raza" ("the race") as an inclusive term that encompasses all Latinos. However, it is nearly impossible to find one word to describe all people descended from cultures as diverse as those in Europe, Latin America, and a much greater spread of races. Similarly, to speak of "Latino" folklore is like speaking of "European" folklore: it is a vast term.

Latino and Chicano cultures are, like other immigrants' cultures, fully American. One can go very wrong reading old-country writers, like Mexico's Octavio Paz, who mistakes Mexican Americans for Mexicans living in the United States who have somehow forgotten who they are. Rather, *he* cannot understand what they have become: Americans. The vital new language, dress, and folklore *del este lado* ("of this side of the border") creatively revise materials *del otro lado* ("of the other side of the border," a common Chicano expression). When Chicano poet Jose Antonio Burciaga appears on a talk show in Mexico, he is asked, in confusion, "Are you Mexicano?" and has to reply, "Yes, but I am also *gabacho,*" an American. Indeed, Burciaga is replying not with the Mexican word *gringo,* but with a word from *calo,* the vital new Spanish-English tongue of Americanized Latinos. Words change, moving *del otro lado* to *este lado,* and not only words change. Figures like Emiliano Zapata and Pancho Villa, who in Mexican literature can appear as violent bandits, become Robin Hoods and Patrick Henrys in Mexican-American literature.

They become politicized, in fact. The legend of the Aztec's homeland, Aztlán, is a case in point. The Aztecs, before the period of their empire, had been a nomadic hunting tribe that made its way south, about 1200 C.E., to the Valley of Mexico. These nomads kept the tradition of a northern homeland, Aztlán, a land of milk and honey, never located, a garden of Eden similar to no place now known in the Southwest. The legend plays no important role in Mexican folklore, but in contemporary Mexican-American lore, Aztlán is famous and emotionally important. If Aztlán is north, who is to say it was not within current borders

Gloria Anzaldúa's works, such as Borderlands/La Frontera: The New Mestiza Writes *(1987), which draws upon "borderlands" folklore and mythology, have illuminated the Chicano experience in the United States.*

of the United States? If so, Mexican Americans have actually returned home, and Octavio Paz and the Mexicans are living in a foreign country. In the hands of an activist like Rudolfo Anaya, Aztlán even means that Mexican Americans are actually an indigenous people returning to their ancestral homeland, which is "occupied," in Anaya's phrase, by a foreign invader. The poet Virgil, acting on much slighter evidence than exists for Aztlán, fashioned for the Romans a national epic designed to outrival that of the Greeks, and nationalism fueled many nineteenth-century European folklore revivals, even Alfred, Lord Tennyson's epic, which raised King Arthur from obscurity. The process continues.

The many existing folklore studies favor Texas and New Mexico Hispanos and above all the rural experience—almost as if Latinos and Chicanos lose their character in the urban barrios and are less worthy of study. Yet 88 percent of Latinos and Chicanos now live in metropolitan areas, though only 75 percent of other Americans do.

Jesus Contreras and George Leonard

See also Anaya, Rudolfo Alfonso; Legend; Paredes, Américo

✿✿✿✿✿✿✿✿✿✿✿✿✿✿✿✿✿

References

Anaya, Rudolfo. *Bless Me, Ultima.* Berkeley, Calif.: Tonatiuh, Quinto Sol, 1972.

Paredes, Américo. "The Folk Base of Chicano Literature." In *Modern Chicano Writers,* ed. T. Ybarra Fausto and J. Sommers. Englewood Cliffs, N.J.: Prentice-Hall, 1979.

———. "Folklore, Lo Mexicano, and Proverbs." *Aztlán: The Chicano Journal of the Social Sciences and the Arts* (13 (1982): 1–11.

LEACH, MACEDWARD (1892–1967)

MacEdward Leach devoted his academic career to the study of multiform artistic traditions—the medieval romance, balladry, and folk song in general. He relished a good story, well told, whether in manuscript or print, sung or recited, old or new. Where these stories came from and how they became what they are were questions that led him first to the library and then to the field.

Raised in Illinois, Leach was educated at the University of Illinois and the University of Pennsylvania, where he spent almost his entire professional life. Trained as a medievalist, over time he began to feel a particular affinity for the continuing oral materials—märchen, legends, ballads, and songs—that had had incarnations in identifiable works of medieval art. His own developing interests led him to bring like-minded persons into his orbit, and they established a separate department devoted to the study of folklore and folklife at the University of Pennsylvania. Simultaneously, he nourished the American Folklore Society, serving for many years as its secretary. He was committed to the establishment of multiple institutional bases for the study of folklore and folk traditions.

His early work, most particularly his edition of *Amis and Amiloun* (1937), beautifully illustrates where he began—with an interest in popular literature as preserved in medieval manuscripts, their sources and analogues. In studying the romance, which describes an ideal friendship, he found himself in dialogue with earlier folklorists—Jacob and Wilhelm Grimm, Theodor Benfey, Alexander Krappe, Gordon Hall Gerould, Joseph Bédier, Emmanuel Cosquin, Johannes Bolte, Georg Polivka, Edwin Sidney Hartland, and Antti Aarne—as he explored where the chanson de geste, which had immediately preceded the romance itself, had come from, identifying "The Two Brothers" (AT 303) and "The Faithful Servitor" (AT 516, "Faithful John") as likely sources.

Although he had only read the romance, Leach clearly had a sense of its orality when he wrote in his edition of *Amis and Amiloun:* "The twelve-line stanza here is sometimes monotonous, and occasionally it becomes a jumble; on the other hand, it is often spirited and swift and adequate; especially in passages of direct discourse is this true. Here and there through the poem are passages of charming music." Some 20 years later, in an edition of William Caxton's *Paris and Vienne* (1957), Leach talked about a new kind of story emerging at the end of the Middle Ages—"of the here and now rather than of the far away and long ago ... in prose." In each case he was dealing with materials that existed in multiple versions and with multiple analogues.

When he turned his attention to another kind of popular literature, the ballad—often associated with the Middle Ages—the nature and number of versions existing simultaneously through and in time expanded: in manuscript, print, and oral tradition. If, as an undergraduate student at the University of Illinois, he had once sung and danced, barefoot, to ballads on the green under the tutelage of his teacher Gertrude Schoepperle, his awareness of the living socialization of ballads and folk songs was infinitely enriched by field trips to Labrador, Newfoundland, Nova Scotia, Jamaica, and Virginia—perhaps inspired by his association at the University of Pennsylvania with the anthropologist Frank Speck. In collecting ballads and folk songs, he experienced a context and a humanity that were impossible in his study of the romances but that added to his ability to hypothesize about the contexts and human involvements in such past artistry.

His editions of romances and ballads attest to a knowledge that flowered in the classroom where he himself became the master storyteller, weaving a kind of magic that compelled students to seek out other versions—in manuscript, print, and oral tradition—and which made the popular artistry of the past and present live and resonate. He became a special redactor of materials old and new, whether romance or legend, and he excelled in spinning tales about his own experiences, at home and in the field—experiences that, like his teaching, revealed a warm human being who both knew and performed the narrative art, recognizing its many transformations as well as its transformative power. His teaching nurtured the study of oral and written literature and educated a generation of students/scholars who have continued his work, as testimony to the narrative art of a man whom many have called a gentleman and a scholar.

Mary Ellen Brown

See also Ballad; Romance; Tale-Type

✵✵✵✵✵✵✵✵✵✵✵✵✵✵✵✵✵

References

Leach, MacEdward, ed. *Amis and Amiloun*. London: Early English Text Society, 1937.

———. *The Ballad Book*. New York: Harper, 1955.

———. *Paris and Vienne*. London: Early English Text Society, 1957.

Leach, MacEdward, and Tristram P. Coffin, eds. *The Critics and the Ballad*. Carbondale: Southern Illinois University, 1961.

"MacEdward Leach, 1892–1967." *Journal of American Folklore* 81 (1968): 97–120.

Legend

Legend is a conversational narrative whose reported events are set in historical (as opposed to myth's cosmological) time and whose telling makes possible debate concerning the "real world" occurrence and/or efficacy of the events, characters, folk beliefs, and/or folk customs described. Many legends are migratory—that is, their variants are widely known across different geographical areas. For this reason, as well as the fact that legends deal typically with the ambiguous and the unusual, their plots, character types, and motifs can provide a sense of both familiarity and strangeness for those literary works and films that draw upon them. Nevertheless, modern-day adaptations are often tied only loosely to folkloric tradition.

Deriving from the Latin word *legenda* ("to read"), legends were originally narratives about the lives of saints and were read aloud during medieval Christian church services. An oral religious legend still circulating today is that of St. Christopher (the patron saint of travelers) who, as his name indicates (Christopher = Christ-bearer), is said to have carried the Christ child across a swollen river. Written literature that employs the character type of that saint, sometimes sarcastically, includes Vernon Lee's (Violet Piaget's pen name) story "St. Eudaemon and His Orange-Tree" (1904) as well as similar stories by Richard Garnett (1835–1906) and Anatole France (1844–1924). Other written literature has expanded upon individual folk religious motifs—for instance, those concerning miracles as used by Swedish author Selma Lagerlöf in her story "The Legend of the Christmas Rose" (1910); requests for aid from a spiritual benefactor as in Mexican-American writer Sandra Cisneros's "Little Miracles, Kept Promises" (1991); or the appearance of signs of divine presence as in the John Dufresne magic realism story "The Freezer Jesus" (1988).

Heroic legends have also contributed characters and plot sequences to literature and film. One of the oldest of these legend-and-adaptation sets constitutes the Arthurian cycle, which has furnished material for works such as Thomas Malory's prose romance *Le Morte d'Arthur* (written 1469–1470, published 1485), T. H. White's *The Sword in the Stone* (1939), and John Boorman's film *Excalibur* (1981). Likewise, folk stories of Robin Hood, Maid Marian, and the band of merry men have formed the basis (in however general a way) for various films, among them the classic adventure film *The Adventures of Robin Hood* (1938) or more recently *Robin Hood, Prince of Thieves* (1991), while rumor-like legend narratives speculating on events surrounding the death of President John F. Kennedy provided the focus for Oliver Stone's film *JFK* (1991).

Long a staple of hearth fire and campfire narrative, ghost stories have enjoyed considerable popularity. Notable works produced during the heyday of literary ghost stories (the mid-1800s through the 1920s) include Charles Dickens's *A Christmas Carol* (1843), which popularized interest in the idea of the Christmas ghost, and Henry James's *The Turn of the Screw* (1898), whose plot turns disturbingly among the possibilities that ghosts indeed intend evil toward children, that the governess is mad and is hallucinating the ghosts, or that the governess herself is the one possessed and is being manipulated into tormenting the children. James plays effectively with readers' hesitation among these possibilities, among others, thus invoking folk legend's tendency to raise the question of ambiguity.

Written literature has also borrowed a range of extranatural figures from folk legend. In contrast to John Polidori's early story "The Vampyre" (1819), Bram Stoker's novel *Dracula* (1897) more closely adapted Eastern European folk beliefs (such as destroying a vampire by decapitating it) and has exerted considerable influence on twentieth-century treatments. In recent years, proliferating interest in the vampire has resulted in the fictionalizing of a variety of vampire types, some of which show only slight similarities to the creatures of European tradition. An example is found in fantasist Jewelle Gomez's novel *The Gilda Stories* (1991), in which an African-American lesbian vampire recompenses her blood donors by bestowing on them edifying dreams.

Other legendary beings that have garnered attention are the werewolf, as in Angela Carter's "The Were Wolf" (1977), which makes the predator-victim relationship ambiguous—has the shape-shifter or the human preyed more devastatingly upon the other?—the zombie, which in some recent manifestations has acquired the trait of cannibalism—as is illustrated in horror author Poppy Z. Brite's story "Calcutta, Lord of Nerves" (1992) and in the cult classic film *The Night of the Living Dead* (1968)—despite the fact that zombies are rarely associated with cannibalism in folk belief; Sasquatch, or Bigfoot, a staple character of supermarket tabloids but occasionally a symbolic figure in literary fiction, as in Ron Carlson's story "Bigfoot Stole My Wife" (1987), in which a husband's belief in Bigfoot helps him avoid emotional responsibility for his wife's leaving him; and the bosom serpent, which in Nathaniel Hawthorne's story "Egotism" (1843), as well as in the *Alien* trilogy of films (1979, 1986, 1992), preys upon the protagonist's psyche as well as (according to tradition) upon his or her physical body.

Contemporary or urban legends—stories that deal with the tensions of modern-day life—have also provided material to film and written literature. Horror films often encourage viewers' emotional involvement by emphasizing the malicious creativity of the crazed attacker/murderer villain, a character type also found in folk legend. Films employing such a villain include *When a Stranger Calls* (1979), which adapts the legend plot of "The Babysitter," and *Candyman* (1992), which borrows from the legend/teenage slumber party ritual of "Mary Whales."

Other adaptations include the films *Smokey and the Bandit* (1979) and *Every Which Way but Loose* (1978), which contain episodes resembling the story of "The Driver's Revenge" against motorcycle gangs; an episode of the television series *LA Law* on May 11, 1989, which adapted the motif of "The Urine in the Beer"; Hugh Mills's novel *Prudence and the Pill* (1966), which borrows from the tale of "The Substituted Contraceptive Pills"; and Elizabeth Jane Howard's story "Mr. Wrong" (1973), which combines various elements from the legends of "The Vanishing Hitchhiker," "The Death Car," and "The Killer in the Back Seat." In its different manifestations, folk legend has offered written literature and film material for a range of sometimes inspirational, sometimes threatening, and sometimes bizarre characters and story plots. Many modern adaptations, though, owe more to their creators' imagination than they do to the details of folkloric tradition.

Danielle M. Roemer

See also Arthurian Tradition; Bunyan, Paul; Dracula; Henry, John; Robin Hood; *Song of Roland*; Trolls; Urban Legends

✱✱✱✱✱✱✱✱✱✱✱✱✱✱✱✱✱

References

Brunvand, Jan H. "Legends and Anecdotes." In *The Study of American Folklore*, 3d ed., pp. 158–185. New York: W. W. Norton, 1986.

———. *The Vanishing Hitchhiker: American Urban Legends and Their Meanings*. New York: W. W. Norton, 1981.

DeVries, Jan. *Heroic Song and Heroic Legend*. London and New York: Oxford University Press, 1963.

Loomis, C. Grant. *White Magic: An Introduction to the Folklore of Christian Legend*. Cambridge: Harvard University Press, 1948.

Melton, J. Gordon. *The Vampire Book: An Encyclopedia of the Undead*. Detroit: Visible Ink Press, 1994.

LEPRECHAUN

A solitary fairy in Irish folklore, the leprechaun looks like a tiny old man and is generally described as a crafty shoemaker who lives in a remote place and guards buried treasure. If captured and threatened with violence, the leprechaun may reveal the hiding place of his gold; however, he almost always escapes with his treasure intact, vanishing when he tricks his human captor into looking away momentarily or otherwise defeating even the most careful precautions. An account is commonly given of a man who prevails so far as to be led to a single ragwort plant in his own field, under which a treasure is buried. He releases the leprechaun in order to mark the spot with a scrap of red cloth and leaves to fetch a spade. When he returns moments later, he finds the field filled with ragworts marked with identical red scraps.

The word *leprechaun* is probably derived from the Old Irish *lu-chorpan*, "little body." It has also been said to derive from *leith bhrogan*, the "one-shoemaker," because the character is generally found working on only one shoe. On the other hand, his cobbling vocation itself is alternatively explained as the result of the corruption in folk etymology of *lu-chorpan* into a form meaning "half-brogue."

In Ireland, especially in County Cork, the leprechaun is identified with the *clúracán* or *cluricaun* ("elf" or "sprite"), another tiny, old fairy and guardian of hidden treasure who cares for beer barrels and wine casks in the wine cellar he inhabits. The *clúracán* may be a distinct, though related, fairy or a leprechaun after hours, who has given up the day's cobbling for a nightlong, drunken, sheep-riding spree. Likewise, the *ganconer* or *gancanagh* may be related to the

The miniature, mischievous leprechaun, an important figure in Irish folklore.

leprechaun, though the *ganconer* is described as an idle smoker known principally for making love to shepherdesses. The *fir darrig* ("red man") is a larger, solitary fairy known for its mischievousness, or even malevolence, and its red color. "Leprechaun" is sometimes taken as representative of all such fairies.

The leprechaun is frequently said to wear buckled shoes, a leather apron, drab clothes, and a cocked hat or red cap. This description accords with a tradition common to the British Isles that solitary fairies dress in red while "trooping" fairies wear green. Other sources, however, dress the leprechaun in green from head to toe. Although his stature is not recorded with particularity, some sources would have him as small as six inches in height, or as tall as two and a half feet. Leprechauns appear in numerous works including Katharine Briggs's *A Dictionary of Fairies* (1976), James Stephens's *The Crock of Gold* (1912), and W. B. Yeats's *Fairy and Folk Tales of Ireland* (1973).

Lorraine Walsh

See also Briggs, Katharine; Legend; Stephens, James; Victorian Fairy Lore; Yeats, William Butler

✳✳✳✳✳✳✳✳✳✳✳✳✳✳✳✳✳

References

Briggs, Katharine. *A Dictionary of Fairies*. London: Allen Lane, 1976.

Croker, Thomas Crofton. *Fairy Legends and Traditions of the South of Ireland*. Delmar, N.Y.: Scholar's Facsimiles and Reprints, 1983.

Wilde, Lady Jane Francis. *Ancient Legends, Mystic Charms, and Superstitions of Ireland*. New York: Lemma, 1973.

LIFE STORY

A life story is a person's own story of his or her life; it is usually told in the first person and is composed of many episodes rather than a single incident. Storytellers do not orally compose such stories as uninterrupted and coherent multiepisodic narratives; instead, they create their narratives with the help of an interviewer or independently as a written autobiography. Jeff Todd Titon (1980) argues that it is important to view the life story as a self-contained fiction, and he thus distinguishes it from such other genres as biography, oral history, and family story, as well as the life history that is so significant for gaining cultural information in anthropological research. The life story emerges as an interviewer poses questions to the storyteller, and it is usually the interviewer's editing skills that determine the final form such a story will take.

Although they are both forms of personal narrative, the life story and the personal experience story differ markedly in terms of length, number of episodes, and authorship. The shorter personal experience story relates a single incident and is the independent creation of the storyteller. In contrast, the life story is a collaborative project. Folklorists such as Elliott Oring (1987) and Barbara Kirshenblatt-

Gimblett (1989) emphasize, as does Titon, the role of the interviewer and the storyteller's objective in conveying a coherent "voice" that matches his or her self-image. Other researchers such as Charlotte Linde and Elaine Lawless (1993) see life stories as creating interwoven strands or blocks of meaning that allow storytellers to express certain ideas they consider essential lessons from their lives. As in all personal narratives, life stories serve to demonstrate and sometimes to directly articulate the values, attitudes, and beliefs that are a part of the storyteller's worldview.

David Stanley (1979) draws attention to the role of life stories in personal novels, and his thesis is developed in a variety of contexts in a 1992 publication on personal narrative in literature. Writers in the same issue of *Southern Folklore Quarterly* examine the role of the life story in such works as Herman Melville's *The Confidence Man* (1857), William Faulkner's *The Reivers* (1962), Zora Neale Hurston's *Mules and Men* (1935), and Mary McCarthy's *Memories of a Catholic Girlhood* (1957).

A classic work that uses the life story as its essential structure is Charlotte Brontë's *Jane Eyre* (1847). Early in the book, Brontë relates (in the voice of Jane, the narrator and the protagonist) the story of Jane's experience in "the red room" in which she sees a light pass through the room and faints as she believes the light is her uncle's ghost. This frightening childhood experience is crucial in establishing the reader's insight into Jane's passionate and rather superstitious personality, a personality that becomes more intense as Jane grows into adulthood. The reader is thus prepared for Jane's readiness to listen to fortune-tellers, her fondness for lonesome ballads, and her belief in telepathy. The novel is made more complex by the reader's awareness that much of the "story" in the book draws upon Charlotte Brontë's own life. The relationship between the life story and the novel in particular is a significant issue in literary history.

Sandra K. Dolby

See also Faulkner, William; Genre; Hurston, Zora Neale; Melville, Herman; Personal Experience Story; Storytelling

✳✳✳✳✳✳✳✳✳✳✳✳✳✳✳✳✳

References

Dolby (Stahl), Sandra K., and Danielle Roemer, eds. "The Personal Narrative in Literature." *Western Folklore* 51 (1992): 1–107.

Kirshenblatt-Gimblett, Barbara. "Authoring Lives." *Journal of Folklore Research* 26 (1989): 123–149.

Lawless, Elaine. *Holy Women, Wholly Women: Sharing Ministries of Wholeness through Life Stories and Reciprocal Ethnography.* Philadelphia: University of Pennsylvania Press, 1993.

Oring, Elliott. "Generating Lives: The Construction of an Autobiography." *Journal of Folklore Research* 24 (1987): 241–262.

Stanley, David H. "The Personal Narrative and the Personal Novel: Folklore as Frame and Structure for Literature." *Southern Folklore Quarterly* 43 (1979): 107–120.

Titon, Jeff Todd. "The Life Story." *Journal of American Folklore* 93 (1980): 276–292.

LITERARY BALLAD

The so-called literary ballad is a poem written in imitation of folk ballads. A number of British and American writers have written literary ballads, especially since the last years of the eighteenth century. Literary ballads imitate the language and poetic conventions of traditional ballads (though these are not uniform throughout traditional balladry).

Early interest in the ballad on the part of the literate elite was generated particularly by writers and literary scholars. Bishop Thomas Percy's *Reliques of Ancient English Poetry* (1765) was an especially influential book in stimulating this trend. Although folk ballads are songs, they were not always recognized as such, and they appeared in early published collections as poems divorced from the context of singing. Important early editors of folk-ballad collections like Percy and Sir Walter Scott—who published his own *Minstrelsy of the Scottish Border* in 1802–1803—also "improved" the ballads they received from their sources, that is, they edited them like written poems. Hence, ballads came to be thought of by many people as poems.

Ballads—particularly certain ballads like "Sir Patrick Spens" and "Barbara Allen"—entered the English literary canon. Indeed, anthologies of English literature published in recent years still include ballads, usually offered as examples of medieval poetry (despite the fact that the individual ballads so presented actually may have originated well after the Middle Ages, though the ballad form itself is medieval in origin).

Folk ballads attracted literary attention in part because of their presumed medieval origins and the fascination the Middle Ages held for the romantic age. Many literary ballads are attempts to duplicate the flavor of folk ballads, and thus they re-create the themes, settings, and language of the earlier songs, using stories set in the historical past and deliberately archaic language. A literary ballad may be a virtual rewriting of a traditional ballad (such as Allan Cunningham's "The Bonnie Bairns," which echoes "The Cruel Mother") or be more loosely based on one (as is David Mallet's "William and Margaret" upon "Fair Margaret and Sweet William"). Or the connection may be looser still with the use of general ballad characteristics (such as the use of a "dramatic" structure, that is, the telling of the story through much dialogue and in definable "scenes" and metrical forms common to folk ballads) or the use of themes or episodes from one or more traditional ballads.

Poets have also written literary ballads with modern stories and the absence of archaic language, in some cases based on broadside rather than traditional folk ballads. W. H. Auden even imitates the broadside convention of providing a well-known tune for a newly printed ballad when he notes that his "Let Me Tell You a Little Story" should be sung to the tune of "St. James' Infirmary." There have also been modern literary ballads that are humorous or that parody ballads or earlier literary ballads. Rudyard Kipling's "The Fall of Jock Gillespie" uses a title and dialect suggestive of the border ballads (those stemming from the historical conflicts along the English-Scottish border), but it tells a humorous story of modern times. Henry Duff Traill's "After Dilettante Concetti" pokes fun at Dante Gabriel Rossetti's literary ballad "Sister Helen."

The term *ballad* has sometimes been incorporated into the titles of works of prose fiction, as in Carson McCullers's short story "The Ballad of the Sad Café." Such usage stems from some connection the author is making with the kinds of stories told in ballads or with the folk milieu of ballad singing. Such works of fiction, of course, are not literary ballads, but they do represent another influence balladry has had upon literary narrative.

Frank de Caro

See also Ballad

✳✳✳✳✳✳✳✳✳✳✳✳✳✳✳✳✳

References

Friedman, Albert. B. *The Ballad Revival: Studies in the Influence of Popular on Sophisticated Poetry*. Chicago and London: University of Chicago Press, 1961.

Hustvedt, S. B. *Ballad Books and Ballad Men*. Cambridge: Harvard University Press, 1930.

Laws, G. Malcolm, Jr. *The British Literary Ballad: A Study in Poetic Imitation*. Carbondale and Edwardsville: Southern Illinois University Press, 1972.

LA LLORONA

Legends about La Llorona, or "the weeping woman," are found in parts of the U.S. Southwest, Mexico, and Central America. A Mexican and Chicano (originally pre-Hispanic) legend gaining wide currency circa 1550 in Mexico City, the figure is frequently conflated with La Malinche, the Aztec interpreter-traitress and consort of the Spanish conquistador Hernán Cortés, and with such indigenous personages as Tlazoltéotl, Cihuacóatl, and Cihuateteo.

In life, her name was María (Luisa in some renderings), a lowborn and beautiful campesina who fell in love with the noble Don Muño Montes Claros. After she bore him three children, Don Muño left her for a woman of his own class. Grieving madly, La Llorona drowned her children. The apparition seeks "replacements," predatorily and perpetually, in wayward children; or alternately, in several versions she is, like Cain, held accountable to heaven until she finds the "missing" progeny. She is regularly associated with the *motifeme*, or paired function, of water, as she is said to haunt streams and rivers by night, lamenting, *Ay, mis hijos!* ("Oh, my children!"). She appears invisible but for her face or has a hollow death's head. Near-limitless variations attribute to her the countenance of a bat or a horse, shiny blade fingernails, long black hair, and a white dress. To many victims, she looms sirenlike, rapturously beautiful. But her society spells certain doom: to those to whom she even speaks, death or insanity comes swiftly. She is generally considered a man hater, and revenge figures in most versions of the legend.

La Llorona is seen as the *anima*, or dark side, to images of motherhood held dear in Western society, among them the Holy Virgin. The myriad stories—primarily oral—surrounding the phantom La Llorona play on the deepest cultural insecurities of loss, retribution, sequestration and abandonment, parental impotence, family violence, and, from an impressionable child's perspective, punishment from a predatory shadow figure. La Llorona has long been useful as a cautionary monster: a pedagogical and moral tool in maintaining sexual innocence (as a sentinel superintending adolescent rites of initiation); obedience to parental authority (as a boundary-maintenance spook like the Bogeyman to keep children within their own home territory); the conjugal status quo (as a warning against wayward husbands' libidos); and vigilant motherhood (as a deterrent to child neglect).

Signs with the icon of La Llorona are used in the Southwest near bodies of water to alert people to the dangers of drowning. Quite commonly, too, she is held up as a warning to young girls not to seek marriage above one's station and to children not to cry. Kin to the *robachicos* ("child stealer"), *el Cuco* ("bogeyman"), or even the modern *chupacabras* ("goat-sucker"), La Llorona is a perceived supernatural threat to a sacred cultural institution: the Hispanic family unit. A type of femme fatale like Seneca's Medea or a fallen woman in the mold of Eve or Lilith, she functions as a roving figurehead of the world at large with all its attendant temptations, imperfections, and snares; that is, a projection of any number of human fears, but especially those involving hearth and home.

Unlike, for example, Picasso's visions of a woman mourning, La Llorona's suffering usually is not conceived sympathetically in the popular consciousness, although there are renditions of the wailing woman such as Octavio Paz's alignment of her with the *madre sufrida mexicana* ("long-suffering Mexican mother"); versions casting her as a martyr, "jilted" lover, or mother; and literary treatments, as in Alma Luz Villannueva's story, in which the wanderer turns heroine: La Llorona changes her children into fish to save them from a great flood. Chicana and Chicano writers such as Lucha Corpi and Rudolfo Anaya have used the image to great advantage in exploring ideas such as self and other, cultural fusion, the problem of origins, and womanhood. Many people see La Llorona as a symbol of the Chicanos, whose children become "lost" to assimilation, bias, and violence. La Llorona can be a source of strength, as in Sandra Cisneros's *Woman Hollering Creek* (1991), and a rallying point for cultural criticism, as in the work of Yvonne Yarbro-Bejarano, in which the *llorona* ("weeper") is instead a *gritona* ("shouter").

R. Kelly Washbourne

See also Anaya, Rudolfo Alfonso; Cisneros, Sandra; Legend

✳✳✳✳✳✳✳✳✳✳✳✳✳✳✳✳✳

References

Anaya, Rudolfo. "La Llorona, El Kookooee, and Sexuality." *Bilingual Review* 17 (1992): 50–55.

Kearney, Michael. "La Llorona as a Social Symbol." *Western Folklore* 28 (1969): 199–206.

Rebolledo, Tey Diana. *Women Singing in the Snow: A Cultural Analysis of Chicana Literature.* Tucson: University of Arizona Press, 1995.

Villannueva, Alma Luz. *Weeping Woman: La Llorona and Other Stories.* Tempe, Ariz.: Bilingual Press, 1994.

West, John. *Legendary Ladies of Texas.* Dallas: E-Heart Press, 1981.

LOATHLY LADY

The loathly lady, a woman whose exceedingly unattractive physical appearance is transformed into one of great beauty, appears in several medieval folktales. The best known literary permutations of this story in English are John Gower's tale of Florent in *Confessio Amantis*, Geoffrey Chaucer's "Wife of Bath's Tale," and the anonymous tail-rhyme romance "The Wedding of Sir Gawain and Dame Ragnell."

In stories of the loathly lady, a hero encounters a repulsive female who is described either simply as a loathly hag or as one whose repulsive appearance is grotesquely exaggerated. For instance, in "The Wedding of Sir Gawain and Dame Ragnell," Ragnell's "face was red, her nose snotted, her mouth wide, her teeth yellow, her eye rheumy, her teeth hung over her lips, and her cheeks were as fat as a woman's hips. Her neck was long and thick, her hair clotted and snarled. Her shoulders were a yard broad, and her breasts were a load for a strong horse. She was formed like a barrell. No tongue can adequately describe how foul she was, but she was ugly enough."

In most tales, the loathly lady offers to grant a wish to the hero, but only on the condition that he will have some sort of sexual contact with her, the request ranging from a kiss to a consummated marriage. When the hero accepts the offer (often after others have rejected it), she transforms into an exceedingly beautiful woman who may also present the hero with gifts of power or wealth. The loathly lady apparently has her origins in twelfth-century Irish tales. She reveals herself as the personified Sovereignty of Ireland, and the hero's acceptance of her wins him (or his descendants) the kingship of Ireland.

English stories usually connect the transformation of the loathly lady with the hero's granting her sovereignty in their marriage. In

Chaucer's "Wife of Bath's Tale," King Arthur's court condemns a knight for rape; his life will be spared only if he can answer the question "What do women most want?" On the verge of forfeiting his life, the knight encounters a loathly lady who offers to give him the answer if he will marry her. He agrees and wins his life with the answer "Sovereignty in marriage." The hag then insists on the promised marriage, and on their wedding night, she reveals herself to the reluctant groom as a beautiful woman. She then gives the knight a final test: he must decide whether his bride will be either loathly and faithful or beautiful and probably faithless. Unable to decide, he leaves the decision to her; having received sovereignty in their marriage, the bride elects to be both beautiful and faithful. The plots of Gower's tale of Florent and "The Wedding of Sir Gawain and Dame Ragnell" are similar.

David Sprunger

See also Chaucer, Geoffrey; *Gawain and the Green Knight, Sir*

✳✳✳✳✳✳✳✳✳✳✳✳✳✳✳✳✳✳

References
Eisner, Sigmund. *A Tale of Wonder: A Source Study of the Wife of Bath's Tale*. New York: Burt Franklin, 1969.

Hahn, Thomas, ed. *Sir Gawain: Eleven Romances and Tales*. Kalamazoo: Western Michigan University, Medieval Institute Publications, 1995.

Hall, Louis, ed. and trans. *The Knightly Tales of Sir Gawain*. Chicago: Nelson-Hall, 1976.

Maynadier, G. H. *The Wife of Bath's Tale: Its Sources and Analogues*. London: David Nutt, 1901.

LOCAL COLOR

The use of detailed descriptions of features (including geography, customs, dialect, food, clothing, building types, and other material artifacts) peculiar to or characteristic of a region in a work of literature is referred to as local color. "Regions" described by local-color writers can be as large as the U.S. South or New England or as small as Faulkner's Yoknapatawpha County in Mississippi. Frequently cited local-color writers include the English writers Thomas Hardy (Wessex) and Rudyard Kipling (India) and Americans Bret Harte (the West), Mark Twain (the Mississippi region), George Washington

Cable and Kate Chopin (Louisiana), E. W. Howe and Hamlin Garland (the Midwest), Sarah Orne Jewett and Mary E. Wilkins Freeman (New England), Charles W. Chesnutt (North Carolina and Ohio), Edward Eggleston (Indiana), and Joel Chandler Harris (the Old South).

Critics sometimes use the term *local color* disparagingly to imply that a work has nothing to offer but quaint descriptions of eccentric characters and strange customs, but it is also used in recognition of an author's careful attention to detail and evocation of a thoroughly fleshed-out ethos. In some works, local color seems added on, almost as an afterthought or a bonus to make up for the work's defects; in the best local-color works, however, setting, character, local customs, and plot are inextricably intertwined (see, for example, George Washington Cable's "Belles Demoiselles Plantation").

Folklorists have most often approached local-color literature as a depository of folklore, including folk speech (dialect, proverbs, riddles, colloquialisms, etc.), folk customs, and folk narratives (see, for example, Baker 1973). Other kinds of study are more rare; for example, Joe Arpad (1973) has traced the cross-fertilization between oral and written sources in one strand of southwestern humor, the fight story.

Local-color writers, with their emphasis on ordinary people, humble lives, and true-to-life landscapes, had an important influence on the emergence of American literary realism and naturalism. But local-color and literary realism are not necessarily realistic in a strict sense. Local-color writers' use of eye dialect (spelling words in unusual ways to evoke the sound of a spoken dialect, as "Ten t'ousand dollah for dis house?") and homey descriptions makes it tempting to assume that they are presenting accurate depictions of local folklife, but this assumption is not always valid. One goal of local-color writing is the more-or-less accurate depiction of a real way of life, but there are other goals as well. One obvious example is humor. The humorists of the old Southwest, who described their subjects in great detail, were generally well-educated outsiders who looked on local characters with a degree of fond derision; their descriptions are often affected both by this attitude and by their goal of creating humorous fiction. Perhaps less obvious is the bias created by sentimentality, such as is found in the works of Jewett and Freeman. Although we can learn much from local-color works about customs, attitudes, and dialects, we should not simply treat such works as documentaries; what seems realistic is not necessarily real.

Kenneth D. Pimple

See also Chesnutt, Charles Waddell; Dialect; Hardy, Thomas; Harris, Joel Chandler; Twain, Mark

✳✳✳✳✳✳✳✳✳✳✳✳✳✳✳✳✳

References

Arpad, Joe. "The Fight Story: Quotation and Originality in Native American Humor." *Journal of the Folklore Institute* 10 (1973): 141–172.

Baker, Ronald L. *Folklore in the Writings of Rowland E. Robinson.* Bowling Green, Ohio: Bowling Green University Popular Press, 1973.

Brown, Caroyn S. *The Tall Tale in American Folklore and Literature.* Knoxville: University of Tennessee Press, 1987.

West, Victor Royce. *Folklore in the Works of Mark Twain.* University of Nebraska Studies in Language, Literature, and Criticism, no. 10. Lincoln: University of Nebraska Press, 1930.

LOCAL POETS

Local poets are those who, through the medium of unsung poetry, express or reflect the concerns, sentiments, or aesthetics of their community. Like local-song composers, these poets use the literary conventions of their society to create works for public performance. Whether orally composed or written, whether recited or silently read, the single most important quality of the local poet's work is that the audience is made up of others in the poet's community. The poetry itself may take any form acceptable within the poet's culture—from rhymed and metrically constrained poetry to entirely free verse—and may employ metaphor, simile, personification, or any other poetic device.

Such poets are usually found in communities with a strong sense of cohesion, and these communities may range from small rural villages to large urban neighborhoods. As part of their function, local poets may be called upon by their neighbors to commemorate important community events, such as weddings and anniversaries. They may recite their work at the celebration itself (or have it recited by a local orator), present a written version to the honorees, or publish the poem in a community newspaper. However the poem is performed, it becomes a part of a commemorative or celebratory ritual within the community. Likewise, local poets are often asked to write obituary verses to accompany community death rituals, and the poem might be read at the funeral service, be published along with the obituary, or even appear on the grave marker.

Beyond serving an important function at rituals, local poets are among the people who document the community as a whole by composing verses of a topical nature related to the locality: poems about local disasters, poems of praise for the accomplishments of community members, satirical verses directed against those who merit community censure, poetic descriptions of events that are outside the poet's locality but that are, nevertheless, of interest to community members. As well, local poets often write evocative pieces that describe the region or landscape of the community, its occupations and industries, or its history—these poems sometimes become local anthems.

Although the talents of most local poets are recognized only within the boundaries of their communities, their poetry is nevertheless a part of the greater tradition of literature within any given culture. Local poets generally draw upon literary traditions from outside their area, for example, by copying the styles of poetry they recall from school readers. Some will attempt to broaden their audience by publishing outside their immediate area, whether in regional newspapers or through vanity press publications. In doing so, local poets cross the line from the intimacy of folk poetry, where poet and audience share the same microculture, to the mass-mediated world of popular poetry.

Of course, all poets begin, to some degree, as local poets, even if their aspirations extend beyond their community. For example, Robert W. Service's evocative poems of the Yukon may have originally served as anthems for his neighbors in Dawson City, but they soon gained international attention; his poetry eventually reentered folk performance through the talents of recitation tellers, as well as influencing many local poets to copy his style. Thus, local poetry is part of the continuous interplay between local, national, and international traditions that make up the entirety of literature.

Michael Taft

See also Burns, Robert

✳✳✳✳✳✳✳✳✳✳✳✳✳✳✳✳✳✳✳

References

Greenhill, Pauline. *True Poetry: Traditional and Popular Verse in Ontario*. Montreal: McGill-Queen's University Press, 1989.

Greenhill, Pauline, ed. *Folk Poetry/Poesie Populaire. Canadian Folklore Canadien* 15:1 (1993): special issue.

Renwick, Roger deV. *English Folk Poetry: Structure and Meaning*. Philadelphia: University of Pennsylvania Press, 1980.

Service, Robert W. *Collected Poems of Robert Service*. New York: Dodd, Mead and Company, 1940.

Taft, Michael. *The Bard of Edam: Walter Farewell, Homesteader Poet*. North Battleford, Sask.: Turner-Warwick, 1992.

LOMAX, JOHN AVERY (1867–1948)

The American folk-song collector John Avery Lomax cofounded the Texas Folklore Society and was twice president of the American Folklore Society (1912, 1913). For some 30 years, he was a tireless collector of folk songs, and together with his son Alan, he contributed more than 10,000 songs, recorded in the field, to the Archive of American Folk Song (now the Archive of Folk Culture) of the Library of Congress. Following in the footsteps of the English folk-song and dance student Cecil J. Sharp, Lomax collected American folk songs of the West and South at about the same time Phillips Barry, also a student of folk song, was doing similar work in the Northeast. Their work helped convince ballad scholars of the existence of a living tradition of American folk song. Lomax's classic *Cowboy Songs and Other Frontier Ballads* (1919) was a pioneer work in American folklore in presenting to the public this genre of oral literature.

In the 1930s and 1940s, Lomax and his son Alan traveled through the U.S. South collecting folk songs and published (among other works) *American Ballads and Folk Songs* (1934), *Negro Folk Songs as Sung by Lead Belly* (1936), and *Folk Song: U.S.A* (1947). Lomax also published a popular autobiography, *Adventures of a Ballad Hunter* (1947). Through his books and many recordings, Lomax helped create popular interest in (and a market for) cowboy songs, African-American songs, and other folk songs of the United States.

Lomax also had an important impact on the study of occupational and regional folklore. Born in Mississippi and raised in Bosque County, Texas, partaking of both the post–Civil War South's desire to regain its regional pride and an emerging sense of American nationalism, he sought the spirit of Texas in its folk songs. He found in the cowboy the perfect symbol of the American common man and American romantic nationalism.

Lomax's greatest fame probably stems from his promotion of Huddie Ledbetter (known as "Lead Belly" or "Leadbelly"), "discovered" by the Lomaxes in the Louisiana State Penitentiary in 1933. Leadbelly was a talented performer, but his reputation as a black convicted murderer befriended by white folklorists titillated white audiences and pandered to the stereotypes held by whites. Lomax's widest influence probably stems from his collections of cowboy songs; along with an array of other apologists for the West, Theodore Roosevelt, Owen Wister, and Frederic Remington, Lomax helped define the American West in the popular imagination and elevate the American cowboy to mythic status.

Kenneth D. Pimple

See also Regional Folklore

✳✳✳✳✳✳✳✳✳✳✳✳✳✳✳✳✳

References

Lomax, John Avery. *Adventures of a Ballad Hunter*. New York: Macmillan, 1947.

———. *Cowboy Songs and Other Frontier Ballads*. New York: Macmillan, 1919.

———. *Negro Folk Songs as Sung by Lead Belly*. New York: Macmillan, 1936.

McNutt, James Charles. "Beyond Regionalism: Texas Folklorists and the Emergence of a Post-Regional Consciousness." Ph.D. dissertation, University of Texas at Austin, 1982.

LÖNNROT, ELIAS (1802–1884)

Physician, folklorist, professor, dictionary maker, and creator of the Finnish national epic, the *Kalevala*, Elias Lönnrot was born on April 9, 1802, in the isolated parish of Sammatti in southern Finland. The son of a local tailor, he rose from obscurity to a position of central importance in the Finnish national awakening. Unfitted by disposition for the tailor's trade and driven by a passion for learning, Lönnrot began his formal education in 1814, supported by relatives and a local chaplain. At the time, he spoke only Finnish and struggled at the outset to learn Swedish, the language spoken by the educated and ruling classes in his country. A diligent student, he overcame his difficulties, received a good classical education, and eventually mastered many languages. In 1822, Lönnrot entered the University of

Turku in Finland; in the spring of 1827, he passed the examination for the degree of candidate of philosophy. The university was destroyed by fire in the same year, and in the following year, it was transferred to Helsinki. Lönnrot continued his studies there, earning a degree in medicine in 1832.

During the first decades of the nineteenth century, the romantic nationalistic ideas of Johann Gottfried Herder (1744–1803) made their way into Finland. These ideas held that to survive as a nation, each nation must develop its own cultural identity based on the language and poetic traditions originating in its past and surviving in the present among the unlettered folk of the countryside. During his school years, Lönnrot, inspired by these beliefs, had turned his attention to folklore. In 1827, relying on everything published on the subject before that time, he published a slim academic dissertation on Väinämöinen, the principal hero of Finnish epic poetry.

In the spring of 1828, while on vacation from the university because of the recent fire and resolved to add to his nation's meager store of traditional poetry, Lönnrot traveled to the eastern province of Karelia and collected a sizable number of folk songs, which he published in four parts as *The Kantele, or, Old and Later Poems and Songs of the Finnish People* (1829–1831). This expedition was to be the first of 11 extensive collecting trips he would take during his lifetime, traveling some 13,000 miles through backwoods country, mostly on foot, and collecting thousands of lines of folk poetry. In 1831, Lönnrot and a group of like-minded friends founded the Finnish Literature Society to promote the study and development of Finnish language and literature. Lönnrot, who served as the society's first secretary, received its first stipend to continue his collecting efforts.

After leaving the university, Lönnrot took a position as district doctor in the remote northeastern city of Kajaani. From there, sometimes on an extended leave of absence, he made numerous collecting trips into the hinterlands of both Finnish and Russian Karelia. He soon began arranging and rearranging the poems he collected, working them through several redactions and moving always toward a larger, composite epic whole. To his friends, he wrote that he would not quit collecting until he could match half of Homer and that he hoped future generations would value the Finnish epic as highly as the Gothic peoples esteemed the *Edda* and as much as the Romans esteemed, "if not quite Homer, then at least Hesiod" (Lönnrot Manuscript Collection). On February 28, 1835, Lönnrot sent his completed manuscript, the *Kalevala*, to the Finnish Literature Society for publication.

After still more collecting by himself and by a new generation of young scholar-patriots inspired by his example, Lönnrot published an expanded version of the epic in 1849. The publication of the *Kalevala* more than filled Lönnrot's hopes. Although few of his educated contemporaries spoke Finnish well enough actually to read the work, the epic nonetheless bolstered the Finns' national self-esteem and proved, at least to their satisfaction, that Finland had had a glorious past, that the Finns possessed a literary masterpiece worthy of emulation, and that the Finnish language deserved to become the national language, a language of culture and education.

Drawing on his rich field collections, Lönnrot published a number of other important works: the *Kanteletar* (1840), a compilation of lyrical folk poems; *Proverbs of the Finnish People* (1842); *Riddles of the Finnish People* (1844); *Ancient Incantation Poems of the Finnish People* (1880); and his monumental *Finnish-Swedish Dictionary* (1866–1880, two volumes). He also worked hard to raise the educational level of his countrymen, supported and contributed to a developing press, and from 1836 to 1840 published his own periodical, *Mehiläinen* [The bee].

In 1853, Lönnrot was named professor of Finnish language at the University of Helsinki. He retired in 1862 to his native parish, Sammatti, and died on March 19, 1884, a national hero.

William A. Wilson

See also *Edda, Poetic*; *Edda, Prose*; Epic; Herder, Johann Gottfried; Homer; *Kalevala*; Nationalism

✳✳✳✳✳✳✳✳✳✳✳✳✳✳✳✳✳✳

References

Antti, Aarne. *Elias Lönnrot: Elämä ja toiminta*. 2 vols. Helsinki: Finnish Literature Society, 1931–1935.

Lönnrot Manuscript Collection, Finnish Literary Society, Helsinki.

Maijamaa, Raija, ed. *Elias Lönnrot: Valitut teokset*. 5 vols. Helsinki: Finnish Literature Society, 1990–1993.

LORD, ALBERT BATES (1912–1991)

A Slavicist, folklorist, comparatist, and collector of southern Slavic oral poetry, Alfred Bates Lord was cooriginator (with Milman Parry) of the oral-formulaic theory. Initially Parry's research assistant in their joint fieldwork with oral epic singers from 1933, Lord assumed leadership after his mentor's death in 1935. He was to transform what had been a laboratory exercise—employing the southern Slavic analogy to confirm Homeric oral tradition—into a multidisciplinary field that now treats more than 130 ancient, medieval, and modern traditions (summary in Foley 1992). Trained in both classics and comparative literature, Lord focused on southern Slavic, ancient and Byzantine Greek, Old English, Old French, Russian, Latvian, Albanian, Central Asian, Finnish, and biblical studies. Through his innovative scholarship, the direction that Parry had mapped out was to develop far beyond the original conception, taking on an identity as one of the major twentieth-century movements in folklore, literature, and anthropology.

In 1949, Lord completed the doctoral dissertation that was published as *The Singer of Tales* in 1960. Basing his model for traditional oral epic on the southern Slavic performances he had experienced, and drawing comparisons not only with Homer but also with medieval European vernacular materials (English, French, and Greek), he significantly enlarged Parry's vision for comparative study. Lord fully elaborated the dynamics of the recurrent phrase or formula ("a group of words which is regularly employed under the same metrical conditions to express a given essential idea") and narrative type-scenes or themes ("groups of ideas regularly used in telling a tale in the formulaic style of traditional song") (Lord 1960, p. 68). He also described story patterns, or tale-types, like the Odysseus story that was known not only in southern Slavic but in Albanian, Turkish, Russian, English, and other traditions. What is more, he furnished examples of formulaic and thematic structure for all five of the poetries and offered interpretations of the involved works based on an understanding of the idiom in which they were composed. Because of its foundational content, his book has served as the comparative manifesto for studies in oral tradition.

The basis for Lord's far-reaching scholarship lay principally in his and Parry's fieldwork in the former Yugoslavia, begun in

1933–1935 and continued by Lord in 1950–1951 and later. From the Milman Parry Collection of Oral Literature, an archive of recordings of southern Slavic oral traditions containing more than a half-million lines of epic as well as a substantial sample of traditional oral lyric (called "women's songs"), Lord contributed two landmark publications during the 1950s: the first volumes in the ongoing series *Serbocroatian Heroic Songs* (*SCHS*), chronicling the epic tradition of Novi Pazar (a region in present-day Bosnia), and *Serbo-Croatian Folk Songs* (1951), with Béla Bartók, an edition and translation of lyric songs. Further volumes of *SCHS* have appeared, but none is more important than Lord and David Bynum's edition and translation of *The Wedding of Smailagić Meho* (1974), a work dictated to Parry and Lord in 1935 by the unlettered master-singer Avdo Medjedović and totaling 12,311 lines, about the length of Homer's *Odyssey*.

In addition to these major, seminal works, Lord contributed more than 70 articles on a wide variety of topics, selectively sampled in his *Epic Singers and Oral Tradition* (1991) and exhaustively listed in his obituary in the *Journal of American Folklore*. His legacy consists most essentially in having furnished a comparative methodology for oral-formulaic theory.

John Miles Foley

See also Balkan Folklore and Literature; Homer; *Iliad*; *Odyssey*; Oral-Formulaic Composition and Theory; Parry, Milman; Tale-Type; Theme

✳✳✳✳✳✳✳✳✳✳✳✳✳✳✳

References

Foley, John Miles. "Obituary: Albert Bates Lord (1912–1991)." *Journal of American Folklore* 105 (1992): 157–165.

———. *The Theory of Oral Composition: History and Methodology*. Bloomington: Indiana University Press, 1992 (1988).

Lord, Albert B. *Epic Singers and Oral Tradition*. Ithaca, N.Y.: Cornell University Press, 1991.

———. *The Singer of Tales*. Cambridge: Harvard University Press, 1960.

Lord, Albert B., and Béla Bartók. *Serbo-Croatian Folk Songs*. New York: Columbia University Press, 1951.

LÜTHI, MAX (1909–1992)

A German literature and folktale scholar, Max Lüthi worked on "high literature," including works on Shakespearean drama (*Shakespeares Draman* [1966] and *Shakespeare, Dichter des Wirklichen und des Nichtwirklichen* [1964]), and comparisons of high literature and folk literature (*Volksliteratur und Hochsliteratur: Menschenbild—Thematik—Formstreben* [1970]). His work on folk literature encompasses the *Sage* ("legend"), the *Legende* ("saint's legend"), and other forms of oral narrative, but his most important work is dedicated to the *Märchen* ("fairy tale," "folktale," "wonder tale").

Lüthi's work reveals a deep love for the märchen along with painstaking scholarship and rare erudition. His approach to the märchen is textual and literary rather than ethnographic or historical; his focus is on the tales themselves—their artistic and aesthetic qualities and the characteristics that define the genre—rather than the people who tell them, the contexts in which they are told, or the circumstances under which they were developed. In two of his greatest works, *Das europäische Volksmärchen: Form und Wesen* [The European folktale: Form and nature (1947)] and *Das Volksmärchen als Dichtung: Ästhetik und Anthropologie* [The fairytale as art form and portrait of man (1990)], Lüthi describes the stylistic characteristics that define the European märchen, much as Russian formalist Vladimir Propp described its structural characteristics.

In *The European Folktale* (1982), Lüthi describes with great clarity and authority the following major characteristics: one-dimensionality (*Einedimensionalität*), depthlessness (*Flächenhaftigkeit*), abstract style or single-strandedness (*Einsträngigkeit*), isolation and universal interconnection (*Allverbundenheit*), and sublimation and all-inclusiveness. In characterizing the märchen as one-dimensional, for example, Lüthi points out that the märchen hero makes no real differentiation between the supernatural and the everyday; by contrast, the hero of the *Sage* will be baffled or frightened by the apparition of a witch. As Lüthi puts it: "Everyday folktale characters do not feel that an encounter with an otherworld being is an encounter with an alien dimension. It is in this sense that we may speak of the one-dimensionality (*Einedimensionalität*) of the folktale."

Lüthi also published a pair of more popular books: *Es war einmal: Vom Wesen des Volksmärchens* [Once upon a time: On the nature of fairy tales (1964)] and *So leben Sie noch Heute: Betrachtungen zum*

LÜTHI, MAX

Volksmärchen (1989), collections of essays taken from a series of radio broadcasts he made.

Kenneth D. Pimple

See also *Märchen*; Propp, Vladimir I.

✻✻✻✻✻✻✻✻✻✻✻✻✻✻✻✻✻

References

Lüthi, Max. *The European Folktale: Form and Nature*. Trans. John D. Niles. Bloomington: Indiana University Press, 1982.

———. *The Fairytale as Art Form and Portrait of Man*. Trans. Jon Erickson. Bloomington: Indiana University Press, 1984.

———. *Once Upon a Time: On the Nature of Fairy Tales*. Trans. Lee Chadeayne and Paul Gottwald. Bloomington: Indiana University Press, 1976.

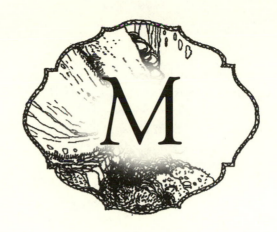

MACNEILL, MÁIRE (1904–1987)

The Irish folklorist Máire MacNeill graduated from the National University of Ireland in Celtic studies and became a member of the Irish Folklore Commission when it was founded in 1935. She also trained in Swedish folklore methods at Uppsala University. Drawing on the oral tradition gathered by the Irish Folklore Commission in response to a 1942 questionnaire on harvest customs, historical evidence, and literary texts from Old Irish—principally *Cath Maige Tuired, Oidheadh Chloinne Tuireann,* and *Baile an Scáil* to the contemporary folktales told about Balor and Lugh and the Tuatha Dé Danaan—MacNeill produced *The Festival of Lughnasa* (1962). This work was her magisterial study of a popular Irish festival celebrating the beginning of harvest, the most famous expression of which is the annual pilgrimage on the last Sunday of July to Croagh Patrick, Ireland's holy mountain in County Mayo. Examining 195 sites of these gatherings, MacNeill discovered survivals of the Celtic festival in honor of Lugh, and she traced its myths in the legends and customs associated with the festival's nineteenth- and twentieth-century observances, observances that replaced the pagan elements with Christian tradition.

Lughnasa's documentation of the close coexistence of pagan and Christian as well as the survival of Lughnasa customs—hill gatherings, berry picking, and especially dancing—inspired Irish playwright Brian Friel's award-winning *Dancing at Lughnasa,* a memory play set in Donegal at harvesttime in 1936. The play's program notes pay direct tribute to MacNeill's work.

MacNeill left the Irish Folklore Commission in 1949 and moved to Boston. She was visiting lecturer in Irish folklore at Harvard University in 1964 and 1965 before she returned to Ireland in 1967 to translate two folklore classics from the Irish—Seán Ó hEochaidh's collections of fairy legends and *Fairy Legends from Donegal* (1977), with the Irish text edited by Séamas O Catháin and the English translation by MacNeill. "Eoin Óg agus an Mhaighdean Mhara," one of Ó hEochaidh's legends translated by MacNeill as "The Sea Girl and Eoin Óg," provides the metaphor for the Seamus Heaney poem "Maighdean Mara," which the poet dedicated to Ó hEochaidh. MacNeill's translation of Séamus Ó Duilearga's collection of a Kerry storyteller, *Leabhar Sheáin I Chonaill, Seán O Conaill's Book: Stories and Translations from Iveragh,* followed in 1981.

MacNeill's last major work, *Máire Rua, Lady of Lemaneh,* published posthumously in 1990, compares the tradition surrounding the best known character in County Clare folklore with the facts of her life preserved in the O'Brien family records, particularly *The Inchiquin Manuscripts* and other contemporary documents. MacNeill separated the version of the sovereign goddess myth from the historical Máire Rua to reveal a shrewd businesswoman who protected her heirs' interests despite the political and religious turmoil of seventeenth-century Ireland.

Maureen Murphy

See also Celtic Literature; Festival; Legend; Myth

✳✳✳✳✳✳✳✳✳✳✳✳✳✳✳✳✳

References

Almqvist, Bo. "Dr. Máire MacNeill-Sweeney (1904–87). In Memoriam." *Béaloideas* (1988): 221–223.

———. "Máire MacNeill Sweeney, 1904–1987." *Clare Association Yearbook* (1988): 28–29.

MacNeill, Máire. *The Festival of Lughnasa.* Dublin: Comhairle Bhéaloideasa Éireann, 1983 (1962).

"Máire MacNeill Sweeney (1904–1987): Scholar." In *National Gallery of Ireland, Acquisitions 1986–1988,* pp. 60–61. Dublin: National Gallery of Ireland, 1988.

Murphy, Maureen. "Máire MacNeill (1904–1987), an Appreciation." In Máire MacNeill, *Máire Rua, Lady of Leamaneh.* Whitegate, Ireland: Ballenahella Press, 1990.

MACPHERSON, JAMES (1736–1796)

A Scottish poet and historian, born a poor farmer's son in the Highland village of Ruthven, James Macpherson achieved international renown as the supposed translator of the Ossianic poems, which appeared in *Fragments of Ancient Poetry* (1760), *Fingal* (1761), and *Temora* (1763). Macpherson claimed that the two epics, "Fingal" and "Temora," as well as numerous shorter poems, were the work of a third-century Scottish bard, Ossian, and that Macpherson himself had collected the poems on journeys to the Scottish Highlands and Western Isles. Accusations of forgery surfaced almost immediately, eventually embroiling Macpherson in a bitter argument with Samuel Johnson, but they did little to damage the poems' popularity in Europe and in America. Although it has since been determined that the bulk of the poems have no discernible traditional source, Macpherson did in fact draw many characters and episodes from traditional Scots Gaelic heroic ballads.

The Ossianic poems appeared less than 20 years after the Battle of Culloden Moor, and they strongly evoke the sense of a dying people passing, perhaps forever, into the mists of oblivion. An aged Ossian sits and sings of the past to those who will hear him, recalling the heroic deeds of his father, Fingal, and the strong but sensitive warriors of Morven. Although modified to suit contemporary sentimental tastes, Macpherson's depiction of Ossian concurs with traditional portrayals of the bard, the last of his people, telling tales of the Fenian warriors to St. Patrick. Interestingly, Macpherson chose to "translate" Ossian's poems into a measured prose that imitates many of the rhythms of Scots Gaelic ballads. And in passages where Macpherson actually borrowed from a discoverable source, the translation appears remarkably faithful by eighteenth-century standards.

But it is obvious that Macpherson significantly amplified and altered the traditional Ossianic material. Among other accusations, he is often faulted for confusing plots and characters from the Ulster cycle of stories with Fenian lore; he even includes a brief and extremely distorted version of the Irish Táin in the second book of *Fingal*.

Macpherson was among the first to popularize Scottish folklore material in high literary and artistic circles, and his international success no doubt encouraged writers like Sir Walter Scott to use Scottish lore in their literary productions. Macpherson's poetry, admired by such important political and cultural figures as William Blake, Samuel

Taylor Coleridge, Johann Wolfgang von Goethe, and Napoleon, helped to mold the spirit and genius of the romantic generation. Furthermore, the controversy surrounding the Ossianic poems stimulated folklore research in the nineteenth century as interested parties went to the Highlands seeking the truth of the poems' origins. Macpherson himself was most likely responsible for the discovery of "The Book of the Dean of Lismore," a sixteenth-century manuscript that contains nearly 30 Gaelic ballads, many about Ossian and other Fenian characters. Although Macpherson's editorial practices were dubious at best, his influence on nineteenth-century literary tastes and antiquarian interests should not be overlooked.

Melanie K. Hutsell

See also Cuchulain; Fakelore; Ossian; Scott, Sir Walter

✳✳✳✳✳✳✳✳✳✳✳✳✳✳✳✳✳✳

References

Fitzgerald, Robert P. "The Style of Ossian." *Studies in Romanticism* 6 (1966): 22–33.

Grobman, Neil R. "James Macpherson, Ossian, and the Revival of Interest in Oral Bardic Traditions in Eighteenth-Century Scotland." *Midwestern Journal of Language and Folklore* 6 (1980): 51–55.

Murphy, Peter T. "Fool's Gold: The Highland Treasures of Macpherson's Ossian." *English Literary History* 53 (1986): 567–589.

Thomson, Derick S. *The Gaelic Sources of Macpherson's "Ossian."* Aberdeen University Studies no. 130. Edinburgh: Oliver and Boyd, 1952.

Maggio

Maggio, a genre of Italian sung popular theater, is performed by amateur troupes in northern Tuscany and, with slightly different conventions, in southern Emilia. The name derives from an original association with May Day, but nowadays this type of theater is performed during July and August. With a vociferous audience encircling the outdoor performance space, the play, typically including stylized sword fighting, is presented using few props, no scenery, and unvarying traditional costumes. Written texts are enacted with the aid of a promoter who is onstage and are accompanied by a violin, guitar, or piano accordion.

Texts are composed in three main verse forms. Octosyllabic lines (arranged in four- or five-line stanzas rhyming abba or abbcc) make up most of the script, while for moments of dramatic import two special metrical forms are used: the classic "ottava" (eight hendecasyllabic lines rhyming abababcc) and the "arietta" (four heptasyllabic lines, the last truncated, rhyming abbc). Each of these metrical types is associated with a different traditional melody, performed in a highly melismatic style that results in significant differences between renditions by different singers.

Maggio meters demonstrate links to Hispanic and Italian literary and popular genres. The octosyllabic quatrain is the standard meter of the Spanish literary verse romance, of seventeenth-century Spanish drama, and of Hispanic-derived popular theater genres in Central and South America and the Philippines. The hendecasyllabic ottava occurs in Italian literary verse romances, such as Ariosto's *Orlando furioso*, as well as in other kinds of central and southern Italian popular song.

Maggio scripts make liberal use of metrical formulas and display a high degree of redundancy in plot and character. Many traditional *maggio* plots derive from narratives circulating in cheap printed editions in the nineteenth and early twentieth centuries. The stock of written texts, which is still being added to, can be traced back to a variety of sources, including traditional scripts circulating in manuscript form, literary classics, opera plots, and television films.

For example, the *maggio* script *I paladini di Francia* [The French paladins], performed by the Gorfigliano company in 1988, derives from Andrea da Barberino's fifteenth-century Tuscan prose romance *I reali di Francia* [The French royal family]. A popular traditional *maggio* plot, *Pia de' Tolomei*, the tragic story of a Sienese noblewoman mistreated by her husband and imprisoned in the malaria-ridden Maremma marshes, is mentioned in Dante's *Purgatorio* (canto V, line 133). Seven *maggio* companies have presented different versions of this story in Tuscany in the 1980s and 1990s.

It is common for *maggio* scripts to be extensively adapted for each production by deleting or adding scenes and characters according to the number of players in the company and their vocal capabilities. Revisions are always made with performance in mind rather than with the aim of producing a coherent literary text.

Linda Barwick

See also Performance

✳✳✳✳✳✳✳✳✳✳✳✳✳✳✳✳✳
References

Barwick, Linda. "The Filipino *Komedya* and the Italian *Maggio*: Cross-Cultural Perspectives on Related Genres of Popular Music Theatre." In *Masks of Time: Drama and Its Contexts*, ed. A. B. Gibbs, pp. 71–108. Canberra: Australian Academy of the Humanities, 1992.

D'Ancona, Alessandro. *Origini del teatro italiano*. 2 vols. Rome: Bardi, 1966 (1891).

Magrini, Tullia. "Identità del Maggio drammatico." In *Il Maggio drammatico: Una radizione di teatro in musica*, ed. T. Magrini, pp. 7–37. Bologna: Edizioni Analisi, 1992.

Venturelli, Gastone. "Le aree del Maggio." In *Il Maggio drammatico: Una tradizione di teatro in musica*, ed. T. Magrini, pp. 45–128. Bologna: Edizioni Analisi, 1992.

Malory, Sir Thomas (d. 1471)

English literature would be much impoverished if Sir Thomas Malory had not spent so many years in prison. He was accused and often indicted (if not actually convicted) of horse and cattle rustling; of assault, burglary, robbery, and rape (of the same woman twice); of removing large sums of money, jewels, and other valuables from the Cistercian Abbey of Combe, near Coventry; and of bushwhacking and attempting to assassinate Humphrey Stafford, duke of Buckingham. While incarcerated, Malory translated, or "reduced to English," a collection of stories about King Arthur and his noble knights that Malory had found in French and English literary sources and to which he freely added the oral traditions about Arthur that survived in the countryside. Malory's manuscript was among the first books published in England by the printer William Caxton, and *Le Morte d'Arthur* [The death of King Arthur (1485)] became the fundamental storehouse of all information on King Arthur known to the English-speaking world.

Although Malory's literary sources derived from different peoples and different epochs, they retained the traces—often rationalized, modernized, inconsistent, and misinterpreted—of their origins in the imagination of the folk among whom they must have originated. The Irish, Welsh, French, and Germans have variously valid claims for these origins, often influenced by the mythological tales

¶Here foloweth the fyrth boke of the noble and wo꜓thy p꜓ynce kyng Arthur.

¶How fy꜓ Launcelot and fy꜓ Lyonell departed fro the courte fo꜓ to feke auentures / ꜡ how fy꜓ Lyonell lefte fy꜓ Launcelot fleppynge ꜡ was taken. Capitulū.j.

Hone after that the noble ꜡ wo꜓thy kyng Arthur was comen fro Rome into Englande / all the knyghtes of the roūde table refo꜓ted vnto p̄ kyng and made many iuftes and turneymentes / ꜡ fome there were that were good

knyghtes / whiche encreafed fo in armes and wo꜓fhyp that they paffed all they꜓ felowes in p꜓oweffe ꜡ noble dedes ꜡ that was well p꜓oued on many . But in efpecyall it was p꜓oued on fy꜓ Launcelot du lake . Fo꜓ in all turneymentes and iuftes and dedes of armes / bothe fo꜓ lyfe and deth he paffed all knyghtes ꜡ at no tyme he was neuer ouercomen but yf it were by treafon o꜓ enchauntement. Sy꜓ Launcelot encreafed fo meruaylouſly in wo꜓fhyp ꜡ honour / wherfo꜓e he is the firſt knyght p̄ the frenſhe booke maketh mencyon of / after that kynge Arthur came from Rome / wherfo꜓e quene Gueneuer had hym in grete fauour aboue all other knyghtes / and certaynly he loued the quene agayne aboue all other ladyes and damoyſelles all the dayes of his lyfe / and fo꜓ her he
i iii

A page from Sir Thomas Malory's Morte d'Arthur *[The death of King Arthur], printed by Wynken de Worde in 1529.*

of classical antiquity and the Bible: Arthur's desire to kill all male children born on May Day, for example, is reminiscent of the biblical slaughter of the innocents by King Herod. Morgan le Fay, who shares characteristics with the Germanic Valkyrie, probably descended both from Morrigan, a man-devouring, Celtic lamia and prophetess, and from Matrona, a Continental Celtic mother and water goddess (who also gave her name to the river Marne). Lancelot may ultimately derive from the Welsh sun god Lug and the Welsh warrior Llwch Llawwynnawc or Llenlleawc (which the Bretons, or French, under the influence of the name "Lancelin" translated as Lancelot), and he was probably the hero of an independent and widely diffused folktale (involving the theft of an infant by a water fairy and the rescue of a queen from an otherworld prison), which was subsequently attached to the Arthurian material.

The variety of folkloric sources often led to conflicting characterizations. Kay, for example, first appears as the false claimant to the throne, then becomes the trusted adviser to the king, and finally appears as the jester/mocker figure. Lancelot, Balin, Torre, Gareth (known as Beaumains), La Cote Male Tayle, and Arthur himself all share characteristics of the ugly duckling or male Cinderella—a knight of such inauspicious beginnings that his subsequent successes are shocking. Malory's sources drew upon more than one version of the Holy Grail, which at various moments in the narrative is visible or invisible, contains Christ's blood, heals Lancelot's madness, and feeds the knights of the Round Table, each according to his desire.

Other matters more commonly associated with folk literature—such as disguise, shape-shifting, mistaken identity, false pretenders, literal fools, fatherless children, rash boons, taboos, and percipient dreams—are all present in the text. Among the most famous are the recognition tasks: Arthur pulls the sword from the stone to become the greatest earthly king in Christendom; Balin delivers the dolorous blow that lays waste three kingdoms and wounds the fisher king, who can only be cured by the purest knight in the world; and Galahad, the pure knight, pulls Balin's sword from a stone to become the most triumphant knight in the spiritual realm. Among the most portentous are the fraudulent sexual invasions that rely upon transformation and the children that are subsequently born of such concourse: Uther, disguised by Merlin as the duke of Tintagel, rapes Igraine, and Arthur, the great king, is born. Lancelot, twice beguiled by Dame Brusen, copulates with Elaine, and Galahad, the spiritual knight who finds the Holy Grail, is born. Perhaps in the same vein, Arthur sleeps with his half sister, Margawse, and Mordred, the traitor who destroys civilization, is born.

In Malory's *Morte d'Arthur*, we find a compilation of folk motifs and matters, characters and situations, folktales and folklore all in the service of a mythic story about the glorious rise and catastrophic fall of Arthurian civilization.

Jerome Mandel

See also Arthur, King; Arthurian Tradition; Camelot

✳✳✳✳✳✳✳✳✳✳✳✳✳✳✳✳✳

References

Field, P. J. C. *The Life and Times of Sir Thomas Malory*. Cambridge, Eng.: Brewer, 1993.

McCarthy, Terence. *Reading the Morte D'arthur*. Cambridge, Eng.: Brewer, 1988.

Spisak, James W., ed. *Studies in Malory*. Kalamazoo, Mich.: Medieval Institute Publications, 1985.

Text, bibliography, biographical material on Malory are available at <http://www.luminarium.org/medlit/malory.htm> or, more generally, at <http://www.georgetown.edu/labyrinth>.

Vinaver, Eugene. *The Works of Sir Thomas Malory*. 3d ed. Rev. P. J. C. Field. Oxford: Oxford University Press, 1990.

MÄRCHEN

According to Jacob and Wilhelm Grimm's *Deutsches Wörterbuch* [German dictionary (1852–1960)], Märchen (a diminutive of *Mär* ["an account"]) means, more broadly, a fictional tale (Latin, *fabula*). Märchen is one of the most basic of the many different terms that have been used in order to separate the vast body of diverse traditional narratives into more manageable genres. In his *Verzeichnis der Märchentypen* [Index of tale types (1910)], Antti Aarne established three major divisions: animal tales *(Tiermärchen)*, real tales (*eigentliche Märchen*, now translated as "ordinary folktales"), and humorous tales or jests *(Schwänke)*. The *eigentliche Märchen* include, in addition to magic tales (fairy tales), religious tales, romantic tales (novelle), and tales of the stupid ogre. Märchen is sometimes used in the very narrow sense of "fairy tale." Its singular form is the same as its plural, and it has the advantage that it is easily modified: *Volksmärchen* ("folktales") can be distinguished from *Buchmärchen* ("book tales") and *Kunstmärchen* ("artistic tales" or "literary tales").

As a technical term, märchen can be confusing because of its broader and narrower senses. From the time of the Grimms' *Kinder- und Hausmärchen* [Children's and household tales (1850)], German editors have compiled märchen collections by mixing fairy tales, children's tales, humorous tales, and animal tales and including tales from Europe as well as all parts of the world. Following German cultural historian André Jolles (1874–1946), the idea of the märchen is sometimes defined (in a circular and rather mystical way) by the spiritual concern (*Geistesbeschäftigung*) that the folktale evidences as opposed to the different concerns of the myth, legend, jest, etc. (see Ranke 1967). In this respect, the salient quality of the märchen is that its free-flowing fantasy removes it from the constraints of reality. Märchen is a word with many shifting resonances, some of which are not reliable even for all of Europe. The content and style of folktales are to some extent regional: the German *Märchen* is not exactly the same as the French *conte populaire* or the Russian *skazka*. Just as can happen when the particular significance of the term *fairy tale* is pushed too far, arguments over which tales are the real märchen, or which characteristics of the märchen are essential and which are accidental, quickly become unpleasantly idiosyncratic.

Because folktales are so various, generalizations about them can be very difficult to formulate and defend. Once it is clear which tales are being discussed, however, people writing in English can usually use English terms. For example, if *fairy tale* seems too vague or too literary, *magic tale* (AT 300–749) is more specific. Moreover, the English word *folktale* has the advantage that it implies traditionality, which is essential to the definition of folklore.

Christine Goldberg

See also Aarne, Antti; Fairy Tale; Folktale; Genre; Grimm, Jacob and Wilhelm; Legend; Myth

✳✳✳✳✳✳✳✳✳✳✳✳✳✳✳✳✳

References

Aarne, Antti. *Verzeichnis der Märchentypen*. Folklore Fellows Communication no. 3. Helsinki: Academia Scientiarum Fennica, 1910.

Leyen, Friedrich von der. *Die Welt der Märchen*. 2 vols. Düsseldorf: E. Diederichs, 1953–1954.

Lüthi, Max. *The European Folktale: Form and Nature*. Bloomington: Indiana University Press, 1984.

———. *Märchen*. 7th ed. Zurich: Manesse, 1989.

Oberfeld, Charlotte, ed. *Wie alt sind unsere Märchen?* Regensburg, Germany: Erich Röth, 1990.

Ranke, Kurt. "Einfache Formen." *Journal of the Folklore Institute* 4 (1967): 17–31.

Marie de France

Marie de France, a woman writing in Old French during the second half of the twelfth century, is best known for her 12 Breton *lais*, or short verse romances. Despite numerous efforts, scholars have been unable to determine Marie's historical identity. All they agree upon is that she was from France, lived in England, was knowledgeable about court life, had a good education, and was able to compose verse and translate Latin into French.

Marie's name is attached to her work only in a single thirteenth-century manuscript that contains the 12 *lais*, a collection of Aesop's fables, and a poem on the purgatory of Saint Patrick. Internal evidence suggests that these works are all by Marie: she is identified as Marie in the prologue to the lay "Guigemar," and a colophon at the end of the collection of fables refers to her French origin. Some scholars, however, dispute definite attribution of any of the works except the fables to Marie.

Marie claimed to be the first writer to translate and collect Breton *lais*, rhymed verse narratives whose plots were supposedly drawn from Celtic materials. Like others of the genre, Marie's tales are usually set in Britain or Brittany, and the plots often rely on the magical and the marvelous. Marie's *lais* are notable for their sensitive treatment of women in marriage and in love outside of marriage.

Although scholars generally agree that the *lais* were not composed in this order, the Harley Manuscript opens with a general prologue and presents the *lais* in the following sequence: In "Guigemar," a knight encounters many obstacles, including a magic ship and a magically knotted shirt, before winning his true love. In "Equitan," a king loves his steward's wife, but when they conspire to kill the steward, both die instead. In "Le Fresne" [The ash tree], a princess is abandoned at birth but is eventually reunited with her family. In "Bisclavret" [The werewolf], a knight's unfaithful wife and her lover conspire to trap him forever in his werewolf shape. In "Lanval," a knight falls in love with a fairy princess but is forbidden to reveal her existence to other mortals.

In "Deus Amanz" [Two lovers], a king sets an impossible task for his daughter's suitors, only to have the daughter and her lover die upon completing it. In "Yonec," a closely guarded princess is courted by a knight who can transform himself into a hawk. In "Laüstic" [The nightingale], a woman uses a nightingale as a ruse to communicate with her beloved, but her cruel husband traps and kills the bird. In "Milun," a son and father, each fighting incognito, nearly slay each other. In "Chaitivel" [The unfortunate one], a woman's four suitors fight in a tournament; three die and the fourth is wounded and left impotent. In "Chevrefoil" [The honeysuckle], Tristan summons Isolt to a secret rendezvous by leaving a carved stick along a roadway. In "Eliduc," the longest of the *lais*, a knight's loyalties are torn between two women and two lords.

Marie's work apparently enjoyed considerable popularity in the Middle Ages. Denis Piramus, a contemporary of Marie, wrote in his *Life of St. Edmund the King* that counts, barons, knights, and ladies of the English court desired to hear Marie's writings read aloud over and over. Assorted tales (often incomplete) appear in several Old French manuscripts and in the *Strengleikar*, a collection of Old French works translated into Old Norse.

David Sprunger

See also Aesop's Fables

✳✳✳✳✳✳✳✳✳✳✳✳✳✳✳✳✳

References
Marie de France. *The Lais of Marie de France*. Trans. and ed. Robert Hanning and Joan Ferrante. Durham, N.C.: Labyrinth Press, 1978.
———. *The Lais of Marie de France*. Trans. and ed. Glyn S. Burgess and Keith Busby. Harmondsworth, Eng.: Penguin, 1986.

MELVILLE, HERMAN (1819–1891)

The fiction writer and poet Herman Melville was born in New York City. However, in 1830 he moved to Albany, New York, with his family and worked intermittently as a clerk and schoolmaster until 1839, when he joined the crew of a merchant vessel bound for Liverpool, England. That journey, together with a trip down the Mississippi River by steamboat in 1840 and a whaling voyage to the South Pacific from 1841 to 1844, brought Melville into contact with the people, places, and cultures he later revisited, imaginatively, in many of his works.

Particularly important from a folkloristic perspective are his books *Typee* (1846), *Omoo* (1847), *Mardi* (1848), *Redburn* (1849),

White Jacket (1849), *Moby-Dick* (1851), and *The Confidence Man* (1857). In *Moby-Dick* alone, Melville dramatizes, describes, or alludes to almost every conceivable form of folk expression through his fictional persona Ishmael, who describes from the perspective of a cultural insider the language and customs of the nineteenth-century whale fishery; quotes traditional proverbs, weather lore, and supernatural beliefs; discourses on scrimshaw and other folk arts; and recounts tales, legends, and myths that have close analogues in the standard motif and type indexes.

Although it is sometimes possible to identify and classify specific borrowings or appropriations from folk tradition, the boundaries between folklore and fiction are often blurred. For example, Ahab's symbolically charged act of nailing a doubloon to the mast of the *Pequod* as a reward for the first lookout to spot Moby Dick seems purely a literary invention, but it is based on a commonplace whaling custom noted in the logs of various ships. Conversely, the "trepan" or "head mending" stories represented in *Mardi* as true accounts of Polynesian surgical practices are variants of a European wonder tale known as "The Three Doctors," which in this context has the genre markings and performance features of a tall tale. And the latter scene is just one of many literary re-creations or simulations of folkloric processes and performances, other notable examples being the "skylarking" events in *Redburn*, *White Jacket*, and *Moby-Dick* and the succession of con games or scams on which *The Confidence Man* is based.

The functions of folkloric phenomena in Melville's fiction are almost as varied as the forms in which they are expressed and the contexts in which they are situated. When the narrator of *Omoo* shares with his audience a story he has heard about "a horse's hoof with the shoe on having been fished up out of the pickle of one of the casks," he is simply emphasizing through the comic hyperbole of a whopper the deplorable condition of the ship's provisions. But the seemingly local allusion to the legend of the Flying Dutchman at the beginning of *Mardi* resonates throughout the novel as the narrator's Pacific journey becomes a "chartless voyage" over an "endless sea." By contrast, the "legends of the whale fishery," as Ishmael characterizes them in *Moby-Dick*, are for the most part imaginative inventions in the form of personal or supernatural legends repeated in variant versions throughout the novel. Rather than cohering in a single archetypal pattern, as a number of critics have argued, these stories—together with the historical, scientific, and philosophical narratives with which they are frequently combined—reveal the relative nature of "truth" and the indeterminacy of absolute meaning.

As these few examples suggest, Melville was neither the folklife recorder that early scholars believed him to be nor the mythographer envisioned by later critics. Rather, he was an artist of extraordinary versatility and insight who understood more clearly than any other writer of his time that folklore is not a set of static genres but a powerful medium for personal, cultural, and literary expression.

James W. Kirkland

See also Legend; Motif; Myth; Proverbs; Supernatural; Tale-Type; Tall Tale

✳✳✳✳✳✳✳✳✳✳✳✳✳✳✳✳✳✳

References

Babcock, C. Merton. "Melville's Proverbs of the Sea." *Western Folklore* 11 (1952): 254–265.

Cannon, Agnes. "Melville's Use of Sea Ballads and Songs." *Western Folklore* 23 (1964): 1–16.

Grobman, Neil. "The Tall Tale Telling Events in Melville's *Moby-Dick*." *Journal of the Folklore Institute* 12 (1975): 19–27.

Kirkland, James W. "A New Source for the 'Trepan' Scenes in Melville's *Mardi*." *English Language Notes* 30 (1993): 39–47.

MERMAID

The mermaid, or "sea woman," is usually associated with coastal areas, though these legendary humanoid, supernatural creatures can also live in lakes, rivers, and streams. Although the mermaid of current popular culture is a hybrid—half woman and half fish—mermaids are also described in Western folklore as completely human or as shape-shifting seals. As a protectress of the sea and its creatures, the divine mermaid still receives presents and prayers from sailors and fishermen in many parts of the world.

As the empirical worldview of the Western industrial age waxed and supernatural beliefs retreated to rural hamlets, the mermaid in literature and Victorian art became a winsome, hybrid creature of languid loveliness. At this point, the mermaid emerged as a symbol in Western literature, invoking the cultural myths of the indiscrim-

Mermaids take on a myriad of roles in folk literature, from protectress of the sea to enchantress.

inate female sexual appetite or presexual purity. Recent criticism has paid particular attention to the mermaid's appearance in T. S. Eliot's *The Waste Land* (1922). Passing mention has been made to William Shakespeare's *Midsummer Night's Dream*, William Butler Yeats's "The Mermaid," and Herman Melville's *Moby-Dick*. In these works, mermaids are regarded as an indication of elements of nostalgic fantasy or, alternately, as the failure of the modern imagination. Psychoanalytic interpretations consider the mermaid to be a symbol of either released or repressed womanhood; feminist criticism adds victimization.

Hans Christian Andersen's fairy tale, "The Little Mermaid," recently revived in a film by Disney, incorporated Danish mermaid legends in a religious tract for children. In J. M. Barrie's *Peter Pan*, mermaids add an atmosphere of fantasy in a world of perpetual innocence. Similarly, other works of children's literature—such as L. Frank Baum's *The Sea Fairies* and C. S. Lewis's *Voyage of the Dawn Treader*—include mermaids as denizens of enchantment, visible primarily to children, and utterly separate from accepted reality. Modern popular drama and films like *Mr. Peabody and the Mermaid* usually dwell on issues of gender, male midlife crisis, and impossible love. Henrik Ibsen used the mermaid in an 1888 play, *The Lady from the Sea*, to discuss the constrictive hold of social convention on the individual. The films *Splash* and Disney's *The Little Mermaid*, produced in the 1980s, have a focus on romance and therefore have much in common with traditional mermaid folktales collected at the beginning of the twentieth century.

Indeed, it is important to note that mermaids may not be symbols in literature in regions where mermaid legends still thrive.

There are a few mermaid studies that do not divorce the mermaid from her belief community—the best examples are of Cornish, Mexican, and Russian uses of mermaid lore in literature—and such studies indicate that a mermaid's appearance in a piece of literature mobilizes a set of beliefs about the known and unknown worlds. A careful analysis of the mermaid in literature will first consider the depth of the author's connection to a particular mermaid tradition. Mermaids are well defined in folk tradition as their description, powers, and abilities are restricted by the parameters of belief. When the belief tradition fails or fades, the mermaid is then set adrift for appropriation as a symbol for concepts and concerns prevalent in a culture. This is the reason mermaids as symbols in the larger Western mythos are constantly being redefined and reinterpreted.

The enigma of the mermaid in a scientific world has perplexed mermaid scholars and authors alike and has spawned several explanations. The dominant theory accounting for the existence of mermaid legends in the West posits that seafarers mistook the manatee, a docile but homely creature resembling a walrus, for a lovely mermaid. Evidently the manatee's habit of perching upright on rocks while nursing its young was thought sufficient to confuse seasoned sailors. Because the manatee is a warm-water mammal and most Western mermaid legends have been collected in northern European coastal areas—from Scotland to Scandinavia—it has been suggested that the many accounts of mermaid sightings by respected sea captains and naturalists actually refer to a "now extinct type of unusually human-like species of seal" (Eberhart 1983).

Cynthea L. Ainsworth

See also Andersen, Hans Christian; Folktale; Legend; Myth; Siren

✸✸✸✸✸✸✸✸✸✸✸✸✸✸✸

References

Beck, Horace. *Folklore and the Sea.* Middletown, Conn.: Wesleyan University Press, 1973.

Berman, Ruth. "Mermaids." In *Mythical and Fabulous Creatures: A Source Book and Research Guide*, ed. Malcolm South, pp. 133–145. New York: Greenwood Press, 1987.

Eberhart, George M. *Monsters: A Guide to Information on Unaccounted for Creatures.* New York: Garland, 1983.

Riehl, Joseph E. "Procter, Lamb, and Eliot: Mermaids Calling Each to Each." *Charles Lamb Bulletin* 58 (1987): 47–54.

MINNESANG

Minnesang ("love song"), a German musical and poetic tradition, appeared in the mid-twelfth century under the strong influence of Provençal troubadours and their art. The Hohenstaufen emperor Frederick I, called Frederick Barbarossa (reign 1152–1190), and his wife, Beatrice of Burgundy, were patrons of the French tradition and encouraged its growth in Austria. The German minnesingers, however, also drew themes and music from Gregorian musical tradition, the erotic "goliard" (student who wandered around Europe as an itinerant scholar), and folk traditions to develop a uniquely German art. As the artistic expression of an international cultural movement, *Minnesang* later became important to the romantics, who considered themselves members of a similar movement. But *Minnesang* was also the first German vernacular "high art," and thus focused romantic concerns on finding a distinctly German spirit and expressive style.

Strictly speaking, *Minnesang* refers exclusively to courtly love, but the term is usually used to designate Middle High German lyric poetry on a variety of topics, including love songs, topical commentary, and religious songs (called *Lieder, Sangsprüche,* and *Leiche,* respectively). Enough texts survive for scholars to distinguish regional and historical styles, but musical notations are incomplete at best. *Minne* musical and lyric composition, though complex, was less rigidly structured than its French counterpart, making German melodies more difficult to reconstruct from later transcriptions. This situation is unfortunate since music and verse were inseparable in their original context.

Descriptions of *Minnesänger* ("minnesingers") and their performance styles have been drawn from medieval manuscript illustrations and literary sources, especially Gottfried von Strassburg's "Tristan." *Minnelieder* were probably performed solo, with instrumental music generally being saved for preludes, interludes, or postludes (but perhaps accompanying the songs in some cases). The use of fiddles was especially popular, though many other stringed instruments were also used, as were wind and perhaps percussion instruments. *Minnesang* is also defined in terms of public performances and courtly participants. Performance occasions ranged from small court dinners to large public festivals, for which the noblest composers hired others to sing.

Minnesänger came from a range of social classes and may even have included women, but they were typically landless, "unfree" knights with other duties. They often traveled and were paid for performances, and many assumed names that emphasized either their hopes for payment or their image as wandering pastoralists. *Minnesänger* were highly trained, though not always literate or able to write music. They were expected to compose poems and music, to sing well in several languages, and to play several musical instruments. Composition was an elite insider's art, one that was governed by a complex set of principles.

The Crusades and the Holy Roman Empire declined while cities and commerce grew, and *Minnesang* came to reflect these changes. By the death in 1318 of the last traditional minnesinger, Heinrich von Meissen (also called Frauenlob, or Praise Women), the tradition had inspired citizen guilds whose accomplished members were called *Meistersänger* ("master singers"). In the late fourteenth century, Meistersinger Johannes Hadlaub collected one of the largest and earliest collections of *Minnelieder,* many of which were already rare. Older *Minnesang* became the stuff of legends like *Sängerkrieg auf der Wartberg* [Singers' battle at Wartberg], an apocryphal legend dating from the fourteenth century about a contest between Walther von der Vogelweide, Heinrich von Ofterdingen, and Wolfram von Eschenback. German literature, especially folk and religious songs and love poetry, followed *Minnesang* conventions for centuries, and *Minnesang* themes and imagery are still reflected in both elite and popular art.

Clover Williams

See also Ballad; Romance

✳✳✳✳✳✳✳✳✳✳✳✳✳✳✳✳✳

References

Lang, Paul Henry. *Music in Western Civilization.* New York: W. W. Norton, 1941.

McMahon, James V. *The Music of Early Minnesang.* Columbia, S.C.: Camden House, 1990.

Rose, Ernst. A *History of German Literature.* New York: New York University Press, 1960.

MODERN LANGUAGE ASSOCIATION OF AMERICA (MLA)

The Modern Language Association of America (MLA) is the oldest and largest scholarly organization in the United States dedicated to the study of modern languages and literature. Founded in New York City at Columbia University in 1883, the organization has grown from the approximately 40 founders to over 25,000 members as American higher education has shifted from classical to modern languages and literatures and as the United States has tried to understand and deal with other cultures around the world.

The MLA focuses its attention on literature and literary research in a number of ways. The association itself is organized primarily by national literature (American, English, Italian, German, French) and is then subdivided by literary periods. There are also a few special interest areas within literary research: interdisciplinary approaches, bibliography, translation. The Modern Language Association has published a scholarly journal devoted to literary research, *Publications of the Modern Language Association (PMLA)*, since 1884, and since 1922 it has compiled and published annual bibliographies of contributions to literary studies. The MLA also has had an active publishing program, including new editions of literary works as well as aids to scholarship (bibliographies, concordances, surveys) and pedagogy.

When the Modern Language Association was formed, there was no clear distinction between folklore—especially folk narrative—and literature. In fact, early volumes of *PMLA* included studies of Louisiana French folktales and Russian animal tales. When the MLA became large enough to organize and name divisions in the 1920s, no language group set up a folklore division; nevertheless, folklore was the central topic for a group that focused on popular literature until late 1962. Folklore was also a regular area of the annual bibliography, first as a subdivision of each national literature and later as a wholly separate subfield and volume.

For a long period, the American Folklore Society held its annual meetings alternately with the American Anthropological Association and the Modern Language Association, but as the American Folklore Society developed its own identity and met on its own, folklore topics largely dropped out of *PMLA* and the folklore-related groups within the MLA largely disappeared. Today, however, several folklore-related discussion groups are active in the

MLA, there are usually many conference presentations dealing with aspects of oral literature(s), and the American Folklore Society, as an affiliated organization, can sponsor several sessions at MLA conventions.

Quite a few scholars have played important roles in both American folkloristics and the Modern Language Association. Alcée Fortier, George Lyman Kittredge, Louise Pound, and Archer Taylor served as presidents of both societies, and other folklorists have served the MLA in executive roles: Francis B. Gummere, John A. Lomax, C. Grant Loomis, and Francis Lee Utley. There are certainly others—from Francis James Child to Stith Thompson, Wayland D. Hand, and Albert Lord—who have contributed substantially to both fields without serving in national positions in either organization.

The MLA has particular significance since most people who teach folklore or literature do so within academic departments of modern languages and literatures, and the association has become the chief professional organization for those involved in language and literature study.

Eric L. Montenyohl

See also Child, Francis James; Hand, Wayland D.; Kittredge, George Lyman; Lomax, John Avery; Lord, Albert Bates; Taylor, Archer; Thompson, Stith; Utley, Francis Lee

✳✳✳✳✳✳✳✳✳✳✳✳✳✳✳✳✳

References

Fisher, John H. "Remembrance and Reflection: *PMLA* 1884–1982." *Publications of the Modern Language Association* 99 (1984): 398–407.

Montenyohl, Eric L. "Folklore Studies in the Modern Language Association." *Midwestern Folklore* 17 (1991): 110–124.

Parker, William Riley. "The MLA, 1883–1953." *Publications of the Modern Language Association* 68 (1953): 3–39.

Zielonka, Alfred Walter. "The Modern Language Association of America, 1883–1960: An Historical Account of Selected Activities." Ph.D. dissertation, State University of New York at Buffalo, 1964.

Zumwalt, Rosemary. *American Folklore Scholarship: A Dialogue of Dissent.* Bloomington: Indiana University Press, 1988.

MOMADAY, NAVARRE SCOTT (1934–)

Navarre Scott Momaday, a Kiowa Indian, combines traditional, folkloristic elements of American Indian culture with modern, Western artistic and literary forms. Numerous awards (including a Pulitzer Prize for fiction in 1969 for *House Made of Dawn*) and decades of critical praise have established him as one of the greatest American writers: he deserves credit for the renaissance in American Indian literature. Momaday bridges and merges cultures in artistic expressions—embodying the folkloristic principle of dynamism of tradition, learning from and connecting to his past, and innovating and shaping the future.

Momaday often weaves traditional myths and legends of his ancestors into his stories, so that in many cases they become integral to his imagery and messages (*The Way to Rainy Mountain* [1969], *The Names: A Memoir* [1977], and *The Ancient Child* [1989]). *The Way to Rainy Mountain* may be the best representation of why his work is of interest to folklorists, as in that work he combines myth, history, personal experience narratives, anecdotes, and poetry to provide a rich account of the Kiowa people. The book was illustrated by his father. Momaday uses various media (fiction, nonfiction, poetry, and drama) to express his visions and paints, teaches, and is a notable raconteur. His work as a painter and a storyteller links him to traditional Kiowa media of artistic expression.

Family connection is one of the typically Native American elements of Momaday's work. His fascination with his Kiowa roots (through his father) began when he was a child. He often uses traditional American Indian narratives, symbols, ceremonies, characters, and themes in his writing, many of which he has experienced, collected, or observed. Momaday concerns himself with the act of imagining oneself, as a human, or as an American Indian, which both he and his one-eighth Cherokee mother find "essential" (see *The Names: A Memoir*). Momaday's writing consistently addresses such issues as emerging identity, particularly in terms of Native Americans in the late twentieth century. The character Abel in *House Made of Dawn* struggles to find his way as does Set (which means "bear" in Kiowa) Lockman in *The Ancient Child*. A half-Kiowa Indian raised primarily in the Euramerican world, Set visits relatives in Oklahoma and receives a sacred medicine bundle. The medicine confuses Set until a "full Indian"—half Kiowa, half

Navajo—woman helps him complete his transformation into what one might call his true self.

Momaday's consciousness was shaped by the Native Americans he lived among, both in the Southwest (where he was raised, where Abel lives, and where Set has his transformation) and the Plains (especially Oklahoma, home of his Kiowa relatives). Momaday's tribal name, *Tsoai-talee* [Rock Tree Boy], connects him to a place sacred in Kiowa legend, Devils Tower in the Black Hills of South Dakota (known to the Kiowa as Rock Tree). The bear from the etiological Kiowa legend associated with Devils Tower lives in Momaday's imagination and in much of his work.

Place also looms in Momaday's imagination and work. He often dwells lovingly on descriptions of landscape, especially the Kiowa homeland in the Plains. Vivid and powerful descriptions of nature aid Momaday's attempt to imagine a traditional worldview. Connection to the land, and a deep appreciation of it, are the hallmarks of the numerous Native American writers since Momaday's success opened the way for them. His success definitely inspired others and made literary critics and publishers accept Native Americans as viable writers.

Momaday's profound imaginative ability—sometimes compared to that of Franz Kafka, James Joyce, William Faulkner, and magical realists—enables him to express other realities so convincingly that he often persuades his readers of the possibility of such transformations, metaphors, and fluidity. Like the characters in his books, Momaday lives among several cultures: Indian and Euramerican; traditional and modern; Kiowa, Western, and American; folk and academic (Ph.D. Stanford 1963, and English professor for almost 30 years). His creative endeavors express something fundamental about traditional and modern Native American cultures but also about the existential dilemmas of identity and being that are more universal. Momaday's successful and productive negotiation among cultures and traditions makes his works resonate with many members of our increasingly multicultural world.

Mary Magoulick

See also Faulkner, William; Joyce, James; Legend; Myth; Personal Experience Story

✳✳✳✳✳✳✳✳✳✳✳✳✳✳✳✳✳

References

Momaday, N. Scott. *The Ancient Child*. New York: Doubleday, 1989.
———. *House Made of Dawn*. New York: Harper and Row, 1968.

———. *The Names: A Memoir.* New York: Harper and Row, 1977.

———. *The Way to Rainy Mountain.* Albuquerque: University of New Mexico Press, 1969.

Woodard, Charles L. *Ancestral Voices: Conversations with N. Scott Momaday.* Lincoln: University of Nebraska Press, 1989.

MONOGENESIS

Monogenesis refers to the theory that there is a single origin for any traditional narrative, which is a major tenet of the historic-geographic method. Adherents propose that each story, or tale-type, has its own history and that the oral transmission of any original text created variants which could lead back to a hypothetical ur-form, or archetype, of the tale. Usually, the earliest version of a tale is preserved in written literature, sometimes in quite ancient texts. Even earlier oral versions may have derived from the original tale, which may be reconstructed through comparative historical-geographical analysis.

Strict adherence to the principle of monogenesis has often been challenged. Various theories maintain the possibility of polygenesis (many beginnings) in certain cases. Narratives could emerge independently at different times and places because of universal rituals surrounding the life cycle of humans everywhere. Proponents of a myth-ritual theory of narrative believe that ritual origins operate apart from historical incidence, that ritual becomes drama, and that drama becomes narrative. Carl Jung and his followers argue that a collective unconscious inherited by people everywhere creates a superorganic collection of archetypes, which in turn lead to the creation of universally known mythic characters and events.

Some supporters of the basic principle of monogenesis for folk narrative have favored a more complex view. Carl Wilhelm von Sydow (1878–1952), an eminent Swedish folklorist, challenged a strict interpretation of monogenesis. His writings modified the thinking of many scholars by showing that regional subtypes, or oicotypes of the international tale-types, had their own separate histories and that those histories figured more importantly than a hypothetical single origin in antiquity.

Monogenesis remains the most accepted theory among folklorists for explaining the existence of multiple versions of the complex tales, such as märchen. Simple tales and smaller narrative units, such as episodes and motifs (the smallest narrative unit), can be created independently, and the diffusion of narrative texts through oral transmission is the process by which most tales have been disseminated. This process of diffusion is sometimes marked by the recording of a written version in literature by a known "author." Although we may never know for certain the single origin of a particular narrative, we can see that traditional tales are retold in oral versions and written literature.

Kenneth A. Thigpen

See also Historic-Geographic Method; Jung, Carl Gustav; Motif; Ritual; Sydow, Carl Wilhelm von; Tale-Type

✳✳✳✳✳✳✳✳✳✳✳✳✳✳✳✳✳

References

Kiefer, Emma Emily. *Albert Wesselski and Recent Folktale Theories.* Folklore Series no. 3. Bloomington: Indiana University Publications, 1947.

Krohn, Kaarle. *Die folkloristische Arbeitsmethode.* Oslo, Norway: The Institute for Comparative Research in Human Culture, 1926. Trans. Roger L. Welsch as *Folklore Methodology.* Austin: University of Texas Press, 1971.

Sydow, Carl Wilhelm von. *Selected Papers on Folklore.* Copenhagen: Rosenkilde and Bagger, 1948.

Thompson, Stith. *The Folktale.* New York: Holt, Rinehart and Winston, 1946.

Moraga, Cherríe (1952–)

Writer, poet, playwright, and lesbian activist, Cherríe Moraga was born in Whittier, California, and educated at San Francisco State University (M.A. 1980). Moraga's is an important presence in contemporary Chicano intellectual culture, for she gives voice to the persistent censure gay men and lesbians face in Mexican-American communities. As the daughter of an Anglo father and a Mexican mother, Moraga's narratives portray her personal attempts to integrate a mixed-race cultural heritage with a lesbian identity. In her original collection of writings, *Loving in the War Years* (1983), Moraga's concerns led her to examine the legendary Mexican figure of La Malinche ("the betrayer") in a lengthy essay entitled "A Long Line of Vendidas" ("women who sell out their people"). "The concept of betraying one's race through sex and sexual politics is as common as corn," Moraga states, and no folk legend illustrates the concept more than that of La Malinche.

Based on the historical person of Malintzin Tenepal—the young Aztec princess who in 1519 became the translator, adviser, and mistress to the Spanish conqueror of Mexico, Hernán Cortés—the legend of La Malinche locates the betrayal and conquest of the indigenous peoples of Mexico in the supposed untrustworthiness of female sexuality. This narrative, Moraga and other Chicana feminist theorists contend, passes on a legacy of ambivalence and misgivings about female sexuality to contemporary Mexican-American women. It encourages them to suspect one another of treachery and to place the men in their lives always before themselves. In short, La Malinche supports the notion of male supremacy. Ever aware of the relationships between sexual politics and racial identity, Moraga exposes the misogyny that structures the myth of La Malinche at the same time that she sympathetically reexamines the historical context in which the person, Malintzin, made choices that Moraga argues persuasively are comprehensible.

Moraga is also one of the first and most important compilers of political and creative writing by women of color. She coedited with Gloria Anzaldúa *This Bridge Called My Back: Writings by Radical Women of Color* (1981) and edited *Cuentos: Stories by Latinas* (1983).

Krista Comer

See also Latino and Chicano Folklore and Literature; Legend

✳✳✳✳✳✳✳✳✳✳✳✳✳✳✳✳✳✳✳

References

Gomez, Alma, and Mariana Romo-Carmona, eds. *Cuentos: Stories by Latinas*. New York: Kitchen Table Women of Color Press, 1983.

Herrera-Sobek, María, and Helena María Viramontes. *Chicana Creativity and Criticism: Charting New Frontiers in American Literature*. Houston: Arte Público, 1988.

Horno-Delgado, Asuncion, et al., eds. *Breaking Boundaries: Latina Writing and Critical Readings*. Amherst: University of Massachusetts Press, 1989.

Moraga, Cherríe, and Gloria Anzaldúa, eds. *This Bridge Called My Back: Writings by Radical Women of Color*. Watertown, Mass.: Persephone Press, 1981.

Morrison, Toni (1931–)

An African-American writer born in Lorain, Ohio, to George and Ramah Willis Wofford, Toni Morrison received her B.A. degree from Howard University in 1953 and her M.A. from Cornell in 1955. She has been an editor at Random House; has taught at Texas Southern University, Bard College, Howard University, and Yale University; and more recently has been the Robert F. Goheen Professor in the Humanities at Princeton University. Her fiction includes *The Bluest Eye* (1970), *Sula* (1975), *Song of Solomon* (1977), *Tar Baby* (1981), *Beloved* (1987), and *Jazz* (1992). Morrison received the National Book Critic's Circle Award for *Song of Solomon* and the Pulitzer Prize for Fiction for *Beloved*.

Morrison "saturates" her fiction with folklore, using gossip, music, celebrations, and the tales of her mother and father and aunts. In her emphasis on the transmission of the tale, its orality as well as its content, she follows in the tradition of Zora Neale Hurston. For Morrison, to write is to "hook" the reader/"listener" into participation with the tale itself, using a technique similar to the call and response of the black preacher. In her first novel, *The Bluest Eye*, storytelling itself is as important as the stories told of the great black migration shortly before World War II, the exodus from the rural sharecropper South to the so-called promised land of the urban, ghettoized North.

Although Morrison uses a number of folktales in each of her novels, generally she tends to concentrate on one or two, varying, modifying, reshaping them: the "blinking" black man tale, which becomes an extended "nigger" joke in *Sula*; the flying Africans and the singing

Nobel prize–winning author Toni Morrison infuses her fiction with the folklore of her African-American heritage.

bones in *Song of Solomon;* the "pitch" of the trickster figure in *Tar Baby*. Perhaps *Beloved* reveals Morrison's most complex use of folklore to date: in its story of demonology (slavery itself), it is a ghost tale, a ghostly tale, the polyvocal story (stories) of "Sixty Million / and more." This novel, so rich in the telling, with its admixture of history, folklore, biblical myth, music, and celebration, was followed by *Jazz*, with its balladlike structure, its singer-narrators, its blues-like story loops lacking closure, its riffs and improvisations—all strategies of rehearsing and replaying the tale of the woman (and man) wronged.

Morrison's use of folklore questions its meaning in the very retelling and reshaping of the tales and culture of her people. Conscious of the interplay between storytelling and audience response, she says: "It [the language] must not sweat. . . . It is the thing that black people love so much—the saying of words" (LeClair 1981, p. 27). In Morrison's work, the language does not sweat, it sings.

Josie Campbell

See also Hurston, Zora Neale; Orality

****

References

Awkward, Michael. *Inspiriting Influences: Tradition, Revision, and Afro-American Women's Novels*. New York: Columbia University Press, 1989.

Harris, Trudier. *Fiction and Folklore: The Novels of Toni Morrison*. Knoxville: University of Tennessee Press, 1991.

LeClair, Thomas. "The Language Must Not Sweat: A Conversation with Toni Morrison." *New Republic*, March 21, 1981, 25–28.

Watkins, Mel. "Talk with Toni Morrison." *New York Times Book Review*, September 11, 1977, 48–50.

Motif

A motif is a memorable and recognizable element within a composition. Folk narratives consist of such traditional elements, and beginning in the nineteenth century, folklorists looked for multiple examples of motifs in order to discover their various forms and distributions. Even as early folktale scholars concentrated on tale-types, it was evident that there were traditional episodes and descriptive details that belonged in different tales. American folktale scholar Stith Thompson found that Native American tales were configured not so much as integral tale-types, but as incidents that might be strung together in different patterns. Similarly, French folktale scholar Emmanuel Cosquin, in looking for Asian analogues to Western tales, was often able to trace episodes (which he called themes) more effectively than complete tales.

In order to provide access to analogous narrative material from all parts of the world, Thompson devised the *Motif Index of Folk Literature*, which he first published in six volumes between 1932 and 1936. He defined a motif as the smallest element in a tale having the power to persist independently in tradition. This definition did not satisfy all of his critics, so, in answer to the question, What is a motif? he explained:

> Certain items in narrative keep on being used by storytellers; they are the stuff out of which tales are made. It makes no difference exactly what they are like; if they are actually used in the construction of tales, they are considered to be motifs. As a matter of fact, there must be something of particular interest to make an item important enough to be remembered, something not quite commonplace. (Thompson 1955, p. 7)

Thompson's list of motifs does not pretend to be complete. He designed the numbering system to accommodate additional material, and scholars frequently identify new material that should be included in the index when it is next revised.

The concept of motif came to folklore from literary criticism, which in turn had taken it from art and music. The word implies motivation, a moving force, but many of the items listed in the *Motif Index* are static. Thompson chose to be inclusive in order to cover a great amount of material with as little difficulty as possible. He wrote:

> Sometimes the interest of a student of traditional narrative may be centered on a certain type of character in a tale, sometimes on an action, sometimes on attendant circumstances of the action. Hence I have endeavored to use all the elements of tales that have in the past been objects of special study and similar elements that are likely to serve as such objects in the future. (Thompson 1955, Vol. 1, p. 11)

Structuralists prefer to separate action motifs from characters and attendant circumstances. Thus, Russian folklorist Vladimir

Propp distinguished functions from characters, and American folk-lorist Alan Dundes introduced the term *motifeme*, an action motif as defined from within a particular narrative.

Christine Goldberg

See also Cosquin, Emmanuel; Historic-Geographic Method; Propp, Vladimir I.; Tale-Type; Theme; Thompson, Stith

✳✳✳✳✳✳✳✳✳✳✳✳✳✳✳✳✳✳

References

Ben-Amos, Dan. "The Concept of the Motif in Folklore." In *Folklore Studies in the Twentieth Century*, ed. Venetia Newall, pp. 17–36. Woodbridge, Eng.: Brewer; Totowa, N.J.: Rowman and Littlefield, 1980.

Dundes, Alan. "From Etic to Emic Units in the Structural Study of Folktales." *Journal of American Folklore* 75 (1962): 95–105.

Lüthi, Max. "Motiv, Zug, Thema aus Sicht der Volkserzählungsforschung." In *Elemente der Literatur*, ed. Adam T. Bisanz and Raymond Trousson, vol. 1, pp. 11–24. Stuttgart: Kröner, 1980.

Thompson, Stith. *Motif Index of Folk Literature*. 6 vols. Bloomington: Indiana University Press, 1955–1958 (1932–1936).

———. *Narrative Motif-Analysis as a Folklore Method*. Folklore Fellows Communication no. 161. Helsinki: Academia Scientiarum Fennica, 1955.

Muir, Edwin (1887–1959)

The Scottish poet, translator, and critic Edwin Muir sought in his work to reconcile his rural childhood in the Orkney Islands with the family tragedies and sense of entrapment in a spiritual and industrial wasteland that he experienced when he moved as an adolescent to Glasgow. This progression is described in *The Story and the Fable* (1940) and later reworked as the first part of *An Autobiography* (1954).

With the support of his wife, teacher and novelist Willa Anderson Muir, he moved in 1919 to London where he helped to edit the magazine *The New Age*. He also embarked on a period of psychoanalysis, which released some of the powerful imagery that found its way into his poetry. A period in Prague from 1921 to the outbreak of World War II led to his "rediscovering the world of life" and a new maturity of creativity: "I began to write poetry at thirty-five instead of at twenty-five or twenty" (Muir 1987). He and Willa also first translated Franz Kafka's work into English and became involved in the work of PEN, an international association of poets, playwrights, essayists, editors, and novelists.

Autobiography, interwoven with classical mythology, creates a powerful, allusive, and personal yet universal symbolism throughout Muir's work. The sense of a lost idyll, the island Eden of his childhood, took on wider significance after the devastation of Europe in two protracted wars. Some of his finest poetry appears in the collection *One Foot in Eden* (1956), in which he rehearses some of his most potent themes, creation and creativity, and explores them through a fusion of Christian and classical mythology. Landscapes of inescapable loss and ruin are peopled by figures like Oedipus and Persephone, who are condemned to bring grief by actions they are compelled to take. A recurrent image is Penelope, who, like the poet, "wove and unwove a web all day / That might have been a masterpiece" (Butter 1991, p. 224). The same collection also offers, in the much-anthologized "The Horses," the hope of a new world in which humanity and the animal world can cooperate harmoniously, "their coming our beginning" (Butter 1991, p. 226).

Muir's European perspective led him away from some of the developments in Scottish writing in the mid-twentieth century, as is shown by his own somewhat acerbic view of the bleakness of Scottish culture in *Scottish Journey* (originally published in 1935): "This land was songless" (Muir 1979, p. 38). After the publication of Muir's *Scott and Scotland* (1936), this view of the use of Scots language in poetry led to conflict with the Scottish poet Christopher Murray Grieve (pseudonym Hugh MacDiarmid). However, Muir was greatly drawn to the traditional Scottish ballads and the storytelling traditions of his childhood, and much of his poetry is influenced by ballad meter and structure. Before his death, he proposed a full-length work on the ballads, which was finally undertaken by Willa Muir and published as *Living with the Ballads* (1965); it is still a stimulating entry to ballad study.

Elaine Petrie

See also Ballad; Grieve, Christopher Murray; Myth; Scottish Literature; Storytelling

✳✳✳✳✳✳✳✳✳✳✳✳✳✳✳✳✳

References

Butter, Peter, ed. *The Complete Poems of Edwin Muir*. Aberdeen: Association for Scottish Literary Studies, 1991.

McCulloch, Margery. *Edwin Muir: Poet, Critic, and Novelist*. Edinburgh: Edinburgh University Press, 1993.

Muir, Edwin. *An Autobiography*. London: Hogarth Press, 1987 (1954).

———. *Scottish Journey*. Edinburgh: Mainstream Publishing, 1979.

MUNRO, ALICE (1931–)

The Canadian fiction writer Alice Munro was born in Wingham, Ontario, received her B.A. from the University of Western Ontario, and has thus far published nine collections of short stories and a quasi-novel entitled *Lives of Girls and Women* (1971). Her earlier fiction, which uses many aspects of the bildungsroman, stayed close to her own experience, concentrating on her childhood, the lives of married and divorced women, and the world of Huron County, Ontario, where Munro grew up and where she has lived since the mid-1970s. In recent collections, however, she has moved away from her own experience to exercises in historical re-creation. Munro's fiction has been acclaimed for its ability to present ordinary events with a magical intensity and clarity. Her intricately constructed stories juxtapose disparate narratives, and the reader is left to sort out the connections among them. The stories are informed by a feminist understanding of sexual relations but make an ironic rather than an overt critique of patriarchal power.

Canadian folklorist Carole Carpenter has noted that Canadians of English, and to a lesser degree Scottish, descent neglect and even deny their own folklore, a term they associate with "ethnic" groups outside the mainstream of Canadian culture. Munro does not employ folklore in any conventional sense, but because of her acute sensitivity to the speech patterns and unconscious assumptions of her often rural characters she is a superb recorder of Anglo-Scottish, Protestant Canadian folkways. In one of her earliest stories, "Walker Brothers Cowboy" (*Dance of the Happy Shades* [1968]), the child narrator is fascinated and puzzled by the phrase "She digs with the wrong foot," used by her aunts to designate a Catholic. More typically, Munro shows her characters' consciousness as embedded in a web of texts drawn from all levels and aspects of culture: a working-class father reciting to himself a passage from *The Tempest*, for example, in "Royal Beatings" (*Who Do You Think You Are?* [1978]).

Munro is particularly sensitive to the meanings of clothing and music. In "Accident" (*Moons of Jupiter* [1982]), which takes place in a small Ontario town in 1943, she gives a careful and complete description of the heroine's clothes ("fashionable for that year") and records the pieces being prepared by the school choir for its Christmas concert ("He Shall Feed His Flock," "The Huron Carol," "Hearts of Oak," "The Desert Song," and "The Holy City"). Such culturally significant catalogs and such precise references to the details of particular times and places give Munro's fiction an almost anthropological character. In this sense, Munro could be called the best folklorist among Canadian writers. Although critics have as yet paid little attention to Munro's use of tall tales, riddles, fairy tale motifs, and other transformed elements of traditional folklore, her fiction is rich in such material. For example, wild men (and women) and trickster figures recur throughout her work, the most striking example being Milton Homer, a "simple" man who plays a pivotal role in *Who Do You Think You Are?*

Besides her skill in choosing the telling detail, Munro shows a constant interest in storytelling. In "Royal Beatings," the heroine not only turns her own life into dramatic fantasies but is intrigued by tales of the beatings given by townsfolk to a local butcher who may have had incestuous relations with his daughter. Munro's fiction plays constantly with the paradox of stories as both revelations and concealments, "open secrets," as the title of her 1994 collection would have it. Her careful attention to the surface of Anglo-Canadian culture, combined with her postmodern sense that subjectivity is the function of various competing discourses, gives Munro's fiction a double aspect, at once realistic and metafictional, which allows her to record with unusual insight the complex interactions of consciousness and culture.

Douglas Freake

See also *Bildungsroman*; Fairy Tale; Shakespeare, William; Storytelling; Tall Tale; Trickster; Wild Man; Women

✳✳✳✳✳✳✳✳✳✳✳✳✳✳✳✳✳

References

Carpenter, Carole. *Many Voices: A Study of Folklore Activities in Canada and Their Role in Canadian Culture.* Ottawa: National Museums of Canada, 1979.

Carscallen, James. "Alice Munro." In *Profiles in Canadian Literature,* 2, ed. Jeffrey M. Heath, pp. 73–80. Toronto: Dundurn Press, 1980.

Fowler, Rowena. "The Art of Alice Munro: The Beggar Maid and Lives of Girls and Women." *Critique: Studies in Contemporary Fiction* 25 (1984): 189–198.

Hoy, Helen. "'Alice and Janet': Alice Munro's Metafiction." *Canadian Literature* 121 (1989): 59–83.

MYTH

Folklorists define myth as a sacred narrative, originating in oral tradition, that focuses on interaction of the human and divine worlds. Unfortunately, a widely held assumption that myth means "false belief" perpetuates ethnocentric deprecation of another group's or culture's serious, value-laden narratives. Because everyday language easily ignores folklore scholarship, however, it is probable that myth will continue to appear in contexts unrelated to narratives, divinity, or a culture's principal value system. Journalists will therefore continue to write of "the myth of supply-side economics," politicians of "the myth of the American dream," literary theorists of "the myth of origin of the English language," and so on.

If folklorists could control language use, myth would refer to an oral prose narrative regarded as sacred and true within the society that tells it, set in the remote past in a world unlike the present one. In anthropologist William Bascom's tripartite classification of oral prose narratives, myth is distinguished from legend, which is told as true about sacred or secular matters in the recent, historical past, and is distinguished also from folktale, which is fictional and ahistorical. This set of definitions brings comparative order to masses of cross-cultural materials and also has counterparts in indigenous systems of classification. In the early twentieth century, for example, the anthropologist/sociologist Bronislaw Malinowski found among Trobriand Islanders three kinds of narratives: *liliu,* which are true and sacred and serious; *libwogwo,* which refer to events and persons in the recent past; and *kukwanebu,* performed as leisure-time entertainment.

Sacred narratives occur in the oral verbal art of nearly every culture known, dating as far back in time as records exist. The word *myth* itself, however, did not enter English until 1830. Related terms like "mythical" and "mythological" were used several centuries earlier and persisted through the Middle Ages in Latin compilations like the *Mitologiae* of Fulgentius (c. 550 C.E.). Myth came into English directly from Late Latin *mythos* or *mythus;* so did its cognates including the French *mythe,* Spanish *mito,* German *Mythe,* and Russian *Muo.* In the early Christian era, *mythos* was adopted from the Greek as a synonym for the word *fabula* ("story," "tale"). Thereafter, though basically neutral, both terms were sometimes applied to Greco-Roman narratives that were specifically regarded as fictional, compared to the sacred narratives that were told as true within Christian society.

Origin myths are found in most cultures worldwide; this scene depicts Hebrew beliefs about human creation.

Earlier, *mythos* had entered Late Latin as a transliteration of a Greek word with a range of meanings all positing oral speech, though not necessarily narrative: word, saying, story, fiction, and so on. In its very earliest uses, according to commentator Richard P. Martin, 155 of 167 occurrences of *mythos* in the *Iliad* refer to speech acts, that is, to authoritative oral words that cause something to happen (e.g., commands, threats, boasts, proposals, prayers).

Authoritative fascination with the twice-adopted word myth has surely caused something to happen during past centuries in Europe. During the eighteenth and nineteenth centuries, universities began subdividing into academic specialties, whereupon each relevant discipline developed its own approach, which was too often presented as exclusively correct and universally applicable to all mythologies. Anthropologists at first connected myths to rituals, but they now investigate each myth's function within its specific society. Literary critics and art historians analyze individuals' creative reworkings of mythological sources, folklorists document cross-cultural comparisons of motifs and entire narratives, and psychologists link myths to dreams and to shared human experiences of birth and childhood. Classical scholars reconsider familiar mythological texts, taking into account new developments in archaeology and in textual scholarship for other ancient societies besides Greece and Rome.

Along with classicists, present-day theologians and historians of religion can claim continuity with their medieval predecessors' efforts to establish relationships between Christian myths and the sacred narratives of previous and parallel cultures. For a millennium and a half, Christian educators confronted the problem articulated by Augustine of Hippo (354–430 C.E.) by seeking ways to justify the teaching of Virgil, Ovid, and other tellers of pagan myths. One solution was allegory: for example, the lengthy *Ovide moralisé* (c. 1300) assigns Christian meanings to each character and situation in Ovid's *Metamorphoses*. Academic theologians now eschew allegory. Like the classicists, they now consider familiar narratives (from the Bible) in light of new discoveries in archaeology and various ancient societies' verbal art. However, some recent writers for popular audiences reinvent the wheel by proposing one-to-one allegorical translations of myths, or even literal interpretations—that everything said to have happened really did happen—resembling those credited to Euhemerus of Messene (c. 300 B.C.E.).

Given the long history of interpretation and the longer history of telling myths in just the much-studied European culture alone, and given the realization that parallel developments in non-Western cultures must be considered on their own terms rather than wrenched into alignment with Europe, it seems unlikely that there will soon be one limited definition of myth agreeable to all academic disciplines. Users of the term should tread cautiously in the meantime, ever aware that one person's false belief may well be another person's sacred narrative.

Betsy Bowden

See also Frazer, James George; Freud, Sigmund; *The Golden Bough*; Jung, Carl Gustav; Motif; Structuralism

✳✳✳✳✳✳✳✳✳✳✳✳✳✳✳✳✳

References

Dundes, Alan, ed. *Sacred Narrative: Readings in the Theory of Myth*. Berkeley: University of California Press, 1984.

Feldman, Burton, and Robert D. Richardson. *The Rise of Modern Mythology, 1680–1860*. Bloomington: Indiana University Press, 1972.

Martin, Richard P. *The Language of Heroes: Speech and Performance in the Iliad*. Ithaca, N.Y.: Cornell University Press, 1989.

Morford, Mark P. O., and Robert J. Lenardon. *Classical Mythology*. 4th ed. White Plains, N.Y.: Longman, 1991.

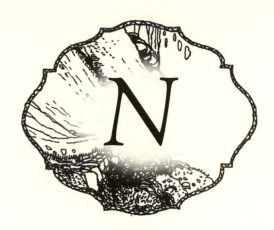

NAMES

Both storytelling in the folk-cultural register and literary narration are essentially engaged with the creation of true, or at least believable, chunks of a past that never was while the onomastic, or naming, strategies employed in the creation of such pasts, both in terms of time and space, differ significantly. Since the folktale past is not just ahistorical but also acartographic, the use of identifying place-names is inappropriate and therefore rare. A sequence of events that "once upon a time" took place "beyond the beyond" or "in a part of the country where strangers seldom came" or "on the edge of a forest" does not require, is in fact not expected, to be accurately located (and therefore locatable) through recognizable names, indeed through any names at all. The spatial dimension of a folktale past is not namable, unless namelessness may be considered a kind of naming, too.

By contrast, the believability of historical and contemporary legends, their claim to veracity, depends in no small measure on allegedly accurate dates and verifiable named places. For instance, events in 10 randomly chosen *Sagen* (numbers 201–210) in the Grimm brothers' collection are supposed to have happened, respectively, in Halberstadt, at the Visper River, in Dassel, in Schartfeld, in Cologne, near Altenburg, in Schiltach (on April 10, 1533), in Schwarzenstein, in Saxony, and after the battle of Ditmar. Likewise, most versions of the "Vanishing Hitchhiker" legend are associated with a specific location—frequently, and not unnaturally, with a named street or road.

These toponymic characteristics of the two folk narrative genres are not paralleled by the naming practices concerning the protagonists in folktales and legends. It could, in fact, almost be claimed that the reverse is true, for it is in the legends that the main characters are usually unnamed, unless a historical personality is involved. The actions in the same 10 *Sagen* already quoted are ascribed to the citizens (of Halberstadt), a shepherd, a diver/farmer, a monk and a knight (as well as Emperor Henry IV), builders and their wives (in an alternative version, the builder is called Master Gerhard), the master of the house, a woman innkeeper, a very wealthy maiden, and 12 foot soldiers. Not surprisingly, the persons who encounter the vanishing hitchhiker (herself or himself also nameless) are normally not named but are referred to as "one of my girlfriend's best friends and her father"; a traveling man; a friend of the narrator; "a fellow I know"; Mike, the cab driver; people; Mr. and Mrs. Robert Nuddin; young men; a young man; a taxi driver; a priest; a woman; a friend's "fiancé and her aunt who's a nun"; "someone Miss Packard knew, unfortunately I cannot remember the person's name"; and an unnamed narrator of a first-person story. It is, as has often been demonstrated, part of the nature of such legends that the bizarre events they relate are told of an unnamed friend of a friend (the FOAF syndrome).

Folktale protagonists and other characters are also often nameless—a man; a woodcutter and his wife; a fisherman, a wife, and a king; twelve princesses and a nobleman; a gentleman, his wife, a godmother, and a prince, etc.—or bear generic names like Jack, Tom, and Will. When they are named, their names tend to be apt and more often than not express part of their nature, particularly in the way the world sees them: Little Red Riding Hood, Snow White, Cinderella, John the Bear, Tom Thumb, Rapunzel, Parsilette. Such names are like onomastic clothes that outwardly proclaim who their bearers are.

This tendency also applies when appearances are deliberately intended to deceive, as when persecuted innocent heroines disguise themselves, temporarily and expediently hiding their aristocratic nature under demeaning coverings like Allerleirauh (All-Kinds-of-Fur), Katie Woodencloak, Cap o' Rushes, Rashiecaat, Donkey Skin, Catskin, Tattercoats, and other sisters in distress (AT 501B). The fact that both the nameless and the named characters are unidentifiable outside the folktales in which they are actors goes without saying; one cannot recognize a person in an unrecognizable place at an unrecognizable time, and listeners to, or readers of, folk narratives have no expectations in this respect.

Literary authors, on the other hand, have all these options available in addition to several other onomastic tactics reflecting the naming practices of their own culture or of the cultural settings of their stories. These authors are at liberty to choose individual names for the purpose of identifying places and persons within the covers of the fiction they are writing, as well as to select modes of presenting them in relationship to other names. They may, for example, decide to infiltrate fictitious names of characters of their own invention into a society defined by the presence of names of historical persons or smuggle invented place-names into a nomenclature of real names of places. Such attempts almost inevitably lead to the fictionalizing of the actual names and the actualization or factualization of the fictitious ones. Literary retellings or reshapings of folk narratives rely heavily on a transfer of names from the original stories to their literary adaptations, especially in their titles. Such onomastic references may, however, also be made in titles of art literature that are only vaguely related to the folktales in question, either in theme or in plot—as, for instance, some of Ed McBain's detective novels, which are set in Florida and feature the lawyer Matthew Hope as the main sleuth, have the titles *Goldilocks, Rumpelstiltskin, Beauty and the Beast, Jack and the Beanstalk, Snow White and Rose Red, Cinderella.*

The giving and using of names are as essential human traits as telling stories and listening to them. It is not surprising, therefore, that names are such central ingredients in all narrative performances in all cultural registers. Sometimes it might even be claimed that names tell their own stories.

W. F. H. Nicolaisen

See also Folktale; Folktale Adaptations; Grimm, Jacob and Wilhelm; Legend

✳✳✳✳✳✳✳✳✳✳✳✳✳✳✳✳✳✳

References

Nicolaisen, W. F. H. "Literary Names as Texts: Personal Names in Sir Walter Scott's *Waverley*." *Nomina* 3 (1979): 29–39.

———. "Names and Narratives." *Journal of American Folklore* 97 (1984): 259–272.

———. "Names as Intertextual Devices." *Onomastica Canadiana* 68 (1986): 58–66.

———. "Names in Derivative Literature and Parodies." *Literary Onomastics Studies* 14 (1987): 49–67.

———. "An Onomastic Vernacular in Scottish Literature." In *Scotland and the Lowland Tongue*, ed. J. Derrick McClure, pp. 209–218. Aberdeen: Aberdeen University Press, 1983.

———. "The Past as Place." *Folklore* 102 (1991): 3–15.

Narayan, Rasipuram Krishnaswami (1906–)

Rasipuram Krishnaswami Narayan has been one of the leaders of what can be identified as the folklore movement in the English literature of India. "I like telling stories," Narayan stated in an interview in 1976, adding that if he had not become a writer he would have become a storyteller. Narayan established a folksy style of storytelling with the publication of his first novel, *Swami and Friends*, in 1935. After writing 13 more novels, four short-story collections, three sets of legends drawn from the Hindu scriptures, two travelogues, four essays, and one autobiographical account, he remains the acclaimed father figure of contemporary Indian English fiction. His work also represents a link between folklore and literature.

Narayan's stories take the reader to Malgudi, a fictional town located somewhere between the two southern Indian cities of Madras and Mysore where he grew up and has lived all his life. His stories are all about common people whose lives are touched by something uncommon. The folk base for Narayan's fiction is traceable to his childhood and his grandmother who told him stories of gods and demons from the *Ramayana*, the *Mahabharata*, the puranas, and the jātakas. Myths and legends of the Tamil-speaking Madras area where he grew up also had a strong impact on his fiction. The grandmother, the village storyteller, and the learned swami who interpreted the scriptures shaped Narayan's imagination as he turned to these oral traditions in molding his art.

Consciously and subconsciously, Narayan has sought a folk aesthetics to govern his fictive world of folk characters. Most apparent is the mythic theme that is dominant in his religious legend collection, *Gods, Demons, and Others* (1964), *The Ramayana* (1972), *The Mahabharata* (1978), and *Man-Eater of Malgudi* (1945). In recasting popular Hindu myths and legends as his own stories, Narayan infuses a realistic element for his readers inside and outside India. In his 1964 essay "The World of the Story-Teller," Narayan explained that his method was to "allow the original episodes to make their impact on my mind as a writer, and rewrite them in my own terms, from recollection" (Narayan 1964). The gripping drama of fights between great kings and their monstrous enemies, battles between warring factions of ancient royalty, and curses and blessings pronounced by the powerful over the powerless have inspired Narayan to modernize the scriptural myths. Narayan strengthens his mythic connection in *The World of Nagaraj* (1990), in which the protagonist tries to write a book about Narayan, the storyteller in the Hindu pantheon.

The theme of religious life is also significant in the folkloric writings of Narayan. The protagonist in *The Guide* (1958) is the glib-talking ex-convict who walks into a village and is mistaken for a swami with supernatural powers. Narayan draws upon the tradition of ascetics and the role holy men have played in village life to build his plot and develop his characters. The yogi works miracles and performs a rain ritual called *bagirathan*, which involves fasting and prayer to end the drought. Narayan uses the rain ritual and the idea of sainthood perpetuated in rural communities to keep folk religion as an essential ingredient of his fiction. *The Financial Expert* (1953) is the story of ironic twists and turns in the life of a local wizard, Margayya. In the process of portraying the character of the financier whose relations with his son remain rocky, the novelist emphasizes the significance of worshiping Lakshmi, the goddess of wealth. Details of *Lakshmi Puja*, a 40-day propitiation of the goddess, constitute a vital element of the work, juxtaposing the adherence to tradition by the father and the abandonment of tradition by the son.

The survival of rural traditions in urban settings is another focus Narayan develops in a later novel, *The Painter of Signs* (1976). Set in the Malgudi of 1972, the love affair of Rama and Daisy parallels that of King Santhanu and the goddess Ganga in human form found in the first book of the *Mahabharata* and often retold in oral tradition. The myth survives in Narayan's novel through a process of adaptation and integration. "God and Cobbler," which first appeared in *Playboy* (February 2, 1976) and was later included in the short-story collection *Malgudi Days* (1982), is a good example of how Hindu myths have survived in Narayan's works as common knowledge shared by his characters and sometimes by his readers. The survival of another tradition, the belief in spirit possession, is the core idea of Narayan's novel *The English Teacher* (1945), which many critics have found to be autobiographical. If so, Narayan may be making a personal statement about the positive values of folk traditions.

The lure of village life and the permanence of rural folk culture is one more theme Narayan has found invaluable for many of his short stories. "Under the Banyan Tree" (1947) evokes the village tradition of storytelling by the local raconteur, and "Such Perfection," which also appeared in the collection *An Astrologer's Day and Other Stories* (1947), recaptures the belief that the perfection of an idol must have some minor imperfection to avoid the wrath of that deity.

Re-creation and dramatization is the technique Narayan employs in another short story, "Naga," which was first published in the *New Yorker* of August 26, 1972. This story of a snake charmer and his son brings back to life the profession of the snake charmer and some related snake lore. Belief in ghosts, return of the dead to the scene of death, and poltergeist phenomena dominate the plot, character portrayal, and atmosphere in another set of short stories narrated by the local raconteur, whom Narayan identifies as "the talkative man" or T. M., the central figure in his 1986 novel, *Talkative Man*.

Narayan has also adapted stories about Gandhi. Narayan builds on oral accounts of Gandhi's accomplishments, songs, and chants popularized by Gandhi; worship of Gandhi as a god; common interpretations of Gandhi's satyagraha, or "truth force"; and the Gandhian lifestyle emulated by his followers. *Waiting for the Mahatma* (1955) depicts Gandhi's influence on the people of Malgudi, and *The Vendor of Sweets* (1967) explores the emergence of a Gandhi cult and the acceptance of Gandhi as a culture hero.

Southern Indian folklife, particularly its oral traditions, beliefs, and practices to which Narayan was exposed, is re-created in his fiction as part of a twofold process of integration and dramatization. The effect is the emergence of a new art form, one that is unique and appealing to the Indian and non-Indian reader alike. Narayan manages to bridge the gap between folk and literary aesthetics to give shape to what might be called folkloric fiction.

Mohammed S. Ansari

See also Legend; Myth; *Panchatantra*; Storytelling

✳✳✳✳✳✳✳✳✳✳✳✳✳✳✳✳✳✳

References

Ansari, Mohammed. "A Folk Connection: The Folklore Movement in English Literature of India." Ph.D. dissertation, Indiana University, 1986.

Hariprasanna, A. *The World of Malgudi: A Study of R. K. Narayan's Novels.* New Delhi: Prestige Books, 1994.

Iyengar, Srinivasa K. R. *Indian Writing in English.* New Delhi: Sterling Publishers, 1985.

Mukherjee, Meenakshi. *The Twice-Born Fiction: Themes and Techniques of the Indian Novel in English.* New Delhi: Heinemann, 1971.

Narayan, R. K. "The World of the Story-Teller." In Narayan, *Gods, Demons, and Others*, pp. 9–10. New York: Viking Press, 1964.

Pousse, Michel. *R. K. Narayan: A Painter of Modern India.* New York: Peter Lang, 1995.

Walsh, William. *R. K. Narayan: A Manifold Voice.* New York: Barnes and Noble, 1970.

NATIONALISM

A driving force behind the development of folklore studies, nation-alistic studies were in the beginning intimately associated with the efforts of zealous scholar-patriots who collected and studied the lore of the common folk, not just to satisfy their intellectual curiosity or to enlarge their understanding of human behavior, but primarily to lay the foundations on which their emergent nation-states would one day rest. In this movement, the nationalistic attempt to redraw political boundaries to fit the contours of ethnic bodies merged with the romantic emphasis on feeling and intuition, on nature, and on the past as the source of inspiration for the present. The resulting "romantic nationalism" turned researchers toward the golden age of yesteryear, where they would discover historical warrant for the establishment of independent nations as well as models to use in shaping the present and future. These models could be found pri-marily in the ancient folk traditions surviving among the peasant population in the countryside, a population living close to nature, unspoiled by the learning and cosmopolitanism of city life.

It can be shown that romantic nationalistic impulses existed as early as the sixteenth century. After the Reformation, monarchs in England and Sweden, attempting to consolidate power in their own hands, employed chroniclers to search the antiquities of their realms for evidence of a glorious past that would justify the establishment of strong central governments in the present. The impulses can also be seen in the eighteenth-century preromantic and antiquarian move-ments, which intensified interest in antiquities and in the folk who had kept them alive and resulted in works like Thomas Percy's influ-ential *Reliques of Ancient English Poetry* (1765), but the tenets of romantic nationalism are most clearly delineated in the writings of the German philosopher Johann Gottfried Herder (1744–1803).

The period of cultural unity that Herder believed had once existed in medieval Germany had, as a result of decades of war, largely disappeared by his time. The country had become fragmented into 1,800 different territories with an equal number of rulers. Worse still, the people had abandoned their own native cultural forms for foreign models—particularly those of the French. The German nobility had widely imitated the brilliant court life of Versailles, with the unfortu-nate consequence that French ideas and customs had filtered down to the middle classes and had widened the gap between them and the common people. French was the language of refinement and culture, and the German of the common people was considered vulgar. In literature, matters were equally bad. German writers not only used the French language but also based the form and content of their works on French and classical models. All this spelled disaster to Herder. He insisted that Germany must return to its own foundations or Germany was doomed. By showing the German people why building a national culture on native foundations was not only desirable but absolutely necessary, he formulated a set of principles of nationalism that have generally been held applicable to all nations struggling for independent existence.

First, Herder argued that each nation is a distinct organic unit created by its own peculiar environmental and historical circumstances and is different, therefore, from all other nations. The organic structures of these units were reflected in what he called national characters or national souls. Second, he argued that a nation could not survive as a nation unless it remained true to its national character; it must cultivate its own native cultural and artistic traditions along lines laid down by past experience. To introduce foreign elements into a unified organic nation, into the body politic, would ultimately lead to the death of the nation. Third, he argued that the cultural and historical pattern of a people—the national soul—is expressed best in a nation's language and especially in its folk poetry, the loftiest expression to which language could aspire. Folk poems he called "the archives of a nationality" (Herder 9:352), "the imprints of the soul" (Herder 3:29) of a nation. To live in harmony with this nation, to capture its special character and make it their own, the citizenry would have to absorb its poetry and live in accordance with its spirit.

Finally, Herder argued that when the continuity of a nation's cultural development has been interrupted, as it had been in Germany, the only salvation lay in collecting from the common people the lore surviving among them from the time before the break. From this lore, scholar-patriots could put the nation once more in touch with its true national spirit and thus make possible its future development on its own cultural foundations, speaking its own language and creating its own literary forms. In stirring words, Herder issued a call to action: "The voice of your fathers has faded and lies silent in the dust. . . . Lend a hand then, my brothers, and show our nation what it is and is not, how it thought and felt or how it thinks and feels" (Herder 9:530–531).

Herder's clarion call sounded not only in Germany but throughout much of Europe, inspiring nationalistic folklore studies in the Nordic countries (especially Finland and Norway) and in Central and Eastern Europe (especially among the Slavs). Throughout the nineteenth century, patriotic scholars, inspired by nationalistic sentiments, headed into the hinterlands to rescue from oblivion their countries' treasured folk heritages. In the twentieth century, as Third World countries have broken free from their colonial yokes and have focused attention on their own cultural heritages, the same stirring phrases about glorious national pasts and noble destinies that once moved Europeans to action have echoed through Asia and Africa.

In the United States, in words that bear a strong nationalistic imprint, Americanists like Richard M. Dorson have argued that a peculiarly American folklore has sprung from the circumstances of the country's geography and history. In the tales of swashbuckling, homespun American folk heroes can be found, argues Dorson, the genius of the American national character. Other U.S. scholars, turning their attention from the nation as a whole and focusing instead on the different immigrant and ethnic groups that populate the culturally diverse land, have attempted to locate the spirit, or cultural identity, of these groups in their folklore. As have their counterparts elsewhere, they have often found a spirit both noble and ennobling—and they have followed lines laid down long ago by Herder.

We realize today that the pasts to which romantic nationalists turned were, for the most part, mythic pasts, that the great and noble nations they wished to re-create were the products of their own fruitful imaginations. In the nineteenth century, the efforts of these nationalists often brought about salutary results, redressing historical inequities. But in the twentieth century, the movements have often taken on an extremist coloring as researchers have projected their own political ideals onto the past and have then used this imagined, or invented, past to sanction their ideals. In other words, the image of the cultural past supposedly reflected in the mirror of folklore, the image after which loyal citizens or group members are urged to pattern their behavior, will be determined by the political predispositions of the individual holding the mirror.

In nineteenth-century Finland, for example, romantic nationalists, breaking free from centuries of Swedish cultural domination, crisscrossed Finland's backwoods collecting ancient songs. They then used those songs to create a national epic, the *Kalevala*, to underpin the development of a native Finnish literature, to elevate the belittled Finnish language, and, in the process, to lay the foundation of Finland's future independence. Once independence had been achieved, however, intellectual leaders from both ends of the political spectrum interpreted Finnish folk poetry to fit their own views and then, in the name of loyalty to heritage, used this poetry to advocate diametrically opposed courses of political action—the political right to generate in the citizenry a militaristic posture and to argue for an expansionist foreign policy; the political left to counter the ideology of the right and to argue for a classless, communistic society.

In all likelihood, folklore-based nationalism will continue to play an important role in the contemporary world. As newly liberated peoples from the former Soviet Union attempt to constitute or reconstitute themselves as independent nations, many of them, in good Herderian fashion, are seeking in their folklore records of the past historical justification for their present actions. Unfortunately, in these efforts, as folklorist Roger Abrahams points out, "one people's nationalism can be transformed into the means by which other peoples are disenfranchised" (1993, p. 5). In a world rent by ethnic strife and ethnic cleansing, today's cultural/political leaders must determine whether to follow old romantic nationalistic models that worked reasonably well in the previous century but, in their emphasis on unique and pure cultural forms, are potentially divisive, or to seek new models based on cultural pluralism and mutual respect for all peoples.

William A. Wilson

See also Dorson, Richard M.; Herder, Johann Gottfried; *Kalevala*; Percy, Thomas; Romanticism

✳✳✳✳✳✳✳✳✳✳✳✳✳✳✳✳✳✳✳

References

Abrahams, Roger D. "Phantoms of Romantic Nationalism in Folkloristics." *Journal of American Folklore* 106 (1993): 3–37.

Herder, Johann Gottfried von. *Sämmtliche Werke*. Ed. Bernhard Suphan. 3 vols. Hildesheim, Germany: Georg Olms, 1967–1968 (1877–1913).

Wilson, William A. *Folklore and Nationalism in Modern Finland*. Bloomington: Indiana University Press, 1976.

———. "Herder, Folklore, and Romantic Nationalism." *Journal of Popular Culture* 6 (1973): 819–835.

———. "Richard M. Dorson as Romantic-Nationalist." *Journal of Folklore Research* 26 (1989): 36–42.

NATIVE AMERICAN WRITING

Many contemporary Native American writers, like other writers who are aware of oral tradition, often incorporate folklore in their writing. They use folk beliefs or the description of folk items and ceremonies; they incorporate material from myths, legends, tales, or oral history; and finally, they approximate the oral storytelling situation in writing.

Leslie Marmon Silko uses folk beliefs as well as the description of folk items and ceremonies in her novel *Ceremony* (1977). Her protagonist, Tayo, believes that his cursing the jungle rain has caused drought in his native New Mexico; his conviction derives from the general Native American belief that all of nature is connected. Silko's novel also includes a description of a Navajo-derived sandpainting and the ceremony, used to help heal the protagonist, that revolves around the sandpainting. In *House Made of Dawn* (1968), N. Scott Momaday contextualizes his novel through descriptions such as those of the rooster pull for the Feast of Santiago and the ceremonies performed in the pueblo of Walatowa on the first and second of August of each year.

Examples of another use of folklore—the incorporation of material from myth, legend, or tale—occur in both Louise Erdrich's and Silko's works. In *Tracks* (1988), Erdrich uses a character from myth, Nanabozho, as a template for one of the novel's narrators, Nanapush, and she also incorporates the legend of the water monster, Misshepeshu, who resides in Lake Matchimanito and serves as the character Fleur's spirit helper. For the plot of her short story "Yellow Woman" (1974), Silko uses a legend from her native Laguna Pueblo. In *Ceremony*, however, she uses a slightly different technique, incorporating myth and legend as poetic texts running parallel to the prose story of the protagonist. Further examples of blurring and mixing genres include James Welch's use of items of oral history as well as written history in *Fools Crow* (1986).

Most interesting among the various types of interplay between folklore and literature are the means some Native American writers use to approximate, in print, the oral storytelling situation. Momaday does so particularly in the "Night Chanter" section of *House Made of Dawn*, in which the character Benally speaks in the second person and in a very conversational style and tone. In *Love Medicine* (1984), Erdrich places the reader in the community through stories

Contemporary Native American writers use oral history, myths, and legends, like the warrior legend depicted here.

by six different first-person narrators using omniscient and limited-omniscient narration. The different narrators corroborate, provide different viewpoints on, or question the stories of other members of the community, giving the reader a sense of the process of oral storytelling. In similar fashion, Erdrich uses two narrators in *Tracks*, one of whom addresses a third person, Lulu, directly. Erdrich's expanded version of *Love Medicine* (1993) has the effect of making readers conscious of a continuing community and gives them a sense of their continuing participation in that community.

Contemporary Native American writers use folklore for a variety of purposes: verisimilitude, symbolism, contextualization, and approximation of the oral performance of storytelling. Like other literary devices, the use of folklore is an important aspect of the work of these writers.

Kathleen E. B. Manley

See also Erdrich, Louise; Momaday, Navarre Scott; Silko, Leslie Marmon; Trickster

✳✳✳✳✳✳✳✳✳✳✳✳✳✳✳✳

References

Manley, Kathleen E. B. "Decreasing the Distance: Contemporary Native American Texts, Hypertext, and the Concept of Audience." *Southern Folklore* 51 (1994): 121–135.

Owens, Louis. *Other Destinies: Understanding the American Indian Novel.* Norman: University of Oklahoma Press, 1992.

Ruoff, A. LaVonne Brown. *American Indian Literatures: An Introduction, Bibliographic Review, and Selected Bibliography.* New York: Modern Language Association of America, 1990.

Silko, Leslie Marmon. "Language and Literature from a Pueblo Indian Perspective." In *English Literature: Opening up the Canon,* ed. Leslie Fiedler and Houston A. Baker, Jr., pp. 54–72. Selected Papers from the English Institute, 1979, new ser., no. 4. Baltimore: Johns Hopkins University Press, 1981.

NAUMANN, HANS (1886–1951)

The Germanist Hans Naumann was known in literary circles primarily for his work with old German literature: *Boethius,* the *Ludwigslied,* an Old High German reader, studies of folk songs, and collections of märchen and proverbial sayings. His impact on the literary world pales, however, in comparison to his influence on *Volkskunde* (roughly, "folklore"). He is remembered in literature and in folklore as the author of *Primitive Gemeinschaftskultur* [Primitive communal culture (1921)] and *Grundzüge der deutschen Volkskunde* [Basic characteristics of German folklore (1922)]. In those two works, Naumann introduced the controversial ideas for which he is best known: "No matter how trivial a detail it may be, [one must ask if] it is an item of primitive communal good [*primitives Gemeinschaftsgut*] that has come from below, or of sunken cultural goods [*gesunkenes Kulturgut*] that has come from above" (Naumann 1922, p. 2).

Naumann thus divided the creators of the works he investigated into a progressive, intellectually cultured, and inspiring upper stratum and a stagnant and receptive lower stratum. This approach countered the long-standing romantic theory that the folk make up a creative community. The reaction to these concepts initiated a fundamental and unprecedented discussion about the objects and the goals of *Volkskunde,* and the response was both positive and negative.

Naumann's conceptualization of the folk was not original. Similar ideas can be found in the writings of other writers of the period; the Swiss Eduard Hoffmann-Krayer, in 1902, distinguished between a political nation (*populus*) and a social civilization (*vulgus in populo*). In contrast to cultural history, which investigated the "individual-civilizational moment" of culture, *Volkskunde* was concerned with the "general-stagnating cultural moment" in the *vulgus*. From this theoretical construct of social dynamics, Hoffmann-Krayer drew his conclusion that the folk do not produce but rather reproduce. It was, however, the French ethnologist and philosopher Lucien Lévy-Bruhl who seems to have had the most direct influence on Naumann. In the work *Les Fonctions mentales dans les sociétés inférieures* [Mental functions in inferior societies (1910)], which appeared in German translation as *Das Denken der Naturvölker* (1921) shortly before Naumann's *Grundzüge*, Lévy-Bruhl drew obvious parallels between the thoughts, beliefs, and cult world of the "primitives" and similar expressions in the folklife of the so-called culture folk. Lévy-Bruhl saw a rigid distinction between the complex thinking of the natural folk and the logical thinking of the "culture folk."

Virtually all German, Austrian, and Swiss literary and folklore scholars of the day responded to Naumann's ideas, through lengthy reviews of his books but also through articles that refuted his conceptualizations. Early on, the response was positive; during the 1920s, however, several theoretical articles appeared that countered Naumann's theses. In Austria, for example, Viktor von Geramb modified Naumann's cultural dynamics of trickling down by searching for "special manifestations" in a "mother stratum" that was to be distinguished from the individualized cultural world of the "daughter strata." A professor of folklore at the University of Berlin, Julius Schwietering, presented a concept of historical-social positions and called for an exact investigation of folk goods in their own context, including both their meaning and their function.

Hans Naumann was a popular figure and a dynamic speaker, which led to guest professorships abroad. He was thus known more widely than just in the German-speaking world as the man who had introduced a fundamentally new theory of the folk and of *Volkskunde*; hindsight makes it clear that Naumann's theory also had political ramifications.

He became a member of the National Socialist Party in 1922. In 1932, he published his *Deutsche Nation in Gefahr* [German nation in danger], a study that clearly reveals his affinity to the rapidly growing fascist ideology. In June 1932, Naumann joined over 50 German and Austrian professors in support of national socialism. Throughout most of the 12 years of the Third Reich, he seemed to be a model Nazi. At first Naumann profited from his party membership, and in 1934, he was named the rector of the University of Bonn. By February 1935, however, he had been abruptly deposed as rector because he had not "behaved appropriately" in actions being taken by the regime against the theologian Karl Barth and the literary figure Thomas Mann. The Gestapo seized remaining copies of the third edition of Naumann's *Grundzüge* and most likely destroyed them. He continued to speak out for the party and particularly for Hitler. Finally, Naumann was removed from his university position, and his life was in danger. Ironically, he was denied permission by the British authorities in the postwar years to return to his professorate. He petitioned repeatedly for reinstatement but died before it was granted.

James R. Dow

See also *Märchen*; Proverbs

✳✳✳✳✳✳✳✳✳✳✳✳✳✳✳✳✳✳

References

Naumann, Hans. *Grundzüge der deutschen Volkskunde.* Leipzig: Quelle and Meyer, 1922.

———. *Primitive Gemeinschaftskultur.* Jena, Germany: Eugen Diederichs, 1921.

Schirrmacher, Thomas. *"Der göttliche Volkstumsbegriff"* und der *"Glaube an Deutschlands grosse und heilige Sendung":* Hans Naumann als Volkskundler und Germanist im Nationalsozialismus: Eine Materialsammlung mit Daten zur Geschichte der Volkskunde an den Universitäten Bonn und Köln. 2 vols. Bonn: Verlag für Kultur und Wissenschaft, 1992.

Schmook, Reinhard. *"Gesunkenes Kulturgut—primitive Gemeinschaft": Der Germanist Hans Naumann (1886–1951) in seiner Bedeutung für die Volkskunde.* Vienna: A. Riegelnik, 1993.

———. "Zu den Quellen der volkskundlichen Sichtweise Hans Naumanns und zu den Reaktionen der Fachwelt auf dessen 'Grundzüge der deutschen Volkskunde' in den 20er und 30er Jahren." In *Beiträge zur Wissenschaftsgeschichte der Volkskunde im 19. und 20. Jahrhundert,* ed. Kai Detlev Sievers, pp. 73–90. Neumünster, Germany: Karl Wachholtz Verlag, 1991.

Ziegler, Matthes. "Folklore on a Racial Basis: Prerequisites and Tasks." In Hannjost Lixfeld, *Folklore and Fascism: The Reich Institute for German Volkskunde,* ed. and trans. James R. Dow, pp. 178–189. Bloomington: Indiana University Press, 1994.

NEKRASOV, NIKOLAY ALEKSEYEVICH (1821–1878)

The Russian poet and publicist Nikolay Alekseyevich Nekrasov was born in Podolia in the Ukraine. His aristocratic Polish mother was disowned by her father for marrying a Russian officer, and the latter settled his family on his paternal estate on the Volga near Yaroslavl. Educated until the age of 11 by his mother, to whom he wrote his first poems, Nekrasov was then placed by his father, a provincial police chief who was harsh on family and serfs alike, in a Yaroslavl school. Nekrasov was expelled five years later for writing satirical poems attacking the school's administrators, and at age 16, his father sent him to St. Petersburg to enroll in the court military academy. He attempted to enter the University of St. Petersburg instead, failed his entrance examinations, and was disinherited by his father. Nekrasov survived in St. Petersburg by tutoring, proofreading, and writing reviews while auditing literature classes at the university.

Nekrasov destroyed his first published poems when they were attacked by the leading critic of the emerging radical intelligentsia, Vissarion Belinsky. Belinsky later praised and published Nekrasov's literary essays after he accepted the critic's uncompromising views on art and society. In 1846, Nekrasov's poetry began to appear regularly in the influential literary journal *Sovremmeni* [The contemporary],which he purchased, edited, and published until it was shut down in 1864. In 1847, his portrayals of Russian peasants, together with Ivan Turgenev's *Zapiski ekhotnika* [Sportsman's sketches], found an audience that served the political interests of the radical intelligentsia. In an age of realist prose, Nekrasov emerged as Russia's leading poet, but his "civic poetry" was praised by the radicals more for its correct content than for its mixed style. Its focus on Russia's continuing social and political problems after serfdom was officially abolished in 1862 and was valued more than his employment of multiform poetic systems of a rich Russian oral tradition.

Although Nekrasov's more conventional lyrical poems often continued the classical tradition in Russian poetry, his best turned away from the poetry of the mind to the "poetry of the heart," a move thus characterized and praised in the 1850s by Nikolai Chernyshevsky, another major critic among the radicals. Nekrasov's more subjective poems, in which he successfully combined the spirit of both lyrical and narrative genres in Russian folklore, include literary masterpieces as well as fragments that made their way into the tradition of Russian folk songs. The erratic rhythm and obvious, syntactic rhymes in "The Peddlers," especially when sung with musical accompaniment, are true to their folk models. In perhaps his most popular poem, "Frost, the Red-Nosed," Nekrasov embedded the mood of ritual songs as a family laments the death of a young peasant. Additionally, he used the rhymes of children's game songs, remembered after the funeral by the exhausted widow while she freezes to death cutting firewood in the white, realistic stillness of the Russian forest. In a long narrative poem, "The Women," Nekrasov dramatized the personal tragedy of the wives of two Decembrists, lasting symbols of the political protest in czarist Russia, who choose to leave their families behind and follow their exiled husbands into the frozen forests, the "holy silence" of Siberia, a frightful place where the Russian and the human spirit live on.

Beginning in 1867, Nekrasov published his poems in the journal *Otechostvennye Zapiski* [Notes of the fatherland], which he bought and edited together with Mikhail Saltykov (pseudonym N. Shchedrin, the only other major literary personality in the 1860s and 1870s who was never alienated by the radicals. Although Nekrasov's career as a publisher brought him financial security, he never abandoned his chronicling of patriarchal and provincial life, particularly the endless suffering of women and those at the bottom of Russia's social ladder.

Between 1866 and 1878, he wrote but did not complete his novel-length narrative poem "Who Is Happy in Russia?" The poem's rich dialogue and the commonplace scenes of peasant life reveal the emotions of the poet. Building tonic, unrhymed lines, he uses the spirit of traditional poetic devices found in the satirical and epic poems of wandering *skomorokhi* ("clown-minstrel") and in his heroes' archaic lexicon and colloquial speech, folk formulas, epithets, sayings, and riddles. Nekrasov's grief over his own mother's suffering and early death and his anger evoked by the social and political abuses he was surrounded by in Yaroslavl and St. Petersburg influenced the major themes of his best narrative poems. His attempts to compose "nonpoetic poetry" successfully tapped the native roots of traditional songs and later influenced works of Russian symbolist and futurist poets.

John Kolsti

See also Russian Folk Lyric Song; Style

✳✳✳✳✳✳✳✳✳✳✳✳✳✳✳✳✳

References

Birkenmayer, Sigmund S. *Nikolaj Nekrosov: His Life and Poetic Art*. The Hague: Mouton, 1968.

Bristol, Evelyn. *A History of Russian Poetry*. Oxford: Oxford University Press, 1991.

Nekrasov, N. A. *Poems by Nikolas Nekrassov*. Trans. Juliet M. Soskice. London: Oxford University Press, 1936.

———. *Red-Nosed Frost*. Boston: Ticknor and Company, 1886.

———. *Who Can Be Happy and Free in Russia?* Trans. Juliet M. Soskice. Westport, Conn.: Hyperon Press, 1997 (1917).

Terras, Victor, ed. *Handbook of Russian Literature*. New Haven and London: Yale University Press, 1985.

NIBELUNGENLIED

Germany's greatest epic—the *Nibelungenlied*—was recorded sometime around the year 1204, but portions of it had existed in oral tradition for at least 750 years. Before that date, two major stories formed the basis for the literary document: the historical happenings of the great barbarian migrations in the fourth and fifth centuries (350–500) and the vast body of heroic legendry surrounding both the Low German hero Siegfried and the Nibelungs, ostensibly the people from northern regions of *Nebel* ("fog"). Variants of the epic are found in Germany as well as in most of the Nordic countries in the *Eddas*, the *Thidrekssaga*, the *Völsungasaga*, and heroic songs. Identifiable historical figures like Attila the Hun and Ostrogothic kings are blended into the heroic sagas surrounding Siegfried, Kriemhilde, the Burgundian royal family in Worms on the Rhine, and Brünhilde.

The story is that of Siegfried who courts and marries the beautiful Kriemhilde; Brünhilde, who is married to King Gunther of Worms, becomes jealous; the king's liege Hagen engages in deception; Siegfried is slain; Kriemhilde marries Attila and takes revenge on her family for causing Siegfried's death. Much that was in oral tradition concerning the Nibelungs is not included in the three extant manuscripts, particularly the youth of Siegfried. The text alludes to such elements as dragons, giants, and dwarfs and specifically incorporates water nixes, treasure hordes, magical capes and belts, heroic tasks, a sword placed between a man and a woman, and a bleeding

The thirteenth-century Nibelungenlied *recorded centuries of Germanic oral tradition, such as the legend of Siegfried slaying the dragon Fafnir.*

wound after death that reveals Siegfried's murderer. Three motifs, however, are central to the final version of the story: Siegfried's cloak of invisibility (*Tarnkappe*) acquired from the dwarf Alberich, Siegfried's fabulous strength and his incredibly sharp sword Balmung, and most important, the spot of vulnerability that Siegfried acquired when a linden leaf fell on his shoulder while he was bathing in the blood of the dragon Fafnir that he had just slain.

There is good reason to believe that legends associated with many of the central episodes in the *Nibelungenlied* existed in songs sung by *skops* ("singers") to Germanic tribesmen. In the treatise *Germania* (98 B.C.E.), the Roman historian Tacitus refers to the fact that songs are one way of remembering the past; an Old High German text, the *Hildebrandslied*, recorded around the year 800, gives clear evidence of such heroic songs; and there are other examples of ancient Germanic songs in alliterative verse that record the deeds of Siegfried and the Burgundians.

By 1816, Karl Lachmann, building on theories associated with Homeric origins, had developed his *Liedertheorie* ("song theory") in which he suggested that the *Nibelungen* epic was little more than an aggregation of ballads circulating in oral tradition. Meanwhile, Jacob Grimm saw remnants of Germanic mythology and heroic legendry in the Märchen, and even stated: "[Briar Rose] lies sleeping in a castle surrounded by a wall of thorns, until the right prince before whom the thorns give way, sets her free, *is the sleeping beauty* [emphasis added], who according to the old Norse saga, is surrounded by a wall of flames through which no one can force his way but Sigurd, who wakens her" (Hunt 1944, p. 405).

Today we realize that a skilled poet blended historical personages with well-known and widespread traditional motifs and entire legend cycles to create a major literary work of the Germanic world. The legacy of the *Nibelungenlied* is found in stone and wood carvings throughout that world, the famous *Ring* operas of Richard Wagner, classic movie versions produced by one of Germany's best known early film directors, Fritz Lang, and more recently, a comic book version.

James R. Dow

See also Grimm, Jacob and Wilhelm; Legend; *Märchen*

✳✳✳✳✳✳✳✳✳✳✳✳✳✳✳✳✳✳

References

Bartsch, Karl, ed. *Das Nibelungenlied*. 18th ed. Wiesbaden: F. A. Brockhaus, 1965.

Bauml, Franz H. *A Concordance to the Nibelungenlied, Bartsch–de Boor Text.* Leeds, Eng.: W. S. Maney and Sons, 1976.

Bekker, Hugo. *The Nibelungenlied: A Literary Analysis.* Toronto: University of Toronto Press, 1971.

Borghart, Kees Hermann Rudi. *Das Nibelungenlied: Die Spuren des mündlichen Ursprungs in schriftlicher Überlieferung.* Amsterdam: Rodopi, 1977.

Hunt, Margaret, trans. *Grimm's Fairy Tales: Complete Edition.* Rev. James Stern. New York: Pantheon, 1944.

Lang, Fritz, director. *Siegfried* (1924) and *Kriemhilde's Revenge* (1925). Films.

Thomas, Roy, and Gil Kane with Jim Woodring and John Costanza. *Richard Wagner's The Ring of the Nibelung.* New York: D. C. Comics, 1991.

NIGRA, COSTANTINO (1828–1907)

A diplomat and poet, Costantino Nigra also published the first systematic study of the Italian ballad (*canzone epico-lirica*) in a series of articles dating from 1854 and culminating in his 1888 *Canti popolari del Piemonte* [Popular songs of Piedmont]. This latter work included texts, variants, and philological discussions of 153 distinct ballads as well as examples of other songs such as lullabies and the short lyrical songs termed *strambotti* and *stornelli*. Nigra drew not only on his own collection but also on the collections and expertise of his wide circle of acquaintances, both Italian and international (Nigra corresponded with the most influential international ballad scholars, including Francis James Child, Gaston Paris, and Svend Grundtvig). The volume includes comparative texts from other regions of Italy and discusses similar ballads in other European traditions. For example, *Il testamento dell'avvelenato* [The poisoned man's testament] (Nigra 26) is equivalent to "Lord Randal" (Child 12) while *Un'eroina* (Nigra 13) is related to "Lady Isabel and the Elf-Knight" (Child 4). Nigra's work has been an essential reference for subsequent publications of collections of Italian ballads, which frequently use the same ordering.

Nigra's view of "popular poetry" (as he called "song") was fundamentally concerned with metrics and linguistic forms, which he saw as being determined by particular ethnic groups within the emergent Italian nation. Connecting race to language and language to particular genres of popular song, Nigra believed that a popular song emerges and spreads among people with the same ethnic-racial substratum: for example, the Celtic-romance northern Italians created and sang mainly ballads while the Italic-romance races of central and southern Italy created and sang lyrical songs in *strambotto* or *stornello* form. Furthermore, the content of songs corresponded to racially determined aesthetic sentiments, so the prosaic northerners preferred historical ballads and abstract thought while the lyrical songs of the passionate southerners were concerned with matters of the heart. As a diplomat and politician, Nigra used these theories to bolster claims that northern Italy was a more appropriate seat than Rome for the capital of Italy, since northerners were more temperamentally suited to government and administration.

Nigra gave pride of place in his volume to the ballad *"Donna lombarda"* [Woman from Lombardy (Nigra 1)], which recounts the story of an adulterous wife foiled in an attempt to poison her husband with the head of a snake cooked in wine. After the deception is revealed, often by the miraculous intervention of their infant son, the wife is either forced to drink the poison herself or is beheaded by her outraged husband. Although the first written documentation of the song is dated 1838, Nigra argued that popular oral tradition had accurately conserved over many centuries the story of the adultery and death of Rosmunda, queen of the Longobards, at Ravenna in 573, as recounted in the ninth-century chronicles of Paolo Diacono and Agnello di Ravenna. Later scholars rejected Nigra's theory, arguing on stylistic grounds that the subject matter and form of the song could date no earlier than the nineteenth century. *"Donna lombarda,"* which is still sung in Italy today, is one of the few Italian ballads known to have spread internationally, French-language versions having been recorded in both France and Canada.

Linda Barwick

See also Ballad; Child, Francis James; Comparative Method

✳✳✳✳✳✳✳✳✳✳✳✳✳✳✳✳✳✳

References

Barwick, Linda. "Critical Perspectives on Oral Song in Performance: The Case of Donna Lombarda." Ph.D. dissertation, Flinders University of South Australia, 1986.

Cocchiara, Giuseppe. "I 'Canti popolari del Piemonte'." In Costantino Nigra, *Canti popolari del Piemonte*, vol. 1, pp. vii–xxiii. Turin: Einaudi, 1957.

Nigra, Costantino. *Canti popolari del Piemonte*. 2 vols. Turin: Einaudi, 1957 (1888).

Nō (Noh)

Nō (Noh) is a kind of musical dance drama that was formed in four-teenth-century Japan by combining musical and dance elements from ancient religious rituals with acrobatic, juggling, and magic entertainments. The two great actor-playwrights who brought together these disparate elements to form the nō drama as we know it today were Kan'ami (1333–1384) and his son Zeami (1363–1443). Their establishment of a school of nō was greatly facilitated in 1374 when they received the official support of Shōgun Ashikaga Yoshi-mitsu (1358–1408), the military ruler of Japan at the time.

Scholars generally classify the 240 extant plays in the repertoire in two ways. The first system divides the plays into two groups depending on the role of the *shite* ("main protagonist"): *mugen nō* consists of plays in which the *shite* is a god, ghost, or demon who appears in a dream, and the second group, *genzai nō*, consists of plays in which the *shite* is from the world of ordinary experience.

The second and more common form of classification organizes the plays according to their order of presentation in a formal program of *nō*. In a complete *nō* cycle, five plays are presented and each of the plays in the cycle has a specific content and characters. The first group of plays (*waki nō*), consisting of approximately 30 plays, are plays whose main character is a deity. The dramatic action of these plays focuses on the origin stories of Shinto shrines or praises the attributes and powers of specific gods. The second group (*asura nō*), with 16 plays, focuses on the spirits of dead warriors killed in battle who wander around the countryside seeking peace and release for their souls. In this group of plays, the spirit of the warrior usually meets a mendicant Buddhist priest, relates the story of his death, and seeks prayers from the priest to release him from his personal hell.

The third group (*katsuramono*), with 38 plays, features women, or at times the spirits of plants, as the main protagonists. These plays are thought to contain some of the classic expressions of *yūgen*, a term of great importance in Japanese aesthetics that combines the feeling of elegant beauty, sad beauty, the essence of humanity, and/or the profound mysterious meaning of the universe. The fourth group, with 94 plays, is composed of a number of subgroups including *kyōranmono* ("madness plays") and *onrȳmono* ("revengeful ghost plays"). This group contains some of the most dramatic and often performed plays in the repertoire. The fifth group (*kiri nō*) contains

53 plays in which the *shite* role features nonhumans, for example, demons, monsters, or goblins.

The abundance of plays that deal with gods, the spirits of the dead, and nonhumans has been used by a number of scholars, among them Benito Ortolani, to argue for a close connection between the role of female shamans, shamanistic possession, shamanistic communication with spirits of the dead, early religious drama, folk beliefs, myth, and legend and the early development of *nō*.

Richard W. Anderson

See also *Bunraku*

✳✳✳✳✳✳✳✳✳✳✳✳✳✳✳✳✳

References

Keene, Donald. *Twenty Plays of the Nō Theatre*. New York: Columbia University Press, 1970.

Ortolani, Benito. *The Japanese Theatre: From Shamanistic Ritual to Contemporary Pluralism*. Princeton, N.J.: Princeton University Press, 1995.

Shimazaki, Chifumi. *Restless Spirits from Japanese Noh Plays of the Fourth Group: Parallel Translations with Running Commentary*. Ithaca, N.Y.: Cornell University East Asia Program, 1995.

———. *Warrior Ghost Plays from the Japanese Noh Theater: Parallel Translations with Running Commentary*. Ithaca, N.Y.: Cornell University East Asia Program, 1993.

Waley, Authur. *The Nō Plays of Japan*. Rutland, Vt.: Charles E. Tuttle Company, 1976.

Yasuda, Kenneth. *Masterworks of the Nō Theatre*. Bloomington: Indiana University Press, 1989.

Nursery rhymes

Nursery rhymes are a genre of folk poetry with numerous subtypes, including counting-out rhymes, riddles, dandling rhymes, and lullabies. Although origins can be difficult to determine, most British nursery rhymes seem to come from the seventeenth and eighteenth centuries. Attempts by scholars to connect nursery rhymes with historical events or personages have been largely inconclusive. Prince Cole, who lived in Britain in 3 B.C.E., is not necessarily the same as "Old King Cole" of the popular rhyme. Similarly, the rhyme "Ring Around a Rosie" need not, as many people assume, be a veiled account of troubles during the plague years in England. Katherine

Nursery rhymes like "Old King Cole," familiar to many British and American children, are sometimes identified as a form of folk poetry dating to seventeenth-century England.

Elwes Thomas, author of *The Real Personages of Mother Goose* (1930), has linked Bo-Peep with Mary Stuart, queen of Scots; Simple Simon with King James I of England; and both Old Mother Hubbard and Little Tommy Tucker with Cardinal Wolsey, who served as an adviser to King Henry VIII. Nursery rhyme dissemination occurred to some extent through printed ballads in the seventeenth century but also took place through oral transmission.

The first printed collection of nursery rhymes, *Mother Goose's Melody*, appeared between 1781 and 1791; its compiler was either John Newbery, his stepson, or his grandson. This finely bound and illustrated volume, which includes 16 of William Shakespeare's songs, apparently served as the model for the first American *Mother Goose* published by Isaiah Thomas of Worcester, Massachusetts, in 1785. Two other important U.S. editions are from the Boston publishing house of Munroe and Francis: *Mother Goose's Quarto, or Melodies Complete* (1825) and *The Only True Mother Goose's Melodies* (1843). Since the early 1800s, there have been many published collections and analyses of nursery rhymes, including James O. Halliwell's *The Nursery Rhymes of England* and Sabine Baring-Gould's *A Book of Nursery Songs and Rhymes* (1895).

Since nursery rhymes are widely known and loved, it is not surprising that they have frequently appeared in works of literature. Some of their earliest inclusions are in plays, such as Francis Beaumont's *Knight of the Burning Pestle* and Ben Jonson's *The Masque of Oberon* (1616). A reference to a book of riddles in Shakespeare's play *The Merry Wives of Windsor* (1602) indicates that Shakespeare had some familiarity with nursery rhymes. Among later dramatists' works are W. S. Gilbert's *Harlequin Cock Robin and Jenny Wren* (1866) and Agatha Christie's *The Mousetrap* (1954). In addition to the latter play, structured around the rhyme "Three Blind Mice," Christie wrote several novels with nursery rhyme themes (e.g., *Ten Little Indians* [1946] and *Pocket Full of Rye* [1958]). In each of these mystery novels, a well-known nursery rhyme provides a pattern for sinister surprises that culminate in murder.

Other contemporary novels that take their titles from nursery rhymes include Robert Penn Warren's *All the King's Men* (1946), Ken Kesey's *One Flew over the Cuckoo's Nest* (1962), and Jonathan Kellerman's *When the Bough Breaks* (1985). The presumed familiarity of readers with the rhymes gives contemporary authors an opportunity to develop symbols and metaphors that people can easily understand. In addition, rhymes sometimes furnish the means for introducing and delineating characters, as in Rumer Godden's *In This House of Brede* (1969). Parodies of familiar nursery rhymes, while common in oral tradition, are less common in literature.

Elizabeth Tucker

See also Ballad; Riddle; Shakespeare, William

✳✳✳✳✳✳✳✳✳✳✳✳✳✳✳✳✳✳

References

Campbell, Joseph. *The Hero with a Thousand Faces*. Princeton, N.J.: Princeton University Press, 1968.

Kreyling, Michael. *Figures of the Hero in Southern Narrative*. Baton Rouge: Louisiana State University Press, 1987.

Pearson, Carol. *The Female Hero in American and British Literature*. New York: Bowker, 1981.

Thomas, H. Nigel. *From Folklore to Fiction: A Study of Folk Heroes and Rituals in the Black American Novel*. New York: Greenwood Press, 1988.

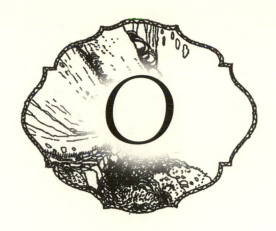

Oates, Joyce Carol (1938–)

The American fiction writer Joyce Carol Oates was born in Millersport, New York, and received her elementary education there in a one-room schoolhouse. She attended Syracuse University, graduating as valedictorian; earned her M.A. in English from the University of Wisconsin; and taught at the University of Windsor, Canada, from 1968 through 1978. In 1978, Oates moved to Princeton, New Jersey, where she resides today, teaching in Princeton University's creative writing program. Oates exhibited a gift for storytelling early in life and has fine-tuned that gift in the printed pages of more than 50 volumes of novels, short stories, plays, poetry, and criticism. Much of Oates's creative work blurs the lines between established literary genres and invites interdisciplinary studies, as her short story "Where Are You Going, Where Have You Been?" (1966) and her novel *Bellefleur* (1980) illustrate.

Inspired by *Life* reporter Don Moser's piece "The Pied Piper of Tucson" about a teenage serial killer in Arizona, Oates's short story "Where Are You Going, Where Have You Been?" is perhaps her best known and most widely studied work to date. A pivotal piece in her career, it is still the subject of vigorous and diversified criticism, much of which centers on the story's relationship to women's cautionary narratives, doomed maiden legends, coming-of-age parables, and "happy ending" fairy tales, fantasies, and myths.

Bellefleur, thematically like much of Oates's fiction, deals with the human desire to control, manipulate, and ultimately reshape one's surroundings. And yet, unlike much of the work preceding it, *Bellefleur* seeks to disrupt our notions of chronological time and linear history, so much so that readers are forced to make their own connections and meanings out of the limitless possibilities presented

461

to them. In this sense, as scholars have noted, the novel's style and vision are much like the crazy quilt, Celestial Timepiece, that the character Aunt Mathilde works on and discusses in the chapter of the same name. Aunt Mathilde's quilting instructions, "Feel this square, now feel this one, . . . and now this one—do you see? Close your eyes. . . . Do you understand?" point to a way of reading the novel itself. Like the quilt, only careful reflection can enable the pieces of the novel to come together as a whole to create meaning. Like other women writers, Oates sees the quilt as a metaphor for her own mode of creative expression. As a matter of fact, the chapter's title, "Celestial Timepiece," is also the title of a poem in which she illustrates her understanding of the relationship between quilting and the female literary tradition.

Although *Bellefleur* is Oates's most explicit adaptation of the quilt aesthetic, her work as a whole operates in much the same way—with myriad swatches of American life, seamless joinings of literary genres, and unique patternings of tradition and experimentation. Her seemingly inexhaustible store of creativity makes her one of the preeminent writers in the United States today.

Karen E. Beardslee

See also Legend; Myth; Quilting

****

References

Nodelman, Perry. "The Sense of Unending: Joyce Carol Oates's *Bellefleur* as an Experiment in Feminine Storytelling." In *Breaking the Sequence: Women's Experimental Fiction*, ed. Ellen G. Friedman and Miriam Fuchs, pp. 250–264. Princeton, N.J.: Princeton University Press, 1989.

Showalter, Elaine. *Sister's Choice: Tradition and Change in American Women's Writing*. Oxford: Clarendon Press, 1991.

Showalter, Elaine, ed. *"Where Are You Going, Where Have You Been?" Joyce Carol Oates*. New Brunswick, N.J.: Rutgers University Press, 1994.

Wesley, Marilyn C. *Refusal and Transgression in Joyce Carol Oates' Fiction*. Westport, Conn.: Greenwood Press, 1993.

ODYSSEY

The *Odyssey* is an ancient Greek epic poem composed around 700 B.C.E. and, like the *Iliad*, is attributed to a bard named Homer. Its subject is the return of the hero Odysseus from Troy to his own kingdom

Odysseus returns to Ithaka after winning the Trojan war, in this painting of the climactic scene from the Greek epic poem the Odyssey.

of Ithaka after the conclusion of the Trojan War (c. 1200 B.C.E.). Greek forces had besieged the Trojans for 10 years before finally overcoming them and accomplishing their object, the retrieval of Helen (wife of King Menelaos of Sparta, who had deserted her family for the Trojan prince Paris). Thereupon, the victors sailed back to their homes and families in Greece, but various adventures and obstacles delayed Odysseus's return. In the meantime, a pack of aggressive suitors had begun spending their days in his palace, bullying his son Telemachos and pressing his wife, Penelope, to wed one of them. In the tenth year after the war, Odysseus reached Ithaka and, disguised as a beggar, tested the loyalty of his household. In concert with his son, he brought about the destruction of the arrogant and dangerous suitors, regained his estate, and was reunited with his wife.

The story of Odysseus's return was one branch of a complex of interrelated Greek legends having to do with the Trojan War, legends that circulated both as prose narratives and as epic songs. Homer assumes his audience's prior acquaintance with the story, and his function is not so much to acquaint his listeners with unknown events as it is to relate mostly familiar events pleasurably and artfully. The story itself was set toward the end of the heroic age, or, in archaeological terms, the late Bronze Age, about five centuries before the time of the poem's composition.

The legend of Odysseus is noteworthy for the many international oral narratives it incorporates, including the story of the soldier who returns home just in time to prevent the remarriage of his wife ("The Homecoming Husband" [AT 974]), a narrative that is found in the epic traditions of other peoples as well. Also included in the Odysseus legend is the widespread folktale of the tricking of a one-eyed ogre by a clever hero ("The Ogre Blinded" [AT 1137]).

There are frequent representations within the *Odyssey* of oral storytelling by ordinary persons as well as of the performance of epic song by professional bards. Homer himself, as the twentieth-century scholars Milman Parry and Albert Lord have demonstrated, was an oral poet, part of a once-flourishing tradition of Greek oral poetry in which bards composed (or, more accurately, recomposed) songs in live performance. It is uncertain, however, what kind of ancient social occasion might have prompted so long a song, which, even if performed in installments, would require almost 20 hours of singing, nor what prompted someone to record it in writing. To judge from modern experiments, it seems most likely that the singer was induced to do a special performance for a scribe in which he dictated rather than sang his composition. Whatever the motive, the case is not unique, since other epic songs from other nations and times have also been written down by anonymous scribes.

William Hansen

See also Epic; Homer; *Iliad*; Lord, Albert Bates; Oral-Formulaic Composition and Theory; Parry, Milman

✳✳✳✳✳✳✳✳✳✳✳✳✳✳✳✳✳

References

Foley, John Miles. *The Odyssey, Beowulf, and the Serbo-Croatian Return Song.* Berkeley and Los Angeles: University of California Press, 1990.

Hansen, William. "Homer and the Folktale." In *A New Companion to Homer,* ed. Ian Morris and B. B. Powell, pp. 442–462. Leiden: Brill, 1996.

Lord, Albert B. *The Singer of Tales.* New York: Atheneum, 1960.

Samter, Ernst. *Volkskunde im altsprachlichen Unterricht: Ein Handbuch.* Vol. 1, *Homer.* Berlin: Weidmann, 1923.

OEDIPUS

The story of Oedipus was a fertile one for Greek literature, which used the hero's ignorance of his own birth as a paradigm for the limits of human knowledge, an ironic literalization of the Apollonian dictum to know oneself first and foremost. The story is briefly narrated in Book 11 of the *Odyssey*; it formed the basis of a lost epic, *Oidipodeia*; and it inspired a number of treatments on the tragic stage, of which that of Sophocles has overshadowed all others. The casting of Oedipus as an intellectual hero in *Oedipus the King* (c. 432 B.C.E.) entails a unique complex of thematically related elements: the riddle of the Sphinx, the pervasive role of Apollo, and the metaphorical interplay of sight and knowledge as dramatized by the confrontation with the blind seer Teresias at the beginning of the play and the ultimate self-blinding of an Oedipus who now also knows the truth (there is no blinding in the *Odyssey* version). In keeping with this theme, and in contrast to most of the other analogues, the crimes are in this version of the story less important than the catastrophic process of their revelation.

The tale-type of which Oedipus is the earliest and most famous actualization (AT 931) can be defined by two narrative components: (1) the exposure of a child, motivated either by a prophecy of some dire future event or by some problematic aspect of his conception (e.g., incest or illegitimacy), and (2) the survival of the child and his subsequent unwitting acts of patricide and maternal incest. In some cases, the exposed infant is somehow mutilated as well. Apart from the story of Oedipus, the tale is notably applied to medieval legendary biographies of Judas Iscariot, and other analogues have been collected from much of the rest of the world.

The mutilation motif provides some positive evidence for the existence of an underlying folk tradition linking the ancient and medieval material. In virtually all the non-Greek versions in which mutilation is present, it is either localized on the upper body or not localized at all; furthermore, it is an organic part of the narrative, functioning subsequently as a means of recognition. The application of this motif to the ankles or feet of Oedipus looks very much like a contextually determined adaptation of a traditional element, in this case merely to etymologize the hero's name (as if it means "Swellfoot"); significantly, Oedipus's mutilation is *narratively* superfluous, being largely unnecessary to establish his identity. Outside the Greek tradition, it is rarely the foot that is the mutilated part.

Seemingly related in some way is AT 933, best known for its application to the legendary Pope Gregory, which contains both the exposure and incest but commonly omits the patricide and concludes with the ultimate penance and exaltation of the hero, generally in a religious framework (e.g., elevation to the papacy or sanctification). The Russian formalist Vladimir Propp linked this tale with the later career and death of Oedipus, as dramatized in Sophocles' *Oedipus at Colonus*, a suggestion further pursued by Lowell Edmunds.

Robert Mondi

See also Freud, Sigmund; Greece, Ancient; Motif; *Odyssey*; Propp, Vladimir I.; Tale-Type

✳✳✳✳✳✳✳✳✳✳✳✳✳✳✳✳✳

References

Edmunds, Lowell. *Oedipus: The Ancient Legend and Its Later Analogues*. Baltimore: Johns Hopkins University Press, 1985.

Edmunds, Lowell, and Alan Dundes, eds. *Oedipus: A Folklore Casebook*. Madison: University of Wisconsin Press, 1995 (1983).

OICOTYPE

An oicotype (variant spellings: oikotype, ecotype) is a localized form of a widespread traditional narrative, custom, or belief. The term is most commonly used in reference to narrative forms. Tales of the same main type can be formed into special regional types not only in different countries but also in the different cultural districts of a single country. When members of a particular culture group, whether geographically, linguistically, ethnically, politically, or otherwise defined, encounter a tale and incorporate it into the group repertoire, the dynamic process of oicotypification is activated. Members of the group adapt the tale to make sense within the group's physical and social environments, value system, and aesthetic sensibilities. Elements of the content, style, and structure of folkloric forms are changed to fit the culture in typical ways. Thus, an oicotype is characteristic of the culture group that has adapted it. Looking at the way in which features of folklore are characteristic of their social habitat helps to elucidate the connection between the lore and the folk.

The term *oicotype* was borrowed from botanical science and first introduced into the discipline of folklore by the Swedish philologist and folklorist Carl Wilhelm von Sydow (1878–1952) in 1934. Essays in his 1948 anthology *Selected Papers on Folklore* discuss the oicotype, and in one of them, "Geography and Folktale Oicotypes," he explains his appropriation of the term:

> In the science of botany oicotype is a term used to denote a hereditary plant-variety adapted to a certain milieu (seashore, mountain-land etc.) through selection amongst hereditarily dissimilar entities of the same species. When then in the field of traditions, a widely spread tradition, such as tale or legend (i.e., sagn), forms certain culture districts, the term oicotype can also be used in the science of ethnology and folklore. (von Sydow, 1948)

Von Sydow's notion that when tales travel they assume local form and his consideration of the ways physical and sociocultural contexts could influence the traditional texts they surround were innovative in their time. He offered the concept of oicotype as an alternative to the way his contemporaries in the historic-geographic, or Finnish, school thought about tales. A primary aim of the Finnish school was to construct hypothetical ur-forms—possible original exemplars—of international tale-types. Von Sydow was more interested in actual local redactions of international tale-types as part of a natural, living whole. Like the members of the Finnish school, von Sydow was interested in the migration and diffusion of tales. However, while the Finnish school adherents described the almost effortless automigration of tales, von Sydow stressed that it was difficult to transfer tradition to new surroundings. He had an empirical interest in the social matrix within which diffusion occurs.

Although the study of oicotypes has not claimed a major place in folklore scholarship, several scholars have built and expanded upon von Sydow's concept of oicotype. Von Sydow stressed the isolation of the culture group and time depth as necessary conditions for the development of oicotypes; later scholars did not deem these to be necessary. More significantly, later scholars not only identified oicotypes but also analyzed them. If oicotypes are shaped by the force that a group's social and aesthetic value systems exert upon traditions, an analysis of oicotypes should in turn reveal the group's values. The

American folklorist Roger Abrahams used this method in his 1963 study of a corpus of oicotypes from an urban black community, *Deep Down in the Jungle*. The development of American scholarship on the oicotype is chronicled and discussed by Timothy Cochrane in his 1987 article "The Concept of Ecotypes in American Folklore."

Ilana Harlow

See also Historic-Geographic Method; *Märchen*; Sydow, Carl Wilhelm von; Tale-Type

✳✳✳✳✳✳✳✳✳✳✳✳✳✳✳✳✳

References

Cochrane, Timothy. "The Concept of Ecotypes in American Folklore." *Journal of Folklore Research* 24 (1987): 33–55.

Sydow, Carl W. von. *Selected Papers on Folklore*. Copenhagen: Rosenkilde and Bagger, 1948.

Ong, Walter (1912–)

Professor emeritus of humanities in psychiatry at St. Louis University, Walter Ong is the author of dozens of books and articles such as *The Presence of the Word: Some Prolegomena for Cultural and Religious History* (1967); *Fighting for Life: Contest, Sexuality, and Consciousness* (1981); and *Orality and Literacy: The Technologizing of the Word* (1982). Ong is a major figure in the study of how orality, literacy, and technology affect literature and society. His writings cover a vast area of scholarship from ancient to modern languages and literature and extend to philosophical discourses on the nature of language and criticism of contemporary culture.

Ong was born in Kansas City, Missouri, on November 30, 1912. After studying Latin, Greek, English, and history at St. Stanislaus Seminary, in Flourissant, Missouri, where he entered the Jesuit Order, he received a licentiate in philosophy and an M.A. in English in 1940 from St. Louis University. He went to Paris on a Guggenheim fellowship in 1950 to do research for his dissertation on Peter Ramus, which resulted in a two-volume Harvard publication, *Ramus, Method, and the Decay of Dialogue* and *Ramus and Talon* (1958). In 1970, he became professor of humanities in psychiatry and in 1981, university professor of humanities at St. Louis University.

Ong differentiates oral and literate cultures in terms of thought and worldview, identifying certain characteristics that define orally based thought. For example, he contends that oral cultures employed additive rather than subordinate styles in narration and that repetitions flourish as functional elements without appearing to be simply redundant. Oral cultures lean toward conservatism over time and are aggregative rather than analytic in their organization of knowledge. Ong further argues that writing structures knowledge at a distance from the reality of world events, whereas the oral mind comprehends actions on a more immediate level. For this reason, agonistic qualities emerge more dynamically in oral narratives, and oral style thus appears more empathic and participatory than objectively distant; the oral mind is situational and does not function in a world of abstractions. As a result of these characteristics, the oral style tends toward homeostasis, maintaining a relative uniformity or stability as prescribed by the values of the given society.

Ong also observes vestiges of orality in written literary works, referring to these traces as evidence of "oral residue" or "secondary orality," in which the characteristics of orality mentioned above manifest themselves even though the text is clearly a product of literacy. This persistence demonstrates that literacy cannot completely extinguish all aspects of orality from a given cultural tradition.

Anastasios Daskalopoulos

See also Orality; Style

✳✳✳✳✳✳✳✳✳✳✳✳✳✳✳✳✳

References

Lumpp, Randolph F. "Walter Jackson Ong, S.J.: A Biographical Portrait." *Oral Tradition* 2 (1987): 13–18.

Ong, Walter J. *Interfaces of the Word: Studies in the Evolution of Consciousness and Culture*. Ithaca, N.Y.: Cornell University Press, 1982 (1977).

———. *Orality and Literacy: The Technologizing of the Word*. London: Routledge, 1991 (1982).

———. *The Presence of the Word: Some Prolegomena for Cultural and Religious History*. New Haven: Yale University Press, 1967.

———. *Rhetoric, Romance, and Technology: Studies in the Interaction of Expression and Culture*. Ithaca, N.Y.: Cornell University Press, 1971.

OPERA DI PUPI

The *Opera di Pupi*, or marionette theater, is one of at least three interrelated traditions that present the Carolingian cycle, which deals with the exploits of Charlemagne and his Paladins, to working-class Sicilian audiences. Other major purveyors of that cycle are the Sicilian popular press and the *contastorie*, storytellers who declaim the exploits of Charlemagne, Orlando, and Rinaldo in the public squares of major Sicilian cities.

The *Opera di Pupi* is a relatively recent tradition, first appearing in Sicily in the early nineteenth century. In its infancy, the *Opera di Pupi* was based upon farces inspired by the commedia dell'arte, but even in its formative years, probably under the influence of the declamatory art of the *contastorie*, it began to add chivalric materials to the repertoire until today the Carolingian cycle, presented in approximately 270 hour-long episodes, makes up the bulk of the repertoire. In order to create combat-ready marionettes, the puppeteers not only began constructing ornate suits of armor for their puppets but also exchanged the string that maneuvered the puppet's right hand (the hand that wields the sword) with an iron rod. The resulting innovations transformed the characteristic farcical brawls of the *vastoni* (singular, *vastone*), comedic characters representative of the Sicilian working classes, into epic battles that at times culminated in such theatrics as the hewing of an opponent in two or even a beheading.

The puppeteers did not give up their *vastoni* as chivalric materials came to more and more dominate their repertoire; they instead allowed them to comment upon, burlesque, and even insert themselves into the epic arena. Perhaps inevitably, the *vastoni*, as representatives of the Sicilian people, became juxtaposed to the knights who became, by virtue of that juxtaposition, the symbol of the Sicilian aristocracy. The *Opera di Pupi* thus became almost incidentally politicized. Further incursions into epic were made by saints and bandits, the lives of whom were also part of the puppeteers' repertoire, until the epic configuration of knight, *vastone*, saint, and bandit became a comment on the Sicilian social configuration of noble, commoner, priest, and mafioso. Orlando, who too often takes on the behavior of the saint, is not the ultimate hero of the *Opera di Pupi*. The hero is Rinaldo, who takes on the attributes of a bandit and is in fact nicknamed the mafioso.

The fact that the *Opera di Pupi* is still to be seen in Sicily despite the considerable competition offered by television and film is owing to both the resiliency of the puppeteers and the efforts of the International Museum of Marionettes in Palermo, Sicily. The museum, under the direction of Janne Vibaek and Antonio Pasqualino, has amassed not only a fine collection of puppets and the wealth of folk arts associated with the *Opera di Pupi* but also an extensive collection of video and audio recordings of numerous puppet plays.

Michael Buonanno

See also Charlemagne; *Commedia dell'arte*; Epic

✳✳✳✳✳✳✳✳✳✳✳✳✳✳✳✳✳✳

References

Buonanno, Michael. "The Palermitan Epic: Dialogism and the Inscription of Social Relations." *Journal of American Folklore* 103 (1990): 324–333.

Pasqualino, Antonio. *L'Opera dei Pupi.* Palermo: Sellerio Editore, 1970.

Pitre, Giuseppe. "Le tradizioni cavalleresche popolari in Sicilia." *Usi e costumi, credenze, e pregiudizi del popolo Siciliano* 1 (1889): 121–341.

ORAL-FORMULAIC COMPOSITION AND THEORY

Oral-formulaic theory is a major approach to the study of oral tradition and works with roots in oral tradition that prescribes a specialized language or idiom as the basis of composition in performance. Also known as the Parry-Lord theory after its founders (Milman Parry and Albert Lord), this approach puts a premium on the utility of patterned phraseology (formulas), typical narrative scenes (themes), and large-scale organization (story patterns) in providing ready solutions to the performer's ongoing challenge of maintaining fluent, intelligible composition. In addition to applying the theory to living traditions, chiefly poetry, scholars have retrospectively analyzed ancient and medieval works to determine the extent of their dependence on such paradigms and, in some cases, their "oral" or "literary" character. With typical structures demonstrated in more than 130 separate language areas, the most pressing question has become how to interpret works composed in this specialized idiom.

The oral-formulaic theory began with Milman Parry's pioneering studies of the Homeric epics, the *Iliad* and *Odyssey*, which reveal systematic patterning behind the recurrence of particular phrases, especially noun-epithet expressions like *podas ôkus Achilleus* ("swift-footed Achilleus") and *thea glaukôpis Athênê* ("goddess bright-eyed Athena"). Instead of explaining the great epics as either conglomerate editions of smaller poems (according to the analyst school) or as the personal and individual achievements of a single genius (the unitarian school), Parry argued that a poetic diction as systematized as the language of the Homeric poems must be the legacy of generations of bards, who perfected the idiom over centuries. His fundamental insight was that the language of Homer was traditional.

The core of Parry's theoretical proposal was the formula, which he defined as "an expression regularly used, under the same metrical conditions, to express an essential idea" (Parry 1971, p. 1), and which he eventually enlarged beyond the noun-epithet phrase to include any metrically determined unit of Homeric diction. Thus, for example, recurrent expressions for speech-introduction (e.g., "And so he/she spoke") were shown to combine with recurrent names for mortals or gods to produce predictable—and in terms of the oral-formulaic theory, useful—hexameter lines.

For Parry, utility in formulaic diction derived from the participation of individual phrases in larger, generative "formulaic systems," groups of items fitting the same metrical slot that are also related by common semantic and syntactic features. Although this aspect of the poetic idiom gave the composing poet a flexibility in line-to-line construction, the simplicity of the diction was attributed to an overall "thrift"—"the degree in which [a formulaic system] is free of phrases which, having the same metrical value and expressing the same idea, could replace one another" (Parry 1971, p. 276). Formulaic language was therefore understood as serving the poet's needs, not only in providing ready solutions, but in productively limiting compositional options.

This approach began as an analytical procedure to prove the traditional nature of ancient Greek texts, but Parry, under the influence of his mentor, Antoine Meillet, and of Matija Murko, a Slavic ethnographer and philologist familiar with southern Slavic epic poetry from his own fieldwork, soon added the criterion of "orality" as a necessary implication of the traditional character of verse making. In order to confirm his hypothesis of an oral tradition from which the Homeric poems stemmed, Parry and his assistant, Albert Lord, undertook a large-scale fieldwork expedition to the former Yugoslavia in 1933–1935 (continued by Lord in 1950–1951 and later) to study the living phenomenon of the southern Slavic oral traditional epic at firsthand. They recorded acoustically or by dictation more than half a million lines of epic from preliterate *guslari* ("bards"; those who play the *gusle*, a single-stringed lute). The work is now deposited in the Milman Parry Collection of Oral Literature at Harvard University, and Lord and David Bynum have published selections of it in the 1953 series *Serbocroatian Heroic Songs (SCHS)*.

Aside from writing a few short papers, Parry did not live to carry out the comparative analysis of Homer and the southern Slavic epic that he had envisioned. After his death in 1935, Lord assumed responsibility for that planned enterprise and, in fact, moved well beyond the original analogy to make the oral-formulaic theory a truly multidisciplinary undertaking.

The most influential of Lord's writings, in many respects the touchstone for the entire field, is *The Singer of Tales*, completed as his dissertation in 1949 and published in 1960. This book uses the *guslar* in performance as a model for Homer—and also for Anglo-Saxon, Old French, and Byzantine-Greek narrative poets. In addition to illustrating formulaic composition in southern Slavic songs, the *Iliad* and the *Odyssey*, the Song of Roland, *Beowulf*, and the song of the hero *Digenis Akritas*, he described narrative units called "themes," or "groups of ideas regularly used in telling a tale in the formulaic style of traditional song" (Lord 1960, p. 68). These included, for example, such typical actions as arming a hero, readying a horse, and summoning guests to a wedding or battle. He also identified "story patterns" that were coextensive with the work as a whole, the most familiar example being the "return song," essentially the story of the *Odyssey* that also appears in Turkish, Bulgarian, Albanian, Russian, medieval English, and other traditions. At every level, the key concept is multiformity, the mutability of phraseological or narrative patterns within limits, as an aid to composition in performance.

In the wake of the publication of *The Singer of Tales*, the Parry-Lord theory underwent vigorous translation to Old English, Middle English, Old French, Hispanic, and American folk preaching, biblical studies, and scores of other areas; it also continued to expand into the area of ancient Greek. A history of the comparative methodology is available in John Miles Foley's *The Theory of Oral Composition* (1988) as well as the annotated bibliography in his *Oral-Formulaic Theory and Research* (1985), with updates in the journal *Oral Tradition*.

With formulas, themes, and story patterns identified in traditions worldwide, new questions began to arise about the implications of the oral-formulaic theory for interpretation, especially in relation to texts with extensive prior critical histories, such as the Homeric poems. One of the central tenets of the approach, as originally stated, held that a certain percentage of formulas and formulaic systems constitute proof of the ultimately oral provenance of a given text, independent of any supporting testimony for that claim. The reasoning proceeded from the criterion of utility: if a poet had regular recourse to ready-made diction and narrative patterns, then he or she was composing traditionally, and thus orally. Quantitative measurement of this sort did not take into account the inevitable differences among languages, traditions, or genres, nor did it consider the persistence of the formulaic idiom after the introduction of writing.

Indeed, as the oral-formulaic theory has been applied to more and more traditions, many of them still living, it has become increasingly apparent that the absolute dichotomy of oral versus written does not fit the evidence. Manuscript works that presumably represent freestanding compositions by individual authors still show extensive use of the formulaic language, and different rules govern the structure and texture of formulas and themes from one language to another, or even from one genre to another. Additionally, the issue of performance and all that it entails has come to the fore: oral tradition presents many channels for communication (linguistic, paralinguistic, and nonlinguistic), only a limited number of which are reflected in what we conventionally reduce to a transcribed text. Many of these newer challenges are confronted in Foley's *The Singer of Tales in Performance* (1995).

John Miles Foley

See also Balkan Folklore and Literature; *Beowulf*; Homer; *Iliad*; Lord, Albert Bates; *Odyssey*; Parry, Milman; *Song of Roland*

✳✳✳✳✳✳✳✳✳✳✳✳✳✳✳✳✳✳

References

Foley, John Miles. *Oral-Formulaic Theory and Research: An Introduction and Annotated Bibliography*. New York: Garland, 1985.

———. *The Singer of Tales in Performance*. Bloomington: Indiana University Press, 1995.

———. *The Theory of Oral Composition: History and Methodology*. Bloomington: Indiana University Press, 1992 (1988).

Lord, Albert B. *The Singer of Tales*. Cambridge: Harvard University Press, 1960.

Parry, Milman. *The Making of Homeric Verse: The Collected Papers of Milman Parry.* Ed. Adam Parry. Oxford: Clarendon Press, 1971.

Parry, Milman, Albert B. Lord, and David E. Bynum, collectors, eds., and trans. *Serbocroatian Heroic Songs (Srpskohrvatske junacke pjesme).* Cambridge and Belgrade: Harvard University Press and the Serbian Academy of Sciences, 1953–.

Oral history

Oral information about the past and the recording of that information—that is, oral history—represent a very old method of historical research (Herodotus talked to veterans of the Persian wars to obtain information for his famous history of the fifth century B.C.E.), but the term *oral history* is a recent one and interest in oral history as a discrete methodology is a recent development. Although oral historical information can be recorded simply by manual notation, oral history today is generally understood to involve the use of audiotapes or even camcorders.

The work of the Columbia University historian Allan Nevins was highly influential in the establishment of oral history as a distinct methodology, and the modern study of oral history is often traced to the founding of the Columbia Oral History Archives in 1948. Oral history became important as historians recognized that the conditions of modern life made such documents as letters and diaries less common than formerly. Thus, the makers of history were to be interviewed and their responses to interviewers' questions—their knowledge of events—were to be put on tape.

Projects in oral history have varied, but often the people interviewed have been important persons able to comment upon significant political or economic developments. One of the most celebrated books based on oral history techniques, for example, was T. Harry Williams's Pulitzer Prize–winning biography of Louisiana governor Huey Long (1969). Williams interviewed notable politicians and commentators to obtain information for his interpretation of this populist whose brief career had a powerful impact on democracy in the United States.

However, there is also a strain of oral history that looks at ordinary people and the social developments affecting them, a concentration that is central to folklorists. Several volumes by the Chicago journalist Studs Terkel that have focused on the oral history of such topics as the Great Depression and race relations in the United States as remembered by ordinary men and women have been very popular.

Folklorists become involved in oral history in several ways. They have sometimes endeavored to record the historical memories of members of folk cultures or participants in folk processes or events. And some of the oral genres they have studied, such as the legend and personal narrative, convey information about the past. Folklorists often have been interested in determining the extent to which historical traditions pass on accurate knowledge about past events, and even when such traditions pass on unverifiable or inaccurate information, the folklorists may learn about people's attitudes toward history or about the communities that possess the traditions.

In considering historical traditions, folklorists must take into account the formal characteristics of the relevant genres; and they must be concerned with those genres as types of oral literature and take into account their oral literary features. Historical traditions have sometimes been incorporated into literary works, for example, by Sir Walter Scott. As local oral history projects have become widespread, they occasionally have become elements in narrative literature.

Frank de Caro

See also Legend; Personal Experience Story; Scott, Sir Walter

✳✳✳✳✳✳✳✳✳✳✳✳✳✳✳✳✳✳

References

Allen, Barbara, and William Lynwood Montell. *From Memory to History: Using Oral Sources in Local Historical Research*. Nashville: American Association for State and Local History, 1981.

de Caro, Frank. "Oral History and Folklore." In *Oral History and Community History*, pp. 15–40. Baton Rouge: Louisiana Library Association, 1985.

Dorson, Richard M. *American Folklore and the Historian*. Chicago: University of Chicago Press, 1971.

Smith, Lee. *Oral History*. New York: Ballantine, 1983.

Williams, T. Harry. *Huey Long*. New York: Knopf, 1969.

ORALITY

Orality refers to the state or quality of being spoken and heard, and three phases of orality have been identified by scholars. The first refers to oral communication that is uninfluenced by writing technologies. In the second phase, sometimes referred to as primary orality, oral communication becomes associated with written representations or symbols. In each society, such representations—beginning with hieroglyphics and cuneiform—evolved at different times into alphabetic representation of sound or writing. Societies that had such technology learned to organize linearly, to catalog using lists, and as a result, to think differently. Progressing to a new manner of thought and speaking, societies enter the third phase, or secondary orality. In this phase, individuals internalize the writing process and begin thinking in terms of words and alphabetic sounds rather than in terms of images that symbolize concepts and ideas. In the late twentieth century, even if a culture does not communicate at the level of secondary orality, it has probably been influenced by the products of such a culture.

Historically, folklorists have focused attention on groups within cultures that are characterized as being in the secondary orality phase and who are isolated in three primary ways: culturally, regionally, and economically. These so-called folk groups are thought to be composed of the persons within a society who are the least affected by the dominant, popular communication technologies of the time period.

The study of orality and its relationship to the production of literature, whether oral or written, has been influenced by work on the epic and the development of the concept of oral-formulaic composition. In describing the performance of the living epic tradition in Yugoslavia, the work of the scholars Milman Parry and Albert Lord has had enormous impact on the study both of folklore and of literature.

Using the oral-formulaic process, the oral poet learns, composes, and transmits songs orally and merges these three activities so that they are different "facets" of the composition process. Scholars have suggested that works such as Homer's *Iliad* and *Odyssey*, as well as the Old English *Beowulf*, were originally performed using oral formulas.

Other scholars have been concerned with the omissions that occur when oral speech is preserved by modern recording technologies and subsequently presented on the printed page. Noting that the written text does not offer an opportunity to indicate techniques of emphasis and other kinds of clarification common to oral speech, a number of folklorists have begun employing particular transcriptive techniques, such as Dell Hymes's ethnography of speaking. It is hoped that this kind of transcription system will aid in the transfer to the printed page of some of the environmental factors and kinesic attributes that help to contextualize the spoken word. This approach may provide the scholar with techniques to realize the lived reality more accurately.

Some folklorists have focused on the ways orality has been used by literary artists and have often provided insights into a group's beliefs, structure, and values. Seminal in this area is Carl Lindahl's *Earnest Games* (1987), which reveals how the folklore of medieval times informed Geoffrey Chaucer's *Canterbury Tales*.

Rachel Gholson

See also *Canterbury Tales*; Chaucer, Geoffrey; Lord, Albert Bates; Oral-Formulaic Composition and Theory; Parry, Milman; Transcription

✳✳✳✳✳✳✳✳✳✳✳✳✳✳✳✳

References

Foley, John Miles. *Oral-Formulaic Theory and Research: An Introduction and Annotated Bibliography*. New York: Garland, 1985.

Hymes, Dell, and John J. Gumperez, eds. "The Ethnography of Communication." *American Anthropologist* 66:6 (1964): 127–132.

Lord, Albert Bates. "Characteristics of Orality." *Oral Tradition* 2:1 (1987): 54–72.

Ong, Walter J. *Orality and Literacy: The Technologizing of the Word*. New York: Routledge, 1982.

ORPHEUS

Orpheus is the singer-poet of Greek mythology whose music was said to be so alluring that it could tame wild animals and even trees and stones followed him when he played his lyre. The oldest extant source of his name is a fragment of sixth-century B.C.E. poetry by Ibycus in which he is called "famous Orpheus," indicating that he had probably existed in the oral tradition since archaic times. The

Orpheus charms the King of Hades with his music in order to return his bride, Eurydice, to life on Earth in this representation of the sixth-century B.C.E. Greek myth.

meaning of Orpheus's name and his origin are unknown, but he reportedly came from Thrace (Bulgaria). His father was either a king, Oiagreus, or Apollo, the Greek and Roman god of prophecy, music, and poetry. His mother is identified as a muse, usually Calliope, the Greek muse of eloquence or of epic poetry. He was worshiped in a hero cult, but never as a god.

The best known story about Orpheus describes his descent into the underworld to return his bride, the nymph Eurydice, to life. The tale gets its normal form from two Latin poems, Virgil's *Fourth Georgic* and Books 10 and 11 of Ovid's *Metamorphoses*, both dating to the second half of the first century B.C.E. In both poems, Eurydice dies from treading on a poisonous snake, but in Virgil's account, that happens on her wedding day as she flees from a rapist, Aristaeus, the god of beekeeping. Both versions relate Orpheus's grief at the loss of his wife; his entry into the realm of Hades by enchanting Charon and Cerberus with his music; his failure to obey Persephone's injunction not to look back at Eurydice until both are safely on earth; and his death and dismemberment at the hands of angry Thracian women. Ovid tells us that these followers of Bacchus killed Orpheus because, after his ascent, he refused to play the lyre for women but only for young boys. Virgil says they killed him because they were jealous of his love for his wife. Both tell that his still-singing head and his lyre were carried off by the river Hebrus. In Ovid, the head landed on the island of Lesbos, where it continued to sing until Apollo silenced it by sending both Orpheus and Eurydice to the Islands of the Blessed. According to Virgil, Orpheus's head may be singing still.

Apollonius Rhodius's *Argonautica* (second century B.C.E.) tells of Orpheus's travels with Jason and that Orpheus's song saves the crew of the *Argo* from the lure of the sirens. As a mythological patron of all the arts of the Western world, Orpheus appears, for example, in the poetry of John Milton, Rainer Maria Rilke, Guillaume Apollinaire, Arthur Rimbaud, and Muriel Rukeyser; in paintings and sculptures by Odilon Redon, Gustave Moreau, Marc Chagall, Paul Klee, and Auguste Rodin; in operas by Christoph Gluck, Geoffrey Burgon, Claudio Monteverdi, Jacques Offenbach, and Phillip Glass; and in ballets by Igor Stravinsky and George Ballanchine. Orpheus is also the subject of films: *Orpheé* (1950) by Jean Cocteau; *Black Orpheus* (1959), set in Rio de Janeiro during carnival; and *The Fugitive Kind* (1960) and *Orpheus Descending* (1990), both based on plays by Tennessee Williams.

Orphism, a religious philosophy dating to the sixth century B.C.E. that may have had some connection with the descent story, focused on rituals to help the dead escape from being reborn into another human life. The discovery of many "Orphic cosmogonies" (i.e., cosmological text purportedly composed by adherents of the sect or by Orpheus himself) has both facilitated and problematized scholarship on Orphism.

Liz Locke

See also Folktale; Ritual

✳✳✳✳✳✳✳✳✳✳✳✳✳✳✳✳✳

References

Guthrie, W. K. C. *Orpheus and Greek Religion.* Princeton, N.J.: Princeton University Press, 1993 (1935).

Kosinski, Dorothy M. *Orpheus in Nineteenth-Century Symbolism.* Ann Arbor, Mich.: University Microfilms Inc. Research Press, 1989.

Lee, M. Owen. "Orpheus and Eurydice: Myth, Legend, and Folklore." In *Classica et Mediaevalia*, vol. 26, pp. 402–412. Copenhagen: Libraire Gyldendal, 1965.

Linforth, Ivan M. *The Arts of Orpheus.* Berkeley: University of California Press, 1941.

Segal, Charles. *Orpheus: The Myth of the Poet.* Baltimore and London: Johns Hopkins University Press, 1989.

OSSIAN

A character in the Ossianic or Fenian cycle of Irish and Scottish folklore, also called Oisín or Oiséan, Ossian is often depicted as a poet and singer and is the son of Fionn mac Cumhaill, the cycle's central figure. Fionn leads the *fianna,* a band of male warriors and hunters who roam the countryside seeking adventure, and tales of Fionn and his *fianna* are preserved both in a literary and in an oral tradition, the latter surviving still in the Gaelic-speaking areas of Ireland and Scotland. Each tradition may have influenced the other throughout the centuries, and both traditions together make up the body of Fenian material.

An important Irish Ossianic text of the twelfth century, "Acallamh na Senórach," or "The Colloquy of the Old Men," postulates the survival of Ossian and another member of the *fianna* until the time of St. Patrick and is largely a pastiche of stories told to St. Patrick about Fionn mac Cumhaill and his men. The narrative development exemplified in "The Colloquy of the Old Men" eventually earned Ossian an important and honored place in Fenian lore. In Scotland, a series of popular heroic ballads arose around the concept of an anachronistically aged Ossian telling tales of the *fianna* to the Irish saint. "The Book of the Dean of Lismore," a manuscript dating from the sixteenth century, preserves many of these Scots Gaelic ballads, and others have been collected up until the present time.

In the eighteenth century, the Scottish poet James Macpherson first brought Ossian and the Fenian lore to the attention of an international reading public. He published three volumes of poems—*Fragments of Ancient Poetry* (1760), *Fingal* (1761), and *Temora* (1763)—which he declared contained the genuine compositions of Ossian, a Scottish bard who was the son of a third-century king named Fingal. Macpherson claimed to have collected these poems, two of which were epics, in the Highlands of Scotland and then translated them from the Gaelic into measured English prose. In truth, the majority of the material was spurious, but Macpherson's Ossianic poems were immensely popular.

Like the Ossian of the Scots Gaelic heroic ballads, Macpherson's Ossian is an old man who has outlived his generation and become at last the sole survivor of his culture. He sings to those who will listen in an attempt to preserve memories of the past. Containing many characters and incidents from the heroic ballads, Macpherson's poems heavily reflect contemporary sentimental tastes and the deep sense of cultural loss following the Highland defeat at the Battle of Culloden Moor less than 20 years before the poems' publication.

The controversy surrounding Macpherson's Ossianic poems ultimately piqued the curiosity of scholars who traveled in the nineteenth and twentieth centuries to the Gaelic-speaking areas of Ireland and Scotland seeking the real Ossian in the songs and tales of Fionn mac Cumhaill and his *fianna*.

Melanie K. Hutsell

See also Fakelore; Macpherson, James

✳✳✳✳✳✳✳✳✳✳✳✳✳✳✳✳✳✳

References
Meek, Donald E. "The Gaelic Ballads of Scotland: Creativity and Adaptation." In *Ossian Revisited*, ed. Howard Gaskill, pp. 19–48. Edinburgh: Edinburgh University Press, 1991.

O hOgáin, Dáithí. *Fionn mac Cumhaill: Images of the Gaelic Hero*. Dublin: Gill and Macmillan, 1988.

Thomson, Derick S. "Macpherson's Ossian: Ballads to Epics." In *Fiannaíocht: Essays on the Fenian Tradition of Ireland and Scotland*, ed. Bo Almqvist, Séamus O Catháin, Pádraig O Héalaí. Dublin: Folklore of Ireland Society, 1987.

Ó SÚILLEABHÁIN, SEÁN (SEAN O'SULLIVAN) (1903–1996)

An internationally noted authority on Irish folk tradition, Seán Ó Súilleabháin (Sean O'Sullivan) began collecting folktales in County Kerry where he worked as a primary schoolteacher. In 1935, Ó Súilleabháin was chosen as archivist of the newly formed Coimisiún Béaloideasa Éireann [Irish Folklore Commission]. Through his studies at the University of Uppsala's Landmåls Folkminesarkivet (Dialect and Folklore Archive), he adopted the methodology of Herman Geyer, Ivan Liljeblad, and Aake Campbell to the collecting and cataloging of Irish folktales. In 1937, Ó Súilleabháin created a guidebook for collectors, based on the Swedish system, entitled *Láimhleabhar béaloideasa* [Folklore handbook]. Expanded and republished in English in 1942 as *A Handbook of Irish*

Ó Súilleabháin, Seán (Sean O'Sullivan)

Folklore, this volume quickly became the "bible" of folklore collectors as it covers a breadth of folkloric concerns and aspects of collection including categories and examples of folktales, questions to elicit and authenticate material, and techniques for acquiring story variants. Despite the thoroughness of the collecting guidelines, however, Ó Súilleabháin admitted the limitations of written accounts—"The voices, with their many modulations, are silent on the page; the audience is absent; only the pattern of the narrative and the procession of motifs remain" (Ó Súilleabháin 1966, p. xxxvii).

Ó Súilleabháin, like other students of Irish folklore, felt that Irish traditional tales were in danger of disappearing, and he realized their importance both as the repository of Irish cultural heritage and as a link to European culture. Through the offices of the Irish Folklore Commission, local collectors were trained in Ó Súilleabháin's system and appointed to collect tales in their districts. The commission also invited the participation of primary school pupils from the 26 Irish counties, and between 1937 and 1938, more than half a million of the over 1.5 million pages of material in the commission's archives were collected by the schoolchildren. Ó Súilleabháin carefully preserved these documents separately from those acquired by the commission's regular collectors.

A second key volume by Ó Súilleabháin, published in 1963 with Reidar Th. Christiansen, was *The Types of the Irish Folktale*. This volume contains a comprehensive classification and the manuscript location of the over 43,000 tales and variants of the Irish Folklore Commission's holdings gathered up to 1956. In his work as archivist, Ó Súilleabháin found that Irish tales could be classified into roughly three groups: tales that were indigenous to the Gaelic-speaking regions of Ireland and Scotland, tales with "distinctive patterns" that used well-known folkloric motifs, and international tales shared by a number of countries. Ó Súilleabháin also published stories selected from the commission's collection in *Folktales of Ireland* (1966), *The Folklore of Ireland* (1974), and *Legends from Ireland* (1977).

Other volumes are likewise important for their treatment of other forms of folklore. In *Irish Folk Custom and Belief* (1968), Ó Súilleabháin included prayers, charms, and even local history, suggesting as well that "folk belief is a correlative of the sciences of higher cultures. It tries in its own way to find answers to many questions about life and the world in general" (Ó Súilleabháin 1968,

p. 12). Additional works include *Caitheamh Aimsire ar Thórraimh* (translated as *Irish Wake Amusements*) (1967) and *Storytelling in Irish Tradition* (1973).

Sylvia McLaurin

See also Belief; Folktale

✳✳✳✳✳✳✳✳✳✳✳✳✳✳✳✳✳✳

References

Ó Súilleabháin, Seán. *A Handbook of Irish Folklore*. Detroit: Singing Tree Press, 1970.

———. *Irish Folk Custom and Belief*. Hatboro, Penn.: Folklore Associates, 1968.

———. *Irish Wake Amusements*. Cork: Mercier Press, 1967.

Ó Súilleabháin, Seán, ed. and trans. *Folktales of Ireland*. Chicago: University of Chicago Press, 1970.

Ó Súilleabháin, Seán, and Reidar Th. Christiansen. *The Types of the Irish Folktales*. Folklore Fellows Communication no. 188. Helsinki: Academia Scientiarum Fennica, 1966.

OTHELLO

The renowned Venetian general Othello is among William Shakespeare's most memorably tragic characters. From the beginning of Shakespeare's play *Othello* (1604–1605), the Moor is racially and culturally differentiated from the local Venetians, but he is able to idealize those differences and make them seem exotic in romantic life stories. As the play progresses, however, Othello falls from his initial laudable station, and he comes to distrust the world around him. Othello's struggle is a personal quest for self-knowledge, and in that struggle his personal narratives become central—reflecting the manner by which he presents and later discovers his own identity.

Othello is an accomplished narrator, proficient in telling stories that reach into an extended past in order to create a connected picture of his personal history. Because of his notable past and because of his age, at the beginning of the play that bears his name, Othello is in a position of comfortable achievement. His public identity seems already firmly established by the accumulation of memorable accomplishments, and his autobiographical narrations—the authorial

Shakespeare explored the uses of narrative in constructing cultural and personal identity through the character of Othello the Moor, depicted here narrating his heroic exploits.

renderings of his own life—tend to be highly retrospective in looking back onto a successful military career.

Othello performs personal narratives at strategic moments to shape his own identity. But in the course of this play he makes a discovery, learning in the end that his true identity does not really tally with his narratively constructed public image. The tragedy of *Othello* unfolds with this discovery, coincident with the deterioration of what may be called Othello's narrative ego.

Iago, Othello's antagonist, contravenes Othello's narrations with a different sort of storytelling, one that is marked by equivocation and innuendo and accomplishing much by what is left "unsaid." The comfortable sphere of control that Othello had created with his life stories begins to slip away from him as he searches for objective truth and tangibility in the false reports of Iago. The Moor finds himself immersed uneasily in the "real" world of disappointment, a transition brought on as he retreats from telling his own story and attempts instead to fill out the details of someone else's.

In the final scene of the play, Othello manages to resume his familiar narrating stance with its accompanying reflection into the past. The moment of his suicide and final narration are coterminous, and he becomes for that instant the personification of evil in the image of the despised Turk. The fact that Othello now willingly turns Turk himself, telling a story in which he identifies with the Turk even while he returns to his glorious military past, bespeaks the confusion that the play's action has caused him. Narration can no longer restore order out of chaos, as it previously could, and his final attempts at resolution with narration are ambivalent at best.

For all his efforts of self-fashioning and refashioning with life stories, Othello's narrative maneuvers falter. He becomes so utterly alienated from the world around him that tales of personal history can lead only to death, not to public approval and triumph as before.

Charles Greg Kelley

See also Personal Experience Story; Shakespeare, William; Storytelling

✳✳✳✳✳✳✳✳✳✳✳✳✳✳✳✳✳

References

Dolby (Stahl), Sandra. *Literary Folkloristics and the Personal Narrative*. Bloomington: Indiana University Press, 1989.

———. "The Oral Personal Narrative in Its Generic Context." *Fabula* 18 (1977): 18–39.

Hardy, Barbara. "The Personal Narrative as Folklore." *Journal of the Folklore Institute* 14:1–2 (1977): 9–30.

———. "Shakespeare's Narrative: Acts of Memory." *Essays in Criticism* 39:2 (1989): 93–115.

Titon, Jeff Todd. "The Life Story." *Journal of American Folklore* 93 (1980): 276–292.

Walker, Janelle. "A Perspective on the Use of Personal Texts in Folklore." *Folklore Historian* 12 (1995): 29–38.

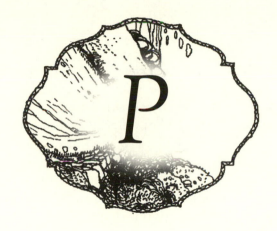

*P*AESE DI CUCCAGNA

The *paese di Cuccagna*, (Italian) land of Cockaigne, or *pays de Cocaigne* (French), is a mythic land of plenty where rivers run with wine (ale or milk), food falls like manna from heaven, work is banished, and no one ever grows old. In its many permutations over the centuries and across continents, the land has acquired many names: Lubberland (England), *Schlaraffenland* (Germany), land of Prester John (Hungary), Oleana (Norway), *Panigons* (France), Eldorado, Nowhere, and so forth. The myth represents one of the most persistent desires for a return to a lost earthly paradise, a folk version of utopia projected through the stomach rather than the mind. It is a "poor man's paradise" or a "collective dream of the hungry masses" and calls for the satisfaction of basic needs: food, rest, shelter, and sexuality.

In Italy, this myth becomes a strictly sensual paradise and essentially a gastronomic utopia, reflecting, through the inversion principle, a reality of want that spans the fourteenth to the twentieth centuries. The land of plenty is actually the land of hunger. The heightened popularity of the concept in the sixteenth and eighteenth centuries coincided with periods of recurring acute famine. Yet new ingredients are continuously added to the *cuccagna* "cauldron" itself as it comes to assimilate features of the tall tale, the pilgrim's travel tale, geographic myths coinciding with the age of discoveries, topsy-turvy land *(Il mondo alla rovescia)*, and the carnivalesque. Indeed *cuccagna* has come to be associated in the popular mind with feasting and survives in this reduced sense in many Italian dialects. On public piazzas today it still survives as *l'albero di Cuccagna*, a ritual remnant in the form of a greased pole with prosciutto and cheese (among other prizes) hanging at the top. In eighteenth-century Naples, rococo marvels of food—*macchine della cuccagna* ("Cockaigne machines")—ephemeral, edible architecture, were assembled before the royal palace, and on each of the four Sundays of carnival they were attacked and dismantled by a frenzied, famished crowd.

Although one of the earliest written attestations of a land of Cockaigne may be found in the thirteenth-century French fabliau (*fabliau de Cocagne*), it made its appearance in Italian letters under the altered name of *Bengodi* in Boccaccio's *Decameron* (Book 8, 3) when the simpleton Calandrino is duped into believing in a place where a cauldron sits atop a parmesan-cheese mountain spewing forth tortellini and macaroni all day long, which roll down the mountain and land in a pool of rich capon broth. Although each author or teller adds new details to the *cuccagna* type of landscape, the essentials of the Italian depiction are the cheese mountain, a prison for those who wish to work—for, as the banner reads in this topsy-turvy land, *chi più dorme più guadagna* ("he who sleeps most, earns most")—and sometimes a palace of pleasure (depicted in many iconographic representations on broadsides).

The *cuccagna* theme was extremely fertile in oral circulation, judging from the myriad representations of *cuccagna* in the broadside press in the form of prints, songs, board games, and so forth, yet it surfaces in literary form less frequently. A list of Italian authors who make reference to this mythic land would be tedious, but some illustrious names follow: Giovanni Boccaccio, Folengo, Calmo, and Aretino. Works actually featuring *cuccagna* in their titles are Carlo Goldoni's *Il paese della Cuccagna* (1750) and Matilde Serao's *Il paese di Cuccagna* (1891), in which Naples is the land of Cockaigne and *cuccagna* is used as a metaphor for the lottery mania.

Cuccagna seems to have survived well into the twentieth century—the immigrant's America, for instance, was also known as a *paese di Cuccagna*, a place where the streets were paved with gold and no one would go hungry again—but the idea seems to have persisted longest in children's literature. Pinocchio's *paese dei Balocchi* ("toyland") may represent a child's version of *cuccagna*, as might the magic pasta pot in Tomie de Paola's *Strega Non[n]a: An Old Italian Tale* (1975) or, more recently, in Judy and Ron Barrett's *Cloudy with a Chance of Meatballs* (1978), which posits:

> If food dropped like rain from the sky, wouldn't it be marvelous? Or would it? It could after all, be messy. And you'd have no choice. What if you didn't like what fell?

Or what if too much came? Have you ever thought of what it might be like to be squashed flat by a pancake?

Luisa Del Giudice

See also Boccaccio, Giovanni; Croce, Giulio Cesare; Tall Tale

✳✳✳✳✳✳✳✳✳✳✳✳✳✳✳✳✳

References

Camporesi, Piero. *Il paese della fame*. Bologna: Il Mulino, 1978.

Cocchiara, Giuseppe. *Il paese di Cuccagna*. Turin: Einaudi, 1956.

Fortunati, Vita, and Giampaolo Zucchini, eds. *Paesi di cuccagna e mondi alla rovescia*. Florence: Alinea, 1989.

Rammel, Hal. *Nowhere in America: The Big Rock Candy Mountain and Other Comic Utopias*. Urbana and Chicago: University of Illinois Press, 1990.

Richter, Dieter. *Schlaraffenland: Geschichte einer populären Phantasie*. Cologne, 1984. Italian translation, *Il paese di Cuccagna: Storia di una utopia popolare*. Florence: Diederichs, 1989.

Rossi, Vittorio, ed. "Il paese di Cuccagna nella letteratura italiana." In *Le lettere di messer Andrea Calmo*, appendix 2, pp. 398–410. Turin: Loescher, 1888.

PANCHATANTRA

Known from Java to Iceland, the *Panchatantra* is one of the most famous and most translated books in world literature—some 200 versions of it exist in over 50 languages. Since the original has been lost, its initial form is not known, and there is no proof as to exactly when it was written or by whom. Sanskritist Franklin Edgerton's research indicates that the work was composed in India somewhere between 100 and 500 C.E.; there is no accurate way of dating the work other than to say it was created earlier than the sixth century C.E., since it was translated into Pahlavi, a literary language of Persia, about 531 C.E.

As the title indicates, the *Panchatantra* [Five books] consists of five independent books. Each book has its own frame tale and includes a number of fables usually told by the characters in the framing story. A frame narrative preceding the first book ties the five books together. This short introduction tells about a king who entrusts his three sons to a wise Brahman, Vishnusharmen, who composes five books of fables, makes the princes memorize them, and as promised, teaches them the art of practical living within six months. Since then, according to the introduction, the *Panchatantra* has circulated the world educating the young.

The *Panchatantra* illustrates a materialistic philosophy developed simultaneously in India in more technical treatises, and its fables present a realistic philosophy of life, of which the basic doctrine is "the big fish eat the little fish." Dealing with practical reason and economics, the book aims to develop the complete person in practical affairs and serves as a handbook for success in gaining, exercising, and maintaining power and wealth. Although it encourages faithful relationships with relatives, friends, and superiors, the *Panchatantra* is Machiavellian in its political philosophy and illustrates a pragmatic strain in Indian culture that is often overlooked in favor of mysticism.

Although the elaborate use of framing narratives to present a number of traditional tales indicates that the *Panchatantra* was compiled from oral stories, philologist Norman Brown compared modern Indian folktales with variants found in older Indian versions of the *Panchatantra* and concluded that most of its fables did not originate in Indian folklore but entered it from elsewhere. Since oral literature and written literature are mutually influential, though, most likely many of the stories in the *Panchatantra* were in the oral tradition before the work was initially written; however, since collections of Indian folktales are relatively recent, it is not certain that the tales were popular among the people until after the *Panchatantra* was well known.

Regardless of whether the individual stories in the work were derived from the oral tradition, no parallel to the structure of the *Panchatantra* has been found in oral tradition. The framing narratives and the didactic application of the individual fables indicate that the work was created either by an artist or, through communal re-creation, by several independent artists. The many folktales in the work show that a number of international tales are at least as old as 500 C.E., and the many early translations of the work suggest how some folktales were spread over much of the world.

Ronald L. Baker

See also Fable; Frame Tale

✳✳✳✳✳✳✳✳✳✳✳✳✳✳✳✳✳

References

Benfey, Theodor. *Pantschatantra: Fünf Bücher Indischer Fabeln, Märchen, und Erzählungen.* 2 vols. Leipzig: F. A. Brockhaus, 1859.

Brown, W. Norman. "The Pañcatantra in Modern Indian Folklore." *Journal of the American Oriental Society* 39 (1919): 1–54.

Edgerton, Franklin. *The Panchatantra Reconstructed.* 2 vols. New Haven, Conn.: American Oriental Society, 1924.

Penzer, N. M., ed. *The Ocean of Story.* 10 vols. Delhi: Motilal Banarsidas, 1968 (1926).

Ryder, Arthur W., trans. *The Panchatantra.* Chicago: University of Chicago Press, 1925.

PAREDES, AMÉRICO (1915–)

The folklorist, mentor, novelist, journalist, and poet Américo Paredes was born to humble ranchers in Brownsville, Texas; earned a Ph.D. at the University of Texas, Austin, in 1956; and became one of the twentieth century's first influential Mexican-American scholars. An early collection of poetry, *Between Two Worlds* (1991), suggests the bicultural and binational identities that would have a profound impact on Paredes's professional pursuits and commitments. Paredes is best known for *With His Pistol in His Hand* (1958), a groundbreaking study of a widely circulated corrido (narrative folk song or ballad) about the Texas-Mexican folk hero, Gregorio Cortez. The book is as imaginative as it is scholarly. In its consideration of the history, people, and folkways of the Texas-Mexican border country, and in its sympathy for Texas-Mexican cultural dilemmas, the study is an original and a model for subsequent scholarship.

The legendary incident memorialized in the corrido occurred in 1901 when a non-Spanish-speaking Texas sheriff, accompanied by an Anglo translator, went to question the Mexican ranch hand Cortez about a missing horse. The inept translator misinterpreted Cortez's response. In the ensuing confusion, the sheriff drew his gun, Cortez's brother drew his own, the sheriff shot the brother, and Cortez shot the sheriff. Because of the experiences of Texas Mexicans with the inequalities of Anglo due process, Cortez fled, and through skill, luck, and the aid of Mexican sympathizers, he eluded hundreds of pursuing Texas Rangers over thousands of miles. Finally safe in Mexico, he heard that his family was imprisoned for his "crime" and gave himself up. A protracted trial followed in which Cortez won his freedom.

In Gregorio Cortez, Paredes saw a folk hero who embodied

Texas-Mexican resistance to Anglo-Texan regional dominance. To Texas Mexicans in south Texas, the Texas Rangers symbolized an unjust authority that was widely suspected of being behind the unlawful dispossession of properties belonging to Mexicans. By out-smarting the rangers, Cortez inverted the racial stereotype of the passive and dumb Mexican and instead demonstrated native intelligence and courage. A study of the corrido reveals not only the tale's specific conflict but also the broader political and cultural conflicts between peoples whose coexistence came about not through consent, but through war and treaty. The corrido preserves the cultural values of the Texas-Mexican community at a time of continued disenfranchisement of landowners and nonlandowners alike. As a text about the tensions inherent in Anglo-Mexican relations, *With His Pistol in His Hand* serves as a template for the concerns of later Mexican-American poets, novelists, political activists, and literary critics.

In 1983, a film version of the book appeared. The screenplay was written by the Chicano novelist Victor Villaseñor, and the film was directed by the documentary filmmaker Robert H. Young and featured Edward James Olmos as Gregorio Cortez. Border folklore, Paredes argued, is the backbone of a Mexican-American literary tradition, a reminder of the past as well as evidence of a continuing cultural integrity.

Paredes also wrote widely about other legends, tales, and ballads of Mexican-American culture; translated and edited many books on Mexican folktales; and wrote *The Urban Experience and Folk Tradition* (1971) and *Mexican-American Authors* (1976). He directed the Folklore Center at the University of Texas, Austin, from 1957 to 1970 and thereafter directed Mexican-American studies there. He became professor emeritus in 1985.

Krista Comer and José Aranda

See also Ballad; *Corrido*

✳✳✳✳✳✳✳✳✳✳✳✳✳✳✳✳✳✳

References

Calderón, Hector, and José David Saldivar. *Criticism in the Borderlands: Studies in Chicano Literature, Culture, and Ideology*. Durham, N.C.: Duke University Press, 1991.

Paredes, Américo. *With His Pistol in His Hand: A Border Ballad and Its Hero*. Austin: University of Texas Press, 1958.

Saldivar, Ramón. *Chicano Narrative: The Dialectics of Difference*. Madison: University of Wisconsin Press, 1990.

PARRY, MILMAN (1902–1935)

A classicist, comparatist, and collector of south Slavic oral epic poetry, Milman Parry was cooriginator (with Albert Bates Lord) of the oral-formulaic theory. Parry began as a student of the Homeric *Iliad* and *Odyssey* who sought to answer the so-called Homeric question by demonstrating that these epics were the creation not of a single gifted individual, but of a centuries-old tradition of verse making. Between 1933 and 1935, Parry and Lord led field expeditions to the former Yugoslavia, specifically to study and record the oral performances of preliterate epic singers *(guslari)* in order to test the further thesis that such a traditional poetry must also be orally composed and transmitted. Parry's many influential publications and the Milman Parry Collection of Oral Literature at Harvard University, which contains more than half a million lines of southern Slavic epic recorded in the field, stand as testimony to his pioneering enterprise.

Parry's first crucial insight was that Homer's formulaic diction—most readily observable in the consistent use of noun-epithet phrases like "rosy-fingered dawn" or "swift-footed Achilleus"—constituted a specialized, inherited variety of ancient Greek that served the generations of epic singers as a ready medium for tale telling. In both Parry's M.A. and D.Litt. theses, he demonstrated the complex patterning of this special idiom, defining the formula as "an expression regularly used, under the same metrical conditions, to express an essential idea" and noting that the diction was programmatically thrifty in normally containing only one metrically acceptable way to name a person or deity in any grammatical case in the Homeric hexameter line (Parry 1971, p. 276). He also began to describe a corresponding unit of narrative, later called "the theme" by Lord, that constituted an expressive idiom at the level of scenes or actions.

Under the particular influence of Antoine Meillet, his mentor at Paris, and Matija Murko, a Slavic ethnographer and philologist who spent his summers studying the *guslari*, Parry evolved the theory that the formula was the touchstone of not only traditional but oral composition. He detailed these views, the core of his theoretical contribution, in two articles published in 1930 and 1932 ("Studies in the Epic Technique of Oral Verse-Making, I" and "II").

But Parry was not only a theorist, and it was typical of what he styled his "literary anthropology" that he saw the next step as a journey to then-Yugoslavia to test his hypothesis in the living laboratory of still extant oral epic song. With the assistance of native speaker (and *guslar*) Nikola Vujnović, Parry and Lord made acoustic or dictated records of dozens of live performances by singers from various regions, the most talented of them being Avdo Medjedović of Bijelo Polje in Montenegro, who, though unable to read or write, dictated two epics that are each about the length of the *Odyssey*.

Although Parry did not live to write the comparative study of oral poetry that he envisioned, or to publish selected south Slavic epics in the original and English translation (both projects undertaken and completed by Lord in later years), Parry's groundbreaking explanation of the special idiom of the traditional oral epic provided a new and extremely powerful answer to the Homeric question. It also was eventually to give rise to the oral-formulaic theory, which has affected more than 130 separate areas to date, from biblical studies and Chinese philosophy to the contemporary art of the American folk preacher.

John Miles Foley

See also Balkan Folklore and Literature; Homer; *Iliad*; Lord, Albert Bates; *Odyssey*; Oral-Formulaic Composition and Theory

✳✳✳✳✳✳✳✳✳✳✳✳✳✳✳✳✳

References

Foley, John Miles. *The Theory of Oral Composition: History and Methodology*. Bloomington: Indiana University Press, 1992 (1988).

———. *Traditional Oral Epic: The* Odyssey, Beowulf, *and the Serbo-Croatian Return Song*. Berkeley: University of California Press, 1993 (1990).

Lord, Albert Bates. *Epic Singers and Oral Tradition*. Ithaca, N.Y.: Cornell University Press, 1991.

———. *The Singer of Tales*. Cambridge: Harvard University Press, 1960.

Parry, Milman. *The Making of Homeric Verse: The Collected Papers of Milman Parry*. Ed. Adam Parry. Oxford: Clarendon Press, 1971.

Parry, Milman, Albert B. Lord, and David E. Bynum, collectors, eds., and trans. *Serbocroatian Heroic Songs (Srpskohrvatske junacke pjesme)*. Cambridge and Belgrade: Harvard University Press and the Serbian Academy of Sciences, 1953– .

PERCY, THOMAS (1729–1811)

Thomas Percy, bishop of Dromore, is remembered for his *Reliques of Ancient English Poetry,* a collection of old ballads, poems, romances, and songs that became the most influential book of the romantic period and the foundation document of the ballad revival. This collection of ballad poetry was published in 1765 and was based on an old folio manuscript that Percy saw lying on the floor and being used by the maids to light the fires: "This very curious old Manuscript in its present mutilated state, but unbound and sadly torn & c., I rescued from destruction, and begged at the hands of my worthy friend Humphrey Pitt" (*Reliques* 1, p. lxxxii). The *Reliques,* however, is by no means a reprint of the large folio—only one-fourth of the printed texts were extracted from it and included—but the published collection mirrors the poetic diversity of the manuscript itself: Robin Hood ballads; historical ballads derived from garlands; metrical romances; poetry from the time of the Tudors and Stuarts; some traditional pieces; and some modern ballad imitations.

Percy offered his *Reliques of Ancient English Poetry* almost apologetically. The songs and poems, he explained, are not "labors of art" but "effusions of nature": they are "the barbarous productions of unpolished age" (*Reliques* 1, p. 1) and as such are artless but graceful, simple but pleasing. Being effusions of nature, these songs of the ancient minstrels were thought rude and deficient in the higher beauties of art. Thus, they needed to be collated, complemented, and corrected prior to publication. Once polished, they would appeal to the heart of the lover of ballad poetry. Furthermore, they would also be of interest to the historian, since the *Reliques* reveals the first efforts of ancient genius and exhibits the customs and opinions of remote ages.

Although Percy's collection of ancient English poetry was intended for "the reader of taste and genius" and "the judicious antiquary" (*Reliques* 1, p. 6), the affecting simplicity and artless beauties of the old ballads also struck a chord with the general public, and when the *Reliques of Ancient English Poetry* was published in 1765— in the wake of the Scottish poet and historian James Macpherson's work on the Ossianic poems in 1760—they were met with great acclaim. Percy's ballad poetry was seen to be a corrective of the "polished" poetry of the day, and *Reliques of Ancient English Poetry* proved an enormous success in England, Scotland, and indeed, the rest of

Europe. Sir Walter Scott acknowledged his indebtedness to Percy and so did William Wordsworth, who claimed that English poetry had been "absolutely redeemed" by the publication of the *Reliques*.

Within a year of the book's publication, poems from the *Reliques* were translated into German and had a profound effect on the Sturm und Drang literary movement in Germany. Johann Gottfried Herder, and later Jacob and Wilhelm Grimm, elaborated on Percy's distinction between the poetry of nature (i.e., the poetry of the people) and the poetry of art, laying the foundation for an independent folklore genre.

Despite the book's far-from-homogeneous collection of material, the *Reliques* served as a role model for many ballad collections and editions in the eighteenth and nineteenth centuries, including those by Sir Walter Scott, and perhaps surprisingly, Francis James Child. Although Percy was not a field collector in any sense of the word, he gathered many ballads and songs from various sources. He took great care, however, to distinguish his ballads from the broadsides that were commonly sung and hawked in the streets. Unlike modern ballad scholars, Percy was not interested in the music or the singers, nor did he show much awareness of the songs' traditional habitat. To him, the ballads were decidedly poems.

Joseph Ritson, Percy's most adamant critic, took no issue with this opinion; he was, however, infuriated by Percy's views on the minstrels and his claim to have published from an ancient manuscript. Although Ritson admitted that the (supposedly) old texts were "beautiful, elegant and ingenious" (Furnivall and Hales 1, pp. xvii–xix), he questioned the very existence of the folio manuscript and accused Percy of being a liar and a forger. Percy was hurt by these—unfounded—accusations, but he did not feel obliged to disclose the folio manuscript. Distancing himself from the publication of the *Reliques* in later life—not wanting his professional title of "bishop" used in connection with ballad poetry—it was left to the scholars Frederick J. Furnivall and Francis James Child more than 100 years later to secure the folio manuscript for the public. Not surprisingly, Percy's theories on ballads and his editorial practices have come into disrepute today, but it cannot be denied that no other single book has given a greater impetus to the study and collecting of ballads than Bishop Percy's *Reliques of Ancient English Poetry*.

Sigrid Rieuwerts

See also Ballad; Child, Francis James; Grimm, Jacob and Wilhelm;

Herder, Johann Gottfried; Macpherson, James; Ossian; Romance; Romanticism; Scott, Sir Walter

****

References

Friedman, Albert B. *The Ballad Revival: Studies in the Influence of Popular on Sophisticated Poetry.* Chicago: University of Chicago Press, 1961.

Furnivall, Frederick J., and John W. Hales, eds. *Bishop Percy's Folio Manuscript: Ballads and Romances.* 3 vols. London: Trübner, 1867–1868.

Herder, Johann Gottfried. "Auszug aus einem Briefwechsel über Ossian und die Lieder alter Völker (1773)." In *Herder's Sämmtliche Werke,* ed. Bernhard Suphan, vol. 5, pp. 159–207. Berlin: Weidermann, 1881.

Macpherson, James. *Fragments of Ancient Poetry: Collected in the Highlands of Scotland and Translated from the Galic or Erse Language.* Edinburgh: Hamilton and Balfour, 1760.

Percy, Thomas. *Reliques of Ancient English Poetry: Consisting of Old Heroic Ballads, Songs, and Other Pieces of Our Earlier Poets Together with Some Few of Later Date.* 3 vols. London: Dodlsey, 1765.

Percy Folio Manuscript. British Museum Add. MSS. 27879, c. 1650.

PERFORMANCE

Performance, in its most prominent usage in contemporary folkloristics, is a framed mode of communication in which aesthetic considerations are brought to the fore. The performer assumes responsibility to the audience, not only for the content of the communication, but also for the way in which it is presented. Norms for the manner of presentation vary according to culture, group, genre, situation, and other factors, as do the means for indicating the beginning of performance. Performance may be an attribute of a specific genre or event, or it may be optional; it may be sustained or touched upon fleetingly; its terms may even be negotiated during the course of the performance.

Richard Bauman's influential formulation, building on the work of Dell Hymes, emerged as part of the shift during the 1960s and 1970s toward the analysis of folklore in its social and cultural context. When performance is employed by folklorists, it does not necessarily involve, although it need not preclude, acting or playing a part or giving an oral rendition of a written text. It does, however, retain the connotations that a performance is intended to entertain while exposing both performer and material performed to public view, heightened scrutiny, and evaluation of the manner in which the performance is carried out.

The focus on performance has fostered and stimulated important changes in the practice and focus of folklore study and has remained one of the most influential paradigms within folkloristics since the mid-1970s as exploration of its implications continues. Given that in performance theory the realm of the aesthetic is seen as being constituted by and recognizable from a behavioral move into the performance frame, this approach eliminates reliance upon ethnocentric, elite, or Western notions of "art." Performance theory thus supplied the theoretical grounding for an expanded notion of what constitutes folklore—based on the recognition of locally recognized and emerging genres—as well as for a shift in disciplinary emphasis away from formal genre definition and the historic-geographic search for ur-texts (original, first texts) and toward an interest in the functional analysis of individual, contextualized, aesthetic expressions.

The notion of the folkloric performance as emergent from its context encouraged folklorists to reconceptualize tradition as a process rather than a determinate object or quality, since each new rendition of a traditional form both enacts continuity and challenges the possibility of maintaining a tradition unchanged. Attention to the formal attributes of verbal art and its essence as live performance has revivified the study of ethnographic and ancient texts, as scholars recognize poetic structuring and dramatic action in texts formerly conceived of as only prose narratives.

Performance theory and its ramifications within folkloristics have likewise had a significant impact on the study of folklore and literature. Fundamentally, from this perspective literature and vernacular verbal art can no longer be seen as being different in kind, only in degree. Both are performances, that is, attempts to display communicative competence as defined by a particular audience, to call attention to the way the discursive presentation is done, to reach communicative goals while responding to the group's aesthetic expectations, to enhance experience, and to invite evaluation of the effectiveness of the attempt. Scholars have recognized the practical interdependence of oral and written transmission in many traditions and have realized, in subsequent elaborations of performance theory, that the very features that constitute and distinguish oral performances make them more cohesive and more textlike—and thus expose them to be more readily decontextualized and used in other contexts.

The performance approach steers the study of folklore and literature away from the simple enumeration and identification of examples of folklore in literary works toward other issues, issues that are broadly functional, rhetorical, and semiotic. The folk performer, the ethnographer (or the folklorist who collects and presents folklore), the literary author, and the characters in the literary work are all seen as analogously although not identically mobilizing the discursive resources available to them and employing traditionalizing practices to create modes of textual authority.

Patricia E. Sawin

See also Bakhtin, Mikhail Mikhailovitch; Historic-Geographic Method; Oral-Formulaic Composition and Theory

✳✳✳✳✳✳✳✳✳✳✳✳✳✳✳✳✳

References

Bauman, Richard. *Verbal Art as Performance*. Rowley, Mass.: Newbury House, 1977.

Bauman, Richard, and Charles L. Briggs. "Poetics and Performance as Critical Perspectives on Language and Social Life." *Annual Review of Anthropology* 19 (1990): 59–88.

Lewis (Brown), Mary Ellen B. "The Study of Folklore and Literature: An Expanded View." *Southern Folklore Quarterly* 40 (1976): 343–351.

Preston, Cathy Lynn, ed. *Folklore, Literature, and Cultural Theory: Collected Essays*. New York: Garland, 1995.

Stoeltje, Beverly J., and Richard Bauman. "The Semiotics of Folkloric Performance." In *The Semiotic Web 1987*, ed. Thomas A. Sebeok and Jean Umiker-Sebeok, pp. 585–599. Amsterdam: Mouton de Gruyter, 1988.

PERI ROSSI, CRISTINA (1941–)

Born in Montevideo in 1941, the Uruguayan poet and novelist Cristina Peri Rossi studied humanities at the University of Montevideo and originally worked in her native country as a journalist and teacher of literature. She began her writing career quite early, publishing her first book of stories, *Viviendo* [Living], in 1963. Because of her political activities, she was forced to flee her native country in 1972—at the time, she was 30 years old and had published five books. Since then, Peri Rossi has resided in Barcelona, Spain, where she has continued to publish stories, novels, and poetry that are noted for their linguistic play, eroticism, and political commitment. Her writing deals with many crucial themes, most notably identity, representation, exile, love, political oppression, and sexuality.

Cristina Peri Rossi's work is decidedly international, urban centered, and intellectual, often without any direct reference to her native country. Her narratives are populated by such "high culture" motifs as the museum and the dictionary and by such postmodern characters as a generic, contemporary Everyman named only Equis ("X"). Yet, while contemporary, metropolitan, and literary society occupies center stage in Peri Rossi's writing, she has also said that what most interests her as a writer is the anguish and anxiety caused by the urban denizen's loss of an organic unity with the natural world. In the process of portraying that loss, Peri Rossi's work also displays certain characteristics that align it with more folkloric traditions. Features often associated with fairy tales and mythic modes that appear in Peri Rossi's narratives include the journey motif, riddles, allegorical structure, fantasy, and representations of initiation and marriage rituals.

The journey is the central motif of Peri Rossi's most important work to date, her novel *La nave de los locos* [The ship of fools (1995)]. This text documents the wayward itinerary of the anonymous yet endearing Equis as his travels take him to a series of real places, such as Toronto and Madrid, as well as to symbolic, mythical spaces, such as La Isla ("The Island"), and abstract, unnamed sites, such as *La Ciudad de A* ("the city of A"). Equis's quest throughout this endless journey is ultimately for a new sense of community in the face of dispersion and marginalization. The fragmentary portrayal of this journey is interspersed and contrasted with descriptions of a medieval tapestry that depicts the biblical story of the creation and the origin of man. Another notable aspect of this novel is its portrayal of several riddles that are presented to Equis in dreams. The first riddle has to do with the initiation of Equis's quest while the last involves an enigmatic question posed by a king to the princes and knights who desire to marry his daughter. Several critics have analyzed these riddles and their significance to the novel.

The allegorical strain in Peri Rossi's work, which is certainly predominant in *La nave de los locos*, also appears in many of her short stories. In *Indicios pánicos* [Signs of panic (1970)], an earlier work comprising poems, vignettes, stories, and other fragmentary writings that prefigure the authoritarian regime which would take power in 1972, there are several pieces that could be characterized as allegorical tales, including "El Prócer" [The leader], in which a statue of one of the nation's forefathers comes alive and attempts to come to terms with the contemporary political scene. A later collection of short stories, *La rebelión de los niños* [The children's rebellion (1980)], provides a critical view of contemporary society through the eyes of children, a frequent technique used by Peri Rossi. In this collection, allegory also plays a role, especially in the final story "La rebelión de los niños," which is a fable about political repression and resistance. A more recent collection, *Una pasión prohibida* [A forbidden passion (1986)], also contains several stories that read like fables or allegories. For example, the first story narrates, with considerable humor and biting satire, the reception of an angel who inadvertently falls to earth.

Mary Beth Tierney-Tello

See also Fable; Myth; Riddle; Ritual

✳✳✳✳✳✳✳✳✳✳✳✳✳✳✳✳✳

References

Kaminsky, Amy. *Reading the Body Politic: Feminist Criticism and Latin American Women Writers*. Minneapolis: University of Minnesota Press, 1993.

Kantaris, Elia. "The Politics of Desire: Alienation and Identity in the Work of Marta Traba and Cristina Peri Rossi." *Forum for Modern Language Studies* 25:3 (July 1989): 248–264.

Mora, Gabriela. "Enigmas and Subversions in Cristina Peri Rossi's *La nave de los locos*." In *Splintering Darkness: Latin American Women Writers in Search of Themselves*, ed. Lucía Guerra-Cunningham, pp. 19–30. Pittsburgh: Latin American Literary Review Press, 1990.

Tierney-Tello, Mary Beth. "Exile and New Dream of Symmetry: Cristina Peri Rossi's *La nave de los locos*." In Mary Beth Tierney-Tello, ed., *Allegories of Transgression and Transformation: Experimental Fiction by Women Writing under Dictatorship*, pp. 173–208. Albany: State University of New York Press, 1996.

PERRAULT, CHARLES (1628–1703)

Charles Perrault's contribution to folklore and literature lies in his 11 fairy tales. Three are verse tales, published separately: *Patient Griselda* (1691), *The Ridiculous Wishes* (1693), and *Donkeyskin* (1694). The others are prose tales, cumulatively entitled *Histories or*

"Puss in Boots" was one of Charles Perrault's eight prose tales published in 1697 that later became widely known as the Tales of Mother Goose.

Tales of Past Times—or, as they later came to be known, *Tales of Mother Goose*—published in 1697. This collection includes Perrault's most famous tales: "Sleeping Beauty," "Little Red Riding Hood," "Bluebeard," "Puss in Boots," and "Cinderella," along with the lesser known "The Fairies," "Hop o' My Thumb," and "Rickey with the Tuft." Although Perrault was not the first French writer of fairy tales, nor were his tales intended only for a child audience, his are the ones most familiar to today's children.

A poet, scholar, and lawyer with family connections in high places, for many years Perrault held a favorable political bureaucratic position under Louis XIV. In 1671, he was appointed to the prestigious Académie Française, and while an active member of the academy, Perrault engaged in a famous series of literary debates known as "the quarrel between the ancients and the moderns," which in part concerned the legitimacy of writing popular works such as fairy tales. His stance eventually made an enemy of the poet Nicolas Boileau-Despréaux, and Boileau later caustically denigrated Perrault's prose tales. Later, when the first edition of the Mother Goose tales was published, the title page carried the initials "P. P.," implying that the tales were the product of Perrault's son, Pierre. Many critics now believe that this ruse was simply the elder Perrault's way of avoiding further recriminations.

The oral telling of original fairy tales was a popular pastime of the royal court and literary salons of seventeenth-century France, and while Perrault undoubtedly drew on a large oral folk tradition in creating his tales, he also had some literary precedents: literary analogues in Latin, German, Italian, and even French literature existed for many of his tales. Several of his contemporaries were also composing literary fairy tales in the 1690s, nearly all of them women.

Perrault, of course, did not claim to be presenting genuine "tales of the folk" verbatim; the language, humor, and descriptive details of his stories reflect the seventeenth-century upper-class and court society that he knew intimately, not the peasant class. In the mode of his role model, the French poet Jean de La Fontaine, each story ended with a moral, an element that Perrault considered essential to the value of the tale but which is more often than not omitted by modern retellers. Rather than trying to preserve oral tales heard in the nursery or by the fireside, Perrault was advancing the modernist cause by melding popular motifs and style with the literary elements admired in his day. That he did so with such deft vividness and conciseness is a tribute to his skill as an author, a talent for which his perennial audiences, both children and adults, have been grateful.

Martha Hixon

See also Fable; *Märchen*

✳✳✳✳✳✳✳✳✳✳✳✳✳✳✳✳✳

References

Barchilon, Jacques, and Peter Flinders. *Charles Perrault*. Boston: G. K. Hall, 1981.

Opie, Iona, and Peter Opie. *The Classic Fairy Tales*. New York and Toronto: Oxford University Press, 1974.

Perrault, Charles. *The Complete Fairy Tales of Charles Perrault*. Trans. Neil Philip and Nicoletta Simborowski. New York: Clarion, 1993.

———. *The Fairy Tales of Charles Perrault*. Trans. Angela Carter. London: Victor Gallancz, 1977.

Zipes, Jack. "Introduction." In Jack Zipes, ed., *Spells of Enchantment: The Wondrous Fairy Tales of Western Culture*, pp. xi–xxx. New York: Viking, 1991.

PERSONAL EXPERIENCE STORY

The personal experience story is a prose narrative relating a personal experience; it is usually told in the first person, and its content is nontraditional. The plot of the story is based on an actual event—a single episode—in the life of the storyteller, and thus it is considered to be a "true" story rather than a fictional one. Unlike most folklore, a personal experience story is not passed down through time and space, nor is it kept alive through variation from one teller to another. Instead, even as oral performances, such stories are often considered the property of the person who had the experience and created the story in the first place. They are creative pieces that tap into tradition only as they draw upon conventional notions of what is story-worthy or thematically relevant and upon the broad outlines of the genre itself.

Proof of the traditionality of the genre is found in the many clearly traditional genres that must, to be effective, disguise themselves as personal experience stories—genres such as tall tales, first-person jokes, or catch tales, in which the storyteller is "lying" but pretends to be relating an experience he or she really did have. The

504

personal experience story itself is so common that for many years it was neglected by researchers studying oral narratives.

As oral narratives, personal experience stories are found in a variety of contexts, from conversations around a kitchen table to television talk shows, from informal work breaks to more formal settings, such as a classroom or business meeting. People who tell personal experience stories expect to entertain or impress their listeners. Although the plots of the stories are not traditional, most demonstrate common and often humorous themes of discomfiture, depict exaggerated character traits, or offer lessons in behaviors to avoid or emulate.

Because such stories are so very common in real life, the performance of oral personal narratives is often re-created in literature. One of the earliest literary presentations of such a performance is in the Sumerian epic *Gilgamesh* (c. 2000 B.C.E.), a narrative pieced together from ancient tablets that records the storyteller's own single-episodic adventures during his reign as king of Uruk. More recent literature, especially novels, often makes use of the personal experience story.

A classic work that uses the genre to good effect is Mark Twain's *Adventures of Huckleberry Finn* (1884). For example, after Jim and Huck have been on the island awhile, Huck decides to visit the shore and find out what people were saying about his supposed murder. He then tells how he dresses up like a girl and stops at a little shanty on the Illinois side of the river. The woman in the house talks to him for some time but eventually "tests" him to see if he is really a girl by throwing a lump of lead into his lap. Huck claps his legs together to catch the lump and thus reveals that he is a boy and not used to wearing a dress. This "test" happens to be a traditional motif (H1578.1.4.1), but the narrative in which it is embedded is a typical "theme of discomfiture" experience story. Twain is able to include it as a realistic part of the story because the tradition of the personal experience story is so familiar to his readers.

Earlier in the same work, Huck tells of an incident involving Tom Sawyer and Jim. Jim is sleeping, and Tom decides he must play a trick on Jim. He steals Jim's hat from his head and hangs it in a tree above him; then he leaves a nickel behind in payment for some candles. Jim wakes up and claims that witches put a spell on him and rode him all over the state, leaving the hat and the nickel as evidence. The beauty of this passage is that it illustrates one of the common themes of such stories—the account of a practical joke. In addition, it expands into another related category, the memorate, which is a personal experience story involving the supernatural. Jim's belief that he was "ridden by witches" is a well-known one, and stories abound of experiences similar to the one Jim soon relates to his friends. The added bonus in Twain's account is his discussion of the process by which Jim's story becomes increasingly exaggerated over time.

The personal experience story is an oral genre that is closely tied to literature from ancient times to the present. Fiction writers have found it an indispensable aid in presenting realistic plot incidents in a form long enjoyed by readers and storytellers alike.

Sandra K. Dolby

See also Genre; Storytelling; Style; Tall Tale; Twain, Mark

✳✳✳✳✳✳✳✳✳✳✳✳✳✳✳✳✳✳

References

Bauman, Richard. *Story, Performance, and Event.* Cambridge: Cambridge University Press, 1986.

Dolby (Stahl), Sandra K. *Literary Folkloristics and the Personal Narrative.* Bloomington: Indiana University Press, 1989.

———. "The Oral Personal Narrative in Its Generic Context." *Fabula* 18 (1977): 18–39.

Dolby (Stahl), Sandra K., and Richard M. Dorson, eds. "Stories of Personal Experience." *Journal of the Folklore Institute* 14 (1977): 5–126.

Honko, Lauri. "Memorates and the Study of Folk Belief." *Journal of the Folklore Institute* 1 (1964): 5–19.

Piñon, Nélida (1937–)

Born in Rio de Janeiro to Spanish parents, the Brazilian writer Nélida Piñon has written eight novels and three collections of short stories, which often explore the legends and myths of Spain (especially Galicia) and of her native Brazil. For Piñon, myth—along with language and memory—is at the heart of literary production. She is especially interested in how myths are absorbed and transformed in the collective imagination. Piñon has said that she wanted to be a writer when she was eight years old and, indeed, that she could never conceive of her existence except as an act of creation. It is not surprising, then, that the myth of creation occupies such a prime position in her narratives, perhaps most explicitly in her novels *Fundador* [Founder] and *A casa da paixão* [The house of passion (1972)], both of which are vivid examples of the dense, highly symbolic prose for which she is noted.

Piñon's writings consistently touch on themes of creation, passion, the sacred, the erotic, the oppression of women, and more recently, history. For Piñon, passion is an elemental force that exceeds rationality. Indeed, in many of her works she seems intent on representing such an intangible and inexplicable force, causing some critics to accuse her of being too "hermetic." Her style does often tend to the abstract and allegorical, and her narratives are frequently highly experimental in terms of form. Lately, she has turned to the historical saga in *A república dos sonhos* [Republic of dreams (1989)] and to social criticism in *A doce canção de Caetana* [Caetana's sweet song (1992)]. Both of these texts, which have been translated into English, draw more heavily on realist techniques such as description of place and character, making them in some ways more accessible than some of her earlier work.

Myth is especially important in *A casa da paixão*, a novel that has been studied from the perspective of Jungian theories. Throughout the narrative, which lies somewhere between bildungsroman and psychosexual fable, the protagonist (Marta) struggles for her sexual autonomy, forming a sensual relationship with the sun, rebelling against her incestuously desirous father (Pai), and resisting the father's understudy and supplanter (Jerônimo). After a complex series of transformations, Marta ends up entering into a mythic sexual union with Jerônimo. In the text, ritual plays a central role, and much of the drama revolves around the protagonist's sexual initiation, her sensual relationship to the natural world (most notably the sun), and her struggle against the marriage rites imposed on her by her authoritarian father. The fusion of the sacred and the erotic and the act of creation itself are both important aspects of the narrative.

Myth and legend are also incorporated, albeit in a very different way, in *A república dos sonhos*. This expansive novel narrates four generations of a Brazilian family descended from Madruga, an immigrant from Galicia. Although Brazil's contemporary reality is often prominent as the foreground, the narrative moves back and forth between the remembered stories, legends, and traditions of Galicia and the effect those dreams and myths have on the lives of Madruga's family. The importance of the African heritage of Brazil and the myths of progress and industry, which inform the foundational fable of the young country, as well as the Old World influences, which continue to exert their force, are all enmeshed in this saga, which skillfully blends the personal and the political, internal emotions and external realities.

Politics, while often obliquely present in many of Piñon's narratives, is perhaps most explicitly explored in her collection of stories *Calor das coisas* (1980), which contains representations of political repression and torture. Another work with political resonances is *A doce canção de Caetana*, which takes place in a small town in Brazil in 1970. This text, while narrating the trials and tribulations of the staging of an opera, provides a shrewd critique of the political illusions generated by the regime.

The rebellion of women against patriarchal, authoritarian forces comes up in several of Piñon's works, most notably in *A casa da paixão* and *A força do destino* [Force of destiny (1977)]. The latter work, a parody of the nineteenth-century opera with the same name by Giuseppe Verdi, narrates the struggle of the tragic lovers against the woman's father and brother while also emphasizing and problematizing the process of literary production itself through the introduction in the story of a character/author named Nélida Piñon.

Mary Beth Tierney-Tello

See also *Bildungsroman;* Jung, Carl Gustav; Legend; Myth; Ritual; Women

✳✳✳✳✳✳✳✳✳✳✳✳✳✳✳✳✳

References

Moniz, Naomi Hoki. *As viagens de Nélida.* Campinas, Brazil: Editora de UNICAMP, 1993.

Pratt, Annis. *Archetypal Patterns in Women's Fiction.* Bloomington: Indiana University Press, 1981.

———. "Spinning among Fields: Jung, Frye, Lévi-Strauss, and Feminist Archetypal Theory." In *Feminist Archetypal Theory: Interdisciplinary Revisions of Jungian Thought,* ed. Estella Lauter and Carol Schreier Rupprecht. Knoxville: University of Tennessee Press, 1985.

Tierney-Tello, Mary Beth. "Defiance and Its Discontents: Nélida Piñon's *A casa da paixão.*" In Mary Beth Tierney-Tello, ed., *Allegories of Transgression and Transformation: Experimental Fiction by Women Writing under Dictatorship,* pp. 29–77. Albany: State University of New York Press, 1996.

Poe, Edgar Allan (1809–1849)

The fiction writer, poet, and critic Edgar Allan Poe is the most familiar of American writers and the most enigmatic. His works appear in virtually every American literature anthology; his most popular tales and poems have been repeatedly reproduced in films, theatrical productions, and other artistic media; and certain details of his life—the early deaths of his mother and his wife, his turbulent relationship with his foster father John Allan, his alleged addiction to opium and alcohol, the mysterious circumstances of his death—have been repeated so often in biographies, documentaries, and classrooms that they have passed into popular tradition. Yet many popular conceptions of Poe are based on misconceptions and out-right lies perpetrated by his literary executor, Rufus Griswold. Poe's literary productions include not only such Gothic tales as "Ligeia" and "The Fall of the House of Usher" but tales of ratiocination, hoaxes, comic burlesques and satires, literary criticism, and even a philosophical treatise on the origins of the universe.

Although Poe rarely depicted folk communities or attempted to render in realistic detail the language and traditions of particular groups, folklore nonetheless plays a significant role in a number of his works. The American tradition of the confidence game, closely aligned with "skylarking," "yarn spinning," "lying," and other aspects of tall-tale performance, finds expression in essays such as "Diddling" (the folk term for a con or scam) as well as in such apparently serious stories as "Facts in the Case of M. Valdemar," in which Poe gulls his readers into accepting his purely fictitious account of a medical hypnosis experiment as actual fact. Legends of phantom ships such as the Flying Dutchman—widely known in both folklore and popular fiction—merge with ostensibly realistic accounts of nautical adventure in "Ms Found in a Bottle" and *The Narrative of Arthur Gordon Pym* (1838) to create liminal worlds between reality and fantasy, life and death, reason and madness. And folk beliefs—particularly those associated with animals, birds, and insects—simultaneously assert and question the reality of supernatural agency in stories such as "The Black Cat," "The Raven," and "The Gold Bug."

A representative example of Poe's literary recontextualization of folkloric material is "The Tell-Tale Heart." Cast in the form of a dramatic monologue narrated by a convicted murderer on the eve of his execution, this story has affinities with both the folk memorate (an oral account of a first-person experience with the supernatural) and the "criminal's goodnight" formula of the broadside ballad. But its most powerful folkloric dimension is "the evil eye," the central element in a folk "event" or "drama" that has been played out for thousands of years in communities all over the world. In the fictional context, this pattern is manifest in the narrator's fear and loathing of the old man's eye ("It was not the old man who vexed me but his evil eye"), in the paradoxical attribution of malign power to a man who is old and frail, in the protective measures adopted by the narrator to meet the perceived threat, and ultimately, in the symbiotic relationship between the "overlooker" (the person believed to have the evil eye) and the victim.

Where or when Poe learned of the evil eye and other folkloric phenomena is uncertain, but this much is clear: his understanding of this subject was broad as well as substantive, and he repeatedly drew upon that knowledge to satirize human gullibility and pretension, to blur the boundaries between the natural and the supernatural, to explore the recesses of the mind, and to dramatize how supernatural belief systems affect both interpersonal relationships and individual behavior.

James W. Kirkland

See also Ballad; Legend; Performance; Tall Tale

✳✳✳✳✳✳✳✳✳✳✳✳✳✳✳✳✳

References

Lynch, James J. "The Devil in the Writings of Irving, Hawthorne, and Poe." *New York Folklore Quarterly* 8 (1952): 111–131.

Pry, Elder R. "A Folklore Source for 'The Man That Was Used Up.'" *Poe Studies* 8 (1975): 46.

Reilly, John. "The Lesser Death-Watch and 'The Tell-Tale Heart.'" *American Transcendental Quarterly* 2 (1969): 3–9.

Twitched, James. "Poe's 'The Oval Portrait' and the Vampire Motif." *Studies in Short Fiction* 14 (1977): 387–393.

Varnado, S. L. "Poe's Raven Lore: A Source Note." *American Notes and Queries* 7 (1968): 35–37.

POLYPHEMUS

The Polyphemus tale can be most broadly characterized as the story of an ogre who is incapacitated and outwitted by blinding. In some cases, this act is facilitated by the creature being one-eyed (congenitally or otherwise), in which case the single eye is poked out with a sharp object; in cases where he has two eyes, some other stratagem is generally employed. In many variants, the ogre is cannibalistic. Well over 200 analogues of this tale have been collected from Africa, Europe, and Asia; the two best known early versions are those found in the ninth book of the *Odyssey* and the third voyage of Sinbad in the *Arabian Nights*.

In the *Odyssey*, Polyphemus is identified as a Cyclops, and the account assumes a single eye. The necessity for the blinding is motivated by the imprisonment of Odysseus and his men in a cave whose entrance is blocked by a huge rock that only Polyphemus can move; killing him outright would save them from being eaten but leave them to starve to death. A number of deceptions are combined in their escape, cumulatively attesting to Odysseus's ingenuity: Polyphemus is made drunk; the men slip out of the cave hidden under sheep (in many versions they wear animal skins); and final escape is guaranteed by Odysseus's foresight in telling Polyphemus that his name is Nobody.

The episode ends with an illustrative example of the contextualization of a folkloric element in an epic setting. A common ending to the tale is the so-called ring sequel, in which the ogre carries out a trick of his own: he gives the hero a ring that turns out not only to be nonremovable but also capable of speaking, which it does at the command of its blinded master to reveal the location of the fleeing hero. In the *Odyssey*, it is Odysseus himself, his epic pride balking at the anonymity that is the price of the Nobody trick, who shouts out, revealing both his location and his true name. The former imperils their escape, as Polyphemus hurls boulders in the direction of the voice; through the latter, Odysseus motivates the wrath of Polyphemus's father, Poseidon, which is needed for the larger narrative context.

There are two developments in postepic literature. The humorous potential of the tale was exploited in a number of comedies now lost, as well as in Euripides' *Cyclops*, the only fully preserved satyr play. At the same time, there was a trend toward a more sympathetic portrayal of Polyphemus, a romanticizing of "the wild man." This romanticization is already hinted at in the *Odyssey*, especially in the pathetic address of the blinded creature to his favorite ram; it is more pronounced in the *Cyclops*, where the fact that Odysseus and his men are *not* imprisoned in the cave renders the blinding an act of malicious vengeance rather than a means of escape; it is most fully developed in the Hellenistic romance of Polyphemus and Galatea, in which a love-stricken Polyphemus is cruelly rejected by a nymph because of his ugliness. The story can be found in the eleventh idyll of Theocritus and the *Metamorphoses* of Ovid.

Robert Mondi

See also Greece, Ancient; Homer; *Odyssey*; Wild Man

✳✳✳✳✳✳✳✳✳✳✳✳✳✳✳✳✳

References

Glenn, Justin. "The Polyphemus Folktale and Homer's *Kyklopeia*." *Transactions of the American Philological Association* 102 (1971): 133–181.

Mondi, Robert. "The Homeric Cyclops: Folktale, Tradition, and Theme." *Transactions of the American Philological Association* 113 (1983): 17–38.

PONIATOWSKA, ELENA (1933–)

Although born in Paris and only arriving in Mexico with her family when she was eight years old, Elena Poniatowska has immersed herself in Mexican culture in her work as a journalist, essayist, and novelist. Growing up in Mexico City, Poniatowska spoke predominantly French and English with family and friends but learned Spanish— including many proverbs and Mexican popular expressions that later found their way into her writings—from the domestic help of her upper-class family's home. Through her writing, and especially through her extensive use of the interview mode, Poniatowska has transformed herself from the daughter of wealthy, transnational parents into a passionately Mexican, literary advocate of the poor and marginalized classes.

In Poniatowska's many works of fiction and nonfiction, the link with folklore is perhaps best examined through the idea of oral history, which has been at the center of many of her literary and journalistic endeavors. Several of her most important works to date are actually montages of oral testimony that the author solicited from various personages. *La noche de Tlatelolco: Testimonios de historia oral, Gaby Brimmer* [The night of Tlatelolco: Oral history testimonials, Gaby Brimmer (1979; co-authored with Gaby Brimmer herself)]; *Fuerte es el silencio* [Strong is the silence]; and *Nada, nadie* [Nothing, nobody (1995)] are all works of nonfiction that use the interview as a central methodology. The author acquired her skills as an interviewer on the job as a journalist for the Mexico City *Excélsior*. She also worked briefly for the anthropologist Oscar Lewis, editing interviews he had compiled, an experience she says influenced the writing of her testimonial novel *Hasta no verte, Jesús mío* (1964).

The use of the interview not only lends the structure of oral history to her works but also means that a significant amount of the folklore of Mexican culture is recorded as content. A prime example is *Hasta no verte, Jesús mío*, which recounts the life of Jesusa Palancares, a poor woman living in Mexico City's slums who told her story to the author over a period of several years. Jesusa's difficult childhood in Oaxaca, her fighting in the Mexican revolution (1910–1930), and her involvement in spiritualism are all portrayed in rich detail, giving the reader a glimpse of some of the beliefs and customs of Mexico's more marginalized groups.

Poniatowska's other works of fiction are often more autobiographical in nature. For example, her collection of short stories *De noche vienes* [You come at night] and her novel *La "flor de lis"* [The iris] detail the lives of women as they struggle against the limitations imposed on them by the patriarchal Mexican society.

In other texts, even in those in which the interview is not of prime importance, Poniatowska constructs her fiction around the lives of historical figures. For example, in *Querido Diego, te abraza Quiela* [Dear Diego, I hug you (1986)], the author composes 12 fictional letters from the artist Angelina Beloff to her ex-lover Diego Rivera. Poniatowska's work *Tinísima* (1998) uses the life of the photographer and activist Tina Modotti as a point of departure.

Mary Beth Tierney-Tello

See also Oral History; Proverbs, Women

❋❋❋❋❋❋❋❋❋❋❋❋❋❋❋❋❋

References

Franco, Jean. *Plotting Women: Gender and Representation in Mexico*. New York: Columbia University Press, 1989.

Jörgenson, Beth E. *The Writing of Elena Poniatowska: Engaging Dialogues*. Austin: University of Texas Press, 1994.

Shaefer, Claudia. *Textured Lives: Women, Art, and Representation in Modern Mexico*. Tuscon: University of Arizona Press, 1992.

Steele, Cynthia. *Politics, Gender, and the Mexican Novel, 1968–1988*. Austin: University of Texas Press, 1992.

POSTMODERNISM

Postmodernism is a term that is often employed to refer to cultural production of the late twentieth century characterized by features like pastiche, fragmentation, and the blending of elite, folk, and popular cultures. Appearing in print as early as the 1930s, the term has come into wider usage since the 1960s. In the 1970s, philosopher Jean-François Lyotard argued that the postmodern is characterized by a lack of grand totalizing narratives. Literary critic Frederic Jameson said it is a periodizing concept that connects new features in culture with the consumer society of the late twentieth century; it can be used to describe everything from the fiction writings of William Burroughs, Thomas Pynchon, and Ishmael Reed to the architectural design of the Bonaventure Hotel in Los Angeles.

Jameson is one of the most influential theorists of the postmodern; not only is his work cited in analyses that focus on literature and popular culture, but his concepts are also used in discussions of the folk elements of culture. For example, folklore scholar José Limón's ethnographic readings of Mexicano legends, barbecues, and barroom polkas draw on Jameson's vision of the postmodern. Even with the attention given to the blending of levels of culture in definitions of the postmodern, approaches like Limón's that focus on the folk culture are rare. Much postmodern theorizing ignores or only indirectly references the folk level of culture; Jameson's definitions of the postmodern tend to emphasize "high culture" and "popular culture."

However, folklore is a part of the blending of cultural levels that is often identified as a defining feature of the postmodern. Folklore scholar Frank de Caro points out that folklore is culturally pervasive; he also argues that folklore can appear in postmodern novels as readily as it does in the literature produced by regional writers. To illustrate his point, he traces the uses of folklore in Jay McInerney's novel *Story of My Life* (1988), which de Caro describes as a postmodern novel because of its self-reflexiveness, self-regarding irony, and demonstration of the crossover between elite, folk, and popular arts. Other scholars have also examined the workings of folklore in postmodern literature. Folklorist Mark Workman describes the focus of Samuel Beckett's *Endgame* (1958) as "postmodern family folklore" and says that in the play, the characters think and love in fragments and exchange broken-down versions of more traditional narrative forms like personal experience narratives.

There is one particular controversial critical approach to reading literature and culture that is often loosely associated with postmodern theorizing: deconstruction, which usually involves reading a text against itself—an approach used to demonstrate that meaning is provisional and variable and that texts are unstable. However, deconstruction is not alone in its recognition of these factors; long before it appeared on the theoretical landscape, the study of folklore had concerned itself with the variability and multiplicity of narratives (like folktales and legends) and other folk forms as well. The emphasis of folklore studies on performance also indicates a continuing attention to the provisional and variable nature of cultural products and productions.

One of the most commonly voiced critiques of deconstruction and other postmodern theorizing focuses on the jargonistic language practitioners often employ—what folklorist Henry Glassie calls "tricky diction" and the postmodern tendency to "stew in words." This same critique is succinctly expressed in a folk form—a joke.

What do you get when you cross a member of the Mafia
    with a deconstructionist?
An offer you can't understand.

Folklore-based analyses of culture often rely on fieldwork and provide close readings of specificities. While arguing that theories of the postmodern have important implications for the study of contemporary folklore, folklore scholar John Dorst also says that folklore's ethnographic expertise and sensitivity to cultural specificities are much needed additions to many postmodern approaches to texts and other cultural products.

Jeanne B. Thomas

See also Folktale; Legend; Performance; Personal Experience Story

✳✳✳✳✳✳✳✳✳✳✳✳✳✳✳✳✳✳

References

de Caro, Frank. "The Three Great Lies: Riddles of Love and Death in a Postmodern Novel." *Southern Folklore* 48 (1991): 235–254.

Dorst, John D. "Postmodernism vs. Postmodernity: Implications for Folklore Studies." *Folklore Forum* 21 (1988): 216–220.

Glassie, Henry. "Postmodernism." *Folklore Forum* 21 (1988): 221–224.

Jameson, Frederic. "Postmodernism and Consumer Society." In *Postmodernism and Its Discontents: Theories, Practices*, ed. E. Ann Kaplan, pp. 12–39. London: Verso, 1988.

————. "Postmodernism; or, The Cultural Logic of Late Capitalism." *New Left Review* 146 (1984): 53–92.

Limón, José E. *Dancing with the Devil: Society and Cultural Poetics in Mexican-American South Texas*. Madison: University of Wisconsin Press, 1994.

Lyotard, Jean-François. *The Postmodern Condition: A Report on Knowledge*. Minneapolis: University of Minnesota Press, 1984.

Thomas, Jeannie B. "Out of the Frying Pan and into the Postmodern: Folklore and Contemporary Literary Theory." *Southern Folklore* 51 (1994): 107–120.

Warshaver, Gerald D. "On Postmodern Folklore." *Western Folklore* 50 (1991): 219–229.

Workman, Mark. "Folklore in the Wilderness: Folklore and Postmodernism." *Midwestern Folklore* 15 (1989): 5–14.

POSTSTRUCTURALISM

Insofar as folklore is governed by a ceaseless necessity to differ from itself, it may be said to be always susceptible to poststructuralist analysis. Folklore, the quintessentially traditional form of human behavior, could not be a meaningful or viable component of culture were it not also as dynamic as it is conservative. Both the conservatism and dynamism of folklore are manifested in performance, which at one and the same time reaffirms existing conventions of enactment while realigning those conventions to accord with the always shifting circumstances that make every performance inevitably unique.

That dualistic aspect of folklore harkens back to the distinction made by Ferdinand de Saussure between *langue* and *parole*: every speech act strains against the very pattern that makes its production possible in the first place. The emergent quality of folk performance also resonates with the fundamental tenet of poststructuralism derived from Saussure's distinction between signifier and signified: whereas he regarded them as theoretically separate but practically united, poststructuralists have emphasized the gap between the two elements of the sign, which results in the ultimate deferral of meaning. The implication of this insight for folklore is that no matter how opportune or fitting a performance may appear to be, it could always be more so.

This poststructuralist perspective admittedly does not bear equally on all forms of folklore—folk houses, for instance, typically endure over long periods of time and provide deep gratification, spiritual and physical, for their inhabitants. The more ephemeral the folklore, however, or the more volatile the situation to which it is a response, the more likely it is to be comprehended by poststructuralist critique. This situation is perhaps especially true of those folk narratives or literary texts that seek to name or identify a person or character. No story—with the exception of stories perceived as myths—could ever be utterly adequate to the task of conveying the full being of the speaker or subject it purports to describe (the equivalent, as Mikhail Bakhtin put it, to picking oneself up by one's own hair), and yet that is precisely the implicit goal of every personal experience narrative. A further implication of this claim is that the very notion of "the full being" of a person is itself problematic given that to a great extent, we know and define ourselves through language. The folk subject, situated within a stable community, might indeed possess an apparent fixity lacking in more mobile outsiders, but fixity is not identical to essence. If every retelling is a new telling, then at least to some extent it is a new self that performs it.

Whereas structural studies of folklore emphasize the iterability of folk performances, poststructuralism emphasizes the difference inherent in even the most faithful iteration. It is difference that makes new meaning possible while holding that very possibility in abeyance. Ample evidence of this shift in perspective is provided by the study of the folktale. Although each analyst formulated a different kind of method, both the formalist Vladimir Propp's and the structuralist Claude Lévi-Strauss's analyses of tales were based on the same premise of a static corpus of replicated texts.

Their analyses are in stark contrast to the contemporary use to which many traditional tales are being put in postmodern literary reworkings of them. Stories such as "The Bloody Chamber" by Angela Carter employ what folklorist Cristina Bacchilega refers to as "self-reflexive magic mirrors" in order to reveal the traditionally submissive, passive, or dependent-subject positions of women in folklore and the alternative positions imagined by "multiply[ing] narrative and gender possibilities."

As the above example suggests, even though poststructuralism and folklore may appear to be antithetical to one another, poststructuralism can actually serve to illuminate one of the most vital aspects of folklore: its capacity to accommodate and contribute to the creation of the ever-changing circumstances of its use.

Mark E. Workman

See also Bakhtin, Mikhail Mikhailovitch; Carter, Angela; Performance

✳✳✳✳✳✳✳✳✳✳✳✳✳✳✳✳✳

References

Bacchilega, Cristina. *Performing Wonders: Fairy Tales, Gender, and Narrativity.* Philadelphia: University of Pennsylvania Press, 1997.

Barthes, Roland. "From Work to Text." In *Textual Strategies: Perspectives in Post-Structuralist Criticism*, ed. Josue V. Harari, pp. 73–81. Ithaca, N.Y.: Cornell University Press, 1979.

Workman, Mark E. "Tropes, Hopes, and Dopes." *Journal of American Folklore* 106 (1993): 171–183.

Prague Linguistic Circle

The Prague Linguistic Circle united a group of Czech and Russian emigré scholars, but speakers from abroad were also often invited to its sessions. The circle owed its existence to the initiative of linguists and philologists Wilém Mathesius (1882–1945) and Roman Jakobson (1896–1982) and met for the first time in 1926. Jakobson, whose favorite areas of research at that time were the language of poetry and phonetics, wanted to revive the traditions of the Moscow Linguistic Circle and found a willing ally in Mathesius.

After emigrating from Russia, Jakobson was influenced by N. S. Trubetzkoy (1890–1938), and the result of their joint efforts was the creation of phonology, a branch of linguistics that examines sounds of speech from the point of view of their function in the process of communication rather than as articulatory and acoustic entities. This approach to phonetics tied in with the ideas underlying Russian formalism, another trend indebted greatly to Jakobson. Although Trubetzkoy lived in Vienna, he became one of the most prominent members of the Prague circle. The members of the circle first appeared as a group at two international congresses in 1928 and 1929, and the publication of *Travaux du Cercle Linguistique de Prague* [Work of the Prague Linguistic Circle] made their ideas widely known; volume 7 of the *Travaux* consisted of Trubetzkoy's posthumous book *Grundzüge der Phonologie* [The bases of phonology].

A functional view of linguistic and literary phenomena is a cornerstone of structuralism, and the Prague brand of structuralism turned out to be especially long-lived. Its impact on the humanities was considerable between the two twentieth-century world wars, and it increased greatly after Jakobson settled in the United States. Phonology was the dominant theme of the Prague circle in the period 1926–1939, and those members who devoted themselves primarily to phonology (Bohumil Trnka, Josef Vachek) made their mark quite early. Important works were also written by L'udovít Novák, Vladimír Skalička, and Pavel Trost. The doctrine of the Prague circle has its roots in the teachings of I. A. Baudouin de Courtenay and Ferdinand de Saussure, but Saussure, though he recognized the systemic nature of language at any given moment of its development, did not extend his ideas to language history. That was done by the members of the Prague circle, who were the first to formulate the principles of historical phonology and apply them to Slavic, Germanic, and Romance materials. Trubetzkoy's interest in the use of phonetic means in morphology culminated in the emergence of morphology as a special branch of linguistics.

Most works by the members of the Prague circle treated phonology and morphology, but other aspects of language were not neglected. The circle's initial program presupposed an in-depth study of dialectology, the formation of the literary norm (the standard), and the language of poetry, among other things. Besides Jakobson, these problems were developed by Sergei (Serge) Kartsevskii, Bohuslav Havránek, and Jan Mukařovsky. Mukařovsky's works gained international currency after the war, but the best of them were written in the 1930s. Jakobson's and Petr Bogatyrev's research into oral tradition resulted in major contributions to structural folklore.

The death of Trubetzkoy (1938) and Jakobson's flight from Czechoslovakia after its occupation by German troops (1939) dealt a severe blow to the Prague Linguistic Circle. During World War II, the circle continued to function, but the *Travaux* ceased to appear. During the first years of Soviet domination of Czechoslovakia, structuralism led a precarious existence at best. When the circle was resurrected, it was a new body despite some continuity ensured by the presence of several former participants. There is every reason to speak about today's Prague school as being loyal to its past, but the Prague circle barely survived World War II.

Anatoly Liberman

See also Propp, Vladimir I.; Russian Formalism; Structuralism
✻✻✻✻✻✻✻✻✻✻✻✻✻✻✻✻✻

References

Garvin, Paul. *Prague School Reader on Esthetics, Literary Structure, Style*. Washington, D.C.: Georgetown University Press, 1964.

Matejka, Ladislav. *Sound, Sign, and Meaning: Quinquagenary of the Prague Linguistic Circle*. Ann Arbor: University of Michigan, Department of Slavic Languages and Literatures, 1976.

Steiner, Peter. *The Prague School: Selected Writings 1926–1946*. Austin: University of Texas Press, 1982.

Vachek, Josef. *Prague School Reader in Linguistics*. Bloomington: Indiana University Press, 1964.

PRE-SOVIET PROSE AND FOLKLORE IN RUSSIA

Relations between folklore and literature in Russia are enormously rich and complex. An illiterate subculture continued to exist in Russia well into the nineteenth century, but church and state were long hostile to this subculture and did not let it merge with the literate mainstream of Russian culture. Czar Ivan IV (1530–1584) is reported to have employed professional storytellers, but he never thought of having their stories recorded for posterity. Nevertheless, folk traditions do appear in medieval Russian literature, almost entirely the domain of pious monks. The "Russian Primary Chronicle" (c. 1113) has episodes that read like sagas; for example, the tale of the death of Prince Igor in 945 at the hands of backwoods tribesmen and the cruel vengeance taken on them by Olga, Igor's crafty widow. The story is rife with motifs that are clearly fictitious and ancient (one is found as early as the fifth century).

The lives of Russian saints occasionally depart from the canon of Byzantine lives and introduce motifs taken from magic folktales. The life of Saints Peter and Fevroniya of Murom is essentially a version of the folktale of the wise woman of the people who manipulates her royal consort. The life of St. Mercury of Smolensk has the

A Kholui lacquer depicts the twelfth-century Russian tale of Prince Igor battling for his life.

holy warrior return from battle against the Tatar invaders carrying his own head—like the heroes of various folk traditions elsewhere, including St. Denis, patron saint of France.

In the fifteenth and sixteenth centuries, some folk traditions appeared in manuscript, always with an air of moral edification. Only in the seventeenth century did literature as entertainment gain a foothold, as numerous Western romances, mostly tales of the chivalry type, were translated, usually from the Polish. The most popular of these were the "Tale of Prince Bova" and the "Tale of Brave Duke Peter of the Golden Keys." The first of these goes back, via the Croatian version, to the Italian romance in verse *Buovo d'Antona*, which in turn goes back to a thirteenth-century French epic, *Beuves d'Hanston*. The second of the tales came from a Polish version of the French *Roman de Pierre de Provence et de la belle Maguelonne de Naples*. These and several other imported romances almost immediately became Russian folktales, later went through innumerable printings as chapbooks, and eventually entered Russian "high" literature in works by some major writers, including Aleksandr Pushkin (1799–1837).

The seventeenth century also has records of satirical and moral tales that can be traced to the *Facetiae* of Poggio Bracciolini, the *Gesta Romanorum*, the *Magnum speculum exemplorum*, the *Historia septem sapientum Romae*, and other international sources. Many of these tales then turned up in folklore and in chapbooks and were reintroduced into "high" literature. For example, "The Tale of Czar Agei and How He Suffered for His Pride" (from the *Gesta Romanorum*) became a folktale and a chapbook and eventually a story by Vsevolod Garshin (1855–1888). Czar Agei is cured of his pride when he strips off his clothes to swim a river and an angel takes them and assumes his shape, leaving him a naked beggar. In the eighteenth century, Russian folktales began to be collected, quite unsystematically, to be printed in popular editions such as *Grandma's Promenades* and *Medicine against Melancholy and Insomnia*. Both of these works had many subsequent editions.

The romantic period brought with it a sustained scholarly interest in folklore and eventually produced large collections of various genres. *Russian Folktales* (1936) by Alexander Afanasiev (1826–1871) became a classic. The study of folklore, then as later, was also an ideological battlefield. Collectors, students, and admirers of folklore tended to be conservative Slavophile nationalists, and progressive Westernizers were disappointed at not finding in the Russian folktale any of the sentiments that might bear out the validity of their own populist mystique.

In the nineteenth century, the teller of tales was still a presence in rural areas, and a Russian writer's first contact with fiction was often through the folktale, heard from a nurse or a peasant serf. Yet at the same time, literature—the tales of Pushkin and Nikolay Gogol (1809–1852), for example, but also *The Count of Monte-Cristo* by Alexandre Dumas (1802–1870)—kept being made into folktales. Scholars looking for alleged sources of "The Viy" by Gogol mostly found versions that were obviously derived from Gogol's story, not vice versa.

Russian romanticism developed a distinct "folkloric" genre. Not only did poets write lyrics in the style and meter of the folk song, but prose writers, too, produced stories and even novels that took the reader into the world of the folk epic or folktale. For instance, Alexander Weltmann's novel *Kashchei the Deathless* has a Russian squire engage in a long and futile pursuit of Kashchei, a malevolent and elusive spirit whose soul is hidden in a Chinese box of magic identities, in the mistaken assumption that Kashchei had abducted his wife. The sources of Russian romantic "folklorism" were, however, diverse. Pushkin, Gogol, Weltmann, Antony Pogorelsky, Vladimir Odoevsky, and others rather indiscriminately used Russian and international folklore as well as the tales of non-Russian authors such as Charles Perrault, Ludwig Tieck, E. T. A. Hoffmann, and Washington Irving, among others.

Following the example of Western writers (for instance, Sir Walter Scott's *Tales of My Landlord* [1816], some Russians tried to impersonate a narrator of the people, among them, Gogol in some of his stories included in *Evenings on a Farm near Dikanka* (1926), Vladimir Dahl in *Russian Fairy Tales: First Group of Five*, and Fyodor Dostoyevsky in "An Honest Thief." This technique, eventually dubbed *skaz* (from *skazat'*, "to tell") by the formalists of the 1920s, was developed to perfection by Nikolay Leskov, whose story "The Lefthanded Craftsman" combines a popular flair with consummate virtuosity.

Among the great novelists of the nineteenth century, Lev (Leo) Tolstoy (1828–1910) was the greatest user of folklore. Many of his 30 or so stories in *Tales for the People*, written for the moral edification of the uneducated, are based on folk traditions, some of them very old. The story "Three Hermits" (who are so simple they can't even memorize the Lord's Prayer but so holy they can walk on water) dates back at least to the sixteenth century. Fyodor Dostoyevsky (1821–1881), too, occasionally introduced folk traditions into his novels, including "The Onion" in *The Brothers Karamazov* (1878–1880).

Victor Terras

See also Bylinas; Chapbook; Folktale; Fool in Christ; Gogol, Nikolay Vasilyevich; Motif; Russian Ballad; Russian Folk Lyric Song

✳✳✳✳✳✳✳✳✳✳✳✳✳✳✳✳✳✳

References

Afanas'ev, Aleksandr. *Russian Fairy Tales*. Trans. Norbert Gutterman, folkloristic commentary by Roman Jakobson. New York: Pantheon, 1973.

Oinas, Felix J. "Collection and Study of Folklore in Tsarist Russia." In *Handbook of Russian Literature*, ed. Victor Terras, pp. 139–142. New Haven: Yale University Press, 1985.

Propp, Vladimir. *Morphology of the Folktale*. Trans. L. Scott. Austin: University of Texas Press, 1968.

Sokolov, Yu M. *Russian Folklore*. Trans. C. Ruth Smith. Detroit: Folklore Associates, 1971.

Propp, Vladimir I. (1895–1970)

The Russian scholar Vladimir I. Propp was the first to apply formalist methods to the study of folklore. Propp graduated from the University of St. Petersburg (later Leningrad) in his native town in 1917 and joined the faculty of Leningrad University in 1932 as a language teacher and a folklorist. His chief works deal with the structure and origin of the fairy tale, with the history of the heroic epic, with the origins of ritual folklore, and with the poetics of folk poetry. He took part in the formalist movement that flourished in Russia between 1917 and 1927 and represented a major reorientation in literary and artistic theory. With an emphasis on the importance of form over content, of text over context, and a disdain for scientific positivism, the formalist movement was viewed with disfavor by those in power during the Stalinist period and went into eclipse in the years following 1927.

At the beginning of the Stalinist period, Propp published his *Morfologiia skazki* [Morphology of the folktale], in which he postulated a common form for the Russian wonder tale (tales involving magic, Aarne's types 300–749). This form described the action of the story and was divided into 31 episodes, or functions, which always followed each other in the same order, though all did not need to be present in each story. The weakness of such an approach, as with the formalist position in general, was that it tended to ignore historical and social influences on the tales, but Propp sought to remedy this in his next major work, *Istorisheskie korni volshebnoj skazki* [The historical roots of the folktale]. In this work, he examined the evolution of Russian tales from a hunter-gatherer past, a past containing such elements as exogamy, human sacrifice, and initiations. These ritual aspects of early society became preserved in later folktales.

Elsewhere, Propp elaborated this concept, stating that folktales had originally been an integral part of ritual but that belief in the efficacy of the rite declined with time, causing the tales to lead an independent life, though their reality was still that of the hunter-gatherer. Cause and effect did not exist, time was completely subjective, and such categories as subject and object, singular and plural, did not exist as we know them. The tales were thus born of a clash of two ages, the civilized present and the primitive past. The old and the benign became dangerous, hybrids such as dragons were invented, and plots became unrealistic.

Propp's work remained largely unrecognized outside the Soviet Union until it was translated into English in 1958. Since then it has inspired several important studies in both folklore and anthropology. Propp's importance lies in providing the first systematic and rigorous study of a common narrative form for folktales and in suggesting that narratives existed as wholes rather than as mere collections of contextual borrowings. More than this, Propp, and those who have followed his lead, have raised the possibility of a common form for all narrative, oral or written, and this idea has potential consequences of great interest for the study of literature.

Peter Gilet

See also Epic; Fairy Tale; Folktale; Russian Formalism; Structuralism

✳✳✳✳✳✳✳✳✳✳✳✳✳✳✳✳✳✳

References

Bremond, Claude. "Posterité Sovietique de Propp." *Cahiers de littérature orale 2* (1977): 25–59; 3 (1977): 118–168.

Propp, Vladimir. *Morphology of the Folktale*. Trans. L. Scott. Austin: University of Texas Press, 1968.

———. *Theory and History of Folklore*. Trans. A. Y. Martin and R. P. Martin. Minneapolis: University of Minnesota Press, 1984.

PROVERBS

Proverbs are concise traditional statements of apparent truths with currency among the folk. More broadly stated, they are short, generally known sentences of the folk that contain wisdom, truths, morals, and traditional views in metaphorical, fixed, and memorizable form and which are handed down orally from generation to generation. Although proverbs are recognizable through such "markers" as structure, shortness, metaphor, and style (i.e., alliteration, rhyme, parallelism, ellipsis, etc.), their actual traditionality and currency will always have to be established before they can in fact be called "proverbs." This requirement differentiates proverbs from such literary genres as aphorisms, epigrams, maxims, quotations, and slogans. This same requirement, however, does not mean that quotations like Ralph Waldo Emerson's "Hitch your wagon to a star" or Theodore Roosevelt's "Speak softly and carry a big stick" might not have become proverbial through repeated use; many English speakers, for example, do not recall or know the respective authors.

Although proverbs like "The early bird catches the worm" or "No pain, no gain" are complete thoughts that can stand alone, such sub-genres as proverbial expressions ("To add fuel to the fire"), proverbial comparisons ("As flat as a pancake"), proverbial exaggerations ("Not to trust someone any further than one can throw a bull by the tail"), and twin (binary) formulas ("Safe and sound") are but fragmentary metaphorical phrases that must be integrated into a sentence. Humorous or satirical reactions to the wisdom or didacticism of proverbs have found expression in so-called wellerisms, which follow a triadic structure of (1) a statement (often a proverb), (2) an identification of the speaker, and (3) an explanatory situation, as for example, "'One good turn deserves another,' as the dog said, chasing his tail."

It should be no surprise that proverbs have been of interest to folklorists and literary historians alike. Verbal folklore in the form of fairy tales, legends, jokes, and proverbs plays a major role both in regional literature and in the true masterpieces of national and world literatures. Studies of the type "the proverbial language in the works of X" abound in large numbers. Especially in the nineteenth century and the first half of the twentieth, scholars did an impressive job of identifying proverbs in various literary works and produced more or less annotated lists of texts without contexts. The identification of proverbs often did not include information essential to informed interpretation, such as by whom, when, where, and why proverbs were used. The identification of proverbial language in literary works, however, did lead to major historical proverb dictionaries, such as those by Bartlett Jere Whiting and F. P. Wilson, which list proverbs and their variants from classical or at least medieval literature right through to modern times.

The works of many authors have been investigated for their inclusion and use of proverbs, and these investigations have not been restricted to the particularly "folksy" literature of a rural area, to any particular genre of literature, or to any specific historical period. Some of the best literary proverb studies deal with such world authors as Chrétien de Troyes, Geoffrey Chaucer, François Rabelais, William Shakespeare, Miguel de Cervantes (Saavedra), Johann Wolfgang von Goethe, Ralph Waldo Emerson, Charles Dickens, Lev Nikolayevich Tolstoy, George Bernard Shaw, Bertolt Brecht, and Agatha Christie. Additionally, works of philosophical and religious essays and political speeches as well as almanacs have been investigated for their rhetorical proverb use, as, for example, works by Plato, Aristotle, Marcus Tullius Cicero, Martin Luther, Michel Eyquem de Montaigne, Benjamin Franklin, Otto von Bismarck, Vladimir Ilich Lenin, Adolf Hitler, and Winston Churchill. Monographs and articles on the proverbs used by such individual authors abound. And there are several studies in which scholars look at the bigger picture of proverbs used by various authors during an entire historical period, providing a more comprehensive understanding of the social and cultural significance of proverbs.

Although prose and dramatic works have received considerable attention, the lyrical genre has been treated with much less vigor. There have been a few isolated investigations of the integration of proverbs in the 305 ballads edited by Francis James Child and in German, Greek, and English folk songs. Recently, there have also been signs of interest regarding the quite frequent use of proverbs in popular songs, from the librettos of musicals to the lyrics of mood music, blues, country western tunes, and even the latest hits of rock and roll. There is definitely such a genre as "proverb songs," which not only carry the proverb in the title but repeat the proverbial wisdom as a leitmotiv throughout the stanzas. The song "Faint Heart Never Won Fair Lady" from Sir W. S. Gilbert and Sir Arthur Sullivan's musical *Iolanthe* (1882) and Bob Dylan's memorable hit "Like a Rolling Stone" readily come to mind.

There is also, however, a hitherto quite ignored subgenre of "proverb poems." Alice Cary's "Hoe Your Own Row," Emily Dickinson's "Which [bird in the hand] Is Best?," Robert Frost's "Mending Wall," Arthur Guiterman's "Proverbial Tragedy," Carl Sandburg's "Good Morning, America," W. H. Auden's "Leap Before You Look," and Susan Fromberg Schaeffer's "Proverb" are all proverb poems in which the authors have used traditional proverbs or deliberately changed antiproverbs to express social and human concerns. Carl Sandburg's epic poem *The People, Yes* (1936) abounds in proverbs to bring alive the different languages and cultures of the immigrants in Chicago. But all of this is nothing new at all, for François Villon wrote his "Ballade des proverbes" in the fifteenth century, and, in fact, medieval minstrels employed proverbs in their lyrics. John Heywood wrote 600 *Epigrams upon Proverbs*, and John Gay included dozens of proverbial comparisons in his "A New Song of New Similes," which found its anonymous counterpart in the proverb poem "Yankee Phrases" a hundred years later in the United States.

Wolfgang Mieder

See also Chaucer, Geoffrey; Child, Francis James; Dickens, Charles; Dylan, Bob; Gay, John; Goethe, Johann Wolfgang von; Shakespeare, William; Taylor, Archer; Wellerisms

✽✽✽✽✽✽✽✽✽✽✽✽✽✽✽✽✽✽

References

Barbour, Frances M. *A Concordance to the Sayings in Franklin's "Poor Richard."* Detroit: Gale Research Company, 1974.

Carnes, Pack, ed. *Proverbia in Fabula: Essays on the Relationship of the Fable and the Proverb.* Bern: Peter Lang, 1988.

Colombi, Maria Cecilia. *Los refranes en el Quijote: Texto y contexto.* Potomac, Md.: Scripta Humanistica, 1989.

Mieder, Wolfgang. *American Proverbs: A Study of Texts and Contexts.* Bern: Peter Lang, 1989.

———. *International Proverb Scholarship: An Annotated Bibliography.* 3 vols. New York: Garland, 1982–1993.

———. *Proverbs Are Never out of Season: Popular Wisdom in the Modern Age.* New York: Oxford University Press, 1993.

Mieder, Wolfgang, and George B. Bryan. *Proverbs in World Literature: A Bibliography.* New York: Peter Lang, 1996.

Pfeffer, J. Alan. *The Proverb in Goethe.* New York: Crown Press, 1948.

Rölleke, Heinz, ed. *Das Sprichwort in den "Kinder- und Hausmärchen" der Brüder Grimm.* Bern: Peter Lang, 1988.

Schulze-Busacker, Elisabeth. *Proverbes et expressions proverbiales dans la littérature narrative du moyen âge français: Recueil et analyse.* Paris: Honoré Champion, 1985.

Taylor, Archer. *The Proverb.* Intro. and biblio. by Wolfgang Mieder. Bern: Peter Lang, 1985 (1931).

Whiting, Bartlett Jere. *Chaucer's Use of Proverbs.* New York: AMS Press, 1973 (1934).

P'U SUNG-LING (1640–1715)

P'u Sung-ling was a short-story writer of the early Ch'ing period in China. He was a native of Shandong Province, and lived during the transition from the Ming dynasty (1368–1644) to the Ch'ing dynasty (1644–1912). He studied for the imperial examinations and aspired to official status but only attained a lower degree. He then directed his literary talents to writing short stories based upon the traditional written *ch'uan-ch'i* ("legendary tale"). P'u Sung-ling's *Liao-chai chih-i* (translated as *Strange Stories from the Leisure Studio* or, as in Herbert Giles's translation, *Strange Stories from a Chinese Studio*) was written in the period from 1679 to 1707 and published posthumously in 1766. It is one of the most popular collections of Chinese short stories and remains a valuable source of Chinese folklore and belief in the supernatural.

In the preface to his work, P'u states that he collected stories from people passing by his roadside pavilion to drink tea and tell stories. Many of the stories do derive from Ming and Ch'ing dynasty folk legends; however, a number of them can be traced to written sources of traditional tales or *ch'uan-ch'i* that had circulated in various forms since the T'ang dynasty (618–907).

Liao-chai has become the most accessible source of traditional tales of this genre because of its comprehensiveness—164 tales in total—and P'u's concise style of retelling the tales for a literary audience. The majority of legends contained in the work are ghost legends or tales of the appearance of fox spirits in human, often feminine, transformations. These transmigrations of the soul of animals and even insects become ideal earthly lovers who help the good attain wealth and fortune but bring fitting retribution upon the bad. Dream motifs are also an important element derived from folk belief in this collection. Other folklore motifs in P'u's work are those of grateful animals, hidden treasure, supernatural marriages, and resuscitation of the dead. The fox legends in particular can still be found in the legend stock of people from this area of China. Contemporary writers, the film industry, and television have also been attracted by the popularity of such legends and have used them in various ways, but P'u Sung-ling's quiet, economical suspense and tender humor are largely missing in these highly sensationalized versions.

Interpretations of P'u Sung-ling's work often give allegorical significance to the plots of reward and retribution. The beliefs in the supernatural are those of the traditional Buddhist and folk Taoist religions, not of Confucianist ethics, however, especially in light of Confucius's prohibition against speaking of gods and spirits, things beyond this world of which one does not know. The tales of corrupt officials are often interpreted as registering protest in disguised form against the Manchu rulers. Under such oppression, supernatural aid from the spirit world was viewed as the only way one could achieve success and good fortune.

Besides being a master of the short story, P'u also wrote folk songs, essays, and poetry as well as works on medicine and agriculture. Scholars have varying opinions about whether or not a popular novel entitled the *Hsing-shih yin-yuan chuan* [Marriage to awaken the world] written in the early T'ang dynasty can be attributed to him.

Patricia Haseltine

See also Belief; *Ch'uan-ch'i*; Legend; Motif

✳✳✳✳✳✳✳✳✳✳✳✳✳✳✳✳✳

References

Chang, Chun-shu, and Hsueh Lun (Lo) Chang. "The World of P'u Sung-ling's *Liao-chai chih-i*: Literature and the Intelligentsia during the Ming-Ch'ing Dynastic Transition." *Journal of the Institute of Chinese Studies of the Chinese University of Hong Kong* 2:2 (1973): 401–423.

Giles, Herbert F. *Strange Stories from a Chinese Studio*. London, 1880.

Hom, Marlon Kau. "The Continuation of Tradition: A Study of *Liaozhai zhiyi* by Pu Songling (1640–1715)." Ph.D. dissertation, University of Washington, 1979.

Muhleman, James V. "P'u Sung-ling and the *Liao-chai chih-yi*: Themes and Art of the Literary Tales." Ph.D. dissertation, Indiana University, 1978.

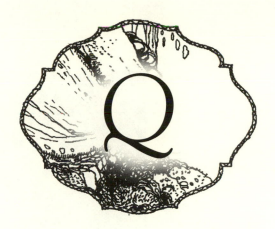

QUILTING

Quilting was introduced into the American colonies from Europe and became a widespread women's folk craft, especially among Anglo and African Americans. The traditional quilt's three layers—a top of pieced or appliquéd patchwork or solid fabric, an insulation ("batting"), and a lining—are bound with a running stitch ("quilting") or by tying with strong thread ("tacking" or "knotting"). The traditional or improvisational patterns of the quilt and the quilt-making process, with its language and aesthetics, are specialized vehicles of women's communication that serve as motif and metaphor in fiction, poetry, and literary theory.

Mirroring daily life, quilts themselves function symbolically in literature. Eliza Calvert Hall's *Aunt Jane of Kentucky* (1898) presents quilts as memory objects—family albums and diaries holding her own personal narratives—and as metaphors for living and explaining predestination and free will. Receiving detailed critical attention in works such as Barbara Christian's anthology, Alice Walker's short story "Everyday Use" (1973) explores the utilitarian and decorative functions of quilts, which symbolize family heritage and tradition, mark rites of passage, and function as a boundary, or curtain, separating the traditional and modern worlds.

Writers unfamiliar with the quilt-making process often stereotype it as communal because of the quilting bee, which symbolizes the community of women in Whitney Otto's *How to Make an American Quilt* (1991), featuring a contemporary California quilting group. However, traditional quilt-makers frequently work alone, especially when piecing quilt tops. In Susan Glaspell's "A Jury of Her Peers" (1917), piecing a Log Cabin quilt is a lonely woman's creative outlet that also covers up major evidence that she murdered her husband.

For another wife, in a short story by Sylvia Townsend Warner (1984), the making of a Widow's Quilt expresses the woman's wish for her husband's death, and the quilt becomes symbolic of the domestic drudgery that ultimately kills her. In both stories, only women can read the quilt-makers' hidden messages; men remain oblivious.

The metaphor of piecing offers writers and critics a nonhierarchical model for assembling disparate plots, chapters, stories, and poems into whole "verbal quilts," such as Lucille Clifton's 1987 *Quilting* poems. And critics

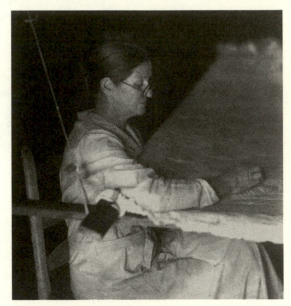

Quilting is a folk art that serves many purposes, including recording cultural and family heritage, and the often communal process of quilt-making has also served as a forum for sharing traditional knowledge as well as gossip.

have employed piecing as a paradigm of a female aesthetic and creative process to illuminate seemingly fragmented writing. Noting the recognition the 1970s brought to women artists, Elaine Showalter and Elaine Hedges explore continuities between the needle and pen. Showalter's central work on nineteenth- and twentieth-century women authors, *Sister's Choice* (1991), uses quilt patterns and piecing to analyze works including Harriet Beecher Stowe's *Uncle Tom's Cabin* (1852), Alice Walker's *The Color Purple* (1982), and Joyce Carol Oates's poem "Celestial Timepiece."

More recent articles and doctoral dissertations apply quilting metaphors of binding and fragmentation as well as aesthetics involving patterns and improvisation to describe individual, family, and generational relationships and the creation and depiction of community and culture in novels by Toni Morrison, Eudora Welty, and Gloria Naylor. Reflecting the continuing interest in and the vitality of traditional and contemporary quilt-making, these feminist studies and even an on-line bibliography of fiction involving quilting represent the proliferation of quilting as a multivalent symbol with layers of function and meaning.

Susan Roach

See also Morrison, Toni; Oates, Joyce Carol; Personal Experience Story; Walker, Alice; Welty, Eudora; Women

✳✳✳✳✳✳✳✳✳✳✳✳✳✳✳✳✳✳✳✳

References

Christian, Barbara, ed. *"Everyday Use": Alice Walker*. New Brunswick, N.J.: Rutgers University Press, 1994.

Elsley, Judy. *Quilts as Text(iles): The Semiotics of Quilting*. New York: Peter Lang, 1996.

Ferrero, Pat, Elaine Hedges, and Julie Silbur. *Hearts and Hands: The Influence of Women and Quilts in American Society*. Nashville: Rutledge Hill Press, 1996 (1987).

Hedges, Elaine. "The Needle or the Pen: The Literary Rediscovery of Women's Textile Work." In *Tradition and the Talents of Women*, ed. Florence Howe, pp. 338–364. Urbana: University of Illinois Press, 1991.

Roach-Lankford, Susan. "Quilts." In *Decorative Arts and Household Furnishings in America: An Annotated Bibliography*, ed. Kenneth L. Ames and Gerald W. R. Ward, pp. 257–264. Winterthur, Del.: Henry Francis du Pont Winterthur Museum, 1989.

Showalter, Elaine. *Sister's Choice: Tradition and Change in American Women's Writing*. Oxford: Clarendon Press, 1991.

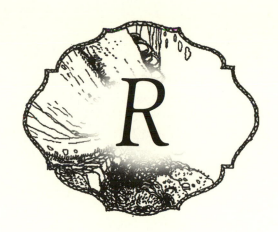

RABELAIS, FRANÇOIS (1494–1553)

Successively a monk, doctor, professor of anatomy, and curate, François Rabelais is the author of *Pantagruel* (1532, henceforth P), *Gargantua* (1534, henceforth G), the *Tiers livre* [Third book] (1546, henceforth Book 3), and the *Quart livre* [Fourth book] (1548, henceforth Book 4). A fifth book consists of discarded sketches and spurious additions. Learned, unpredictable, and possessed with a genius for exploiting languages (P, chap. 9), Rabelais is the most difficult of the French canonical writers (Book 3, chap. 35). He is also France's most eloquent spokesman for classical culture and wisdom (P, chap. 8) and Renaissance humanism (G, chap. 50). He based his most fantastic-seeming inventions on real events and steered his most fantastic voyages (Book 4) to real places. A comic fantasy of a war of cake peddlers, for instance (G, chaps. 26–51), refers to a local feud in Touraine involving his father. To some readers Rabelais is an allegorist, to others a smut master, to others a freethinker. His works move playfully between real and imagined worlds and between sense and nonsense. Throughout, his work draws on folk culture, transforms folk materials, and imitates folk practices.

Folk materials are constantly transformed. Medieval childlore provided Rabelais with Gargantua's rhyme on what the privy says to its users (G, chap. 13) and a list of 217 games (G, chap. 22). The trickster Panurge's discussion by sign language (3, chap. 20) is an international tale-type (AT 924, motif H607). The motto of the utopian Abbey of Thélème, *faictz ce que vouldras*, "Do what you will" (G, chap. 57), which Rabelais drew from contemporary talk and writing, becomes an ethical program. The giant Gargantua, growing out of both traditional giant legends and the folktale "John the Bear" (AT 301B), becomes universal man, and his interminable periods of

535

sleep echo the bear's hibernation. From the lore of the learned, Rabelais took Latin proverbs to parody (G, chap. 9); throughout, he parodied the Bible. On the motif of frozen words (X1623.2), which he derived from Plutarch (46–125 C.E.) and Castiglione (1475–1529), he built an allegory of the Renaissance revival of Plato's (428–348 B.C.E.) teaching (Book 4, chaps. 55–56).

Imitating folklore practices, Rabelais framed many stories into his books (P, chaps. 21–22; Book 4, chaps. 12–15; chaps. 45–47; see also Keller [1963]). He addressed his audience like an oral performer, sometimes in riddles (prologues to P and Book 3). Indeed, *Gargantua* ends with a pretended obscene riddle (G, chap. 58), which led Claude Gaignebet (1986) to read the succeeding books as esoteric knowledge. Rabelais put folk play on the page, for instance, the contest between carnival and Lent (Book 4, chaps. 29–42; see also Kinser [1990]). Carnival, indeed, now seems Rabelais's major imitation of folklore. To the Russian philosopher-critic Mikhail Mikhailovitch Bakhtin (1895–1975), Rabelais's work celebrates the popular-festive life in the Middle Ages and the Renaissance. Carnival life is expressed in the language of the marketplace, forms and images drawn from folk festivals, and an aesthetic of grotesque realism that emphasizes the body.

Lee Haring

See also Bakhtin, Mikhail Mikhailovitch; Festival; Riddle; Tale-Type

✳✳✳✳✳✳✳✳✳✳✳✳✳✳✳✳✳

References

Bakhtin, Mikhail Mikhailovitch. *Rabelais and His World*. Trans. Helene Iswolsky. Cambridge: Massachusetts Institute of Technology Press, 1968.

Gaignebet, Claude. *A plus hault sens: L'ésotérisme spirituel et charnel de Rabelais*. 2 vols. Paris: G. P. Maisonneuve et Larose, 1986.

Keller, Abraham C. *The Telling of Tales in Rabelais: Aspects of His Narrative Art*. Analecta Romana. Frankfurt am Main: Vittorio Klostermann, 1963.

Kinser, Samuel. *Rabelais's Carnival: Text, Context, Metatext*. The New Historicism, Studies in Cultural Poetics. Berkeley: University of California Press, 1990.

RANK, OTTO (1884–1939)

Otto Rank, a Viennese psychoanalyst, was the first academic, as distinct from physician, in Sigmund Freud's circle. Rank's doctoral dissertation, *Grundzüge einer Psychologie des dichterischen Schafens* [The incest theme in literature and legend (1912)], demonstrated the considerable cross-cultural importance of the twin themes of the Oedipus complex, incest and patricide, as motifs of folklore and literature. Together with psychoanalyst Hans Sachs, Rank contributed the editorial manifesto "The Significance of Psychoanalysis for the Humanities," to the first issue of Freud's journal *Imago*. Rank interpreted myths as unconscious productions whose manifest contents are accepted religiously as true, despite their self-evident irrationality, for aesthetic and other emotionally compelling reasons that remain wholly unconscious.

In Rank's view, the manifest content of myths is as accidental and meaningless as the manifest content of dreams, and may similarly be ignored by interpreters. Rank applied his theory of myths in *The Myth of the Birth of the Hero* (1914), in which he detected the presence of the Oedipus complex in the infantile hero's hardships and subsequent relations with female characters and male villains. In *Der Doppelgänger* [The double (1914)], Rank explained tales of doppelgängers, or doubles, and discorporeal souls as narcissistic fantasies. Rank also produced a volume of collected essays on myth, *Psychoanalytische Beiträge zur Mythenforschung* [Psychoanalytic contributions to myth research]. After two decades as one of Freud's most devoted supporters, Rank developed independent theories of neurosis and broke with the Freudian school. His major contributions on folklore belong to his Freudian period.

Dan Merkur

See also Freud, Sigmund; Myth

✳✳✳✳✳✳✳✳✳✳✳✳✳✳✳✳✳

References

Rank, Otto. *The Double: Psychoanalytic Study.* Trans., ed., and intro. Harry Tucker, Jr. Chapel Hill: University of North Carolina Press, 1971.

———. *The Incest Theme in Literature and Legend.* Trans. Gregory C. Richterg, intro. Peter Rudnytsky. Baltimore: Johns Hopkins University Press, c. 1922.

———. *The Myth of the Birth of the Hero and Other Writings.* Ed. Philip Freund. New York: Vintage Books, 1959.

———. *Psychoanalystische Beiträge zur Mythenforschung.* Leipzig: Internationaler Psychoanalytischer Verlag, 1919.

Ranke, Kurt (1908–1985)

Born in Blankenburg, Germany, on April 14, 1908, Ranke studied German, history, and church history between 1927 and 1933 at the universities of Bonn, Munich, and Kiel. At the last institution, he earned his doctorate in February 1933 with a dissertation on AT303, "The Two Brothers" (published as Folklore Fellows Communication [FFC] 114 in 1934). After a year as an editorial assistant on Jacob and Wilhelm Grimm's German dictionary, he was appointed to a position in the German Department of the University of Kiel, earning his *venia legendi* (his right to teach at university level) in 1938 with a monograph on the veneration of the dead in Indo-European cultures (not published until 1951 as FFC 140). Although appointed to a lectureship at Kiel in 1940, World War II and its aftermath prevented Ranke from effectively taking up the position until 1948. At that time, he immediately resumed his career as a publishing scholar, with a strong emphasis on folk narrative studies. In 1960, he moved to the chair of *Volkskunde* (folklore) at the University of Göttingen where he gathered a remarkable team around him. After many productive years, after his retirement in 1973, and having become a respected elder statesman in the profession, he died in Göttingen on June 6, 1985.

Twenty-six of Ranke's most influential and groundbreaking publications were gathered together and made accessible in a volume entitled *Die Welt der einfachen Formen* [The world of simple forms (1978)], which was dedicated to him on his seventieth birthday. Ten years earlier, colleagues and students had celebrated his sixtieth birthday with an extensive festschrift, *Volksüberlieferung* [Folk tradition (1968)], which also contains a detailed critical discussion of Ranke's most seminal writings. As an editor, Ranke produced a three-volume edition of Schleswig-Holstein folktales (1955–1962), an edition of the *Folktales of Germany* in the series Folktales of the World (1966), and an anthology devoted to *European Anecdotes and Jests* (1972).

Although the list of his publications is awe-inspiring, his most lasting scholarly legacy will consist of three important achievements: the creation of the journal *Fabula* in 1958; the founding of the International Society for Folk Narrative Research in 1959 (both during his tenure in the chair of folklore at the University of Kiel); and, after his move to Göttingen, the establishment and continuing publication of the multivolume *Enzyklopädie des Märchens* [Encyclopedia of fairy tales (1977)], for which he served as both editor in chief and the contributor of 82 significant articles.

To many people, especially in the English-speaking world, Ranke is perhaps best known as an anthologizer, editor, planner, and organizer, but those more extensive and visible endeavors may well obscure the real quality of the mind of the man, as expressed, for instance, in his sensitive and sensible "Observations on the Nature and Function of the Märchen" (1958), his lifelong wrestling with Jolles's notion of "Simple Forms" (1965), or his illuminating comments on "Oral and Literary Continuity" (1969). Although Ranke remained comfortable within the scholarly ideology and conceptual framework of the historic-geographic method, he derived from the successful completion of his dissertation a keen interest in the substance, theories, and issues of folk narrative research in general. In his search for the creative impulses that operate behind the diverse kinds of folk narrative, what mattered to Ranke was the discovery of the imaginative shaping individual or the actualization of the communal spirit and soul in the poetic individual. All in all, Ranke was, indeed, a giant during some of the most difficult times for the development of *Volkskunde* in a German academic setting.

W. F. H. Nicolaisen

See also *Einfache Formen;* Folktale; Grimm, Jacob and Wilhelm; Historic-Geographic Method; International Society for Folk Narrative Research

✳✳✳✳✳✳✳✳✳✳✳✳✳✳✳✳

References

Ranke, Kurt. *Folktales of Germany*. Chicago: The University of Chicago Press, 1966.

———. *Indogermanische Totenverehrung*, vol. 1. Folklore Fellows Communication no. 140. Helsinki: Academia Scientiarum Fennica, 1951.

———. *Die Welt der einfachen Formen*. Berlin and New York: de Gruyter, 1978.

———. *Die zwei Brüder: Eine Studie zur vergleichenden Märchenforschung*. Folklore Fellows Communication no. 114. Helsinki: Academia Scientiarum Fennica, 1934.

Ranke, Kurt, et al. *Enzyklopädie des Märchens: Handwörterbuch zur historischen und vergleichenden Erzählforschung*. Berlin and New York: de Gruyter, 1977– .

RECEPTION AESTHETICS

Reception aesthetics translates as *Rezeptionsästhetik*, a term that gained currency in the 1960s when German critics began to take account of contradictory reactions to literary works. The writings of Martin Heidegger, Hans-Georg Gadamer, and Jürgen Habermas contributed to this theory, which asserts that literature produces a work only when it is actualized. Thus, the reader or hearer comes to constitute the reality of text or performance. Central contributions are the view of Roman Ingarden (1893–1970) that representation in literature is incomplete until completed by a reader, and the reintroduction by Hans Robert Jauss (1921–) of history into literary interpretation.

Reception aesthetics transposes into literature the focus on communication that began to sweep through anthropology, mathematics, linguistics, computing, and folklore after World War II. Communication theory declares that a literary or folklore text, regarded simply as a message with formal characteristics, cannot itself contain meaning, as contended by Anglo-American "new" criticism. One needs to know the relations among the text, the sender, and the receiver, whose reception of the message crucially determines its meaning. Although all language has a "directive" function ("Call me Ishmael"), certain linguistic and folkloric forms occur only when that effort is paramount. Attention to the directive function of language illuminates the performance of such a folklore genre as the proverb or aphorism ("Many hands make light work") and the figurality ("signifying") in African and African-American literature and folklore.

Among theories of folklore, reception aesthetics most closely parallels the performance approach, which mandates a close study of the complex events in which folklore is communicated to an audience. If, as Wolfgang Iser (1926–) contends, the meaning of a literary text is created only at the time of reading, then meaning in folklore comes into existence only at the time it is performed. The interaction between performer, behavior, and hearer provides empty spaces in the work that must be filled by the receiver. When a member of the audience thus creates the meaning of a folktale, the only reality of that meaning is particular, indeed "idiosyncratic." Similarly, if, as Jauss asserts, "tradition [in literature] is incapable of perpetuating itself by itself, it presupposes a response" (Jauss 1982, p. 64), then tradition in folklore has no time depth. It presupposes continual communication. If every act of cultural production and reception occurs in the social, historical, and economic context of small-group communication, both reception aesthetics and performance study call for a rigorously empirical, indeed microscopic, program of research.

Lee Haring

See also Folktale; Performance; Proverbs

✳✳✳✳✳✳✳✳✳✳✳✳✳✳✳✳✳✳

References

Bauman, Richard. *Verbal Art as Performance.* Prospect Heights, Ill.: Waveland Press, 1977.

Ingarden, Roman. *The Cognition of the Literary Work of Art.* Trans. Ruth Ann Crowley and Kenneth Olson. Evanston, Ill.: Northwestern University Press, 1973.

Iser, Wolfgang. *Prospecting: From Reader Response to Literary Anthropology.* Baltimore: Johns Hopkins University Press, 1989.

Jauss, Hans-Robert. *Toward an Aesthetic of Reception.* Trans. Timothy Bahti. Minneapolis: University of Minnesota Press, 1982.

RECONTEXTUALIZATION

Recontextualization refers to the process that takes place when discourse that has been extracted, or decontextualized, from one context is recentered, or recontextualized, to fit within a new context. The terms *decontextualization* and *recontextualization* emerged from recent studies in folklore, linguistic anthropology, and related disciplines that emphasize agent-, practice-, or performance-centered approaches to the study of expressive forms in social interaction. Understood as two facets of a single process, these terms highlight the dialectic between the socially given and the emergent in the practice of social life, and they therefore provide a productive analytical framework for addressing questions about historical and intertextual dimensions of discourse production and reception.

Implicit in recontextualization, as in the related contextualization, is the recognition that texts and contexts are interdependent. Recontextualization is therefore not a matter of injecting fixed, traditional texts into the flow of discourse. Texts do not become meaningful by virtue of juxtaposition with a specific contextual surround. Rather, text and context must be understood as emergent achievements of performance. In order for a text to be meaningful and interpretable, performers must actively contextualize their performance with respect to the dynamics of the performance event, establishing links to relevant aspects of the situational context, event participants, past performances, interpretive conventions, cultural values and beliefs, and the physical environment. Approaching discourse through the concepts of decontextualization and recontextualization, therefore, focuses attention on (1) how performers creatively transform and adapt discourse from previous events—in terms of form, function, style, content, indexical grounding, meaning, and so on—to fit the goals and needs of the current performance event; (2) how performers create interpretive frameworks and suggest meanings by establishing intertextual links and continuities with past performances; and (3) what texts bring with them when they are recontextualized in a new setting.

The concepts of decontextualization and recontextualization also provide productive insight into a number of topics of perennial interest to scholars of oral and written literature. Traditionality, for example, can be viewed as a symbolic construction invoked during recontextualization through establishing links with previous performances and variant texts (e.g., "I remember my father telling me this story" or "I've heard many versions of this story").

Similarly, genre can be understood as a product of choices in presenting a text in such a way as to elicit intertextual links that evoke the associations and interpretive strategies of a particular genre. Generic recontextualization is partly achieved through formal and stylistic patterning of the performance. Metanarrative framing also plays a significant role in this process (e.g., "Once upon a time," "I swear on my granny's grave this is a true story," or "May I never see my children again if I'm telling you a lie!").

These concepts also afford insight into scholarly practices themselves. Anytime a text is extracted from one ethnographic, historical, or literary context and placed into a folktale collection, radio broadcast, or scholarly article, an act of decontextualization and recontextualization has taken place. The decontextualization/recontextualization framework highlights questions about the historical and scholarly conventions that govern this act. For example, folklorists now scowl at the once-common practice of blending fragments or multiple performances to create "complete" ballad texts for publication. Similarly, scholars now demand word-for-word transcriptions where summaries were once acceptable.

Donald Braid

See also Ballad; Folktale; Genre; Performance; Style

✳✳✳✳✳✳✳✳✳✳✳✳✳✳✳✳✳

References

Bauman, Richard. "Contextualization, Tradition, and the Dialog of Genres: Icelandic Legends of the *Kraftaskáld*." In *Rethinking Context,* ed. Charles Goodwin and Alessandro Duranti, pp. 125–145. Cambridge: Cambridge University Press, 1992.

———. "The Nationalization and Internationalization of Folklore: The Case of Schoolcraft's 'Gitshee Gauzinee.'" *Western Folklore* 52 (1993): 247–269.

Bauman, Richard, and Charles Briggs. "Poetics and Performance as Critical Perspectives on Language and Social Life." *Annual Review of Anthropology* 19 (1990): 59–88.

Briggs, Charles L. "Metadiscursive Practices and Scholarly Authority in Folkloristics." *Journal of American Folklore* 106 (1993): 387–434.

Silverstein, Michael, and Greg Urban. *Natural Histories of Discourse*. Chicago: University of Chicago Press, 1996.

REGIONAL FOLKLORE

Regional folklore is that body of folklore material—ballads, legends, tales, songs, crafts, art, food, etc.—that is tied to and collected from a specific regional group. Although isolating geographic features may serve to create the most recognizable regional groups, other barriers—social, psychological, linguistic—work in much the same way, creating a relative privacy that fosters a sense of community which preserves traditions both unique and essential to the group. Thus, regional groups include, for instance, not only the mountaineers of the Cumberlands and the Ozarks, but the Pennsylvania Dutch and the Louisiana Creoles. As folklorist and historian Richard Dorson pointed out, regional folklore often includes items common to many regions, in local versions. But "region-specific" folklore—items that do not appear and are not understood outside the region—should be at the heart of any regional folklore study, for these items most clearly reflect the group ethos.

At least from the time of Washington Irving, regional folklore has been the subject and the substance of much American literature. Regional folklore permeates the works of such local-color artists as Hamlin Garland and Mark Twain, yet these authors depict regions from the outside, using the "folk" (and their folkways) to entertain their readers. Those authors referred to as American regionalists, on the other hand, whose works were once viewed as romantic and idealistic, go beyond simply portraying a region to understanding the region via an understanding of the region's folklore and vice versa. Hence, these writers provide regional folklorists with their best literary sources.

The regionalist folk aesthetic finds expression in a wide variety of American writings. For instance, the nineteenth-century novel by Caroline Kirkland, *A New Home, Who'll Follow* (1839), and the sketch collections by Sarah Orne Jewett, *The Country of the Pointed Firs* (1886), and Zitkala-Sa, *American Indian Stories* (1921), are unique blendings of ethnography and realist fiction, works that emphasize the importance of local practices to the maintenance of everyday life in a frontier village, the New England coast, and the Yankton Reservation, respectively. The modern poetry of Sterling Brown not only reflects the author's immersion in southern black folklife but testifies to the importance of culturally specific traditions in the formation of both an individual and a group consciousness.

With the inclusion of multiethnic literatures, contemporary literature is experiencing what could be termed a "regionalist renaissance." For the contemporary creations of such authors as Lee Smith (*Oral History* [1983]), Leslie Marmon Silko (*Ceremony* [1977]), Roberta Fernandez (*Intaglio: A Novel in Six Stories* [1990]), Amy Tan (*The Joy Luck Club* [1990]), and Stuart Dybek (*The Coast of Chicago* [1990]) seem to argue that regional folk culture is not only alive and well but absolutely necessary to group survival. By situating the worlds of their texts within their own regional groups, these and other regionalist authors chronicle folklore realistically, intelligently, and sympathetically; regional folklorists can in turn discover troves of folklore in such regional works.

Karen E. Beardslee

See also Silko, Leslie Marmon; Twain, Mark

✳✳✳✳✳✳✳✳✳✳✳✳✳✳✳✳✳

References

Dorson, Richard M., ed. *Handbook of American Folklore*. Bloomington: Indiana University Press, 1983.

Fetterley, Judith, and Marjorie Pryse, eds. *American Women Regionalists 1850–1910*. New York: W. W. Norton, 1992.

Flanagan, John T., and Arthur Palmer Hudson, eds. *Folklore in American Literature*. New York: A. S. Barnes and Company, 1958.

Hoffman, Leonore, and Deborah Rosenfelt, eds. *Teaching Women's Literature from a Regional Perspective*. New York: Modern Language Association, 1982.

McWilliams, Carey. *The New Regionalism in American Literature*. Seattle: Folcroft Library Editions, 1971.

Renaissance, English

In England, the Renaissance is a period from William Caxton's introduction of printing (1476) to the beginning (1649) or end (1660) of the Commonwealth. Literary critics often characterize English Renaissance literature as a period of borrowing from French, Italian, and especially classical sources. Poets, dramatists, and essayists adopted subjects, themes, and forms from ancient Greek and Latin literature to express the English experience. But alongside this interest in the classics grew a sense of national pride, born of England's success in international affairs and its new separation from the rest of Europe with regard to religion. Nationalism produced a certain appreciation for English culture, and this appreciation extended to English folklore—stories, legends, songs, dramas, etc.—that originated from the English people themselves. One cannot, however, decide the question of literary antecedents for Renaissance literary works as an either-or binary between classics and folklore; rather, the combination of influences produced some of the Renaissance's best works.

Universally recognized as a Renaissance poetic masterpiece, Edmund Spenser's *The Fairie Queene* (1595) consciously imitates classical epic poetry, especially Virgil's *Aeneid,* in form and allusions (for example, the tale of a man imprisoned inside a tree—canto 2 in Spenser—parallels a similar story in the *Aeneid* [Book 3]); however, the poem's intent is the glorification of British virtue and the British queen. Therefore, Spenser enlivened the classical tale with British names and places and borrowed most of his heroes from British legends, especially those of King Arthur and St. George, legends that existed in both literary sources and in the oral tradition.

But other reasons besides pride in country brought folklore into the literary consciousness of Renaissance England. The invention of printing made works in the vernacular increasingly available, and a subsequent rise in vernacular literacy resulted in a much larger audience for these works. What might be termed collections of folklore became available in print to stimulate the imaginations of both writers and their public, and many of these collections went through several printings, testifying to their popularity. Nationalism influenced, to a certain extent, the collection and the popularity of folklore miscellanies. William Camden's *Britannia* (1586), often credited with being the earliest work of British folklore, offered a nationalistic justification for folklore pursuits, or the study of "antiquities": "to acquaint the World with *Britain*, that ancient Island; that is, to restore Britain to its Antiquities, and its Antiquities to Britain" (Dorson 1968, p. 2). Camden's work cataloged not only material available from written sources, but also oral testimony from the inhabitants of the regions under study.

Often the most popular collections examined religious subjects: some chronicled, for instance, stories of witchcraft or demonic activity in the city and countryside or offered remedies for ills caused by the presence of the evil one. The popularity of these works was related to the religious uncertainty of the period, beginning with Henry VIII's break with Rome; continuing with the ensuing conflicts between Catholics, Anglicans, Protestants, and the various separatist and reformist movements; and reaching an apex in the brief overthrow of the monarchy and institution of a Puritan theocracy (1649–1660).

Samuel Harsnett's *Declaration of Egregious Popishe Impostures* (1603), the source of Edgar's inventory of devils as Tom o' Bedlam in William Shakespeare's *King Lear* (1605), reflects the anti-Catholic sentiment that was prevalent (and periodically written into law) during the reign of Elizabeth I. Harsnett's work recounts a series of exorcisms conducted illegally by Catholic priests in 1585, an account based on the stories told by the priests and four of the individuals exorcised. Harsnett probably intended his work to discredit the priests and the Catholic Church, but despite the work's polemic thrust, he produced a sort of primitive ethnography that in many ways parallels contemporary anthropological accounts of exorcisms. King James I himself produced a treatise on *Daemonologie* (1599), which elucidated demonic activity by bringing together insight on the subject from both theology and folk legend.

The age of the Renaissance in England paralleled that nation's age of exploration, and undoubtedly the discoveries and the adventures of explorers such as Sir Walter Raleigh, Sir Francis Drake, and Henry Hudson inspired the Renaissance imagination. The discovery of new worlds also gave birth to a curiosity about the customs and habits of heretofore-unheard-of peoples. In 1589, Richard Hakluyt assembled some of the accounts of the early English explorers into *The Principal Navigations, Voyages, and Discoveries of the English Nation*, which, in addition to relating the seafaring adventures of the early explorers, described firsthand their ethnographic observations of the cultures they encountered in the New World.

Captain John Smith of the Jamestown colony learned the language and customs of the native inhabitants of Virginia in order to survive in that strange world and wrote several treatises extolling life in the Virginia colonies and describing native customs and stories of encounters in great detail. Some of Smith's stories have passed into folklore via his writings, such as the story of his rescue by Pocahontas. Accounts such as Smith's, however, functioned mainly as propaganda, written to lure colonists and investors. Descriptions of native cultures often perpetuated the idealized concept of "the noble savage," a being who, by virtue of his or her simplicity, lived closer to the ideals of ancient Greece and Rome or to Christian virtue than did the members of the decadent European civilization. In order to sell these idealized images of the New World, outright fictionalizations were not uncommon. The immensely popular travel novels of the seventeenth and eighteenth centuries (e.g., Daniel Defoe's *Robinson Crusoe* [1719] or Jonathan Swift's *Gulliver's Travels* [1726]) descended from such accounts. Thus the travelogue, a literary genre that has enjoyed great success in subsequent periods of English literature, developed from a folkloric interest in the cultures of the newly discovered exotic lands and peoples.

The Renaissance genre that was perhaps most influenced by folklore, however, was drama—a not-unpredictable assumption, since drama appealed to a large segment of the population, literate and illiterate, gentry and peasant. The performance nature of drama also contributed to its close interaction with folklore, for folklore shares this essential nature—a story is told, a ballad is sung, a proverb is related. Early Renaissance drama continued the medieval dramatic traditions, genres indebted to traditional folklore in both content and performance method. Towns, merchant and craft guilds, and clergy still cooperated to stage cycle plays as celebrative spectacles for various Christian festivals, especially Easter.

Cycle plays, or mystery plays, combined a group of smaller pageants or scenes and staged them in succession, often on moving wagons, to tell one of the major stories of the Bible, such as the life of Jesus or the events of Genesis and Exodus. Tradition designated to each guild a fixed segment of the story to stage: a cycle performed in Yorkshire, for instance, began with the tanners' play of the creation of heaven and earth and ended with the mercers' version of the Last Judgment, a total of 59 segments in the entire cycle. The plays rarely followed the scripture "to the letter"; rather, the performers incorporated the oral legends and traditions associated with various biblical events into their plays (e.g., Mrs. Noah), often for comedic results, and occasionally resulted in charges of secularization and blasphemy. However, the plays served their functions: to entertain and to teach the biblical stories to a largely nonliterate, non-Latin-speaking audience.

Other medieval dramatic forms flourished well into the Renaissance and beyond. The morality plays, which encouraged virtues and discouraged vices by portraying them as abstract allegories, also continued throughout the period, often written and performed by clergy for teaching purposes. Saints' plays combined canonical and traditional elements to dramatize the lives of the saints, although records of such plays from later than the fifteenth century are rare, probably owing to the anti-Catholic bias arising out of the Reformation. Mummers' plays, such as the "dumb show" in *Hamlet* that exposes the treachery of Claudius, are usually classed as a courtly genre, but the antecedents of these plays were traditional folk genres involving disguise of the players, words subordinated to action (or missing entirely), and a plot consisting of heroic combat, a death, and a resurrection. Finally, Robin Hood plays drew their characters and plot from the stories of a legendary hero and formed an integral part of May festivals for English villages well into the seventeenth century.

The later Renaissance drama most familiar to modern audiences, such as the plays of William Shakespeare, Christopher Marlowe, and Ben Jonson, although perhaps more indebted to classical influences for form, also adopted folk themes and motifs in order to appeal to a wide-ranging audience. In fact, one can turn to almost any scene of a Shakespearean play and discover numerous references to folk customs, legends, and beliefs.

Numerous folklore sources, themes, and motifs besides the supernatural also appear in Renaissance drama, although many of them may have come to the playwrights through literary sources originally based on folklore. Scholars constantly bicker over the difficult question of whether or not a playwright had actually read, had access to, or needed access to a possible written source.

Catherine Quick

See also Arthur, King; Bible; Faust Legend; Hamlet; *King Lear;* Legend; Shakespeare, William; *The Taming of the Shrew*

✳✳✳✳✳✳✳✳✳✳✳✳✳✳✳✳✳✳

References

Brody, Alan. *The English Mummers and Their Plays: Traces of Ancient Mystery.* Philadelphia: University of Pennsylvania Press, 1970.

Cocchiara, Guiseppe. *The History of Folklore in Europe.* Trans. John N. McDaniel. Philadelphia: Institute for the Study of Human Issues, 1981.

Dorson, Richard M. *The British Folklorists: A History.* Chicago: Chicago University Press, 1968.

Goodman, Jennifer R. *British Drama before 1660: A Critical History.* Boston: Twayne Publishers, 1991.

Mississippi Folklore Register 7 (1976). Special issue on Shakespeare and folklore.

RICHMOND, W. EDSON (1918–1994)

Although primarily a folklorist and ballad scholar, W. Edson Richmond was also an accomplished teacher of and researcher in the history of the language and of literature. At the end of his life, he was professor emeritus of English and folklore at Indiana University. During his career, he served on the editorial boards and as editor of a number of literary and folklore journals, was acting chair of Indiana University's Folklore Institute, chaired the awards committee of the Chicago Folklore Prize, and received numerous fellowships and awards, including election to the Norwegian Academy of Sciences and Letters.

Richmond's scholarly interests encompassed onomastics, dialectology, medieval and comparative literature, linguistics, and most particularly the ballad—that most literary of oral genres. His journal articles interrogated some of the assumptions generally held: that ballads are sung, that they arose in the Middle Ages, that they lack refrains. His examination of the Child ballads and parallel Scandinavian materials led him to contradict the givens; he suggested that some ballads circulated in oral tradition without being sung, that there are few records of medieval balladry, and that two-thirds of the English-language ballads lack refrains. He also tackled other issues concerning ballads, most particularly those surrounding the question of variation. Although most scholars had addressed the issue of change in oral transmission, Richmond pointed out that variation results not only from human memory but also from conscious attempts to explain what seemed unclear as well as from scribal error in written transmission. Throughout his career, he returned to the historical record to seek particular illustrations. That interest in past scholarship culminated in the publication of *Ballad Scholarship: An Annotated Bibliography* (1989), a work that remains a lasting legacy to his long interest in balladry.

Richmond also participated in the classification of ballad materials, most particularly Scandinavian materials, and worked toward the creation of typologies that would enable comparative study. In more than 25 essays and hundreds of reviews, he offered a mediating perspective on ballad lore.

Bruce A. Rosenberg

See also Ballad; Child, Francis James; Scandinavian Folk Literature

✱✱✱✱✱✱✱✱✱✱✱✱✱✱✱✱

References

Edwards, Carol L., and Kathleen E. B. Manley, eds. *Narrative Folksong: New Directions*. Boulder, Colo.: Westview Press, 1985.

Jonsson, Bengt R., Svale Solheim, and Eva Danielson with Mortan Nolsoe and W. Edson Richmond. *Types of the Scandinavian Medieval Ballad: A Descriptive Catalogue*. Oslo: Universitets Forlaget, 1978.

Richmond, W. Edson. *Ballad Scholarship: An Annotated Bibliography*. New York: Garland, 1989.

RIDDLE

The riddle has been defined by folklorist John McDowell as an "interrogative ludic routine," a question and answer exchanged not for information, but in play. The answer is known to the questioner, who poses the riddle as a challenge; "the riddlee" must come up with an acceptable solution.

The riddle plays in the zone between wit and knowledge and is often used as a challenge: Venda women in South Africa judge the intelligence of prospective husbands by posing riddles, just as the queen of Sheba tested Solomon with "hard questions." In many cultures, the riddlee is expected to guess the answer and, based on cultural background and the information contained in the question, is able to arrive at an acceptable solution. In others, the answer is more arbitrary, and the solution can only be reached by prior knowledge. In such cases, the riddle is not so much problem as password, as is the case when riddles are used in initiation rituals. Often the questioner has the power to reject a proffered solution and decree another; on other occasions, as when the sphinx challenged Oedipus, the correct guess must be respected. Riddling sessions may be contests of power as well as contests of wit.

Ordeal by riddle is familiar in folktales and in literary narratives influenced by tradition, from the Iranian epic *Shahnameh* to Puccini's opera *Turandot* (AT 851). A widely distributed tale-type—AT 927—features "the neck riddle," so called because a neck depends on it. A condemned prisoner wins his or her freedom by posing a riddle to the judge, who cannot answer it because the solution is rooted in the private experience of the poser. Samson used a similar narrative riddle in his wager with the Philistines; another example is Rumpelstiltskin's "What is my name?"

The true riddle, typical of oral riddling sessions, is often based on a metaphor with a "block element": the question defines the solution in terms of something both similar and dissimilar ("No doors there are to this stronghold, but thieves break in to steal the gold—answer, an egg."). Broad cultural oppositions such as nature/culture or animate/inanimate are linked in riddles, and the effect is often to "naturalize" a cultural situation, as in Finnish riddles that compare women to household objects and men to agricultural tools or fertile women to fruit-bearing trees. Such riddles suggest an ordered universe of correspondences; thus, it is not surprising to find the riddle widely used in the socialization of children. The Christian catechism, with its fixed questions and answers, is one outgrowth of a pedagogic technique used since the time of the Babylonians. Other religions have more fully developed the didactic potential of the genre: in the Hindu Vedic hymns, riddles postulate cosmological relationships.

Sometimes a riddle's content is more disruptive, and the mixing of categories is not harmonious, but disturbing. It is significant that riddles are often told during times of transition: on the nights of harvest, during wakes for the dead, and during courtship. In many cultures, young people force awareness upon the object of their affections by posing a riddle that suggests an obscene solution (e.g., the Tuscan "You stick it in hard, you take it out soft—answer, spaghetti"). The same technique was used by the English novelist Jane Austen in her nineteenth-century novel *Emma* in more euphemistic form: Mr. Elton writes Emma a charade for which the solution is "courtship."

Riddles often go beyond mild provocation to address truly upsetting questions. A significant group of riddles queries one of the foundations of the nature/culture distinction: the incest taboo. The riddle with an incestuous relation as its solution (for example, "The branch's leaf is like the root / the father eats the mother's fruit") may be found in William Shakespeare's play *Pericles* and in numerous world folktales; it also underlies the more innocent riddle of the sphinx. The real riddle occupying Oedipus throughout Sophocles' play is that of his own origin, and the prophet Tiresias poses it to him continually in "riddling speech." The answer to the riddle is unspeakable, making it a double neck riddle: both Pericles and Oedipus condemn themselves as much by success as by failure to reach a solution.

The riddling form of oracle and prophecy is a kind of neck riddle in reverse: here, the solution is enacted in the subsequent narrative. In Shakespeare's play *Macbeth*, the witches present to Macbeth the apparently insoluble paradoxes of Birnam Wood coming to Dunsinane and a man not born of woman. In the course of the plot's unfolding, these riddles are tragically answered.

In modern Western culture, the riddle plays most frequently upon its own medium: language. What children know as riddle today is usually a conundrum, the solution of which stands in a punning rather than in a metaphorical relation to the question ("What's black and white and red all over?—answer, a newspaper."). The riddling of children today plays with the apparent arbitrariness of language and of the other cultural systems they are forced to learn. The Mad Hatter's famous conundrum, "Why is a raven like a writing-desk?" receives no answer in the course of the Alice books but is left as a tease, echoed when Alice frequently complains of the enigmatic character of other questions posed to her by adults in the narrative. The surrealists carried Lewis Carroll's play with the tricky relationship of representation and reality—a major concern of twentieth-century art and philosophy—further by playing a riddle game in which an object known only to the riddler has to be described in terms of another; for example, a terrier in terms of a flowerpot or a rainbow as the Rue de la Paix.

The concerns of oral and literary riddles are not so different, and the use of riddles in traditional and literary narratives closely echoes that of everyday life. On rare occasions, we find the riddle elaborated poetically as an end to itself: such are the famous Anglo-Saxon riddles of the Exeter Book. Most often, though, the riddle's play with the relationships between categories becomes a way to negotiate relationships between people.

Dorothy Noyes

See also Oedipus

✳✳✳✳✳✳✳✳✳✳✳✳✳✳✳✳✳

References

Abrahams, Roger D. *Between the Living and the Dead*. Folklore Fellows Communication no. 225. Helsinki: Academia Scientiarum Fennica, 1980.

———. "The Literary Study of the Riddle." *Texas Studies in Literature and Language* 14 (1972): 177–197.

Bryant, Mark. *A Dictionary of Riddles*. London: Routledge, 1990.

McDowell, John H. *Children's Riddling*. Bloomington: Indiana University Press, 1979.

Taylor, Archer. *The Literary Riddle before 1600*. Berkeley and Los Angeles: University of California Press, 1948.

Ritual

According to Alan Richardson (1983), "Rituals are regular, repetitive, rule-determined patterns of symbolic behavior, performed by one or more people, that utilize any or all of the following components: language, action, visual imagery, personification and characterization, specific objects imbued with meaning, and music." In the approaches of the English anthropological school of comparative mythology, the theories of myth and those of ritual become closely intertwined. Borrowed in part from philology, the comparative study of languages, this method draws on the early anthropologist E. B. Tylor's notion of unilinear cultural evolution in which cultures are seen to move through stages from savagery and barbarism to civilization. Relics of beliefs and practices survive from one cultural stage to another, and through study of these remnants, the original can be discovered or reconstructed. The idea that folklore—beliefs, customs, and narratives to these scholars—evolved as society did led to an understanding of the interrelatedness of myth and ritual.

A nineteenth-century preoccupation with origins and survivals of this earlier time led to a search for the rituals believed to precede the myth. The "myth-ritual theory," derived from the work of James George Frazer, in his 12-volume work *The Golden Bough* (1890), maintained that certain literary forms such as poetry, drama, and myth are the products of a gradual verbalization of religious rites and rituals as they had been traditionally or historically practiced and performed. When the original sense of these rituals was forgotten or lost, myths, tales, songs, poetry, and drama were attempts to recover the meaning. Such assumptions have proved problematic, and the concept of cultural evolution has been drastically revised. Although much myth, poetry, and drama may have come from the verbalization of ritual, these scholars failed to address the question of where these early rituals and rites came from.

The tendency in academic circles to focus on the question of what came first, the myth or the ritual, has been largely set aside, as in the work of the French anthropologist Claude Lévi-Strauss; what is important is the way in which myth and ritual function in both literature and in life, separately and in concert. For Lévi-Strauss, myth functions at the conceptual level and ritual at the performance level. In a more recent period, with the focus on the performed aspect of narrative and literature, as in Victor Turner's work, ritual is seen as the content of the drama rather than as the source. However, practitioners of ritual theory, especially when associated with archetypal criticism—as in Northrop Frye's interpretation of William Blake's work as coherent myth in *Fearful Symmetry* (1947)—still subscribe in various ways to the idea of myth as the verbalization of ritual. The intersection of ritual and literature lies then, on the one hand, in the search for survivals of ritual in literary forms and, on the other hand, in recognizing that rituals, as parts of life, necessarily find their way into literature where they can be studied independently of theories of their origin.

Amanda Carson Banks

See also Archetype; Frazer, James George; Gunkel, Herman; Lang, Andrew; Myth

✳✳✳✳✳✳✳✳✳✳✳✳✳✳✳✳

References

Bascom, William. "The Myth-Ritual Theory." *Journal of American Folklore* 70 (1957): 103–114.

Frazer, James George. *The Golden Bough: A Study in Magic and Religion.* 2d ed. London: Macmillan, 1900.

Frye, Northrop. *Fearful Symmetry: A Study of William Blake.* Princeton, N.J.: Princeton University Press, 1947.

Gaster, Theodore. "Myth and Society." *Numen* (1954): 184–212.

Richardson, Alan, and John Bowden, eds. *The Westminster Dictionary of Christian Theology.* Philadelphia: Westminster Press, 1983.

Turner, Victor. *Dramas, Fields, and Metaphors: Symbolic Action in Human Society.* Ithaca, N.Y.: Cornell University Press, 1974.

RITUAL MURDER

Ritual murder is a folk belief, expressed in legend, rumor, gossip, or ballad, claiming that members of a disliked group have secretly murdered a vulnerable member of the majority, typically a male child. In some versions of the narrative, the ritual is described in detail, but typically it is merely alleged that the victim's blood is needed for some purpose or that the murder itself serves as a form of initiation.

Because of the frequent presence of the motif of blood in ritual murder accusations, ritual murder and the blood libel legend largely overlap, although in some ritual murder accusations, blood is not mentioned. Blood libel legends are a subtype of ritual murder accusations, and these legends focus on anti-Semitic charges that Jews were using Christian blood for their rituals; classic use of such legends appears in the accounts of the murders of William of Norwich and Hugh of Lincoln. The most prominent literary account of both motifs is surely Geoffrey Chaucer's "Prioress's Tale." The theme can be traced as far back as the fifth century, and folklorist Bill Ellis (1983) has demonstrated that similar Roman tales attacked Christians in the early Christian era.

The most frequent ritual murder narratives in contemporary Western cultures involve a "mutilated boy," typically murdered by castration in the restroom of an urban or a suburban shopping center. Most of these narratives claim that the murderers were older boys of a different race. For African-American narrators, the murderers are white; for Euramericans, the victim is white. In South Africa under apartheid, colored gangs were supposedly the killers of white children. Although these accounts typically provide only sketchy motivation for the crime, the fact that castration is invariably involved suggests some measure of ritual action, perhaps an unstated connection to Jewish circumcision practices. On occasion, the murder is directly linked to gang initiation.

These rumors and legends are situated within the political and social circumstances of contemporary society just as surely as the classic blood libel tales were situated within an earlier nexus of belief. The location of many ritual murder stories in the restrooms of large shopping centers speaks to the perceived dangers of anonymous public spaces. The fact that the victim is a child newly separated from his mother speaks to the concern about a lack of oversight of one's children in a hostile world. Even the illusion of control and safety that a shopping center encourages is misleading.

Ritual murder narratives are similar to another class of narratives recounting the abduction or near abduction of an innocent, usually young girl. In these accounts, also frequently set in shopping centers—or sometimes in boutiques—a girl is drugged, disguised, and sold into prostitution, only saved, in some versions, by an observant mother.

The murder of an innocent child fills an audience with horror, and to achieve this response, the stories rely on standards of cultural plausibility. Shopping center murders are perceived as the sort of act that might reasonably, if tragically, occur, given what we "know" about the groups of malefactors who populate our world.

Gary Alan Fine

See also Chaucer, Geoffrey; Urban Legends

✳✳✳✳✳✳✳✳✳✳✳✳✳✳✳✳✳✳

References

Brunvand, Jan H. *The Choking Doberman and Other "New" Urban Legends.* New York: W. W. Norton, 1984.

Dundes, Alan, ed. *The Blood Libel Legend: A Casebook in Anti-Semitic Folklore.* Madison: University of Wisconsin Press, 1991.

Ellis, Bill. *"De legendis urbis:* Modern Legends in Ancient Rome." *Journal of American Folklore* 96 (1983): 200–208.

Ridley, Florence H. "A Tale Told Too Often." *Western Folklore* 26 (1967): 153–156.

ROBIN HOOD

Robin Hood is the best known outlaw of medieval England. His exploits in Barnesdale and in Sherwood Forest—stealing from the rich and giving to the poor, battling the evil sheriff of Nottingham, and falling in love with the aristocratic Maid Marian—have become part of the common heritage of the English-speaking world. The student of literature can find Robin Hood treated or mentioned by such notable poets and playwrights as William Langland, Michael Drayton, John Dryden, Ben Jonson, William Shakespeare, and Alfred, Lord Tennyson. Novelists, too, such as Sir Walter Scott and Alexandre Dumas, have featured Robin Hood as a central character. Even more numerous are books for children, the most important of which is probably Howard Pyle's illustrated version of the Robin Hood stories (1833). Indeed, tales of Robin Hood in almost every narrative and dramatic genre have flourished since the mid-fourteenth century, and they continue to do so today.

One of the most obsessive aspects of the study of Robin Hood by scholars has been the attempt to historicize him. It is likely that Robin Hood, if he existed at all, did so in the thirteenth and early fourteenth centuries. Unfortunately, he was not mentioned by any medieval historian or writer as a contemporary figure. By the time he is mentioned at all, he is legendary: the first reference to a Robin Hood whom we know to be the famous outlaw finds him already the subject of popular "rymes." Many attempts have been made to argue for particular individuals, places, and dates on which to pin the Robin Hood legend. Most notable among these are the arguments by Yorkshire antiquarians Joseph Hunter, P. Valentine Harris, J. W. Walker, and historian J. C. Holt. Although the attempts are altogether fascinating, the evidence is quite scanty, and the subject will probably never be considered closed.

It is perhaps more fruitful to trace the development of the legend of Robin Hood. This avenue of inquiry has been explored both by Holt and by Stephen Knight, who traces the legend down to modern movies and television shows. In the Robin Hood legend as we know it today, elements of both noble and popular versions of the story mingle with the inventions of various important authors. The resulting story makes Robin a good and noble man who is victimized on the basis of race and because of his loyalty to his king against an

A nineteenth-century lithograph depicts Robin Hood, a legendary fourteenth-century English folk hero known for stealing from the rich and giving to the poor.

unjust usurper. He becomes an outlaw, performs good deeds, and is eventually rewarded by the return of his property.

The earliest Robin Hood texts are poems. Although many were included by Harvard professor and ballad scholar Francis James Child in his canon of popular ballads, it is unclear whether they were written or composed orally, sung or spoken, or of popular or elite origin. In this sense, they stand at the nexus of literature, popular culture, and folklore. In the earliest of these Robin Hood ballads, Robin is a yeoman, outlawed for reasons unspecified, who inhabits a greenwood and robs passersby. The audience addressed by these early ballads was also yeomen, a term that covered a wide range of men below the rank of esquire—members of what we would today consider the middle class. As the tales themselves changed, however, they spread from the middle classes both upward and downward.

In the fifteenth century, Robin Hood and Little John were adopted as characters in the May games. These festive events, common all over England, included performances of song, dance, and drama. It seems that in this environment, Robin first became a character in plays involving Maid Marian and Friar Tuck, originally independent characters. Since successful dramatic performances often needed noble patronage, Robin's story began to adapt itself to noble tastes. The dramatists popularized the notion that Robin was a displaced noble and that he lived during the regency of the usurper Prince John, while Richard I was away at the Crusades and then in captivity in Austria. Some people identified Robin as the earl of Huntington, others called him the baron of Locksley.

At the same time, Robin Hood ballads were continuing to flourish. The diffusion of the ballads through minstrel performances in such places as markets and taverns and the increasing availability of cheap literature (broadsides and chapbooks) through the advent of printing kept the materials alive.

Although, as early as 1521, Robin was said to rob only the rich and, occasionally, to help the poor, it was not until 1795 that his lawlessness was held up as a model of virtuous behavior. Joseph Ritson, the compiler of an important anthology of Robin Hood ballads, preceded this work with an essay on the life of Robin Hood. Influenced by his political belief in the ideals of the French Revolution, Ritson called Robin both virtuous and patriotic. He portrayed Robin as a champion of the poor and oppressed against rich overlords, because "all opposition to tyranny is the cause of the people" (Ritson 1972 [1823], p. xiii). The second edition of Ritson's work (1823) was abridged for children so that the morals of Robin Hood could be imparted to England's youth.

A related theory concerning Robin was put forth by Ritson's friend and adviser, Sir Walter Scott. According to that theory, Robin was a Saxon baron being oppressed by the Norman ruling class. According to modern commentators, including Holt, it is anachronistic to think that Saxons and Normans existed as two separate aristocratic groups in opposition to one another during the reigns of Richard and John. Indeed, it is to Scott's novel *Ivanhoe* (1820) that we must attribute the first appearance of this idea in connection with Robin Hood.

There has been no loss of popularity for Robin Hood in the twentieth century. Countless novels, films, and television programs continue to introduce the outlaw to modern audiences. His widespread appeal is largely owing to the ambiguities of his situation; since we do not know his true identity, authors have been free to speculate and to cast him in various different roles to appeal to different groups. Through this process, a character has been created who is both noble and popular. Since he has been placed in the regime of an unlawful and cruel usurper, his lawlessness has become loyalty, his thievery has become rebellion, his violence has become justice. From being an outlaw, he has been made a hero. No doubt his exploits will continue to entertain people for many years to come.

Stephen Winick

See also Ballad; Child, Francis James; Legend; Performance; Scott, Sir Walter; Shakespeare, William

✳✳✳✳✳✳✳✳✳✳✳✳✳✳✳✳✳

R**eferences**

Child, Francis J. *The English and Scottish Popular Ballads*. 5 vols. New York: Dover, 1965 (1882–1898).

Dobson, R. B., and J. Taylor. *Rymes of Robyn Hood: An Introduction to the English Outlaw*. Pittsburgh: University of Pittsburgh Press, 1976.

Holt, J. C. *Robin Hood*. New York: Thames and Hudson, 1982.

Knight, Stephen. *Robin Hood: A Complete Study of the English Outlaw*. Cambridge, Mass.: Blackwell, 1994.

Ritson, Joseph. *Robin Hood: A Collection of All the Ancient Poems, Songs, and Ballads, Now Extant, Relative to That Celebrated English Outlaw: To Which Are Prefixed Historical Anecdotes of His Life*. Totowa, N.J.: Rowman and Littlefield, 1972 (1823).

ROMANCE

From the late twelfth century C.E., when the Old French cognate of the word first occurred, until the early nineteenth century, *romance* usually meant a loosely defined genre of narrative verbal art—in the vernacular language rather than in Latin, episodic rather than cumulative in structure, and in content often sending an individual protagonist into the wilderness to combat forces foreign to everyday life. Never used precisely, around 1800 the term's derivative, "romantic," became associated with the temperament of avid readers of mass-marketed prose romances. By a convoluted extension thereafter, the collective term came to include nonnarrative poetry expressing some emotional state within an individual poet's psyche.

It was not until the turn of the twentieth century that implications of unfulfilled sexual passion became firmly attached to the term *romance*. This latest aura of meaning arose from academic attention to selected passages in medieval verse romances. Scholars wrenched from context scattered incidents involving heterosexual intrigue, then stretched and molded them to align with late Victorian social ideals. In fact, though, across the centuries romance heroes have expended far more energy riding good horses and killing bad men than rescuing fair damsels in distress, who typically turn out to be sole heirs to their respective fathers' lands.

Etymologically, *romanz* refers to the Romance vernacular, that is, the oral dialect of ordinary speech in those parts of Europe once governed from Rome. By the twelfth century, local vernaculars had become fully distinct from Latin, the written language of official culture. The first instance of the term *romanz* labels one of five episodic verse narratives composed around 1170–1182 by Chrétien de Troyes: *Eric and Enide*, *Cligès*, *Yvain (The Knight of the Lion)*, *Lancelot (The Knight of the Cart)*, and the unfinished *Perceval (The Story of the Grail)*. The prologue to *Cligès* has fueled scholarly debate about oral and written genres of medieval literature, for in it Chrétien states that the *histoire* (traditional story? credible history?) comes from a very old *livre* ("book") from which he has taken the *contes* (stories? incidents? adventures?) to make this *romanz*.

Among the five verse narratives by Chrétien, all except *Cligès* focus on King Arthur and his knights of the Round Table. Thus, the earliest exemplar demonstrates neatly that Arthurian content is neither necessary nor sufficient for the medieval genre *romanz*. Just decades after Chrétien's lifetime, his compatriot Jean Bodel specified three distinct subjects for *romanz*: the matter of France (legends surrounding the ninth-century emperor Charlemagne), the matter of Rome (stories from classical antiquity about Troy, Alexander the Great, and so on), and the matter of Britain (Arthuriana). In addition, each region of Europe had verse narratives glorifying its own local heroes. In medieval England, the deeds of Guy of Warwick far outshone those of King Arthur. Indeed, only two major Arthurian romances survive in the Middle English language, besides those translated from known French sources: the "Wife of Bath's Tale," by Geoffrey Chaucer, and *Sir Gawain and the Green Knight*, both from the fourteenth century. The structure of each poem is smoothly interlocked, however, not at all episodic. Both also diverge in other features from the norm of their assigned genre.

In these two Middle English works and elsewhere, present-day scholars may be using the term *romance* in senses that are more honorific than generic. Medievalists tend to apply romance to Arthurian narratives in most but not all European vernaculars, unless several scholars agree that an item seems unromantic to them (as the chronicle or epic *Brut*, by Layamon, written in Middle English around 1200). Episodic narratives with no Arthurian characters but with definite French underpinnings may also earn the laudatory label "romance." For example, *Floris and Blauncheflur* is first preserved in two Old French versions around 1150, then a Middle English one around 1250, plus versions in vernaculars from Provence, Germany, Scandinavia, Italy, Greece, Spain, and Portugal.

As the major exception, works in Celtic languages are seldom thought of as romances no matter how closely they resemble Chrétien's five prototypes. Most strikingly, the earliest Arthurian narrative extant in any language sends its hero questing on episodic adventures to prove himself worthy of marriage to a giant's daughter. *Culhwch and Olwen* is in Welsh prose, not verse. However, many prose narratives in non-Celtic languages are normally called romances.

Miguel de Cervantes (Saavedra), for example, was mocking the rambling prose romances so popular five centuries later in Spain and throughout Western Europe when he wrote *Don Quixote* in 1605, and it is sometimes implied that the genre died of humiliation in the wake of his work. On the contrary, romance remained standard recreational reading, displaced only gradually by the novel. Moreover, mockery had appeared all along. Eleventh-century Welsh audiences may well have laughed at *Culhwch and Olwen*, and parodic exaggeration also occurs in one of the earliest romances in the dialect of French spoken in England, Anglo-Norman: *Ipomedon*, by Hue of Roteland (c. 1180). Thus, the film *Monty Python and the Holy Grail* (1975) attains a peak but stands neither as innovation nor as the end point of the genre of romance.

Retrospective definitions of romance have been skewed by scholarly demands for high moral seriousness in worthwhile literature and by other unstated assumptions: that French literature sets the standard for vernacular verbal art, that the romantic movement sets the standard for introspective poetry, that legendary twelfth-century knights regarded sexual intercourse with attitudes appropriate to nineteenth-century learned gentlemen, and so on. In future scholarship, awareness of the term's ever-shifting applications and connotations may encourage more conscientious definition of medieval and other genres, based upon extant evidence rather than academic agenda. For now, it can be stated definitively that romance means *Cligès* by Chrétien de Troyes.

Betsy Bowden

See also Arthur, King; Arthurian Tradition; *Gawain and the Green Knight, Sir*; Loathly Lady

✳✳✳✳✳✳✳✳✳✳✳✳✳✳✳✳✳

References

Crane, Susan. *Insular Romance: Politics, Faith, and Culture in Anglo-Norman and Middle English Literature*. Berkeley: University of California Press, 1986.

Ramsey, Lee C. *Chivalric Romances: Popular Literature in Medieval England*. Bloomington: Indiana University Press, 1983.

Stevens, John. *Medieval Romance: Themes and Approaches*. New York: W. W. Norton, 1974.

Varty, Kenneth. "Medieval Romance." In *The New Princeton Encyclopedia of Poetry and Poetics*, ed. Alex Preminger and T. V. F. Brogan, pp. 751–754. Princeton, N.J.: Princeton University Press, 1993.

ROMANCE OF REYNARD

The *Romance of Reynard* is a collection of tales with the central character of Reynard, a sly fox with human traits. The original 15 tales were written between 1174 and 1205 and have been attributed to the French author Pierre de St. Cloud. Widely read and added to in the centuries following, examples can be found in manuscripts whose origins are particularly concentrated in northeastern France, the Low Countries, Scandinavia, England, and northern Germany. In France, the character of Reynard became so popular that his name became the standard word for fox.

Scholars have determined a number of possible sources for St. Cloud's tales of Reynard. In the mid-twelfth century, a scholar from Ghent wrote the Latin poem "Isengrimus." This poem, with its animal characters with human traits, reveals some similarities with the *Romance of Reynard*. Bestiaries, a popular form of literary production of the time, emphasized animals and their traits, often to convey moral messages. The idea of learning from animals has affinities with St. Cloud's use of animal characters to satirize his society. The Reynard stories, it is thought, could also be related to the beast fables that had been extremely popular in parts of Europe. The most famous name associated with such fables is Aesop.

More generally, the use of animal characters for didactic purposes had a long tradition in the Middle East—the Byzantine Empire, for example, was home to many such tales—and it is possible that this tradition influenced the writing of the original Reynard tales. Arabic translations of Sanskrit fable collections were popular in Iberia in the thirteenth century, and, while obviously not serving as sources for St. Cloud's earlier tales, their existence points out that tales about trickster animal figures like Reynard the Fox were very common in Europe as well as in many other parts of the globe.

Folklore research reminds us that stories about trickster animals like the fox are common in China, Japan, India, South America, and Africa. In Chinese tales, foxes can transform themselves or become invisible and therefore must be appeased. Tales about foxes making deals with scholars for the latter's advancement have also been recorded.

The animal tale is one of the most widespread forms of folklore. Although at times the trickster animal might be a coyote, as in Native American stories, or a rabbit or spider, as in African-American ones, the similarities reveal an interconnectedness between European storytelling traditions and similar traditions the world over. This interconnectedness has been pointed out by the producers of a motif and tale-type index for the Reynard the Fox stories, which documents their close connections to non-European folklore forms.

Within Europe, a number of later authors created their own versions of various Reynard stories. Geoffrey Chaucer (1344–1400) used one in his "Nun's Priest's Tale," William Caxton (1422?–1491) published an English version (*The History of Reynard the Fox*) in 1481, and the German author Johann Wolfgang von Goethe (1749–1832) used the character of Reynard in his 1794 story "Reinecke Fuchs."

The first major modern edition of *Romance of Reynard* was published in the 1820s. The members of an international society specializing in research of beast epics (International Beast Epic Society) devote much attention to questions dealing with the various versions of the Reynard stories.

Joseph F. Patrouch

See also Aesop's Fables; Chaucer, Geoffrey; Epic; Fable; Romance; Trickster

✳✳✳✳✳✳✳✳✳✳✳✳✳✳✳✳

References

Foulet, Alfred, ed. *Le Couronnement de Renard, poème du treizième siecle*. Princeton, N.J.: Princeton University Press, 1929.

Smith, Richard Edwin. *Type-index and Motif-index of the Roman de Renard*. Uppsala, Sweden: Ethnologiska Institutionen, 1980.

Terry, Patricia, ed. *Renard the Fox*. Boston: Northeastern University Press, 1983.

ROMANCERO

The traditional Spanish *romances* ("ballads") composed during the Middle Ages were published in *romanceros* ("songbook collections") in the sixteenth century. These anonymous ballads are musical compositions of two eight-syllable hemistiches per line, in assonant rhyme form, without strophic division. Modified through variants, the poems were diffused orally by popular tradition and professional minstrels throughout Spain and its dominions, from the New World to North Africa.

There have been two schools of thought on ballad formation: the neotraditionalists, led by Ramón Menéndez Pidal, believe the ballads to have fragmented from longer Spanish epics, with the poems' reduction in length over time accounting for their expressive economy and the abrupt transitions and endings. The individualist school, initially constituted by Joseph Bédier, Benedetto Croce, and Leo Spitzer, attributes the ballads' origins to a new artistic consciousness that created a novel poetic style. The first Spanish ballads date from the early fourteenth century; recently, however, some scholars, noting similarities in form and content, have attempted to link a twelfth-century mozarabic poem *(jarcha)* with the *romancero;* such a connection would necessitate a revision of the current views on ballad composition.

Ballads are usually divided by their subject matter: historical events, as narrated in the ballad cycles centering on King Rodrigo and the Cid *(romances históricos);* border clashes between Moors and Christians *(fronterizos);* political uprisings and battles *(noticieros);* biblical and mythological topics *(novelescos);* and themes from European legends, refashioned in such cycles as those on Charlemagne and his court *(carolingios).* Other categories depend on both the poems' chronology, marking the difference between popular and traditional, and their style. Scholars thus differentiate among traditional "primitive" ballads *(romances viejos),* traditional ballads reworked by minstrels *(eruditos),* and popular ballads composed by minstrels *(juglarescos).* Ballads circulated in chapbooks, such as those sung by blind men *(romances vulgares),* are considered to bridge the written and oral traditions.

Spanish balladry is distinguished by its archaic vocabulary and spelling and by its creative mixture of verb tenses combining past, present, and future verb forms. This flexibility allows the singer a means of rendering diverse temporal planes and of communicating them directly to the public. In the ballad of Count Arnaldos, for example, the singer recites, "Thus spoke the Count Arnaldos / you'll hear clearly what he'll say." The oral tradition makes effective use of repetitions and parallelisms, both for their aesthetic value and for their aid as mnemonic devices. Alliterative word formations in such ballad lines as "Me, I'm the Mooress Moraima," convey musicality and establish a subjective viewpoint while parallel lines proffer a formulaic diction that helps propel the narrative forward.

All ballads before the first decades of the sixteenth century comprise the *romancero antiguo,* or old ballad tradition; the subsequent *romancero nuevo,* or new balladry, influenced by the written collections of the oral tradition, was composed in the early modern period by such well-known poets as Lope de Vega, Francisco de Quevedo, and Luis de Góngora, and in this century by Federico García Lorca, primarily as literary texts.

Transmitted orally through the centuries, the old ballad tradition may still be heard in Spain's rural areas, in Latin America, in Portugal's Tras Os Montes region, and—with numerous thematic and language changes—in those countries with a strong population of Sephardic Jews, such as Greece, Morocco, Turkey, and the United

States. Further, the traditional ballad's ability to re-create itself according to changing cultural and historical circumstances, as in the Spanish civil war ballad on the execution of the republican heroes García and Galán, has allowed it to remain a vibrant oral force.

Anne J. Cruz

See also Ballad; Cervantes (Saavedra), Miguel de; Chapbook; Epic; Legend; Tradition

✳✳✳✳✳✳✳✳✳✳✳✳✳✳✳✳✳✳✳

References

Alvar, Manuel. *El Romancero: Tradicionalidad y pervivencia*. Barcelona: Planeta, 1970.

Catalán, Diego. *Siete siglos de Romancero (historia y poesía)*. Madrid: Gredos, 1969.

Díaz Viana, Luis. *El Romancero*. Madrid: Anaya, 1990.

Foster, William David. *The Early Spanish Ballad*. New York: Twayne Publishers, 1971.

Menéndez Pidal, Ramón. *Estudios sobre el Romancero*. 2 vols. Madrid: Espasa Calpe, 1973.

ROMANTICISM

As a historical movement, romanticism engendered what we call folklore and confirmed its separation from literature, thus paving the way for the rediscovery and appropriation of folklore by literary authors. Nostalgia led romantics to prize old tales and associate them with childhood; the press of industrialism and decline of agriculture led them to value peasant life as folkloric.

Romanticism rejoiced in asserting, indeed creating, national culture under the flag of a return to roots. James Macpherson (1736–1796), the most popular English-language poet after William Shakespeare, composed works he attributed to Ossian, a Gaelic-language poet. Macpherson's supposed discovery of a Scottish national epic embodied the romantic nationalism that begat the study of folklore. His wildly enthusiastic reception all over Europe spoke for an idea whose time had come: the voice of the folk. Ossian's great advocate in Germany was Johann Gottfried von Herder (1744–1803), who avowed that poetic ability was not confined to an elite and that the highest poetic expressions came from archaic culture. Archaic poetry, including that in the Old Testament, must be studied and read; a nation's artistic achievements must grow from the folk.

Herder's advocacy of "natural" poetry (archaic, Ossianic, ballad) led him to jumble together poems of very diverse origins in his *Volkslieder* [Folksongs (1778–1779)]. His conceptions of purity and anonymity were taken over in *Des knaben Wunderhorn* [The boy's magic horn (1802–1808)], a collection of "natural" poetry by the German writers Achim von Arnim and Clemens Brentano in which the authentic essence of the German nation was sought and found. By this supposed return to the roots of national culture, romanticism enlarged the cultural and literary horizons of Europe.

In the same direction, researchers into Jacob (1785–1863) and Wilhelm (1786–1859) Grimm's language and narrative led their readers to lump together the *Nibelungenlied*, the Eddic poems, and *Beowulf* with tales, chapbooks, and songs of known authors because all were purely Teutonic. Similarly in Scotland, a generation after the small farmers had been displaced by sheep and the Jacobites had been defeated in the dreadful Battle of Culloden Moor (1746), Sir Walter Scott (1771–1832) nostalgically advocated the Jacobite cause by collecting, publishing, and imitating Scottish folk poetry. Scott's hugely popular Waverly novels (1814–1832]) portrayed Scotland as remote, isolated, and politically irrelevant, and he became a representative of important romantic tendencies. Among these were a desire to escape from the actuality of an industrializing Europe and a preference for outdoor scenes to indoor scenes. Hence, it was through Scott's antiquarian, nostalgic pictures of Highland life and Robert Burns's rewritings of folk-song lyrics that readers came to learn of Scottish folklife. The folklore used in romantic literature nearly always comes from such mediated, edited sources.

Other European literatures also underwent the influence of folklore. In France, the influences of Jean-Jacques Rousseau (1712–1778) and of Bernardin de Saint-Pierre's novel *Paul et Virginie* (1787) led to the collecting of Breton and other regional lore and the literary use of folklore by the nineteenth-century writers George Sand and Victor Hugo. In Italy, Giovanni Berchet (1783–1851) translated Spanish folk poetry and wrote *Romanze* (1834) under its influence while Giacomo Leopardi (1798–1837) manifested the influence of folkloric nationalism. Hungary's greatest romantic poet, Sándor Petöfi (1823–1849), declared that popular poetry was the only real poetry.

Imitation of folk lyrics by these poets, as by William Wordsworth (1770–1850) and Samuel Taylor Coleridge (1772–1834), the latter most notably in "Rime of the Ancient Mariner," enlivened the appropriation of folklore. Imitation continued through the literary ballads of Oscar Wilde ("A Ballad of Reading Gaol") and A. E. Housman, as well as the literary fairy tales of Hans Christian Andersen. Other themes of romanticism—its medievalism, mystery, and supernaturalism; the rebellious attitudes, extreme sensitivity, and enthusiasm of a Lord Byron—do not reflect the content of folklore. Rather, they correspond to the adventuresome impulse to collect folklore and the expectation that its novelty will impress "nonfolk" readers as foreign and exotic.

Lee Haring

See also Andersen, Hans Christian; Arnim, Achim von; *Beowulf*; Brentano, Clemens; Burns, Robert; Chapbook; *Edda, Poetic*; Epic; Goethe, Johann Wolfgang von; Grimm, Jacob and Wilhelm; Herder, Johann Gottfried; Macpherson, James; Ossian; Scott, Sir Walter

✳✳✳✳✳✳✳✳✳✳✳✳✳✳✳✳✳✳

References

Brown, Mary Ellen. *Burns and Tradition*. Urbana: University of Illinois Press, 1984.

Cocchiara, Giuseppe. *The History of Folklore in Europe*. Trans. John N. McDaniel. Philadelphia: Institute for the Study of Human Issues, 1981 (1952).

Ehrenpreis, Anne Henry. *The Literary Ballad*. London: Edward Arnold, 1966.

Marcell, David W. "Fables of Innocence." In *Handbook of American Folklore*, ed. Richard M. Dorson, pp. 73–78. Bloomington: Indiana University Press, 1983.

Zipes, Jack. *The Brothers Grimm: From Enchanted Forests to the Modern World*. New York: Routledge, 1988.

ROSSETTI, CHRISTINA GEORGINA (1830–1894)

The British Victorian secular and religious poet and younger sister of the poet and painter Dante Gabriel Rossetti, Christina Georgina Rossetti is most famous for her narrative poem, *Goblin Market* (1862). Reared in a rich Anglo-Italian cultural environment, she was exposed to folklore early and retained her interest in it. The Rossetti family knew Thomas Keightly (1789–1872) and his folktale collection, *The Fairy Mythology* (1828). The family was related by marriage to Anna Eliza Bray, author of *The Tamar and the Tavy* (1836) and collector of Cornish lore, and by blood to the infamous Dr. John Polidori, Lord Byron's physician and fellow contributor to vampire lore.

Goblin Market utilizes and transforms materials on the "fairy fair"—in which appealing merchandise is found to be illusory—and on "fairy food"—the prohibition against eating what supernatural creatures offer—to shape a tale of temptation, sacrifice, and regeneration. The "little goblin men," with their grotesque human and animal natures, appear to be the creations of Rossetti's own imagination. In general, she was more involved with ghosts than goblins, as manifested by her many poems in which the former appear. These are of two varieties: Gothic pseudo-folk ballads and less traditional poems that seem touched by religious or personal convictions. Of the ballad imitations, the most successful are "The Hour and the Ghost," which employs the motif of the demon lover, and "Lord Thomas and the Fair Margaret," a folk ballad of death and the maiden. An actual belief in revenants may distinguish such chilling poems as "The Poor Ghost," "The Ghost's Petition," and "A Chilly Night," in all of which ghostly visitors bring meaningful, if painful, messages from the world of the dead. Still other poems, like "At Home" and "After Death," show the poet casting herself in the role of the ghost and returning to view the earthly world.

Although better known for her lyrics, Rossetti wrote numerous literary folk ballads, including unusual poems like "Jessie Cameron" (1866) with its peasant narrator and folkloric flavor, as well as more conventional ones like "Sister Maude" (1862) and "Noble Sisters" (1862), which utilize the motif of the jealous sibling. Rossetti also deserves attention for her unconventional, acerbic fairy tales collected in *Commonplace* and in *Speaking Likenesses* (1872).

Carole Silver

See also Ballad; Victorian Fairy Lore

✳✳✳✳✳✳✳✳✳✳✳✳✳✳✳✳✳✳

References

Briggs, Katharine M. "Goblin Market." In *An Encyclopedia of Fairies*. New York: Pantheon, 1976.

Duffy, Maureen. *The Erotic World of Faery*. London: Hodder and Stoughton, 1972.

Rossetti, Christina. *Complete Poems: A Variorum Edition*. 3 vols. Ed. R. W. Crump. Baton Rouge: Louisiana State University Press, 1979–1990.

ROURKE, CONSTANCE MAYFIELD (1885–1941)

Constance Mayfield Rourke was a pioneering scholar who led an attempt to discover the nature and source of the American character. Writing at a time when most of her colleagues questioned the idea of a significant and unified culture in the United States, she set out to prove in her work that she had

> no quarrel with the American character; one might as well dispute with some established feature in the natural landscape. Nor can it be called a defense. Someone has said that a book should be written as a debt is gratefully paid. This study has grown from an enjoyment of American vagaries, and from the belief that these have woven together a tradition that is various, subtle, sinewy, and scant at times but not poor. (Rourke 1986)

That quotation from her major work, *American Humor: A Study of the National Character*, written in 1931, encompasses the main lines of Rourke's work. A freelance writer throughout her life, she set out to define the meanings and significance of American culture, providing in *American Humor* an understanding of the general materials from which our society has developed. As she indicated, the lineage was complicated and not subject to a dogmatic interpretation, but three main sources combined in syncretic fashion to compose the basic forms of our character: the Yankee, the backwoodsman, and the Negro:

> The three figures loomed large, not because they represented any considerable numbers in the population, but because something in the nature of each induced an irresistible response. Each had been a wanderer over the land, the Negro a forced and unwilling wanderer. Each in a fashion of his own had broken bonds, the Yankee in the initial revolt against the parent civilization, the backwoodsman in revolt against all civilization, the Negro in a revolt which was cryptic and submerged but which none the less made a perceptible outline. (Rourke 1986)

With the sense of comedy an underlying and cohesive element, Rourke thus suggested some of the roots of and resources for American literature.

In *The Roots of Culture* (1942), published posthumously, she recognized the ideas of Johann Gottfried Herder, whose work had been of interest to American writers Ralph Waldo Emerson and Walt Whitman, pointing out that among Herder's European followers, "a mild nostalgia quickly took the place of Herder's bold creative concept of the folk as a living wellspring of poetry and song." She emphasized his notion "that history should portray the many layers of the culture of peoples rather than the peaks of achievement."

Rourke's other studies were to be developed in a multivolume history of American culture, but her death prevented the realization of that goal. She left sufficient materials, however, including studies of the early American theater, Davy Crockett, John James Audubon, and Charles Sheeler (both as photographer and painter), to fulfill her main goal of revealing the complex and wide-ranging movement of American thought. Her work remains as a major repudiation of the idea that the United States has no aesthetic tradition of its own. She followed in the steps of Emerson, who had maintained that "we have listened too long to the courtly muses of Europe." That democratic message, she knew, needed to be passed on to each new generation of Americans.

Gene Bluestein

See also Herder, Johann Gottfried

✻✻✻✻✻✻✻✻✻✻✻✻✻✻✻✻✻

References

Rourke, Constance. *American Humor: A Study of the National Character*. Ed. W. T. Lhamon, Jr. Tallahassee: University of Florida Press, 1986 (1931).

Rubin, Joan Shelley. *Constance Rourke and American Culture*. Chapel Hill: University of North Carolina Press, 1980.

RUSALKA

A female supernatural being found among eastern Slavs, the *rusalka* (plural, *rusalki*; called *rusalka mavka* or *bohynia* [plural, *mavki bohyni*] among the Ukrainians) usually lives in water and may have a fish tail like a mermaid, though many *rusalki* have legs and emerge from the water, especially at night, to dance circle *khorovod* ("dances") in the fields or to sit in trees, combing their hair and singing. *Rusalki* are associated with the unquiet dead. They are said to be the souls of maidens who committed suicide by drowning because they were pregnant out of wedlock. These maidens, like others who died before their time, are forced to live out what would have been their natural life span as specters. *Rusalki* may also be the souls of children who were cursed or killed by their mothers or who died before they could be baptized. Although children appear in narratives about the origin of *rusalki*, most *rusalka* stories are about adult women.

Rusalki are described as being young and beautiful in Ukrainian and southern Russian memorates, fabulates, legends, and literary works. They are often pictured as seducing young men, luring them to a lake or river with their singing, and then drowning them by tickling them so they cannot stay afloat. Northern Russian sources describe *rusalki* as old and ugly, sometimes with green hair and breasts of iron, which they use to beat their male victims. Literary works share the depiction of the *rusalka* as in Nikolay Mikhaylovich Karamzin's "Bednaia Liza" [Poor Lisa (1792)], Mikhail Yuryevich Lermontov's "Taman" section of *Geroi nashego vremeni* [The hero of our time (1840)], Grigory Rasputin's "Zhivi I pomni" [Live and remember (1974)], and other literary works.

Rusalki are usually considered part of an unclean force, *nechistaia sila*, especially by Christian writers. A more neutral designation assigns them to lower mythology along with devils, demons, and homestead, field, and forest spirits. It is likely, however, that *rusalki* belong in a different category and are remnants of a prehistoric goddess religion. Evidence suggesting that *rusalki* developed out of ancient goddesses—like Mokosh, the goddess of moisture, and Rozhanitsa, the goddess of birth—includes their association with crop fertility and the role they play in the cycle of agrarian ritual.

Crops are said to grow with special vigor wherever *rusalki* dance their *khorovod*; during the seventh week after Easter, villagers would try to entice *rusalki* to walk in their fields and, afterward, ceremonially lead them back to their watery homes so they would pose no danger to the young men who needed to do the plowing and sowing. Young, unmarried women played a special role in the seventh-week festival, one of them sometimes enacting the role of a *rusalka*, a role that could also be assigned to a straw-filled dummy or a specially cut and decorated birch tree. If the *rusalka* was a tree or a dummy, she was often sacrificed by drowning or burning or by being torn apart and scattered in the fields. References to this practice, as well as to *Semik*, an all-girl celebration held in the forest on the seventh

Thursday after Easter when young women pledge eternal friendship and tell fortunes, appear in literary works.

Natalie Kononenko

See also Belief; Legend; Mermaid

❋❋❋❋❋❋❋❋❋❋❋❋❋❋❋❋❋❋

References

Ivanits, L. *Russian Folk Belief*. New York: M. E. Sharpe, 1989.

Kononenko, Natalie. "Mermaids (*Rusalki*) and Russian Beliefs about Women." In *New Studies in Russian Language and Literature*, ed. Anna Lisa Crone and Catherine V. Chvany, pp. 221–238. Columbus, Ohio: Slavica Publishers, 1986.

Zelenin, Dmitri K. *Ocherki russkoi mifologii: Umershie neistestvennoiu smertiiu i rusalki*. Moscow: Indrik, 1995 (1916).

RUSSIAN BALLAD

The Russian ballad falls into two distinct categories: the folk ballad and the literary ballad. The term *ballad* has been used only fairly recently for the Russian folk ballad, known to its singers as "songs" or "poems." Having peaked in the fourteenth through the seventeenth centuries, this genre is characterized by its everyday family thematics and the predominantly tragic outcome of its conflicts. In contrast to the lyric song, the folk ballad has a defined or "complete" plot, and the events have a stronger tragic nature. As in the Russian epic folk song, the bylinas, the swiftly moving episodes of a ballad's single conflict find expression in third-person narrative, using the past tense with delayed, slower action in the present or future tense. Switches to dialogue or monologue underscore moments of high tension. Realistic motives far outnumber the fantastic ones. Unlike the longer bylinas, in which the tragic occupies an insignificant place, the ballad's thematics, plot, and motifs enforce its tragic nature through poetic devices such as foreshadowing, dreams, and evil omens.

Characters clearly divide into the positive and the negative: the victim is often a maiden or young wife; the perpetrator of evil is often a husband, brother, or mother-in-law. Although evil usually triumphs, the positive heroes, who consistently perish young, are eventually the moral victors. Frequent topics include Tatar or Turkish oppression, captivity, incest, and family jealousy. Antithetical structure condemns evil through contrast with good, allowing the narrator to remain unobtrusive. Folk ballads lack nature scenes, elaborate descriptions, or portraits of characters, whose defining epithet, however, remains constant.

Composed in tonic verse without rhymes, stanzas, or refrains, the Russian folk ballad achieves dynamism through an abundance of verbs. Avoiding explanation for actions imbues the atmosphere with mystery and suspense, which is often augmented by magical symbolism and the ballad's crux—allegory. The greater stability of story over character is exhibited by the frequency of nameless and typical personages known only for their family standing and relations. The Russian folk ballad began to wane at the end of the eighteenth and beginning of the nineteenth centuries.

The Russian literary ballad emerged on the basis of Western European romantic ballads and a newly created interest in Russian folklore that began with the publication of the collections by Mikhail Chulkov (1743–1792) and Mikhail Popov (1742–1790) in the late eighteenth century. Often originating as free translations or renditions of English, German, and other ballads, the literary ballad retained non-Russian character names but often added Russian color for settings and motifs. The literary ballad's stanzas fall into quatrains with alternate rhymes (rhyming couplets are rare); its meter is mostly ternary meters and sometimes iambic. Created for reading, it could be longer than the folk ballad; for singing, the literary tradition composed romances.

The earliest published example is Nikolay Mikhaylovich Karamzin's (1766–1826) *Raisa*, with sources in David Mallet's *William and Margaret* (1723) and the work of Gottfried August Bürger (1747–1794). As in the folk ballad, it lacks an introduction and its conclusion is cursory, but hyperbole appears in emotive descriptions of nature, characters, and action as well as in emotional interruptions of narrative in the form of interjections. Karamzin's emphasis on the heroine's psychology and his intense use of epithets were emulated by later writers. His ballad, *Alina*, set as an eighteenth-century idyll, interrupts the narrative with discursive observations.

Russia's greatest popularizer of the literary ballad, Vasily Zhukovsky (1783–1852), translated and imitated Western European sources in over 40 ballads. Through his artistic genius, he transformed his sources into rival works of art in the Russian tradition, incorporating certain themes and motifs as well as other aspects of folk tradition. He expanded the narrative, put greater emphasis on setting and characters, allowed interruptions and moralizing, and imbued natural and supernatural settings with local color. Typically, Zhukovsky retained mere outlines of Western plots, such as in the nine ballads from the German poet Johann Schiller, which he infused with generalized or Russianized settings and characters. Bürger's ballad *Lenore* found varying solutions in Zhukovsky's three versions, *Liudmilla*, *Lenora*, and *Svetlana*, with the latter employing a high number of Russian folk elements such as divination.

Johann Wolfgang von Goethe's *Der Erlkönig* spawned Katenin's *The Wood Sprite*, A. K. Tolstoy's (1817–1875) "Where the Vines Bend over the Whirlpool," and Bella Akhnadulina's (b. 1937) "The Rider-Garden" in the twentieth century. James Macpherson's work on Ossian was a popular model for many, most notably for Aleksandr Pushkin (1799–1837) and Nikolai Gumilev (1886–1921). Pushkin's *Bridegroom*, which is based on Russian fairy tales and the work of the brothers Grimm, combines the speed and suspense of the ballad with elements of the fairy tale in which the heroine prevails over the murderous bridegroom. Romanticization of the Caucasus found reflection in Mikhail Lermontov's (1814–1841) *Tamara*, which is based on Georgian sources. A. K. Tolstoy perfected the horror ballad in "The Wolves," using historical settings of Kievan Russia, as in Pushkin's "Song of the Wise Oleg," and of ancient Moscow. Tolstoy's most famous ballad, *Vasilii Shibanov*, is taken from Karamzin's *History of the Russian State*.

At the turn of the century, several Russian symbolists—Valery Briusov (1873–1924), Konstantin Balmont (1867–1943), and Aleksandr Blok (1880–1921) in particular—echoed John Keats's "La Belle Dame sans Merci." Under the influence of Pushkin's ballad "The Demons," which creates atmosphere rather than relating a story, the literary ballad becomes shorter and more fragmentary in the later poets, but nowhere as brilliantly as in the quasi-ballads of Anna Akhmatova (1889–1966), who presents a setting of suspense and horror without a definable story or plot. These pieces stand in stark contrast to her long ballad in blank verse *By the Very Edge of the Sea* and her two shorter ballads, "In the Forest" (based on Keats's "Isabella, or The Pot of Basil") and "The Gray-Eyed King." The Soviet period produced the ballads of Nikolai Tikhonov (1896–1979) in rhyming couplets extolling communist bravery, like the "Ballad of Nails," and Sergey Yesenin's (1895–1925) "Ballad of the Twenty-Six," which extols Soviet martyrs in choppy isometric rhythm. Decreased visibility and greater formal freedom seem to be the lot of the literary ballad at present, giving rise to the poet as bard—Vladimir Vysotskii (1938–1986) and Bulat Okudzhava (b. 1924).

Sonia I. Ketchian

See also Akhmatova, Anna; Ballad; Bylinas; Grimm, Jacob and Wilhelm; Macpherson, James; Ossian; Russian Folk Lyric Song

✳✳✳✳✳✳✳✳✳✳✳✳✳✳✳✳✳✳

References

Katz, Michael R. *The Literary Ballad in Early Nineteenth-Century Russian Literature.* Oxford: Oxford University Press, 1976.

Ketchian, S. "The Balladic Poems of Anna Akhmatova." *Transactions of the Association of Russian-American Scholars in the U.S.A.* 23 (1990): 175–192.

———. "In the Forest with Anna Akhmatova and John Keats." *Keats-Shelley Journal,* forthcoming 1999.

Pein, Annette. *Schiller and Zhukovsky: Aesthetic Theory in Poetic Translation.* Mainz: Liber Verlag, 1991.

RUSSIAN FOLK LYRIC SONG

The type of Russian folk song that is most numerous and widespread is the *pesenka* ("little song"), called by folklorists "lyric song" to differentiate it from the many other folk genres. The word *lyric* is not meant to suggest some direct outpouring (older songs of this type avoid the first person) but rather to indicate the centrality of emotion as subject: love, longing, grief.

Ballads, laments, and cradle songs can be quite close to the emotional focus of the lyric song, which is true also of certain ritual songs, especially those connected with the folk wedding tradition. The lines delineating the genres are not at all clear, particularly with regard to diction, stylistic features, and metaphor. There are a great many points in common even between epics and lyric songs. Ballads were not even considered separate from lyric songs until the mid-nineteenth century, and then they were called by scholars "lower epics." Some dancing and game songs seem almost indistinguishable from the lyric.

What all the older genres share in common are the assumptions, customs, and concerns of Old Russia peasant life on the estate, what is called the "old patriarchal way of life." Even in those genres that are obviously removed from the original milieu—soldiers' songs, bandits' songs, carters' and bargers' songs—there is typically a harkening back to the home village, the family, the home.

By the second part of the nineteenth century, the comparatively long and complex traditional song forms began to be abandoned in favor of a newer, shorter form called the *chastushka*. This became the most popular of the folk-song types and the only one still being generated in large numbers. The thematics of the *chastushka* can draw on all the subjects mentioned above, plus those from the modern, urban, and industrial world, even politics. Since these *chastushki* originated as short dancing songs and are most closely related to the earlier dancing/game lyrics, they tend to have more regular meter and rhyme. As in the case of the lyric song, love songs represent the most frequent group; these are thought of especially as a woman's or a young girl's genre.

The form is usually four lines, sometimes six; a particular instance is the two-liner, which is called a *stradanie*, meaning "suffering." This type derives from the old lyric song tradition in which the woman perceives love as pain and loss, married life as a woeful trial, the husband unattractive and cruel, his family spiteful and demanding, the neighbors nosy and gossiping. (There are of course a great many happy songs, but the impression is that the sad ones predominate.) The beloved is a "bright falcon" (part of an elaborate system of bird and plant imagery), young and handsome, but unattainable: he may be fickle and abandon the woman, or he may be conscripted and have to leave her, or the husband and his family may present obstacles.

There is a name for the view of life and love as suffering—it is called *zhenskaia dolia*, a "woman's lot." Certain songs reflect this point of view as in the lyric below:

> The flowers flowered in the field, but faded;
> My beloved loved me, but he left me.
> Oh, he's left me, my sweetheart, but not for long.
> Ah, just for a wee while, oh, just one little hour;
> A little hour seems to me a whole little day;
> A little hour seems to be a whole little week;
> The little week seems like the whole month of May.

It is not surprising that the rich resources of the lyric song (as well as other genres of folk poetry) have been tapped by many literary figures; particularly interesting in this regard are Russia's two great women poets, Marina Tsvetaeva and Anna Akhmatova. Because of the readily recognized conventions of the folk lyric, a poet has only to signal a connection with the genre in order to introduce a whole rich frame of reference and meaningful associations into a poem, which in itself may have no direct relation to the Russian folk at all. Often, the interesting tension between the sophistication of the literary poet and borrowing from the folk singer creates the aesthetic effect of the poem. This is sometimes the case with Anna Akhmatova.

Sam Driver

See also Akhmatova, Anna; Ballad; Russian Ballad; Women
✳✳✳✳✳✳✳✳✳✳✳✳✳✳✳✳✳✳

References

Alexander, Alex E. *Russian Folklore: An Anthology in English Translation*. Belmont, Mass.: Nordland, 1975.

Reeder, Roberta. *Down along the Mother Volga: An Anthology of Russian Folk Lyrics*. Intro. Vladimir Propp. Philadelphia: University of Pennsylvania Press, 1975.

————. "Folk Song." In *Handbook of Russian Literature*, ed. Victor Terras. New Haven: Yale University Press, 1985.

Sokolov, Iu. M. *Russian Folklore*. Hatboro, Pa.: Folklore Associates, 1966.

RUSSIAN FORMALISM

Russian formalism is the doctrine that was espoused by a group of scholars active in St. Petersburg (Leningrad) and Moscow roughly between 1915 and 1930. Their centers were the Petersburg OPOJAZ (Obshchestvo izucheniia poeticheskogo iazyka, that is, Society for the Study of Poetic Language) and the Moscow Linguistic Circle. The formalists set out to study literature as art rather than as an expression of human psychology or a reflection of social reality. Hence, their emphasis on narrative technique and the peculiarities of language in prose and poetry, as well as formalism, the unfortunate name that has often been interpreted as indifference to the message of literature.

The aim of the formalists was to show that literature cannot be dissected into content and form and that what is traditionally called form is the essence of artistic endeavor. The best known participants in the movement were Roman Jakobson (who emigrated after the revolution), Viktor Shklovskii, Iurii Tynianov, Boris Eikhenbaum, and Boris Tomashevskii. Some of their students also became distinguished scholars; among them, Boris Bukhshtab and Lidiia Ginzburg deserve special mention. Vladimir Propp had to fight the accusation of formalism all his life, but it is the ideas of Russian formalism that underlie his *Morphology of the Folktale* (1928).

The reception of formalism on the part of the literary establishment was predictably hostile, the more so as all the proponents of the new trend were very young and inclined to dismiss the achievements of their predecessors as irrelevant. The Zeitgeist ("spirit of the time") was on their side, however, for the intellectual climate of the early twentieth century favored constructivism in literature and art. The formalists drew their inspiration from Russian futurist poetry, notably from Velimir Khlebnikov and Vladimir Maiakovskii's interest in the "self-sufficient word." Jakobson was the main connecting link between the poets and the scholars. The formalists' iconoclastic spirit frequently carried them away, but the study of numerous Russian and foreign authors soon taught them the true complexity of their subject. It so happened that after the revolution the group confronted not conservative scholarship but the Communist Party, which looked upon literature only as a means for promulgating communist values and did not tolerate art divorced from ideology. Such big guns as Leon Trotsky, Nikolay Bukharin, and Anatoly Lunacharsky wrote critical articles on formalism. No formalist was arrested, but the movement came to an end.

The formalists believed that a system of devices rather than imagery characterizes literature as a special type of human creativity. The artist's main goal is to "defamiliarize" an image, that is, to make it "look strange," as though seen for the first time, and to this end the device is often deliberately exposed to view ("laid bare"). This is close to what is called *Verfremdung* ("estrangement, alienation") in German. According to the formalists, every contrivance serves literature insofar as it destroys the identity of a literary text and ordinary speech and thereby prevents "automatization." They taught that literature is governed by its own laws and that artistic forms die when they use up their potential and become "automatic." Then talentless descendants of the great take over, and the time comes for the avant-garde to have its say. With such premises the formalists analyzed a huge corpus of Russian poetry, as well as the works by Nikolay Gogol, Leo Tolstoy, and many others.

Their method yielded excellent results when applied to highly structured texts and texts written in a particularly idiosyncratic style. Poetry and folklore belong to the first group. The formalists realized early on that many texts from oral tradition are reducible to a predictable sequence of motifs. Their immediate predecessor in this respect was A. N. Veselovskii, but only Vladimir Propp showed that fairy tales tend to follow a rigid, almost unalterable scheme. Among the "idiosyncratic" authors, besides Gogol and Tolstoy, Lawrence Sterne, Charles Dickens, and O. Henry attracted Shklovskii's special attention.

In Russia, the formalists' writings were vilified for over two decades, and the word *formalistic* remained a term of abuse in the contributions of the regime's stalwarts for 30 more years. Despite official resistance, beginning in the late 1950s, the formalists became an object of intense study and admiration. Shklovskii, Bukhshtab, and Ginzburg lived long enough to see their cause at least partly vindicated. In the West, the formalists' legacy was not forgotten thanks to the teachings of Roman Jakobson and indirectly through René Wellek and the doctrine of new criticism.

Anatoly Liberman

See also Prague Linguistic Circle; Propp, Vladimir I.; Structuralism

✳✳✳✳✳✳✳✳✳✳✳✳✳✳✳✳✳

References

Erlich, Victor. *Russian Formalism*. New Haven: Yale University Press, 1981 (1955).

Mateika, Ladislav, and Krystyna Pomorska, comps. *Readings in Russian Poetics*. Ann Arbor: University of Michigan Press, 1978.

Pike, Christopher, trans. *The Futurists, the Formalists, and the Marxist Critique*. London: Ink Links, 1979.

SANDBURG, CARL (1878–1967)

The American poet, biographer, children's writer, and singer and compiler of folk songs Carl Sandburg was born in Galesburg, Illinois, to Swedish immigrant parents. At 13, he quit school to work at several odd jobs in Galesburg: driver of a milk wagon, porter in a barbershop, worker in a brickyard. Then he rode boxcars across the country before serving eight months in the Spanish-American War. After the war he worked his way through Lombard College in Galesburg, became a traveling salesman for a short time, and finally settled in as a newspaper writer and editor, notably for the *Chicago Daily News* (1917–1932). Active in socialist politics, he was a labor reporter for the *Milwaukee Leader,* worked for the Social-Democratic Party in Wisconsin, and served as secretary to Milwaukee's first socialist mayor (1910–1912).

Although Sandburg published a small pamphlet of poems, *Reckless Ecstasy,* in 1904, his first major collection was *Chicago Poems* (1916), followed by *Cornhuskers* (1918), *Smoke and Steel* (1920), and other collections celebrating ordinary people in agricultural and industrial America. His *Complete Poems* (1950) won a Pulitzer Prize, as did the last four volumes of his six-volume biography of Abraham Lincoln published in 1939. Finding the raw material of poetry in the language of common people for his long prose and free-verse poem *The People, Yes* (1936) and other works, he attempted to record the many voices of Americans in their own words. Daniel Hoffman claims that "*The People, Yes* seems to sprawl like the prairies themselves. Some of its sections read like the published proverb collections of the American Dialect Society" (Hoffman 1953, p. 135).

Besides looking to the folk for the speech and sayings in his poetry, Sandburg drew on other aspects of American culture that he considered folklore, such as the Paul Bunyan material. Sandburg also wrote the foreword to Benjamin A. Botkin's *Treasury of American Folklore,* which he called "nothing less than an encyclopedia of the folklore of America" that gives "something of the feel of American history" and "breathes of the human diversity of these United States" (Botkin 1944, pp. v–vi). Sandburg, himself, was a singer and compiler of American folk songs, many of which he learned from hoboes and workers when he was hopping trains across the West. He published songs "gathered by the compiler and his friends from coast to coast and from the Gulf to Canada" (Sandburg 1927, p. vii) in *The American Songbag* (1927) and *The New American Songbag* (1950). He claimed he talked about poetry and art and read his poetry at about two-thirds of the state universities in the United States and, accompanying himself on guitar, always concluded the programs "with a half- or quarter-hour of songs, giving verbal footnotes with each song" (Sandburg 1927, p. ix). Some of the songs he sang are available on recordings.

Folklorists hunting for motifs in Sandburg's poetry may be disappointed since many of them apparently came from popularizers rather than straight from the folk, but Sandburg's poetry nevertheless owes much to the folk, as it was strongly influenced by folk speech, populist values, and communal experiences. In fact, in all of his work—his biography of Lincoln, his poetry, and his folk songs—he expressed the thoughts and feelings of ordinary Americans.

Ronald L. Baker

See also Botkin, Benjamin A.; Bunyan, Paul; Motif; Proverbs

✵✵✵✵✵✵✵✵✵✵✵✵✵✵✵✵✵

References

Botkin, Benjamin A. *A Treasury of American Folklore: Stories, Ballads, and Traditions of the People.* New York: Crown, 1944.

D'Alessio, Gregory. *Old Troubadour: Carl Sandburg with His Guitar Friends.* New York: Walker, 1987.

Hoffman, Daniel G. *Paul Bunyan: Last of the Frontier Demigods.* Philadelphia: University of Pennsylvania Press, 1952.

———. "Sandburg and 'The People': His Literary Populism Reappraised." *Antioch Review* 10 (1950): 265–278.

Niven, Penelope. *Carl Sandburg: A Biography.* New York: Scribner, 1991.

Sandburg, Carl. *The American Songbag.* New York: Harcourt Brace Jovanovich, 1927.

———. "Foreword." In B. A. Botkin, *A Treasury of American Folklore,* pp. v–vi. New York: Crown, 1944.

SATAN

Satan, or the devil, is the fallen angel and adversary of God who has personified evil in folklore and literature since biblical times. Variously represented as a serpent, goat, dog, crow, and other beasts and birds, the satanic figure seems to have originated in early pagan cults in Persia. Satan frequently takes the form of an attractive man with horns, pointed ears, flashing eyes, cloven hooves, and a tail. Some of these physical features derive from Greek mythology, in which the goat-footed deity Pan and the satyrs combine human and animal characteristics. The seductive powers of Satan emerge strongly in folk narrative, the ballad, and literature (Motif D1386.2, "Demon Lover"). Among Satan's numerous names are Old Nick, Old Scratch, Old Horny, Old Hairy, the Black Bogey, and the Foul Fiend.

In certain books of the King James Bible, Satan bears the alternative names of Lucifer ("light-bearer," Isa. 14:12) and Beelzebub (Matt. 12:24). Satan's first Old Testament persona is that of a serpent whose mission is to corrupt Adam and Eve (Gen. 3:1–5). It is not until the New Testament that we hear of the war in heaven that resulted in Satan's fall (Luke 10:18). The Gospels mention a legion of demons to which Satan belongs, intensifying the Bible's portrayal of martial conflict.

Characterizations of Satan in medieval literature emphasize extreme, dramatic evil. In the *Inferno* (1933), Dante placed Satan in the innermost circle of hell, frozen in a foul lake of ice, as punishment for the sin of treachery. Two centuries later, in Heinrich Kramer and Jacob Sprenger's *Malleus maleficarum*, Satan takes the form of a versatile, conniving fiend who will stop at nothing to corrupt human beings, especially women. He holds witches in thrall, demanding worship and sacrifices; children, who are especially vulnerable to his dictates, may be seriously injured or killed. Many portions of the *Malleus* seem to have come from local legends. One account tells of a nun who innocently eats a piece of unblessed lettuce, only to discover that she has eaten Satan (Motif G303.16.2.3.4). The lustful, manipulative Satan who appears in the *Malleus* provided a strong incentive for witch hunting in the late Middle Ages.

John Milton's *Paradise Lost* (1667) gives us one of the finest literary portrayals of Satan. Instead of following the tradition of a unilaterally evil satanic figure, Milton imbued his central character

Satan (from The Devil Walk *by Thomas Landseer, London, 1831) has personified evil in folklore and literature since biblical times.*

with tragic dignity. Tortured by thoughts of lost happiness and lasting pain, Satan bravely fights an invincible deity, deciding to reign in hell rather than to serve in heaven. Some medieval mystery plays (especially the Eger Passion Play of 1516) include relatively positive, rebellious Satans that may have served as prototypes for Milton's tragic hero.

Further tragedy develops in the devil-compact stories that began with Johan Spies's *Historia von Dr. Johann Fausten* published in 1587. Based on the occult activities of an individual born in the late fifteenth century, this chapbook tells of Faust selling his soul to the devil and getting carried away to the nether regions. Many versions of the Faust story circulated as oral legends in the sixteenth century, and the variety of devil-compact stories is clear from such tale-types as "The Devil's Contract" (AT 756B) and "The Devil's Riddle" (AT 812). The motif "Man Sells Soul to Devil" (M211) appears cross-culturally in many oral narratives. Sometimes the meeting with the devil takes place at a crossroad; alternatively, it may occur within a magic circle.

Christopher Marlowe's drama *The Tragical History of Dr. Faustus* (1604) presents a powerful devil who amuses Faust for a while but then demands—and receives—his pay. More than a century later, Johann Wolfgang von Goethe's *Faust* (Part 1 in 1808 and Part 2 in 1832) presented a tragic hero whose deep desire for knowledge drives him to sign his soul away to the attractive, seductive devil, Mephistopheles. An important deviation from Marlowe's pattern is the fact that Goethe's Faust achieves redemption, thwarting the fiend who tried to lead him astray with a woman and other temptations.

Many nineteenth-century authors of the romantic movement portrayed Satan as a rebellious, free-spirited individual whose power and energy reflected their own inclinations. Lord Byron's poem *Heaven and Earth* characterizes Satan as a spirited rebel who has very good reasons for defying God. In Percy Bysshe Shelley's *Prometheus Unbound* (1820), Satan becomes an inspiring benefactor for humankind. The French romantics, including Victor Hugo and Alfred de Vigny, and the German Heinrich Heine enlarged the scope of satanic portraits from this prolific era.

Twentieth-century literature offers a variety of Satans and satanic figures. The devil in George Bernard Shaw's *Man and Superman* (1905) is a feisty, cantankerous creature who complains at length about the state of the world. By the mid-twentieth century, popular novels were reflecting the prevalence of legends and rumors about satanic cults and witches bound to do Satan's bidding. Ira Levin's *Rosemary's Baby* (1967) is one good example of this genre. In this novel, an innocent young wife makes the horrifying discovery that Satan has impregnated her with his child, aided by a cult of evil, manipulative witches (Motif T539.3, "Woman Impregnated by Demon," and Motif T556, "Woman Gives Birth to Demon").

Fantasy literature, with its emphasis upon good struggling with evil, provides fertile ground for satanic figures. J. R. R Tolkien's cruel warlord Sauron in *The Lord of the Rings* (1954–1956) is closely analogous to Satan. Less closely related but similar is the dark, mysterious Darth Vader in George Lucas's novel *Star Wars* (1985), the printed version of the first of a series of movies. In numerous other fantasy novels as well, the main advocate of evil bears a striking resemblance to the archfiend.

The "demon lover" characterization flourishes in romantic novels such as Anya Seton's *Dragonwyck* (1944) while the presence of a sinister, evil figure pervades such horror novels as Stephen King's *The Stand* (1978). In spite of the scientific advancements of the twentieth century, it seems clear that Satan continues to inspire fear, fascination, and moral quandaries that come to the surface in symbiotic folklore and literature.

Elizabeth Tucker

See also Faust Legend, Ritual Murder; Witchcraft

✳✳✳✳✳✳✳✳✳✳✳✳✳✳✳✳✳

References

Langton, Edward. *Satan, a Portrait: A Study of the Character of Satan Throughout the Ages.* New York: Gordon Press, 1976.

Rudwin, Maximilian. *The Devil in Legend and Literature.* New York: AMS Press, 1970.

Russell, Jeffrey Burton. *The Devil in the Middle Ages.* Ithaca, N.Y.: Cornell University Press, 1984.

Victor, Jeffrey S. *Satanic Panic: The Creation of a Contemporary Legend.* Chicago: Open Court Publishers, 1993.

Woods, Barbara Allen. *The Devil in Dog Form: A Partial Type Index of Devil Legends.* Berkeley: University of California Press, 1959.

SCANDINAVIAN FOLK LITERATURE

In early Norse historiography, in Snorri's sagas of the kings of Norway, and in Saxo Grammaticus's *Gesta Danorum*, folklore is used as a historical source; in Olaus Magnus's sixteenth-century *Historia de gentibus septentrionalibus*, it is used in an account of cultural history. The deliberate use of folklore in belles lettres did not start until the romantic period, when folk literatures, especially ballads and fairy tales, were accepted by the cultural elite as literary genres in their own right. Important early editions of ballads include those by Adolf Iwar Arwidsson, Erik Gustaf Geijer, and Arvid August Afzelius in Sweden; Magnus Brostrup Landstad and Sophus Bugge in Norway; Venceslaus Ulricus Hammershaimb and Hans C. Lyngbye in the Faroes; and Knud Lyne Rahbek, Rasmus Nyerup, Werner Hans

Fredrik Abrahamson, and Svend Grundtvig in Denmark. Editions of fairy tales include those by Peter Christen Asbjørnsen and Jørgen Moe in Norway; Konrad Maurer and Jón Árnason in Iceland; Gunnar Olof Hyltén-Cavallius and Georg Stephens in Sweden; and Grundtvig in Denmark. These editions were later supplemented by hundreds of regional and national collections.

Several of the early collections of folklore, such as Andreas Faye's *Norske sagn* (1832), were expressly intended as raw material for poets, and the influence of folk poetry on literature can be seen with respect to both form and content. Paraphrases and retold versions became popular at the end of the eighteenth century. Jørgen Moe, who together with P. Chr. Asbjørnsen published the classical Norwegian edition of fairy tales, initially wanted to use fairy tales following the model of the German poet Ludwig Tieck. Hans Christian Andersen's artistic tales are based on the structure and narrative style of fairy tales.

With romanticism, folk poetry attained a strong position in literature because of the interest in national identity and in the polarity of man and nature and hence, "nature myth." In Norwegian neoromanticism, folk poetry acquired great significance in psychological analysis.

The literary historian Mogens Brøndsted claims that neoromanticism was folk tradition's "last concerted revival in Nordic literature" (Brøndsted 1980, p. 113), but one can also consider the local poetry of the twentieth century to be the great folkloristic period in Nordic literature. A characteristic feature of nineteenth-century authors is that, as representatives of elite culture, they knew folk poetry from secondary sources and incorporated it in their cultural program. A long series of authors with backgrounds in peasant culture concentrated on descriptions of rural localities and small towns, seeing tradition as a stabilizing factor: in Norway, Per Sivle; in Denmark, representatives of "the great generation" such as Jeppe Aakjær, Johan Skjoldborg, Johs. V. Jensen, and Martin Andersen Nexø; in Sweden, Selma Lagerlöf, Erik Axel Karlfeldt, and in modern times Vilhelm Moberg and Astrid Lindgren, who is also an innovator of an oral fairy tale style. Occasional proletarian writers also use the oral narrative tradition, including Jan Fridegård and Oskar Braaten. The fundamental issue is territoriality and identity. Several recent authors have based their novels on comprehensive studies of historical and folkloristic sources, especially Sigrid Undset, Sigurd Hoel, Alfred Hauge, Moberg, and Ulla Isaksson.

In modern literature, tradition is no longer used to build up an identity based on the past; it is used instead to understand the "everyday myths" of contemporary culture in a present and future perspective. Through all the variations in literary trends, folk poetry has always served to demonstrate contemporary culture.

Reimund Kvideland

See also Anderson, Walter; Ballad; *Märchen*

✳✳✳✳✳✳✳✳✳✳✳✳✳✳✳✳✳✳

References

Brøndsted, Mogens. "Folklorens afspejlinger i nordisk skønlitteratur." *Tradisjon* 10 (1980): 103–115.

Gustavsson, Per, ed. *Astrid Lindgren och folkdikten*. Stockholm: Carlsson, 1996.

Schön, Ebbe, ed. *Folklore och litteratur i Norden*. Nordic Institute of Folklore Publications no. 17. Stockholm: Carlsson, 1987.

Sehmsdorf, Henning K. "Myth, Folk Tradition, and Norwegian Literature." *Papers in Scandinavian Studies* 5 (1992): 85–103.

———. "The Romantic Heritage: Ibsen and the Use of Folklore." In *Nordische Romantik*, ed. O. Bandle et al., pp. 162–167. Basel, 1991.

SCHILLER, JOHANN CHRISTOPH FRIEDRICH
(1759–1805)

Primarily known in the literary world as a classicist who created some of the most enduring pieces of German drama and lyrics, particularly ballads, Johann Christoph Friedrich Schiller, much like his contemporary Johann Wolfgang von Goethe, reveals romantic traits in his literary affiliations. Schiller was also a writer and interpreter of significant historical periods; he wrote, for example, major studies on the *Abfall der vereinigten Niederlanden* [Revolt in the United Netherlands (1788)] and a *Geschichte des dreissigjährigen Krieges* [History of the Thirty Years War (1790)]. He also wrote philosophical and aesthetic treatises: *Über Anmut und Würde* [On grace and dignity (1793)] and *Über das Erhabene* [On the sublime].

In 1797, Schiller and Goethe challenged each other to a so-called *Balladenjahr* ("ballad year"). Both drew their sources not, as one might expect, from folk song, but more from regional and international legends. Schiller's ballads tend not to reflect local color to the same degree as those by Goethe, and Schiller's are more distinctly literary in tone. The themes vary: in the "Kraniche des Ibykus" [The cranes of Ibykus], a murder is avenged; in "Der Taucher" [The diver] and "Der Handschuh" [The glove], there is a scathing indictment of irresponsible rulers; "Das Lied von der Glocke" [The song of the bell] deals with a creative act while "Der Kampf mit dem Drachen" [The battle with the dragon] suggests that self-denial is more important than courage.

Schiller's most obvious relationship to folklore can be seen in his epic drama *Wilhelm Tell* (1802), his last drama before his untimely death. The source for this epic was a collection of legends that had been woven together into an historical account in Aegidius Tschudi's *Cronica Helveticon* (1569). One Schiller critic refers to *Tell* as a "fairy tale, a folk legend, a myth transposed to the stage" (Simons 1981, p. 143). Indeed, the play does follow the pattern of a monomyth: a hero with unusual talents lives in an afflicted world, which is again made right after a supreme ordeal. William Tell's talents are supremely tested several times in the course of the play, but most obviously in the apple-shooting scene.

Like all mythical or legendary heroes, Tell must be tested. He shoots the apple off his son's head, escapes from the tyrant Gessler, slays him, and is praised by the folk who are thus rescued. Tell's first feat is accomplished by his own talent; for the second, he needs supernatural assistance in the form of a storm; in the third, the forces of good clearly overcome evil, and the tyrant is slain.

In the German-speaking world, many of the pronouncements of *Wilhelm Tell* have become widely known, everyday proverbial expressions: *Der kluge Mann baut vor* ("a wise man makes plans"; line 274), *Die Unschuld hat im Himmel einen Freund* ("innocence has a friend in heaven"; line 324), *Was Hände bauten, können Hände stürzen* ("what hands built, can be destroyed by hands"; line 387), *Die Schlange sticht nicht ungereizt* ("a snake does not strike without cause"; line 429), *Der Starke ist am mächtigsten allein* ("the strong person is mightiest alone"; line 437), and *Die Axt im Haus erspart den Zimmermann* ("the axe at home saves the carpenter"; line 1514).

Not only have Schiller's proverbial sayings made their way into everyday German speech, but his play *Wilhelm Tell* has produced its own *folklorismus* and his ballads have engendered a kind of adolescent metafolklore. *Wilhelm Tell* is produced regularly not only in Switzerland but also in Swiss settlements abroad—such as New Glarus, Wisconsin. His well-known ballad "Der Taucher" is known by virtually all school-age children in a short version: *"Der Taucher —gluck, gluck und weg war er"* ("The diver—gurgle, gurgle, and he was gone").

James R. Dow

See also Ballad; Folklorism; Goethe, Johann Wolfgang von; Legend; Proverbs

✳✳✳✳✳✳✳✳✳✳✳✳✳✳✳✳✳✳

References

Mieder, Wolfgang. "'Der Apfel fällt weit von Deutschland': Zur amerikanischen Entlehnung eines deutschen Sprichwortes." *Der Sprachdienst* 25:6 (1981): 89–93.

———. "'Zitate sind des Bürgers Zierde': Zum Weiterleben von Schiller-Zitaten." *Muttersprache* 95:5–6 (1985): 284–306.

Schiller, Friedrich. *Sämtliche Werke*. Ed. Gehard Fricke. Munich: Hanser Verlag, 1958–1959.

Simons, John D. *Friedrich Schiller*. Twayne World Authors Series 603. Boston: Twayne Publishers, 1981.

Thomas, Calvin. *The Life and Works of Friedrich Schiller*. New York: Henry Holt, 1901.

Wiese, Benno von. *Friedrich Schiller*. 4th ed. Stuttgart: Metzler, 1978.

SCORZA, MANUEL (1928–1983)

The Peruvian poet, novelist, political activist, and publisher of *Populibros*—popular editions of world literature—Manuel Scorza was forced to leave Peru several times because of his involvement in politics. In the 1940s he was in exile in Mexico. In the late 1960s, because of his involvement in an Andean peasant uprising, Scorza moved to France and taught at the Ecole Normale de Saint-Cloud.

Initially known as a poet (*Las imprecaciones* [1955], *Los adioses* [1960], *Poesía amorosa* [1960], *Desengaños del mago* [1961], *Réquiem para un gentilhombre* [1962], *El vals de los reptiles* [1970]), Scorza has become one of Latin America's most important writers because of his five-novel *La guerra silenciosa* [The silent war], which is based on the Andean peasant and miners' 1962 uprising against the U.S. corporation, Cerro de Pasco.

Scorza's novelistic cycle is a chronicle of the epic struggle of Andean peasants and miners in the central Andes fighting against neocolonialism as well as against a feudal system inherited from colonial days. All the events narrated are at once historical and mythical. As Scorza once stated, his fiction obsessively revolves around the innumerable, recurrent massacres that constitute Peruvian history, and the characters in his novels are real—in this sense, his novels are testimonies—yet, at the same time, the testimonial coexists with the mythical and the oneiric. Scorza thus asserted that his novels are "dream machines." His greatest literary invention was the appropriation and incorporation of postcolonial Andean myths as structuring elements of his narratives. His works fit into the "neoindigenist" current of Latin American literature, and his novels have been translated into more than 25 languages.

Silvia Spitta

See also Epic; Myth

✳✳✳✳✳✳✳✳✳✳✳✳✳✳✳✳✳

References

Aldaz, Anna-Marie. *The Past of the Future: The Novelistic Cycle of Manuel Scorza*. New York: Peter Lang, 1990.

Myers, Doris, ed. *Lives on the Line: The Testimony of Contemporary Latin American Authors*. Berkeley: University of California Press, 1988.

SCOTT, SIR WALTER (1771–1832)

Sir Walter Scott, a prolific author, is best known for his "Waverley novels" (1814–1832), many of which reflect his interest in "popular antiquities." He was also editor of the *Minstrelsy of the Scottish Border* (1802–1803), largely a collection of Scottish oral materials. His interest in such matters went back to his childhood, particularly to his pleasant visits to his grandparents' farm. As a young Edinburgh lawyer, he went on annual "raids" into Liddesdale in the Scottish Borders in quest of ballads and other antiquities in the company of Robert S. Shortreed, the sheriff substitute for Roxburghshire. Practically all the ballads he "collected" in Liddesdale, however, came from a manuscript given to him by a Doctor Elliot of Cleughhead in Liddesdale. The *Minstrelsy* drew from printed, manuscript, and oral sources and included thoughtful introductory commentaries to individual texts. The overall introduction dealt with questions concerning the historicity of many of the ballad stories and their literary qualities.

In keeping with the prevalent opinion of the times, Scott took it for granted that ballad "originals" deteriorate when "passing through the mouths of many reciters." Thus, he thought it his editorial duty to emend and, if necessary, extend the basic ballad variants to counteract the flaws that had resulted from various "corrupting" and "fragmenting" factors such as forgetfulness, omission, interpolation, alteration, and recomposition. Editorial "authenticity" was therefore achieved through the provision of as full a story as possible.

It is not, however, the *Minstrelsy* that best illustrates Scott's attitudes toward folk tradition but rather the Waverley novels, especially those whose action takes place in Scotland or involves Scottish characters. Scott's depiction of the folk in these novels goes far beyond the occasional inclusion of a storyteller, a singer of ballads, a fiddler, a fortune-teller, a purveyor of proverbs and sayings, or dancers around the maypole. Also, to him folk-cultural behavior is not a matter of social stratum or cultural level but rather what might be called "register." For Scott, "folk" only exist as individuals, or rather, folk-cultural behavior is displayed by certain appropriate individuals at certain appropriate times, by some more often and more consistently than by others. Scott the novelist never ceased to be Scott "the folklorist."

W. F. H. Nicolaisen

See also Ballad; Scottish Literature

✳✳✳✳✳✳✳✳✳✳✳✳✳✳✳✳✳

References

Boswell, George W. "Supernaturalism in Scott's Novels." *Mississippi Folklore Register* 8:2 (1974): 187–199.

Nicolaisen, W. F. H. "The Folk in Literature: Some Comments on Sir Walter Scott's Scottish Novels." *Kentucky Folklore Record* 28 (1982): 48–60.

———. "Scott and the Folk Tradition." In *Sir Walter Scott: The Long-Forgotten Melody*, ed. Alan Bold, pp. 127–142. London: Vision Press, 1983.

———. "Sir Walter Scott: The Folklorist as Novelist." In *Scott and His Influence*, ed. J. H. Alexander and David Hewitt, pp. 169–179. Aberdeen: Association of Scottish Literary Studies, 1983.

Truten, Jack. "Folklore and Fiction." *Studies in Scottish Literature* 24 (1991): 226–234.

SCOTTISH LITERATURE

The languages of Scotland are Scots (also previously called Lallans or Lowlands, which is closely related to English); Scottish Standard English; (Scottish) Gaelic, a Celtic language closely related to Irish; as well as the same variety of English that is spoken in England. French, Norse, and Old Welsh have also had historic influence. Throughout Scottish literary history, a Scottish folk tradition has existed side by side with Continental and English literary influences, and has been especially important in times of increased Scottish nationalistic sentiment.

Very little early literature produced in Scotland survives beyond the early medieval Old Welsh *Gododdin*, a few pre-tenth-century Gaelic manuscripts, and about 150 partial or complete Gaelic bardic poems of the mid-fifteenth to mid-seventeenth centuries that were preserved in later manuscripts. Many early Scots and Gaelic poems are political, historical, and anti-English, praising enduring national heroes (such as Robert Bruce and William Wallace). Others are metrical romances. Poets writing in Scots from the fourteenth to the early sixteenth centuries—including the poet William Dunbar; Robert Henryson, writer of verse fables; and Gavin Douglas, translator of the *Aeneid (Eneados)*—are often called the makars ("makers," i.e., poets) or sometimes "the Scottish Chaucerians"; the late fifteenth century was a literary golden age. The earliest known surviving literary prose works in Scots (translations on chivalry) also date from that time.

The sixteenth century was the century of an important English military victory at Flodden that presaged great social change. At this time, religious and political allegories and polemics were written while earlier folk and courtly poetry was written on religious themes. Prose was still written primarily in Latin. Sir David Lindsay, or Lyndsay, author of the play *Ane Pleasant Satyre of the Thrie Estaitis in Commendatioun of Vertew and Vituperatioun of Vyce* (1552), once ranked alongside the later Robert Burns in popularity. Gaelic literature of this period is generally anonymous.

James VI of Scotland wrote poetry and with his court poets, the "Castalian band," sought a poetic renaissance on the European and English models. He became James I of England in 1603, succeeding Elizabeth I. The Highlands were still Gaelic-speaking; Gaelic poetry was both formally bardic and increasingly colloquial and stress based. Some work of women poets of the seventeenth and eighteenth centuries survives.

The centuries-old ballad forms continued in Scots and Gaelic, with themes of politics, news (especially of the English-Scottish border country), magic, custom and belief, and (especially tragic) love. There were also "waulking songs" and other work songs. Most prose was religious. There were collections of folk and fairy lore (e.g., Robert Kirk's *The Secret Commonwealth of Elves, Fauns, and Fairies* [1691]).

The eighteenth century saw the Scottish Enlightenment (it was the age of the philosopher David Hume and the economist Adam Smith); romanticism and "Celtomania"; the Ossianic controversy over a supposedly authentic Gaelic epic; and a resurgence of interest in the "old Scots makars" and poetic tradition, including anthologies and imitations and completions of ballad fragments. The lairds' Gaelic harpers and bards diminished along with the traditional social structure after the unsuccessful Jacobite rising of 1745 (led by Bonnie Prince Charlie) and the English victory at the Battle of Culloden Moor in 1746. Many Gaelic speakers emigrated, especially to eastern Canada, where Scottish folklore, music, and the Gaelic language have been preserved to some degree into the twentieth century.

Political and nationalistic poetry was, understandably, especially prominent (e.g., Alasdair Mac Mhaighstir Alasdair, or Alexander MacDonald), although Mac Mhaighstir Alasdair and other poets such as Donnchadh Bàn Mac-an-t-Saoir (Duncan Bàn Macintyre) also celebrated nature. Robert Burns wrote poems and songs in Scots and in Standard English, often describing contemporary rural life, and he collected folk songs. James Boswell, the biographer of Samuel Johnson, and the novelist Tobias Smollett are famous in English literature. Sir Walter Scott was important as a poet, novelist, and collector of folklore and ballads.

Because of the socially devastating nineteenth-century Highland clearances (the evicting of rural tenant families in favor of sheep farming) and the economic success of the Industrial Revolution in the Lowlands, many more Gaelic speakers moved to Lowland cities or emigrated. Varied literary reactions included the popular Gaelic protest poems of Màiri Nic a' Phearsain (Mary Macpherson), the "kailyard" ("cabbage-patch") school of sentimentalized "realistic" fiction (e.g., the early James Barrie, creator of Peter Pan), and the mystical "Celtic twilight" (e.g., William Sharp, writing as Fiona Macleod). Folklore, especially Gaelic, was collected (e.g., Andrew

Carmichael's *Carmina Gadelica*). Prose was the main literary medium in English and Scots, poems and songs were largely written in Gaelic. The novelist, short-story writer, and poet Robert Louis Stevenson helped revive the literary stature of Scots.

The twentieth century has been called a "Scottish Renaissance," especially with respect to poetry; and literary and cultural revival has been a conscious goal since the 1920s. Poets such as Somhairle MacGill-Eain (Sorley Maclean) in Gaelic, Edwin Muir in English, and Hugh MacDiarmid (Christopher Murray Grieve) in Scots and English are both traditional and experimental, and their work often reflects contemporary ideologies and events as well as history and legend. Novels (e.g., *A Scots Quair* [1932–1934]) by James Leslie Mitchell, writing as Lewis Grassic Gibbon) and short stories have also been important. Interest in folk materials and motifs as a symbol of what is uniquely Scottish has continued.

Pamela S. Morgan

See also Ballad; Burns, Robert; Celtic Literature; Grieve, Christopher Murray; Muir, Edwin; Ossian; Scott, Sir Walter

✳✳✳✳✳✳✳✳✳✳✳✳✳✳✳

References

Thomson, Derick. *An Introduction to Gaelic Poetry*. 2d ed. Edinburgh: Edinburgh University Press, 1990.

Watson, Roderick. *The Literature of Scotland*. Macmillan History of Literature. Houndmills and London: Macmillan, 1984.

Withers, Charles W. J. *Gaelic in Scotland, 1698–1981: The Geographical History of a Language*. Edinburgh: John Donald Publishers, 1984.

Sermon

A sermon is a discourse designed for religious instruction or persuasion. Although it figures in many religious traditions, the sermon has had particular importance in the Judeo-Christian heritage, where it comprises part of the "liturgy of the word." In some Christian contexts, it provides the focal point for corporate religious exercises, which subordinate other expressions of religiosity to the sermon.

Many sermonizers speak from prepared, written texts; thus the sermon has a long history as a literary genre reaching back to the

The folk sermon draws upon folk composition methods and themes; this nineteenth-century engraving depicts a revivalist preacher giving a sermon on the levee in St. Louis, Missouri.

prophetic books of the Old Testament, the teachings of Jesus recorded in the Gospels such as the Sermon on the Mount, and the works of patristic writers such as Saint Augustine. The writing and publishing of sermons have often been part of a cleric's responsibility. Sermons written by the seventeenth-century poet and priest John Donne, for example, fill 10 volumes in the current standard edition, and preachers continue to publish their written sermons in periodicals and in book-length collections. Paralleling its manifestation as written literature, the sermon has also existed as a form of folk literature in at least two contexts: when it is delivered orally and spontaneously and when it becomes the target of parody.

Bruce Rosenberg first identified the formulaic nature of the oral sermon. His studies, which focus primarily on African-American preachers, reveal that oral sermonizers may use methods similar to those that Milman Parry and Albert Lord identified among Yugoslavian epic singers. During an often informal apprenticeship, when they listen to sermons preached by respected elders, folk preachers absorb a set of formulaic patterns and phrases as well as thematic structures into which they can insert those patterns as they preach spontaneously, breaking into rhythmic chants at climactic moments in their performances. Folk preachers stress that they chant their sermons under the influence of spiritual forces, which lead them to select the appropriate versions of formulas for their sermon topic and for their immediate audience. Rosenberg shows that the same preacher delivering what he identifies as the same sermon on different occasions may incorporate different formulas that enable him to expand or contract components of his thematic outline for the sermon. Gerald L. Davis has refined Rosenberg's ideas by also focusing on the sermons of African-American preachers. Jeff Todd Titon and Elaine J. Lawless have extended the oral-formulaic approach to folk sermon composition and performance to preachers from other ethnic traditions. Lawless's work has focused specifically on women preachers.

Folk sermons of the type studied by Rosenberg and other folklorists have figured in many literary depictions of preachers. Twentieth-century American examples include the sermon by Daddy Grace that concludes William Styron's *Lie Down in Darkness* (1951), sermons preached by the title character and others in Sinclair Lewis's *Elmer Gantry* (1927), and the "priest of the sun" sermon delivered by Kiowa peyotist John Tosamah in N. Scott Momaday's *House Made of Dawn* (1968). Frequently, though, authors have not been sensitive to the stylistic features of oral composition and performance but have focused primarily on content, which may be used ironically to highlight a discrepancy between the pious sentiments of the sermon and the impiety of the preacher.

A more ambitious adaptation of the tradition of the oral sermon is the collection of poems by James Weldon Johnson entitled *God's Trombones* (1927). Johnson uses both the style and the idiom of African-American traditional preaching to recast stories from the Old Testament in a format that captures what folklorists have called the "Bible of the folk," renderings of canonical narratives in a way that makes them more immediate and accessible to a particular audience.

Early in the development of Christianity, the mock sermon emerged as a folk parody of the high seriousness of liturgical discourse. Paralleled by similar devices in pre-Christian ceremonialism such as the Saturnalia, a mock sermon might occur in festive contexts such as during carnival or the Feast of Fools, as noted in the work of M. M. Bakhtin. Perhaps the most well-known literary adaptation of the mock sermon is that preached by Friar John to the inhabitants of the Abbey of Theleme in François Rabelais's *Gargantua* and *Pantagruel*. The sermon with which Geoffrey Chaucer's pardoner interrupts his contribution to the *Canterbury Tales* might be considered to be in the mock sermon tradition, and Victor Hugo exemplified the genre in his historical novel *Notre Dame de Paris* (1831). Twentieth-century mock sermons include those preached by Hazel Motes, who hopes to attract converts to his Church of Christ without Christ, in Flannery O'Connor's *Wise Blood* (1951).

William M. Clements

See also Bakhtin, Mikhail Mikhailovitch; Chaucer, Geoffrey; Momaday, Navarre Scott; Oral-Formulaic Composition and Theory; Rabelais, François

✴✴✴✴✴✴✴✴✴✴✴✴✴✴✴✴✴

References

Bakhtin, M. M. *Rabelais and His World*. Trans. Helene Iswolsky. Cambridge: Massachusetts Institute of Technology Press, 1968.

Davis, Gerald. *I Got the Word in Me and I Can Sing It, You Know: A Study of the Performed African-American Sermon*. Philadelphia: University of Pennsylvania Press, 1985.

Lawless, Elaine J. *Handmaidens of the Lord: Pentecostal Women Preachers and Traditional Religion*. Philadelphia: University of Pennsylvania Press, 1988.

Rosenberg, Bruce E. *Can These Bones Live? The Art of the American Folk Preacher*. Urbana: University of Illinois Press, 1988.

Titon, Jeff Todd. *Powerhouse for God: Speech, Chant, and Song in an Appalachian Baptist Church*. Austin: University of Texas Press, 1988.

SHAKESPEARE, WILLIAM (1564–1616)

Arguably the most renowned author of all time, William Shakespeare penned many works that have been praised as masterpieces of English literature. Keenly attuned to the literary conventions of his day, Shakespeare adopted those conventions with skill. In *Titus Andronicus* (1590), for example, Shakespeare emulated conventional Senecan-style tragedy. The work is patterned after earlier revenge plays and heavily influenced by Thomas Kyd's *The Spanish Tragedy* (1584). And Shakespeare provides us with a rendition of the pastoral romance, another literary convention, as late as *The Winter's Tale* (1610–1611). With the advancement of his career, Shakespeare's use of convention became more intricate, and his later plays reflect a more carefully crafted style and greater structural complexity. Still, the underlying force of much of his artistry lay in the use and manipulation of traditional materials. Shakespeare and folklore can be viewed from a variety of perspectives: the dramas as repositories of individual items of folklore, folklore as source material, the incorporation of folkloric situations and contexts, and Shakespeare's possible role as ethnographer.

Shakespeare incorporated into his dramas many items of folklore—individual texts from folk tradition such as snatches of folktales and ballads as well as the so-called minor genres like proverbs, riddles, and other examples of folk speech. The identification of such items has been the controlling agenda in many studies of folklore in Shakespeare—as part of an attempt to chart the history of a given play or to reconstruct the literary history of a folklore genre. The most productive studies examine the items of folklore within their larger dramatic context, interpreting as well as identifying folkloric elements.

Hamlet (1600–1601), for example, is packed with popular adages of the sixteenth century and offers a wealth of material for proverb hunters. Nowhere in *Hamlet* is the proverb lore more apparent than in Act I, scene iii, the famous scene in which Polonius imparts fatherly advice to his departing son Laertes. (Many of the aphorisms in Polonius's speech have prototypes in Renaissance proverb collections, all influenced to some degree by Desiderius Erasmus's immensely popular *Adagia* [1500].) In the lengthy string of proverbs, Polonius counsels his son:

> Give thy thoughts no tongue,
> Nor any unproportioned thought his act.
> Be thou familiar, but by no means vulgar.
> . . . Beware
> Of entrance to a quarrel, but being in,
> Bear't that th' opposed may beware of thee.
> Give every man thine ear, but few thy voice,
> Take each man's censure, but reserve thy judgement.
> Costly thy habit as thy purse can buy,

But not expressed in fancy, rich, not gaudy,
For the apparel oft proclaims the man. . . .
. . . Neither a borrower nor a lender be,
For loan oft loses both itself and friend,
And borrowing dulleth th' edge of husbandry.
This above all: to thine own self be true,
And it must follow, as the night the day,
Thou canst not then be false to any man. (I, iii, 59–80)

This counsel points ironically to Polonius's own character flaws, which are evident throughout the play. Unable to follow the advice himself, Polonius is far from discreet, judicious, and diplomatic, as he charges Laertes to be; and most assuredly he is not true to others—or himself. So Shakespeare employs these proverbs with dramatic strategy: the traditional wisdom invoked by Polonius is contradictory and self-indicting—a means by which truth and logic, already clouded in this complex play, are further confounded.

Shakespeare also drew upon old folktales as source material, which is not surprising, for many tales are, in effect, distilled dramas, with opposing characters thrown into dramatic conflict and an always pervading sense of story. Exposed to the tales from written sources such as chapbooks and other plays, or just as likely from oral retellings, Shakespeare manipulated the plots of the tales for his dramatic purposes.

Antti Aarne and Stith Thompson's *The Types of the Folktale* (1964) is an effective resource for evaluating the extent to which Shakespeare drew upon traditional tales. *Cymbeline* (1609–1610), for example, is related to the tale-type "The Wager on the Wife's Chastity" (AT 882). The play incorporates central elements of that tale-type, from the wager on the wife's chastity and token of infidelity secured by a devious merchant (Jachimo) to the husband's leaving home and the final reconciliation between husband and wife.

Many scholars have assumed that Shakespeare patterned the story of *Cymbeline* solely after "Bernabò of Genoa," from Giovanni Boccaccio's *Decameron* (Book II, Section 9), based on certain similarities between the two works. However, there are enough dissimilar details and entire episodes added or omitted in *Cymbeline* to suggest a plot source altogether different from the *Decameron*: Shakespeare's inclusion of the exchange of gifts that will serve as identifying tokens, the confrontation of the seducer, and an ending of reconciliation; none of these elements appears in Boccaccio. Moreover, in "Bernabò" there is no analogous character to Shakespeare's Cloten. *Cymbeline* might have as easily been modeled after some lost written source (which itself drew upon AT 882) or perhaps even some oral version of the tale. *Cymbeline* also incorporates central episodes from "Snow White" (AT 709): the play and this tale overlap in their inclusion of a jealous stepmother, a compassionate executioner, a maligned maiden, a house of robbers, poisoning attempts, aid of the robbers, resuscitation, and final reconciliation. It seems hardly possible that Shakespeare could create in his play the same plot sequence as "Snow White" and do so entirely independent of the tale.

Shakespeare also presents folkloric situations within staged social contexts in many of his plays. *Hamlet*, for instance, is itself a literary version of an old legend, but the play also incorporates legend situations that feature characteristic disputes over veracity. The ambiguities that come from the underlying polemic of truth and believability figure in Hamlet's philosophical and ethical quandaries.

In *1 Henry IV* (1597–1598), Falstaff's storytelling mirrors another folk tradition. His frequent bawdy exchanges with Prince Hal and their rowdy compatriots in the Boar's Head Tavern suggest the patterns of the tall-tale contest: conscious comical lying and exaggeration, first-person narration, formulaic repetition, and mock acceptance by the listeners, all occurring within a predominantly male group. Although the tall tale is sometimes considered primarily an American narrative genre, it clearly has European precursors, and Falstaff is a prototype of the frontier braggarts and colorful yarn spinners of the American tradition. The occasions of lying in *1 Henry IV* define the social climate of misrule surrounding Falstaff, which sometimes clarifies and sometimes confounds Hal's internal conflict of identity. These matters reinforce the play's larger tensions of truth and falsehood, responsibility and honor.

Every literary work is in a sense a production of its culture, and it is no slight to Shakespeare's particular genius to recognize his drama as a creation of, and valuable depiction of, Elizabethan and Jacobean culture—thus pointing to the ethnographic significance of his work. For example, *Twelfth Night* (1599–1600) illuminates the festive attitudes associated with the Elizabethan observance of the feast of Epiphany, the twelfth day of the Christmas season. Originally intended to commemorate various sacred events in the life of Christ, over time Epiphany became linked in folk practice with the pagan holiday Saturnalia, which was characterized by riotous behavior and ritual reversal of the natural order. Although the feast day is not referred to explicitly in the play, *Twelfth Night* clearly captures the spirit of Epiphany in Shakespeare's time. The unrestrained revels of Sir Toby Belch and his friends, the perplexing fusion of the serious and comic, and especially the gender reversals of the central plot, all typify the licentious, topsy-turvy world of the festival.

The enchanting literary and theatrical appeal of Shakespeare's dramas cannot be denied. Within that larger artistic framework are all sorts of folk texts, traditions, and authentic portrayals of folkloric contexts; often these instances of folklore are connected to the heart and soul of the plays.

Charles Greg Kelley

See also Ballad; Festival; Folktale; *King Lear; Othello;* Proverbs; Riddle; Tale-Type; Tall Tale; *The Taming of the Shrew*

✳✳✳✳✳✳✳✳✳✳✳✳✳✳✳✳✳✳✳

References

Brunvand, Jan Harold. "The Folktale Origin of *The Taming of the Shrew*." *Shakespeare Quarterly* 17 (1996): 345–359.

Gorfain, Phyllis. "Riddling as Ritual Remedy in *Measure for Measure*." In *True Rites and Maimed Rites: Ritual and Anti-Ritual in Shakespeare and His Age*, ed. Linda Woodbridge and Edward Berry, pp. 98–122. Urbana: University of Illinois Press, 1992.

Johnson, W. Stacey. "Folklore Elements in *The Tempest*." *Midwest Folklore* 1 (1951): 223–228.

Kelley, Charles Greg. "A Folkloric Analysis of Narrative Contexts in Shakespeare." Ph.D. dissertation, Indiana University, 1996.

Rosenberg, Bruce A. *Folklore and Literature: Sibling Rivals*. Knoxville: University of Tennessee Press, 1991.

Wood, James O. "Lost Lore in *Macbeth*." *Shakespeare Quarterly* 24 (1973): 223–226.

Silko, Leslie Marmon (1948–)

The novelist, poet, short-fiction author, and essayist Leslie Marmon Silko is of mixed Laguna/Plains Indian, Mexican, and white ancestry. Born in Albuquerque, New Mexico, and raised on the Laguna Pueblo Reservation, she published her first story, "The Man to Send

Rain Clouds," in 1969, the same year she graduated from the University of New Mexico with a B.A. in English. In 1977, Silko published her first novel, *Ceremony*, to considerable critical acclaim. The novel was preceded by a poetry collection, *Laguna Woman* (1974), and followed by three other book-length works: *Storyteller* (1981), *Almanac of the Dead* (1991), and the self-published *Sacred Water* (1993). Her stories have been widely anthologized. Silko has been a leading figure in the Native American renaissance—a literary and artistic movement that began in the late 1960s among Native Americans who ground their work in native verbal art and cultural traditions.

Instead of yearning for a precontact and allegedly ideal past or, on the other hand, rejecting the past for a Euramerican-dominated present, Silko's fiction recognizes the identity-confirming power of native tradition in contemporary life. That is the subject of her story "Yellow Woman" (1974). The story's female Navajo protagonist finds herself enacting the traditional tale of Yellow Woman's sexual tryst with a man who is not her husband. Turning between but not yet integrating myth and secular life during much of the story, the woman finally rediscovers her identity within tradition. She realizes that her abduction by and voluntary indiscretion with the man represent a localized enactment of timeless pattern: she has been simultaneously both Yellow Woman who was kidnapped by a *ka'tsina* spirit and a late-twentieth-century wife and mother who went outside marriage to satisfy her need for independence and passionate involvement. Likewise, in *Storyteller*, Silko emphasizes the guiding and sustaining power of tradition, but here she stresses the role of the storyteller as a crucial agent of that power. Pursuing storytelling through various means (family stories, photographs, biographical vignettes, retellings of traditional tales), Silko stresses the dynamic interconnectedness of native past and native present.

Further, in the novel *Ceremony*, Silko celebrates the healing power in the native tradition's adaptability to contemporary circumstance. As William M. Clements has argued, "While Laguna culture remains distinct and viable, it does so through its flexibility and ability to incorporate and shape outside influences" (Clements 1994, p. 197). This potential for adaptability—this willingness to deal with "the other"—is illustrated, for example, in the very structure of *Ceremony*, in which Silko interweaves Laguna myth with the life experiences of the novel's protagonist. She shows how the alienated half-breed and World War II veteran, Tayo, learns to recommit to

Laguna values and thereby to heal himself spiritually and emotionally. He does so by entering sacred time through the contemporary enactment of myth. However, this enactment is not a nostalgic repetition of rituals from the past. Instead, as the native healer Betonie tells Tayo in *Ceremony*, flexibility is crucial: "At one time, the ceremonies as they had been performed were enough for the way the world was then. But after the white people came, . . . it became necessary to create new ceremonies. I have made changes in the rituals. . . . only this growth keeps the ceremonies strong." In short, native tradition (as well as the individual who chooses to operate within it) must adapt to new circumstances in order to survive and to heal.

Danielle M. Roemer

See also Native American Writing

✳✳✳✳✳✳✳✳✳✳✳✳✳✳✳✳✳

References

Clements, William M. "Leslie Marmon Silko." In *Dictionary of Literary Biography. American Novelists since World War II*, vol. 143, pp. 196–205. 3d ser. Detroit: Gale Research, 1994.

Graulich, Melody, ed. *"Yellow Woman," Leslie Marmon Silko*. New Brunswick, N.J.: Rutgers University Press, 1993.

Seyersted, Per. *Leslie Marmon Silko*. Boise, Idaho: Boise State University Press, 1980.

Silko, Leslie Marmon. *Yellow Woman and a Beauty of the Spirit: Essays on Native American Life Today*. New York: Simon and Schuster, 1996.

Singer, Isaac Bashevis (1904–1991)

Isaac Bashevis Singer was a Jewish-American writer, born in Poland, whose more than 20 volumes—including novels, short stories, memoirs, and tales for children—were designed to "prevent time from vanishing." Although he left Poland in 1935 to take up permanent residence in New York City, Singer continued to write exclusively about the Yiddish-speaking Jews of his native country—the many who perished in the Holocaust and the few who survived to emigrate to the United States. As the only Yiddish writer to reach a mass audience—albeit via the English translations in which he increasingly collaborated—Singer all but single-handedly preserved a dying language and a shattered culture.

Satan in Goray (1935), Singer's first novel, written in Poland, employs a blend of Jewish folklore with a surreal mise-en-scène, which became the trademark of his most popular fiction. The remote setting, the archetypal *shtetl* ("village"), the fanatical messianism, and the grotesque imagery (e.g., the *dybbuk*, or "evil spirit") of *Satan in Goray* recur not only in Singer's 1962 novel, *The Slave*, but also in some of his most haunting short stories, including "The Destruction of Kreshev," "Zeidlus the Pope," and "The Gentleman from Cracow." Satan, omnipresent in Goray, presiding over "The Destruction of Kreshev" and "Zeidlus the Pope" as narrator, and assuming the outwardly pleasing form of the title character in "The Gentleman from Cracow," runs amok in Singer's fiction when Jews distort or abrogate their belief in God. Because Singer's typical Jewish apostates are disaffected intellectuals, he invokes the pietistic simplicity of *dos kleine menshele*—"the little" or "insignificant man" of Yiddish folklore—as the behavioral ideal, most famously in "Gimpel the Fool," which in Saul Bellow's translation won for Singer the modernist cachet and mainstream acceptance accorded to no other Yiddish writer.

If Singer was most famous for demonic stories in the manner of *Satan in Goray,* those represent only one facet of his achievement. Of equal importance is his realistic fiction, beginning with *The Family Moskat* (1950), his first novel written in the United States. Densely populated and epic in scope, *The Family Moskat* and its immediate successor, *The Manor* (1967)—so long that its English version was eventually published in two volumes, *The Manor* and *The Estate* (1969)—recall the massive family chronicles of the nineteenth century that culminated in Thomas Mann's *Buddenbrooks*. But Singer's most immediate inspiration was the example of his revered elder brother, I. J. Singer, whose masterpiece, *The Brothers Ashkenazi*, is cited specifically in the dedication to *The Family Moskat*. Despite their radically different styles, *The Family Moskat* and *The Manor* echo *Satan in Goray* in valorizing the network of customs and rituals that comprise traditional Jewish belief. The family chronicles clarify Singer's reliance on the biblical parable of the prodigal son for the moral scaffolding of his fiction. In these and succeeding novels, moral tension is generated in protagonists who typically deviate from Jewishness, recognize the error of their ways, and try to decide whether and how to return to the fold.

As the son of a rabbi and of a mother descended from generations of rabbis, Singer, who briefly attended rabbinical seminary himself, only to exchange traditional Judaism for modern secularism, was ideally positioned to evoke the prodigal-son scenario. Two of his most radically successful prodigals are the protagonists of *The Magician of Lublin* (1960) and *The Penitent* (1983): the former walls himself apart from the world; the latter flees the world for the ultra-orthodox Meah Shearim district of Jerusalem. In regaining their Jewishness, both reenact the ancient Jewish role of the *baal tschuve* ("one who returns").

Fantastic or realistic, Singer's fiction is, therefore, above all moral. As such, it conflates Jewish folklore and Jewish history to achieve not merely a parochial but a universal moral resonance that won Singer the 1978 Nobel Prize for Literature.

Lawrence S. Friedman

See also Epic; Legend; Local Color

✳✳✳✳✳✳✳✳✳✳✳✳✳✳✳✳✳✳

References
Alexander, Edward. *Isaac Bashevis Singer*. Boston: Twayne Publishers, 1980.
Buchen, Irving H. *Isaac Bashevis Singer and the Eternal Past*. New York: New York University Press, 1968.
Friedman, Lawrence S. *Understanding Isaac Bashevis Singer*. Columbia: University of South Carolina Press, 1988.

SIREN

Appearing as mythological creatures in Homer's *Odyssey*, sirens called to sailors from their remote island, promising a glimpse of the future and other unspecified delights. Sailors were so eager to engage the sirens that, heedless of safety, they destroyed their own ships on the treacherous rocks surrounding the island. What the sirens actually promised the sailors is rarely translated from the original, and popular belief has come to associate "the siren's call" with either a penetrating screech, which maddens the victim to the point of fatal recklessness, or a mysterious and lovely singing, which seduces the hearer to his own destruction.

The *Odyssey* does not describe the siren's physical form, but classical vase paintings commemorating the Homeric episodes depict creatures resembling harpies—with fish tails held at right angles behind their bodies. Few legends or tales mention flying sirens, but they are not uncommon in Western art. Because of their association with haunting melodies and doomed sailors, "siren" became synonymous with "mermaid" in the Middle Ages, when sirens were described in legend and bestiaries as fish women, acquiring a mirror and a comb as part of their paraphernalia. "Siren" continues to be synonymous with "mermaid" in some parts of the world. "Sirens" have also inspired the shrill horns on emergency vehicles and early warning systems. Modern versions of the legend combine a predatory femininity with a deadly voice of an exquisite character, which causes men to go mad: for example, the Lorelei.

Cynthea L. Ainsworth

See also Legend; Mermaid; *Odyssey*

✳✳✳✳✳✳✳✳✳✳✳✳✳✳✳✳✳

References

Berman, Ruth. "Sirens." In *Mythical and Fabulous Creatures: A Source Book and Research Guide*, ed. Malcolm South, pp. 147–153. New York: Greenwood Press, 1987.

Hamilton, Edith. *Mythology.* New York: New American Library, 1969.

Tripp, Edward. *The Meridian Handbook of Classical Mythology.* New York: Meridian, 1974.

Song of Roland

Chanson de Roland, or *Song of Roland,* is a medieval French epic recounting the defeat by Muslim forces of a rear guard of Charlemagne's army as it returned through the Pyrenees mountains between France and Spain. The historical record from about 830 shows that on August 15, 778, Eggihard, Charlemagne's steward; Anselm, count of the palace; and Roland, duke of the Marches of Brittany—"together with a great many more"—died in battle against the Muslims and that it was impossible for Charlemagne to take revenge on the enemy. Somehow, details of this historic event had grown into legend and the *Chanson de Roland* by the eleventh century.

In *Chanson de Roland,* Charlemagne, 36 years old at the time of

A representation of the scene in the French medieval epic Song of Roland *where Roland, Charlemagne's nephew and rear guard, was overtaken by the Muslim forces.*

the historical event, evolved into a 200-year-old monarch, and Roland was elevated to being Charlemagne's sister's son, a bond of high importance in medieval chivalric culture. *Chanson de Roland* also introduces a villain, Ganelon, who for unspecified reasons hates Roland and betrays him to the enemy. Roland, who commands Charlemagne's rear division as the army returns to France, has orders in the event of trouble to blow his horn as a signal for the main army to return and assist him. When the enemy troops—tipped off by Ganelon—attack in overwhelming numbers, Roland waits until his forces are almost completely destroyed before he summons Charlemagne's army by blowing the horn so powerfully that he bursts the blood vessels in his head. The army returns to find Roland and his companions slain, but in another significant departure from the historical record, the troops go on to slaughter the Saracen forces.

In its transformation of the historical events into an elaborate piece of literary art, *Chanson de Roland* falls into the genre of chanson de geste, or "song of great deeds," emphasizing themes of chivalric heroism, especially in the face of overwhelming odds. Composed in lines of approximately 10 syllables, grouped in stanzas of unequal length, and bound together by assonance, the text reflects sophisticated technical skill.

The early poem survives in a single manuscript from the eleventh century, the Oxford Manuscript. Evidence suggests, however, that it was widely known and enjoyed throughout the Middle Ages, and French versions of *Chanson de Roland* appear in several manuscripts from the thirteenth through the fifteenth centuries. The Normans supposedly sang of Roland for inspiration during the Battle of Hastings in 1066, and throughout Europe, there exist texts in Norse, German, and Italian that contain versions of *Chanson de Roland* or fill the gaps in Roland's biography.

A study of language and structure in *Chanson de Roland* led the Harvard scholar Albert Lord to suggest in his book *The Singer of Tales* (1960) that the epic had been produced by oral-formulaic composition. Later scholars have concurred that the poem uses formulaic elements but have not agreed whether or not *Chanson de Roland* evolved from the oral-formulaic tradition.

David Sprunger

See also Charlemagne; Epic; Oral-Formulaic Composition and Theory

✳✳✳✳✳✳✳✳✳✳✳✳✳✳✳✳✳

References

Lord, Albert B. *The Singer of Tales*. Cambridge: Harvard University Press, 1960.

Owen, D. D. R. *The Legend of Roland: A Pageant of the Middle Ages*. London: Phaidon, 1973.

The Song of Roland. Trans. Glyn Burgess. Harmondsworth, Eng.: Penguin, 1990.

Soto, Pedro Juan (1928–)

The Puerto Rican novelist, short-story writer, playwright, and university professor Pedro Juan Soto has made a major contribution to Latin American literature by incorporating Puerto Rican life in the United States into his work. Most particularly his work is inhabited by characters associated with the Puerto Rican barrio in New York City. Although Soto did not initiate this trend, his international recognition through literary prizes (e.g., Cuba's Casa de las Américas, awarded in 1982) corroborates the acceptance of the Latino world on North American soil as a geographical extension of Latin America and, therefore, as desirable material for mainstream Hispanic literature.

In Puerto Rico, Soto is also well known as an outspoken advocate of independence. His notoriety increased when his son, Roberto Soto Arriví, a university activist, was killed in a police raid in 1978 while he was allegedly trying to bomb a communication tower. The incident received international notice because of speculation that higher government offices (both U.S. and Puerto Rican) had previous knowledge of the subversive attack and that, in fact, an undercover agent might have encouraged the students' plan.

Pedro Juan Soto went to New York City in 1946 as a student at the University of Long Island, where he received a B.A., and he stayed in New York until 1954, when he finished his M.A. at Columbia University. This experience has been pivotal in his literary development. Later he wrote: "I hate the city of New York intensely, and I love it with equal intensity." This conflict is a theme of his short-story collection *Spiks* (1956), named after the derogatory label given to Puerto Ricans in New York. In *Spiks*, Soto offers a realistic picture of the so-called Nuyoricans, or inhabitants of Spanish Harlem.

In his saga of the poor Puerto Rican generations, Soto depicts this new society, not fully Puerto Rican and not fully American, as the product of urban life in the United States. Because Soto's approach is clearly sociological in his sketching of Puerto Rican ghetto culture, his characters display qualities of interest to the folklorist. For instance, language usage becomes an important stylistic device as the characters reflect cultural dichotomies in the Spanish-English code-switching known as "Spanglish." The fight to preserve Puerto Rican ethnicity and Hispanic traditions against American, Protestant-related urban values becomes a constant struggle for the alienated characters.

Soto's novels explore problems of Puerto Rican ethnic alienation as characters have to accept the American dream as their only choice. Erratic behavior, a sort of cultural schizophrenia, eventually follows this disassociation from Puerto Rican values. One example is the violence of Usmaíl, an illegitimate light-skinned mulatto whose white American father had seduced Usmaíl's illiterate black mother with false promises; Usmaíl finally revolts against the ideal of Anglo supremacy by killing an American serviceman. Another character, Eduardo, the Nuyorican of *Ardiente suelo, fría estación* [Hot land, cold season (1961)], recognizes after a trip to Puerto Rico that his bicultural nature is the source of his identity problem. In an interesting turn of events, Soto's most recent novel, *Un oscuro pueblo sonriente* (1982), depicts the life of Americans holding professional posts in Puerto Rico and emphasizes the failure of their efforts to turn their Puerto Rican setting into an American environment.

Soto's influence in and firsthand knowledge of North American immigration make him an ideal recorder of the construction of continental Puerto Rican popular culture. Soto's works stand out for their contribution to the preservation of contemporary Puerto Rican folklore, both on the island and in the mainland United States.

Rafael Ocasio

See also Dialect

✳✳✳✳✳✳✳✳✳✳✳✳✳✳✳✳✳

References

Fernández, José B. "Soto, Pedro Juan." In *Biographical Dictionary of Hispanic Literature in the United States: The Literature of Puerto Ricans, Cuban Americans, and Other Hispanic Writers*, ed. Nicolás Kanellos, pp. 299–305. New York: Greenwood Press, 1989.

Foster, David William. "Soto, Pedro Juan." In *A Dictionary of Contemporary*

Latin American Authors, p. 98. Tempe: Center for Latin American Studies, Arizona State University, 1975.

Ryan, Bryan, ed. "Soto, Pedro Juan." In *Hispanic Writers*, pp. 446–447. Detroit: Gale Research, 1991.

Soto, Pedro Juan. "The City and I." In *Literature and the Urban Experience*, ed. Michael C. Jaye and Ann Chalmers Watts, pp. 185–191. New Brunswick, N.J.: Rutgers University Press, 1981.

SOYINKA, WOLE (1934–)

The Nigerian playwright, poet, novelist, critic, and 1986 Nobel laureate Wole Soyinka attended Government College and University College in Ibadan, Nigeria. From 1954 to 1960, he lived in England, where he received an honors degree in English language and literature from the University of Leeds and trained with the Royal Court Theatre in London. After he returned to Nigeria in 1960, he lectured at the universities of Ibadan, Ife, and Lagos, where he was also involved in theatrical productions and established two theater companies. From August 1967 to October 1969, he was imprisoned because of his political activity during the Nigerian civil war. While in prison, he translated D. O. Fagunwa's *The Forest of a Thousand Daemons* (1968) from Yoruba to English. After being released, Soyinka left Nigeria and held various teaching positions outside the country, but between 1976 and 1985, he returned to Nigeria to teach at the University of Ife. Since 1985, he has held visiting professorships at several universities, including Yale and Cornell. Throughout, he has continued to write poems, plays, autobiographies, and works of criticism.

Unlike his Yoruba counterparts, D. O. Fagunwa and Amos Tutuola, Soyinka has concentrated less on the folkloric secular aspects of Yoruba culture and more on the sacred, what Soyinka calls the "cthonic realm," in which the artist is engaged in the simultaneous acts of creation and destruction. But he has also been influenced by the chanting, proverbs, praise-name epithets, and comic slapstick used in Yoruba folk drama. Elements of Yoruba oral poetic forms, such as *ijala* (the poetry of hunters and blacksmiths), *oriki* ("praise poems"), and *ege* ("funeral dirges") inform many of Soyinka's poems and plays. In *Kongi's Harvest* (1967) as well as in many other plays, variations on or imitations of traditional proverbs occur throughout, as, for example, "The pot that will eat fat / Its bottom must be scorched."

Within a satirical or an allegorical framework, Soyinka often uses Yoruba *orisha* ("gods") and mythic structures to draw parallels to contemporary Nigerian situations and to unmask corruption and hypocrisy. In particular, Soyinka employs Ogun—the god of iron, of the crossroads, of hunters—to represent duality, the creative and destructive forces in the world. The long poems "Idanre" and "Ogun Abibiman," as well as the play *The Road* (1965), contain embodiments of Ogun in addition to other Yoruba mythological figures. In his play *A Dance of the Forests* (1963), Soyinka tried to merge Yoruba traditions of festival drama with European traditions of dialogue drama. In *Dance* and other plays, Soyinka deals with the Yoruba concept of *egungun*, ancestors who link the living with the dead and are powerfully present in the *egungun* masquerades during the annual festivals.

Besides his creative work, which draws on Yoruba themes and motifs (of which the examples above provide only a small representation), Soyinka has written several critical essays expounding his position on ritual drama and clarifying his mythopoetic methods. In his essay "The Fourth Stage: Through the Mysteries of Ogun to the Origin of Yoruba Tragedy," Soyinka elaborates his ideas about Yoruba ritual drama, defined by Yoruba metaphysics, which creates a transcendental reality or "fourth space." He argues that African literature reflects human experience through the social vision of the author.

Despite charges by some African critics, particularly the so-called decolonist group, that his work is overly influenced by European literary models, Soyinka has displayed an unceasing commitment to preserving Yoruba culture by exploring Yoruba mythic structures and explicating the Yoruba tragic model of transition and transcendence.

Sue Standing

See also Myth; Tutuola, Amos

✿✿✿✿✿✿✿✿✿✿✿✿✿✿✿✿✿

References

Coger, Greta M. K. *Index of Subjects, Proverbs, and Themes in the Writing of Wole Soyinka*. New York: Greenwood Press, 1988.

Katrak, Ketu. *Wole Soyinka and Modern Tragedy*. London: Greenwood Press, 1986.

Maja-Pearce, Adewale, ed. *Wole Soyinka: An Appraisal*. Oxford: Heinemann, 1994.

Ojaide, Tanure. *The Poetry of Wole Soyinka*. Lagos: Malthouse, 1994.

Soyinka, Wole. *Myth, Literature, and the African World*. Cambridge: Cambridge University Press, 1976.

Wright, Derek. *Wole Soyinka Revisited*. New York: Twayne Publishers, 1993.

STEINBECK, JOHN (1902–1968)

American author John Steinbeck's 1930s novels are often concerned with rural, uneducated, regional, or ethnic groups, the "folk" of popular imagination, and it is in these novels that he makes the greatest use of folklore, especially in *Tortilla Flat* (1935), *In Dubious Battle* (1936), *Of Mice and Men* (1937), and *The Grapes of Wrath* (1939). Steinbeck's concept of the folk is more idealized and romantic than that of professional folklorists, but his methods of research were analogous to those of folklore field-workers.

The major characters in *Tortilla Flat* are Mexicanos who live in a village environment on the outskirts of Monterey, California. These people, of "Spanish, Indian, Mexican, and assorted Caucasian bloods," are depicted as simple, innocent, pleasure-loving, and religiously superstitious. Steinbeck's portrayal of them reveals more about the mainstream culture's image of a minority folk group than it does about the actualities of Mexican-American village life.

Steinbeck maintained his interest in agrarian people in *In Dubious Battle*, a more overtly political novel about striking migrant fruit pickers, and in *Of Mice and Men*, whose two main characters are itinerant farmworkers. He continued to portray rural people in a sentimental and romantic light, which can be seen especially in the character of Lennie, the mentally retarded farmhand in *Of Mice and Men*.

Steinbeck's concern with oppressed migrant farmworkers culminated in his best known novel, *The Grapes of Wrath*, the story of a displaced Oklahoma farm family, the Joads, and their trek to California in search of a better life. He presents a complex picture of the dynamics of folk culture in this novel, drawing on a wide range of folklife materials: family stories, local-character anecdotes, folk beliefs, customs, proverbs, foodways, jokes, folk music and dance, legends, and folk ideas. Here, he more effectively uses folklife to achieve his literary purposes than in the earlier novels. For example, he has a five-page detailed description of a traditional hog butchering, which suggests the importance of communal cooperation within the microcosm of family life.

Steinbeck seems especially attuned to the nuances of performance contexts and how shifts of context can alter the meaning of folk expression. A good example occurs when Tom Joad tells a local anecdote to preacher Jim Casy as they walk down the road toward the Joad farm. The story is about bashful Willy Feeley who takes a heifer to be bred with a neighbor's bull. Watching the animals breed, he begins to feel "purty fly," and says to the neighbor's daughter, "I wisht I was a-doin' that," to which she replies, "Why not, Willy? It's your heifer." Later in an "interchapter" about Route 66, the same basic story is told by a truck driver to a waitress in a diner, except that this time the story is about an anonymous "little kid" and the waitress responds with "harsh screeching laughter" instead of the soft laughter of Jim Casy. In the first context, the story is a local anecdote and suggests the closeness of a community in which everyone knows everybody; in the second context, the story is a joke that reveals the distance of relationships in a modern, mobile society. Steinbeck uses the details of performance context to reinforce one of the major contrastive themes of the novel.

Steinbeck used journalistic methods to gather material from migrant workers in California, but his descriptions of observing and living with the workers also suggest a similarity with the ethnographic methods of folklorists. He became fluent in the performance techniques of the traditional agrarian folk society so he could more accurately represent the dynamics of their interaction in ways that enhanced his literary purposes. There are still elements of sentimental romanticism toward agrarian folk culture, but there is a better balance with the hardships and everyday textures of life in such a culture, which makes *The Grapes of Wrath* Steinbeck's best and most popular novel.

Patrick B. Mullen

See also Labor Folklore and Literature; Local Color

✳✳✳✳✳✳✳✳✳✳✳✳✳✳✳✳✳✳

References

Astro, Richard, and Tetsumaro Hayashi, eds. *Steinbeck: The Man and His Work.* Corvallis: Oregon State University Press, 1973.

Lisca, Peter. *The Wide World of John Steinbeck.* New Brunswick, N.J.: Rutgers University Press, 1958.

Mullen, Patrick B. "American Folklife and *The Grapes of Wrath*." *Journal of American Culture* 1 (1978): 742–753.

Steinbeck, Elaine, and Robert Wallsten, eds. *Steinbeck, a Life in Letters.* New York: Viking, 1975.

STEPHENS, JAMES (1880–1950)

Like other Irish literary figures, James Stephens is as much a part of lore as his own characters. Evasive about the facts of his personal life, Stephens contributed to his own myth by offering mostly incorrect dates for the major events in his life, even claiming to have been born the same year as James Joyce, 1882, when he was actually born in 1880. Much of the scholarship on Stephens has concentrated on his "whimsicality," a label that has caused some of his biographers and critics to neglect the authenticity of his works, which celebrate the elemental, if contradictory, components of the Celtic ethos.

At the height of his career, Stephens was considered the equal of William Butler Yeats, John Millington Synge, and other luminaries of the Irish renaissance. This acclaim was owing in part to his skillful renditions of Celtic legends that were the genesis and undergirding of that renaissance.

Winner of the Polignas and the Tailteann Festival prizes, Stephens wrote both fiction and nonfiction—poetry, drama, essays, novels, short stories, and redactions of ancient saga literature. Stephens appears to have worked backward from the product to the source, publishing a love story, *The Charwoman's Daughter* (1912); a unique work (and his most famous), *The Crock of Gold* (1912); a volume of short stories, *Here Are Ladies* (1913); an adventure story, *The Demi-gods* (1914); and a report on the Easter Rebellion, *The Insurrection in Dublin* (1916), before writing three works that are specifically based on Gaelic saga material—*Irish Fairy Tales* (1920), *Deirdre* (1923), and *In the Land of Youth* (1924). Unlike Yeats, Stephens concentrated on saga material only after his reputation had been made in the modern mode; his poetry—collected in *Insurrections* (1909), *The Hill of Vision* (1912), *Songs from the Clay* (1915), and *The Adventures of Seumas Beg* (1915)—however, illustrates a bardic lyricism.

In part because of his connections with the Yeats circle, Stephens saw in the ancient tales of Ireland the ethnic heart of a proud yet suppressed culture. Like other members of the Celtic renaissance, he was keenly interested in the reinstitution of Gaelic as the national language of Ireland. He learned to read Gaelic to a satisfactory degree, though he never learned to speak it well.

The political upheavals of the early 1900s must have seemed to Stephens, as to the other artists of the period, a rebirth of national spirit for which the accompanying blood and pain of parturition were expected, though nonetheless traumatic. In a letter to Lady Isabella Augusta Gregory dated August 18, 1920, Stephens wrote, "Bathing in the past, in the strange and beautiful was never so necessary as in these horrible times" (Finneran 1974, p. 254). Stephens believed Celtic stories to be the worthy subjects of literary endeavor for patriotic reasons, to ground the nation in a dignified if quasi historicity. Moreover, his association with the Irish theosophists and a thorough reading of the works of William Blake taught him to find in the saga stories connections among Celtic beliefs and those of other cultures, correlations that he reprised in his prose and poetry. Although Stephens's literary output was in decline in the last years before his death in 1950, he retained in himself and in his commentaries for the BBC (British Broadcasting Company) a clear and natural vision of indigenous Celticism.

Sylvia McLaurin

See also Celtic Literature; Gregory, Lady Isabella Augusta; Legend; Yeats, William Butler

✳✳✳✳✳✳✳✳✳✳✳✳✳✳✳✳✳✳

References

Finneran, Richard J., ed. *The Letters of James Stephens*. New York: Macmillan, 1974.

Martin, Augustine. *James Stephens: A Critical Study*. Totowa, N.J.: Rowman and Littlefield, 1977.

Russell, George (pseudonym, A. E.). *Imaginations and Reveries*. Dublin: Maunsel, 1915.

STOKER, BRAM (1847–1912)

Bram (Abraham) Stoker, best known as the author of *Dracula*, was born in Dublin, Ireland, in November 1847, the third of seven children born to Abraham and Charlotte Thornley Stoker. His father was a poorly paid civil servant, his mother a social worker who wrote about women and poverty for the Dublin newspapers. He was bedridden until the age of seven and was deeply affected by his mother's vivid, often frightening, stories of both Irish tradition and a cholera epidemic of her childhood.

At Trinity College in Dublin, Stoker excelled in sports and was a head officer in both the historical and the philosophical societies.

His first speech was titled "Sensationalism in Fiction and Society." He also devoted himself to the theater and to defending Walt Whitman's poetry against charges of obscenity. Stoker graduated in 1868 with honors in science and began working as a government clerk and drama critic for the *Dublin Mail*. He began a friendship with the actor Henry Irving in 1876, after having written a rave review of Irving's work.

In December 1878, Stoker married Florence Balcombe, a famous beauty who had been courted by Oscar Wilde (a college friend of Bram's). The Stokers moved to Glasgow, where Henry Irving had taken over the Lyceum Theatre and had formed his own company. Bram managed the theater until Irving's death in 1905. In 1879, the couple's only child, Noel, was born. The Stokers established a fashionable weekly salon in their home, and Stoker pursued simultaneous careers as a legal solicitor and an author of books, essays, and short stories.

Dracula, published in 1897 and dedicated to the novelist and childhood friend Hall Caine (nicknamed Hommy-Beg), was Stoker's fourth book. The first, in 1879, had been a reference work for civil servants. The second, *Under the Sunset* (1882), was an author-subsidized collection of bizarre literary fairy tales; and a romance, *The Snake's Pass* (1890), concerned conflicting legends of treasure in an Irish bog. After *Dracula*, Stoker published several less successful novels, including *Miss Betty* (1898), *The Mystery of the Sea* (1902), *The Jewel of Seven Stars* (1903), *The Man* (1905), *Lady Athlyne* (1908), *The Lady of the Shroud* (1909), and *Lair of the White Worm* (1910). He also wrote two nonfiction books, a two-volume *Personal Reminiscences of Henry Irving* (1906), and *Famous Imposters* (1910), in the latter sketching several (mostly female) cross-dressers. Stoker researched most of his work, but never so extensively nor so successfully as for *Dracula*.

Seventy-eight pages of Stoker's research notes for *Dracula* (found in the 1970s and housed in the Rosenbach Museum in Philadelphia) mention 24 French and English books, including folkloristic and historical studies as well as works on animal behavior, meteorology, medicine, and psychology. He crafted characters using Italian physicist, physician, and early criminologist Cesare Lombroso's psychophysiology and literary precedents (including *King Lear*). Stoker also explored materials in the British Museum and may have discussed his work with Arminus Vambery, a Hungarian folklorist and professor of oriental languages in Budapest. And Stoker conducted fieldwork: in Whitby, England, where most of the novel takes place, he studied local records and dialect and recorded beliefs and narratives about storms, shipwrecks, and burials.

Bram Stoker died on April 20, 1912, after a long illness. His ambiguously worded death certificate has suggested tertiary syphilis to some biographers, but that is speculative. Bram Stoker was never famous, but perhaps his obscurity proves his skill. Dracula was created so well that he has assumed a life and legacy of his own.

Clover Williams

See also Dracula; *King Lear*

✶✶✶✶✶✶✶✶✶✶✶✶✶✶✶✶✶

References

Farson, Daniel. *The Man Who Wrote Dracula: A Biography of Bram Stoker*. New York: St Martin's Press, 1976.

Leatherdale, Clive. *The Origins of Dracula: The Background to Bram Stoker's Gothic Masterpiece*. London: William Kimber, 1987.

Ludlam, Harry. *A Biography of Dracula: The Life Story of Bram Stoker*. London: Foulsham, 1962.

Storytelling

Modern storytelling, often called professional storytelling, is a consciously developed art in which trained tellers perform before audiences of children and adults. This art began to develop in the late nineteenth century and expanded rapidly as librarians and teachers received formal training in the presentation of stories for children. Their primary sources were printed collections of tales such as those by Charles Perrault, the Grimm brothers, and Hans Christian Andersen.

Children formed the primary audiences until the 1970s, when storytelling began a rapid expansion. Today, there are storytelling centers, groups, and festivals in almost every state of the United States and each of the provinces and territories of Canada, and indeed throughout the world. Storytelling is still popularly seen as being primarily for children, but concerts, festivals, and workshops for adults are now the mainstay of many professional performers.

Modern storytelling has always relied very heavily on tales in printed collections, not only those mentioned above, but also newer collections from all areas of the world. In earlier decades, printed

Storytelling has been a tradition across diverse cultures and ages, as this picture of an Algerian storyteller attests.

texts were primary. Teachers and librarians emphasized published collections and used traditional stories as a means of encouraging children to read. One researcher, Richard Alvey (1974), has described how this narrow approach to storytelling ironically led to a slow decline, beginning in the 1940s when recorded tales on phonograph records began to be widely popular. Alvey noted that storytelling for children had ebbed considerably by the early 1970s.

A single modest festival in a small southern town began to turn the tide. The first storytelling festival took place in 1973 in Jonesborough, Tennessee, featuring a handful of tellers who came from a variety of backgrounds. These included narrators whose tales arose in oral tradition from their own families as well as tellers with library and educational training. There were also professional humorists and a few performers with theater-oriented training. This blend of oral and literary traditions has continued as a model for story festivals across North America.

This newer form of storytelling, centering on adult-oriented concerts and festivals, is popularly called "the storytelling revival." Proponents sincerely, but erroneously, see themselves as the descendants of a romanticized ancient art of oral narration. Many have neither knowledge of nor experience with any authentic oral tradition, relying heavily on literary sources removed from the living context of storytelling as a face-to-face exchange within a community of tellers. Tellers often perform recitations of original literary works written for children or adults. There are also small theatrical groups that offer dramatic productions of folktales.

Folklorists have tended to fault such storytelling as unauthentic because it does not arise from a specific oral tradition. However, modern storytelling can be seen in a more creative light, as an oral art form in its own right.

Kay Stone

See also Andersen, Hans Christian; Grimm, Jacob and Wilhelm; Perrault, Charles

❋❋❋❋❋❋❋❋❋❋❋❋❋❋❋❋

References

Alvey, Richard. "The Historical Development of Organized Storytelling to Children in the United States." Ph.D. dissertation, University of Pennsylvania, 1974.

Birch, Carol, and Melissa Heckler. *Who Says? Essays on Pivotal Issues in Contemporary Storytelling*. Little Rock, Ark.: August House, 1996.

Sobol, Joseph. "Jonesborough Days: The National Storytelling Festival and the Contemporary Storytelling Revival Movement in America." Ph.D. dissertation, Northwestern University, 1994.

Stone, Kay. *Burning Brightly: New Light on Old Tales Told Today*. Peterborough, Ont.: Broadview Press, 1998.

———. "Once Upon a Time Today: Grimm Tales for Contemporary Performers." In *The Reception of Grimms' Fairy Tales: Responses, Reactions, Revisions*, ed. Donald Haase, pp. 250–268. Detroit: Wayne State University Press, 1993.

STRAPAROLA, GIAN FRANCESCO (c. 1480–c. 1557)

An Italian author about whose life little is known, Gian Francesco Straparola was the author of the two-volume *Le piacevoli notti* [The entertaining nights], which appeared in Venice in 1550 and 1553. A collection of 75 novellas and 73 riddles, it presents them as told by a set of men and women relaxing at the Venetian suburb of Murano over the course of the last 13 nights of the Venetian Carnival—a framing device that is based on Giovanni Boccaccio's *Decameron*. Among the novellas are 20 folktales, including the first appearance in literature of "Puss-and-Boots" and "Beauty and the Beast," which were adapted by Giambattista Basile for his collection the *Pentamerone* (1634). *Le piacevoli notti* was quickly translated into Spanish and had several Spanish imitators, resulting in early collections of Spanish folktales. The work was also used as a source by William Shakespeare and Jean-Baptiste Molière.

Because of its place in the sequence of folktale collections, *Le piacevoli notti* has been included in studies on the transformation of folktales through literary media. Applying the morphological theory of Vladimir Propp, an attempt has been made to develop a morphological scheme for a set of tales based on their commonalities as they appear in several collections. This attempt fails despite a clear literary-historical trail, because the tales have been removed from oral tradition and successively transformed to address a new middle-class audience— the emphasis on personal efficacy and empowerment of characters being evidence of this class-based change. The interaction of class mores and values with local social structures as reflected in the changes within the tales is indicative of the development of popular culture.

John Cash

See also Basile, Giambattista; Boccaccio, Giovanni; *Decameron*; Folktale; Propp, Vladimir I.; Riddle; Shakespeare, William

✱✱✱✱✱✱✱✱✱✱✱✱✱✱✱✱✱

References

Larivaille, Paul. *Le Réalisme du merveilleux: Structures et histoire du conte*. Centre de Recherche de Langue et Littérature Italienne, Documents de Travail et Prépublications no. 28. Nanterre: Université Paris, 1982.

———. *Perspectives et limites d'une analyse morphologique du conte: Pour une révision du schéma de Propp*. Centre de Recherche de Langue et Littérature Italienne, Documents de travail et Prépublications no. 2. Nanterre: Université Paris, 1979.

Pozzi, Victoria Smith. *Straparola's Le piacevoli notti: Narrative Technique and Ideology*. Los Angeles: University of California, 1981.

Senn, Doris. "*Le piacevoli notti* (1550/53) von Giovan Francesco Straparola, ihre italienischen Editionen und die spanische Übersetzung, *Honesto y agradable entretenimiento de damas y galanes* (1569–81) von Francisco Truchado." *Fabula* 34:1–2 (1993): 45–65.

Straparola, Gian Francesco. *The Nights of Straparola*. Ed. W. G. Waters. London: Lawrence and Bullen, 1894.

STRUCTURALISM

Structuralism was an intellectual movement that flourished in the early and middle decades of the twentieth century. It arose in reaction to earlier literary criticism, which had tended to reduce a work of art to its social and historical environments. Structuralism, however, held that a work of art was an entity in itself with its own particular structure. This structure, it was said, was the proper object of literary criticism and could be studied without reference to any social or historical influences.

Structuralism and formalism are closely related intellectual movements, the former usually being considered a development of the latter. Formalism first appeared as such in Russia between 1917 and 1927. The revolution of 1917 was an intellectual as well as a political liberation, and under Lenin, in the first years of the Soviet state, writers, thinkers, poets, and critics explored a new approach to art. The study of art was no longer to be seen as a postscript to the statements made by science, as it had been in the bourgeois culture of the past, but was to be the object of its own science.

Russian formalism produced two separate schools in the 1920s: the Moscow Linguistic Circle and the St. Petersburg Obshchestvo Izucheniia Poeticheskogo Iazyka (OPOJAZ) [Society for the Study of Poetic Language]. While the Moscow group saw poetry as language in its aesthetic function and the historical development of artistic forms as having a sociological basis, the St. Petersburg group was less compromising, asserting the autonomy of poetry from language in general and the autonomy of the work of art from its social setting. An offshoot of the Russian formalism movement, the Prague Linguistic Circle, also appeared at this time in Czechoslovakia.

In its early phase in Russia, the formalist debate was concerned primarily with poetry and with the poetic use of language, yet it also had implications for prose works and even for oral narrative (folktales). In particular, it demanded that the literary critic should adopt the morphological method, emphasizing the literary work as a unity made up of its constituent parts. Russian formalist Vladimir Propp took up this idea in his study of folktales and stated that the first step in any analysis was to establish the morphology of the tale(s), since without this structure there was no point in attempting any historical study, for the scholar had to know how the parts of the tale related to the whole before comparing that whole with religion, myth, and history.

Russian formalism was to have a short life. It began as an enthusiastic rejection of that bourgeois positivism which had flourished in the nineteenth century, a positivism that gave priority to the novel over the poem, to referential language over poetic language, to the object over the word referring to it, to the content of a text over the texture of the verbal sign. In France, the symbolist and dadaist movements of the late nineteenth and early twentieth centuries had already rebelled against this distorted view of art, and Russian formalism continued the revolt. In 1924, however, Lenin died. Stalin replaced him, and the formalist movement went into eclipse, since Stalinists were as distrustful in their own way of artistic autonomy as the bourgeoisie.

Outside Russia, formalism spread, especially after the first translation into English of Propp's *Morphology of the Folktale* in 1958. Formalism was to inspire such major writers as Roland Barthes and Tzvetan Todorov, and in particular, through the inspiration of Propp, the movement was to result in a proliferation of new theories concerning narrative structures.

Scholar Claude Bremond, for instance, examined a large body of folktales, basing his analysis on a series of triads. A. J. Greimas reduced Propp's 31 functions to 21, by the use of oppositions similar to those proposed by Claude Lévi-Strauss, and attained a much higher level of abstraction than Propp. These and other scholars followed a line of enquiry that emphasized the syntagmatic axis of a narrative: its sequence of events. Yet narrative can also be ordered in the paradigmatic dimension, where the choices made in each of the syntagmatic episodes are subject to analysis.

The structuralist scholar whose work in this direction is best known is Claude Lévi-Strauss. Myths, he said, were the product of the mind's natural tendency to group phenomena by opposites. The oppositions thus generated were resolved by a middle term, which participated in both of the others. The characteristic of myth was that it performed this operation using concrete tokens rather than an abstract philosophical language, arranging the oppositions like chords in a piece of music and reiterating them again and again in different ways to get its effect.

Formalism was a revolt against the dominance of the positivist mentality in art, and its success led to the exploration, in the middle decades of the twentieth century, of many interesting paths of inquiry, especially in the field of narrative. Yet, in the end, formalism proved to be open to the same sort of narrowness as its theoretical predecessors. If they denied the quite legitimate autonomy of a work of art from its environment, then formalism, in its extreme forms, could deny equally legitimate environmental influences upon that same work of art. No doubt, it was this narrowness that inspired the poststructuralism current in academic circles since the 1970s—a poststructuralism whose focus has once more turned, through the mediation of such positions as Marxism and feminism, from the text of the work of art to its context.

Peter Gilet

See also Myth; Poststructuralism; Prague Linguistic Circle; Propp, Vladimir I.; Russian Formalism

✳✳✳✳✳✳✳✳✳✳✳✳✳✳✳✳✳✳

References

Bremond, Claude. "Morphology of the French Folktale." *Semiotica* 2 (1970): 247–276.

Greimas, Algirdas Julien. *Semantique structurale*. Paris: Larousse, 1966.

Lévi-Strauss, Claude. *Structural Anthropology*. Trans. C. Jakobson and B. G. Schoef. New York: Basic Books, 1963.

Propp, Vladimir. *Morphology of the Folktale*. Trans. L. Scott. Austin: University of Texas Press, 1968.

Todorov, Tzvetan. *The Poetics of Prose*. Trans. R. Howard. Ithaca, N.Y.: Cornell University Press, 1977.

STURT, GEORGE (1863–1927)

George Sturt, also known as George Bourne, wrote eight books describing in intimate and affectionate detail the folklife of Farnham, England, which went in Sturt's lifetime from servicing rural trades to being a suburban retreat for London's professional classes. Sturt was born into a wheelwright's family, but his father's death, when George was 21, obliged him to give up teaching school (forgoing, he feared, his literary aspirations) to try to become a wheelwright himself in order to support his mother and sisters and out of loyalty to the craftsmen who depended on the business. His discovery of the unsuspected depths of the traditional knowledge of wheelwrights is the theme of *The Wheelwright's Shop* (1923).

Sturt's writings have been quietly influential in anthropology and cultural criticism, contributing to anthropologist Robert Redfield's formulation of "the folk society" and to literary critic F. R. Leavis's "organic community." Sturt's achievement lies elsewhere, however: as an ethnographer who anticipated such late-twentieth-century developments as occupational folklife and a mode of writing that reflexively questioned his own preconceptions and authority to write about a culture not entirely his own.

His first literary success was *The Bettesworth Book* (1901), a series of conversations with Frederick Grover, an older man who worked as his gardener. This book, and *Memoirs of a Surrey Labourer* (1907), are remarkable for the degree to which Sturt allows Grover's voice to predominate. The books explore a rural working-class man's choice of conversational narratives and the attitudes and worldview embodied in them. Sturt listened attentively and transcribed the talk of such men, from memory and in convincing detail. The reader encounters Grover directly.

Sturt wrote a journal of daily events, including such conversations with Grover and the men in the wheelwright's shop, for 37 years. A journal encourages a revising of opinion as new perceptions arise, and as Sturt drew heavily on the journal for his books, they have a characteristically modest, reflective, and exploratory quality.

Change in the Village (1912), which influenced Redfield, is Sturt's most overtly political work in that it details the oppressive effects of gentrification on the hamlet outside Farnham to which he had moved. Middle-class newcomers, including himself, were imposing their own values upon their working-class neighbors. As a socialist he felt guilty being an employer and the beneficiary of a system in which a majority endured less civilization so that a minority might enjoy more. A reader of nineteenth-century art critics and cultural analysts John Ruskin and William Morris, Sturt admired craft knowledge, knowing its satisfactions at firsthand, yet he felt that it was too dearly bought when it narrowed opportunities for education and wider experience. Although he regretted the passing of traditional industries, he would not go back.

At 53 he was paralyzed by a stroke and thus confined to family reminiscences. *William Smith, Potter and Farmer* (1919), *A Farmer's Life* (1922), and *A Small Boy in the Sixties* (1927) show his determination to go on writing about local vernacular culture: the organic fit between a region, its people, and the things they make while "civilizing" it.

Martin Lovelace

See also Labor Folklore and Literature

✳✳✳✳✳✳✳✳✳✳✳✳✳✳✳✳✳

References

Fraser, John. "Reflections on the Organic Community," *Human World* 15–16 (1974): 57–74.

Keith, W. J. *The Rural Tradition: A Study of the Non-Fiction Prose Writers of the English Countryside*. Toronto: University of Toronto Press, 1974.

Sturt, George. *The Journals of George Sturt*. Ed. E. D. Mackerness. 2 vols. Cambridge: Cambridge University Press, 1967.

———. *The Journals of George Sturt, "George Bourne," 1890–1902*. Ed. Geoffrey Grigson. London: Cresset, 1941.

STYLE

In its most general sense, style refers to a characteristic mode or manner of expression, a conventionalized, formally constituted orienting framework for the production and reception of discourse. More precisely, style is a constellation of systematically related, co-occurrent formal features that contrast with other such constellations. Considerations of style always imply dimensions of contrast between or among alternatives. The bases on which styles are distinguished, and thus on which the contrasts among them become salient, are many, varying from one speech community to another and from one historical period to another. The orders of style that have figured significantly in the conception and study of folklore, however, are relatively limited.

Attention to style in folklore derives from the roots of the discipline in eighteenth-century philology. Questions concerning the origin and evolution of literary forms, the foundations of literary greatness, the distinctiveness of national literatures, and the consequences of literacy were of central importance. Most influential in this regard for the development of folklore was the German philosopher of culture Johann Gottfried Herder. Synthesizing and extending the earlier work of such figures as Thomas Blackwell, Robert Wood, Robert Lowth, and Hugh Blair, Herder sought to identify the distinctively national styles that characterized the poetry of the world's people. In his emphasis on national, culturally founded expressive styles, Herder promulgated a conception of style as rooted in the collectivity, which has remained the dominant perspective in folklore ever since. Herder also provides a place for the individual folk poet as stylistic exemplar, insofar as such individuals give voice to the collective genius or the spirit of their people. Herder laid the foundations of a relativist, comparativist perspective of folk poetics keyed most centrally to the distinctiveness of national styles, the stylistic patterns that distinguish the folklore of one nation or people from another, but open to the consideration of individual style as well.

As more contemporary folklorists have extended their conception of the social base of folklore to other collectivities besides the nation, the collectivist view of style has been adapted accordingly. Melville Jacobs, for example, in the Boasian tradition of linguistically oriented Americanist anthropology, has traced an expressive style that was shared by a number of Native American peoples in the Northwest Coast culture area as a result of extensive culture contact. This poetic style, which Jacobs characterizes as terse, spare, parsimonious, and elliptical, selects for description only a lean range of rapidly moving actions, events, and narrative circumstances.

Beyond its "transnational" scope, Jacobs's work illustrates as well the extension of stylistic analysis beyond simple characterization of a collective folk style into the investigation of form-function-meaning interrelationships. The laconic and elliptical style of the Northwest Coast, Jacobs suggests, has significant implications for the reception and interpretation of folklore in performance: the information conveyed directly by the "terse delineation and speedy action" of the performance is interpretively extended and fleshed out by the invocation on the part of the audience of an extensive store of associational meanings and understandings (Jacobs 1959, pp. 266–272). Thus, the expressive experience is far more densely meaningful than the text alone would suggest. Folklorist and classicist John Miles Foley advances a rich interpretive framework for Serbo-Croatian oral epic based upon similar principles.

At the same time that investigations of communal style can transcend the boundaries of a single people, they can be narrowed in scope to consider dimensions of stylistic contrast within the nation, keyed to factors of social differentiation, as between regional, occupational, or other subcultures. A case in point is the current burgeoning interest in gender-based styles. American folklorists Joan Radner and Susan Lanser, for example, identify a characteristically female expressive style in the folklore of women, which they term *coding*. The coding style is suffused with devices of indirection and disguise, including metaphor, substitution of third-person others for the first-person "I," ellipses, litotes, passive constructions, euphemisms, and qualifiers, which serve the structuring and communicative capacities of spoken language as the oral-aural medium of performance. Although Radner and Lanser draw examples specifically from the discourse of Anglo-American women, their delineation of the coding style stands as an important contribution to comparativist perspectives on style.

The distinctive qualities of spoken language and oral poetics and the differences between spoken and written language and literature were of central concern to eighteenth-century philologists, part of the philosophical discourse in which the advent and spread of literacy were touchstones of modernity. Within this intellectual context, scholars like Blackwell, Lowth, and Herder ascribed the formal qualities of premodern literary forms—from Homeric epics to the Old Testament to folk songs—to the oral-aural medium in which they were created. Thus developed the notion of a distinctively oral style—formulaic, polysyndetic, iterative—keyed to the exigencies of oral performance and the capacities of spoken language as a medium of communication. Danish folklorist Axel Olrik's epic laws of folk narrative, anthropologist Franz Boas's theory of verbal art, and the Parry-Lord theory of oral-formulaic composition are among the more influential theoretical formulations shaped by this line of inquiry.

The relationship between spoken and written language is also centrally implicated in the problem of rendering oral folklore in print. As understandings of oral stylistics have become more rigorous and nuanced in formal terms, the intersemiotic translation of oral performance to the printed page has become a more complex and considered undertaking. The pioneering efforts of student of ethnopoetics Dennis Tedlock and linguistic anthropologist Dell Hymes, under the rubric of ethnopoetics, to render the stylistic organization of oral performances visible on the printed page have enhanced both the aesthetic experience of reading published texts and the acuity of analytical methods for the study of oral style.

Richard Bauman and Jennifer Schacker-Mill

See also Epic; Ethnopoetics; Herder, Johann Gottfried; Homer; Oral-Formulaic Composition and Theory

✳✳✳✳✳✳✳✳✳✳✳✳✳✳✳✳

References

Bauman, Richard. *Story, Performance, and Event: Contextual Studies of Oral Narrative*. Cambridge: Cambridge University Press, 1986.

Boas, Franz. *Primitive Art*. New York: Dover, 1955 (1927).

Foley, John Miles. *Immanent Art: From Structure to Meaning in Traditional Oral Epic*. Bloomington: Indiana University Press, 1991.

Hymes, Dell. *"In Vain I Tried to Tell You": Essays in Native American Ethnopoetics*. Philadelphia: University of Pennsylvania Press, 1981.

———. "Ways of Speaking." In *Explorations in the Ethnography of Speaking*, ed. Richard Bauman and Joel Sherzer, pp. 433–451. Cambridge: Cambridge University Press, 1989 (1974).

Jacobs, Melville. "Areal Spread of Indian Oral Genre Features in the Northwest States." *Journal of the Folklore Institute* 9 (1972): 10–17.

———. *The Content and Style of an Oral Literature*. Chicago: University of Chicago Press, 1959.

Lord, Albert. *The Singer of Tales*. Cambridge: Harvard University Press, 1960.

Olrik, Axel. *Principles for Oral Narrative Research*. Trans. Kirsten Wolf and Jody Jensen. Bloomington: Indiana University Press, 1992.

Radner, Joan N., and Susan S. Lanser. "Strategies of Coding in Women's Cultures." In *Feminist Messages*, ed. Joan N. Radner, pp. 1–29. Urbana: University of Illinois Press, 1993.

Tedlock, Dennis. *The Spoken Word and the Work of Interpretation*. Philadelphia: University of Pennsylvania Press, 1983.

SUPERNATURAL

Anything that cannot be explained rationally by means of modern science is said to be paranormal or supernatural. A wide variety of topics, including ghosts, witchcraft, second sight, fairies, werewolves, vampires, curses, magic, omens, and prophecies are covered by the term *supernatural*. These subjects turn up repeatedly in legends and folktales, that is, believers tell narratives in which supernatural elements are presented as fact while nonbelievers include them in stories they present as fiction, to be told simply for entertainment, but not necessarily for laughter. Supernatural creatures are not always bad: some, such as vampires, werewolves, and trolls, are generally evil, but others, such as elves, brownies, and fairies, are often helpful.

It is commonly believed that many of the supernatural creatures popular in European folklore are not found in the United States, but, even so, legends about "bearwalkers" and other shape-shifters, zombies, and even werewolves have been collected in the New World; legends about Bigfoot seem to be a fusion of ancient European wild man traditions with Native American beliefs about hairy apelike beings. Furthermore, a vast amount of lore about witches and ghosts has been reported in the United States. These matters suggest the possibility that narratives about European supernatural beings are more common in North America than is generally believed. The failure to turn up large numbers of such tales in the United States may reflect nothing more than the biases or assumptions of collectors.

Supernatural lore is found not only in informal oral tradition but in formal literature as well. William Shakespeare's plays, for example, are filled with ghosts and witches. Much of the horror in the Gothic tale of terror that reached its height of popularity in the nineteenth century, and in the late twentieth century still had a large following, was based on supernatural elements. This genre was presaged by the British writer Horace Walpole's *The Castle of Otranto* (1764); its first American practitioner of any note, Charles Brockden Brown, produced several books in this style four decades later. Better known to modern audiences are Johann Christoph Friedrich Schiller, Christoph Martin Wieland, and Johann Wolfgang von Goethe, all important names in literary history who helped establish a craze for this type of fiction.

Throughout the nineteenth century, horror fiction dominated the literary market in much of the world, and contributions were made by such authors as Edgar Allan Poe, Washington Irving, and Nathaniel Hawthorne in the United States; Aleksandr Sergeyevich Pushkin in Russia; and Ernst Theodor Amadeus Hoffman in Germany. In many respects, the most influential piece of horror fiction was Bram Stoker's *Dracula* (1897), which was based on folk traditions about corpses that rise up out of the tomb and suck the blood of the living. Stoker's creation, particularly as interpreted by Bela Lugosi in the 1931 film *Dracula*, has greatly shaped modern vampire lore.

W. K. McNeil

See also Dracula; Folktale; Ghosts; Goethe, Johann Wolfgang von; Hawthorne, Nathaniel; Legend; Poe, Edgar Allan; Schiller, Johann Christoph Friedrich; Shakespeare, William; Stoker, Bram; Wild Man

✳✳✳✳✳✳✳✳✳✳✳✳✳✳✳✳✳✳

References

Barber, Paul. *Vampires, Burial, and Death*. New Haven: Yale University Press, 1988.

Briggs, Katharine. *An Encyclopedia of Fairies: Hobgoblins, Brownies, Bogies, and Other Supernatural Creatures*. New York: Pantheon Books, 1976.

Hill, Douglas, and Pat Williams. *The Supernatural*. New York: New American Library, 1974 (1965).

Kittredge, George Lyman. *Witchcraft in Old and New England*. New York: Atheneum, 1972 (1929).

Parson, Coleman O. *Witchcraft & Demonology in Scott's Fiction*. Edinburgh and London: Oliver and Boyd, 1964.

SYDOW, CARL WILHELM VON (1878–1952)

The Swedish folklorist and literary scholar Carl Wilhelm von Sydow was a professor and held the first chair of folklore at Lund University in Sweden; he also founded the journal *Folkminnen och Folktanker* [Folk mentality and folk psychology]. He was known for his controversial views on the study of folk narrative and folk belief, and for his partially successful attempt at establishing an international terminology for use in folkloristics. Throughout his writings, von Sydow emphasized the importance of fieldwork and direct observation of folk traditions in their natural context in order to provide reliable facts upon which abstract theories may be based. His work advanced the study of traditional storytelling communities, illuminating the oral sources of the literary folktale.

In his lectures and articles about folk belief, Sydow confronted the prevailing view, based on the writings of Wilhelm Mannhardt and James G. Frazer, that folk customs and beliefs are survivals of pre-Christian mythology. These scholars, wrote Sydow, only read books about customs and usually failed to observe the customs in practice. They therefore misinterpreted activities that were simply pranks, "youthful frolic," jokes, or even deliberate inventions of the people. For example, stories of a demon or a witch hiding in the final sheaf of grain, told at harvesttime, were not related to ancient fertility cults; rather, the stories were invented by adults to keep children from trampling the crops (1948, pp. 89–105).

The contemporary canonical theories on the diffusion of folktales were also an object of Sydow's criticism. In his essay "On the Spread of Tradition," he attacked the shortcomings of the assumption that tales have a life independent of people. Scholars had failed to study the "biology of tradition"—the complex interrelations among a tradition, the community in which the tradition exists, and the performers of the tradition. Folktales do not travel; it is their performers, the "active bearers of tradition," who travel and are responsible for the diffusion of tales over broad distances (Sydow 1977 [1948], pp. 89–105).

Related to Sydow's theories on diffusion, but less controversial, was his attempt to establish an international terminology for the comparative study of folk traditions, especially folk narratives. Among the terms advocated by Sydow that are still used today is oicotype (also spelled ecotype)—a regional form of an internationally known narrative; an oicotype has acquired unique ethnic, cultural, or historical characteristics as a result of isolation in a given geographical area. The *memorate*, a category of legends, denotes stories people tell about "individual, purely personal experiences." The *fabulate*, also a form of legend, refers to stories about real events that have passed into widespread tradition and have been "transformed by the inventive fantasy of the people." Less currency was gained by Sydow's other terms for folklore genres, among them the *dite*, a tradition that is "not narrative, belief, knowledge, or fiction," for example, the saying "It is sinful to walk backward" (Sydow 1977 [1948], pp. 44–99, 106–145).

Carl Wilhelm von Sydow is remembered today as a teacher who, according to the Swedish scholar Orvar Löfgren, "managed to be an angry young man well into his older days," stimulating students to challenge the canons and clichés of their times (*Nordic Institute of Folklore Newsletter* 2 [1993]:14). The Department of European Ethnology at the University of Lund holds annual memorial lectures in his honor.

Guntis Smidchens

See also Frazer, James George; Tradition

✳✳✳✳✳✳✳✳✳✳✳✳✳✳✳✳✳

References
Berg, Gösta. "Carl Wilhelm von Sydow." In *Biographica: Nordic Folklorists of the Past: Studies in Honor of Jouko Hautala*, ed. Dag Strömback et al., pp. 171–188. Copenhagen: Nordisk Institut for Folkedigtning, 1971.
Sydow, Carl W. *Selected Papers on Folklore*. New York: Arno Press, 1977 (1948).

SYNGE, JOHN MILLINGTON (1871–1909)

The Irish playwright and folklorist, and the youngest son of a peaceful Anglo-Irish Protestant home, John Millington Synge studied the Irish language at Trinity College (Dublin) and later in Paris as well as music in Germany. Absorption in Irish prepared him well for an 1896 meeting with William Butler Yeats, who counseled him: "Go to the Aran Islands. Live there as if you were one of the people themselves; express a life that has never found expression" (Yeats 1961, p. 299). Synge made five visits to those remote western islands, and his affection for the peasants fused with his reticence in a tender ethnography, *The Aran Islands* (1907). For the new Irish dramatic movement he wrote *The Shadow of the Glen* (1903), *Riders to the Sea* (1904), and *The Well of the Saints* (1905) as well as *The Tinker's Wedding* (1905), a bitter farce never performed in his lifetime. *The Playboy of the Western World* (1907) caused demonstrations because of its supposed denigration of an Irish peasantry idealized by nationalists. Synge lived two years after that work was published, working against time and ill health on *Deirdre of the Sorrows* (1910), the tragedy of Ireland's great mythological heroine (put in final form by Yeats and Lady Isabella Augusta Gregory).

Combining the old-fashioned "Cromwellian English" lingering in the Aran Islands with direct translation from Irish, Synge universalized the islanders. Although Irish folklore was not his only source, Synge drew plots and dialogue from his folklore fieldwork. The poor, primitive-seeming peasantry of Aran perfectly conformed to contemporary conceptions of "the folk." The islanders opened to the playwright a world before bourgeois individualism, in which tiny communities preserving folk belief, custom, and speech still relied on the resources of tradition. Synge's ethnography is animated by a delight in the exceptional and the strange. It is easy to infer, from the parallels between *The Aran Islands* and the plays, that Synge was a true realist, but as an ethnographer he often looked to the daily life of Aran for the source of a ceaselessly renewed, sometimes puzzling synthesis of realism and fantasy, rudeness and nostalgia, quotation and elaboration.

As a playwright, Synge transmitted the "perpetual translation" of Irish folk speech into English. He used the vernacular so effectively that each time the word *shift* was heard in *The Playboy of the Western World*, it was a signal for demonstration. A more emphatic proof of the political importance of language cannot be found. But

Synge was no ideologue. Language was not merely Synge's medium; it was the subject matter, says one critic, and became signified instead of signifier. Through language, Christy becomes a playboy, wins Pegeen's heart, and affirms his triumph at the end, realizing a part of himself that he has not known. Synge's most daring experiment in heightening creolized speech was to put peasant language in the mouths of mythological characters in *Deirdre of the Sorrows*, which most pervasively of all his plays embodies his fascination with mutability, mortality, and endless yearning.

Lee Haring

See also Gregory, Lady Isabella Augusta; Yeats, William Butler

✳✳✳✳✳✳✳✳✳✳✳✳✳✳✳✳✳

References

Kiberd, Declan. *Synge and the Irish Language*. Totowa, N.J.: Rowman and Littlefield, 1979.

Kopper, Edward A., Jr., ed. *A J. M. Synge Literary Companion*. New York: Greenwood Press, 1988.

Saddlemyer, Ann. *J. M. Synge and Modern Comedy*. Dublin: Dolmen, 1967.

Yeats, William Butler. *Esssays and Introductions*. New York: Macmillan, 1961.

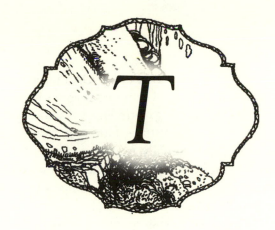

TAIWANESE OPERA

Taiwanese opera (*Ke-Chai Hsi*) is a musical performance of Chinese historical legend or traditional romance in a Minnan dialect. Combining the singing of arias and folk songs with stylized movement and acrobatics, it has developed since Chinese migrated to the island, mainly from the coastal areas of the mainland, during the Ming and Ch'ing dynasties. Taiwanese opera is said to have begun with amateur troupes from the area of I-lan and later spread to other parts of the island. It has become one of the best representatives of a still-flourishing local Chinese opera, as are Hakka Opera and Cantonese Opera. Local opera is distinguished from the Beijing Opera mainly in its use of *Nan-kuan* ("southern style") music and local songs, but *Pei-kuan* ("northern style") music, as in Peking Opera, is usually also performed by contemporary Taiwanese opera troupes.

Traditionally, local opera troupes perform for Buddhist and folk Taoist temples on the birthdays of the deities, for clan observances, and on other special festival occasions. In the 1960s, some troupes were successful enough to enter onto the stages of indoor theaters in the cities, and some performers became popular stars. Since the 1970s, Taiwanese opera has developed a form appropriate to the media of television, and currently, Taiwanese operas are performed in the national theater of Taipei. The Ming Hua Yuan Troupe, active as a traveling family troupe for several generations, has attained professional status by performing for paying audiences, rather than for private patrons or temple organizations, and it has gone abroad on tour. In the folk opera, improvisation according to an orally transmitted scenario has been the norm; however, with increased professionalism and literacy, scripts are now available.

In Taiwanese opera, as in the Beijing Opera, the roles are divided into age, sex, and status groups. Costumes represent traditional Ch'ing dynasty dress, and face-painting distinguishes famous historical figures and their dignity or moral rectitude. However, troupes are composed of both men and women, usually from the same family, and women play the roles of young heroes as well as those of male elders. An especially gifted actress who plays male roles is Yang Li-Hua, who has been a favorite for two decades in the opera produced for television audiences. The role of women in this opera is in sharp contrast to the tradition of male impersonation found in late-nineteenth- and early-twentieth-century Beijing Opera.

The musical instruments used are those found in other forms of southern Chinese folk music and can be divided into wind, percussion, reed, and string instruments. Whereas in the Beijing Opera the instruments are usually located to one side of the stage, symmetry, common to other folk arts in China, is maintained in the local Taiwanese opera performances by having the percussion instruments to one side of the stage and the other instruments on the opposite side. Symmetry of movement and staging is also more pronounced in the local operatic form, but is largely absent in the professional productions on the stage and on television.

A field study carried out in 1975–1977 by Patricia Haseltine revealed that in the repertoires of two troupes, the Wang Ting Troupe and the Ming Hua Yuan Troupe, there was a proliferation of identifiable Thompson folk motifs and a number of folktale types. Such types as "The Three Stolen Princesses" (AT 301), "The Man on a Quest for His Lost Wife" (AT 400), "The Swan Maiden" (AT 465C), "The Extraordinary Companions" (AT 513–514), "Faithful John" (AT 516), "The Strong Woman as Bride" (AT 519), "The Prophecy" (AT 930), and "Foolish Bridegroom" (AT1685) were found in the scenarios of the troupes' street and temple performances. As in the Chinese variants of these tales, the themes emphasized in the dramas were the Confucian virtues of faithfulness, filiality, chastity, and brotherhood. Whereas the matter of some plays consisted of traditional historical legends of China, occasionally a troupe director-manager devised more contemporary plots. In such cases, traditional motifs were still applied, even though they were combined with new ones in a new story.

Patricia Haseltine

See also Chinese Opera; Dialect; Folktale; Legend; Motif; Performance

✳✳✳✳✳✳✳✳✳✳✳✳✳✳✳✳✳
References

Aarni, Antti, and Stith Thompson. *The Types of the Folktale: A Classification and Bibliography*. Folklore Fellows Communication no. 184. Helsinki: Academia Scientiarum Fennica, 1964.

Haseltine, Patricia. "Folk Enactment in Taiwanese Local Opera." Ph.D. dissertation, Indiana University, 1979.

Mackerras, Colin. *Chinese Theater: From Its Origins to the Present Day*. Honolulu: University of Hawaii Press, 1983.

———. "The Growth of the Chinese Regional Drama in the Ming and Ch'ing." *Journal of Oriental Studies* 9:1 (1971): 1–30.

Young, Lung-chang. "The Dynamics of Popular Culture: Regional Theaters in Kiangsu." *Journal of Popular Culture* 7 (1973): 51–67.

TALE-TYPE

A tale-type is a recurring pattern of narrative plot elements or motifs. It is not a story itself but a basic outline that is common to, and abstracted from, the many variants of a widespread tale. There have been many oral and literary redactions of traditional tales by peoples in various countries and eras. The pattern of motifs in each of these redactions enables us to identify them as variants of a single story or tale-type. Although there is a recognizable family resemblance among variants, they are not identical. Often the details that fill out the basic plot are quite different.

The term *tale-type* is associated with the Finnish school founded by Finnish folklorists Julius (1835–1888) and Kaarle (1863–1933) Krohn. When Kaarle Krohn noted that tales in various national archives had remarkably similar plotlines, he formulated the concept of tale-type. His student, Antti Aarne (1867–1925), used this concept to develop a system for the classification of the international folktale. This resulted in Aarne's 1910 index, *The Types of the Folktale (Verzeichnis der Märchentypen)*, later expanded upon by the American folklorist Stith Thompson (1885–1976) in 1928 and again in 1961. The index assigned a number to each of over 2,000 Indo-European tale-types, and folklorists often refer to international tales by their Aarne-Thompson, or AT, number.

All the tales that Aarne grouped together as a type were assumed to have had historical contact with each other. That is, the similarity between the tales resulted from diffusion of an archetypal tale that had originated in one country. The Finnish school attempted to trace the geographical and chronological diffusion of the tale-type back to its original time and place of origin by studying all known literary and oral forms of the tale.

Dated literary versions of tales shown to represent an early or late form of the tale were helpful for scholars interested in determining the tale-type's age since the original oral version was deemed the most complete. For example, in his book *The Folktale* (1946) Thompson explains that since the version of the tale of Cupid and Psyche found in Apuleius's writings of the second century C.E. is a more highly developed form of the tale than that told in modern Europe, the date of the archetype must be well before the common era. One of the most exhaustive studies of a tale-type is Walter Anderson's work on "Emperor and Abbot" (AT 922). Anderson found 571 versions, over 150 of which were literary, and placed the oral origin in the seventh century, finding literary versions dating back to the ninth century.

The Finnish school also reconstructed the hypothetical archetype or ur-form (original form) of tale-types. The Finnish method follows the classical philological program, and, indeed, the classical philologist Karl Lachmann (1793–1851), often cited as the father of modern textual criticism, used similar methodology in his efforts to reconstruct classical works of Greece and Rome. Lachman assembled all extant texts of a given work, compared them closely, and corrected imperfections to restore the work to what he determined was its original form.

The Finnish school has been criticized, partially because it highlights the phenomenon of similarity among international texts and often neglects the equally fascinating phenomenon of variation among those texts. Still, the study of variants as a tale-type should not overshadow interest in the astounding persistence of the general type.

Ilana Harlow

See also Anderson, Walter; Historic-Geographic Method; Krohn, Leopold Kaarle; Oicotype; Sydow, Carl Wilhelm von

✻✻✻✻✻✻✻✻✻✻✻✻✻✻✻✻✻

References

Anderson, Walter. *Kaiser und Abt*. Folklore Fellows Communication no. 42. Helsinki: Academia Scientiarum Fennica, 1923.

Krohn, Kaarle. *Folklore Methodology*. Trans. Roger L. Welsch. Austin: University of Texas Press, 1971.

Roberts, Warren E. *The Tale of the Kind and Unkind Girls*. Berlin: De Gruyter, 1958.

Thompson, Stith. *The Folktale*. Berkeley: University of California Press, 1977 (1946).

TALL TALE

The tall tale is a humorous folk narrative that uses outrageous exaggeration within the frame of a realistic story—in certain situations, in order to perpetuate a hoax. There are also many performance contexts in which the storyteller is already known for his or her reputation as a liar. Mody Boatright (1961) has pointed out that the tall tale involves more than mere exaggeration and that it employs a number of artistic devices such as "ludicrous imagery" to involve and entertain the audience. Texas storyteller Ed Bell told of the time he caught 15–20 big fish in a fog so thick that when the fog lifted he found himself 10 miles from the nearest water. He had the reputation of being "the biggest liar on the Texas coast."

The tall tale is usually associated with American literature, but it finds expression in a wide range of world literatures, from Philippe d'Alcripe's sixteenth-century text *La Nouvelle fabrique des excellents traits de vérité* [The new factory of excellent drafts of truth] and R. E. Raspe's eighteenth-century *Baron Münchhausen's Narratives of His Marvellous Travels and Campaigns in Russia*, to the modern fabrications of Gabriel García Márquez's *One Hundred Years of Solitude* (1970) and Ishmael Reed's *Yellow Back Radio Broke Down* (1969). These examples also illustrate the variety of ways tall tales can be adapted to literature: d'Alcripe's attempt to render accurately orally told tales on the printed page, Raspe's rewriting of Baron Münchhausen's tales in a high literary style, Márquez's transformation of fantastic exaggeration into magic realism, and Reed's satiric send-up of American heroes from an African-American perspective. As with most folklore forms, the history of the tall tale is a complex interweaving of oral and literary influences that has complicated the task of defining the genre.

At least from the time of d'Alcripe's collection of French tales, the tall tale has been intimately connected with a teller who is often presented as the hero of the story. The tall-tale hero is sometimes confused with the legend hero, especially in American folklore and literature. The differences are significant, since the legend is a serious belief genre and the tall tale is a fictional and humorous one, although it uses realistic devices in order to "set up" the listener. The confusion is partially owing to the fact that the characteristics of the tall tale and legend hero overlap in American folklore. Davy Crockett was a legendary hero in that he was a historical figure and belief stories were told about his exploits, but he also used the tall tale as a means of promoting himself.

Another area of confusion is between the tall tale, a narrative form, and tall talk, nonnarrative folk language. A character in literature may boast of his exploits (the boasting tradition is usually associated with men in American folklore) in a stylized fashion and also be a tall-tale hero. The American legendary hero Mike Fink was a braggart who engaged in tall talk and told tall tales with himself as hero, but every tall-tale storyteller does not necessarily use tall talk. Ed Bell told numerous tall tales about himself, but he eschewed tall talk.

Tall tales go back to the time of the colonies in American literary history, with Benjamin Franklin using them to hoax readers of a London newspaper, but perhaps the greatest literary use of the tall tale came in the early nineteenth century and the southwestern humorists. Such writers as Thomas Bangs Thorpe, George Washington Harris, and Augustus Baldwin Longstreet employed frontier folklore, including the tall tale, in their sketches and stories published in such newspapers as the *Spirit of the Times*, and they established a precedent for Mark Twain's uses of frontier humor.

Tall tales, tall talk, and tall-tale heroes have continued to be used in literature in various ways. One of the most important techniques has been in the literary representation of the folk storytelling context as a means of manipulating the narrative frame. Mark Twain was a master of this technique, using the eastern gentleman as narrator to set up the local western storyteller in order to evoke humor and comment on regional differences in such stories as "The Notorious Jumping Frog of Calaveras County" and "The Story of the Old Ram." The American tall-tale hero is updated by Ishmael Reed in a story from *Yellow Back Radio Broke Down*: the Loop Garoo Kid mixes tall talk, ludicrous imagery, African-American voodoo, and Old West clichés with references to cars, talk shows, and multinational corporations in order to satirize contemporary American society. The tall tale is alive in twentieth-century literature but with decidedly self-conscious modern twists.

Patrick B. Mullen

See also Twain, Mark

✳✳✳✳✳✳✳✳✳✳✳✳✳✳✳

References

Boatright, Mody C. *Folk Laughter on the American Frontier*. New York: Collier Books, 1961.

Brown, Carolyn S. *The Tall Tale in American Folklore and Literature*. Knoxville: University of Tennessee Press, 1987.

Cohen, Hennig, and William B. Dillingham, eds. *Humor of the Old Southwest*. Boston: Houghton Mifflin, 1964.

Mullen, Patrick B. *I Heard the Old Fishermen Say: Folklore of the Texas Gulf Coast*. Austin: University of Texas Press, 1978.

Thomas, Gerald. *The Tall Tale of Phillipe D'Alcripe*. St. John's, Newfoundland: Memorial University, 1977.

THE TAMING OF THE SHREW

The Taming of the Shrew, a comedy by William Shakespeare, written about 1596 and published in the folio of 1623, is based in part on a widespread folktale known by the same title. In the folktale example (AT 901), the shrewish wife is tamed when her husband kills his dog and his horse for their disobedience and threatens to do the same to her if she opposes him. Later, the husband tests his wife's changed behavior by forcing her to agree to absurd statements, and finally, he wins a wager on his wife's obedience when she comes at once when called while the wives of two other men delay. Similar to AT 901, and sometimes joined with it, is "The Lazy Cat" (AT 1370), in which a husband beats his cat (or an inanimate object) for not working while forcing his wife to hold that which is being beaten, thus simultaneously being beaten herself. (AT 1370 is related to Child 277, "The Wife Wrapt in Wether's Skin.")

A profusion of early "shrewish wife" stories—more-or-less similar to each other—and an anonymous English play, "The Taming of a Shrew" complicate the question of the origin of Shakespeare's plot. One interesting text is in Don Juan Manuel's collection *El Conde Lucanor* [Count Lucanor], written about 1335 and published in Spanish in 1575 but not translated into English until the nineteenth century. One chapter contains the standard tamed-wife plot, and another chapter describes forcing a wife to agree to absurdities.

The subplot of Shakespeare's play was adapted from a literary source, and the setting of the play is Italy. Only the taming plot derives from the folktale. It centers on the husband's—Petrucchio's—tormenting and taming his wife, Katharina, by outdoing her in shrewishness. The horse-killing episode of the folktale is relegated to offstage action in the play and is summarized in a speech by Petrucchio's servant; the action is modified by having the master irrationally beat the *servant* after the bride's horse stumbles. Katharina is forced to agree with Petrucchio's absurd statements when they travel to visit her father; in the wager scene, she comes immediately when called, and she kisses her husband at his command to do so.

Shakespeare's source for the taming plot was most likely an oral text of the folktale rather than any published text. The presence of such an oral tradition is suggested by the preponderance of AT 901 versions from northern Europe and especially by a particularly complete text that appeared in *The Tatler* in 1710. Although described by essayist, playwrite, and politician Richard Steele (1672–1729) as a story he learned from "a family wherein I was several year an intimate acquaintance . . . in Lincolnshire" (*The Tatler*, September 30, 1710), this version was denounced by Samuel Johnson in his edition of Shakespeare as a plagiarism from the play. Comparative study suggests the opposite—that Shakespeare's own taming plot borrowed from an English oral tradition of which *The Tatler* version is a late example, authentic in all its details although somewhat literary in style.

In the United States, Shakespeare's comedy inspired the musical *Kiss Me Kate*, and in modern oral tradition, AT 901 survives as a joke—referring to the wife's first transgression in the same words used to warn the stumbling horse—with the punch line, "That's once!"

Jan Harold Brunvand

See also Shakespeare, William; Tale-Type

❋❋❋❋❋❋❋❋❋❋❋❋❋❋❋❋❋

References

Brunvand, Jan Harold. "The Folktale Origin of *The Taming of the Shrew*." *Shakespeare Quarterly* 17 (1966): 345–359.

———. *The Taming of the Shrew: A Comparative Study of Oral and Literary Versions*. New York: Garland, 1991.

———. "The Taming of the Shrew Tale in the United States." In *The Study of American Folklore: An Introduction*, 2d ed., Jan Harold Brunvand, ed., pp. 360–371. New York: W. W. Norton, 1978.

TAYLOR, ARCHER (1890–1973)

Archer Taylor was a scholar of folklore, Germanic studies (late medieval to early modern literature and culture), bibliography, and book production. The list of his writings is lengthy and shows the wide range of his interests. Taylor was educated at Swarthmore College in languages and literatures with an emphasis in German, received a master's degree in German in 1910 from the University of Pennsylvania, and received his Ph.D. in German from Harvard in 1915, with a dissertation on the Wolfdietrich epics. During his career, he taught at Pennsylvania State University, Washington University in St. Louis, the University of Chicago, and the University of California at Berkeley.

His work in folklore began at Washington University when he began contributing to journals such as *Modern Language Notes, Modern Philology,* and the *Journal of American Folklore*. While at Chicago, he introduced folklore into the fields of study for the doctorate in the Department of Germanic Languages and helped build up the library collections, including holdings in Middle High German literature. His literary and comparative work in folklore focused especially on proverbs, riddles, folk songs and ballads, and folktales. His publications on proverbs and riddles alone include collections or studies of material (and this list is by no means exhaustive) from Scotland, Ireland, Wales, England, Armenia, Turkey, Italy, India, Mongolia, Japan, ancient Rome, and the United States—from California, Michigan, the Ozarks, and North Carolina as well as riddles among Native Americans and transplanted groups such as the Poles in Michigan.

One of the founders of the California Folklore Society and the society's journal, *California Folklore Quarterly* (now *Western Folklore*), Taylor also was one of the founders and editors of the journal *Proverbium*. Beginning in 1945, he published bibliographical guides on the history of books and of libraries; collected early volumes both for himself and for various libraries; and served on the general-bibliography staff of the Modern Language Association of America. He was elected to numerous offices in professional societies and was the recipient of honorary degrees and twice a Guggenheim Fellow. He had a justly deserved reputation for offering help, generosity, and hospitality—entertaining in the book-lined rural California house he and his wife built by hand or in his equally book-lined house in Berkeley Hills. He is still remembered as one of the key figures in American folklore studies: works such as *The Proverb* (1931) and *English Riddles from Oral Tradition* (1951) continue to be regarded as classics.

Pamela S. Morgan

See also Epic; Modern Language Association of America (MLA); Proverbs; Riddle

✳✳✳✳✳✳✳✳✳✳✳✳✳✳✳✳✳

References

Hand, Wayland D. "Writings of Archer Taylor on Proverbs and Proverbial Lore." *Proverbium* 15 (1970): 4–8.

Loomis, C. Grant, with additional material by Elli Kaija Köngäs and Richard M. Dorson. "Bibliography of the Writings of Archer Taylor." In *Humanoria: Essays in Literature, Folklore, Bibliography, Honoring Archer Taylor on His Seventieth Birthday*, ed. Wayland D. Hand and Gustave O. Arlt, pp. 356–374. Locust Valley, N.Y.: J. J. Augustin, 1960.

Taylor, Archer. *"The Proverb" and "An Index to 'The Proverb.'"* Intro. and biblio. by Wolfgang Mieder. New York: Peter Lang, 1985.

———. *Selected Writings on Proverbs.* Ed. Wolfgang Mieder. Folklore Fellows Communication no. 216. Helsinki: Academia Scientiarum Fennica, 1975.

Zumwalt, Rosemary Levy. *American Folklore Scholarship.* Bloomington: Indiana University Press, 1988.

THEME

A theme is the subject—the fundamental idea—of a text. Folktale scholarship recognizes a hierarchy of theme, tale-type, episode, and motif. The theme is general, such as rich versus poor, appearance versus reality, treachery, or help from otherworldly powers. The tale-type outlines the plot of the story. The separable sections of a complex tale are its motif complexes, or episodes, and the particular details are called motifs. Tale-types that share a common theme often share certain episodes as well; in that case, they belong to a cycle or a complex of tales.

Comparative folktale scholarship has been shaped by scholars of literature, and the idea that old plots are recycled in new literary works continues to fascinate. Thus, English-speaking literary scholars trace the theme of Don Juan, of Faust (a bargain with the devil), or of the quest for the Holy Grail. Germans make a distinction between *Thema* ("theme") and *Stoffe* ("material"). According to German literary scholars Horst Dämmrich and Ingrid Dämmrich:

> Differences among scholars arise in regard to the level of abstraction assigned to a theme. The most ardent supporters of thematic studies believe that themes capture fundamental conceptions of human relationships.
>
> . . . Themes are central organizational units of texts. Themes, figures, motifs, motif sequences, and metaphoric correlates are mutually dependent. (Dämmrich and Dämmrich 1987, pp. 240–241)

In oral-formulaic theory, themes are the typical scenes from which the narrative is built. Some examples are an assembly, the arrival of a messenger, the arming of a hero, and disguise followed by recognition. Names and other details are chosen to fit each story. Thus, any particular story is made up of a series of themes, and the same themes are recycled in different stories.

The definition of themes has been controversial in ballad classification. Phrases such as "emotional core," "plot gist," and "central focus" imply that each ballad type has a single theme. However, such narrative units, when identified, are found to combine together in clusters, and many ballads have more than a single such theme.

Although a theme is supposed to be abstract and a motif is supposed to be concrete, according to dictionary definitions the words can be synonymous. And indeed, particularly if a text is short and its subject is distinctive, the theme might well be a motif in the folkloric sense of the term. Folktale scholar Stith Thompson included many simple tales in his *Motif Index* (1955–1958). If a longer, complex narrative is broken up into sections, the theme of each part is likely to be a motif: many folktale episodes were assigned motif numbers, and others deserve to have them. Thus, defining the theme of a work is a matter of interpretation and is more or less subjective. What to one observer looks like a theme, another calls a motif.

Christine Goldberg

See also Motif; Oral-Formulaic Composition and Theory; Tale-Type

✳✳✳✳✳✳✳✳✳✳✳✳✳✳✳✳✳✳

References

Christiansen, Arthur. *Motif et thème*. Folklore Fellows Communication no. 59. Helsinki: Academia Scientiarum Fennica, 1925.

Dämmrich, Horst, and Ingrid Dämmrich. *Themes and Motifs in Western Literature: A Handbook.* Tübingen: Francke, 1987.

Foley, John Miles. *The Theory of Oral Composition.* Bloomington and Indianapolis: Indiana University Press, 1988.

Frenzel, Elisabeth. *Stoffe der Weltliteratur: Ein Lexikon.* 7th ed. Stuttgart: Alfred Kröner, 1988.

Long, Eleanor. "Ballad Classification and the 'Narrative Theme' Concept." In *Ballad Research,* ed. Hugh Shields, pp. 197–213. Dublin: Folk Music Society of Ireland, 1986.

THOMPSON, FLORA (1876–1947)

Flora Thompson is best known for her trilogy *Lark Rise to Candleford* (1939–1943). Set in the 1880s, her childhood in the hamlet of Lark Rise (Juniper Hill, Oxfordshire) and adolescence in the small town she called Candleford embody a transition from ancient to modern in rural English life. The books combine the earnestness of autobiography—Laura, the heroine, is transparently Thompson's childhood self, Flora Timms—with the objectivity of the novel. They have been used as ethnography by folklorists, questioned as an account of social conditions by historians, and enjoyed by a wide number of readers who find Thompson's intimate account of rural folklife engrossing and credible.

The works' persuasiveness lies in the details: minor and mundane, they combine to form the most densely textured account of vernacular culture in the canon of English rural literature. This texture is particularly achieved through speech: we hear people talking throughout, and there is hardly a page on which some proverbial phrase is not quoted, summoning an attitude and creating an atmosphere. Laura, a withdrawn child (like many autobiographers), is depicted as overhearing gossip or attracting confidences because of her quietness. She gives the impression of having been present at every cultural scene she describes, from children's play and schooling to women's and men's respective ways of talking about sex, an uncanonical topic in this literature. Most of the material is taken from memory, but other rural-life books may have had more influence than is apparent: the title of the last chapter honors George Sturt's *Change in the Village* (1912).

The material cannot all have been from personal recollection given that Thompson began *Lark Rise* when she was 50 years old, 30 years after leaving Oxfordshire. Her method in reassembling these memories can be seen in her last novel, *Still Glides the Stream*, in which an older woman revisits her native village, talks to survivors from her childhood era, and gains "details she had forgotten, or had not known . . . their varying viewpoints threw crosslights on happenings already in her mind" (Thompson 1948, p. 16). Her reminiscences were thus qualified by ethnographic interviews.

Folklorist Roger deV. Renwick draws on *Lark Rise to Candleford* for its contextual account of public-house singing and to support his reading of a symbolic code of folk metaphor in English folk poetry. Debora G. Kodish, another folklorist, finds material on women's artful gossip, and the social historian Barbara English argues that Thompson constructed "a past which never really existed" by suppressing details of death, illness, and exploitative working conditions. Nevertheless Thompson was not a naive retailer of "the merrie England myth"; she sought a balanced view of the good and bad in the old way of life. Her own life was not a perfectly happy one, whether at Juniper Hill or after, and the story told between the lines is of the disappointments, rebuffs, and disillusionments of a sensitive and clever girl in a culture that derided learning and saw cleverness as harmful to the chances of a working-class girl or boy.

Martin Lovelace

See also Sturt, George

✳✳✳✳✳✳✳✳✳✳✳✳✳✳✳✳✳

References

English, Barbara. "*Lark Rise* and Juniper Hill: A Victorian Community in Literature and History." *Victorian Studies* 29:1 (1985): 7–34.

Kodish, Debora G. "Moving towards the Everyday: Some Thoughts on Gossip and Visiting as Secular Procession." In *Folklore Papers of the University Folklore Association* no. 9, pp. 93–104. Austin: University of Texas at Austin, 1980.

Lane, Margaret. "Flora Thompson." *Cornhill Magazine* 1011 (1957): 145–165.

Pickering, Michael. "Popular Song at Juniper Hill." *Folk Music Journal* 4 (1984): 481–503.

Renwick, Roger deV. *English Folk Poetry: Structure and Meaning*. Philadelphia: University of Pennsylvania Press, 1980.

Thompson, Flora. *Lark Rise* (1939); *Over to Candleford* (1941); *Candleford Green* (1943): all issued as *Lark Rise to Candleford*. London: Oxford University Press, 1945; London: Penguin Modern Classics series, 1973.

———. *Still Glides the Stream*. London: Oxford University Press, 1948.

Thompson, Stith (1885–1976)

Arguably "the father of American folklore," Stith Thompson was for the five decades before his death the best known of American folklorists and the most influential force in the field. One cannot study American folklore without coming across his name innumerable times and always in important contexts.

He was born in Kentucky; attended Butler University, the University of Wisconsin (M.A.), and the University of California; and earned his Ph.D. from Harvard in 1914. His dissertation, "European Borrowings and Parallels in North American Indian Tales," was directed by the illustrious George Lyman Kittredge, and the experience was to influence the rest of Thompson's professional life. Harvard was, at the time, a leading center for the study of folklore in America, and at the time, folklore study was based in the English Department. Kittredge, himself a student and colleague of the ballad scholar Francis James Child, was a distinguished scholar of medieval and Renaissance literature and knowledgeable about folklore. Thompson learned a great deal about those literary areas from his mentor, and his book *The Folktale* (1946) is laced with examples from medieval literature.

Thompson went to Indiana University in 1921 to teach courses in literature and folklore and there began efforts to establish folklore as a university subject. His efforts culminated in the formation of the country's first folklore Ph.D. program at Indiana in 1953, and since that time, many distinguished folklore scholars have graduated from that university. Simultaneously, Thompson worked to establish folklore courses and programs at other universities around the country, and from them, as well, other prominent folkloric scholars have been produced. In these ways, he helped established folklore study as a serious American discipline.

During his decades at Indiana University, he edited and saw through publication *The Types of the Folktale* (1964) and the monumental *Motif Index of Folk Literature* (1955–1958). These works alone would have established him as his nation's leading folklore scholar, but he also published *European Tales among the North American Indians* (1919), *Tales of the North American Indians* (1929), *The Folktale* (1946), and *One Hundred Favorite Folktales* (1968). The influence of his dissertation in several of these volumes is obvious.

Thompson introduced many American folklorists to the theories and methods of analysis being done on the folktale by the Finns, thus introducing the American scholarly community to European folktale scholarship. His lengthy and detailed essay on the Indian "Star Husband Tale" demonstrated the historic-geographic method to an English-speaking North American audience, and his editions of the folktale types and the motif index provided the tools that enable this research to be performed.

When the focus of folklore scholarship shifted in the 1950s away from a study of the folkloric item as text-based entity to the folkloric transmission act as a communicative event, Thompson's research, his scholarly editions, and his influence began to decline. Nevertheless, his contributions have been enormous; no other American scholar has been as important or as influential.

Warren Roberts

See also Aarne, Antti; Historic-Geographic Method; Kittredge, George Lyman

✳✳✳✳✳✳✳✳✳✳✳✳✳✳✳✳✳

References

Thompson, Stith. *European Tales among the North American Indians*. Colorado Springs: Colorado College, 1919.

———. *The Folktale*. New York: Dryden Press, 1946.

———. *Motif Index of Folk Literature*. 6 vols. Rev. ed. Bloomington: Indiana University Press, 1955–1958.

———. *Tales of the North Americans Indians*. Cambridge: Harvard University Press, 1929.

Thompson, Stith, and Antti Aarne. *The Types of the Folktale: A Classification and Bibliography*. Folklore Fellows Communication no. 184. Helsinki: Academia Scientiarum Fennica, 1964.

*T*HE THOUSAND AND ONE NIGHTS

The Thousand and One Nights, or, *1001 Nights*, or, more accurately, the *Thousand Nights and a Night* (Arabic, *"Alf layla wa-layla"*), is a medieval Arabic frame tale mentioned in ninth-century commentaries, although the earliest extant manuscript dates from the fourteenth century. The framing story of Shahrazad, who narrates stories night after night to escape the wrath of her tyrannical husband Shahrayar, is believed to have had its roots in Persian tradition, where it was known as *Hazar afsaneh* [Thousand stories].

In The Thousand and One Nights, *Shahrazad escapes the wrath of her tyrannic husband Shahrayar by continuously telling stories; this medieval collection of folk stories, such as "Aladdin," "Ali Baba," and "Sinbad," has influenced literature worldwide.*

The stories within *1001 Nights* come from a variety of sources, both written and oral, and most have analogues in other traditions. The fourteenth-century manuscript, recently edited by Muhsin Mahdi, is also the shortest of the versions, containing 40 stories spread over 271 nights. Nineteenth-century versions contain many more tales and a greater variety as well, including fables and fairy tales in addition to the folktales and romances of earliest versions. In fact, most of the stories that have been most popular in the West—"Aladdin," "Ali Baba," "Sinbad"—were late additions. Most scholars agree that the later Arabic versions of the *1001 Nights* have been influenced not only by the continuing oral storytelling tradition, but also by European translations. In the nineteenth century, particularly, there was a great effort made to stretch the collection out to include precisely 1,001 nights, even though the medieval Arabic 1001 merely represented a large number.

Antoine Galland translated the *1001 Nights* into French in 1704, and since then the story has enjoyed popularity as a literary work in the West. Many translations into English were made in the nineteenth century, and the work subsequently known as the *Arabian Nights* has had a profound impact on European and American literature since that time. Diverse authors—John Barth, Jorge Luis Borges, Samuel Taylor Coleridge, Joseph Conrad, Charles Dickens, James Joyce, Edgar Allan Poe, Marcel Proust, Alfred, Lord Tennyson, H. G. Wells, William Butler Yeats, and others—have been drawn to the *1001 Nights* not only because of its complex structure as a frame tale, which can accommodate any number of smaller narratives, but also because of the European fascination with the East. Translators sought exotic tales to supplement the existing Arabic texts, and some were rumored even to have written the works themselves and represented them as having Arabic sources.

In the Arab world, however, the *1001 Nights* has until very recently received little scholarly attention because it was considered more a product of the folk tradition. Emerging from oral storytelling, the language of the *1001 Nights* is colloquial, as until the twentieth century, formal prose was reserved for scholarly and philosophical writings rather than fiction. Even though the *1001 Nights* has often been demeaned as containing insignificant stories "fit for only women and children," it has maintained its popularity in the oral tradition from the ninth century to the present. The *1001 Nights* has played important roles in both the folk and literary traditions as a conduit for oral tales across linguistic and cultural boundaries, as the inspiration for other medieval frame tales, and as the raw material for many imaginative prose works, both in the East and the West. Through its diverse ancestors and descendants, it epitomizes the interaction between folk and literary narrative.

Bonnie D. Irwin

See also Frame Tale; *Märchen*

✳✳✳✳✳✳✳✳✳✳✳✳✳✳✳✳✳✳

References

Haddawy, Husain, trans. *The Arabian Nights, Based on the Text of the Fourteenth-Century Syrian Manuscript Edited by Muhsin Mahdi*. New York: W. W. Norton, 1990.

Irwin, Robert. *The Arabian Nights: A Companion*. New York: Penguin, 1994.

Mahdi, Muhsin. *The Thousand and One Nights*. Leiden: E. J. Brill, 1995.

Pinault, David. *Story-Telling Techniques in the Arabian Nights*. Leiden: E. J. Brill, 1992.

TOLKIEN, J. R. R. (JOHN RONALD REUEL)
(1892–1973)

A philologist, scholar of Anglo-Saxon and Middle English literatures, and novelist, J. R. R. (John Ronald Reuel) Tolkien was born
in Bloemfontein, South Africa. He was taken to England at the age
of four, was subsequently educated there, and later became a professor at Oxford University. His fame as a novelist came from his
heroic-quest trilogy, *The Lord of the Rings* (1954–1955). Set in the
fictional world of Middle-earth and chronicling the struggle between
good and evil forces for possession of a magical ring of power, the
trilogy consists of *The Fellowship of the Ring* (1954), *The Two Towers*
(1954), and *The Return of the King* (1955). Tolkien prefaced the story
told in the trilogy with *The Hobbit* (1937), a novel he wrote for his
children. A "prequel," *The Silmarillion* (1977), appeared posthumously in the same year as an authorized biography by Humphrey
Carpenter.

In a famous 1936 lecture (published in 1937 under the title
"Beowulf: The Monsters and the Critics"), Tolkien praised the epic
poem *Beowulf* for its "surveying a past . . . noble and fraught with
a deep significance." Not coincidentally, Tolkien's own works on
Middle-earth suggest a similar sense of depth. One can recognize temporal patterns by reading the trilogy (a story of Middle-earth's Third
Age) in light of *The Silmarillion* (a history of the First and Second
Ages) and thus span a period of over 7,000 years. Tolkien also fostered
a sense of familiarity concerning Middle-earth's cultural environment
by utilizing oral literature, custom, and lore from our own world's
Norse, Scandinavian, Germanic, Celtic, and Anglo-Saxon cultures.

In addition to borrowing generic features of the epic and the
quest narrative, Tolkien dipped into specific works such as the Norse
Elder Edda for the names of 16 of his dwarfs, for the name of the wizard Gandalf, and for adaptable plot elements such as the story of the
warrior Sigurth's taking of the evil dwarf Andvari's corrupting and
doom-bringing golden ring. Like Tolkien's "one ring," this ring was
eventually destroyed by fire along with its last owner. Tolkien's narratives also recall Teutonic and Scandinavian lore of the unquiet
dead; the tradition of named and lineaged weapons (e.g., Aragorn's
sword Andúril); the story of the god Odin's winning out against the
giant Vafthrudnir by asking not an actual riddle, but a question to
which only Odin knew the answer (which parallels the tale in *The*

TOLKIEN, J. R. R.

Hobbit of hero Bilbo Baggins asking the inappropriate question "What have I got in my pocket?" of his opponent Gollum during their riddle duel); and, as an echo of poetic kennings, the association of individual characters with multiple names and titles (e.g., Gandalf as "Mithrandir," "the Grey Pilgrim," etc.).

From European oral narrative in general, Tolkien borrowed the character types of the knight hero (Aragorn), the unlikely hero (Frodo), the princess (Arwen), and the monster (e.g., trolls) as well as developing versions of nature deities (e.g., Tom Bombadil, the Ents). From Celtic lore in particular, he patterned his elves after the Sidhe, remnants of the Irish Tuatha Dé Danaan who, though diminished in power, still retained earthly existence. As with Tolkien's elves and the land of Valinor, the Sidhe eventually left earth to return to their homeland, Tir na nOg. Other elements allude to works of Anglo-Saxon literature: Tolkien's goblin characters, the orcs, are named after the Old English *orcneâs* ("hell-corpses") mentioned in *Beowulf* (line 112). Further, Bilbo's encounter with the dragon Smaug in *The Hobbit* recalls the story in *Beowulf* (lines 2,208–2,845) of the theft of a cup from a dragon's barrow and the dragon's vengeful rampage, which brings about its death. Given such groundings in tradition, Tolkien's modern epic skillfully bridges the literary worlds of the remembered and the invented.

Danielle M. Roemer

See also *Beowulf*; Celtic Literature; *The Dragon Slayer*; *Edda, Poetic*; *Edda, Prose*; Epic; Heroic Pattern; *Nibelungenlied*

✣✣✣✣✣✣✣✣✣✣✣✣✣✣✣✣✣

References

Noel, Ruth S. *The Mythology of Middle Earth.* Boston: Houghton Mifflin, 1977.

Shippey, T. A. "Creation from Philology in *The Lord of the Rings.*" In *J. R. R. Tolkien, Scholar and Storyteller: Essays in Memoriam*, ed. Mary Salu and Robert T. Farrell, pp. 286–308. Ithaca, N.Y.: Cornell University Press, 1979.

———. *The Road to Middle Earth.* 2nd ed. London: HarperCollins.

Tolkien, J. R. R. "*Beowulf*: The Monsters and the Critics." *Proceedings of the British Academy* 22 (1937): 245–295.

TRADITION

Tradition is one of the key concepts in folkloristics, and understanding it has been a preoccupation of folklorists since the beginning of the discipline. Early folklorists thought that tradition was passed on (diffused) through time and space either unchanged or "corrupted" by its bearers and that it consisted of unwritten knowledge (lore) surviving from ancient times into the modern age without much contemporary meaning or function.

Later it was recognized that variation is an integral part of tradition, resulting from the diffusion through oral means or by imitation. It was further recognized that for tradition to survive in a group (folk), it had to have a function. By the 1960s, tradition was generally defined as the passage of oral, gestural, material, and customary lore from one person, place, and generation to another by word of mouth or by imitation.

Tradition was thought to be preserved in societies by the "collective memory" of the group. This idea is a classic reification: groups cannot have memories, only individuals can. Thus, a collective memory cannot exist in the real world. Since Edward Shils (1981) recognized tradition as a process—not just the products produced by it—collective memory can only be recognized as a metaphor for the interaction or negotiation of tradition among group members. Roger Janelli (1976) referred to the reified collective memory as a macrolevel of tradition. Only on the negotiated, performance level, or microlevel, does tradition guide behavior and social interaction. Ways of practicing a specific tradition in the past are remembered, forgotten, changed, preserved, argued, deliberately changed, in short, renegotiated among group members to fit the contemporary context. When the tradition is performed, it is individually remembered by group members as it was practiced and again becomes macrolevel tradition until it is recalled for renegotiation and performance in the future.

From its enculturation by young children, tradition, then, may be considered a process originating as learned behavior. It is not deduced from reason or logic; it is not a part of personal experience learned by oneself; it is not a part of instinctive or inherited genetic behavior. Most of what one learns, one learns from members of one's own society, who pass on great amounts of information. But all behavior learned from others is not traditional, only that which contributes to group identity. Thus, tradition may be defined as learned behavior that contributes to group identity and exists in unstandardized multiple variation.

At the microlevel, tradition exhibits both continuity and change to meet the needs of the specific context of its performance. Thus, through time and over the areas in which a specific tradition has diffused, tradition is dynamic. Modern inventions like writing and various forms of media tend to have a standardizing effect on tradition, minimizing, though not eliminating, the possibilities for variation that exist in the oral tradition. Some folklorists make claims that "real" or "authentic" tradition can exist only in the oral tradition, but the fact is that tradition exists in both oral and printed forms. Another observation is that the older the tradition, the more variation it tends to exhibit. The end product of a traditional form may be unrecognizable from earlier forms of the same tradition.

Although it may be important for the group dynamic to believe that traditions are ancient, some are in fact recent inventions. The difference between fads and traditions may be minimal, though fads may not contribute to group cohesion as strongly as traditions. Shils declares a form to be traditional if it diffuses into a third generation; that is, into a form practiced by a group that did not originate it. So, the concept of generation (usually considered a period of the lifetime of a person between birth and the years of reproduction, roughly 20 to 30 years) may be attached to the performance of a tradition rather than to its performers. Thus, the festival of Halloween may be said to be hundreds of generations old, each season constituting a generation of its performance. Other traditions, like the appearance of Rudolph the red-nosed reindeer, dating only from a 1939 advertising gimmick, may be relatively recent. The importance of tradition as a symbol of group identity overrides its value in antiquity.

One of the most common misconceptions concerning tradition is that it is dying out as it is replaced by modern institutions. This devolutionary theory is meaningless when applied to tradition as a process. It may have some meaning when applied to the products of tradition that may die out when they lose their function in society. The horse-drawn plow, for instance, may cease to be used in the fields as improvements are made in cultivation machinery. Such a product of tradition may survive, however, with an altered function, as when the same horse-drawn plow is preserved in a museum as a symbol of cultural history.

John William Johnson

See also Performance

****

References

Ben-Amos, Dan. "The Seven Strands of Tradition: Varieties in Its Meaning in American Folklore Studies." *Journal of Folklore Research* 21:2–3 (1984): 97–131.

Dundes, Alan. "The Devolutionary Premise in Folklore Theory." *Journal of the Folklore Institute* 6:1 (1969): 5–19.

Handler, Richard, and Jocelyn Linnekin. "Tradition: Genuine or Spurious." *Journal of American Folklore* 97 (1984): 273–290.

Hobsbawn, Eric, and Terence Ranger, eds. *The Invention of Tradition*. Cambridge: Cambridge University Press, 1983.

Janelli, Roger. "Toward a Reconciliation of Micro- and Macro-level Analyses of Folklore." *Folklore Forum* 9 (1976): 59–66.

Shils, Edward. *Tradition*. Chicago: University of Chicago Press, 1981.

TRANSCRIPTION

Transcription, or the translation of folk performances to print, lies at the intersection of folklore and literature. Folklorists and writers trying to preserve the words, sounds, and nonverbal qualities of folk performances in print have devised a number of recording methods. The degree to which folklorists and writers strive to capture the sounds, sights, and contextual features of artistic verbal performances depends on their theories of folklore and their goals. Early literary folklorists, following the European comparative method, sought to discover the historical and geographical spread of a tale. They did not value aesthetic, performative features and thus transcribed only the plots, leaving out recordings of intonations, dialect, gestures, and context. Early anthropological folklorists, seeking to record Native American languages and traditions, transcribed verbatim native languages and then translated them into English. Although a few anthropologists such as Franz Boas, Edward Sapir, and Bronislaw Malinowski strove to transcribe additional nonverbal and contextual features of performances, most neglected to transcribe folklore as aesthetic performance. In reaction to dry scholarly texts, both anthropologists and literary folklorists published popularized versions, rewritten to suit the tastes of a mass reading public. But these popularized versions, while more colorful, could not be depended on as accurate transcriptions.

With the growing availability of film, audio, and video technology, as well as the ethnographic and performance approaches to folklore that developed in the late 1960s and 1970s, folklorists began employing more literary techniques to transcribe performance features. Dialect, one of the most important markers of a speech community, can be represented to some degree with proper use of "literary dialect," or the use of natural language spellings to convey pronunciation. Writers such as William Faulkner, Charles Dickens, and Langston Hughes have skillfully used literary dialect to represent folk speech. In his "A Theory of Literary Dialect," Sumner Ives argues that literary dialect can generally indicate a difference in phonemes, as well as social gradation between characters, pronunciation features, unconventional morphology, and local expressions and names.

The key to a successful use of literary dialect is to make sure that the readers know which dialect the author considers to be standard. For example, since Joel Chandler Harris, the author of the Uncle Remus tales, spoke an r-less dialect, he did not expect that the final r on "Brer" in Brer Rabbit and Brer Fox would be pronounced. Thus, Harris expected "Brer" to be read and pronounced as "bruh," according to Ives. Although literary dialect can convey dialect with some degree of accuracy, another popular respelling technique called "eye dialect" is used in paternalistic, chauvinistic ways to caricature folk speakers. Frontier humorists such as George Washington Harris use respellings that look like dialect but convey no difference in actual sound, such as "tu" (to), "ove" (of) and "conversashun" (conversation) to create humorous dialect characters. Harris's Sut Lovingood stories, or the cartoons of Li'l Abner and Snuffy Smith, are full of such eye dialect.

In addition to transcribing dialect, folklorists and writers often borrow poetic techniques of line breaks and typography to capture nonverbal sounds and movement. Using the breath-pause line breaks of free-verse poets, anthropologist Dennis Tedlock advocates using line breaks to represent the breath pauses of speech. Using small type for soft volume, regular type for normal volume, and capitals for loud volume, Tedlock and others strive to convey vocal dynamics. Italicized comments in the margins are often used to describe important aesthetic features, such as gestures and tones. Sensitive and carefully done transcriptions play a vital role in the transmission of folklore through the print medium.

Elizabeth C. Fine

See also Dialect; Dickens, Charles; Faulkner, William; Harris, Joel Chandler; Performance

✳✳✳✳✳✳✳✳✳✳✳✳✳✳✳✳✳✳

References

Briggs, Charles L. *Competence in Performance: The Creativity of Tradition in Mexicano Verbal Art.* Philadelphia: University of Pennsylvania Press, 1988.

Fine, Elizabeth. *The Folklore Text: From Performance to Print.* Bloomington: Indiana University Press, 1994 (1984).

Ives, Sumner. "A Theory of Literary Dialect." In *A Various Language: Perspectives on American Dialects,* ed. Juanita V. Williamson and Virginia M. Burke, pp. 145–177. New York: Holt, Rinehart and Winston, 1971.

Shorrocks, Graham. "Reflections on the Problems of Transcribing Contemporary Legends." *Contemporary Legend* 2 (1992): 93–117.

Tedlock, Dennis. *Finding the Center: Narrative Poetry of the Zuni Indians.* Trans. Dennis Tedlock. New York: Dial Press, 1972. Reprint, Lincoln and London: University of Nebraska Press, 1978.

TRICKSTER

In the study of folklore, the term *trickster* is customarily reserved for characters combining the roles of the clever deceiver–numskull and transformer–culture hero, although the former aspect appears most definitive of the trickster proper. In this capacity, trickster is depicted as the quintessential sociopath: greedy and selfish, deceitful and thieving, imitative and pretentious, venal and libidinous, peripatetic and shortsighted, intermittently cunning yet ultimately stupid. Frequently anthropomorphic and/or possessed of shape-shifting abilities, tricksters are usually generically male but may be transformatively female or hermaphroditic.

Tricksters typically serve as the subjects of entire tale cycles, which are most often simply series of loosely connected episodes concerning the main character's wanderings as the trickster alternately preys upon, or is himself tricked and victimized by, the other beings he encounters. Curiously, tricksters also figure prominently in the sacred mythologies of many cultures, sometimes as evil destroyers, more often as demiurges whose actions generally (albeit oftentimes unwittingly) benefit humanity, establishing the ordered world from chaos or bestowing upon people basic necessities and survival

The Raven, depicted here in a nineteenth-century cedar mask, is an important trickster figure in the folk traditions of the native peoples of the American Pacific Northwest.

skills (e.g., the secret of fire, frequently transmitted by trickster from gods to mortals)—the gist of the transformer–culture hero role.

Given the trickster's universal, multifaceted qualities, it is hardly surprising that, from a cross-cultural perspective, the trickster label has been applied to an array of characters whose culture-specific significances may or may not justify such simple typing. The issue is cloudier still in the realm of written literature, where, allowing for the many conventional folk tricksters adapted from oral traditions, the trickster type has also been identified with such stock literary personae as the picaro, the bastard, the knight-errant, and the antihero, with the oral trickster cycle likened to such literary forms as the bildungsroman and the picaresque novel. The degree to which many of these parallels represent direct influences or simply reflect universal dualities and complementarities in human experience and expression remains open to question, however, especially given the persuasive argument that the folk trickster merely embodies in one form the more general principal of antithesis as an essential, definitive component of various fundamental sociocultural, psychological, and semantic structures (this tenet, in fact, constitutes a unifying thread in the sundry, ostensibly competing psychoanalytic, structural-functional, and symbolic-semiotic interpretations of the trickster).

Nevertheless, while precise lines of influence are often obscure, there is clearly a long-standing connection between oral trickster tales and written literature, particularly in the Indo-European tradition. Indeed, many of the great European folk tricksters from antiquity through the medieval and early modern periods—for example, the Greek Prometheus, Hermes, or Odysseus or the Norse god Loki—are known largely from literary sources. This interconnection is exemplified by the European animal trickster tale, a genre Stith Thompson, the foremost authority on the Indo-European folktale, traced to four principal sources: (1) the literary fable collections of India; (2) early medieval adaptations or elaborations of Aesop; (3) the medieval cycle of Reynard the Fox, often identified after its best known literary form as the *Roman de Renart*; and (4) purely oral traditions, especially those of Russia and the Baltic states.

It should be remembered that, their literary dimensions aside, the first three categories were themselves heavily indebted to oral traditions. Moreover, many of the tales in the animal cycle were also told of "human" tricksters, as were innumerable other stories found both in oral tradition and in medieval tale collections and Renaissance jestbooks, not to mention the oriental literature upon which these works readily drew. So, for example, trickster's sacred associations were preserved throughout Europe's medieval and early modern eras in the popular tales of rogue friars—Tyl Eulenspiegel in Germany, Pfaffe Amis or Der Pfarrer vom Kalenberg in Austria, the "merry priest" Arlotto in Italy—while even Christ himself sometimes assumed that role, as in the British ballad "The Bitter Withy."

Such conventional tricksters are far less common in the European-American sphere, though there are occasional parallels in such regional types as the clever Yankee or in the tall tales and tall-tale personae modeled after the European Munchausen, strains that in the New World, as in the Old World, circulated both orally and in subliterary forms. However, the most important tricksters in the Americas are those of Native American or African provenience—the tricksters whose tales, in fact, constitute the best known and most widely researched instances of the genre worldwide. Ironically, the best evidence for European animal trickster tales in the New World may come from the Native American and black traditions, where one often finds tales that can be traced through the Reynard cycle to venerable Indic sources.

The best known of the North American Indian tricksters is Coyote, who fills that role in the Southwest, Plains, and Plateau regions as well as in California. Other prominent Native American tricksters include Manabhozo—"the Great Hare" of the central woodlands—and Raven, Blue Jay, and Mink, the trickster-transformers of the Pacific Northwest. Among American blacks, the trickster hare of east, central, and southern Africa dominates the North American tradition while the West African spider Ananse serves as the primary trickster in the Caribbean and South America. The human tricksters of sub-Saharan Africa (e.g., Yo of Benin) are also echoed in New World black tradition, most conspicuously in the character John, the wily slave who continually vies with his Old Marster. Trickster's influence is even observable in African-American music—for instance, in blues music, as the emotional condition/psychological state that names the genre is often personified in terms reminiscent of Eshu-Elegba, the Dahoman trickster deity of entrances and cross-roads, and the philosophical principle of accident.

In contrast to European tradition, literary treatments of Native American and New World black trickster tales are quite recent developments, initially emanating, moreover, from outside the cultures themselves. First appearing during the nineteenth century, such early retellings by outsiders are epitomized by Henry Wadsworth Longfellow's *Song of Hiawatha* (1855), which borrowed the name of a sixteenth-century Iroquois chief but was actually based on the Ojibwa Manabhozo cycle, or Joel Chandler Harris's various Uncle Remus collections, which were largely responsible for popularizing the tales of Brer Rabbit and his cohorts beyond their natural habitat. More recently, trickster (or at least trickster-like) figures have appeared in the works of Native American and African-American authors—for example, some critics detect the trickster archetype behind various characters in the novels of Louise Erdrich or N. Scott Momaday, or in the antiheroic protagonist of Ralph Ellison's *The Invisible Man* (1947)—but often in guises that, once again, seem to question their immediate identification with folk tradition. Or perhaps these perplexities merely offer further testimony of the trickster's extraordinary powers of shape-shifting and deception.

John Minton

See also Aesop's Fables; Ellison, Ralph; Erdrich, Louise; Fable; Folktale; Harris, Joel Chandler; John and Old Marster Tales; Momaday, Navarre Scott; Tall Tale; Thompson, Stith; Uncle Remus

✳✳✳✳✳✳✳✳✳✳✳✳✳✳✳✳✳

References

Babcock-Abrahams, Barbara. "'A Tolerated Margin of Mess': The Trickster and His Tales Reconsidered." *Journal of the Folklore Institute* 11 (1975): 147–186.

Radin, Paul. *The Trickster: A Study in American Indian Mythology*. New York: Schocken Books, 1972 (1956).

Thompson, Stith. *The Folktale*. Berkeley: University of California Press, 1977 (1946).

TROLLS

In Scandinavian folk narrative, trolls are creatures who are usually depicted as gigantic, malicious, dull-witted, ugly, deformed, or animal-like in appearance. Trolls eat or enslave people who wander into their mountainous territory, but those who manage to outwit trolls stand to acquire the treasure—gold or jewels—that trolls hoard. Trolls are particularly antagonistic to Christianity, as is shown in legends about ministers or churches attacked by trolls. Trolls are sometimes depicted as possessing skill as spinners, weavers, or smiths, and they are attracted to beautiful objects and people. Trolls shun the sun and can be destroyed—turned to stone or burst apart—when sunlight hits them.

Trolls can be traced to the medieval Icelandic *Eddas* and sagas, in which they appear as supernatural giants. By the end of the sixteenth century, popular belief in trolls had waned, and thereafter, the creatures appeared only in märchen, fictional ballads, humorous folktales, and etiological legends explaining topographic features.

In Swedish, Norwegian, and Danish folklore, many scholars distinguish between trolls (Swedish/Norwegian *troll*, Danish *trold*) and giants (Swedish *jätte*, Norwegian *jotun*, Danish *jætte*). In Norwegian lore, the two categories are not clearly distinguishable, but in Swedish and Danish lore, a distinction can be made between *jätte*, which resemble the Icelandic trolls, and trolls, which are human-size beings that live in their own communities isolated from human settlements. The activities of Swedish and Danish trolls range from the merely troublesome (invading a household on Christmas Eve) to the dangerous (introducing changelings into the cradle) and overlap with many of the activities ascribed to *jätte* (kidnapping humans, hating Christianity).

Outside of Scandinavia, trolls survive as *trows* in the language and narratives of the Shetland and Orkney Islands, where the transplanted tradition was influenced by Celtic belief in "good folk." *Trows* live in mounds or under the sea. The land-dwelling *trows* are small, dress in green, and have magical powers. The sea-dwelling *trows* appear on the surface of the sea as mermaids or seals and, like selkies, can be enslaved if one possesses their skin.

Although both traditional images of the troll have been employed by writers, the gigantic Norwegian troll, best known by English readers through Scandinavian folktale collections of the mid-nineteenth century, is the image most commonly employed in literature. Peter Christen Asbjørnsen (1812–1885) and Jørgen Engebretsen Moe's (1813–1882) *Norske-Eventyr*, which was translated into English by George Webbe Dasent in 1858 as *Popular Tales from the Norse*, popularized stories such as "East of the Sun and West of the Moon" and "Three Billy Goats Gruff"; these have been retold in numerous nineteenth- and twentieth-century illustrated versions for children. In twentieth-century fantasy literature, trolls appear in J. R. R. Tolkien's *The Hobbit* and *The Lord of the Rings* as malicious, but humorous, grotesques. Tolkien based the creatures on his study of Icelandic sources. In twentieth-century children's literature, trolls employ the full range of traditional characteristics, from dangerous and depraved (see Ursula K. Le Guin's *A Ride on the Red Mare's Back* [1992]) to sociable little folks (see Tove Jansson's moomintroll series).

Jennifer Eastman Attebery

See also *Edda, Poetic*; *Edda, Prose*; Legend; Scandinavian Folk Literature; Tolkien, J. R. R. (John Ronald Reuel)

✳✳✳✳✳✳✳✳✳✳✳✳✳✳✳✳✳✳

References

Amilien, Virginie. "Du texte a l'image: Evolution du troll." *Merveilles-and-Contes* 3:2 (1989): 195–211.

Attebery, Jennifer Eastman. "The Trolls of Fiction: Ogres or Warm Fuzzies?" *Journal of the Fantastic in the Arts* 7:1 (1996): 61–74.

Bruford, Alan. "Trolls, Hillfolk, Finns, and Picts: The Identity of the Good Neighbors in Orkney and Shetland." In *The Good People: New Fairylore Essays*, ed. Peter Narváez. New York: Garland, 1991.

Jonsson, Hjorleifur Rafn. "Trolls, Chiefs, and Children: Changing Perspectives on an Icelandic Christmas Myth." *Nord Nytt* 41 (1990): 55–63.

Motz, Lotte. "The Divided Image: A Study of the Giantesses and Female Trolls in Norse Myth and Literature." *Mankind Quarterly* 27:4 (1987): 463–478.

Puhvel, Martin. "The Mighty She-Trolls of Icelandic Saga and Folktale." *Folklore* 98:2 (1987): 175–179.

Richmond, W. Edson. "Ballad Trolls as Narrative Devices." In *Folklore on Two Continents: Essays in Honor of Linda Dégh*, ed. Nikolai Burlakoff and Carl Lindahl. Bloomington, Ind.: Trickster, 1980.

Tangherlini, Timothy R. "From Trolls to Turks: Continuity and Change in Danish Legend Tradition." *Scandinavian Studies* 67 (1995): 32–62.

TUTUOLA, AMOS (1920–1997)

Born in Abeokuta in western Nigeria, educated in missionary primary schools, and employed as a messenger and storeroom clerk for most of his life, Amos Tutuola has written 10 works of fiction and a compilation of Yoruba folktales, all in English, his second language. Like his Yoruba-language precursor, D. O. Fagunwa, Tutuola has drawn heavily on Yoruba culture in his fiction. His first published novel, and still his best known work, *The Palm-Wine Drinkard and His Dead Palm-Wine Tapster in the Deads' Town* (1952), brought immediate critical acclaim in Europe but generated controversy in Nigeria over Tutuola's debt to Fagunwa, his use of Yoruba oral literature, and his so-called naive English.

Palm-Wine Drinkard, like most of Tutuola's fiction, is a picaresque novel narrated by a hero who undertakes a hazardous quest from the world of the living into the spirit world and back again. Many aspects of the story derive from Yoruba oral literature, including the hero's similarity to folktale protagonists such as the hunter, the trickster, and the magician. Yoruba proverbs, riddles, praise names, myths of origin, and dilemma tales also figure prominently in Tutuola's writing. The "complete gentleman" episode in *Palm-Wine Drinkard*, in which a headstrong young woman follows a handsome man into the forest as his body is dismembered and its "rented" parts returned until there is nothing left but a skull, has its source in a Yoruba tale. Since many different versions of this and other tales exist, scholars find it difficult to document which details Tutuola adapted and which he invented in a given episode. In addition, since Tutuola uses several of the same motifs as Fagunwa, determining their origin is doubly complicated.

Among the Yoruba motifs that Tutuola uses and reuses are stories of enfants terribles (half-bodied babies and *abiku,* "born to die children"), the antelope woman who marries a hunter, magical objects that provide food, the "godmother" figure, animal helpers, and tortoise trickster tales. In the chapter headings of *The Brave African Huntress* (1958) and *Ajaiyi and His Inherited Poverty* (1967), Tutuola cites proverbs, such as "Animals are surplus in the town in which the people have no teeth," and then elaborates on those proverbs in subsequent chapters. With shape-shifting humans, animals who behave like humans, and superhuman ogres and monsters, Tutuola's fiction mirrors the Yoruba belief in the interpenetration of the natural and supernatural worlds. By weaving folktales into larger narrative frameworks, Tutuola's distinctive writing style combines Yoruba syntax and oral storytelling techniques with contemporary English vocabulary and images of modern life such as radios, television, airplanes, bombs, petrol drums, and high heels. His transformations of Yoruba cultural archetypes, along with his extravagant visual imagery and comic hyperbole, make him an inimitable, singular voice among contemporary African writers.

Sue Standing

See also *Märchen;* Motif; Proverbs; Riddle; Soyinka, Wole; Tradition

✳✳✳✳✳✳✳✳✳✳✳✳✳✳✳✳

References

Afolayan, A. "Language and Sources of Amos Tutuola." In *Perspectives on African Literature,* ed. C. Heywood, pp. 49–63. New York: Africana, 1971.

Belvaude, Catherine. *Amos Tutuola et l'univers du conte africain.* Paris: L'Harmattan, 1989.

Irele, Abiola. "Tradition and the Yoruba Writer: D. O. Fagunwa, Amos Tutuola, and Wole Soyinka." In *The African Experience in Literature and Ideology,* pp. 174–197. Bloomington: Indiana University Press, 1990.

Obiechina, Emmanuel N. "Amos Tutuola and the Oral Tradition." In *Language and Theme,* pp. 21–52. Washington, D.C.: Howard University Press, 1990.

TWAIN, MARK (1835–1910)

Generally perceived as the foremost American literary artist of the nineteenth century, Mark Twain also made extensive use of folklore in his writing. Born Samuel Langhorne Clemens in a small,

As one of the foremost writers of the nineteenth century, Mark Twain (shown here dictating his autobiography in 1906) made extensive use of folk culture and folklore in his portrayals of the American South.

slaveholding Missouri frontier village and raised in a burgeoning Mississippi River town, he graduated from his early occupation as typesetter to being a riverboat pilot. When the Civil War broke out, he went west to Nevada, California, and Hawaii, where he learned mining but returned to his first loves, writing and publishing. Throughout his literary career, Twain made wide use of the southwestern tall tale and of Mississippi River lore, especially in his two classic novels of American boyhood, *Tom Sawyer* (1876) and *Huckleberry Finn* (1884), in which he recorded cures for warts, African-American witch legends, and dozens of other examples of folk culture. Twain frequently retold on paper stories he first heard from slaves, on the steamboat, or in the mining camp. Twain went beyond translating oral tales to a written medium; he is credited with the first written use of several thousand words, mostly ethnic or occupational slang such as spunk-water (for rain trapped in a stump), and even his pen name, when sung out by a steamboat leadsman, meant two fathoms of depth, safe water for most boats. Many of these words slipped into national currency by their appearance in his books and stories.

Despite these contributions to the dissemination of folklore through literature, it is a mistake to see Twain as primarily a pen-wielding harvester of oral matter. Throughout his life, Twain was a legendary talker. During the early part of his career as a best-selling author (1866–1873), Twain was even better known as a platform lecturer and visited several hundred towns from the eastern seaboard to California. One of the most popular attractions on the circuit, Twain helped to define American storytelling with his laconic, almost disinterested style, his rambling narratives, his biting asides, and his mounting climaxes. Because he aspired to the literary pantheon centered around Boston's *Atlantic Monthly*, he later resisted the lucrative lecture circuit, which defined him more as a performer than a litterateur. In 1895–1896, however, financial exigencies drove him to undertake a world tour, which brought his remarkable skill as a performer to audiences in Australia, India, and South Africa that were primarily familiar with him as a writer. This tour represented one of the first wholesale exports of living American culture beyond Europe.

Mark Twain was also the first American cultural figure whose fame lasted long enough for him to become a cultural icon. Twain's recognizability helped to develop a national culture above and beyond the regional ones, and as the most widely photographed person and most popular writer in the United States until well after his death, he became a trademark for American humor; pithy epigrams he never wrote or spoke became attributed to him because they sounded like Mark Twain. His continuing significance to American culture depends in large measure on his position between folklore and literature.

Andrew Jay Hoffman

See also Legend; Storytelling; Tall Tale

✳✳✳✳✳✳✳✳✳✳✳✳✳✳✳✳✳✳

References

Fishkin, Shelley Fisher. *Was Huck Black? Mark Twain and African-American Voices*. New York: Oxford University Press, 1993.

Hoffman, Andrew Jay. *Twain's Heroes, Twain's Worlds*. Philadelphia: University of Pennsylvania Press, 1988.

Wonham, Henry B. *Mark Twain and the Art of the Tall-Tale*. New York: Oxford University Press, 1993.

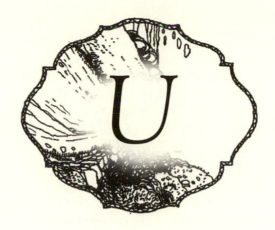

UNCLE REMUS

Uncle Remus is the fictional narrator of a cycle of African-American folktales retold by the Georgian journalist Joel Chandler Harris (1848–1908) that, among other things, recounts the antics of such anthropomorphic animals as Brer Rabbit and Brer Fox. These animal fables are full of observations on human relationships and behavior and, in true folktale fashion, contain as much violence as they do humor. Because of Harris's extremely accurate ear for black dialect, inflection, and storytelling mannerisms, and also because he took great pains to verify that every tale was a genuine African-American story, his Uncle Remus tales are considered among the most significant collections of African-American folklore in the nineteenth century.

The animal trickster tales predominate, but the numerous collections of Uncle Remus stories also include cautionary tales, supernatural stories, and etiological stories as well as songs, pithy sayings, and sketches of contemporary southern life. These tales are linked together by a framework of Harris's own creation: the narrator, an old former slave on a Georgia plantation, tells the tales to the small son of the plantation owners. Although the stories included in the first collection are primarily those Harris remembered hearing at night in the slave quarters of the plantation where he worked as a printer's devil during the Civil War, subsequent Uncle Remus anthologies increasingly relied on tales collected by friends and family members.

The second collection, *Nights with Uncle Remus* (1883), experiments with multiple narrators, friends of Uncle Remus who share in the story swapping, which allowed Harris to re-create a realistic storytelling session and to present variants of the tales he had collected. One of the narrators is a former slave from a coastal Georgia plantation, Daddy Jack, and he speaks in the Gullah dialect that was typical of slaves from the South Seas area. To aid the reader, Harris even included a glossary of the Gullah dialect used in the Daddy Jack's tales.

Despite Harris's claims of being a "recorder only" rather than an author, the Uncle Remus stories are literary folktales, not verbatim records of actual performances. Harris glossed over sexual innuendo—though he retained the unexplained motif of "Miss Meadows and the gals" who are always available when the animals feel the urge to go courting—and never used some authentic tales he considered too ribald for his audiences. Also, his correspondence with friends and collectors indicates that he asked only for outlines of tales, which he put into his own narrative contexts after authenticating them.

Debate has raged over whether the sources of the folklore collected by Harris ultimately lay in Native American, African, or Indian lore. Harris, however, claimed that he had not engaged in any formal ethnographic work. His primary purposes were to preserve what he saw as a fading way of life and to use the portrayal to help heal wounds inflicted on both sides by the Civil War. He shaped his retellings to suit those purposes, and his stories, and the framework that envelops them, repeatedly convey the interdependency of blacks and whites in southern society.

Martha Hixon

See also Folktale; Folktale Adaptations; Frame Tale; Harris, Joel Chandler; Storytelling

✳✳✳✳✳✳✳✳✳✳✳✳✳✳✳✳✳

References

Baer, Florence E. *Sources and Analogues of the Uncle Remus Tales*. Helsinki: Academia Scientiarum Fennica, 1980.

Bickley, R. Bruce, Jr. *Joel Chandler Harris*. Boston: G. K. Hall, 1978.

Brookes, Stella Brewer. *Joel Chandler Harris—Folklorist*. Athens: University of Georgia Press, 1950.

Harris, Joel Chandler. *The Complete Tales of Uncle Remus*. Ed. Richard Chase. Boston: Houghton Mifflin, 1955.

Pederson, Lee. "Language in the Uncle Remus Tales." *Modern Philology* 82 (1985): 292–298.

UNPROMISING HERO

A stock character of the folktale (motif L100), the unpromising hero might seem an unlikely hero because of apparent deficiencies in size, strength, or mental acuity. Other factors in this characterization may be age, gender, birth order (e.g., the third of three children), and socioeconomic status. The unpromising hero's success appeals to readers or listeners because it satisfies their need for wish fulfillment.

Among many unpromising folktale heroes, Tom Thumb (AT 700) triumphs over adversity despite his small size, Cinderella (AT 510A) succeeds with the help of a fairy godmother, the street urchin Aladdin (AT 561) discovers a wonderful lamp, and the young dragon slayer (AT 300) receives magic objects to aid in his quest. Supernatural help is the keynote to success for most of the ill-favored heroes of European folktales. A contrasting example from Native American culture is the Apache/Navaho story of Dirty Boy, who, in spite of seeming dirty and lazy, trains himself to become a famous runner and warrior.

Related to the folktale "The Bear's Son" (AT 301), the epic *Beowulf* features a young hero who, against all odds and with some magical help, defeats the monster Grendel, Grendel's mother, and a dragon. (An alternative view of this conflict emerges in novelist John Gardner's *Grendel* [1971].) Similarly, in the German epic *Nibelungenlied*, young Siegfried slays the dragon Fafnir with a magic sword. In Sir Thomas Malory's *Morte d'Arthur* [The death of King Arthur (1485)], young Arthur finds a sword and becomes king, to almost everyone's surprise. Recent literary versions of Arthur's story include T. H. White's *The Once and Future King* (1958) and Marion Z. Bradley's *The Mists of Avalon* (1982); in the latter, the priestess Morgaine is more of a hero than her half-brother the king.

The Bible contains a number of unlikely heroes: Moses, who is found adrift in the bulrushes by the pharaoh's daughter (motif L111.2.1), becomes a strong leader and lawgiver; David, a small shepherd boy, amazes everyone by slaying the Philistine giant Goliath with his slingshot. Others who survive deadly perils— Daniel in the lions' den and the three young men in the fiery furnace, for example—show that divine protection can make anyone heroic as long as the person's faith is unassailable.

From the eighteenth century on, numerous novels have featured unpromising heroes: Henry Fielding's *Tom Jones* (1749) tells of a foundling who, after many adventures, marries a wealthy woman. The heroes of Charles Dickens's *David Copperfield* (1849–1850) and other novels experience the folktale-based tradition of well-deserved reversal of fortune; so does the central character of Horatio Alger's *Ragged Dick* (1867). Also conforming to this pattern is the heroine of Charlotte Brontë's *Jane Eyre* (1847), as the heroine rises from orphan/servant status to marriage and relative affluence. In Mark Twain's *Huckleberry Finn* (1884), a dirty and ill-educated boy proves himself to be a hero; his companion Jim, once a slave, also assumes heroic proportions.

Of the twentieth-century novels that contain unpromising heroes, many are about characters who seem unlikely to succeed because of their ethnic origin (for example, African-American heroes in Richard Wright's *Black Boy* [1945] and Ralph Ellison's *Invisible Man* [1952] and the Asian-American heroine of Maxine Hong Kingston's *The Woman Warrior* [1976]). There are many feminist novels in which a strong female character excels in spite of expectations for her gender; one of these is Gail Godwin's *The Odd Woman* (1974). It seems clear that the motif of the unpromising hero has exerted a strong influence on the characterization of heroes in British and American literature.

Elizabeth Tucker

See also Arthurian Tradition; *Beowulf*; Bible; Ellison, Ralph; Folktale; Kingston, Maxine Hong; Twain, Mark

✳✳✳✳✳✳✳✳✳✳✳✳✳✳✳✳

References

Bett, Henry. *Nursery Rhymes and Tales: Their Origin and History.* London: Methuen, 1924.

Bornstein, Henry. *Nursery Rhymes from Mother Goose.* Washington, D.C.: Kendall Green Publications, 1992.

One Hundred and One Nursery Rhymes. Folkways Records FC 7730, 1958.

Opie, Iona, and Peter Opie. *Oxford Dictionary of Nursery Rhymes.* Oxford: Clarendon Press, 1951.

Urban Legends

Apocryphal contemporary stories, told as true and usually attributed to a friend of a friend (FOAF), were formerly termed *urban belief tales* and are now also called "contemporary legends," "modern legends," or "modern urban legends." Although neither the subject matter nor the circulation of urban legends is necessarily "urban," the stories usually reflect themes of modern city or suburban life and explore such topics as crime, technology, current events, and celebrities. Some modern urban legends are clearly *not* modern, *not* urban, and *not* always told as true (i.e., as "legends"), but at least some examples of the stories thus classified must fit these criteria, although other versions of modern urban legends may have ancient and/or rural variations and may sometimes be told merely for entertainment, usually in the form of jokes. Still, the term *urban legend* is used by many folklorists, and it has become the generic usage among members of the public and journalists to refer to many of the unverified odd stories that circulate both orally and in print in the modern world.

Although some folklorists in England and the United States collected and studied individual urban legends earlier, Richard M. Dorson focused attention on the whole genre in the last chapter, "Modern Folklore," of his 1959 textbook *American Folklore*. The widespread popularity of urban legends and some areas of interpretation have been suggested in a series of books by Jan Harold Brunvand, *The Vanishing Hitchhiker* (1981), *The Choking Doberman* (1984), *The Mexican Pet* (1986), *Curses! Broiled Again!* and *The Baby Train* (1993). Similar collections of urban legends have been published in England, Scandinavia, Germany, Holland, South Africa, Australia, and elsewhere. Growing from a series of annual seminars that began at the University of Sheffield, England, in 1982, the International Society for Contemporary Legend Research was formed in 1988. The society publishes a newsletter, *FOAFtale News*, and an annual journal, *Contemporary Legend*.

The 10 major headings of the "Type-Index of Urban Legends" included in Brunvand's 1993 book *The Baby Train*—along with a sample story title from each—suggest the range of stories and themes to be found in this urban legend: automobiles ("The Slasher under the Car"), animals ("The Microwaved Pet"), horrors ("The Babysitter and the Man Upstairs"), accidents ("The Exploding Toilet"), sex and scandal ("The Girl on the Gearshift Lever"), crime ("The Kidney Heist"), business and professions ("Red Velvet Cake"), government ("The Wordy Memo"), celebrities ("The Elevator Incident"), and academe ("The One-Word Exam Question"). These and hundreds of other true stories that are too good to be true circulate by word of mouth among adolescents at slumber parties and bull sessions, among office and factory workers during breaks, and among just about everybody at parties, dinners, and other social gatherings. Urban legends also appear regularly in the popular press and are disseminated via photocopies, faxes, and computer links; they are repeated on radio and television talk shows, and sometimes they inspire sitcoms, films, and even serious literature.

Rumors and legends have probably always been a feature of urban life, and sometimes virtually the same "modern" story can be documented from very early writings. For instance, the persistent account of a supposed shopping-mall crime in which a boy is sexually mutilated, even killed, by members of a youth gang has been traced to medieval and classical sources. Geoffrey Chaucer's version of the anti-Semitic "blood libel" version, widespread during the Middle Ages, is "The Prioress's Tale" in the *Canterbury Tales*, and this account of the supposed murder of Hugh of Lincoln in 1255 appears as well in the ballad "Sir Hugh, or, the Jew's Daughter," found as 155 in the edition made by Francis James Child (1882–1898). A description of Syrian Jews ritually torturing and murdering a Christian child appears in a fifth-century source, but folklorist Bill Ellis has shown that anti-Christian versions of the same legend were recorded by Roman lawyers of the second and third centuries C.E. In all of these and many more tellings of the same essential story, the perpetrators of the crime are said to need blood for a religious rite.

Daniel Defoe described the growth and rampant spread of unverified horror stories his *A Journal of the Plague Year* (1722), which describes the ravages of the bubonic plague in London in 1664–1665. Charles Dickens incorporated several legends in his *Pickwick Papers* (1867), including one about an unscrupulous street vendor supposedly selling pies made from kittens. In *The House of the Seven Gables* (1851), Nathaniel Hawthorne recognized the same interaction of oral urban legends with journalism that folklorists still find intriguing, writing: "Tradition . . . sometimes brings down truth that history has let slip, but is oftener the wild babble of the time, such as was formerly spoken of at the fireside and now congeals in newspapers" (Chapter 1).

The numerous appearances of urban legends in literature have barely begun to be cataloged, and the literary effects of such uses largely remain to be analyzed. Such a catalog will be a large one, including such disparate examples as "The Exploding Dog" in Jack London's story "Moon Face" (1902); "Not My Dog" in Lucy Maud Montgomery's *Emily Climbs* (1924); "The Surpriser Surprised" in Carson McCullers's *The Heart Is a Lonely Hunter* (1940); "The Vanishing Hitchhiker" in Carl Carmer's "The Lavender Evening Dress" (from *Dark Trees to the Wind* [1949]); "Alligators in the Sewers" in Thomas Pynchon's novel *V* (1963); "Kitty Takes the Rap" in Toni Morrison's *The Bluest Eye* (1972); "The Crushed Dog" in Tom Robbins's *Still Life with Woodpecker* (1980); "The Dead Cat in the Package" in Yevgeny Yevtushenko's *Wild Berries* (1981); "The Elephant That Sat on the Small Car" in Peter Carey's *Bliss* (1981); "The Choking Doberman" in Hilma Wolitzer's *In the Palomar Arms* (1983); "The Packet of Biscuits" in Douglas Adams's *So Long, and Thanks for All the Fish* (1984); and "The Runaway Grandmother" in Anthony Burgess's *The Piano Players* (1986).

In a rare interpretive study of urban legends and literature, folklorist Bruce Rosenberg analyzed the complex structural and thematic interrelations of several popular legends in the short story "Mr. Wrong" (1979) by the English writer Elizabeth Jane Howard. Distilling a similar analysis of a single legend to its essence, poet Howard Nemerov found the meaning of modern oral literature and of life in his two-stanza poem titled "Poetics." The first stanza repeated a familiar story:

> You know the old story Ann Landers tells
> About the housewife in her basement doing the wash?
> She's wearing her nightie, and she thinks, "Well hell,
> I might's well put this in as well," and then
> Being dripped on by a leaky pipe puts on
> Her son's football helmet; whereupon
> The meter reader happens to walk through
> And "Lady," he gravely says, "I sure hope your team wins."

Nemerov's conclusion interprets such stories:

> A story many times told in many ways,
> The set of random accidents redeemed
> By one more accident, as though chaos
> Were the order that was before creation came.
> That is the way things happen in the world,
> A joke, a disappointment satisfied,
> As we walk through doing our daily round,
> Reading the meter, making things add up.
>   (Nemerov, 1991)

Jan Harold Brunvand

See also Hugh of Lincoln; Legend; Ritual Murder

✴✴✴✴✴✴✴✴✴✴✴✴✴✴✴✴✴

References

Bennet, Gillian, and Paul Smith. *Contemporary Legend: A Folklore Bibliography*. New York: Garland, 1993.

Campion-Vincent, Véronique, and Jean-Bruno Renard. *Légendes urbaines: Rumeurs d'aujourd'hui*. Paris: Éditions Payot, 1992.

Dorson, Richard M. *American Folklore*. Chicago: University of Chicago Press, 1959.

Nemerov, Howard. "Poetics." In *Trying Conclusions: New and Selected Poems, 1961–1991*. Chicago: University of Chicago Press, 1991.

Rosenberg, Bruce A. "Urban Legends: The Modern Folktales." In Bruce A. Rosenberg, ed., *Folklore and Literature: Rival Siblings*, pp. 220–235. Knoxville: University of Tennessee Press, 1991.

Turner, Patricia. *I Heard It through the Grapevine: Rumor in African-American Culture*. Berkeley and Los Angeles: University of California Press, 1993.

Used Words

The term *used words*, or words already used elsewhere, refers to words taken from one context and used in another. Theorists of intertextual works, for example, Julia Kristeva, use the expression "literary reference," which may involve metaliterary speech, stylization, quotation of structures, empirical quotations, allusions, and borrowings, and literary references may index references from literature, culture, philosophy, and mythology. Creative writing also uses folklore, as when a contemporary writer employs folk poetry in his or her own text.

Used words as a term was employed for the first time in contemporary Slovene poetry by the poet Veno Taufer. He was the first to make use of literary references as an organizational procedure and to develop them in all of their variety as type, function, and origin. He was also the first to dedicate his complete collection of songs, *Pesmarica rabljenih besed* [The songbook of used words (1975)], to folk poetry. The interconnections between folk song and literature are clear from the fact that the author consciously chose 33 folk poems from the collection *Slovene Folk Songs* (1971) as the basis for his work on used words.

Taufer suggests that his way of writing poetry consciously touches on folk poetry (in a variety of ways). He has written several poems using folk subjects by employing poetic procedures. For example, the international Orpheus motif is represented in Slovene folk poetry as "Fiddler before Hell." In the folk song, he is called "the ninth king" or "the sad one"; in one instance, the fiddler is even a girl. The fiddler, in order to save his next of kin from hell, goes to hell and back, and souls cling to his long coat in order to be saved. He plays so powerfully and so beautifully that they are saved except for his mother. This is a special Slovene feature; she is excluded because she has committed many sins. In a song bearing the same title, Taufer, in a postmodernistic manner, quotes or assembles new meaning: *"the ninth king* / around him empty / inside him hollow / into a bone / he whistles through and through / *forward backward* / *the ninth king."*

The poetic process unites folklore and literature and establishes at least two levels; a story, motive, or idea, transparently, as in a palimpsest, shines through the deep structure of folkloristic and literary elements. The use of literary references to and from folk poetry unites, interrelates, and integrates two different kinds of poetics. Folk songs, through the employment of their quoted lines and motifs, become fully revived in an environment of contemporary meanings brought into being by the contemporary poet.

The phenomenon of used words in the works of contemporary poets can be defined as a phenomenon of intertextual combination of literary art and other arts, in the present case, literature and folklore. In literary history, the use of quotations and literary allusions was fully exploited by the romantics. In world literature, the incorporation of references is a frequent phenomenon, yet most of the references come from literature, culture, and mythology. T. S. Eliot's *The Waste Land* (1922) is full of allusions and fragments taken from the literatures and myths of European, ancient, and other cultures, as are the works of Ezra Pound, James Joyce, William Faulkner, Mikhail Bulgakov, Jorge Luis Borges, and Umberto Eco. The use and the identification of the literary references, however, require of the writer as well as of the reader a common cultural and literary code, as the used word has to be recognized as such in a contemporary text. Therefore, for instance, a Frenchman cannot recognize Slovene references in a contemporary text unless he knows the Slovene folk songs.

The dialogue between folklore and literature, between one specific folk song and the whole of the folk code, reestablishes an already extant bond between the literary code and folklore in the Slovene (or German, French, Polish, Scottish) cultural tradition, which is accessible to the entire nation in a more or less permanent way. The use of used words from folk poetry in contemporary poetry gives the folk song a different life in the world of the poet's imagination.

Marjetka Golež

See also Joyce, James; Romanticism

✳✳✳✳✳✳✳✳✳✳✳✳✳✳✳✳✳

References

Debeljak, Aleš. *The Imagination of Terra Incognita: Slovenian Writing 1945–1995.* New York: White Pine, 1997.

Genette, Gerard. *Palimpsestes (la littérature ou second degré).* Paris: Seuil, 1982.

Juvan, Marko. "Književne odnosnice v poeziji Vena Tauferja [Literary references in the poetry of Veno Taufer]." *Slavistična revija* [Slavistical review] 33:1 (1985): 51–70.

Kristeva, Julia. *Semantike: Recherches pour une sémanalyse.* Paris: Seuil, 1969.

Popovič, Anton. "Aspects of Metatext." *Canadian Review of Comparative Literature* 3 (1976): 225–235.

UTLEY, FRANCIS LEE (1907–1974)

The folklorist and literary scholar Francis Lee Utley applied the comparative method to topics in medieval studies and also strove to consolidate folklore into a useful academic discipline. Having received his B.A. from the University of Wisconsin in 1929, he earned degrees in English at Harvard (M.A. 1934; Ph.D. 1936), where he studied with George Lyman Kittredge. From 1935 until his death, Utley taught at Ohio State University in the Department of English, where he was given the title of professor of English and folklore. He established a folklore program and archive at Ohio State, which now owns his considerable library (of some 21,000 items). As a teacher, he was much loved, and some of his students (most notably W. Edson Richmond and D. K. Wilgus) went on to become prominent folklorists.

Utley specialized in the traditional background of medieval literature. His work *The Crooked Rib* (1944) demonstrates early (to 1568) British attitudes toward women. He published several works on different aspects of the Flood myth, including a long list of variants of "The Devil in Noah's Ark" (AT 825), a tale for which he wrote the summary in Stith Thompson's 1961 edition of *The Types of the Folktale*. If, as Utley believed, much literature is based on oral or otherwise traditional sources, then the study of folklore must be of central importance to the study of literature.

Comments sprinkled throughout Utley's writings reveal an underlying interest in epistemology (how knowledge can be developed). Although he believed that the investigation of the "life history" (to him, a broad and inclusive concept) of a work was the task of utmost importance to both folklorists and literary scholars, his attitude toward other theories was often generous. He published articles and book reviews on most of the current folklore theories, including myth criticism, structuralism, and the oral-formulaic theory. As early as 1958, he urged that folklore be studied in relation to its cultural context, and as late as 1974, he tried to interest anthropologists in the question of worldwide folktale diffusion. Other articles on subjects of professional interest discuss the definition of folk literature and the status of folklore in higher education in the United States.

As president of the American Folklore Society in 1951 and 1952, Utley bemoaned the quarrelsome division within the society of anthropologists versus literary scholars, believing that different scholarly perspectives result from variations in human temperament. Not surprisingly for a scholar of his professional training, he considered the study of folklore to be an essentially humanistic effort, but he was supportive of and often enthusiastic about the work of anthropologists regarding oral literature. However, he was (justifiably) skeptical of the extremely positivistic stance taken by many contemporary social scientists.

Christine Goldberg

See also Myth; Oral-Formulaic Composition and Theory; Tale-Type; Women

✳✳✳✳✳✳✳✳✳✳✳✳✳✳✳✳✳✳✳

References

Amsler, Mark E. "A Bibliography of the Writings of Francis Lee Utley." *Names* 23 (1975): 130–146.

Finnie, W. Bruce. "In Memoriam: Francis Lee Utley, 1907–1974." *Names* 23 (1975): 127–129.

Wilgus, D. K. "Francis Lee Utley, 1907–1974." *Western Folklore* 33 (1974): 202–204.

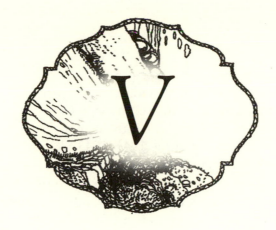

Valdez, Luis Miguel (1940–)

A playwright, actor, director, and activist, Luis Miguel Valdez was born into a family of farmworkers in Delano, California, and educated at San Jose State University. Valdez founded El Teatro Campesino (Farmworkers' Theater) in 1965 to garner public support for California farmworkers. At the time, Delano, California, was witnessing the most sustained labor action in the history of the United Farm Workers, a consumer boycott led by Cesar Chavez and directed against growers of table grapes. The action focused national attention on a range of Mexican-American issues, and *el movimiento* (the Chicano civil rights movement) was born. El Teatro Campesino would play a major role in the consciousness-raising efforts of *el movimiento* and would infuse Chicano ethnic identity with Mexican folkloric rituals and history. Its founding marks the beginning of a renaissance in Mexican-American literary production.

Valdez's theater consisted of a series of *actos*, one-act plays or sets of skits, designed to dramatize the plight of farmworkers. Often simple stories of villains (bosses and farm owners) versus the noble but poor farmworker, Valdez intended that the *acto* should demonstrate social problems while inspiring the audience to political action.

Using popular folk symbols associated with the indigenous cultures of the Aztec and Mayan, most notably that of the mythic homeland Aztlán, El Teatro Campesino aimed to foster a cohesive sense of group identity for the movement's political front. Through the mythic figure of La Llorona, the Aztec woman whose children may have been killed by the invading European army, Valdez downplayed differences between Mexican Americans and highlighted instead a shared history of grievances at the hands of the invaders: land stripped away from its owners, children taken from parents, Mexican culture and indigenous folkways disrespected, all actions unjust and in need of redress. Valdez's ability to muster myth and legend for political ends would be carefully imitated by later activists and writers.

In the late 1970s, Valdez wrote the commercially successful *Zoot Suit,* a play that dramatized the 1942–1943 Sleepy Lagoon incident in East Los Angeles in which a young white man died of injuries sustained at a local swimming hole. Seventeen Mexican-American youths were convicted of manslaughter and assault in a trial widely regarded by Mexican Americans as a fraud, and a wave of anti-Mexican-American sentiment subsequently flared in which "zoot suiters," flamboyantly dressed young Mexican-American men, were the target of attack by police and sailors. Valdez's protagonist, El Pachuco, is the ultimate victor, however, for at the play's end, he reemerges more flamboyantly dressed than ever, a symbol of the ability of Mexican Americans to retain their ethnic identity even during wartime, when pressures to assimilate are highest. In *Zoot Suit,* Valdez preserves the music, dress, and social context of a cultural form indigenous to Mexican-American life.

Krista Comer

See also Legend; La Llorona; Myth

✳✳✳✳✳✳✳✳✳✳✳✳✳✳✳✳✳

References

El Teatro Campesino: The First Twenty Years. San Juan Batista, Calif.: El Teatro Campesino, 1985.

Paredes, Raymund A. "Contemporary Mexican-American Literature, 1960–Present." In *A Literary History of the American West,* ed. J. Gordon Taylor et al. Fort Worth: Texas Christian University Press, 1987.

Sommers, Joseph, and Thomas Ybarra-Frausto. *Modern Chicano Writers.* Englewood Cliffs, N.J.: Prentice-Hall, 1979.

VALENZUELA, LUISA (1938–)

One of the best known contemporary Latin American writers, Luisa Valenzuela is most noted for her innovative use of language and for her concern with politics, especially sexual politics. Indeed, literature and politics have both played a key role in her own life. As the daughter of the Argentine writer Luisa Mercedes Levinson, Valenzuela's exposure to and interest in literature began very early. She started her career as a journalist and has published articles in numerous journals, newspapers, and magazines in Buenos Aires and New York. Her creative work has been very well received and, to date, consists of six novels and several collections of short stories, many of which have been translated into English. Valenzuela's political concerns led her to leave Argentina in 1979, and she lived in voluntary exile, teaching and working in New York City and Mexico City. Recently, however, she returned to Buenos Aires. Her political activities have included work against political repression and censorship with such groups as PEN International (a worldwide organization of poets, essayists, editors, and novelists concerned with literacy issues, support for writers, freedom of speech, and human rights), Amnesty International, and America Watch.

Valenzuela's fiction is consistently politically engaged, often denouncing the oppressive tactics of authoritarianism as well as the repression of and violence against women. For Valenzuela, these two types of domination (both personal and political) are not separate but intimately intertwined, indeed, even mutually supporting. The work in which this interdependence can be most readily observed is her collection of short stories *Cambio de armas* [Other weapons (1985)], which explicitly deals with political repression, torture, desire, and problems of representation as well as gender issues, incorporating the sociopolitical context in such a way that it is inextricably related to sexuality.

The sociopolitical situation of Argentina plays a key role in her other works as well, most notably in *Cola de lagartija* [The lizard's tail (1983)] and *Aquí pasan cosas raras* [Strange things happen here (1979)]. However, the author herself pointed out in an interview that politics became important to her because of the dictatorship in Argentina (1976–1983) but that her primary concern has always been with language and the ways language is "enmasked." Thus, many of the key concerns and motifs of her work—such as myth, censorship, the unconscious, and the use of masks—have to do with identity and how it is formed and transformed through language. For example, her novel *Como en la guerra* [Like in the war (1977)] recounts the protagonist's search for identity through language by using the mythical narrative pattern of the journey.

Folkloric elements are perhaps most prevalent in the collection *Donde viven las águilas* [Up among the eagles (1988)], as several of the stories take place among the ancient peoples of Mexico. Mythical motifs are important in many of the stories, such as "Crónicas de Pueblorrojo" [The redtown chronicles (1988)], which recounts the tale of an Adamic protagonist's ritualistic attempts to name and secure a lost paradise. But while these stories use the images of a seemingly mythical and magical world, and often take the traditionally popular form of the fable, they are ultimately most concerned with language and its dialectical relationship to reality.

Popular culture infiltrates Valenzuela's work since she strives to experiment with linguistic registers and is especially interested in how discourse can both construct and deconstruct its referent. For this reason, she often plays with the cultural materials of myth, legend, and fairy tale. In *Cola de lagartija,* for example, she uses these modes in order to satirize the mythmaking of the most famous political figures of Argentina. Myth also comes into play, as critic Sharon Magnarelli has convincingly shown, in one of the stories in *Cambio de armas*, which can be read as a subversion of the "Sleeping Beauty" fairy tale. Finally, the stories in *Los heréticos* [The heretics (1988)] attempt to deconstruct the myths propagated by Catholicism.

Mary Beth Tierney-Tello

See also Fable; Fairy Tale; Myth; Women

****

References

Castillo, Debra A. "Approaching the Master's Weapons: Luisa Valenzuela." In *Talking Back: Toward a Latin American Feminist Literary Criticism*. Ithaca, N.Y.: Cornell University Press, 1992.

Magnarelli, Sharon. *Reflections/Refractions: Reading Luisa Valenzuela*. New York: Peter Lang, 1988.

The Review of Contemporary Fiction 6:3 (1986) [number entirely dedicated to Luisa Valenzuela's work].

Victorian Fairy Lore

Partially inherited from the romantic era, the Victorian fascination with fairies manifested itself in the collecting of native fairy lore and the use of this material in literature, the visual arts, and drama. Speculation on the origin and nature of fairies and their lore was spurred first by nationalism and the threats posed by the growing

Fairy lore pervaded the literature, visual arts, and drama of the Victorian era, as shown in this drawing by J. A. Fitzgerald.

industrialism, urbanism, and materialism. Later, stimulated by Darwinian thought and advances in the social sciences as well as by interest in occult phenomena, Victorians accumulated and analyzed fairy lore, providing most of the materials available today.

Romantic antiquarians, including Sir Walter Scott, had revived the study of fairy lore and legends or *Sagen* (half-believed tales of elfin activity). To influential volumes like Thomas Keightley's *Fairy Mythology* (1828), Victorians added large quantities of previously uncollected materials native to the British Isles. Important works include J. F. Campbell's *Popular Tales of the West Highlands* (1860–1862), William Henderson's *Folk-lore of the Northern Counties of England* (1866), and John Rhys's *Celtic Folklore, Welsh and Manx* (1901).

Fairy lore—often informed by the growing discipline of folklore—permeated Victorian literature; it pervades the novels of Charles Dickens and Charlotte and Emily Brontë as well as the poetry of William Butler Yeats, Christina Rossetti, William Morris, William Allingham, and Alfred, Lord Tennyson. It profoundly influenced the writing of literary fairy tales and fantasies for both children and adults—including the works of Charles Kingsley, Lewis Carroll, and George MacDonald. The popularity of fairy lore contributed to the rise of a new artistic genre: fairy painting. Noteworthy examples include Richard Dadd's *Fairy Feller's Master Stroke* (c. 1855–1864), Sir Joseph Noel Paton's *Fairy Raid* (1867), and Richard Doyle's illustrations to the book *In Fairyland* (1870). Fairy lore also infiltrated romantic ballet, pantomime, and legitimate theater, culminating in plays like James Barrie's *Peter Pan* (1904).

By the 1880s, increasing interest in the occult had led some people to assert the reality of fairies. Yeats, Sabine Baring-Gould, and Robert Louis Stevenson were among those writers who provided *memorates* (personal accounts of supernatural experiences), and Sir Arthur Conan Doyle defended the authenticity of the controversial Cottingley fairy photographs—pictures of fairies taken by two young girls. Meanwhile, eminent anthropologists and folklorists—including Edward Burnet Tylor, David MacRitchie, and Andrew Lang—were investigating the origins of fairies and their lore. Major theories included the mythological theory (lore is the detritus of ancient myth or the distortion of ancient language), the pygmy theory (fairies and their lore derive from folk memories of dwarflike Mongol invaders later conquered by the Celts), and the survival theory (lore preserves vestiges of the "savage" states of prehistoric culture). Although these theories are now discredited, twentieth-century scholars recognize the importance of the Victorians as investigators, preservers, and systematizers of fairy lore.

Carole Silver

See also Lang, Andrew; Rossetti, Christina Georgina

✱✱✱✱✱✱✱✱✱✱✱✱✱✱✱✱✱✱

References

Briggs, K. M. *The Fairies in English Tradition and Literature*. Chicago: University of Chicago Press, 1967.

Doyle, Sir Arthur Conan. *The Coming of the Fairies*. London: Pavilion, 1922.

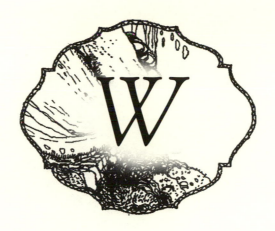

Walker, Alice (1944–)

The award-winning author Alice Walker was born in Eatonton, Georgia, to Minnie Lue and Willie Lee Walker. In 1965, Alice Walker received her B.A. from Sarah Lawrence and in 1972, her Ph.D. from Russell Sage College. Actively involved in the civil rights movement and a consulting editor for *Ms. Magazine*, she has also served as a professor of writing and literature at a number of colleges and universities: Wellesley, Yale, Brandeis, and California at Berkeley. The recipient of numerous awards and honors, Walker was the first black woman to receive the Pulitzer Prize for fiction for her 1982 novel, *The Color Purple*. Presently, she works with Wild Trees Press, which she founded in 1984. Walker's writing includes poetry, stories, and novels, the most notable (in addition to *The Color Purple*) being *The Third Life of Grange Copeland* (1970), *Meridian* (1976), *The Temple of My Familiar* (1989), and *Possessing the Secret of Joy* (1992).

Walker does more than merely speak to or comment on folklore, she "inspirits" her work with it. For Walker, folklore teaches and in teaching helps to save a people. For example, in *The Third Life of Grange Copeland*, Grange teaches his granddaughter the tales of Uncle Remus, both re-creating and reincarnating them, in order to save her life. But Grange is not merely the teller of tales; he analyzes them as he goes along. Although he may see Uncle Remus as a "shag-assed minstrel," at the same time he desires to transform him into what is needed for black people: "a goddam statesman." Not coincidentally, Walker has Grange's desires precisely match the historical changes being attempted at the time through the statesmanship of Martin Luther King. Thus, folklore is not to be analyzed and studied abstractly but to be made use of and lived.

This sense of folkloric tales as being integral to and even salvific of life is not new, of course, and Walker acknowledges a debt to Zora Neale Hurston. An equally strong emphasis on the teller of the tale and its orality is evidenced in all of Walker's work, including *The Color Purple*, which has been criticized as an epistolary novel in the eighteenth-century Anglo tradition; yet epistolarity is used to "render the quintessential black verbal behavior of call-and-response" (Awkward 1989, p. 145). Perhaps Walker's ultimate use of call and response is in *The Temple of My Familiar*, in which Lissie invites us into the temple of *our* familiar, into a dazzling and all-embracing world

Alice Walker, the first African-American woman to win a Pulitzer Prize with her novel The Color Purple *in 1982, infuses her work with folklore as an educational tool.*

telling us tales, literally bodying them forth, and awaiting our response.

Josie Campbell

See also Harris, Joel Chandler; Hurston, Zora Neale; Orality; Uncle Remus

✳✳✳✳✳✳✳✳✳✳✳✳✳✳✳✳✳

References

Awkward, Michael. "*The Color Purple* and the Achievement of (Comm)unity." In *Inspiriting Influences: Tradition, Revision, and Afro-American Women's Novels*, pp. 135–164. New York: Columbia University Press, 1989.

Gates, Henry Louis, Jr. "Color Me Zora: Alice Walker's (Re)Writing of the Speakerly Text." In *The Signifying Monkey: A Theory of African-American Literary Criticism*, pp. 239–258. New York: Oxford University Press, 1988.

Harris, Trudier. "Folklore in the Fiction of Alice Walker: A Perpetuation of Historical and Literary Traditions." *Black American Literature Forum* 11 (Spring 1977): 3–8.

THE WANDERING JEW

The wandering Jew is a legend based on a rebuff or an act of violence a man inflicted on Jesus Christ en route to Calvary: the man's punishment is to wander until Judgment Day. Sources vary about whether he actually shoved Jesus (hence his common name, Botadeo, or "God pusher") or refused him rest, chiding him not to linger with the cross. His most well-known names are Ahasver or Ahasuerus.

The penitent figure is reminiscent of the cast-out Cain, the traitor Judas, and the disobedient Pindola of Buddhist lore, and he is often a conflation of Cartaphilus and Malchus from the Gospel of John. There are relatively stable features of his persona: he is indestructible, restless, taciturn, always standing, possessed of five silver coins at daybreak, forbidden to develop personal ties, and either immortal or self-rejuvenating at the age of 100. Matthew Gregory Lewis's romance *The Monk* (1795) crystallizes many commonplaces of the Jew's morphology: he cannot spend more than two weeks in one place, affects people perversely, wears a burning cross on his forehead, and can converse with the dead. Interpretations are legion: for some people, he represents the hardy, migratory, and persecuted Jewish people; for others, he is a warning against unbelief.

Points of contact with other legends abound. Samuel Taylor Coleridge was inspired by the figure for his immortal mariner, as Johann Wolfgang von Goethe almost certainly was for his Faust. Heinrich Heine refers to the Flying Dutchman, condemned to sail forever for firing on the Lord in defiance, as "the Wandering Jew of the oceans." Other fictional characters, such as Fortunatus and his infinite purse, Cyprian, Manfred, and the wild huntsman all resonate in the Jew as well, and O. Henry's story "Door of Unrest" unites the figure with the Seven Whistlers legend.

A key source for later developments was the 1602 German chapbook, *Ahasver-Volksbuch*; the *Alliterative Morte Arthure*, Friedrich Schiller's *Der Geisterseher* (1789), and Thomas Percy's *Reliques of Ancient English Poetry* all include defining versions. Eino Railo relates that it was C. F. D. Schubart's conception of the Jew (1783) that first took the motif from folklore to artistic literature, wherein the outcast came to be a symbol of *Weltschmerz*, or "world sorrow." In Schubart's conception, the Jew fails at a series of suicidal ventures and then is mercifully granted liberating death.

Characteristic romantic fellow-feeling and pathos appear in William Wordsworth's "Song for the Wandering Jew" (1800): "I feel the trouble, / Of the Wanderer in my soul." A typical view of the wandering Jew as sufferer, for whom imperviousness is torment, is in Percy Bysshe Shelley's posthumously printed work "The Wandering Jew's Soliloquy" (1810) and in the seventh canto of *Queen Mab*. In another interpretation, Eugene Sue's *Le Juif errant* [The wandering Jew], the cobbler Ahasuerus, suffering from an inability to provide for his family, refuses the sufferer and realizes too late the divine charge to repent, to be charitable, and to love. Guillaume Apollinaire's early-twentieth-century approach in *The Wandering Jew and Other Stories* is, by contrast, an ironic, decadent celebration of a life of errantry, lust, wickedness, and carpe diem.

Some nineteenth-century works, like Charles Maturin's *Melmoth the Wanderer* (1892), infused occult, demonic dimensions into the heretofore pathetic figure. Some renderings stressed his longevity over atonement: for example, a protagonist of William Godwin's *St. Leon* (1799), tired of his unnatural eternity, wishes to pass the secrets of the elixir of life to others. Thomas Medwin's poem "The Wanderer" casts the Jew as "the chronicle of time, or age himself." Adding another twist, Rudyard Kipling's hero of "The Wandering Jew," a story in the book *Life's Handicap* (1891), sails east perpetually in an attempt to attain immortality. Some treatments reflect ambivalence. In "Life," the Brazilian master Machado de Assis paints a defiant anti-Christ nature in Ahasver's dialogue with Prometheus, another rebel who likens the Jew's renewable money to Prometheus's liver. Ahasver blames the fallen fire-bringer for having inflicted life on him, whereupon it is revealed to the Jew that he connects the divine and the ephemeral, embodying the hope of a new, higher race.

Works by the Colombian Gabriel García Márquez, such as *One Hundred Years of Solitude* (1970) and "One Day after Saturday," in *No One Writes to the Colonel and Other Stories* (1962), revives the wandering Jew as an impersonal portent of the apocalypse and the transmission of a plaguelike curse. Similarly, Galit Hasan-Rokem notes the Danish folk belief that when the "cobbler of Jerusalem" comes to Denmark, the world ends.

Other contributions to the theme include Nathaniel Hawthorne's "The Virtuoso's Collection," Stefan Heym's *The Wandering Jew*, Enrique Anderson Imbert's "The Magic Book," Samuel Rawet's *Viagens de Ahasverus à Terra Alheia*, Edgar Quinet's *Ahasverus*, David

Pinski's Yiddish play *The Eternal Jew*, Albert Soergel's *Ahasver-Dichtungen seit Goethe*, and Edgar Knecht's *Le Mythe du Juif errant*.

R. Kelly Washbourne

See also Goethe, Johann Wolfgang von; Hawthorne, Nathaniel; Legend

✳✳✳✳✳✳✳✳✳✳✳✳✳✳✳✳✳

References

Anderson, George K. *The Legend of the Wandering Jew*. Providence, R.I.: Brown University Press, 1965.

Baring-Gould, S. *Curious Myths of the Middle Ages*. London: Rivingtons, 1867.

Hasan-Rokem, Galit, and Alan Dundes. *The Wandering Jew: Essays in the Interpretation of a Christian Legend*. Bloomington: Indiana University Press, 1986.

Lowes, John Livingston. *The Road to Xanadu: A Study in the Ways of the Imagination*. Boston and New York: Houghton Mifflin, 1927.

Railo, Eino. *The Haunted Castle: A Study of the Elements of English Romanticism*. New York: Humanities Press, 1964.

Wellerisms

Wellerisms are short oral or literary texts consisting of three parts: a statement (quite often a proverb, proverbial expression, quotation, exclamation, etc.), a speaker who makes this remark, and a phrase or clause that places the utterance in a new light or in an incompatible setting. Most wellerisms follow this triadic structure, the incongruity of which gives them a typically humorous, ironic, or satirical effect, as in the following examples: "'It sure pays to fiddle your time away,' said the violin player as he drew down his $150 a week"; "'Overcome evil with good,' as the preacher said when he knocked a rascal down with the Bible"; "'Let there be light,' murmured the raven-haired beauty as she drew forth the peroxide bottle"; and "'Ruff,' cried the dog as he sat on the cactus." There are shortened texts like "'I'm bored stiff,' said the dead man" as well as longer texts expanded into welleresque dialogues: "'Do you see the point?' asked the needle of the cloth as it passed through it. 'No, but I feel it,' replied the cloth with a groan." The joy and delight in creating one pun after another leads to such strings of wellerisms, in which the speaker of one text is challenged by another.

The origin and history of wellerisms are quite nebulous. Early examples have been found on Sumerian cuneiform tablets as well as in classical Greek and Latin literature. Wellerisms begin to appear in European proverb collections of the sixteenth century, in which many are reduced versions of longer fables, tall tales, and other folk narratives. The most obvious is "'The grapes are sour,' said the fox and couldn't reach them," which is a mere remnant of an Aesopian fable. In English literature, wellerisms appear in the works of the Venerable Bede, Geoffrey Chaucer, William Shakespeare, Ben Jonson, Jonathan Swift, and others. In the United States, Benjamin Franklin cited "'Great wits jump [agree],' says the poet, and hit his head against the post" in August 1735 in *Poor Richard's Almanac*. A more modern author of detective novels, Leslie Charteris, has made frequent use of somewhat suggestive wellerisms with a bishop and an actress as the main characters, such as "'But I'm not nearly satisfied yet,' as the actress said to the bishop."

Wellerisms play a particularly important role in Charles Dickens's novel *Posthumous Papers of the Pickwick Club* (1836–1837). Indeed, since 1839, the name of humorous character Sam Weller has given the genre its internationally accepted designation, "wellerism." In this literary work, wellerisms, with a certain ironic detachment, comment on such themes as marriage, politics, violence, class distinctions, and aggression. They are for the most part quite different from some of the funnier texts that were published in magazines and newspapers in Great Britain and the United States during the period from about 1840 to 1880 when there was literally a "wellerism mania." Although short lists of wellerisms do not appear in today's popular press, they still compete, as a genre of verbal folklore, with jokes, one-liners, puns, and other forms of popular humor. The popularity of wellerisms may have waned, but they have not altogether faded.

Wolfgang Mieder

See also Aesop's Fables; Chaucer, Geoffrey; Dickens, Charles; Proverbs; Shakespeare, William; Tall Tale; Taylor, Archer

✳✳✳✳✳✳✳✳✳✳✳✳✳✳✳✳✳✳✳

References

Baer, Florence E. "Wellerisms in *The Pickwick Papers*." *Folklore* (London) 94 (1983): 173–183.

Loomis, C. Grant. "Traditional American Wordplay: Wellerisms or Yankeeisms." *Western Folklore* 8 (1949): 1–21.

Mieder, Wolfgang. *American Proverbs: A Study of Texts and Contexts*. Bern: Peter Lang, 1989.

Mieder, Wolfgang, and Stewart A. Kingsbury. *A Dictionary of Wellerisms*. New York: Oxford University Press, 1994.

Taylor, Archer. *The Proverb*. Reprint, with intro. and biblio. by Wolfgang Mieder. Bern: Peter Lang, 1985 (1931).

Whiting, Bartlett Jere. "American Wellerisms of the Golden Age." *American Speech* 20 (1945): 3–11.

WELSH LITERATURE

Welsh literature includes works written in Welsh (a Celtic language) and later works written in English (Anglo-Welsh, e.g., works by the poets Henry Vaughan and Dylan Thomas). At various times, medieval Welsh folktales and legends—especially those of King Arthur—have been the basis of movements of national identification and pride.

The earliest extant literature in Welsh—one of the oldest surviving literatures in Western Europe—consists of early medieval heroic and gnomic poetry. Welsh poetry of all periods is highly formal, with strict meters and poetic forms defined by the number of lines in a stanza or the number of syllables in a line, by precise rules of "rhyme" and alliteration within a line (*cynghanedd*, "harmony") and between lines, and by other forms of metrical ornamentation. Bards were socially important in heroic Welsh society, writing elegies, praise poems, and laments for patrons as well as poems on mysticism and nature. The *Gododdin*, the Llywarch Hen cycle, and the other poems of the Cynfeirdd or "early poets," such as Aneirin and Taliesin, are preserved in late medieval manuscripts. There are fragments of prose legal and calendrical texts in Old Welsh; the earliest prose about Wales is in Latin.

Poets writing between c. 1100 and c. 1350 are called Gogynfeirdd ("rather early poets"). Their work is marked by a deliberate archaism of language and frequent allusions to Welsh, classical, and religious legends. Poets writing before the English annexation of Wales in the late thirteenth century are also called "the poets of the princes"; those writing after the end of the Welsh princes are called "the poets of the gentry (or nobility)." From the thirteenth to the seventeenth centuries, such poets, often of high social class themselves, continued to praise their patrons.

One of Wales's most outstanding poets—considered by many to be among the best of the European poets—was the fourteenth-century Dafydd ap Gwilym, who exemplifies the transition from the earlier tradition to a wider European tradition of late medieval poetry with his more personal, lyrical, and often satirical treatment of love, nature, and religion.

Medieval prose literature in Welsh consists of original works as well as of translations and adaptations from English, French, and Latin (pseudo-) histories and romances, which link Welsh literature with the rest of medieval Western Europe and often present familiar folk motifs. The four tales or "branches" of the medieval Welsh work *Mabinogi(on)*, which preserve elements of pre-Christian Celtic mythology, are the most well-known romances, and they were introduced to English readers in the nineteenth-century popular Everyman series translation by Lady Charlotte Guest. The story of King Arthur is among Wales's most important literary contributions, forming from its earliest appearances an important national theme.

In 1536 the Act of Union made the English language the "official" language of Wales after a half-century of increasing bilingualism, and many writers began to imitate English styles. However, traditional Welsh-language poetic meters endured, and the Bible and other religious works were translated into Welsh. New religious prose and poetry were written, as were dictionaries, grammars, and works on classical history. There were new moralistic and religious themes, often expressing personal emotion. A few sixteenth-century plays on biblical or morally didactic themes, similar to English mystery plays, have survived.

In the seventeenth, eighteenth, and nineteenth centuries, antiquarians collected and thereby preserved older texts. Popular "song-book" collections were also common. In the seventeenth century, religious groups such as the Puritans sought to make literacy widespread and printed pamphlets that were read by many people. The important hymn writer William Williams (Pantycelyn) lived from 1717 to 1791. Verse was often written to be sung to particular pieces of music, including English song melodies ("carol poetry"), and "harp stanzas" *(penillion/ penillion telyn)*, verses sung to harp accompaniment, survive, especially in seventeenth-century manuscripts. About 40 eighteenth-century Welsh-language "interludes," versified dramas performed at inns and fairs, are extant, and these present Welsh pseudohistory, ballads, and religious themes or offer social criticism.

The nineteenth century was a time of major social and political change and great literary productivity, especially in the Welsh language. Welsh-language *eisteddfodau* (singular, *eisteddfod*) ("poetical and musical translation"), were revived, resuming an interrupted tradition. Prose writings remained largely theological, although some stories (including folk and fairy tales) were written down and by the end of the century, novels were being written in both Welsh and English. Modern scholarship on Celtic topics began, and the Welsh in Patagonia, who first settled there in 1865, have also contributed to literature in the Welsh language.

The twentieth century has been a period of scholarly and literary revival and nationalism. Poetry is popular, and the National Eisteddfod and local *eisteddfodau* flourish. Short stories, essays, translations, novels, and plays of high quality have been written in great numbers in both Welsh and English (e.g., works by Kate Roberts and Saunders Lewis).

Pamela S. Morgan

See also Arthur, King; Celtic Literature; Legend

✳✳✳✳✳✳✳✳✳✳✳✳✳✳✳✳✳✳

References
Jones, R. M. *Highlights in Welsh Literature*. Swansea and Llandybie, Wales: Christopher Davies, 1969.

Stephens, Meic. *The Oxford Companion to the Literature of Wales*. Oxford: Oxford University Press, 1986.

Welty, Eudora (1909–)

A southern American writer of short stories and novels, Eudora Welty was born in Jackson, Mississippi, and incorporates into her writing southern folkways, a sense of place, and oral tradition along with folktales, legends, and Greek, Roman, and Celtic mythology. She models her writing on the vernacular speech and storytelling conventions of the American South, and her fiction often involves journeys, quests, rituals, and folk motifs. Welty once said in an interview that "folklore and fiction are different branches of the same thing" (Ferris 1977, p. 25). Her works include five novels, five short-story collections, a book of essays, a book of photographs, and an autobiography.

A Curtain of Green and Other Stories (1941) is a collection of her earliest stories, including "A Worn Path." In this story, Phoenix Jackson's journey and quest, along with her name, suggest a mythical dimension. The importance of ritual and action in Welty's fiction, especially private or family ritual, is apparent in these early stories. In "Death of a Travelling Salesman," Prometheus is alluded to by the pivotal phrase and action of the young husband to "borry some fire."

The Robber Bridegroom (1942) contains Welty's most extensive use of folklore forms and motifs. It is a mixture of literary fairy tale, Greek and Roman mythology, folktales, frontier legends, tall tales, fantasy, and frontier realism. Welty's story of Rosamond, the beautiful daughter of a wealthy planter, and Jamie Lockhart, a bandit on the Natchez Trace, suggests not only a tale by the brothers Grimm but also the monster or animal bridegroom tales, such as "Beauty and the Beast," and the tale of Cupid and Psyche from Apuleius of Madaura's second-century work, *The Golden Ass*. Motifs include mistaken identity, the breaking of a taboo, a wicked stepmother, a house in the wood, a magic formula, magic objects, and talismans. Characters from frontier legend and history, such as Mike Fink and the Harp brothers, also appear. The young maiden, however, is more practical than virtuous and values her life over her honor. Much of the humor comes from the reversal of expectations. When Rosamond opens her mouth to speak, lies rather than pearls spill out, enabling her to survive on the frontier. The duality of existence is a major theme, and the doubleness that is typical of folktales is used thematically.

The Wide Net and Other Stories (1943) continues Welty's use of folklore, particularly in the story "Livvie." This story involves the marriage of a girl of 16 to Soloman, an old man on the Natchez Trace. The Trip Around the World quilt pattern contrasts with Livvie's isolation, and the bottle trees are symbolic of Livvie's entrapment and of Solomon's fears that she will be spirited away. In the yard, each branch of the crape myrtle trees ends in a blue or green bottle. A southern black folk belief is that bottle trees protect a home by luring evil spirits into the bottles, where they are trapped.

Delta Wedding (1946) is based partly on legends and stories of the Mississippi Delta region. Quilts and quilting patterns are significant in this work, as well as the customs and rituals of weddings and family celebrations. *The Golden Apples* (1949) uses myth as a structural and thematic device, but there is no strict mythological system to decode. There are parallels between Greek and Celtic mythology and the recurring characters, particularly in "June Recital" and "Shower of Gold." Allusions to mythology include Zeus, Danae, Leda, Perseus, and Medusa as well as the Celtic wandering Aengus. Proverbs are also used in "Shower of Gold."

The Ponder Heart (1954) contains folk humor and tall-tale narration in addition to folk beliefs, such as having a "frizzly hen" in the yard to uncover evil spells. *The Bride of Innisfallen and Other Stories* (1955) includes one story, "Circe," that is based on the enchantress. *Losing Battles* (1970) is a portrayal of southern oral tradition, with old family stories related by family members. It also depicts a southern family reunion as a festival or celebration, along with its rituals and games. *The Optimist's Daughter* (1972) presents the customs and rituals of funerals and associated folk beliefs and omens, such as a bird flying in the house.

The Collected Stories of Eudora Welty (1980) includes "The Demonstrators," which captures the essence of folkways and folk beliefs in a traditional southern community when the civil rights movement was at its height. Welty's works of nonfiction—*The Eye of the Story: Selected Essays and Reviews* (1971), *One Time, One Place: Mississippi in the Depression* (1971), and *One Writer's Beginnings* (1984)—provide valuable insights regarding oral tradition, sense of place, and southern folkways.

Marcia Gaudet

See also *Golden Ass*; Grimm, Jacob and Wilhelm; Legend; Motif; Myth; Quilting; Ritual; Tall Tale

✳✳✳✳✳✳✳✳✳✳✳✳✳✳✳✳✳

References

Ferris, Bill. *Images of the South: Visits with Eudora Welty and Walker Evans.* Memphis: Center for Southern Folklore, 1977.

Kreyling, Michael. *Eudora Welty's Achievement of Order.* Baton Rouge: Louisiana State University Press, 1980.

Prenshaw, Peggy Whitman, ed. *Eudora Welty: Critical Essays.* Jackson: University Press of Mississippi, 1979.

Vande Kieft, Ruth M. *Eudora Welty.* Rev. ed. Boston: Twayne Publishers, 1987.

WESTON, JESSIE LAIDLEY (1850–1928)

Jessie Laidley Weston translated and wrote about medieval European literature, primarily Arthuriana. The British poet T. S. Eliot gave enthusiastic credit and thereby longevity to Weston's best known work, *From Ritual to Romance* (1920). It provided not only the title but also the plan and some of the symbols found in his momentous work *The Waste Land* (1922).

Eliot's footnotes to *The Waste Land* also credit *The Golden Bough* (1890) by James George Frazer, which had likewise inspired Weston. In prose not poetry, *From Ritual to Romance* expresses Weston's imaginative application of the Frazerian worldview to one recurring theme in Arthurian romance: the quest for the Holy Grail. By using historical evidence in ways no longer considered valid by folklorists or anthropologists, Weston created an intriguing scenario wherein the Holy Grail, its guardian the fisher king, and other enigmatic elements of the legend are said to have survived from rituals practiced by mystery cults predating Christianity.

Although Weston did publish one volume each of poems (1896) and short fiction (1900), most of her creative energy went toward the preparation of medieval literature for a popular readership. Her earliest publications, in 1894–1896, honored Richard Wagner: a verse translation of his source *Parzival* by Wolfram von Eschenbach, which was soon followed by a retelling of *Lohengrin* and a synopsis of sources for Wagner's other operas. Between 1897 and 1909, Weston published four book-length studies (on Gawain, Lancelot, "The Three Days' Tournament," and Perceval) and seven volumes of prose translations of Arthurian materials. She continued to produce articles for periodicals and encyclopedias, translations from Middle English, pamphlets denouncing German claims to cultural supremacy, and in 1913 a book that she later reworked into *From Ritual to Romance*. Influential toward that revision were the writings of "the Cambridge group" of anthropologically inclined classicists, especially F. M. Cornford and J. E. Harrison, who had applied Frazerian ideas to ancient Greek drama.

Weston herself never attended university. She was awarded a D.Litt. by the University of Wales in 1923 for her services to Celtic literature, and she cofounded the Lyceum and Halcyon Clubs and held memberships in the Folk-Lore Society, the Quest Society, and Wagnerverein. While at work on another Arthurian book, she died in a London nursing home. Her personal life remains, as she fully intended, a mystery.

Betsy Bowden

See also Arthurian Tradition; Frazer, James George; *The Golden Bough*; Legend; Romance

✳✳✳✳✳✳✳✳✳✳✳✳✳✳✳✳✳

References

Hyman, Stanley Edgar. "Jessie Weston and the Forest of Broceliande." *Centennial Review* 9 (1965): 509–521.

Weston, Jessie L. *From Ritual to Romance*. Foreword by Robert A. Segal. Princeton, N.J.: Princeton University Press, 1993 (1920).

WHITTIER, JOHN GREENLEAF (1807–1892)

John Greenleaf Whittier was an amateur folklorist as well as a gifted poet inspired by folklore. As a young, radical Quaker, he edited and wrote prose for a number of antislavery newspapers and magazines; his early poetry dealt almost exclusively with abolition. After the American Civil War, religion, nature, and New England rural life became the major themes of his poetry, and country poems like *Snow-Bound* (1866) made him the most popular rural New England poet.

Although he had little formal education, he was an avid reader, especially of Robert Burns, who influenced Whittier's art and kindled his interest in folklore. This interest in folklore is reflected in Whittier's first book, *Legends of New England in Prose and Verse* (1831), in "New England Superstitions" (1833), and in *The Supernaturalism of New England* (1847). Although much of the material for his folklore publications came from printed sources, he also collected some traditions from family and acquaintances.

Whittier was interested in folklore mainly as a source for literature. He wrote in the introduction to *The Supernaturalism of New England* that he collected "the present superstitions and still current traditions of New England, in the hope that [they] . . . may hereafter furnish materials for the essayist and poet, who shall one day do for our native land what Scott and Hogg and Burns and Wilson have done for theirs" (Whittier 1847, p. vii). That statement describes his aim in using folklore in his own poetry. Thus, in "Telling the Bees," for instance, he emulates folk-ballad style, incorporates folk belief, and utilizes a common folklore motif of separation and return.

One of many traditional tales and ballads developing the separation and return motif is the British folk ballad "Lord Lovel," with which Whittier's "Telling the Bees" shares the same structure: separation of loved ones, a longing for reunion, return of the departed one, a sign that there is a death on return, and the realization that the loved one at home has died. In the spirit of a folklorist, Whittier annotates in a footnote to the poem the belief that bees will leave their hive if they are not told of a death in the family and if their hive is not covered:

A remarkable custom, brought from the Old Country, formerly prevailed in the rural districts of New England. On the death of a member of the family, the bees were at once informed of the event, and their hives dressed in mourning. This ceremonial was supposed to be necessary to prevent the swarms from leaving their hives and seeking a new home. (Bradley 1974, p. 1519)

In *Legends of New England*, Whittier acknowledged that he set out "to present in an interesting form some of the popular traditions and legends of new England" (Whittier 1831, pref.). He presented regional lore and language not only in his collections of folklore but also in his literary ballads, which metrically, thematically, and structurally were modeled on folk ballads. So successful was he in capturing qualities of the folk-ballad style that few American poets have matched his skill as a writer of literary ballads.

Ronald L. Baker

See also Ballad; Burns, Robert; Legend; Literary Ballad; Motif

✳✳✳✳✳✳✳✳✳✳✳✳✳✳✳✳✳✳

References

Bradley, Sculley, et al. *The American Tradition in Literature*. New York: Grossett & Dunlap, 1974.

Von Frank, Albert J. *Whittier: A Comprehensive Annotated Bibliography*. New York: Garland, 1976.

Whittier, John Greenleaf. *Legends of New England*. Hartford, Conn.: Hanmer and Phelps, 1831.

———. "New England Superstitions." *New England Magazine* (July 1833). Reprinted in *The Supernaturalism of New England*, ed. Edward Wagenknecht, pp. 119–129. Norman: University of Oklahoma Press, 1969.

————. *The Supernaturalism of New England*. London: Wiley and Putnam, 1847.

WILD MAN

A protean form of nature spirit, usually appearing as a hirsute humanoid being that lives in forests apart from civilization, the wild man is found in oral traditions throughout the world. It is one of the oldest folkloric figures in literary texts, a symbol commonly used for exploring culturally specific definitions of humanity.

In its earliest literary manifestations, the wild man motif (F567) embraces such figures as Enkidu in the ancient Sumerian epic *Gilgamesh*; the giants of Genesis in Judeo-Christian tradition; and the satyrs, centaurs, and Cyclops of ancient Greek and Roman mythology. Grendel, of the eighth-century C.E. Anglo-Saxon epic poem *Beowulf*, resembles the hairy apelike giant of Germanic saga, and the wild man's humanity was a persistent theme in medieval encyclopedias and literature.

Augustine of Hippo, in his medieval treatise *The City of God*, pondered theological aspects of humanoid "monstrous races" seen as either a negation of the Christian ideal or part of the deliberate diversity of creation. Bercilak, in the fourteenth-century romance *Sir Gawain and the Green Knight*, is a noble individual whose suggested ancestor is "the green man," a wild man figure from England; but one unnamed wild man in Edmund Spenser's *Faerie Queene* (1590–1596) is bestial, cannibalistic, and incapable of speech. The dangerous, unrestrained sexuality of wild men and wild women was frequently represented in oral tradition, carnival, and iconography and in the literature of the European Middle Ages, but gradually, wild men became a heraldic device, a potent yet domesticated symbolic guardian of nobility.

Literary manifestations of the wild man in modern literature are complicated by the age of exploration and discovery of exotic cultures. European traditions are conflated with descriptions of "savages" as writers explored primitivism in search of humanity's original condition. Hence, Caliban (an anagram for cannibal) in William Shakespeare's play *The Tempest* (1611) is identified as both a wild man and an American Indian. Jonathan Swift's satirical portrait of the hairy Yahoos in *Gulliver's Travels* (1726) is probably based on

European oral tradition and early travel accounts of both apes and African cultures; Yahoos were later reincorporated into the oral traditions of the British colonies. Rather civilized wild men of mixed origins also appear in the golden age dramas of the Spanish Renaissance, as in the comedies of Lope de Vega. Iron Hans, the wild man in one märchen from the Grimm brothers' collection, has become a standard fixture in Western tale collections.

Journalistic accounts of unusual humanoids or people who had "gone wild" by choice or misfortune circulated in the newspapers of the North American frontier; indeed, Davy Crockett is sometimes identified as an American folk hero with wild man qualities. Today, the wild man appears in yet new guises in nature writing and self-help literature, clearly as a vehicle for considering humanity's place in the natural and social world. Bigfoot (Sasquatch, Yeti) appears in popular literature and film but is notable in the writings of Peter Matthiessen and David Rains Wallace as a complex ecological symbol of human interaction with the natural environment. The poet Robert Bly uses the wild man to explore late-twentieth-century expressions of masculinity.

Robert E. Walls

See also *Beowulf*; *Gawain and the Green Knight, Sir*; Grimm, Jacob and Wilhelm; Shakespeare, William

✱✱✱✱✱✱✱✱✱✱✱✱✱✱✱✱✱

References
Bernheimer, Richard. *Wild Men of the Middle Ages: A Study in Art, Sentiment, and Demonology*. Cambridge: Harvard University Press, 1952.
Dudley, Edward, and Maximillian E. Novak, eds. *The Wild Man Within: An Image in Western Thought from the Renaissance to Romanticism*. Pittsburgh: University of Pittsburgh Press, 1972.
Halpin, Marjorie, and Michael M. Ames, eds. *Manlike Monsters on Trial: Early Records and Modern Evidence*. Vancouver: University of British Columbia Press, 1980.

WILDER, LAURA INGALLS (1867–1957)

Although Laura Ingalls Wilder began her writing career as a columnist and an essayist for the *Missouri Realist* in 1911, she is best known for her eight-volume Little House series. Wilder always maintained that while everything in her books was true, the series did not tell the entire truth and should not be taken as a literal history. In fact, the Little House books function as literary retellings of personal experience narratives, describe many aspects of folklife, and reveal much about Wilder's own values and attitudes.

Wilder said repeatedly that her books were really meant as a memorial to her beloved father, Charles Ingalls, and that she wrote *Little House in the Big Woods* (1832) so that another generation of children might enjoy his wonderful stories. The enthusiastic response of her young readers provided the impetus for Wilder to continue the series. Moreover, her acute awareness of her audience led Wilder to eliminate or downplay certain stories that she felt inappropriate for children.

Her choice of subject matter was also undoubtedly influenced by her own reluctance to discuss difficult, unhappy subjects and by her desire to emphasize "the values of hard work, personal stoicism, courage, cheerfulness, family solidarity, and a positive outlook as both survival tools and sources of admirable character" (Adam 1987, p. 98). For instance, Wilder elected not to include the story of Kate Bender in *Little House on the Prairie* (1935), though her daughter, Rose Wilder Lane, did make use of it in her adult novel, *Free Land* (1938). Kate Bender and her two brothers ran the only tavern on the road south out of Independence, Kansas, and they prospered by murdering their guests, stealing their possessions, and burying their bodies in the garden. The Benders' crimes were eventually discovered, and a posse of area residents, including Charles Ingalls, pursued them. After the posse returned, Charles Ingalls said the Benders would never again be found, and Wilder "later formed [her] own conclusions why." Certainly the Bender narrative qualifies as a difficult, unhappy subject, especially since it casts Charles Ingalls in a somewhat unflattering light, and Wilder herself deemed it a story not "fit . . . for a children's book." Furthermore, it does not stress the values and attitudes central to Wilder's series or her own beliefs.

Some controversy surrounds Rose Wilder Lane's involvement in Wilder's work, but it seems unlikely that Lane, rather than Wilder, actually wrote the series. Lane was a best-selling novelist long before her mother began her writing career; and the daughter's portraits of the prairie are far more realistic, even naturalistic, than her mother's. The personal experience narratives the two women selected for their individual works reflect the differences in their audiences, their views of the pioneer experience, and their own values and beliefs.

Debbie A. Hanson

See also Personal Experience Story
✳✳✳✳✳✳✳✳✳✳✳✳✳✳✳✳✳✳

References
Adam, Kathryn. "Laura, Ma, Mary, Carrie, and Grace: Western Women as Portrayed by Laura Ingalls Wilder." In *The Women's West,* ed. Susan Armitage and Elizabeth Jameson, pp. 95–110. Norman: University of Oklahoma Press, 1987.
Anderson, William T., ed. *A Little House Sampler.* New York: Harper and Row, 1988.

WITCHCRAFT

Belief in witchcraft, broadly defined as the possession and practice of supernatural powers, has existed in many cultures from ancient times to the present. In European folklore, the witch has taken the form of an evil personage linked with the devil. Although the evil-minded, destructive crone has been the most common witch figure in European and American folklore, there have also been beautiful, seductive young female witches and young or older male witches. Not all witches in folk tradition are evil; some are benevolent, wise individuals who use their supernatural powers for good. In literature, however, evil witches greatly outnumber those of good intent.

Witches abound in both folktales and legends. Some of the better known witches are cannibals, including the evil occupant of the gingerbread house in "Hansel and Gretel" (AT 327A) and Baba Yaga of Russian folktales, who lives in a house on chicken feet— both of those elderly witches enjoy cooking and eating young children. Hans Christian Andersen's sea witch in "The Little Mermaid" is cruel and destructive to children, and the old witch in "Rapunzel" (AT 310) is unnaturally restrictive with regard to her young charge. Many local legends tell of witches that capture, incarcerate, injure, and eat children. With both folktales and legends emphasizing this kind of witch figure, it is not surprising that it is a common characterization in literature.

The dangerous, child-killing witch is prominent in Heinrich Kramer and Jacob Sprenger's *Malleus maleficarum,* which reflects medieval witch beliefs and served for many years as a handbook for the prosecution of witches. Medieval epic literature also shows awareness of the deadly power of witches, notably in the figure Morgan le

The belief in witchcraft has long been an aspect of European and American folklore as in this eighteenth-century illustration of Shakespeare's three witches from Macbeth.

Fay of the Arthurian cycle. Morgan's characterization takes a different form in Marion Zimmer Bradley's *The Mists of Avalon* (1982), as in that work the priestess Morgaine uses her supernatural powers benevolently until destructive acts become necessary. This novel demonstrates the impact of contemporary neopaganism, or Wicca, which the author used to delineate aspects of goddess worship and spell casting in medieval times.

Among works of literature in the Renaissance, the best known play featuring witches is William Shakespeare's *Macbeth* (1605–1606). The three crones in this play assemble a brew of fearsome ingredients while making prophecies about the future of the central character. Other aspects of belief in witches emerge from three Jacobean plays. Thomas Middleton's *The Witch* (1810) introduces the character Hecate, whose name comes from the underworld goddess of Greek mythology; in this play, Hecate works a spell to impede fertility in a new marriage. *The Witch* was so influential that two of its songs and one dance became part of a revival version of *Macbeth*. An earlier play, John Marston's *The Tragedy of Sophonisba* (1606), explores atrocities attributed to witches in the context of Roman history. The third significant Jacobean play is *The Witch of Edmonton* (1658) by William Rowley, Thomas Dekker, and John Ford. This play dramatizes the transgressions and execution of one Elizabeth Sawyer, who lost her life in the same year that the play first appeared.

More recent plays have examined accusations of witchcraft and their tragic effects. Jean Anouilh's *The Lark* (1955) explores the misunderstandings associated with Joan of Arc's hearing voices, and Arthur Miller's *The Crucible* (1954) dramatizes the allegations by children of witchcraft activity in Salem. In contrast to the Renaissance plays, these works express considerable skepticism toward a literal interpretation of witchcraft.

A great many contemporary novels focus on witchcraft, demonstrating the continuing fascination that this subject has for readers. Ira Levin's novel *Rosemary's Baby* (1967), with its dreadful denouement of the birth of a child begotten by the devil, became an extremely popular film. So did John Updike's *The Witches of Eastwick* (1984), in which beautiful, dangerous witches use their magic in a way that defies all natural laws. Barbara Michael's *Witch* and Anne Rice's *The Witching Hour* are among the numerous other books that have developed the subject of witchcraft in a variety of settings.

Literature for children has included many books about witches. One of the most famous of these is L. Frank Baum's *The Wizard of Oz* (1939). This story, best known by the movie of the same name, features a typically evil, ugly old witch, the wicked witch of the West, as well as a lovely and helpful young witch named Glinda. In C. S. Lewis's *The Lion, the Witch, and the Wardrobe* (1950), there is only one evil witch; her characterization derives some complexity from the fact that she appears to be beautiful and kind but is actually evil and selfish. The idea of the witch as a conniving deceiver comes from Edmund Spenser's character Duessa in *The Faerie Queene*. A kind young woman falsely accused of witchcraft in early America is the heroine of Elizabeth George Speare's *The Witch of Blackbird Pond* (1958). In contrast, "the grand high witch" in Roald Dahl's *The Witches* (1983) is a thoroughly vicious spell-caster whose ambition is to destroy every child in England. The heroine of Liz Rosenberg's *Monster Mama* (1992) appears to be fearsome but actually proves to be a fine person whose son is proud to introduce her to his friends.

It is interesting to see the increase in positive witch figures in contemporary literature. However, many books of recent vintage contain images of dreadful, death-dealing witches that adhere closely to medieval models. This perpetuation of beliefs from the Middle Ages demonstrates the tenacity of folklore of the supernatural, which continues to flourish in a variety of literary forms.

Elizabeth Tucker

See also Andersen, Hans Christian; Arthurian Tradition; Belief; Epic; Folktale; Hecate; Legend; Satan; Shakespeare, William

✳✳✳✳✳✳✳✳✳✳✳✳✳✳✳✳

References

Briggs, Katharine M. *The Witch Figure*. London: Routledge and Kegan Paul, 1973.

Robbins, Rossell Hope. *Encyclopedia of Witchcraft and Demonology*. New York: Crown, 1959.

Russell, Jeffrey Burton. *Witchcraft in the Middle Ages*. Ithaca, N.Y.: Cornell University Press, 1972.

WOMEN

As women writers have emerged into the public arena, particularly in the twentieth century, it has become clear that many of them use folklore in their creative work. For all of them, it has been a vehicle for exploring matters of personal, community, and gendered identity in a literary context; for some, the very act of writing and reading within a community has enabled their engagement with the folk process itself. Although it would be impossible to list here the entire spectrum of published works in this category, the following should indicate the breadth and variety of the field.

Among the most significant and best known users of folklore are those women whose work centers upon life based in their own regional and/or ethnic communities. Zora Neale Hurston, a folklorist and ethnographer as well as a fiction writer, relates nearly the entire narrative of her masterpiece *Their Eyes Were Watching God* (1937) in an African-American idiom, with an eye and ear for local behaviors, situations, and styles; Alice Walker's *The Color Purple* (1982) and Ntozake Shange's *For Colored Girls Who Have Considered Suicide/When the Rainbow Is Enuf* (1977) are similarly firmly rooted in ethnic ways of speaking and the black American social experience. The lives of Chinese and Chinese-American women have been highlighted by means of legend, belief, storytelling, foodways, family, and social relationships by Maxine Hong Kingston in *The Woman Warrior* (1975) and *China Men* and by Amy Tan in *The Joy Luck Club* (1989) and *The Kitchen God's Wife* (1992).

In *Waterlily* (1988), anthropologist Ella Deloria incorporates many of the lifeways of one Sioux community into her narrative. Scottish novelists Nan Shepherd (*The Gowk Storm* [1928]) and Naomi Mitchison (*The Bull Calves* [1947]) employ dialect, ballad text, legend, agricultural, and calendrical customs not only to color the text but as vital thematic elements that drive their work. New Zealander Keri Hulme includes both Anglo and Maori folklore in her Booker Prize–winning *The Bone People* (1984). Joy Kogawa's *Obasan* (1981) employs the immigrant's dual-cultural vision to address the internment of Japanese Canadians during World War II. Edna O'Brien (*The Country Girls* [1960] and *Mother Ireland* [1976]) keeps a firm focus on the details of Irish folk culture in both her fiction and autobiographical nonfiction. Willa Cather's classic novels, including *My Ántonia* (1918), *O Pioneers!* (1913), and *Death Comes for the Archbishop* (1927), draw their strength in part from her sensitivity to the details of the lives of the inhabitants of the American West, particularly of the European immigrants. Many other folk traditions continue to be incorporated into literature by women, notably including but by no means limited to those of Latin America, Jewish communities, Africa, and Scandinavia.

Perhaps because folklore can be so embedded in different aspects of human communication, and also because scholarly conventions concerning the nature of literature have been evolving, the matter of folklore and literature with respect to women goes beyond classical considerations of novel and author, back into prehistory and forward into our own day. Anonymous women storytellers take their place at the origins of the orally performed and transmitted folktale, both secular and sacred, and continue in various ways to assume that role in the family and community. In terms of written literature, as Jack Zipes has discussed in *Fairy Tales and the Art of Subversion* (1983), the seventeenth-century French women writers Marie-Catherine d'Aulnoy, Catherine Bernard, Jeanne-Marie Leprince de Beaumont, and Henriette-Julie de Murat authored some of the classic written versions, loosely based on oral tales, of what ultimately became such fairy tales as "Beauty and the Beast." These same tales continue to inspire new interpretations, variations, and criticisms.

In the nineteenth century, the Grimm brothers collected many of their *Kinder- und Hausmärchen* [Children's and household tales] from women servants. More recently, Ethel Johnson Phelps and Angela Carter have edited collections of folktales from around the world with female protagonists (Phelps, *The Maid of the North* [1981]; Carter, *The Virago Book of Fairy Tales* [1991]); while no one can identify the gender of the oral tellers of all of these tales, their contemporary female editors compiled them with a heightened sensitivity to the significance to audiences of the representation of gender in the fairy tale. Further demonstrating the potential appeal of traditional tales to wide audiences outside their community of origin, Evangeline Walton's four-volume rendition of the Welsh *Mabinogion* cycle became a successful popular paperback series in the 1970s.

In addition to substantial work by women as collectors, translators, and scholars of folktales (e.g., Katherine Luomala in Hawaii, Katharine Briggs in the United Kingdom, Margaret Schlauch for Icelandic and Middle English literature, and Lady Isabella Augusta Gregory in Ireland), women folklorists and anthropologists also move through ethnography to the creation, performance, and analysis of literature, often paying particular attention to issues of gender and ethnicity. Along with the novels of Hurston and Deloria, the folklorist Rayna Green has produced *"That's What She Said"* (1992), a collection of Native American women's poetry and prose including her own creative writing; the storyteller Diane Wolkstein has crafted a translation of the tales and hymns of the great Sumerian goddess *Inanna* (1983) in collaboration with the Sumerologist Samuel Noah Kramer; and Kay Stone performs traditional stories orally as well as writing scholarly material on tales in context. As Susan Glaspell's short story "A Jury of Her Peers" addresses the subversive significance of women's folk culture within patriarchy, so Joan N. Radner and Susan S. Lanser have used Glaspell's story as a springboard to a broader consideration of women's folk coding.

A collective of women scholars, the Personal Narratives Group, has published *Interpreting Women's Lives* (1989), a collection of essays largely concerned with women's written autobiography but also with oral personal narrative—only recently recognized as a folk genre. In an appealing twist, American novelist Alison Lurie's Pulitzer Prize–winning *Foreign Affairs* (1984) has as its protagonist an American woman folklorist who travels to England to collect children's folklore, and the English writer A. S. Byatt's *Possession* (1990), winner of the Booker Prize, relies on a local French legend of the Melusine, as well as the research and descendants of a fictive Breton folklorist, as crucial strands in its complex structure.

Women folklorists have also discerned surprising and telling relationships between women and nonclassical literatures. Janice A. Radway's *Reading the Romance* (1984) explores the complicated links between the writers, readers, and publishers of popular paperback romances while Camille Bacon-Smith has discovered a thriving community of readers of often privately circulated fan literature based on television shows and movies. In addition, the goddess and women's spirituality movements and some Jungian-based psychologies are generating creative literatures and communities joined by those literatures, which heavily invoke folk traditions (including religion, material culture, and life-stage markers) in the name of rediscovering, reclaiming, and furthering women's personal, spiritual, and group identities and values. The enormous variety of published works springing from and uniting these communities range from Judy Grahn's lesbian-feminist poetry to theologian Carol Christ's groundbreaking study of women writers and spiritual quest, *Diving Deep and Surfacing* (1980), to Jungian Clarissa Pinkola Estés's retelling and interpretation of traditional tales in *Women Who Run with the Wolves* (1992).

It is arguable that the marginalization of women as a gender group, and of ethnic women in Western culture by virtue of gender and ethnicity, creates a certain affinity between women writers, women readers, and folklore. Folklore in the contemporary world is, after all and by definition, as much on the fringe of official, mainstream culture as it is close to the hearts of the particular communities to whom it belongs; thus, folklore may provide kinds and degrees of knowledge and perception that might be obscured or unavailable to people who are fully immersed in the majority culture. Hence, the versatility of folklore as a medium for women seeking to write, and for women responding to writing about ethnic, regional, and gender-specific experiences with the voice of authenticity; hence, also, folklore's appeal for women looking outside the mainstream for satisfying creative interaction and freshly meaningful expressions of spirituality. Literature by women and received by women in community helps to offer insight about particularity; about belonging and knowing; about limitations, opportunities, choices, and consequences; and about self in the contexts of gender, group, time, and place.

Jody Davie

See also Briggs, Katharine; Carter, Angela; Cather, Willa; Grimm, Jacob and Wilhelm; Hurston, Zora Neale; Kingston, Maxine Hong; *Märchen*; Walker, Alice; Welsh Literature

✵✵✵✵✵✵✵✵✵✵✵✵✵✵✵✵✵

References

Aptheker, Bettina. *Tapestries of Life: Women's Work, Women's Consciousness, and the Meaning of Daily Experience*. Amherst: University of Massachusetts Press, 1989.

Bacon-Smith, Camille. *Enterprising Women: Television Fandom and the Creation of Popular Myth*. Philadelphia: University of Pennsylvania Press, 1992.

Hollis, Susan Tower, Linda Pershing, and M. Jane Young, eds. *Feminist Theory and the Study of Folklore*. Urbana and Chicago: University of Illinois Press, 1993.

Radner, Joan Newlon, ed. *Feminist Messages: Coding in Women's Folk Culture*. Urbana and Chicago: University of Illinois Press, 1993.

Radner, Joan Newlon, and Susan S. Lanser. "Strategies of Coding in Women's Cultures." In *Feminist Messages: Coding in Women's Folk Culture*, ed. Joan Newlon Radner, pp. 1–30. Urbana and Chicago: University of Illinois Press, 1993.

Stone, Kay F. "The Misuses of Enchantment: Controversies on the Significance of Fairy Tales." In *Women's Folklore, Women's Culture*, ed. Rosan Jordan and Susan Kalcik, pp. 125–145. Philadelphia: University of Pennsylvania Press, 1985.

Weigle, Marta. *Spiders and Spinsters: Women and Mythology*. Albuquerque: University of New Mexico Press, 1982.

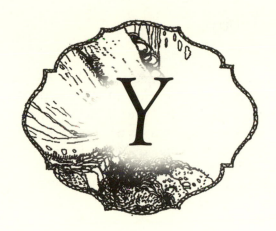

Yeats, William Butler (1865–1939)

Born in Dublin, Ireland, on June 13, 1865, William Butler Yeats was fortunate in at least two ways. First, his father, John Butler Yeats, was a talented and an interesting man. Trained as a barrister, he had become a portrait painter; he was also an admirer of John Locke, someone his son would declare to hate. Members of the Yeats family were known to be good talkers, but it was of his mother, Susan Pollexfen from Sligo, that J. B. Yeats said, "By marriage with the Pollexfens I have given a tongue to the sea cliffs of Sligo." The second stroke of luck William enjoyed was the very place he was born. Ireland, and especially the west of Ireland, was then a treasure of folklore, myths, and legends. Ireland was never invaded by the Romans, and partly because of that fact, its indigenous folklore was allowed to accrete relatively undisturbed until the late nineteenth and early twentieth centuries.

Although his family moved to London when he was two years old, Yeats spent considerable time in Sligo, and he remembered that "she and the fisherman's wife would tell each other stories that Homer might have told." Yeats sat on his mother's lap during the storytelling, and he retained ties to the west of Ireland and its rich, fabulous, and mythic folklore all of his life.

The Yeats family moved back and forth between Dublin and London, and Yeats finished high school in Dublin. Contrary to family tradition, he did not enter Trinity College but enrolled instead at the Metropolitan Art School in Dublin. Although his father, brother, and daughter were painters, Yeats's main benefit from art school was the friendship he formed with George Russell (pseudonym, AE), who is often credited with bringing some focus to Yeats's rather amorphous young searches for meaning. Yeats turned first to

Buddhism, to Mohini Chatterjee for Vedantism, and to Madame Blavatsky for Theosophy; in most of these activities, Russell followed and encouraged Yeats, who dedicated his second book of poetry, *Crossways*, to AE. It is a strange little volume; even the titles to the poems reflect the range of Yeats's interests: "The Indian on God," "The Ballad of Father O'Hart," and in the classical mode, "The Happy Shepherd" followed by "The Sad Shepherd." On the whole, these are good poems, what the poet T. S. Eliot called "anthology" poems.

In *The Rose*, more of the subjects that would occupy Yeats's life emerged. During the 1890s, he became involved in the Dublin Hermetic Society—a quasi-mystical group—and he remained interested in it all his life. He had earlier tried, with Annie Horniman, to found an Irish mystical order—it was to have been centered on an island in Innisfree in the county of Sligo—and "The Lake Isle of Innisfree" is probably the best known poem among his earlier works. We can also see the beginnings of his use of Irish traditional stories in "Cuchulain's Fight with the Sea." Yeats used the characters of Maeve, Emer, Ailill, Cuchulain, Derde, and others from the fifth-century *Tain Bo Cuailnge* [The great cattle raid of Cooney] in both his poetry and his drama.

One of Yeats's most admirable characteristics was his ability to integrate all of his interests so that they complemented each other. In addition to his interest in the myths and legends of the Irish Red Branch cycle, Theosophy, cabalism, and the Hermetic Order of the Golden Dawn (a European cabalistic group), he became involved in Irish nationalism through John O'Leary, an old Fenian with whom Yeats shared rooms for a time. O'Leary gave Yeats books on Irish history, had him speak at the Young Ireland Club, and introduced him to Maud Gonne. Many people think Yeats involved himself in politics because he was passionately in love with Gonne; they tend also to think she was the love of his life. Neither opinion is wholly true. It would have been difficult not to be interested in Irish politics if one were also interested in Irish folklore.

In a way, all of Yeats's interests came together when he became actively involved in drama and made Gonne the central character in the play *Cathleen ni Houlihan*, which is based in Irish folk drama. *The Countess Cathleen* (1892), another folk drama, was dedicated to her, and several of his poems are about her. But Lady Isabella Augusta Gregory—with whom Yeats created the Abbey Theatre—was a most important person in his life. She invited him to her home at Coole Park and, because she understood Gaelic and he did not, took him around the countryside gathering tales and folklore from the Gaelic-speaking preservers of Ireland's history.

Yeats subsequently edited *The Fairy and Folk Tales of Ireland* and published *The Celtic Twilight* (1893), which was eventually included in *Mythologies*. *Mythologies* is subtitled "stories of the supernatural, based on Irish country folklore." Yeats drew constantly from Irish myth and legend and from its indigenous folklore. Augusta Gregory was to him "Mother, friend, sister and brother." She gave him access to the people of the west of Ireland and to the wonders of Italy. No one was more important to him in basic ways with the exception of his wife, George Hyde-lees. A few days after their marriage in 1917, they started an automatic writing project that led to the publication of *A Vision*. In this work, Yeats eclectically attempted to make his own system, or myth, or philosophy.

His early interest in Indian philosophy led to his translation, with Shree Purohit Swami, of *The Ten Principal Upanishads*. He also had come to be interested in Japanese *noh* drama, which informed his *Plays for Dancers*. His motive, he said, was that "some day a play in the form I am adapting for European purposes shall awake once more, whether in Gaelic or in English, under the slope of Silve-na-man or Croagh Patrick, ancient memories."

Yeats wanted to find an ur-folklore, one that binds us all. "Folk Art is, indeed the oldest of the aristocracies of thought, and because it refuses what is passing and trivial, the merely clever and pretty, as certainly as the vulgar and insincere, and because it has gathered unto itself the simplest and most unforgettable thoughts of the generations, *it is the soil where all great art is rooted*," wrote Yeats. This belief carried him through his great books of poetry—*The Tower, The Winding Stair, Words for Music Perhaps*—his *Last Poems*, and his difficult but folkloristically rich plays.

W. B. Yeats died on January 28, 1939. Only one year later, no less a poet than T. S. Eliot said Yeats was "the greatest poet of our time— certainly the greatest in this language, and so far as I am able to judge, in any language." Yeats's grave is in the west of Ireland, which he so loved; it is near Queen Maeve's Knocknarea, where she and her horsemen ride out at night.

Mary Catherine Flannery

See also Belief; Cuchulain; Folktale Adaptations; Gregory, Lady Isabella Augusta; Legend; *Nō (Noh)*

References

Donoghue, Denis. *Yeats*. New York: Viking, 1971.

Eliot, T. S. *On Poets and Poetry*. London: Faber and Faber, 1956.

Jeffares, A. Norman. *W. B. Yeats: A New Biography*. Great Britain: Hutchinson Press, 1988.

Kinahan, Frank. *Yeats, Folklore, and Occultism: Contexts of the Early Work and Thought*. Boston: Unwin Hyman, 1988.

Yeats, W. B. *Collected Plays*. London: Macmillan, 1966.

———. *Yeats's Poems*. Ed. A. Norman Jeffares, appendix Warwick Gould. London: Macmillan, 1989.

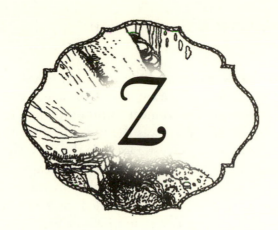

Zhirmunskii, Viktor Maksimovich (1891–1971)

The Russian philologist, linguist, and specialist in written and oral poetry Viktor Maksimovich Zhirmunskii was born in St. Petersburg when it was still the capital of Russia. He remained there after it became the Soviet city of Leningrad, becoming a professor at Leningrad State University in 1919. Zhirmunskii worked at Leningrad State for the whole of his very successful career.

He was an extremely prolific writer. He began with topics of Germanic philology and expanded to studies of Russian poetics, comparative Russian/Western poetics, the history of literature, Turkic linguistics, dialectology, and oral literature. He wrote a number of books, many of which were translated into other languages and became basic sources. Zhirmunskii also contributed to *Sranvnitel'naia grammatika nemetskikh iazykov* [Comparative grammar of the Germanic languages], editing the first four volumes. From 1969 to 1971, he was acting chief editor of the journal *Voprosy iazykoznaniia* [Problems in linguistics], and throughout his career he contributed to numerous collections and studies.

For his efforts, Zhirmunskii was elected a corresponding member of the Soviet Academy of Sciences in 1939 and a full member, or Academician, in 1966. He became a corresponding member of the German Academy of Sciences in Berlin in 1956, the British Academy of Sciences in 1962, the Danish Academy of Sciences in 1967, and the Bavarian Academy of Sciences in 1970. He was also awarded honorary degrees from Oxford University; the University of Krakow, Poland; Humboldt University, Berlin; and Charles University, Prague; and he received the Order of Lenin.

Zhirmunskii's approach to folklore and literature was historical, and he sought to find the real, historical figures behind the characters who appear in epic and song. Like the other Soviet scholars of his day, Zhirmunskii had a Marxist belief in stages of human social development and tried to connect forms of folklore to these stages. What made his work special was the breadth of his knowledge and his efforts to link East and West. He made the West aware of the rich oral traditions of Central Asia and brought increased attention to all Soviet folklore scholarship, especially that focusing on living performers. For his countrymen, he provided information about Western authors, such as Lord Byron and Johann Wolfgang von Goethe, and Western themes, such as the Faust legend, that might otherwise not have been accessible. He tried to show the links between all forms of verbal expression. He sought to place Russian and other Soviet oral and written literature in a world context and to overcome Soviet isolationist tendencies.

Natalie Kononenko

See also Epic; Faust Legend; Legend

✳✳✳✳✳✳✳✳✳✳✳✳✳✳✳✳✳

References

Zhirmunskii, Viktor Maksimovich. *Introduction to Metrics: The Theory of Verse*. Trans. C. E. Brown; ed. with intro. E. Stankiewicz and W. N. Vickery. The Hague: Mouton, 1966.

———. *Narodnyi geroicheskii epos: Sravnitel'no-istoricheskie ocherki* [Heroic folk epic: A comparative historical study]. Moscow: Khudozhestvennaia literatura, 1962.

———. *Selected Writings: Linguistics, Poetics*. Trans. Sergei Ess; comp. Natalya Semenyuk. Moscow: Progress Publishers, 1985.

Zhirmunskii, Viktor Maksimovich, and Nora K. Chadwick. *Oral Epics of Central Asia*. London: Cambridge University Press, 1969.

ILLUSTRATION CREDITS

15 Copyright © Frank Capri, 1994. Courtesy of Archive Photos.
29 North Wind Picture Archives.
54 North Wind Picture Archives.
73 Michael S. Yamashita/Corbis.
92 North Wind Picture Archives.
110 Courtesy of the Dover Pictorial Archive Series.
127 Copyright © Keren Su. Courtesy of Allstock.
136 Corbis-Bettmann.
154 North Wind Picture Archives.
160 North Wind Picture Archives.
168 North Wind Picture Archives.
174 Scala/Art Resource.
193 Christine Osborne/Corbis.
211 North Wind Picture Archives.
247 Print by Utagawa Kuniyoshi. Courtesy of Asian Art & Archaeology Inc./Corbis.
257 Kavaler/Art Resource, NY.
269 From the collection of Carol Rose, photo by David Rose.
275 Library of Congress.
291 Library of Congress.
305 Bhaktivedanta Book, copyright © Trust International 1983.
313 North Wind Picture Archives.
317 Library of Congress/Corbis.
331 Charles & Josette Lenars/Corbis.
346 Kabuki Print by Taiso Yoshitoshi. Courtesy of Asian Art & Archaeology, Inc./Corbis.
352 North Wind Picture Archives.
372 Margaret Randall.
379 From the collection of Carol Rose, photo by David Rose.
405 North Wind Picture Archives.
413 From the collection of Carol Rose, photo by David Rose.
424 Copyright © Horst Tappe, 1993. Courtesy of Archive Photos.
432 Biblia Italiana, Rosenwald Collection, Library of Congress.
446 Archive Photos.
453 North Wind Picture Archives.
459 Print by Walter Crane. Seattle Public Library/Corbis.
463 North Wind Picture Archives.
479 North Wind Picture Archives.
485 Historical Picture Archive/Corbis.

Illustration Credits

INDEX

Index

INDEX

Index

Index

Index

INDEX